Total Quality Management

THIRD EDITION

DALE H. BESTERFIELD

Professor Emeritus, Southern Illinois University

CAROL BESTERFIELD-MICHNA

GLEN H. BESTERFIELD

Associate Professor, University of South Florida

MARY BESTERFIELD-SACRE

Assistant Professor, University of Pittsburgh

Prentice
Hall

Upper Saddle River, New Jersey
Columbus, Ohio

Library of Congress Cataloging-in-Publication Data

Total quality management / Dale H. Besterfield ... [et al.].—3rd ed.
p. cm.
Includes bibliographical references and index.
ISBN 0-13-099306-9
1. Total quality management. I. Besterfield, Dale H.

HD62.15 .T6792 2003
658.4'013—dc21   2002074916

Editor in Chief: Stephen Helba
Executive Editor: Debbie Yarnell
Editorial Assistant: Sam Goffinet
Production Editor: Louise N. Sette
Production Supervision: Carlisle Publishers Services
Design Coordinator: Diane Ernsberger
Cover Designer: Ali Mohrman
Production Manager: Brian Fox
Marketing Manager: Jimmy Stephens

This book was set in Times Roman by Carlisle Communications, Ltd. It was printed and bound by Maple Press. The cover was printed by Phoenix Color Corp.

Pearson Education Ltd.
Pearson Education Australia Pty. Limited
Pearson Education Singapore Pte. Ltd.
Pearson Education North Asia Ltd.
Pearson Education Canada, Ltd.
Pearson Educación de Mexico, S.A. de C.V.
Pearson Education—Japan
Pearson Education Malaysia Pte. Ltd.
Pearson Education, *Upper Saddle River, New Jersey*

10 9 8 7 6 5 4 3 2 1

ISBN: 0-13-099306-9

Preface

This book provides a fundamental, yet comprehensive, coverage of Total Quality Management (TQM). It covers not only the principles and practices, but also the tools and techniques. A practical state-of-the-art approach is stressed throughout. Sufficient theory is presented to ensure that the reader has a sound understanding of the basic concepts. Mathematical techniques are reduced to simple mathematics or developed in the form of tables and charts.

The book will serve the instructional needs of business, education, engineering, health-care, and technology students in higher education institutions. All sizes and types of organizations—service, manufacturing, government, military, construction, education, small business, health care, and nonprofit entities—will find this book an excellent training and reference manual for all personnel.

The book is divided into two parts. Part I covers the principles and practices of TQM. After an introductory chapter, the next six chapters cover the basic TQM concepts of leadership, customer satisfaction, employee involvement, continuous process improvement, supplier partnership, and performance measures.

Part II of the book covers the tools and techniques of TQM. Chapters discuss benchmarking, information technology, quality management systems, environmental management systems, quality function deployment, quality by design, failure mode and effect analysis, products liability, total productive maintenance, management tools, statistical process control, experimental design, and Taguchi's quality engineering.

The authors wish to express their sincere appreciation to Alan Lasley for his contributions on total productive maintenance; Ron Bathje, who drew many of the figures; and Gloria Aiello, who did the index.

We would also like to thank the following reviewers for their valuable input and suggestions: Christopher J. Dewit, Point Park College (PA); Gerard P. Ingold, Point Park College (PA); John Magney, Southern Illinois University–Carbondale; and Roger M. Tripp, ITT Technical Institute (CA).

Dale H. Besterfield
Carol Besterfield-Michna
Glen H. Besterfield
Mary Besterfield-Sacre

Contents

1

Introduction

Definition

Total Quality Management (TQM) is an enhancement to the traditional way of doing business. It is a proven technique to guarantee survival in world-class competition. Only by changing the actions of management will the culture and actions of an entire organization be transformed. TQM is for the most part common sense. Analyzing the three words, we have

Total—Made up of the whole.

Quality—Degree of excellence a product or service provides.

Management—Act, art, or manner of handling, controlling, directing, etc.

Therefore, TQM is the art of managing the whole to achieve excellence. The Golden Rule is a simple but effective way to explain it: Do unto others as you would have them do unto you.

TQM is defined as both a philosophy and a set of guiding principles that represent the foundation of a continuously improving organization. It is the application of quantitative methods and human resources to improve all the processes within an organization and exceed customer needs now and in the future. TQM integrates fundamental management techniques, existing improvement efforts, and technical tools under a disciplined approach.

Basic Approach

TQM requires six basic concepts:

1. A committed and involved management to provide long-term top-to-bottom organizational support.
2. An unwavering focus on the customer, both internally and externally.
3. Effective involvement and utilization of the entire work force.
4. Continuous improvement of the business and production process.
5. Treating suppliers as partners.
6. Establish performance measures for the processes.

These concepts outline an excellent way to run an organization. A brief paragraph on each of them is given here. The next six chapters cover these concepts in greater detail.

1. Management must participate in the quality program. A quality council must be established to develop a clear vision, set long-term goals, and direct the program. Quality goals are included in the business plan. An annual quality improvement program is established and involves input from the entire work force. Managers participate on quality improvement teams and also act as coaches to other teams. TQM is a continual activity that must be entrenched in the culture—it is not just a one-shot program. TQM must be communicated to all people.

2. The key to an effective TQM program is its focus on the customer. An excellent place to start is by satisfying internal customers. We must listen to the "voice of the customer" and emphasize design quality and defect prevention. Do it right the first time and every time, for customer satisfaction is the most important consideration.

3. TQM is an organization-wide challenge that is everyone's responsibility. All personnel must be trained in TQM, statistical process control (SPC), and other appropriate quality improvement skills so they can effectively participate on project teams. Including internal customers and, for that matter, internal suppliers on project teams is an excellent approach. Those affected by the plan must be involved in its development and implementation. They understand the process better than anyone else. Changing behavior is the goal. People must come to work not only to do their jobs, but also to think about how to improve their jobs. People must be empowered at the lowest possible level to perform processes in an optimum manner.

4. There must be a continual striving to improve all business and production processes. Quality improvement projects, such as on-time delivery, order entry efficiency, billing error rate, customer satisfaction, cycle time, scrap reduction, and supplier management, are good places to begin. Technical techniques such as SPC, benchmark-

ing, quality function deployment, ISO 9000, and designed experiments are excellent for problem solving.

5. On the average 40% of the sales dollar is purchased product or service; therefore, the supplier quality must be outstanding. A partnering relationship rather than an adversarial one must be developed. Both parties have as much to gain or lose based on the success or failure of the product or service. The focus should be on quality and life-cycle costs rather than price. Suppliers should be few in number so that true partnering can occur.

6. Performance measures such as uptime, percent nonconforming, absenteeism, and customer satisfaction should be determined for each functional area. These measures should be posted for everyone to see. Quantitative data are necessary to measure the continuous quality improvement activity.

The purpose of TQM is to provide a quality product and/or service to customers, which will, in turn, increase productivity and lower cost. With a higher quality product and lower price, competitive position in the marketplace will be enhanced. This series of events will allow the organization to achieve the objectives of profit and growth with greater ease. In addition, the work force will have job security, which will create a satisfying place to work.

As previously stated, TQM requires a cultural change. Table 1-1 compares the previous state with the TQM state for typical quality elements. This change is substantial and will not be accomplished in a short period of time. Small organizations will be able to make the transformation much faster than large organizations.

TABLE 1-1
New and Old Cultures

Quality Element	Previous State	TQM
Definition	Product-oriented	Customer-oriented
Priorities	Second to service and cost	First among equals of service and cost
Decisions	Short-term	Long-term
Emphasis	Detection	Prevention
Errors	Operations	System
Responsibility	Quality control	Everyone
Problem Solving	Managers	Teams
Procurement	Price	Life-cycle costs, partnership
Manager's Role	Plan, assign, control, and enforce	Delegate, coach, facilitate, and mentor

Gurus of Total Quality Management

Shewhart

Walter A. Shewhart, PhD, spent his professional career at Western Electric and Bell Telephone Laboratories, both divisions of AT&T. He developed control chart theory with control limits, assignable and chance causes of variation, and rational subgroups (see Chapter 18). In 1931, he authored *Economic Control of Quality of Manufactured Product*, which is regarded as a complete and thorough work of the basic principles of quality control. He also developed the PDSA cycle for learning and improvement (see Chapter 6).

Deming

W. Edwards Deming, PhD, was a protégé of Shewhart. In 1950, he taught statistical process control and the importance of quality to the leading CEOs of Japanese industry. He is credited with providing the foundation for the Japanese quality miracle and resurgence as an economic power. Deming is the best-known quality expert in the world. His 14 points provide a theory for management to improve quality, productivity, and competitive position (see Chapter 2). He has authored a number of books including *Out of the Crisis* and *Quality, Productivity, and Competitive Position* as well as 161 scholarly studies.

Juran

Joseph M. Juran, PhD worked at Western Electric from 1924 to 1941. There he was exposed to the concepts of Shewhart. Juran traveled to Japan in 1954 to teach quality management. He emphasized the necessity for management at all levels to be committed to the quality effort with hands-on involvement. He recommended project improvements based on return on investment to achieve breakthrough results. The Juran Trilogy (see Chapter 6) for managing quality is carried out by the three interrelated processes of planning, control, and improvement. In 1951, the first edition of *Juran's Quality Control Handbook* was published.

Feiganbaum

Armand V. Feigenbaum, PhD, argues that total quality control[1] is necessary to achieve productivity, market penetration, and competitive advantage. Quality begins by identifying the customer's requirements and ends with a product or service in the hands of a satisfied customer. In addition to customer satisfaction, some of Feigenbaum's quality principles are genuine management involvement, employee involvement, first-line su-

---

[1] The term total quality control was used rather than TQM during the early years of the movement.

pervision leadership, and company-wide quality control. In 1951, he authored *Total Quality Control*.

Ishikawa

Kaoru Ishikawa, PhD, studied under Deming, Juran, and Feigenbaum. He borrowed the total quality control concept and adapted it for the Japanese. In addition, he authored SPC texts in Japanese and in English. Ishikawa is best known for the development of the cause and effect diagram (see Chapter 18), which is sometimes called an Ishikawa diagram. He developed the quality circle concept (see Chapter 4) in Japan, whereby work groups, including their supervisor, were trained in SPC concepts. The groups then met to identify and solve quality problems in their work environment.

Crosby

Phillip B. Crosby authored his first book, *Quality is Free*, in 1979, which was translated into 15 languages. It sold 1.5 million copies and changed the way management looked at quality. He argued that "doing it right the first time" is less expensive than the costs of detecting and correcting nonconformities. In 1984, he authored *Quality Without Tears*, which contained his four absolutes of quality management. These absolutes are: quality is conformance to requirements, prevention of nonconformance is the objective not appraisal, the performance standard is zero defects not "that's close enough," and the measurement of quality is the cost of nonconformance.

Taguchi

Genichi Taguchi, PhD, developed his loss function concept that combines cost, target, and variation into one metric. Because the loss function is reactive, he developed the signal to noise ratio as a proactive equivalent. The cornerstone of Taguchi's philosophy is the robust design of parameters and tolerances. It is built on the simplification and use of traditional design of experiments. These concepts are described in Chapter 20.

TQM Framework

Figure 1-1 shows the framework for the TQM system. It begins with the knowledge provided by gurus of quality: Shewhart, Deming, Juran, Figenbaum, Ishikawa, Crosby, and Taguchi. As the figure shows, they contributed to the development of principles and practices and/or the tools and techniques. Chapters 2 through 7 provide information on principles and practices, and their titles are given at the bottom of the figure. Chapters 8 through 20 provide information on tools and techniques and their titles are given in the upper right of the figure. Some of these tools and techniques are used in the product and/or

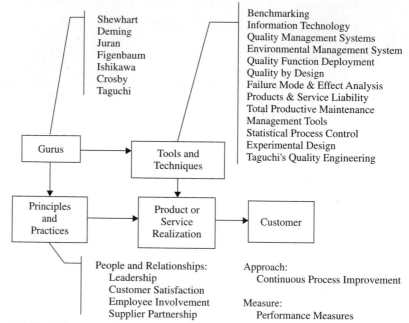

Figure 1-1 TQM Framework

service realization activity. Feedback from internal/external customers or interested parties provides information to continually improve the organization's system, product and/or service.

Awareness

An organization will not begin the transformation to TQM until it is aware that the quality of the product or service must be improved. Awareness comes about when an organization loses market share or realizes that quality and productivity go hand-in-hand. It also occurs if TQM is mandated by the customer or if management realizes that TQM is a better way to run a business and compete in domestic and world markets.

Automation and other productivity enhancements might not help a corporation if it is unable to market its product or service because the quality is poor. The Japanese learned this fact from practical experience. Prior to World War II, they could sell their products only at ridiculously low prices, and even then it was difficult to secure repeat sales. Until recently, corporations have not recognized the importance of quality. However, a new attitude has emerged—quality first among the equals of cost and service. To sum it up, the customer wants value.

TABLE 1-2
Gain in Productivity with Improved Quality

Item	Before Improvement 10% Nonconforming	After Improvement 5% Nonconforming
Relative total cost for 20 units	1.00	1.00
Conforming units	18	19
Relative cost for nonconforming units	0.10	0.05
Productivity increase		(100)(1/18) = 5.6%
Capability increase		(100)(1/18) = 5.6%
Profit increase		(100)(1/18) = 5.6%

Adapted from W. Edwards Deming, *Quality, Productivity, and Competitive Position* (Cambridge, Mass.: Massachusetts Institute of Technology, Center for Advanced Engineering Studies, 1982).

Quality and productivity are not mutually exclusive. Improvements in quality can lead directly to increased productivity and other benefits. Table 1-2 illustrates this concept. As seen in the table, the improved quality results in a 5.6% improvement in productivity, capacity, and profit. Many quality improvement projects are achieved with the same work force, same overhead, and no investment in new equipment.

Recent evidence shows that more and more corporations are recognizing the importance and necessity of quality improvement if they are to survive domestic and world-wide competition. Quality improvement is not limited to the conformance of the product or service to specifications; it also involves the inherent quality in the design of the system. The prevention of product, service, and process problems is a more desirable objective than taking corrective action after the product is manufactured or a service rendered.

TQM does not occur overnight; there are no quick remedies. It takes a long time to build the appropriate emphasis and techniques into the culture. Overemphasis on short-term results and profits must be set aside so long-term planning and constancy of purpose will prevail.

Defining Quality

When the expression "quality" is used, we usually think in terms of an excellent product or service that fulfills or exceeds our expectations. These expectations are based on the intended use and the selling price. For example, a customer expects a different performance from a plain steel washer than from a chrome-plated steel washer because they are a different grade. When a product surpasses our expectations we consider that quality. Thus, it is somewhat of an intangible based on perception. Quality can be quantified as follows:

$$Q = P / E$$

where Q = quality
          P = performance
          E = expectations

If Q is greater than 1.0, then the customer has a good feeling about the product or service. Of course, the determination of P and E will most likely be based on perception with the organization determining performance and the customer determining expectations.

A more definitive definition of quality is given in ISO 9000: 2000. It is defined as the degree to which a set of inherent characteristics fulfills requirements. *Degree* means that quality can be used with adjectives such as poor, good, and excellent. *Inherent* is defined as existing in something, especially as a permanent characteristic. *Characteristics* can be quantitative or qualitative. *Requirement* is a need or expectation that is stated; generally implied by the organization, its customers, and other interested parties; or obligatory.

Quality has nine different dimensions. Table 1-3 shows these nine dimensions of quality with their meanings and explanations in terms of a slide projector.

These dimensions are somewhat independent; therefore, a product can be excellent in one dimension and average or poor in another. Very few, if any, products excel in all nine dimensions. For example, the Japanese were cited for high-quality cars in the 1970s

TABLE 1-3
The Dimensions of Quality

Dimension	Meaning and Example
Performance	Primary product characteristics, such as the brightness of the picture
Features	Secondary characteristics, added features, such as remote control
Conformance	Meeting specifications or industry standards, workmanship
Reliability	Consistency of performance over time, average time for the unit to fail
Durability	Useful life, includes repair
Service	Resolution of problems and complaints, ease of repair
Response	Human-to-human interface, such as the courtesy of the dealer
Aesthetics	Sensory characteristics, such as exterior finish
Reputation	Past performance and other intangibles, such as being ranked first

Adapted from David A. Garvin, *Managing Quality: The Strategic and Competitive Edge* (New York: Free Press, 1988).

based only on the dimensions of reliability, conformance, and aesthetics. Therefore, quality products can be determined by using a few of the dimensions of quality.

Marketing has the responsibility of identifying the relative importance of each dimension of quality. These dimensions are then translated into the requirements for the development of a new product or the improvement of an existing one.

Historical Review

The history of quality control is undoubtedly as old as industry itself. During the Middle Ages, quality was to a large extent controlled by the long periods of training required by the guilds. This training instilled pride in workers for quality of a product.

The concept of specialization of labor was introduced during the Industrial Revolution. As a result, a worker no longer made the entire product, only a portion. This change brought about a decline in workmanship. Because most products manufactured during that early period were not complicated, quality was not greatly affected. In fact, because productivity improved there was a decrease in cost, which resulted in lower customer expectations. As products became more complicated and jobs more specialized, it became necessary to inspect products after manufacture.

In 1924, W. A. Shewhart of Bell Telephone Laboratories developed a statistical chart for the control of product variables. This chart is considered to be the beginning of statistical quality control. Later in the same decade, H. F. Dodge and H. G. Romig, both of Bell Telephone Laboratories, developed the area of acceptance sampling as a substitute for 100% inspection. Recognition of the value of statistical quality control became apparent by 1942. Unfortunately, U.S. managers failed to recognize its value.

In 1946, the American Society for Quality Control was formed. Recently, the name was changed to American Society for Quality (ASQ). This organization, through its publications, conferences, and training sessions, has promoted the use of quality for all types of production and service.

In 1950, W. Edwards Deming, who learned statistical quality control from Shewhart, gave a series of lectures on statistical methods to Japanese engineers and on quality responsibility to the CEOs of the largest organizations in Japan. Joseph M. Juran made his first trip to Japan in 1954 and further emphasized management's responsibility to achieve quality. Using these concepts the Japanese set the quality standards for the rest of the world to follow.

In 1960, the first quality control circles were formed for the purpose of quality improvement. Simple statistical techniques were learned and applied by Japanese workers.

By the late 1970s and early 1980s, U.S. managers were making frequent trips to Japan to learn about the Japanese miracle. These trips were really not necessary—they could have read the writings of Deming and Juran. Nevertheless, a quality renaissance began to occur in U.S. products and services, and by the middle of 1980 the concepts of TQM were being publicized.

In the late 1980s the automotive industry began to emphasize statistical process control (SPC). Suppliers and their suppliers were required to use these techniques. Other industries and the Department of Defense also implemented SPC. The Malcolm Baldrige National Quality Award was established and became the means to measure TQM. Genechi Taguchi introduced his concepts of parameter and tolerance design and brought about a resurgence of design of experiments (DOE) as a valuable quality improvement tool.

Emphasis on quality continued in the auto industry in the 1990s when the Saturn automobile ranked first in customer satisfaction (1996). In addition, ISO 9000 became the worldwide model for a quality management system. ISO 14000 was approved as the worldwide model for environmental management systems.

The new millenium brought about increased emphasis on worldwide quality and the Internet.

Obstacles

Implementation of TQM is described in the next chapter, on leadership. This section gives information concerning the obstacles associated with implementation.

Many organizations, especially small ones with a niche, are comfortable with their current state. They are satisfied with the amount of work being performed, the profits realized, and the perception that the customers are satisfied. Organizations with this culture will see little need for TQM until they begin to lose market share.

Once an organization embarks on TQM, there will be obstacles to its successful implementation. The first eight most common were determined by Robert J. Masters after an extensive literature search and the last obstacle added by the authors.[2] They are given below.

Lack of Management Commitment

In order for any organizational effort to succeed, there must be a substantial management commitment of management time and organizational resources. The purpose must be clearly and continuously communicated to all personnel. Management must consistently apply the principles of TQM.

Robert Galvin of Motorola said that only the CEO can ensure, even in times of great pressure, that quality and customer satisfaction are preserved. In a survey of 188 quality professionals, 66% reported that management's compensation is not linked to quality goals such as failure costs, customer complaints, and cycle time reduction.[3]

---

[2] Robert J. Masters, "Overcoming the Barriers to TQM's Success," *Quality Progress* (May 1996): 53–55.

[3] Nabil Tamimi and Rose Sebastianelli, "The Barriers to Total Quality Management," *Quality Progress* (June 1998): 57–60.

Inability to Change Organizational Culture

Changing an organization's culture is difficult and will require as much as five years. Individuals resist change—they become accustomed to doing a particular process and it becomes the preferred way. Management must understand and utilize the basic concepts of change. They are:

1. People change when they want to and to meet their own needs.
2. Never expect anyone to engage in behavior that serves the organization's values unless adequate reason (why) has been given.
3. For change to be accepted, people must be moved from a state of fear to trust.

It is difficult for individuals to change their way of doing things; it is much more difficult for an organization to make a cultural change.

Management by exhortation and inspiration will fail. Speeches, slogans, and campaigns that are supposed to motivate people are only effective for a short period of time. Impediments to a cultural change are the lack of effective communication and emphasis on short-term results. Organizations that spend more time planning for the cultural aspects of implementing a TQM program will improve their chances of success.[4]

Improper Planning

All constituents of the organization must be involved in the development of the implementation plan and any modifications that occur as the plan evolves. Of particular importance is the two-way communication of ideas by all personnel during the development of the plan and its implementation. Customer satisfaction should be the goal rather than financial or sales goals. Peterson Products, a metal stamping firm near Chicago, improved on-time delivery, which resulted in a 25% increase in sales. Focus on quality and the other goals will follow.

Lack of Continuous Training and Education

Training and education is an ongoing process for everyone in the organization. Needs must be determined and a plan developed to achieve those needs. Training and education are most effective when senior management conducts the training on the principles of TQM. Informal training occurs by communicating the TQM effort to all personnel on a continual basis.

In the study by Tamimi and Sebastianelli previously cited, lack of training in group discussion and communication techniques, quality improvement skills, problem identification, and the problem-solving method was the second most important obstacle.

---

[4] Gary Salegna and Farzaneh Fasel, "Obstacles to Implementing Quality," *Quality Progress* (July 2000): 53–57.

Incompatible Organizational Structure and Isolated Individuals and Departments

Differences between departments and individuals can create implementation problems. The use of multifunctional teams will help to break down long-standing barriers.

Restructuring to make the organization more responsive to customer needs may be needed. Individuals who do not embrace the new philosophy can be required to leave the organization. Adherence to the six basic concepts will minimize the problems over time.

At Spartan Light Metal Products, Inc. in Sparta, IL, product support teams composed of three members from design, quality, and production are assigned to each customer segment.

Ineffective Measurement Techniques and Lack of Access to Data and Results

Key characteristics of the organization should be measured so that effective decisions can be made. In order to improve a process you need to measure the effect of improvement ideas. Access to data and quick retrieval is necessary for effective processes.

Peoples Bank of Bridgeport, CT found that extra inspection, training, and management encouragement did not help a high error rate. Finally the bank investigated the root causes of the problem and corrected them, which virtually eliminated the problem.

Paying Inadequate Attention to Internal and External Customers

Organizations need to understand the changing needs and expectations of their customers. Effective feedback mechanisms that provide data for decision making are necessary for this understanding. One way to overcome this obstacle is to give the right people direct access to the customers. Ingersol Rand of Princeton, NJ had its design team of marketing, engineering, and manufacturing conduct focus groups of customers throughout the country with the result that it was able to develop a new grinder in one-third the usual cycle time.[5] When an organization fails to empower individuals and teams, it cannot hold them responsible for producing results.

Inadequate Use of Empowerment and Teamwork

Teams need to have the proper training and, at least in the beginning, a facilitator. Whenever possible, the team's recommendations should be followed. Individuals should be empowered to make decisions that affect the efficiency of their process or the satisfaction of their customers. Solar Turbines, Inc. flattened its organization by restructuring

---

[5] Willard I. Zangwill, "Ten Mistakes CEO's Make about Quality," *Quality Progress* (June 1994): 43–48.

into work teams and delegating authority to the point of customer contact or to the work performed.

Failure to Continually Improve

It is tempting to sit back and rest on your laurels. However, a lack of continuous improvement of the processes, product, and/or service will even leave the leader of the pack in the dust. Will Rogers said it best, "Even if you're on the right track, you'll get run over if you just sit there." Even though Champion Mortgage's 1998 business volume increased 59%, it continues to address culture, staff, and service issues.[6]

Benefits of TQM

According to a survey of manufacturing firms in Georgia, the benefits of TQM are improved quality, employee participation, teamwork, working relationships, customer satisfaction, employee satisfaction, productivity, communication, profitability, and market share.[7]

TQM is a good investment as shown by a ten-year study by Hendricks and Singhai. They showed that there is a strong link between TQM and financial performance. The researchers selected a group of 600 publicly traded organizations that had won awards for effectively implementing TQM. They then selected a control group similar in size and industry to the award winners. Performance of both groups was compared during the five years prior to the award and five years after winning the award. No difference was shown between the two groups prior to the award. However, as shown below the award group far outstripped the control group during the five-year period after the award.

Description	Control	Award
Growth in Operating Income	43%	91%
Increase in Sales	32%	69%
Increase in Total Assets	37%	79%

The study also showed that stock price performance for the award winners was 114% while the S&P was 80%. In addition, the study showed that small organizations out performed larger organizations. Recent studies have shown that only about 30% of manufacturing organizations have successfully implemented TQM.[8]

---

[6] Mark R. Hagan, "Complacency—the Enemy of Quality," *Quality Progress* (October 1999): 37–44.

[7] Christopher M. Lowery, et. al., "TQM's Human Resource Component," *Quality Progress* (February 2000): 55–58.

[8] Kevin B. Hendricks and Vinod R. Singhai, "Don't Count TQM Out," *Quality Progress* (April 1999): 35–42.

TQM Exemplary Organization[9]

Employing 99,000 workers at 53 major facilities worldwide and based in Schaumburg, Illinois, Motorola is an integrated company that produces an array of electronic products, distributing most through direct sales and service operations. Products include two-way radios and pagers; wireless telephones; semiconductors; and equipment for defense and aerospace applications, data communications, information processing, and automotive and industrial uses.

In 1981, Motorola launched an ambitious drive for a tenfold improvement in the quality of its products and services. They succeeded, and now many of its products are the best in their class. The company's quality goal is simply stated: "Zero defects in everything we do." Motorola's managers literally carry with them the corporate objective of "total customer satisfaction"—it's on a printed card in their pockets. Corporate officials and business managers wear pagers to make themselves available to customers, and they regularly visit customers' businesses to find out their likes and dislikes about Motorola products and services. The information, along with data gathered through an extensive network of customer surveys, complaint hotlines, field audits, and other customer feedback measures, guides planning for quality improvement and product development. Pagers supplied to Nippon Telegraph and Telephone is a major share of that market.

Key initiatives are six-sigma quality and reducing total cycle time. Six sigma is a statistical measure that translates into a target of no more than 3.4 defects per million products and includes customer service. Motorola's cycle-time reduction is even more ambitious; the clock starts ticking the moment the product is conceived. This calls for an examination of the total system, including design, manufacturing, marketing, and administration.

Employees contribute directly through Motorola's Participative Management Program (PMP), which is composed of employees who work in the same area or are assigned to achieve a specific aim. PMP teams meet often to assess progress toward meeting quality goals, identify new initiatives, and work on problems. To reward high quality work, savings that stem from team recommendations are shared. PMP bonuses over the past four years have averaged about three percent of Motorola's payroll. About 40 percent of worker training is devoted to quality matters, ranging from general principles of quality improvement to designing for manufacturability.

---

[9] Malcolm Baldrige National Quality Award, 1988 Manufacturing Category Recipient, NIST/Baldrige Homepage, Internet.

Exercises

1. Describe how the golden rule does or does not influence each of the six concepts of TQM.

2. Of the six basic TQM concepts, which were the most effective in World War II? Explain.

3. Which of the gurus would be the father of quality control? Which had the greatest impact on management? Which is noted for robust design?

4. Select a product or service and describe how the dimensions of quality influence its acceptance.

5. Working as an individual or in a team of three or more people, determine two or more obstacles to implementing TQM in one or more of the organizations listed below:

   (a) Large bank
   (b) Health-care facility
   (c) University academic department
   (d) University nonacademic department
   (e) Large department store
   (f) Grade school
   (g) Manufacturing facility
   (h) Large grocery store

2

Leadership

Definitions

There is no universal definition of leadership and indeed many books have been devoted to the topic of leadership. In his book *Leadership*, James MacGregor Burns describes a leader as one who instills purposes, not one who controls by brute force. A leader strengthens and inspires the followers to accomplish shared goals. Leaders shape the organization's values, promote the organization's values, protect the organization's values and exemplify the organization's values. Ultimately, Burns says, "Leaders and followers raise one another to higher levels of motivation and morality . . . leadership becomes moral in that it raises the level of human conduct and ethical aspiration of both the leader and the led, and thus has a transforming effect on both."[1] Similarly, Daimler Chrysler's CEO Bob Eaton defines a leader as " . . . someone who can take a group of people to a place they don't think they can go." "Leadership is we, not me; mission, not my show; vision, not division; and community, not domicile."[2] As the above illustrates, leadership is difficult to define in anything other than lofty words.

The Malcolm Baldrige National Quality Award has a more grounded definition of leadership in its core values. As stated in its core values and concepts, visionary leadership is:

"An organization's senior leaders should set directions and create a customer focus, clear and visible values, and high expectations. The directions, values, and expectations should balance the needs of all your stakeholders. Your leaders should ensure the creation of strategies, systems, and methods for achieving excellence, stimulating innovation, and building knowledge and capabilities. The values and strategies should help guide all activities and decisions of your organization. Senior leaders should inspire and motivate your entire

---

[1] James M. Burns, *Leadership* (New York: Harper & Row, 1978).

[2] Rick L. Edgeman, et. al., "On Leaders and Leadership," *Quality Progress* (October 1999): 49–54.

workforce and should encourage all employees to contribute, to develop and learn, to be innovative, and to be creative.

Senior leaders should serve as role models through their ethical behavior and their personal involvement in planning, communications, coaching, development of future leaders, review of organizational performance, and employee recognition. As role models, they can reinforce values and expectations while building leadership, commitment, and initiative throughout your organization."

Leadership can be difficult to define. However, successful quality leaders tend to have certain characteristics.

Characteristics of Quality Leaders[3]

There are 12 behaviors or characteristics that successful quality leaders demonstrate.

1. They give priority attention to external and internal customers and their needs. Leaders place themselves in the customers' shoes and service their needs from that perspective. They continually evaluate the customers' changing requirements.

2. They empower, rather than control, subordinates. Leaders have trust and confidence in the performance of their subordinates. They provide the resources, training, and work environment to help subordinates do their jobs. However, the decision to accept responsibility lies with the individual.

3. They emphasize improvement rather than maintenance. Leaders use the phrase "If it isn't perfect, improve it" rather than "If it ain't broke, don't fix it." There is always room for improvement, even if the improvement is small. Major breakthroughs sometimes happen, but it's the little ones that keep the continuous process improvement on a positive track.

4. They emphasize prevention. "An ounce of prevention is worth a pound of cure" is certainly true. It is also true that perfection can be the enemy of creativity. We can't always wait until we have created the perfect process or product. There must be a balance between preventing problems and developing better, but not perfect, processes.

5. They encourage collaboration rather than competition. When functional areas, departments, or work groups are in competition, they may find subtle ways of working against each other or withholding information. Instead, there must be collaboration among and within units.

6. They train and coach, rather than direct and supervise. Leaders know that the development of the human resource is a necessity. As coaches, they help their subordinates learn to do a better job.

---

[3] Adapted from Warren H. Schmidt and Jerome P. Finnigan, *The Race Without a Finish Line* (San Francisco: Jossey-Bass Publishers, 1992).

7. They learn from problems. When a problem exists, it is treated as an opportunity rather than something to be minimized or covered up. "What caused it?" and "How can we prevent it in the future?" are the questions quality leaders ask.

8. They continually try to improve communications. Leaders continually disseminate information about the TQM effort. They make it evident that TQM is not just a slogan. Communication is two way—ideas will be generated by people when leaders encourage them and act upon them. For example, on the eve of Desert Storm, General Colin Powell solicited enlisted men and women for advice on winning the war. Communication is the glue that holds a TQM organization together.

9. They continually demonstrate their commitment to quality. Leaders walk their talk—their actions, rather than their words, communicate their level of commitment. They let the quality statements be their decision-making guide.

10. They choose suppliers on the basis of quality, not price. Suppliers are encouraged to participate on project teams and become involved. Leaders know that quality begins with quality materials and the true measure is the life-cycle cost.

11. They establish organizational systems to support the quality effort. At the senior management level a quality council is provided, and at the first-line supervisor level, work groups and project teams are organized to improve the process.

12. They encourage and recognize team effort. They encourage, provide recognition, and reward individuals and teams. Leaders know that people like to know that their contributions are appreciated and important. This action is one of the leader's most powerful tools.

Leadership Concepts

In order to become successful, leadership requires an intuitive understanding of human nature—the basic needs, wants, and abilities of people. To be effective, a leader understands that:

1. People, paradoxically, need security and independence at the same time.
2. People are sensitive to external rewards and punishments and yet are also strongly self-motivated.
3. People like to hear a kind word of praise. Catch people doing something right, so you can pat them on the back.
4. People can process only a few facts at a time; thus, a leader needs to keep things simple.
5. People trust their gut reaction more than statistical data.
6. People distrust a leader's rhetoric if the words are inconsistent with the leader's actions.

Leaders need to give their employees independence and yet provide a secure working environment—one that encourages and rewards successes. A working environment must be provided that fosters employee creativity and risk-taking by not penalizing mistakes.

A leader will focus on a few key values and objectives. Focusing on a few values or objectives gives the employees the ability to discern on a daily basis what is important and what is not. Employees, upon understanding the objectives, must be given personal control over the task in order to make the task their own and, thereby, something to which they can commit. A leader, by giving the employee a measure of control over an important task, will tap into the employee's inner drive. Employees, led by the manager can become excited participants in the organization.

Having a worthwhile cause such as total quality management is not always enough to get employees to participate. People, (and, in turn, employees) follow a leader, not a cause. Indeed, when people like the leader but not the vision, they will try to change the vision or reconcile their vision to the leader's vision. If the leader is liked, people will not look for another leader. This is especially evident in politics. If the leader is trusted and liked, then the employees will participate in the total quality management cause. Therefore, it is particularly important that a leader's character and competence, which is developed by good habits and ethics, be above reproach. Effective leadership begins on the inside and moves out.

The 7 Habits of Highly Effective People*4

Stephen R. Covey has based his foundation for success on the character ethic—things like integrity, humility, fidelity, temperance, courage, justice, patience, industry, simplicity, modesty, and the Golden Rule. The personality ethic—personality growth, communication skill training, and education in the field of influence strategies and positive thinking—is secondary to the character ethic. What we *are* communicates far more eloquently than what we *say* or do.

A *paradigm* is the way we perceive, understand, and interpret the world around us. It is a different way of looking at people and things. To be effective we need to make a paradigm shift. Most scientific breakthroughs are the result of paradigm shifts such as Copernicus viewing the sun as the center of the universe rather than earth. Paradigm shifts are quantum changes, whether slow and deliberate or instantaneous.

A habit is the intersection of knowledge, skill, and desire. Knowledge is the *what to do* and the *why*; skill is the *how to do*; and desire is the motivation or *want to do*. In order for something to become a habit you have to have all three. The 7 Habits* are a

---

4 This section is adapted from Stephen R. Covey. *The 7 Habits of Highly Effective People*, Simon & Schuster: New York, 1989. © 1989 Stephen R. Covey.

*This section also includes important trademarks of Franklin Covey Co. Used and reprinted with permission from Franklin Covey Co., www.franklincovey.com. All rights reserved.

highly integrated approach that moves from dependency (you take care of me) to independence (I take care of myself) to interdependence (we can do something better together). The first three habits deal with independence—the essence of character growth. Habits 4, 5, and 6 deal with interdependence—teamwork, cooperation, and communication. Habit 7 is the habit of renewal.

The 7 Habits are in harmony with a natural law that Covey calls the "P/PC Balance,"* where P stands for production of desired results and PC stands for production capacity, the ability or asset. For example, if you fail to maintain a lawn mower (PC) it will wear out and not be able to mow the lawn (P). You need a balance between the time spent mowing the lawn (desired result) and maintaining the lawn mower (asset). Assets can be physical, such as the lawn mower example; financial, such as the balance between principal (PC) and interest (P); and human, such as the balance between training (PC) and meeting schedule (P). You need the balance to be effective; otherwise, you will have neither a lawn mower nor a mowed lawn.

Habit 1: Be Proactive*

Being proactive means taking responsibility for your life—the ability to choose the response to a situation. Proactive behavior is a product of conscious choice based on values, rather than reactive behavior, which is based on feelings. Reactive people let circumstances, conditions, or their environment tell them how to respond. Proactive people let carefully thought-about, selected, and internalized values tell them how to respond. It's not what happens to us but our response that differentiates the two behaviors. No one can make you miserable unless you choose to let them.

The language we use is a real indicator of our behavior. Comparisons are given in the table below.

Reactive	*Proactive*
There's nothing I can do.	Let's look at our alternatives.
She makes me so mad.	I control my own feelings.
I have to do that.	I will choose an appropriate response.
I can't.	I choose.
I must.	I prefer.
Things are getting worse.	What initiative can we use?

Habit 2: Begin with the End in Mind*

The most fundamental application of this habit is to begin each day with an image, picture, or paradigm of the end of your life as your frame of reference. Each part of your life can be examined in terms of what really matters to you—a vision of your life as a whole.

All things are created twice—there's a mental or first creation and a physical or second creation to all things. To build a house you first create a blueprint and then construct the actual house. You create a speech on paper before you give it. If you want to have a successful organization you begin with a plan that will produce the appropriate end; thus leadership is the first creation, and management, the second. Leadership is doing the right things and management is doing things right.

In order to begin with the end in mind, develop a personal philosophy or creed. Start by considering the example items below:

Never compromise with honesty.

Remember the people involved.

Maintain a positive attitude.

Exercise daily.

Keep a sense of humor.

Do not fear mistakes.

Facilitate the success of subordinates.

Seek divine help.

Read a leadership book monthly.

By centering our lives on correct principles, we create a solid foundation for the development of the life-support factors of security, guidance, wisdom, and power. Principles are fundamental truths. They are tightly interwoven threads running with exactness, consistency, beauty, and strength through the fabric of life.

Habit 3: Put First Things First*

Habit 1 says, "You're the creator. You are in charge." Habit 2 is the first creation and is based on imagination—leadership based on values. Habit 3 is practicing self-management and requires Habits 1 and 2 as prerequisites. It is the day-by-day, moment-by-moment management of your time.

The Time Management Matrix is diagrammed on the following page. Urgent means it requires immediate attention, and important has to do with results that contribute to your mission, goals, and values. Effective, proactive people spend most of their time in Quadrant II, thereby reducing the time spent in Quadrant I. Four activities are necessary to be effective. First, write down your key roles for the week (such as research manager, United Way chairperson, and parent). Second, list your objectives for each role using many Quadrant II activities. These objectives should be tied to your personal goals or

Time Management Matrix*

	Urgent	Not Urgent
Important	**I** Crises, fire-fighting Pressing problems Deadline driven projects	**II** Prevention, PC Relationship building Recognizing new opportunities Planning, recreation
Not Important	**III** Interruptions, pressing matters Some mail, calls, reports Some meetings, proximate Popular activities	**IV** Trivia, busy work Time wasters Pleasant activities

philosophy developed in Habit 2. Third, schedule time to complete the objectives. Fourth, adapt the weekly schedule to your daily activities.

Habit 4: Think Win-Win*

Win-Win is a frame of mind and heart that constantly seeks mutual benefit in all human interactions. Both sides come out ahead; in fact, the end result is usually a better way. If Win-Win is not possible, then the alternative is no deal. It takes great courage as well as consideration to create mutual benefits, especially if the other party is thinking Win-Lose.

Win-Win embraces five interdependent dimensions of life—character, relationships, agreements, systems, and processes. Character involves the trains of integrity; maturity, which is a balance between being considerate of others and the courage to express feelings; and abundance mentality, which means that there is plenty out there for everyone. Relationships means that the two parties trust each other and are deeply committed to Win-Win. Agreements require the five elements of desired results, guidelines, resources, accountability, and consequences. Win-Win agreements can only survive in a system that supports it—you can't talk Win-Win and reward Win-Lose. In order to obtain Win-Win, a four-step process is needed: (1) see the problem from the other viewpoint, (2) identify the key issues and concerns, (3) determine acceptable results, and (4) seek possible new options to achieve those results.

Habit 5: Seek First to Understand, Then to Be Understood*

Seek first to understand involves a paradigm shift since we usually try to be understood first. Empathic Listening* is the key to effective communication. It focuses on learning how the other person sees the world, how they feel. The essence of Empathic Listening is not that you agree with someone; it's that you fully, deeply understand that person, emotionally as well as intellectually. Next to physical survival the greatest need of a human being is psychological survival—to be understood, to be affirmed, to be validated, to be appreciated.

The second part of the habit is to be understood. Covey uses three sequentially arranged Greek words—ethos, pathos, and logos. Ethos is your personal credibility or character; pathos is the empathy you have with the other person's communication; and logos is the logic or reasoning part of your presentation.

Habit 6: Synergy*

Synergy means that the whole is greater than the parts. Together, we can accomplish more than any of us can accomplish alone. This can best be exemplified by the musical group The Beatles, who as a group created more music than each individual created after the group broke up. The first five habits build toward Habit 6. It focuses the concept of Win/Win and the skills of empathic communication on tough challenges that bring about new alternatives that did not exist before. Synergy occurs when people abandon their humdrum presentations and Win/Lose mentality and open themselves up to creative cooperation. When there is genuine understanding, people reach solutions that are better than they could have achieved acting alone.

Habit 7: Sharpen the Saw (Renewal)*

Habit 7 is taking time to Sharpen the Saw so it will cut faster. It is personal PC—preserving and enhancing the greatest asset you have, which is you. It's renewing the four dimensions of your nature—physical, spiritual, mental, and social/emotional. All four dimensions of your nature must be used regularly in wise and balanced ways. Renewing the physical dimension means following good nutrition, rest and relaxation, and regular exercise. The spiritual dimension is your commitment to your value system. Renewal comes from prayer, meditation, and spiritual reading. The mental dimension is continuing to develop your intellect through reading, seminars, and writing. These three dimensions require that time be set aside—they are Quadrant II activities. The social and emotional dimensions of our lives are tied together because our emotional life is primarily, but not exclusively, developed out of and manifested in our relationship with others. While this activity does not require time, it does require exercise.

In the 7 habits book, Covey states that correct principles are natural laws and that God, the Creator and Father of us all, is the source of them and also the source of our conscience. He submits that to the degree people live by this inspired conscience, they will grow to fulfill their natures; to the degree that they do not, they will not rise above the animal plane.

Ethics[5]

Ethics is not a precept that is mutually exclusive from quality. Indeed, quality and ethics have a common care premise, which is to do right things right.

Definition

Ethics is a body of principles or standards of human conduct that govern the behavior of individuals and organizations. It is knowing what is the right thing to do and is learned when one is growing up, or at a later date during an organization's ethics training program. Ethics can mean something different to different people, especially given an organization's international workforce and the varying cultural norms. Because individuals have different concepts of what is right, the organization will need to develop the standards or code of ethics for the organization.

The Root Causes of Unethical Behavior

Much of the unethical behavior in organizations occurs when:

1. Organizations favor their own interests above the well-being of their customers, employees, or the public.
2. Organizations reward behavior that violates ethical standards, such as increasing sales through false advertising.
3. Organizations encourage separate standards of behavior at work than at home, such as secrecy and deceit versus honesty.
4. Individuals are willing to abuse their position and power to enhance their interests, such as taking excessive compensation for themselves off the top before other stakeholders receive their fair share.
5. Managerial values exist that undermine integrity, such as the pressure managers exert on employees to cover up mistakes or to do whatever it takes to get the job done, including cutting corners.
6. Organizations and individuals overemphasize the short-term results at the expense of themselves and others in the long run; for example behavior is good based on the degree of utility, pleasure, or good received, regardless of the effect on others.
7. Organizations and managers believe their knowledge is infallible and miscalculate the true risks, such as when financial managers invest organizational funds in high-risk options trading.

---

[5] This section is adapted from Dean L. Bottorff, "How Ethics Can Improve Business Success," *Quality Progress* (February 1997): 57–59. © 1997 American Society for Quality. Reprinted with permission.

Tendency toward unethical behavior most likely comes from the interaction of the root causes of pressure, opportunity, and attitude.

Unethical behavior is especially prevalent if employee morale is low. For example, poor working conditions, employee downsizing, unacknowledged good work, and denied promotions can all contribute to an employee's poor attitude.

Ethics Management Program

An ethics management program needs to address pressure, opportunity, and attitude. Managing ethical behavior requires commitment, new policies and procedures, continuous improvement, and investments in appraisal, prevention, and promotion.

The first step is *appraisal*, which is the analysis of the costs associated with unethical behavior. These costs can be divided into the three root causes of pressure, opportunity, and attitude.

- Costs from pressure are those costs from well-intended but unethical decisions made under pressure. They include but are not limited to errors, waste, rework, lost customers, and warranties.

- Costs from opportunity are those costs from intentional wrongdoing. They include but are not limited to theft, overstated expenses, excessive compensation, and nepotism.

- Costs from attitudes are those costs from mistaken beliefs in unethical forms of behavior. They include but are not limited to errors, waste, rework, lost customers, and health care.

In order to obtain these costs, use the information given in the Quality Costs section of Chapter 7.

The second step is *prevention*, which is the development of a system that will minimize the costs. Because management has a good idea of the appraisal costs, this step can proceed concurrently with Step 1.

- Pressure can be addressed by being involved in the development of goals and values and developing policies that allow for individual diversity, dissent, and decision-making input.

- Opportunity can be addressed by developing policies that encourage and protect whistleblowers and require the existence of ombudsmen who can work confidentially with people to solve ethical problems internally.

- Attitude can be addressed by requiring ethics training for all personnel, recognizing ethical conduct in the workplace, requiring performance appraisals to include ethics, and encouraging open discussion concerning ethical behavior issues.

The third step is *promotion*, which is the continuous advertising of ethical behavior in order to develop an ethical organizational culture that is clear, positive, and effective.

- To be clear the philosophy needs to be written, with input from all personnel, and posted. Standardized ethics training should be given to everyone to: (1) teach them how to clarify ethical issues, (2) encourage them to get the facts before acting, (3) encourage them to consider all the consequences before acting, and (4) show them how to test their actions in advance. This testing can be accomplished by asking (1) Is it legal? (2) Is it right? (3) Is it beneficial for all involved? and (4) How would I feel if it was published on the front page of the newspaper?
- To be positive, the culture should be about doing what is right, encouraging principled organizational dissent, and rewarding ethical behavior.
- To be effective, the philosophy must be set and adopted by senior management, with input from all personnel. Senior management should act as they would want others to act and make no exceptions.

Final Comment

Quality is dependent on ethical behavior. Doing what is right in the first place is a proven way to reduce costs, improve competitiveness, and create customer satisfaction. Many companies are hiring ethics consultants to help them achieve their goals.

Unethical behavior by Enron and Worldcom executives in 2002 resulted in bankruptcy for those companies.

The Deming Philosophy[6]

Deming's philosophy is given in his 14 points. Most of these points were given in a seminar for 21 Presidents of leading Japanese industry in 1950. The rest were developed and the original ones modified over a period of three decades.

1. Create and Publish the Aims and Purposes of the Organization

Management must demonstrate constantly their commitment to this statement. It must include investors, customers, suppliers, employees, the community, and a quality philosophy. The statement is a forever-changing document that requires input from everyone. Organizations must develop a long-term view of at least ten years and

---

[6] Adapted from *Out of the Crisis* by W. Edwards Deming by permission of MIT and the W. Edwards Deming Institute. Published by MIT, Center for Advanced Engineering Study, Cambridge, MA 02139. Copyright 1986 by W. Edwards Deming.

plan to stay in business by setting long-range goals. Resources must be allocated for research, training, and continuing education to achieve the goals. Innovation is promoted to ensure that the product or service does not become obsolete. A family organizational philosophy is developed to send the message that everyone is part of the organization.

2. Learn the New Philosophy

Top management and everyone must learn the new philosophy. Organizations must seek never-ending improvement and refuse to accept nonconformance. Customer satisfaction is the number one priority, because dissatisfied customers will not continue to purchase nonconforming products and services. The organization must concentrate on defect prevention rather than defect detection. By improving the process, the quality and productivity will improve. Everyone in the organization, including the union, must be involved in the quality journey and change his or her attitude about quality. The supplier must be helped to improve quality by requiring statistical evidence of conformance and shared information relative to customer expectations.

3. Understand the Purpose of Inspection

Management must understand that the purpose of inspection is to improve the process and reduce its cost. For the most part, mass inspection is costly and unreliable. Where appropriate, it should be replaced by never-ending improvement using statistical techniques. Statistical evidence is required of self and supplier. Every effort should be made to reduce and then eliminate acceptance sampling. Mass inspection is managing for failure and defect prevention is managing for success.

4. Stop Awarding Business Based on Price Alone

The organization must stop awarding business based on the low bid, because price has no meaning without quality. The goal is to have single suppliers for each item to develop a long-term relationship of loyalty and trust, thereby providing improved products and services. Purchasing agents must be trained in statistical process control and require it from suppliers. They must follow the materials throughout the entire life cycle in order to examine how customer expectations are affected and provide feedback to the supplier regarding the quality.

5. Improve Constantly and Forever the System

Management must take more responsibility for problems by actively finding and correcting problems so that quality and productivity are continually and permanently improved and costs are reduced. The focus is on preventing problems before they happen. Variation is expected, but there must be a continual striving for its reduction using control charts. Responsibilities are assigned to teams to remove the causes of problems and continually improve the process.

6. Institute Training

Each employee must be oriented to the organization's philosophy of commitment to never-ending improvements. Management must allocate resources to train employees to perform their jobs in the best manner possible. Everyone should be trained in statistical methods, and these methods should be used to monitor the need for further training.

7. Teach and Institute Leadership

Improving supervision is management's responsibility. They must provide supervisors with training in statistical methods and these 14 points so the new philosophy can be implemented. Instead of focusing on a negative, fault-finding atmosphere, supervisors should create a positive, supportive one where pride in workmanship can flourish. All communication must be clear from top management to supervisors to operators.

8. Drive Out Fear, Create Trust, and Create a Climate for Innovation

Management must encourage open, effective communication and teamwork. Fear is caused by a general feeling of being powerless to control important aspects of one's life. It is caused by a lack of job security, possible physical harm, performance appraisals, ignorance of organization goals, poor supervision, and not knowing the job. Driving fear out of the workplace involves managing for success. Management can begin by providing workers with adequate training, good supervision, and proper tools to do the job, as well as removing physical dangers. When people are treated with dignity, fear can be eliminated and people will work for the general good of the organization. In this climate, they will provide ideas for improvement.

9. Optimize the Efforts of Teams, Groups, and Staff Areas

Management must optimize the efforts of teams, work groups, and staff areas to achieve the aims and purposes of the organization. Barriers exist internally among levels of management, among departments, within departments, and among shifts. Externally, they exist between the organization and its customers and suppliers. These barriers exist because of poor communication, ignorance of the organization's mission, competition, fear, and personal grudges or jealousies. To break down the barriers, management will need a long-term perspective. All the different areas must work together. Attitudes need to be changed; communication channels opened; project teams organized; and training in teamwork implemented. Multifunctional teams, such as used in concurrent engineering, are an excellent method.

10. Eliminate Exhortations for the Work Force

Exhortations that ask for increased productivity without providing specific improvement methods can handicap an organization. They do nothing but express management's desires. They do not produce a better product or service, because the workers are limited by the system. Goals should be set that are achievable and are committed to the long-term success of the organization. Improvements in the process cannot be made unless the tools and methods are available.

11a. Eliminate Numerical Quotas for the Work Force

Instead of quotas, management must learn and institute methods for improvement. Quotas and work standards focus on quantity rather than quality. They encourage poor workmanship in order to meet their quotas. Quotas should be replaced with statistical methods of process control. Management must provide and implement a strategy for never-ending improvements and work with the work force to reflect the new policies.

11b. Eliminate Management by Objective

Instead of management by objective, management must learn the capabilities of the processes and how to improve them. Internal goals set by management, without a method, are a burlesque. Management by numerical goal is an attempt to manage without knowledge of what to do. An excellent analysis supporting this point is given by Castellano and Roehm.[7]

12. Remove Barriers That Rob People of Pride of Workmanship

Loss of pride in workmanship exists throughout organizations because (1) workers do not know how to relate to the organization's mission, (2) they are being blamed for system problems, (3) poor designs lead to the production of "junk," (4) inadequate training is provided, (5) punitive supervision exists, and (6) inadequate or ineffective equipment is provided for performing the required work. Restoring pride will require a long-term commitment by management. When workers are proud of their work, they will grow to the fullest extent of their job. Management must give employees operational job descriptions, provide the proper tools and materials, and stress the workers' understanding of their role in the total process. By restoring pride, everyone in the organization will be working for the common good. A barrier for people on salary is the annual rating of performance.

13. Encourage Education and Self-Improvement for Everyone

What an organization needs is people who are improving with education. A long-term commitment to continuously train and educate people must be made by management. Deming's 14 points and the organization's mission should be the foundation of the edu-

---

[7] Joseph F. Castellano and Harper A. Roehm, "The Problems With Managing By Objectives and Results." *Quality Progress* (March 2001): 39–46.

cation program. Everyone should be retrained as the organization requirements change to meet the changing environment.

14. Take Action to Accomplish the Transformation

Management has to accept the primary responsibility for the never-ending improvement of the process. It has to create a corporate structure to implement the philosophy. A cultural change is required from the previous "business as usual" attitude. Management must be committed, involved, and accessible if the organization is to succeed in implementing the new philosophy. Hillerich & Bradsby Co., the makers of the Louisville Slugger baseball bat, have used Deming's 14 points since 1985 and now have 70% of the professional baseball bat market.[8]

Role of TQM Leaders

Everyone is responsible for quality, especially senior management and the CEO; however, only the latter can provide the leadership system to achieve results. For instance, in the 1980's, General Electric's CEO, Jack Welch, instituted leadership training courses at all levels of the organization. The General Electric training courses taught leadership approaches and models and provided the opportunity for teams to develop solutions to real business problems. Many of the solutions the teams developed were implemented. Jack Welch supported the development of a leadership system whereby quality control leaders were developed at all levels in all functions of the organization, including research, marketing, manufacturing, sales, finance, and human resources. Senior managers need to be provided with the skills to implement quality control techniques and actively participate in the quality council.

Senior management has numerous responsibilities. Senior management must practice the philosophy of Management by Wandering Around (MBWA). Management should get out of the office and visit customers, suppliers, departments within the organization, and plants within the organization. That way, managers learn what is happening with a particular customer, supplier, or project. MBWA can substantially reduce paperwork. Encourage subordinates to write only important messages that need to be part of the permanent record. For example, Kinko's executives perform normal operating duties for two or three days at one location. This approach is an excellent technique for gaining firsthand information.

The idea is to let employees think for themselves. Senior management's role is no longer to make the final decision, but to make sure the team's decision is aligned with the quality statements of the organization. Push problem solving and decision making to the lowest appropriate level by delegating authority and responsibility.

---

[8] March L. Jacques, "Big League Quality," *Quality Progress* (August 2001): 27–34.

Senior managers must stay informed on the topic of quality improvement by reading books and articles, attending seminars, and talking to other TQM leaders. The leader sends a strong message to subordinates when that leader asks if they have read a particular book or article.

The needed resources must be provided to train employees in the TQM tools and techniques, the technical requirements of the job, and safety. Resources in the form of the appropriate equipment to do the job must also be provided.

Senior managers must find time to celebrate the success of their organization's quality efforts by personally participating in award and recognition ceremonies. This activity is an excellent opportunity to reinforce the importance of the effort and to promote TQM. A phone call or handshake combined with a sincere "thank you for a job well done" is a powerful form of recognition and reward. One of the duties of the quality council is to establish or revise the recognition and reward system. In particular, senior management's incentive compensation must include quality improvement performance. Also, provisions must be made to reward teams as well as creative individuals.

Senior managers must be visibly and actively engaged in the quality effort by serving on teams, coaching teams, and teaching seminars. They should lead by demonstrating, communicating, and reinforcing the quality statements. As a rule of thumb, they should spend about one-third of their time on quality.

A very important role of senior managers is listening to internal and external customers and suppliers through visits, focus groups, and surveys. This information is translated into core values and process improvement projects.

Another very important role is communication. The objective is to create awareness of the importance of TQM and provide TQM results in an ongoing manner. The TQM message must be "sold" to personnel, for if they don't buy it, TQM will never happen. In addition to internal efforts, there must be external activities with customers and suppliers, the media, advertising in trade magazines, and interaction with the quality community.

By following the preceding suggestions, senior managers should be able to drive fear out of the organization, break down barriers, remove system roadblocks, anticipate and minimize resistance to change, and, in general, change the culture. Only with the involvement of senior management can TQM be a success.

Implementation

The TQM implementation process begins with senior management and, most important, the CEO's commitment. The importance of the senior management role cannot be overstated. Leadership is essential during every phase of the implementation process and particularly at the start. In fact, indifference and lack of involvement by senior management are frequently cited as the principal reasons for the failure of quality improvement efforts. Delegation and rhetoric are insufficient—involvement is required.

Senior management needs to be educated in the TQM concepts. In addition to formal education, managers should visit successful TQM organizations, read selected articles and books, and attend seminars and conferences. The next step is for senior management to develop an implementation plan.

Timing of the implementation process can be very important. Is the organization ready to embark on the total quality journey? There may be some foreseeable problems, such as a reorganization, change in senior management personnel, interpersonal conflicts, a current crisis, or a time-consuming activity. These problems may postpone implementation to a more favorable time.

The next step is the formation of the quality council. Initiation of these duties is a substantial part of the implementation of TQM. The development of core values, a vision statement, a mission statement, and a quality policy statement, with input from all personnel, should be completed first.

The active involvement of middle managers and first-line supervisors is essential to the success of the TQM effort. They are accountable for achieving many of the organization's performance goals and objectives, and they form enduring links in the communication chain from senior management to the front-line workers. Without middle management's early and active support, the TQM effort could fail. Senior management needs to ensure that managers at all levels have an opportunity, as soon as possible, to develop ownership in the TQM effort and a chance to acquire the insight and skills necessary to become leaders. One way to accomplish this concept is to have a retreat. The retreat will focus on TQM training, leadership skills, and active involvement in the development of the organization's statements.

If there is a union, there should be early discussions with the representatives on TQM. Managers should involve union leaders by sharing with them implementation plans for TQM. As the quality effort progresses, managers and union leaders should work together on quality improvement activities. For example, the United Auto Workers have worked closely with the big three automakers in their TQM activities.

At this stage of the implementation process, it is important to communicate TQM to the entire organization. Communication is important throughout the implementation stage. Communication is necessary to create TQM awareness, interest, desire, and action.

Everyone needs to be trained in quality awareness and problem solving. This training is conducted when the employee is placed on a project team or the work group is ready for the training.

Customer, employee, and supplier surveys must be conducted to benchmark the attitudes of these three stakeholders. Information from these surveys provides ideas for quality improvement projects. The quality council determines the quality improvement projects. In addition the council establishes the project teams and work groups and monitors their progress. The organization has to be patient and not rush the teams for solutions that don't eliminate the root causes. There is often a tendency to rush the implementation process. TECSTAR, a small business, was able to achieve savings of more than $3 million the first year of its TQM program. On the other hand, Karlee, a Malcolm Baldrige

National Quality Award winner, did not achieve results until the third year, but then there was more than a 300% increase in the organization's bottom line.[9]

Quality Council

In order to build quality into the culture, a quality council is established to provide overall direction. It is the driver for the TQM engine.

In a typical organization the council is composed of the chief executive officer (CEO); the senior managers of the functional areas, such as design, marketing, finance, production, and quality; and a coordinator or consultant. If there is a union, consideration should be given to having a representative on the council. Some organizations, such as Friendly Ice Cream of Wilbaham, MA, include front-line representatives from every area. A coordinator is necessary to assume some of the added duties that a quality improvement activity requires. The individual selected for the coordinator's position should be a bright young person with executive potential. That person will report to the CEO.

The responsibility of the coordinator is to build two-way trust, propose team needs to the council, share council expectations with the team, and brief the council on team progress. In addition, the coordinator will ensure that the teams are empowered and know their responsibilities. The coordinator's activities are to assist the team leaders, share lessons learned among teams, and have regular leaders' meetings.

In smaller organizations where managers may be responsible for more than one functional area, the number of members will be smaller. Also, a consultant would most likely be employed rather than a coordinator.

In general, the duties of the quality council are to:

1. Develop, with input from all personnel, the core values, vision statement, mission statement, and quality policy statement.
2. Develop the strategic long-term plan with goals and the annual quality improvement program with objectives.
3. Create the total education and training plan (see Chapter 4).
4. Determine and continually monitor the cost of poor quality (see Chapter 7).
5. Determine the performance measures for the organization, approve those for the functional areas, and monitor them (see Chapter 7).
6. Continually determine those projects that improve the processes, particularly those that affect external and internal customer satisfaction (see Chapter 5).
7. Establish multifunctional project and departmental or work group teams and monitor their progress (see Chapter 4).

---

[9] Laura Struebing and Leigh Ann Klaus, "Small Businesses Thinking Big," *Quality Progress* (February 1997): 23–27.

8. Establish or revise the recognition and reward system to account for the new way of doing business (see Chapter 4).

\ In large organizations, quality councils are also established at lower levels of the corporation. Their duties are similar but relate to that particular level in the organization.\ Initially these activities will require additional work by council members; however, in the long term, their jobs will be easier. These councils are the instruments for perpetuating the idea of never-ending quality improvement.

Once the TQM program is well established, a typical meeting agenda might have the following items:

Progress report on teams.

Customer satisfaction report.

Progress on meeting goals.

New project teams.

Recognition dinner.

Benchmarking report.

Eventually, within three to five years, the quality council activities will become so ingrained in the culture of the organization that they will become a regular part of the executive meetings. When this state is achieved, a separate quality council is no longer needed. Quality becomes the first item on the executive meeting agenda.

Corning's Telecommunications Products Division's (TPD) leadership system or quality council duties is shown in Figure 2-1.

Core Values, Concepts, and Framework

Unity of purpose is key to a leadership system. Core values and concepts provide that unity of purpose. The core values and concepts enable a framework for leaders throughout the organization to make right decisions. They foster TQM behavior and define the culture. Each organization will need to develop its own values. Given here are the core values, concepts, and framework for the Malcolm Baldrige National Quality Award. They can be used as a starting point for any organization as it develops its own.

Visionary Leadership

An organization's senior leaders need to set directions and create a customer orientation, clear and visible quality values, and high expectations. Values, directions, and expectations need to address all stakeholders. The leaders need to ensure the creation of strategies, systems, and methods for achieving excellence. Strategies and values should help

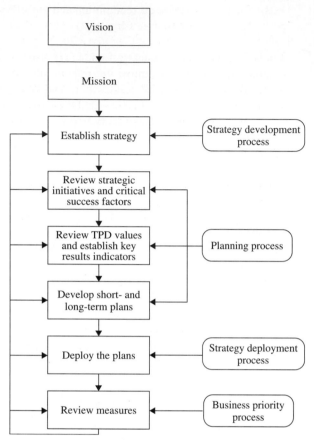

Figure 2-1 Corning TPD's Leadership System
Reproduced, with permission, from Karen Bemowski, "The Journey Might Wander a Bit . . ., But Baldrige Award Winners Armstrong and Corning Find Out that Its Worth It," *Quality Progress* (May 1996): 33–42.

guide all activities and decisions of the organization. The senior leaders must commit to the development of the entire workforce and should encourage participation, learning, innovation, and creativity by all employees. Through their personal roles in planning, communications, review or organization performance, and employee recognition, the senior leaders serve as role models, reinforcing the values and expectations, and building leadership and initiative throughout the organization.

Customer-Driven Excellence

Quality is judged by customers. All product and service characteristics that contribute value to the customer and lead to customer satisfaction, preference, and retention must be the focus of an organization's management system. Customer-driven excellence has both current and future components: understanding today's customer desires and marketplace offerings as well as future innovations. Value and satisfaction may be influenced by many factors throughout the customer's overall purchase, ownership, and service experiences. These factors include the organization's relationship with customers that helps build trust, confidence, and loyalty. This concept of quality includes not only the product and service characteristics that meet basic customer requirements, but it also includes those features and characteristics that differentiate them from competing offerings. Such differentiation may be based upon new or modified offerings, combinations of product and service offerings, customization of offering, rapid response, or special relationships.

Customer-driven quality is thus a strategic concept. It is directed toward customer retention, market-share gain, and growth. It demands constant sensitivity to changing and emerging customer and market requirements and the factors that drive customer satisfaction and retention. It also demands awareness of developments in technology and of competitors' offerings, and rapid and flexible responses to customer and market requirements.

Success requires more than defect and error reduction, merely meeting specifications, or reducing complaints. Nevertheless, defect and error reduction and the elimination of causes of dissatisfaction contribute to the customers' view of quality, and they are important parts of customer-driven quality. In addition, the organization's success in recovering from defects and errors (making things right for the customer) is crucial to building customer relationships and to retaining customers.

Organizational and Personal Learning

Achieving the highest levels of performance requires a well-executed approach to organizational and personal learning. Organizational learning refers to both continuous improvement of existing approaches and adaptation to change, leading to new goals and approaches. Learning needs to be embedded in the way the organization functions. Learning must be (1) a required part of the daily work; (2) practiced at personal and organizational levels; (3) directed at solving problems; (4) focused on sharing knowledge throughout the organization; and (5) driven by opportunities to effect significant change and to do better. Sources for learning include employees' ideas, research and development (R & D), customers' input, best practice sharing, and benchmarking.

Organizational learning can result in (1) enhancing value to customers through new and improved products and services; (2) developing new opportunities; (3) reducing errors, defects, waste, and related costs; (4) improving responsiveness and cycle time performance; (5) increasing productivity and effectiveness in the use of all resources; and (6) enhancing your organization's performance in fulfilling its public responsibilities and service as a good citizen.

Employees' success depends increasingly on having opportunities for personal learning and practicing new skills. Organizations invest in employees' personal learning through education, training, and other opportunities for continuing growth, such as job rotation. On-the-job training offers a cost-effective way to train and to better link training to your organizational needs and priorities.

Personal learning can result in (1) more satisfied and versatile employees who stay with the organization, (2) organizational cross-functional learning, and (3) an improved environment for innovation. Thus, learning is directed not only toward better products and services but also toward being more responsive, adaptive, and efficient—giving your organization marketplace sustainability and performance advantages.

Valuing Employees and Partners

An organization's success depends increasingly upon the skills, knowledge, creativity, and motivation of its employees and partners. Valuing employees means committing to their satisfaction, development, and well-being. Increasingly, this involves more flexible, high-performance work practices tailored to employees with diverse workplace and home life needs. Major challenges in the area of valuing employees include (1) demonstrating your leaders' commitment to your employees' success, (2) recognition that goes beyond the regular compensation system, (3) development and progression within your organization, (4) sharing your organization's knowledge so your employees can better serve your customers and contribute to achieving your strategic objectives, and (5) creating an environment that encourages risk-taking. For example, Southwest Airlines always puts customers second, and employees first. Southwest lives up to its promises to employees, so there is no sense of betrayal to keep people from enthusiastically contributing. It refuses to lay off employees even when airline workers are laid off industry wide. Southwest has the most productive workforce servicing twice the number of passengers per employee of any other airline.

Organizations need to build internal and external partnerships to better accomplish overall goals. Internal partnerships might involve creating network relationships among your work units to improve flexibility, responsiveness, and knowledge sharing. External partnerships might be with customers, suppliers, and education organizations. Strategic partnerships or alliances are increasingly important. Such partnerships might offer entry into new markets or a basis for new products or services. Also, partnerships might permit the blending of your organization's core competencies or leadership capabilities with the complementary strengths and capabilities of partners. For instance, because of Southwest Airlines' spirit of cooperation with co-workers, they requested three advertising companies to work together to develop Southwest's marketing campaign.

Successful internal and external partnerships develop longer-term objectives, thereby creating a basis for mutual investments and respect. Partners should address the key requirements for success, means for regular communication, approaches to evaluating progress, and means for adapting to changing conditions. In some cases, joint education and training could offer a cost-effective method for employee development.

Agility

Success in global markets demands agility. All aspects of e-commerce require and enable more rapid, flexible, and customized responses. Organizations face ever-shorter cycles for the introduction of new and improved products and services, as well as for faster and more flexible response to customers. Major improvements in response time often require simplification of work units and processes and the ability for rapid changeover from one process to another. Cross-trained and empowered employees are vital assets in such a demanding environment.

A major success factor in meeting competitive challenges is the design-to-introduction cycle time. To meet the demands of rapidly changing markets, organizations need to carry out stage-to-stage integration, such as concurrent engineering of activities, from the research concept to commercialization.

All aspects of time performance are critical, and cycle time has become a key process measure. Time improvements often drive simultaneous improvements in organization, quality, cost, and productivity. For example, Southwest Airlines reduced each plane's time at the terminal to ten minutes after a court ruling forced Southwest to sell one of its four planes. The ten-minute turn allowed Southwest to continue its four plane schedule with only three planes and also helped the company achieve the best on-time performance in the airline industry. One less plane translates into a 25% reduction in operating expenses.

Focus on the Future

Focus on the future requires understanding the short- and long-term factors that affect an organization and the marketplace. Pursuit of sustainable growth and market leadership requires a strong future orientation and a willingness to make long-term commitments to key stakeholders. An organization's planning should anticipate many factors, such as customers' expectations, new business and partnering opportunities, the increasingly global marketplace, technological developments, the evolving e-commerce environment, new customer and market segments, evolving regulatory requirements, societal expectations, and strategic moves by competitors. Strategic objectives and resource allocations need to accommodate these influences. A focus on the future includes developing employees and suppliers, creating opportunities for innovation, and anticipating public responsibilities.

Managing for Innovation

Innovation means making meaningful change to improve an organization's products, services, and processes and to create new value for the organization's stakeholders. Innovation should lead an organization to new dimensions of performance. Innovation is no longer strictly the purview of research and development departments; innovation is important for all aspects of your business and all processes. Organizations should be led and managed so that innovation becomes part of the culture and is integrated into daily work.

Management by Fact

Organizations depend on the measurement and analysis of performance. Such measurements should derive from business needs and strategy, and they should provide critical data and information about key processes, outputs, and results. Many types of data and information are needed for performance management. Performance measurement should include customer, product, and service performance; comparisons of operational, market, and competitive performance; and supplier, employee, and cost and financial performance.

Analysis refers to extracting larger meaning from data and information to support evaluation, decision making, and operational improvement. Analysis entails using data to determine trends, projections, and cause and effect relationships that might not otherwise be evident. Analysis supports a variety of purposes, such as planning, reviewing overall performance, improving operations, change management, and comparing your performance with competitors' or with "best practices" benchmarks.

A major consideration in performance improvement and change management involves the selection and use of performance measures or indicators. *A comprehensive set of measures or indicators tied to customer and/or organizational performance requirements represents a clear basis for aligning all activities with your organization's goals.* Through the analysis of data, measures or indicators themselves may be evaluated and changed to better support an organization's goals.

Public Responsibility and Citizenship

An organization's leaders should stress the need to practice good citizenship. Basic expectations to adhere to business ethics and protection of public health, safety, and the environment should be maintained. Protection of health, safety, and the environment includes an organization's operations, as well as the life cycles of products and services. Also, organizations should emphasize resource conservation and waste reduction at the source. Planning should anticipate adverse impacts from production, distribution, transportation, use, and disposal of products. Effective planning should prevent problems, provide for a forthright response if problems occur, and make available information and support needed to maintain public awareness, safety, and confidence.

For many organizations, the product design stage is critical. Effective design strategies should anticipate growing environmental concerns and responsibilities. Organizations should not only meet all local, state, and federal laws and regulatory requirements, but they should treat these and related requirements as opportunities for improvement "beyond mere compliance."

Practicing good citizenship refers to leadership and support—within the limits of an organization's resources—of publicly important purposes. Leadership as a corporate citizen also entails influencing other organizations. For example, an organization might lead or participate in efforts to help define the obligations of its industry to its communities.

Focus on Results and Creating Value

An organization's performance measurements need to focus on key results. Results should be used to create and balance value for your key stakeholders—customers, employees, stockholders, suppliers and partners, the public, and the community. By creating value for key stakeholders, an organization builds loyalty and contributes to growing the economy. To meet the sometimes conflicting and changing aims that balancing value implies, organizational strategy should explicitly include key stakeholder requirements. This will help ensure that actions and plans meet differing stakeholder needs and avoid adverse impacts on any stakeholders. The use of a balanced composite of leading and lagging performance measures offers an effective means to communicate short- and long-term priorities, monitor actual performance, and provide a clear basis for improving results.

Systems Perspective

The Baldrige Criteria provide a systems perspective for managing an organization to achieve performance excellence. The Core Values form the building blocks and the integrating mechanism for the system. However, successful management of overall performance requires organization-specific synthesis and alignment. Synthesis means looking at an organization as a whole and builds upon key business requirements, including strategic objectives and action plans. Alignment means using the key linkages among requirements given in the Baldrige Categories, including the key measures/indicators.

Alignment includes senior leaders' focus on strategic directions and on customers. It means that senior leaders monitor, respond to, and manage performance based on business results. Alignment includes using measures/indicators to link key strategies with key processes and align resources to improve overall performance and satisfy customers.

Thus, a systems perspective means managing the whole organization, as well as its components, to achieve success.

Quality Statements

In addition to the core values and concepts, the quality statements include the vision statement, mission statement, and quality policy statement. Once developed, they are only occasionally reviewed and updated. They are part of the strategic planning process. The utilization of the three statements varies considerably from organization to organization. In fact, small organizations may use only the quality policy statement. Additionally, there may be considerable overlap among the statements. One of the common characteristics of Malcolm Baldrige National Quality Award winners is that all have a vision of what quality is and how to attain it.

Vision Statement

The vision statement is a short declaration of what an organization aspires to be tomorrow. It is the ideal state that might never be reached but which you continually strive to achieve. Successful visions are timeless, inspirational, and become deeply shared within the organization, such as IBM's service, Apple's computing for the masses, Disney theme park's the happiest place on earth, and Polaroid's instant photography.[10] These shared visions usually emerge over time. Ideally, visions are elevated to a cause.

Successful visions provide a succinct guideline for decision-making. Having a concise statement of the desired end provides criteria for sound decision making. Tim Frye of Motorola, Inc. once remarked that he used the company's vision statement when faced with difficult decisions in gray areas that were not covered by company policy.[11] It is important that the leader articulate and act upon the vision and that employees understand the vision and can connect their work with the well-being of the organization. One way to reinforce the significance of the vision statement is to include it (or a portion of it) on employee badges.

An example of a simple, one-sentence vision statement is

We will be the preferred provider of safe, reliable, and cost-effective products and services that satisfy the electric-related needs of all customer segments.

FLORIDA POWER & LIGHT COMPANY

An example of a more elaborate vision statement is

Customers receive what they order without nonconformities, on time in the right quantity, shipped and billed on time.

Suppliers meet our requirements.

Salespeople determine customer needs.

New products or processes are developed to agreed upon requirements, as scheduled, and at lower costs.

People enjoy their work.

The organization makes a profit.

THE AUTHORS

---

[10] Arthur R. Tenner and Irving J. DeToco, *Total Quality Management* (New York: Addison-Wesley, 1992).

[11] John R. Latham, "Visioning: The Concept Trilogy and Process," *Quality Progress* (April 1995): 65–68.

Mission Statement

The mission statement answers the following questions: who we are, who are the customers, what we do, and how we do it. This statement is usually one paragraph or less in length, is easy to understand, and describes the function of the organization. It provides a clear statement of purpose for employees, customers, and suppliers.

An example of a mission statement is

Ford Motor Company is a worldwide leader in automatic and automotive-related products and services as well as the newer industries such as aerospace, communications, and financial services. Our mission is to improve continually our products and services to meet our customers' needs, allowing us to prosper as a business and to provide a reasonable return to our shareholders, the owners of our business.

FORD MOTOR COMPANY

A simpler mission statement is

To meet customers' transportation and distribution needs by being the best at moving their goods on time, safely and damage free.

CANADIAN NATIONAL RAILWAYS

The last statement defined the activities as transportation and distribution rather than as a railroad. Therefore, Canadian National Railways can operate barges, containerized shipments, trucks, aircraft, and ocean-going vessels.

Quality Policy Statement

The quality policy is a guide for everyone in the organization as to how they should provide products and service to the customers. It should be written by the CEO with feedback from the work force and be approved by the quality council. Common characteristics are

Quality is first among equals.

Meet the needs of the internal and external customers.

Equal or exceed the competition.

Continually improve the quality.

Include business and production practices.

Utilize the entire work force.

A quality policy is a requirement of ISO/QS 9000.

A simple quality policy is

Xerox is a quality company. Quality is the basic business principle for Xerox. Quality means providing our external and internal customers with innovative products and services that fully satisfy their requirements. Quality is the job of every employee.

XEROX CORPORATION

A more elaborate quality policy statement is

E. M. Wiegmann is committed to on-time, error-free delivery of products and services, that meet customer expectations 100% of the time. We believe quality is listening carefully to both our employees and our customers, establishing a clear understanding of the requirements before doing anything, and then doing what we have agreed to do, exactly. Quality comes first, profits will follow. A commitment to Total Quality is the best way to ensure a profitable future. Total Quality is a journey rather than a goal. It is a continuous improvement organization.

E. M. WIEGMANN

In summary, the quality statements consist of the core values and concepts given in a previous section, the vision statement, the mission statement, and the quality policy statement. The core values and concepts should be condensed considerably for simplicity and publication.

An example of a statement that includes vision, mission, quality policy, and core values is

Geon has a clear corporate vision . . . To be the benchmark company in the polymers industry through superior performance, demonstrated by:

- Living up to its established principles of excellence in environmental protection, health and safety
- Fully satisfying the expectations of its customers
- Developing and commercializing innovative polymer technology
- Utilizing all resources productively
- Continually improving processes and products
- Generating sustained value for customers, employees, suppliers and investors
- Creating an environment of Trust, Respect, Openness and Integrity

THE GEON COMPANY

Strategic Planning

Many organizations are finding that strategic quality plans and business plans are inseparable. For instance, at Corning, the 1995 Malcolm Baldrige National Quality Award winner, if you ask them to show you their quality strategy, they will show you their business strategy; if you ask them to show you their quality plans, they will show you their business plans. In fact, the term quality is not used too much. The time horizon for strategic planning is for three to ten years, and short-term planning is for one year or less.

Goals and Objectives

Goals and objectives have basically the same meaning. However, it is possible to differentiate between the two by using goals for long-term planning and objectives for short-term planning. The goal is to win the war; the objective is to capture the bridge.

Concrete goals are needed to provide a focus, such as improve customer satisfaction, employee satisfaction, and processes. Goals can force changes in leadership style from reward and punishment to identifying and improving system problems.[12]

Goals must be based on statistical evidence. Without statistical knowledge of the system, goals merely reflect the assumption that slogans, exhortations, and hard work will miraculously change the system. Goals must be definitive, specific, and understandable, using concrete results rather than behaviors or attitudes. The most important characteristic of goals is that they be measurable. Only measurable goals can be evaluated.

Goals must have a plan or method with resources for its achievement. If there is not a cause-and-effect relationship between the goals and the method, then the goal is not a valid one. In addition, a specific timeframe or deadline for achieving the goal should be given.

Goals must be challenging yet achievable. Those individuals, work groups, departments, and functional areas that are affected by the goals should be involved in their development. Stretch goals are satisfactory, provided they are based on benchmark data.[13]

The characteristics of objectives are identical to those given here for goals. They are operational approaches to attain the goals.

Seven Steps to Strategic Planning[14]

There are seven basic steps to strategic quality planning. The process starts with the principle that quality and customer satisfaction are the center of an organization's future. It brings together all the key stakeholders.

1. *Customer Needs.* The first step is to discover the future needs of the customers. Who will they be? Will your customer base change? What will they want? How will the organization meet and exceed expectations?

---

[12] George P. Bohan, "Focus the Strategy to Achieve Results," *Quality Progress* (July 1995): 89–92.

[13] Adapted from John Pessico Jr. and Gary N. McLean, "Manage With Valid Rather Than Invalid Goals," *Quality Progress* (April 1994): 49–56.

[14] Adapted, with permission, from John R. Dew, "Seven Steps To Strategic Planning," *Quality Digest* (June 1994): 34–37.

2. *Customer Positioning.* Next, the planners determine where the organization wants to be in relation to the customers. Do they want to retain, reduce, or expand the customer base? Products or services with poor quality performance should be targeted for breakthrough or eliminated. The organization needs to concentrate its efforts on areas of excellence.

3. *Predict the Future.* Next, the planners must look into their crystal balls to predict future conditions that will affect their product or service. Demographics, economic forecasts, and technical assessments or projections are tools that help predict the future. More than one organization's product or service has become obsolete because it failed to foresee the changing technology. Note that the rate of change is continually increasing.

4. *Gap Analysis.* This step requires the planners to identify the gaps between the current state and the future state of the organization. An analysis of the core values and concepts, given earlier in the chapter, is an excellent technique for pinpointing gaps.

5. *Closing the Gap.* The plan can now be developed to close the gap by establishing goals and responsibilities. All stakeholders should be included in the development of the plan.

6. *Alignment.* As the plan is developed, it must be aligned with the mission, vision, and core values and concepts of the organization. Without this alignment, the plan will have little chance of success.

7. *Implementation.* This last step is frequently the most difficult. Resources must be allocated to collecting data, designing changes, and overcoming resistance to change. Also part of this step is the monitoring activity to ensure that progress is being made. The planning group should meet at least once a year to assess progress and take any corrective action.

Strategic planning can be performed by any organization. It can be highly effective, allowing organizations to do the right thing at the right time, every time.

Annual Quality Improvement Program

An annual program is developed along with a long-term strategic plan. Some of the strategic items will eventually become part of the annual plan, which will include new short-term items.

In addition to creating the items, the program should develop among all managers, specialists, and operating personnel

A sense of responsibility for active participation in making improvements.

The skills needed to make improvements.

The habit of annual improvements so that each year the organization's quality is significantly better than the previous year's.

As pointed out in the section on goals and objectives, operating personnel should be involved with setting objectives, and management should support them with training, projects, and resources. Employees should be asked for suggestions on what they need to improve their process.

Most likely there will be more quality objectives than available resources for accomplishing them. Therefore, those that have the greatest opportunity for improvement should be used. Many objectives will require multifunctional project teams.

Some organizations have well-structured annual quality improvement programs. In organizations that lack those programs, any improvements must come from the initiative of managers and specialists. It takes a great deal of determination by these people to secure results, because they lack the legitimacy and support that comes from an official, structured program designed by the quality council.

Communications[15]

All organizations communicate with their employees in one manner or another. Communications deliver the organization's values, expectations, and directions; provide information about corporate developments; and allow feedback from all levels. It is very important to keep information flowing back and forth between employees and various levels of management. For instance, managers at different levels communicate messages much in the same way as the head football coach communicates to the assistants who call the plays. The assistants assess what is happening on the field and communicate that back to the head coach, who further directs and motivates.

In order for the communication system to be effective, there must be feedback. The culture must encourage two-way communication so that information flows up the ladder as well as down. Communication barriers in an organization need to be removed. Managers should never tell employees not to talk to upper management and can facilitate communication by walking around to allow feedback from employees. A formal system to communicate employee concerns to the appropriate person can be instituted. Improving quality will be hampered if poor communications impedes the flow of information to and from the employees.

Also, the organization must know what message it wants to communicate and what the goals and consequences of the message are before it concerns itself with the various modes to transmit the message. Much has been spent on extensive media that is bankrupt of a substantive message. Communications must be effective and not just information overload. Communications must be evaluated to determine that the message was understood and changed attitudes and behaviors. Surveys can be conducted periodically

[15] This section is adapted from Laura Rubach and Brad Stratton, "Mixing Mediums Is the Message," *Quality Progress* (June 1995): 23–28. © 1995 American Society for Quality. Reprinted with permission.

to determine if the organization's key messages are being understood and supported by the employees.

The organization must have a consistent, congruent message. If there are mixed or contradictory messages, the result is confusion in the organization. All communication must be clear: from top management to supervisors to operators. Focused messages articulated simply, clearly, and repetitively are key.

The purpose of communications is to influence attitudes and behaviors to achieve goals and objectives. Different communication methods are better for different communication needs. Communication is not just providing information, but using the best communication method to motivate people to act upon the message. The available communication methods should be coordinated in a wise manner, being careful not to entirely circumvent the human element of direct communications with impersonal methods. There are two basic communication techniques—interactive and formal.

Interactive

Perhaps the most effective communication allows for discussions between the employees and their supervisor, not just management talking to employees. The immediate supervisor is in the best position to initiate the transfer of information and create discussions on what needs to be improved, how to do it, and why it needs to be done. Indeed, employees consistently report their preferred source of information is their immediate supervisor. The primary communication tool used by Xerox, The Ritz-Carlton Hotel, IBM, Texas Instruments, and many more is face-to-face communications supplemented by newsletters. Motorola, for instance, uses immediate managers to communicate company goals because they know what the information means to the employees on a daily basis and can best answer questions and address employee concerns and ideas. GTE Directories Corporation's vice president and general managers spent the better part of a year on the road to give employees the opportunity for face-to-face contact with headquarters to learn the companies priorities and goals.

There is no one-way to communicate and all supervisors are not equally effective as communicators. Generally, a supervisor's communication will be successful if the supervisor is honest, clear, and inclusive. Communications training programs can also be helpful.

Managers can communicate one-on-one or in a group setting. The group setting would most likely occur at the beginning of the shift and would cover topics such as quality, productivity, schedule, and cost. Brief organizational information might also be imparted at these settings. Meetings of all employees can be held quarterly. These meetings provide the executives the opportunity to explain the "state of the company" and answer questions from employees. Organizations with a large number of employees may need to take the meeting offsite or have the sessions at a number of sites. Another effective communication technique is to have team meetings. These can occur at an informal breakfast or lunch. Questions and answers usually flow freely in these meetings. Interactive communication also occurs electronically by instant messaging and video conferencing.

Formal

Although face-to-face interaction may be a primary communication method, it is best to supplement it with other communication methods to reinforce the message. Formal communication can occur using the printed page or electronics. The most common printed communications are periodic publications such as e-mail or a weekly newsletter. Graphics in the form of charts and diagrams can be used to enhance e-mail and publications. These publications can reach the employees simultaneously and can be targeted to special groups. In multinational organizations, messages must be tailored for different cultures and languages. The Internet can be used for external communications, and the intranet can be used for internal communications. Posted information on the web allows greater individual freedom to obtain information whenever it is needed.

Large, multi-site organizations have found that satellite television can be an effective medium. These programs can be interactive by allowing questions by telephone or fax during the presentation. The presentation should not be too long, and it should be professionally done. These presentations can be videotaped and replayed at other times for the convenience of the employees.

Video is becoming more and more important, because visual messages are a very powerful way to disseminate information. Videos can be produced by the organization, or commercial tapes can be purchased, such as Juran's videotapes on quality. If the organization decides to produce their own videos, they should be professionally done. People are accustomed to television being flashy and full of excitement. A poorly-produced video can distort or dilute the company's message. Producing video is expensive, so there should be an important business purpose for the use of producing a personalized video for an organization. Scripting the information in a video will ensure that no necessary information is left out and that clarity is enhanced. Regardless of the media used, communication has been effective when the employees know as much about the organization as the CEO.

Decision Making

Making poor decisions is one of the deadliest threats to the success of the organization and to one's career. When they act haphazardly without regard to the values and goals of an organization, people fail. In order to make correct decisions, it is best to use the problem-solving method given in Chapter 5.

Leadership Survey

In order to evaluate a manager's performance, a survey of the manager's workers should be taken periodically. On the following page is a manager performance survey used by Xerox.[16]

TQM Exemplary Organization[17]

Xerox Business Systems (XBS), a 14,000-person division of Xerox Corporation, provides document outsourcing and consulting services to businesses worldwide. Document outsourcing services, such as on-site management of mailrooms and print shops, account for 80 percent of revenues. The remainder is derived from "document solutions" —customized services designed to meet customers' specialized requirements for creating, producing, distributing, and storing paper and digital documents. In 1996, XBS provided services at about 2,300 customer locations in the United States. It also serviced 2,000 accounts in 35 foreign countries. XBS has grown into a $2 billion business in less than five years. Revenues and profits have increased by more than 30 percent annually, and XBS's share of the U.S. document-outsourcing market has grown to 40 percent, nearly three times the share of its nearest competitor.

For virtually every business goal, customer requirement, and improvement target, there is an XBS process, measure, and expected result. The division's Senior Leadership Team achieves this clarity of organizational focus through "managing for results"—an integrated planning and management process that cascades action plans into measurable objectives for each manager, supervisor, and front-line associate. The entire process, the company says, is designed to "align goals from the customer's line of sight to the empowered employee and throughout the entire organization."

Yielding five-year and three-year strategic plans and a one-year operating plan, the process attends to the past, present, and future. To encourage organizational learning, for example, the Senior Leadership Team diagnoses the past year's business results and reassesses business practices. The reviews generate the "vital few"—priorities for process and operational improvements. XBS also develops strategic initiatives based on its understanding of the division's strengths and weaknesses as well as its reading of opportunities and threats. This analysis draws on the division's extensive competitive intelligence, "voice of the customer," and "voice of the market" information systems. Other inputs include benchmarking data and storyboarding scenarios, which help the division to refine future customer requirements, anticipate potential risks and challenges, and quantify the resources and action plans necessary to accomplish strategic

---

[16] *Leadership Through Quality: The Way We Work*, Xerox, pages B6–B7.

[17] Malcolm Baldrige National Quality Award, 1997 Service Category Recipient, NIST/Baldrige Homepage, Internet.

Circle the numeral 1, 2, 3, or 4 for each statement based on your perception of your manager's performance. SA—Strongly agree with the statement; A—Agree with the statement; D—Disagree with the statement; SD—Strongly disagree with the statement.

My manager frequently. . .	SA	A	D	SD
1. provides me with honest feedback on my performance	1	2	3	4
2. encourages me to monitor my own efforts	1	2	3	4
3. encourages me to make suggestions	1	2	3	4
4. provides me with an environment conductive to teamwork	1	2	3	4
5. gives me the information I need to do the job	1	2	3	4
6. clearly defines his/her requirements of me	1	2	3	4
7. acts as a positive role model for Leadership Through Quality	1	2	3	4
8. openly recognizes work well done	1	2	3	4
9. listens to Family Group members before making decisions affecting our area	1	2	3	4
10. makes an effort to solve my work-related problems	1	2	3	4
11. encourages the group to work as a team	1	2	3	4
12. informs our department regularly about the state of the business	1	2	3	4
13. displays an understanding of Xerox objectives and strategic directions	1	2	3	4
14. summarizes progress during meetings to seek understanding	1	2	3	4
15. encourages me to ask questions	1	2	3	4
16. asks questions to ensure understanding	1	2	3	4
17. encourages an environment of openness and trust	1	2	3	4
18. behaves in ways which demonstrate respect for others	1	2	3	4
19. makes an effort to locate and remove barriers that reduce efficiency	1	2	3	4
20. ensures regularly scheduled reviews of progress toward goals	1	2	3	4
21. monitors the quality improvement process	1	2	3	4
22. monitors department progress through competitive benchmarks	1	2	3	4
23. rewards those who clearly use the quality improvement process	1	2	3	4
24. sets of objectives based on customer requirements	1	2	3	4
25. uses the quality improvement process	1	2	3	4
26. uses the problem-solving process to solve problems	1	2	3	4
27. treats Leadership Through Quality as the basic Xerox business principle	1	2	3	4

goals. Strategic planning generates a "strategy contract," priorities for investment, and business partnership plans. These are distilled into a human resources plan, an investment plan, and operational plans for each organizational unit, customer account, and employee.

Through XBS's 10-Step Selling Process, on-site services are customized to meet the unique needs of each account. Dedicated account teams develop "standards of performance" according to customer service priorities. These standards, which XBS pledges to meet through its "total satisfaction guarantee," are formalized in operations handbooks developed specifically for each customer.

In addition to leading its competitors in overall customer satisfaction, the XBS division tops the industry in seven of the ten high motivators of customer satisfaction. Performance in all four key categories of customer requirements continues to improve; average scores in 1996 ranged from 8 to 9 on a 10-point grading scale.

Employee satisfaction has increased from 63 percent in 1993 to 80 percent in 1996, which is significantly higher that the average for a peer group of companies.

Exercises

1. Define leadership.

2. Write a plan to implement TQM in a community college.

3. Working as an individual or in a team of three or more people, evaluate one or more of the following organizations concerning the role of the senior managers.

   (a) Large bank
   (b) Health-care facility
   (c) University academic department
   (d) University nonacademic department
   (e) Large department store
   (f) Grade school
   (g) Manufacturing facility
   (h) Large grocery store

4. Select one or more of Deming's 14 points and describe how you would achieve or implement it.

5. Develop a code of ethics for one of the organizations listed in Exercise 3.

6. Visit one of the organizations given in Exercise 3 and determine if they have a quality council or similar structure.

7. If the organization visited in Exercise 6 has a quality council, describe its composition and duties.

8. Working as an individual or in a team of three or more people, determine the quality statements for one or more of the organizations listed in Exercise 3.

9. Write a strategic planning goal and an annual objective.

10. Working as an individual or in a team of three or four people, write a strategic quality plan for one of the organizations listed in Exercise 3.

11. Working as an individual or in a team of three or four people, write an annual quality improvement program for one of the organizations listed in Exercise 3.

12. Working, as an individual or in a team of three or more people, write a communications plan for a small organization and one for a large organization. How do they differ?

13. Write your personal philosophy or creed.

14. Keep a record of your activities including time for a week. Place them in Covey's four quadrants, and analyze the results.

15. Give an example of a Win/Win and Win/Lose situation in your life.

16. Give an example of Covey's Habits 5 and 6.

17. Describe how a supervisor from one of the organizations listed in Exercise 3 measures up to the characteristics of leaders.

18. For one of the organizations listed in Exercise 3 and working as an individual or in a team, modify the leadership survey instrument, conduct the survey, and analyze the results.

3

Customer Satisfaction

Introduction

The most important asset of any organization is its customers. An organization's success depends on how many customers it has, how much they buy, and how often they buy. Customers that are satisfied will increase in number, buy more, and buy more frequently. Satisfied customers also pay their bills promptly, which greatly improves cash flow—the lifeblood of any organization. The organizational diagram in Figure 3-1 best exemplifies just how important the customer is to any organization.

Increasingly, manufacturing and service organizations are using customer satisfaction as the measure of quality. The importance of customer satisfaction is not only due to national competition but also due to worldwide competition. This fact is reflected in the Malcolm Baldrige National Quality Award, where customer satisfaction accounts for 30 percent of the total points. Similarly, customer satisfaction standards are woven

Figure 3-1 **Customer Satisfaction Organizational Diagram**

throughout ISO 9000: 2000. Customer satisfaction is one of the major purposes of a quality management system.[1]

 Total Quality Management (TQM) implies an organizational obsession with meeting or exceeding customer expectations, so that customers are delighted. Understanding the customer's needs and expectations is essential to winning new business and keeping existing business. An organization must give its customers a quality product or service that meets their needs at a reasonable price, which includes on-time delivery and outstanding service. To attain this level, the organization needs to continually examine their quality system to see if it is responsive to ever-changing customer requirements and expectations.

The most successful TQM programs begin by defining quality from the customer's perspective. As defined in Chapter 1, quality means meeting or exceeding the customer's expectations. Dr. Deming added that quality also means anticipating the future needs of the customer. Customer satisfaction, not increasing profits, must be the primary goal of the organization. It is the most important consideration, because satisfied customers will lead to increased profits.

A simplistic definition of customer satisfaction is illustrated by the Teboul model, which is shown in Figure 3-2. The customer's needs are represented by the circle, and the square depicts the product or service offered by the organization. Total satisfaction is achieved when the offer matches the need, or the circle is superimposed on the square. The goal is to cover the expected performance level better than the competitors.

That part of the square that lies within the circle is perceived by the customer as satisfying, and the part of the square outside the circle is perceived as unnecessary. It is important that the organization listen to the "voice of the customer" and ensure that its marketing, design, production, and distribution processes truly meet the expectations of the customer.

Customer satisfaction seems simple enough, and yet it is far from simple. Customer satisfaction is not an objective statistic but more of a feeling or attitude. Although certain statistical patterns can be developed to represent customer satisfaction, it is best to remember that people's opinions and attitudes are subjective by nature.

Because customer satisfaction is subjective, it is hard to measure. There are so many facets to a customer's experience with a product or service that need to be measured individually to get an accurate total picture of customer satisfaction. Whether or not a customer is satisfied cannot be classed as a yes or no answer. Errors can occur when customer satisfaction is simplified too much. The Teboul model, for instance, describes customer satisfaction as the degree to which the customer's experience of a service or product matches her expectations. Using this model, a customer's satisfaction level would be the same if the experience were mediocre in the context of low expectations, or if the experience were superior in the context of high expectations. Customer satisfaction's focus is creating superior experiences, not mediocre experiences.

---

[1] Craig Cochran, "Customer Satisfaction: The Elusive Quarry," *Quality Digest* (November 2001): 45–50.

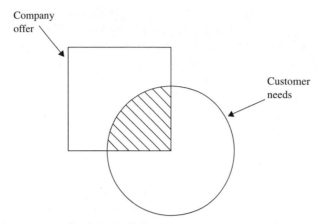

Figure 3-2 Customer Satisfaction Model
Reproduced, with permission, from James Teboul, *Managing Quality Dynamics* (Englewood Cliffs, N.J.: Prentice Hall, Hemel Hampstead, 1991).

Since customer satisfaction is hard to measure, the measurement often is not precise. As with most attitudes, there is variability among people, and often within the same person at different times.[2] Often, due to the difficulty of measuring feelings, customer satisfaction strategies are developed around clearly stated, logical customer opinions, and the emotional issues of a purchase are disregarded. This can be a costly mistake.

Customer satisfaction should not be viewed in a vacuum. For example, a customer may be satisfied with a product or service and therefore rate the product or service highly in a survey, and yet that same customer may buy another product or service. It is of little benefit to understand a customer's views about a product or service if the customer's views about competitors' product or service are not understood. The value customers place on one product compared to another may be a better indicator of customer loyalty. Customer loyalty can be sustained only by maintaining a favorable comparison when compared with competitors.[3] As mentioned before customer satisfaction is not a simple concept to understand or to measure.

Who is the Customer?

There are two distinct types of customers—external and internal. An external customer can be defined in many ways, such as the one who uses the product or service, the one who purchases the product or service, or the one who influences the sale of the

---

[2] Jarrett Rosenberg, "Five Myths About Customer Satisfaction," *Quality Progress* (December 1996): 57–60.

[3] Robert Gardner, "What Do Customers Value," *Quality Progress* (November 2001): 41–48.

product or service. For instance, McDonald's determined the customer to be the child when they introduced their Happy Meals. The child never paid for the meals but the child influenced the sale. Oftentimes, parents purchase lawnmowers and yet the teenage children use the lawnmowers. The identity of the external customer is not always easy to determine.

An external customer exists outside the organization and generally falls into three categories: current, prospective, and lost customers. Each category provides valuable customer satisfaction information for the organization. Every employee in the organization must know how their job enhances the total satisfaction of the external customer. Performance must be continually improved in order to retain existing customers and to gain new ones.

An internal customer is just as important. Every function, whether it be engineering, order processing, or production, has an internal customer—each receives a product or service and, in exchange, provides a product or service. Every person in a process is considered a customer of the preceding operation. Each worker's goal is to make sure that the quality meets the expectations of the next person. When that happens throughout the manufacturing, sales, and distribution chain, the satisfaction of the external customer should be assured.

All processes have outputs, which are used by internal or external customers, and inputs, which are provided by internal or external suppliers. Each supplier performs work that produces some service or product that is used by another customer. As shown by Figure 3-3, each forms a link in the customer/supplier chain, where every chain ends with an external customer and starts with an external supplier. Every employee throughout the organization is part of the chain of internal customers and suppliers.

One basic concept of TQM is an unwavering focus on customers, both internal and external. Most employees know about the external customer or end user but may not think of other employees as internal customers of their output.

In the ideal organization, every employee would have direct contact with customers and be effective at meeting their needs. But the reality is that most employees are shielded from customers by organizational layers. For example, the first-line supervisor in a computer factory may never speak with the businessperson who buys and depends

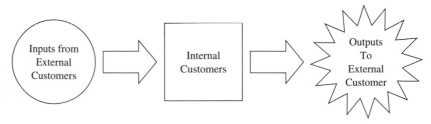

Figure 3-3 **Customer/Supplier Chain**

on the organization's product. However, that supervisor and countless other employees who lack direct contact must still contribute to the businessperson's satisfaction.

The formula for successful internal customer/supplier relationships varies. But it always begins with people asking their internal customers three basic questions:[4]

1. What do you need from me?
2. What do you do with my output?
3. Are there any gaps between what you need and what you get?

The leader's role is to process work through the internal customer-supplier chain by helping workers guarantee that the end product or service fully satisfies the end user. Rather than strive for personal objectives, each individual or group must identify and satisfy the internal customer(s) while fostering a team effort where all people help the organization. Each department must determine what activities are important to both external and internal customers and manage quality every step of the way. All quality management systems start with the basic need of ensuring that the external customer's requirements are adequately documented. Similarly, the organization must document explicitly what each internal customer expects. In addition, clear criteria must be provided for measuring success in meeting the expectations of both internal and external customers.

Customer Perception of Quality

One of the basic concepts of the TQM philosophy is continuous process improvement. This concept implies that there is no acceptable quality level because the customer's needs, values, and expectations are constantly changing and becoming more demanding.

Before making a major purchase, some people check consumer magazines that rate product quality. During the period 1980 to 1988, the quality of the product and its performance ranked first, price was second, and service was third. During the period 1989 to 1992, product quality remained the most important factor, but service ranked above price in importance.

An American Society for Quality (ASQ) survey on end user perceptions of important factors that influenced purchases showed the following ranking:

1. Performance
2. Features

---

[4] George H. Labovitz, "Keeping Your Internal Customers Satisfied," *Wall Street Journal* (July 6, 1987): 12.

3. Service
4. Warranty
5. Price
6. Reputation

The factors of performance, features, service, and warranty are part of the product or service quality; therefore, it is evident that product quality and service are more important than price. Although this information is based on the retail customer, it appears, to some extent, to be true for the commercial customer also.

Performance

Performance involves "fitness for use"—a phrase that indicates that the product and service is ready for the customer's use at the time of sale. Other considerations are (1) availability, which is the probability that a product will operate when needed; (2) reliability, which is freedom from failure over time; and (3) maintainability, which is the ease of keeping the product operable.

Features

Identifiable features or attributes of a product or service are psychological, time-oriented, contractual, ethical, and technological. Features are secondary characteristics of the product or service. For example, the primary function of an automobile is transportation, whereas a car stereo system is a feature of an automobile.

Service

An emphasis on customer service is emerging as a method for organizations to give the customer-added value. However, customer service is an intangible—it is made up of many small things, all geared to changing the customer's perception. Intangible characteristics are those traits that are not quantifiable, yet contribute greatly to customer satisfaction. Providing excellent customer service is different from and more difficult to achieve than excellent product quality. Organizations that emphasize service never stop looking for and finding ways to serve their customers better, even if their customers are not complaining. For instance, at Baptist Hospital in Pensacola, FL, janitors, after cleaning a room, ask if there is anything they can do for the patient. Often patients will have a request for a window shade to be drawn or a door closed.[5]

---

[5] 2000 RIT/USA Today Quality Cup for Health Care.

Warranty

The product warranty represents an organization's public promise of a quality product backed up by a guarantee of customer satisfaction. Ideally, it also represents a public commitment to guarantee a level of service sufficient to satisfy the customer.

A warranty forces the organization to focus on the customer's definition of product and service quality. An organization has to identify the characteristics of product and service quality and the importance the customer attaches to each of those characteristics. A warranty generates feedback by providing information on the product and service quality. It also forces the organization to develop a corrective action system.

Finally, a warranty builds marketing muscle. The warranty encourages customers to buy a service by reducing the risk of the purchase decision, and it generates more sales from existing customers by enhancing loyalty.

Price

Today's customer is willing to pay a higher price to obtain value. Customers are constantly evaluating one organization's products and services against those of its competitors to determine who provides the greatest value. However, in our highly-competitive environment, each customer's concept of value is continually changing. Ongoing efforts must be made by everyone having contact with customers to identify, verify, and update each customer's perception of value in relation to each product and service.

Reputation

Most of us find ourselves rating organizations by our overall experience with them. Total customer satisfaction is based on the entire experience with the organization, not just the product. Good experiences are repeated to six people and bad experiences are repeated to 15 people; therefore, it is more difficult to create a favorable reputation.

Customers are willing to pay a premium for a known or trusted brand name and often become customers for life. Because it costs five times as much to win a new customer as it does to keep an existing one, customer retention is an important economic strategy for any organization. Although it is difficult for an organization to quantify improved customer satisfaction, it is very easy to quantify an increase in customer retention. Investment in customer retention can be a more effective bottom-line approach than concentrating on lowering operational costs. An effective marketing retention strategy is achieved through using feedback from information collecting tools.

Feedback

Customer feedback must be continually solicited and monitored. Customers continually change. They change their minds, their expectations, and their suppliers. Customer feedback is not a one-time effort; it is an ongoing and active probing of the customers' mind. Feedback enables the organization to:

Discover customer dissatisfaction.

Discover relative priorities of quality.

Compare performance with the competition.

Identify customers' needs.

Determine opportunities for improvement.

Even in service industries, such as insurance and banking, customer feedback has become so important that it drives new product development. There are programs to identify and analyze errors, take corrective action, and make ongoing enhancements. All these efforts are justified when the consumers' expectation levels are very high. Effective organizations take the time to listen to the voice of the customer and feed that information back to the idea stage. For instance, listening to the voice of the customer changed how the Internal Revenue Service does business. Previously, the IRS thought that good customer service was mailing tax forms out right after New Year's Day. Then, the IRS asked its customers what good customer service was. The IRS found out that the customers wanted fast refunds and very little contact with the IRS. Now, about 20 million taxpayers can forget using the 1040EZ form and file on their touch-tone phone. There is no contact with the IRS, it takes about six minutes, and the phone system does the math. Refunds are received within 21 days.[6]

Listening to the voice of the customer can be accomplished by numerous information-collecting tools. The principal ones are comment cards, questionnaires, focus groups, toll-free telephone lines, customer visits, report cards, the Internet, employee feedback, mass customization and the American Customer Satisfaction Index.

Comment Card

A low-cost method of obtaining feedback from customers involves a comment card, which can be attached to the warranty card and included with the product at the time of purchase. The intent of the card is to get simple information, such as name, address, age, occupation, and what influenced the customer's decision to buy the product. However, there is very little incentive for buyers to respond to this type of card, and the quality of the response may not provide a true measure of customers' feelings. Generally, people respond only if something very good or very bad has happened. Comment cards are also used in the hospitality industry. Restaurants and hotels provide them at the ends of tables and in hotel rooms. They can even be found on the bottom of restaurant sales re-

---

[6] National Performance Review Staff, "Making the Big U-Turn," *Quality Progress* (March 1996): 59–62.

ceipts. Often, free meals or hotel stays are provided to rectify a poor experience noted on a comment card. Free meals and hotel stays can generate significant customer loyalty provided the organization also fixes the problem.[7]

Customer Questionnaire

A customer questionnaire is a popular tool for obtaining opinions and perceptions about an organization and its products and services. However, they can be costly and time-consuming. Surveys may be administered by mail or telephone. In the form of questionnaires, the customer is asked to furnish answers relating to the quality of products and services. Most surveys ask the customer to grade the question on a one-to-five scale or a one-to-ten scale, where the highest number typically has a description like "highly satisfied." One of the reasons the one-to-five or one-to-ten scale is used is because it easily produces a metric. For example, see Figure 3-4 the Spouse Satisfaction Survey.

Although the "1 to 5" scale is a typical approach to surveys, it probably is not entirely effective. It does not tell the surveyor how important trash removal is relative to other

	Highly Satisfied		Neutral	Highly Dissatisfied	
1. Trash removal	5	4	3	2	1
2. Personal hygiene	5	4	3	2	1
3. Lawn maintenance	5	4	3	2	1
4. Romance	5	4	3	2	1
5. Thoughtfulness	5	4	3	2	1
6. Listening skills	5	4	3	2	1
7. Faithfulness	5	4	3	2	1
8. Respect for mother-in-law	5	4	3	2	1
9. Overall, how satisfied are you with your marriage?	5	4	3	2	1

Figure 3-4 Spouse Satisfaction Survey—Typical Approach
Reproduced with permission of International Management Technologies, Inc., www.imtc3.com, based on Creating a Customer-Centered Culture: Leadership in Quality, Innovation and Speed (1993, Quality Press).

---

[7] Cochran.

Trash removal

1. How often do you expect the trash to be taken out by your spouse?
_____ Not at all _____ Daily _____ When it's full _____ When reminded
_____ When the stench arouses the anger of the neighbors

2. How often would you like the trash to be taken out by your spouse?
_____ Not at all _____ Daily _____ When it's full _____ When reminded
_____ When the stench arouses the anger of the neighbors

3. How often is the trash taken out by your spouse?
_____ Not at all _____ Daily _____ When it's full _____ When reminded
_____ When the stench arouses the anger of the neighbors

4. How satisfied are you with your spouse's trash removal?
_____ Very Dissatisfied _____ Dissatisfied _____ Neutral _____ Satisfied
_____ I fantasize about it

On a scale of 1 to 8, please rank the importance of the following to the
happiness of your marriage, where 1 equals most important.

_____ Trash removal	_____ Thoughtfulness
_____ Personal hygiene	_____ Listening skills
_____ Lawn maintenance	_____ Faithfulness
_____ Romance	_____ Respect for mother-in-law

Figure 3-5 Spouse Satisfaction Survey—The Right Way
Reproduced with permission of International Management Technologies, Inc., www.imtc3.com, based
on Creating a Customer-Centered Culture: Leadership in Quality, Innovation and Speed (1993, Quality
Press).

qualities, nor does it tell the surveyor what the spouse wants or expects. See Figure 3-5
for a better way to do a Spouse Satisfaction Survey.

Although the most detailed and most useful information may come from a mail survey, the results are usually not representative of a normal population. This result occurs
because the only people who will take the time to fill out a survey are those who feel
very strongly about a subject and, therefore, tend to be biased. To further enhance a mail
survey, the survey may be followed up with a phone call to nonresponders.

To make surveys more useful, it is best to remember eight points.

1. Clients and customers are not the same.

2. Surveys raise customers' expectations.

3. How you ask a question will determine how the question is answered.

4. The more specific the question, the better the answer.

5. You have only one chance and only 15 minutes.

6. The more time you spend in survey development, the less time you will spend in data analysis and interpretation.

7. Who you ask is as important as what you ask.

8. Before the data are collected, you should know how you want to analyze and use the data.

Clients are the people for whom you are doing the survey, and customers are the ones who use the product or service. The customers must be surveyed to provide information for the clients to take action. It is important to note that customer satisfaction surveys are different from traditional public-opinion polls. For instance, public-opinion polls are based on respondent anonymity, whereas customers don't necessarily want to remain anonymous. Customer satisfaction surveys need to be sensitive to the management of customer relationships, which is not necessary when doing traditional public-opinion polls. "Customer satisfaction survey respondents are more than survey participants, they are cherished customers of an organization. Their relationship with the organization should be strengthened as a result of the survey, not taxed."[8]

Surveys should focus on what is within the client's abilities or desires to accomplish because surveys do raise customers' expectations. For instance, an employee survey that asks employees what would be a good internal reward system creates expectations in the employee that a reward system will be instituted in some form by the company. If the company has no intention of instituting an employee internal reward system, then this question should not be asked. Raising expectations and then doing nothing only serves to disappoint or anger customers. If at all possible, customer survey participants should be informed of the survey results and the changes implemented to remedy problems.

There are different categories of questions that provide different types of information. For instance, a question that begins with "Do you like Chinese food?" provides information on a customer's feelings or attitudes, whereas a question that asks, "How often do you dine out?" provides information on a customer's behavior. Information on a customer's knowledge about the product can be obtained by a question that has only one correct answer (for instance, "Is there a McDonald's within five miles of your house?"). The type of question asked will determine the type of information received.

Likewise, the more specific the question, the better the answer. If the question asked is too broad, it will provide scattered answers. For example, "How would you improve food?" can produce answers ranging from "reduce the cost" to "cook everything in butter." A more tailored question gives the customer a focus for the kind of information that you are interested in. However, questions should be carefully crafted so that the marketing people do not contaminate the questions (and thereby the answers) with their

---

[8] Terry G. Vavra, "Is Your Satisfaction Survey Creating Dissatisfied Customers?" *Quality Progress* (December 1997): 51.

own thinking. The survey should determine what customers think is important, not what the organization thinks is important.

Customers are giving their most precious commodity when they fill out a survey—their time. The very most a customer will give of their time is 15 minutes. Customers who send back a survey should be thanked profusely for their time. Surveyors sometimes include one dollar along with the survey as a token measure of their gratitude.

When writing a survey, it is best to remember that more multiple-choice questions can be answered in 15 minutes than open-ended questions. To illustrate this point, compare the following multiple-choice question to the open-ended question.

How many times do you dine out in a month?

    a. 1–2 times

    b. 3–5 times

    c. 6–10 times

    d. more than 10 times

The open-ended question requires the customer to calculate the answer, which takes more time. If an exact answer is required, then the open-ended question should be asked even though it takes more time to answer. However, if a good estimate does not compromise your data needs, then the multiple-choice question may be better. Whether the client wants yes or no information or more detailed information will determine the type of questions asked. In summary, how the data is going to be used will determine how the questions will be asked.

Who are asked the survey questions is just as important as what is asked. The customers in a sample should be chosen to best represent the population so that inferences can be made about the population. Customers who can be surveyed are either current customers, past customers, potential customers, or competitors' customers.

Customer surveys should also measure a customer's views of the competition's performance. It is more useful for an organization to know that it has gained points relative to the competition than it is to know that its customers have gone from "somewhat satisfied" to "satisfied." For example, Apple's Macintosh computer has extraordinarily satisfied customers, yet the company's market share continues to decline.[9] A company needs to survey its competitor's customers.

Surveys can be data rich but information poor. The next step is to sift through all the data to get to the useful information. The collected data must be turned into actionable information. The survey analysis must not only identify problems and opportunities; it must also suggest the magnitude of the customer base at risk and the revenue implication of inaction. The final analysis should yield a specific course of action.[10,11,12]

[9] Ken Miller, "Are Your Surveys Only Suitable for Wrapping Fish?" *Quality Progress* (December 1998): 47–51.

[10] Vavra.

[11] Glenda Nogami, "Eight Points for More Useful Surveys," *Quality Progress* (October 1996): 93–96.

[12] Karl Albrecht, "The Use and Misuse of Surveys," *Quality Digest* (November 1994): 21–22.

A second method of administering a survey involves telephoning customers. Almost everyone has a few minutes to answer questions on the telephone. Rapidly changing telecommunications are creating customer information instantly. The Gallup organization has developed an automated, voice-gathering polling service called the Gallup 800 Survey. Organizations can now effectively reach large populations, analyze the results quickly, and determine what their customers are thinking on a near real-time basis. The survey consists of a series of multiple-choice questions that provide information for a customized report, which includes recommendations. Results are available within 24 hours.

Focus Groups

Customer focus groups are a popular way to obtain feedback, but they too can be very expensive. These groups are very effective for gathering information on customer expectations and requirements.

Surveying a focus group is a research method used to find out what customers are really thinking. A group of customers is assembled in a meeting room to answer a series of questions. These carefully structured questions are asked by a skilled moderator, who probes into the participants' thoughts, ideas, perceptions, or comments. The moderator has a clear understanding of the type of information wanted and a plan for obtaining it. Meetings are designed to focus on current, proposed, and future products and services. The people selected to participate have the same profile as the customers that the organization is trying to attract. As an incentive to participate, these people are reimbursed for their time. Focus groups are sometimes used with an organization's employees to examine internal issues.

Imprint analysis is an emerging technique used in focus groups. This is a good way to obtain the intrinsic feelings associated with a product or service. Feelings are not as easily obtained from customer questionnaires, because customers often hold back information on surveys. Word association, discussions, and relaxation techniques can identify a customer's emerging needs, even if the participants are unable to directly articulate those needs. Imprint analysis helps in understanding the human emotions involved in a purchase decision. For instance, a major ice cream company discovered through customer satisfaction surveys that their customers wanted to eat healthier. Before implementing a line of low fat ice cream, the company decided to do an imprint analysis. The imprint analysis discovered that these customers would consume low fat foods and deprive themselves of desserts during the week. But, on the weekends, these same people wanted a super rich ice cream, containing more fat than any ice cream presently on the market. These customers wanted to reward themselves for eating healthy during the week. Needless to say, the ice cream company launched a new, full fat and extra creamy product and sold it at a premium. Their market share increased significantly, creating many loyal customers due to the extra insight that the imprint analysis provided.[13]

---

[13] Cristina Afors and Marilyn Zuckerman Michaels, "A Quick Accurate Way to Determine Customer Needs," *Quality Progress* (July 2001): 82–87.

Toll-Free Telephone Numbers

Toll-free (800/888) telephone numbers are an effective technique for receiving complaint feedback. Organizations can respond faster and more cheaply to the complaint. Such a number does not, however, reach those who decided not to buy the product or those who discovered some likable feature on a competitor's product. Toll-free numbers are in use by at least 50% of all organizations with sales of at least $10 million.

Implementation of toll-free telephone numbers has grown tremendously—in six years, the Cadillac division of General Motors added 24 toll-free numbers. In response to what customers said, Cadillac eliminated deductibles on warranties and pioneered 24-hour roadside service.

Customer Visits

Visits to a customer's place of business provide another way to gather information. An organization can proactively monitor its product's performance while it is in use and thereby identify any specific or recurring problems. Senior managers should be involved in these visits and not delegate them to someone else. However, it is a good idea to take along operating personnel so they can see firsthand how the product is performing. One site visit L-S Electro Galvanizing Company made to its customer, General Motors, produced a surprisingly simple idea. An arrow was needed on the finished 25-ton rolls of steel to show which way the steel unrolled. Previously, GM employees had to guess and often times had to resummon a crane to turn the roll around, which wasted 30 minutes.[14] Another example of a productive customer visit is when U.S. Steel sent an hourly worker, who applied anti-corrosion coating, to the Ford auto plant that used their steel. The worker found flaking zinc and knew there was too much zinc buildup on the edges of the steel. The rods that trimmed the steel were not properly aligned. U.S. Steel also discovered that Ford was wasting steel and money by scraping the bottom sheet of each pile of steel. Ford mistook the harmless white residue on the bottom sheets for rust, when in fact the residue was caused by tremendous pressure from the heavy pile and could easily be wiped off.[15]

The organization should also continually keep informed about new developments in the customer's industry by reading their journals and attending their conferences. Brainstorming sessions with the customers about future products and services should be held at least annually.

Report Card

Another very effective information-gathering tool is the report card. Figure 3-6 shows a typical one. It is usually sent to each customer on a quarterly basis. The data are ana-

---

[14] 1992 RIT/USA Today Quality Cup for Small Business.

[15] 1992 RIT/USA Today Quality Cup for Manufacturing.

QUARTERLY REPORT CARD

To our Customers:

We are continually striving to improve. To assist us in this endeavor, we need your feedback. Would you please grade our performance in each category? The grading scale is

A = Excellent
B = Very Good
C = Average
D = Poor
F = Failing

I. PRODUCT QUALITY   Grade _____
Comments: _____

II. ON-TIME DELIVERY   Grade _____
Comments: _____

III. SERVICE   Grade _____
Comments: _____

IV. OVERALL   Grade _____
Comments: _____

Signed _____ Date _____
Title _____ Organization _____

Figure 3-6 **Sample Report Card**

lyzed to determine areas for improvement. For instance, the University of California in San Diego uses a report card to grade the quality of campus business services, such as the payroll department and the bookstore.[16]

The Internet and Computers

Some managers are beginning to monitor discussions that take place on the Internet to find out what customers are saying about their products. Internet users frequently

---

[16] 1999 RIT/USA Today Quality Cup for Education.

seek advice regarding their everyday activities or activities related to specific interests, hobbies, or sports. Newsgroups, electronic bulletin boards, and mailing lists can be scanned using keyword searches if one knows that a company's product is of interest to participants in certain activities, hobbies, or professions. Ideally, messages that compare a company's products with those of its competitors can be uncovered. In the newsgroups it is best to read the views and discussions of others and not intervene in the discussion with the organization's perspective on the product or service. Intervening will most likely end the discussion. Monitoring Internet conversations is timely, the cost is minimal, and it can be a source of creative ideas. One of the drawbacks of monitoring Internet conversations, however, is that the conversations can be unfocused.[17]

There are even Internet sites that take consumer complaints and compliments about businesses and gives organizations grades based on their ratio of complaints to compliments. Planetfeedback.com also sends letters to companies on behalf of consumers. The organization's web page also provides an easy way for customers to e-mail the company with their thoughts on the organization's products and services.

Computers can be used to detect patterns in seemingly chaotic data. For instance, the sales data from a convenience store chain showed that the peak hours for selling diapers and for selling beer were the same. The diapers were put next to the beer and sales increased for both.[18]

Employee Feedback

Employees are often an untapped source of information. Companies are listening more to the external customer but still are not listening to employees. Employees can offer insight into conditions that inhibit service quality in the organization. Employee groups can brainstorm ideas to come up with solutions to problems that customers have identified.

Although customer research reveals what is happening, employee research reveals why it is happening. Employee feedback should be proactively solicited, instead of checking the wooden suggestion box once a year.[19] For instance, Chrysler regularly surveys employees for issues, because employee surveys are timely compared to customer surveys. When staff members cannot get what they need or have low morale, then they cannot provide good service. Chrysler requires that management share the survey results with employees and uses the findings to make substantial changes.

---

[17] Byron J. Finch, "A New Way to Listen to the Customer," *Quality Progress* (May 1997): 73–76.

[18] Virginia Baldwin Hick, "Technology is Redefining the Meaning of Customer Service," *St. Louis Post Dispatch* (May 1, 1999): Business Section 26.

[19] Stanley G. Aman, "The Essence of TQM: Customer Satisfaction," *Journal of Industrial Technology* (Summer 1994): 2–4.

Mass Customization[20]

The ultimate in customer satisfaction is giving customers exactly what they want. In the past, the price tag for this was prohibitive, but mass customization is a way to provide variety at an affordable cost. Mass customization is a direct result of advances made in manufacturing, such as flexible manufacturing technologies, just-in-time systems, and cycle time reduction. It has been done in the car industry for years. Customers determine what type of seat coverings, color, and stereo system they want. Mass customization is now being used in many other industries. For instance, Levi Strauss customers are measured for jeans, choose the fabric, and choose the pattern at a local store. The custom fit jeans are then manufactured to order at a central factory and sent to the local store. The voice of the Levi Strauss customer is heard at the fabrication stage of production. Dell assembles computers according to each customer's requirements by adding or subtracting components from one of several base systems. In this way, customers get the computer they want at a reasonable price through mass customization at the assembly stage. Modular furniture is a customized product at the delivery stage. Different customers can adapt modular furniture to meet their changing needs long after the initial purchase.

The voice of the customer can be captured in mass customized products by using the hard data of what the customer bought instead of what the customer was thinking about buying. The customer satisfaction information obtained from mass customization can be used to provide more standardized products. The voice of the purchasing customer, however, provides no information about the non-purchasing customer. See Figure 3-7 to better understand the customer's involvement in mass customization.

The American Customer Satisfaction Index[21]

The American Customer Satisfaction Index (ACSI), established in 1994 as a joint project between the University of Michigan and the American Society for Quality, quantifies quality and customer satisfaction and relates them to firms' financial performance. Firms can now measure the value that increased customer satisfaction adds to the bottom line. ACSI looks at products sold in the United States and not just those produced in the United States. In this way, the United States' quality is compared to international quality.

The index is based on findings from telephone interviews from a national sample of about 50,000 households. Survey participants are selected on the basis of having recently

---

[20] This section adapted, with permission, from Rebecca Duray and Glenn W. Milligan, "Improving Customer Satisfaction through Mass Customization," *Quality Progress* (August 1999): 60–66.

[21] Jon Brecka, "The American Customer Satisfaction Index," *Quality Progress* (October 1994): 41–44.

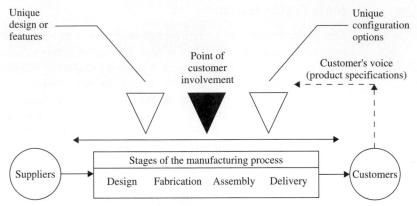

Figure 3-7 Point of Customer Involvement

bought or used a company's product. The index measures eight sectors of the economy, which include more than 40 industries and more than 200 individual companies and agencies. The eight sectors of the economy are:

1. Manufacturing (nondurables)
2. Manufacturing (durables)
3. Retail
4. Transportation, communication, and utilities
5. Finance and insurance
6. Services
7. Public administration and government
8. E-commerce (adopted in 2000)

Each sector has industries, and under each industry are specific companies. For example, under the nondurable manufacturing sector is the industry soft drinks. Under the industry soft drinks are Coca Cola, Pepsi, and various other companies. In 2000, the E-Commerce Sector was added; therefore, these scores are baseline scores. Sector, industry, and company ACSI scores can be found on ASQ's website at www.asq.org. See Table 3-1 for a yearly comparison of scores in the nondurable manufacturing sector and the baseline scores for the E-commerce sector.

The ACSI allows comparisons between individual firms, comparisons between firms and the industry average, and comparisons over time. The ACSI is considered to be one of the forecasts of consumer spending in the United States. There is a strong correlation between ACSI changes in one quarter and changes in consumer spending in the next quarter. Also, according to ACSI, competitive markets get higher satisfaction ratings

TABLE 3-1
National, Industry, and Sector ACSI Scores

	1994	*1995*	*1996*	*1997*	*1998*	*1999*	*2000*	*% Change**
National ACSI**	74.2	77.3	72.2	71.1	72.3	72.1	72.9	(1.8)
Nondurable Manufacturing Sector	**81.6**	**81.2**	**79.0**	**78.5**	**78.8**	**80.0**	**81.0**	**(0.7)**
Soft drinks	86	86	86	83	83	84	86	0
Beer	83	81	79	81	82	79	82	(1.2)
Cigarettes	81	82	77	77	75	76	78	(3.7)
Processed foods	84	84	83	81	81	81	81	(3.6)
Pet foods				83	81	81	83	0
Personal care and cleaning products	84	84	80	82	82	81	84	0
Casual clothing	82	81	78	77	79	79	79	(3.7)
Athletic shoes	79	79	77	74	74	76	79	0
E-Commerce Sector							**73.2**	
Portals							63	
Retail							78	
Auction and reverse auction							72	
Brokerages							72	

*From 1994 to 2000, except pet foods, for which change is measured from 1997 to 2000. This is the first time e-commerce was measured so scores indicated are baselines.
**Third quarter measures for each year except fourth quarter 1994 baseline.

than noncompetitive markets. For instance, government services have the lowest overall customer satisfaction rating.[22]

Using Customer Complaints

For the most part, the information on feedback given in the previous section is proactive. Although complaints are reactive, they are very vital in gathering data on customer perceptions. A dissatisfied customer can easily become a lost customer. Many

---

[22]William Robert Loomies, "QS 9000 Customer Satisfaction is Not Working," *Quality Progress* (July 1999): 54–59.

TABLE 3-2
Survey of Dissatisfied Customers

	COMPLAIN TO		
Product	*Management*	*Front-line*	*No One*
Auto	2%	21%	77%
Mail order	1%	22%	77%
Groceries	1%	15%	84%
Clothing	0%	13%	87%
Home repair	4%	21%	74%
Appliances	0%	12%	88%
Auto repair	1%	28%	71%

organizations use customer dissatisfaction as the primary measure to assess their process improvement efforts.

Table 3-2 shows information from a survey conducted by ASQ of dissatisfied customers. Only about 1.5% took the time to complain to management, about 20% took out their dissatisfaction on front-line personnel, and almost 80% did nothing. This data indicates that it is very easy for management to perceive that customers are satisfied with the product or service. Actually, when satisfied customers are included in the data, the number of formal complaints to management is much lower than 1.5%. Frequently, dissatisfied customers switch to a competitor and don't say anything. For this reason, the customers who don't complain are the ones who should worry an organization the most. The average organization takes its customer base for granted, assuming that no complaints is good news. Every single complaint should be accepted, analyzed, and acted upon, for it represents the tip of the iceberg.

Small organizations have a tremendous advantage in this area, because the top-ranking officer is often in personal contact with key customers. Thus, information on customer dissatisfaction is received into the organization at the highest level, thereby providing a fast response.

Results of another study indicated that more than half of dissatisfied customers will buy again if they believe their complaint has been heard and resolved. Only 20% will buy again if their complaint is heard but not resolved. Fewer than 10% will be repeat buyers when a complaint is not heard. And even though such complaints may not reach the organization's management, they do reach other potential customers.

By taking a positive approach, complaints can be seen as an opportunity to obtain information and provide a positive service to the customer. In reality, the customer is giving the organization a second chance. Some actions organizations can take to handle complaints are as follows:

- Investigate customers' experiences by actively soliciting feedback, both positive and negative, and then acting on it promptly.
- Develop procedures for complaint resolution that include empowering front-line personnel.
- Analyze complaints, but understand that complaints do not always fit into neat categories.
- Work to identify process and material variations and then eliminate the root cause. "More inspection" is not corrective action.
- When a survey response is received, a senior manager should contact the customer and strive to resolve the concern.
- Establish customer satisfaction measures and constantly monitor them.
- Communicate complaint information, as well as the results of all investigations and solutions, to all people in the organization.
- Provide a monthly complaint report to the quality council for their evaluation and, if needed, the assignment of process improvement teams.
- Identify customers' expectations beforehand rather than afterward through complaint analysis.

Ninety percent of all customer contact comes through an organization's front-line employees. A petty complaint voiced to a front-line employee often becomes a major complaint when it gets to the management level.

An organization can save both customers and money by training front-line employees to solve problems directly with customers. Customers want problems solved quickly and efficiently; therefore, employees should know how to handle a wide range of situations that arise in the customer relationship. Customer focus and listening skills are not easily learned. Training becomes a top management priority, because front-line employees must have the skills to encourage customers to discuss their complaints and deal with them. Recognition and reward should be linked to service quality performance and the ability to satisfy customers. Front-line employees should have the responsibility and authority to provide the services necessary to satisfy the customer. For example, a cashier in a restaurant should be empowered to discount the meal price of a dissatisfied customer without seeking management's approval. Management should encourage employees to take risks, make decisions, and not be afraid of making a mistake.

Studies have shown that the better the service at the point of sale, the fewer the complaints and the greater the sales volume. Employees who are dissatisfied with their organization are as noticeable as dissatisfied customers. It's just as important to focus on employee satisfaction as customer satisfaction. A measurement system is necessary to evaluate the improvement in customer satisfaction.

Service Quality

Strategies that have produced significant results in production are often harder to implement in a service environment. Thanks to the teachings of Deming, Juran, and others, significant strides have been made in manufacturing. The same results have been slower in service organizations or service activities in manufacturing.

Customer service is the set of activities an organization uses to win and retain customers' satisfaction. It can be provided before, during, or after the sale of the product or exist on its own. Elements of customer service are:

Organization

1. Identify each market segment.
2. Write down the requirements.
3. Communicate the requirements.
4. Organize processes.
5. Organize physical spaces.

Customer Care

6. Meet the customer's expectations.
7. Get the customer's point of view.
8. Deliver what is promised.
9. Make the customer feel valued.
10. Respond to all complaints.
11. Over-respond to the customer.
12. Provide a clean and comfortable customer reception area.

Communication

13. Optimize the trade-off between time and personal attention.
14. Minimize the number of contact points.
15. Provide pleasant, knowledgeable, and enthusiastic employees.
16. Write documents in customer-friendly language.

Front-line people

17. Hire people who like people.
18. Challenge them to develop better methods.
19. Give them the authority to solve problems.
20. Serve them as internal customers.
21. Be sure they are adequately trained.
22. Recognize and reward performance.

Leadership

23. Lead by example.
24. Listen to the front-line people.
25. Strive for continuous process improvement.[23]

Organization

To ensure the same level of quality for all customers, the organization must record and then communicate to its employees the directions for all tasks. A service quality handbook should be created with the description of each service quality standard. Communicating the service quality standard for each task can be done by formal training, videos, personal coaching, or meetings. Also, intranet sites can be developed so employees can find answers to commonly-asked questions and contact people for more information.

Sometimes, the entire process used by an organization to do business must be changed in order to better serve the customer. For instance, the Florida Estate Tax Division revamped the way they operate by eliminating 50,000 estate tax forms. Florida has many senior residents who were required to file tax forms even if the estate was less than $675,000 and no taxes were owed. The heirs had to wait approximately two weeks to get a tax clearance certificate in order to sell a home or divide up property. Since personnel resources were shifted from these returns to returns where assets were over $675,000, processing time for returns with assets over $675,000 dropped from six months to two weeks.[24]

Other times, physical space must be reorganized to better serve the customer. Harris Methodist Hospital in Fort Worth redesigned its emergency room around the patient. It designed a "quick care" unit for emergency room patients with less serious injuries. The average "quick care" patient now spends 55 minutes in the emergency room instead of 137 minutes. Unfortunately, patients now wonder why treatment is so costly when it took so little time.[25]

Likewise, Belmont University reorganized its physical space to better serve its customers, the students. After many years of student complaints, Belmont created a one-stop Belmont Central where students can add or drop classes, get transcripts, file financial forms, cash checks, and do a myriad of other administrative tasks. Previously, students had to visit several buildings located at opposite ends of the campus to accomplish simple administrative tasks.[26]

---

[23] Adapted from Jacques Horovitz and Chan Cudennec-poon, "Putting Service Quality into Gear," *Quality Progress* (January 1991): 54–58.

[24] 2000 RIT/USA Today Quality Cup for Government.

[25] 1996 RIT/USA Today Quality Cup for Not-For-Profit.

[26] 1997 RIT/USA Today Quality Cup for Education.

Customer Care

An organization should revolve around the customer, because customers are the key to any business. A customer, any customer, should be valued and treated like a friend. Responses to customer complaints should be immediate and should be more than the customer expected to receive. If they are treated with respect customers will simply forgive errors and positively promote the organization. Employees must understand that, as Henry Ford said, "It is not the employer who pays wages—he only handles the money. It is the customer who pays the wages." Employees must please customers, not bosses, management committees, or headquarters. Employees should not follow mind-numbing rules that provide no benefit to the customer.

Fairview-AFX requires its employees to sign a customer code of ethics. It is also given to all customers in order to hold Fairview-AFX employees accountable. Their code of ethics is to:

- Keep promises to customers.
- Return calls to customers in an expedient manner.
- Give customers assistance with their concerns, referring an appropriate staff member for problem-solving action when necessary.
- Treat our customers with respect, courtesy and professionalism at all times.
- Remain aware and evaluate customer satisfaction regularly.
- Continually search for customer-related improvements.
- Deliver service and products quickly and efficiently.
- Give every customer involved and personal attention.
- Maintain a clean and neat appearance, including the workplace, at all times.
- Review and implement customer feedback and suggestions into current procedure when appropriate.
- Engage in any training or education that will enhance our job performance and our commitment to customer care.
- Treat every customer just as we would want to be treated ourselves.[27]

Communication

An organization's communication to its customers must be consistent with its level of service quality. A customer will become dissatisfied if there is a difference between what has been advertised and what has been received. An organization communicates to its customers in many subtle ways. For instance, an organization communicates to its customers even by such means as an employee's telephone manners, or an automated voice

---

[27] 1995 RIT/USA Today Quality Cup for Small Business.

response system that is fast and easy for the customer to use. Customer relationships are based on communication. An organization must listen to its customers and establish a level of trust.

Frequently, the first impression a customer has of an organization is its website. If the organization's website is not customer-friendly, the customer will have a bad first impression. Iomega, the manufacturer of zip drives, improved both the content and the navigation and support tools on the organization's website. Within one year, customer satisfaction increased 40%, problem resolution rate was up 320%, and the cost per solution fell from $10.00 to $0.69.[28]

Front-Line People

Customers are the most valuable asset of any company and should not be referred to employees who have not been properly trained to handle their complaints. Only the best employee is worthy of a company's customers. It is best to remember three things about front-line employees:

1. Hire the best.
2. Develop the best employees into professionals.
3. Motivate the professionals to stay and excel.

To get that "best employee" on the front line, someone with a personality should be hired. For example, in real estate, the most important aspect is location, location, location. In front-line employees, the most important aspect is personality, personality, personality. If employees are not happy, this will be reflected to the customers. Generally, customers are frustrated by small things. Front-line employees need to care, smile, possess a pleasant voice, and thank the customer often for their business. In sum, it's having a positive attitude. Finding good employees who want to serve customers is not an easy task.

Front-line employees also need training. Managers who conduct training classes or participate in class along with employees develop a more effective working relationship and therefore convey the importance of customer satisfaction to new employees.

Of course, front-line employees should possess written and oral communication skills and problem-solving skills, and they should be empowered to resolve complaints. But more importantly, front-line employees should genuinely care for their customers. Customers understand and know when someone empathizes with their feelings and is genuinely trying to help. The ideal is being overly fair with your customers, putting customers before costs. For instance, when a physician found a seam had split on a recently-purchased business suit from an upscale department store, she returned it. Upon returning the suit, the salesperson gave her a 33% discount coupon

---

[28] 2000 RIT/USA Today Quality Cup Finalist for Manufacturing.

for her next purchase because it wasn't fair that she had to take time from her schedule to return the suit. Of course, the physician has been a loyal customer ever since. Ritz Carlton hotel employees may spend up to $2000 to correct a deficiency or rectify a customer complaint.[29]

At Nordstrom, the company policy is simply stated: "Use your good judgment in all situations, keeping in mind that there are strict orders to be obsessed with the customer rather than with Nordstrom's costs." Salespeople at Nordstrom are so obsessed with the customer that when a customer left her airline ticket at the counter of the Nordstrom's women's apparel department, the sales associate took a cab to the airport to locate the customer and deliver the ticket to her.[30] Using good judgment is key to customer relations. Sometimes one customer's needs must be balanced with other customers' needs. For instance, on a commuter flight one passenger wanted to board with a huge elk rack that wouldn't fit through the doorway much less in the carry on luggage compartment. The passenger was irate when the flight attendant, pilot, and baggage handler calmly explained why the elk rack wouldn't fit, as if it needed explaining. Finally, the baggage handler firmly stated that the passenger was either to take her seat or leave the aircraft. The passenger quickly left and the remaining fifteen passengers gave a round of applause. Despite one unhappy customer, the airline was left with fifteen very happy customers.[31]

In summary, front-line people deal with the customers every day. Front-line people are also a valuable source of information; they know better than management what the customer wants. Front-line staff also needs information and support from management to effectively deal with the public. Management can support front-line staff in various ways. For example, management can coach newcomers to help integrate them into the organization quickly. Management can also give front-line people the authority to resolve customer problems. Rewards should be given to encourage front-line employees' efforts.

Leadership by Example

No quality improvement can succeed without management's involvement and, more importantly, commitment. Managers can best show their commitment to service quality by example. Texas Namplate Co. customer-care personnel, including the company president, are available to customers 24 hours a day. Every CEO should be required to spend at least four hours each month behind a service desk. It is hard to understand the customer when you're looking down at him from a 43rd floor window. The American Airlines CEO should have to eat the food he feeds to weary travelers. The General Motors CEO should spend time in a dealer repair shop. Or better yet, the CEO should be

---

[29] Jaclyn R. Jeffry, "Preparing the Front Line," *Quality Progress* (February 1995): 79–82.

[30] Robert Spector and Patrick D. McCarthy, *The Nordstrom Way*, Audio-Tech Business Book Summaries, Vol. 4 No. 8 Sec. 1 (August 1995): 6–7.

[31] Scott Madison Paton, "Unhappy Employees and Unhappy Customers," *Quality Digest* (January 1999): 4.

the customer. For example, the CEO of Harley Davidson rides his bike to work. He commented that if you build motorcycles for a living, you shouldn't ride to work in a Rolls-Royce.[32]

Additional Comments

Gaining new customers can be a lengthy process involving research, targeting, advertising, promotion, and networking. Current customers provide organizations with established business relationships, knowledge and predictability in buying behaviors, and short-term opportunities for expanded sales. Thus, an organization's most likely target for new business is its current customers.

Service quality is an activity; therefore, it can be controlled and improved. Organizations with higher-quality service can charge up to 20% more and still retain customers. Satisfied customers not only continue to patronize the organization, they also add to profits by referring new customers. Referrals can be twice as effective as advertising.

An essential part of customer satisfaction occurs after the sale. Table 3-3 shows various characteristics and expectations.

Many organizations emphasize traditional or reactive service after the sale. Examples include:

Preventive maintenance (service provided according to a prescribed timetable).

Service contract (service provided as required).

No service contract (service requires labor and material billing).

Combinations of the above.

TABLE 3-3
Characteristics and Expectations

Characteristic	Expectation
Delivery	Delivered on schedule in undamaged condition
Installation	Proper instructions on setup, or technicians supplied for complicated products
Use	Clearly-written training manuals or instructions provided on proper use
Field repair	Properly-trained technicians to promptly make quality repairs
Customer service	Friendly service representatives to answer questions
Warranty	Clearly stated with prompt service on claims

---

[32] H. James Harrington, "Looking Down at the Customer," *Quality Digest* (February 2001): 24.

An organization striving to upgrade its service quality must move to the proactive level. Proactive organizations contact their customers and determine their service quality needs and expectations. This information is used to develop the organization's strategy. Management must continually improve the methods for obtaining input from customers to better determine their needs.

For instance, the federal government is improving service quality. Former President Bill Clinton released a report titled, "Putting Customers First '95: Standards for Serving the American People." The 232-page report lists the customer service standards that have been formulated by more than 200 federal government agencies. The standards are designed to please the customers—the American people. For instance, the Occupational Safety and Health Administration (OSHA) promises that inspectors will be respectful and helpful and focus on only the most serious hazards. The Bureau of Labor Statistics promises data any way you want it: from a live person, a recorded message, fax, microfiche, diskette, tape, Internet, or telecommunications device for the deaf. The Internal Revenue Service promises tax refunds due on complete and accurate paper returns in 40 days, or 21 days if the return is filed electronically. Delivering what has been promised builds the American people's confidence that their government can work effectively. After all, if a government office cannot answer the phone and give quick, courteous service, how can it handle defense, commerce, and education?[33]

Although publishing the standards was risky, service in many government offices improved. In 1996, *Business Week* reported that an independent survey of the country's best telephone customer service ranked the Social Security Administration top in the nation.[34]

Translating Needs into Requirements

The Kano model, which is shown in Figure 3-8, conceptualizes customer requirements. The model represents three major areas of customer satisfaction. The first area of customer satisfaction, represented by the diagonal line, represents explicit requirements. These include written or verbal requirements and are easily identified, expected to be met, and typically performance related. Satisfying the customer would be relatively simple if these were the only requirements.

The second area of customer satisfaction represents innovations, as shown by the curved line in the upper left corner of the figure. A customer's written instructions are often purposefully vague to avoid stifling new ideas during conceptualization and product definition. Because they are unexpected, these creative ideas often excite and delight the customer. These ideas quickly become expected.

The third and most significant area of customer satisfaction represents unstated or unspoken requirements, as shown by the curve in the lower right corner of the figure. The cus-

[33] National Performance Review Staff, "Making the Big U-Turn," *Quality Progress* (March 1996): 59–62.

[34] "Top Providers of Telephone Customer Service," *Business Week* (May 29, 1995): 6.

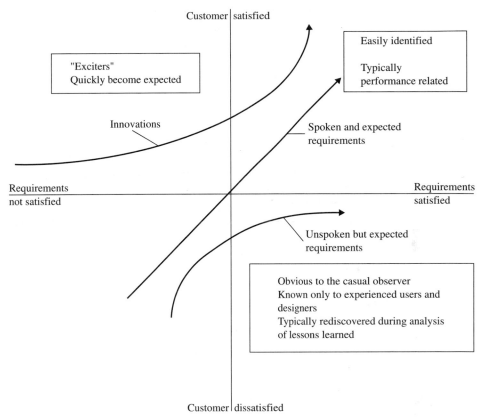

Figure 3-8 Kano Model
Reproduced, with permission, from *Quality Function Development: Implementation Manual for Three-day Workshop* (Allen Park, Mich.: American Supplier Institute, Inc.).

tomer may indeed be unaware of these requirements, or they may assume that such requirements will be automatically supplied. Basic specifications often fail to take real-world manufacturing requirements into account; many merely are based on industry standards or past practice. These implied requirements are the hardest to define but prove very costly if ignored. They may be rediscovered during an after-the-fact analysis of lessons learned.

Realistically, the customer doesn't buy a specification; the customer buys the product or service to fulfill a need. Peter Drucker once said, "Customers don't buy products, they buy results." People don't buy products; they buy transportation or status. Customers are loyal to whatever best helps them achieve their desired outcome.[35] Just meeting a customer's needs is not enough; the organization must exceed the customer's

---

[35] Miller.

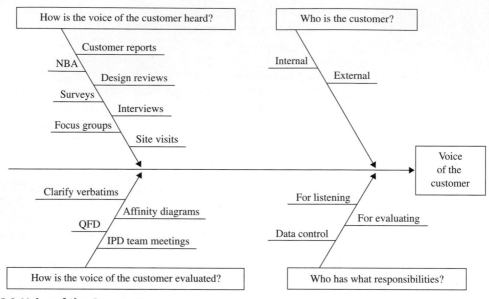

Figure 3-9 Voice of the Customer
Adapted from *Voice of the Customer* (St. Louis, Mo.: McDonnell-Douglas Corporation, 1993).

needs. Figure 3-9, the voice of the customer diagram, summarizes much of the material in this chapter.

Customer Retention

Customer retention is more powerful and effective than customer satisfaction. Customer retention represents the activities that produce the necessary customer satisfaction that creates customer loyalty, which actually improves the bottom line. Customer satisfaction surveys, focus groups, interviews, and observations can help determine what customers think of a service or a product. However, what people say and think is often different from what they do. Customers may be delighted with the tropical oils and aromas in a high-priced, well-advertised hair-care product but still end up buying the generic equivalent. Therefore customer satisfaction should also be measured by using the hard measures of cash register receipts, market share, the level of customer retention, and the number of referrals from customers. The better companies have established a link between customer satisfaction and the bottom line. The analysis identifies the number of customers and the revenue at risk.[36]

---

[36] A. Blanton Godfrey, "Beyond Satisfaction," *Quality Digest* (January 1996): 15.

Customer retention moves customer satisfaction to the next level by determining what is truly important to the customers and making sure that the customer satisfaction system focuses valuable resources on things that really matter to the customer. Customer retention is the connection between customer satisfaction and the bottom line.

Likewise, high employee retention has a significant impact on high customer retention. One way companies can manage customer retention is to pay attention to their present employees and to who they are hiring.[37]

Additional Comments

Improved service frequently carries a cost, so an organization must determine its return on the service investment by determining those elements of service that significantly improve revenues and market share. Diligent use of information-collecting tools and market research will enable an organization to identify those elements most critical to customer satisfaction.

An organization should benchmark (see Chapter 8) the most successful corporations in the industry to determine where it stands relative to its own competitors. Benchmarking will provide information to improve processes and establish realistic goals.

The organization must continually improve the methods of obtaining information concerning the customer's needs and expectations. It is the quality council's responsibility to periodically review the methods.

World-class competitors tend to continually fine-tune their operations to achieve incremental improvements. They know that continuous improvement and customer satisfaction go hand-in-hand. Maximize customer satisfaction and retention, and the financial results will follow.

TQM Exemplary Organization[38]

Merrill Lynch Credit Corporation (MLCC) offers real estate and securities-based consumer credit products—including home financing, personal credit, investment financing, and commercial real-estate financing—to primarily affluent individuals. About 90 percent of its approximately 830 employees, known as partners, are located in MLCC's Jacksonville, FL headquarters.

As part of the Business Planning Process, each July senior managers translate the strategic imperatives into the company's Critical Few Objectives, key performance measures for their CFOs, and specific targets for the next one and three years. For example, a

---

[37] John Goodman, David DePalma, and Scott Broetzmann, "Maximizing the Value of Customer Feedback," *Quality Progress* (December 1996): 35–39.

[38] Malcolm Baldrige National Quality Award, 1997 Service Category Recipient, NIST/Baldrige Homepage, Internet.

CFO to increase process productivity with an aim of increasing shareholder value is measured by the number of days to approve applications, with specific, ambitious, and measurable goals. In turn, these CFOs provide the basis for determining partner performance management plans. By involving all of the firm's partners in providing information for the business planning process, and in regular refinements and progress reviews, MLCC ensures that its plans are fact-based and linked to individual goals and objectives.

MLCC segments its market into several categories of current and potential customers, stratified by their asset levels and age. Working with its parent company, MLCC uses in-depth research to target and deliver appropriate products and services. Its "Voice of the Client" process states customer satisfaction drivers for each client segment and for each of its credit categories. These priority requirements provide the basis for aligning the company's processes and work groups and for identifying indicators and key performance measures for each of its eight core processes. In turn, each of those indicators are tracked and used to identify and put in place improvements in areas having the greatest impact on customer needs and satisfaction.

Information about the customer is truly paramount for MLCC. To ensure that its market research is always current, MLCC continuously evaluates and improves its data on what its clients need and what they might want in the future.

The client data come from an array of sources, ranging from surveys of clients and financial consultants in the field to written or telephone feedback, internal audits, syndicated research, and benchmarking studies. Satisfaction levels of competitors' clients also are used in analyzing client needs. Customer complaints are analyzed in depth, reviewed monthly, and reported back to MLCC regions to identify any sudden changes and to share lessons learned. Negative trends and recurring problems trigger process improvement teams to develop countermeasures and to prevent recurrences. Clients receive acknowledgment of any complaint within two business days, and resolution is received in no more than five business days.

MLCC has impressive results to show that its focus on quality management and performance excellence is a wise investment. Net income rose 100% from 1994 to 1996 and exceeds the industry's average. Return on equity increased approximately 74 percent and its return on assets improved approximately 36 percent in that same period. Key indicators for loan delinquency rates and writeoffs compare favorably with the rest of the industry and are clearly improving—as are the firm's total loan originations, market share in originations, wholesale volume as a percentage of first mortgages, and size of servicing portfolio.

Exercises

1. Define the terms *internal customer* and *external customer*.

2. Is the main concern of most consumers the price of the product or service? Explain.

3. List and explain the six most important factors that influence consumer purchases.

4. What is the best way to improve market share for a product or service?

5. Design a customer satisfaction questionnaire for the following service industries:

   (a) Bank
   (b) Telephone company
   (c) Hospital
   (d) Accounting firm
   (e) Law firm
   (f) Hotel

6. As a manager of a small sporting goods store, describe how you would train front-line employees to handle customer complaints.

7. How does employee satisfaction relate to customer satisfaction?

8. Define quality in two words.

9. Mechanical products, such as cars, break down. Cars often are serviced by the car dealer. How can a car dealer use the service department to encourage future car sales?

4

Employee Involvement

Introduction

Employee involvement is one approach to improving quality and productivity. Its use is credited for contributing to the success enjoyed by the Japanese in the world marketplace. Employee involvement is not a replacement for management nor is it the final word in quality improvement. It is a means to better meet the organization's goals for quality and productivity at all levels of an organization.

Motivation

Knowledge of motivation helps us to understand the utilization of employee involvement to achieve process improvement.

Maslow's Hierarchy of Needs

One of the first and most popular motivational theories was developed by Abraham Maslow. He stated that motivation could best be explained in terms of a hierarchy of needs and that there were five levels. These levels are survival, security, social, esteem, and self-actualization. They are shown in Figure 4-1. Once a given level is satisfied, it can no longer motivate a person.

Relating these needs to motivation, we know that Level 1 (survival) means food, clothing, and shelter, which is usually provided by a job. In the workplace, Level 1 needs include proper lighting, heating/air conditioning, ventilation, phone system, data/voice access, and computer information system.[1] Level 2 (security) can mean a safe place to

---

[1] Brenner, Pamela M., "Motivating Knowledge Workers: The Role of the Workplace," *Quality Progress* (January 1999): 33–37.

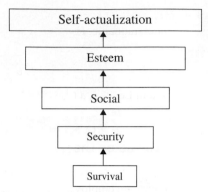

Figure 4-1 Maslow's Hierarchy of Needs

work and job security, which are very important to employees. When the organization demonstrates an interest in the personal well-being of employees, it is a motivating factor. A threat of losing one's job certainly does not enhance motivation. Level 2 is not limited to job security. It also includes having privacy on the job such as being able to lock one's office door or having lockable storage for personal items, as well as having a safe work environment that may include ergonomic adjustable furniture.[2]

Because we are social animals, Level 3 (social) relates to our need to belong. It has been said that cutting someone out of the group is devastating to that individual. Isolation is an effective punishment. Conversely, giving an individual the opportunity to be part of the group by feeling important and needed will motivate that person. If possible, employees should be provided with both formal social areas such as a cafeteria and conference rooms and informal areas such as water coolers and bulletin boards.[3] Being a member of a team is a good way to bring employees into the group. Level 4 (esteem) relates to pride and self-worth. Everyone, regardless of position or job assignment, wants to be recognized as a person of value to the organization. Where possible, employees should be given offices or personal spaces with aesthetics. Business cards, workspace size, and office protocols also provide employees with a certain level of self-esteem within an organization.[4] Seeking advice or input into business or production processes is a good way of telling employees that they are of value. This activity requires giving employees control and freedom of their jobs by providing trust.[5] Level 5 (self-actualization) says that individuals must be given the opportunity to go as far as their abilities will take them. Many organizations have a policy of promoting

---

[2] Brenner.

[3] Brenner.

[4] Brenner.

[5] Brenner.

from within. It is true that some employees do not want to move up the corporate ladder, which is understandable. However, those who do want to move up must know that it is possible.

It is important to note that as employees move up the hierarchy, they will immediately revert back to the previous level if they feel threatened. For example, if an employee is satisfied in Level 3, a rumor of downsizing may cause an immediate return to Level 2.[6]

Herzberg's Two-Factor Theory

Frederick Herzberg extended the general work of Maslow by using empirical research to develop his theory on employee motivation. He found that people were motivated by recognition, responsibility, achievement, advancement, and the work itself. These factors were labeled *motivators*. In addition, his research showed that bad feelings were associated with low salary, minimal fringe benefits, poor working conditions, ill-defined organizational policies, and mediocre technical supervision. These job-related factors were labeled *dissatisfiers* or *hygiene factors*, which implies they are preventable. It is important to realize that dissatisfiers are often extrinsic in nature and motivators are intrinsic. The presence of the extrinsic conditions does not necessarily motivate employees; however, their absence results in dissatisfaction among employees. Absence of motivating factors does not make employees dissatisfied, but when there are motivating factors present, they do provide strong levels of motivation that result in good job performance for the individual and the organization. In general, dissatisfiers must be taken care of before motivators can be actuated. Herzberg's dissatisfiers are roughly equivalent to Maslow's lower levels, and the motivators are similar to the upper levels.[7]

Employee Wants

While management thinks that good pay is the number one want of the employee, survey results show that this factor is usually in the middle of the ranking. Table 4-1 shows employee wants and manager perceptions of employee wants. Employee wants tend to follow the theories of Maslow and Herzberg. It is interesting to note that the managers' perceptions are much different. By involving employees through the use of teams in meaningful work and by providing the proper reward and recognition, managers can reap the advantages of greater quality and productivity along with employee satisfaction. This chapter describes how managers can develop employee motivation and how they can involve their employees through empowerment. If managers are to effectively motivate employees, they must align their actions closer to the motivators.

---

[6] Ann S. Daughtrey and Betty R. Hicks, *Contemporary Supervision* (New York: McGraw-Hill, 1989).

[7] Fred Luthans and Mark J. Martinko, *The Practice of Supervision and Management*, McGraw-Hill Book Company, New York, 1979.

TABLE 4-1
What Employees Want

1 = Top priority
10 = least Priority

Factor	Employee Rating	Manager Rating
Interesting work	1	5
Appreciation	2	8
Involvement	3	10
Job security	4	2
Good pay	5	1
Promotion/growth	6	3
Good working conditions	7	4
Loyalty to employees	8	7
Help with personal problems	9	9
Tactful discipline	10	6

Source: Study by K. Kovich, *Advanced Management Journal,* as reported in the article by Theodore B. Kinni, "Motivating the Unmotivated," *Quality Digest,* March 1993.

Achieving a Motivated Work Force[8]

The building of a motivated work force is for the most part an indirect process. Managers at all levels cannot cause an employee to become motivated; they must create the environment for individuals to motivate themselves. Concepts to achieve a motivated work force are as follows:

1. *Know thyself.* Managers must understand their own motivations, strengths, and weaknesses. This understanding can best be obtained by having peers and employees anonymously appraise the manager's performance. Motivating managers know that the most valuable resource is people and that their success largely depends on employees achieving their goals.

2. *Know your employees.* Most people like to talk about themselves; therefore, the motivating manager will ask questions and listen to answers. With a knowledge of the employees' interests, the manager can help achieve them within the business context. As the manager learns more about the employee, he/she can assist the employee in directing their efforts toward satisfying their goals and well-being. This knowledge will also enable the manager to utilize their strengths.

---

[8] This section adapted, with permission, from Theodore B. Kinni, "Motivating the Unmotivated," *Quality Digest* (March 1993).

3. *Establish a positive attitude*. A positive action-oriented attitude permeates the work unit. Managers are responsible for generating attitudes that lead to positive actions. Feedback should, for the most part (say, 87%), be positive and constructive. Respect and sensitivity toward others is essential to the development of positive attitudes. Asking employees for their opinions concerning job-related problems is an effective way to build a cooperative atmosphere. Managers should treat ideas and suggestions as priceless treasures and implement them immediately whenever possible.

4. *Share the goals*. A motivated work force needs well-defined goals that address both individual and organizational needs. Information on goal setting is given in Chapter 2.

5. *Monitor progress*. The process of goal-setting should include a road map detailing the journey with periodic milestones and individual assignments. Managers should periodically review performance.

6. *Develop interesting work*. Managers should consider altering the employees' assignments by means of job rotation, job enlargement, and job enrichment.

Job rotation permits employees to switch jobs within a work unit for a prescribed period of time. This activity reduces boredom and provides knowledge of the entire process and the affect of the sub-process. Thus, quality consciousness is raised, which may lead to process improvement.

Job enlargement combines tasks horizontally so that the employee performs a number of jobs sequentially. Thus, the employee is responsible for a greater portion of the product or service, which may also lead to process improvement.

Job enrichment combines tasks vertically by adding managerial elements such as planning, scheduling, and inspection. This contributes to the employees' sense of autonomy and control over their work, which may lead to process improvement.

7. *Communicate effectively*. Effective communication provides employees with knowledge about their work unit and the organization rather than "grapevine" information. Communication is covered in greater detail in Chapter 2.

8. *Celebrate success*. Recognizing employee achievements is the most powerful tool in the manager's toolbox. Additional information is given in the recognition and reward section of this chapter.

These eight concepts can be used at all managerial levels of the organization.

Employee Surveys[9]

As described in the previous section, an initial step a manager should take in initiating employee empowerment is to survey their employees to determine their current level of perceived empowerment. Employee surveys help managers assess the current state of

---

[9] This section is adapted from Ronald D. Snee, "Listening to the Voice of the Employee," *Quality Progress* (January 1995): 91–95: and Roger E. Breisch, "Are You Listening," *Quality Progress* (January 1995): 59–62.

employee relations, identify trends, measure the effectiveness of program implementation, identify needed improvements, and increase communication effectiveness. The success of the survey is directly related to the quality of the planning. An organization should not plan, develop, and administer the survey unless managers are willing to use the results and work towards empowering their employees.

The first step is for the quality council to create a multifunctional team with responsibilities as previously described. In addition, the team will determine the objective and develop a plan to communicate results, encourage root cause analysis, and encourage corrective action.

Next, the team will develop the survey instrument using in-house and external expertise. Identifiers such as location, sex, age, seniority, and work unit are absolutely essential to analyze the results. A Likert-type response scale as shown in Figure 4-2 usually provides usable results. If the entire population is not surveyed, then the sampling procedure should be determined for the initial and subsequent ones. The survey is pilot tested and revised as needed.

Other constructs to address in the survey include personality characteristics, management styles, job attitudes, and the work.[10] Examples of each include:

- Personality characteristics—anxiety, self-esteem in the organization, and ability to participate in the organization.
- Management styles—consideration of subordinates, initiating structure, commitment to quality.
- Job attitudes—job satisfaction, social support at work and co-worker's commitment to quality.
- The work—task variety, autonomy and importance.

Several employee empowerment questionnaires exist in the literature.[10,11]

The third step is to administer the survey. This activity begins by communicating to the employees the purpose, schedule of events, and employee expectations. The survey should be administered by an outside group to maintain anonymity. Written comments should be typed with names disguised. Employees should be given time to complete the questionnaire, preferably during normal work hours in a large area such as the cafeteria. Surveys are administered every 12 to 18 months.

Next, the results are compiled and analyzed, and a report is prepared for the quality council in a timely manner. This report is shared with the entire organization, including a mechanism for input of reactions and suggestions.

---

[10] Hayes, Bob E., "How to Measure Empowerment," *Quality Progress* (February 1994): 41–46.

[11] Kontoghiorghes, Constantine and Deborah Dembeck, "Prioritizing Quality Management and Sociotechnical Variables in Terms of Quality Performance," *Quality Management Journal*, Vol. 8, No. 3: 36–48.

Using the rating scheme below, please circle the number that most closely describes how much you agree with the statement.

Rating Scheme:

1 = Strongly disagree	4 = Agree
2 = Disagree	5 = Strongly agree
3 = Neither agree nor disagree	N/A = Not applicable

Statement	Rating
1. There is a strong spirit of cooperation in this organization.	1 2 3 4 5 N/A
2. I know what is expected of me.	1 2 3 4 5 N/A
3. I am treated with respect by my supervisors.	1 2 3 4 5 N/A
4. I am asked for my input.	1 2 3 4 5 N/A
5. I always have what I need to accomplish my job.	1 2 3 4 5 N/A
6. Employees in this organization treat each other with respect.	1 2 3 4 5 N/A
7. I fully understand the goals, policies, and objectives of this organization.	1 2 3 4 5 N/A
8. The actions of management are always consistent with organization goals, policies, and objectives.	1 2 3 4 5 N/A
9. I am well informed.	1 2 3 4 5 N/A
10. I am properly recognized for my contributions.	1 2 3 4 5 N/A
11. My supervisor provides me with feedback on how well I am doing.	1 2 3 4 5 N/A
12. I have all the training I need.	1 2 3 4 5 N/A
13. Employee suggestions and recommendations are welcomed by management.	1 2 3 4 5 N/A
14. Management has a sincere concern for the employees.	1 2 3 4 5 N/A
15. I would like a greater say in how things get done.	1 2 3 4 5 N/A
16. The quality of work by this organization is excellent.	1 2 3 4 5 N/A
17. The working conditions in this organization are excellent.	1 2 3 4 5 N/A
18. This organization has the best reputation of any in this area as a good place to work.	1 2 3 4 5 N/A
19. I thoroughly enjoy my job!	1 2 3 4 5 N/A
20. If I could find another job with the same pay, I would.	1 2 3 4 5 N/A

21. If you had a "magic wand" that could change *one* particular thing, what would you change and why?

_____

_____

22. What is the *one* most important factor that could be improved in order to help you do your job better?

_____

_____

Figure 4-2 Employee Opinion Survey
Adapted, with permission, from G. W. Chase, *Implementing TQM in a Construction Company* (Washington DC: Associated General Contractors of America, 1993).

The last step is to determine areas for improvement. Such areas for improvement will occur at the work unit level, cross boundaries among work groups such as between engineering design and marketing, and cover the entire organization.

By listening to the voice of the employee, the organization can receive feedback to help ensure a thriving TQM effort.

Empowerment

The Manufacturers' Alliance for Productivity and Innovation stated that "[o]rganizations that empower employees as part of their total management effort are twice as likely as other firms to report significant product or service improvement."[12]

The dictionary definition of empowerment is to invest people with authority. Its purpose is to tap the enormous reservoir of potential contribution that lies within every worker. An operational definition follows:

> Empowerment is an environment in which people have the ability, the confidence, and the commitment to take the responsibility and ownership to improve the process and initiate the necessary steps to satisfy customer requirements within well-defined boundaries in order to achieve organizational values and goals.

Empowerment should not be confused with delegation or job enrichment. Delegation refers to distributing and entrusting work to others. Employee empowerment requires that the individual is held responsible for accomplishing a whole task. The employee becomes the process owner—thus, the individual is not only responsible but also accountable. Job enrichment is aimed at expanding the content of an individual's job, whereas empowerment focuses on expanding on the context of the job such as its interactions and interdependencies to other functions of the organization.[13]

In order to create the empowered environment, three conditions are necessary.

1. *Everyone must understand the need for change.* People fear change. The effective communication of why the organization needs to change is critical to success. In addition, people need to understand the role they will play in the change process. Senior management must understand that people change for their own reasons, not for reasons of the organization. People who are older, well educated, highly skilled, and experienced are more likely to accept increased demands and expectations associated with empowerment. In addition, one's perceived internal control (locus of control) contributes to whether or not an employee is receptive to an empowered environment.[14]

---

[12] "News—Employee Involvement Linked to Quality Gains," *Quality Progress* (December 1993): 14.

[13] Dimitriades, Zoe S., "Empowerment in Total Quality: Designing and Implementing Effective Employee Decision-Making Strategies," *Quality Management Journal*, Vol. 8, No. 2 (2001): 19–28.

[14] Dimitriades.

2. *The system needs to change to the new paradigm.* The system needs to change to reinforce and motivate individual and group accomplishments. Individuals and groups must understand that freedom to act and (sometimes to fail) is not only OK but is encouraged. Other contextual factors need to be considered if empowerment is to be successful, such as the role of unions and the type of industry (service or manufacturing). If the union environment is not willing to engage employees in an empowerment culture, success will be difficult.[15]

3. *The organization must enable its employees.* Enablement means providing information, education, and skill. To ask people to change work habits without providing them with the tools for change only increases resistance to the change process. Additional factors that should be considered before determining if organization can enable its employees are strategy and technology.[16] Companies that have a business strategy and technology focus of customization are more likely to embrace empowerment compared to companies whose strategy is that of low-cost and high volume.

There is nothing mystical about empowerment. People generally want to be more in charge of their jobs and careers. After all, they do that successfully in their personal lives every day. Most people appreciate and value the trust and responsibility inherent in an environment that supports empowered people and their actions. When people have the information, education, and skills required to perform in a changed environment, understand their boundaries of empowerment, and realize the necessity for change, their resistance to that change decreases greatly.[17]

A 1993 ASQ/Gallup survey showed that employees feel empowered to:

Stop work in progress 83%

Intervene on customer's behalf 81%

Make exception to procedures 61%

Rework product or service 61%

Replace merchandise 37%

Refund money/authorize credit 26%

Teams

Employee involvement is optimized by the use of teams. Teams, however, are not a panacea for solving all quality and productivity problems, but in most instances, they are effective.

---

[15] Dimitriades.

[16] Dimitriades.

[17] Bob Mann, "Empowerment: An Enabling Process," *Quality Digest* (January 1994): 39–44.

Definition

A *team* is defined as a group of people working together to achieve common objectives or goals. *Teamwork* is the cumulative actions of the team during which each member of the team subordinates his individual interests and opinions to fulfill the objectives or goals of the group. The objective or goal is a need to accomplish something such as solve a problem, improve a process, design a refrigerator, plan a conference, audit a process, or please a customer. It needs to be clearly defined, have milestones set, have resources provided, and use a systematic approach. Members of the team will need to focus on how they relate to each other, listen to the suggestions of others, build on previous information, and use conflict creatively. They will need to set standards, maintain discipline, build team spirit, and motivate each other. Each member of the team has their own history of experience to help achieve the objective. They should have a need to see the task completed, but also the needs of companionship, fulfillment of personal growth, and self-respect.

Why Teams Work

Teams work because many heads are more knowledgeable than one. Each member of the team has special abilities that can be used to solve problems. Many processes are so complex that one person cannot be knowledgeable concerning the entire process. Second, the whole is greater than the sum of its members. The interaction within the team produces results that exceed the contributions of each member. Third, team members develop a rapport with each other that allows them to do a better job. Finally, teams provide the vehicle for improved communication, thereby increasing the likelihood of a successful solution.

Types of Teams

The early history suggests that work simplification efforts by management and labor were most likely the first production-oriented teams. However, the development of quality control circles by the Japanese in 1961 is considered to be the beginning of the use of teams to improve quality. Quality control circles are groups of people from one work unit who voluntarily meet together on a regular basis to identify, analyze, and solve quality and other problems within their area. They choose their own problems and focus on quality-of-work-life and health/safety issues rather than on improving work processes. Often they remain in existence over a long period of time, working on project after project. Quality control circles have been quite successful in Japan and enjoyed some initial success in other countries but not as extensive. A major drawback was a lack of middle management support. Without managers on teams or directly overseeing the teams as a quality council might, members frequently were not able to persuade management to implement their recommendations.

Outside Japan, the popularity of quality control circles has declined; however, this type of team is the progenitor of our present teams. The current types of teams can be divided into four main groups. They may be called by different names and have slightly different characteristics to accommodate a particular organization.

1. *Process improvement team.* The members of a process improvement team represent each operation of the process or sub-process. Usually the scope of the team's activity is limited to the work unit. A team of about six to ten members will come from the work unit and, depending on the location of the sub-process, an external or internal supplier and external or internal customer would be included on the team. During the course of the team's life, additional expertise from other work areas may be added on a permanent or temporary as-needed basis. The life cycle of this type of team is usually temporary—it is disbanded when the objective has been obtained. When the targeted process includes many work units or the entire organization, a cross-functional team may be more appropriate with work unit teams as sub-teams.

2. *Cross-functional team.* A team of about six to ten members will represent a number of different functional areas such as engineering, marketing, accounting, production, quality, and human resources. It may also include the customer and supplier. A design review team is a good example of a cross-functional team. This type of team is usually temporary. An exception would be a product support team, which would be permanent and have as an objective to serve a particular product line, service activity, or a particular customer. This type of team breaks down functional area boundaries.

3. *Natural work teams.* This type of team is not voluntary–it is composed of all the members of the work unit. It differs from quality control circles because a manager is part of the team and the projects to be improved are selected by management. Some employees may opt not to work in teams for a variety of reasons, and managers should anticipate this action and be prepared to help employees become comfortable in the team environment or, alternatively, find work in another unit that still performs work as individuals. Even though "team work" is technically feasible, there may be such resistance that its introduction should be delayed until there has been substantial turnover.

4. *Self-directed/self-managed work teams.* They are an extension of natural work teams without the supervisor. Thus, they are the epitome of the empowered organization—they not only do the work but also manage it. There is wide discretion to organize their work subject to organizational work flow requirements. There is a team coordinator to liaison with senior management, that may rotate among members. The team meets daily to plan their activities, and decisions are usually by consensus. Additional responsibilities may include: hiring/dismissal, performance evaluation, customer relations, supplier relations, recognition/reward, and training. The team must have access to business information in order to plan, control, and improve their processes.

According to a recent survey of *Fortune* 1000 companies, 68% of the companies use self-directed work teams; however, only 10% of the workers are involved in such teams.[18] Developing these types of teams requires not only careful planning and substantial training of the individuals, but also several organizational changes. As a result, many companies begin with a few pilot teams that are implemented slowly to full development over several years.

The following example illustrates the complexity of self-directed work teams. In an electronics plant, a self-directed assembly team handles all aspects of the customer's order: it receives the order, prepares the components, assembles and solders circuit boards, tests the boards, ships the boards, controls inventory levels, and processes all paperwork. Jostens, Inc., manufacturer of class rings, began implementing two self-directed work teams in the fall of 1991. By 1994, 35 such teams were in existence. The company no longer records individual performance; instead, a gain sharing plan and a pay system that rewards team performance has been instituted.[19]

Of course, there is some overlap between these four main types of teams. Also, organizations will modify them to accommodate their culture.

Recognize that the use of teams to empower employees should be done gradually so that acceptance by both management and employees is built on successful results of teamwork. As an organization becomes more comfortable with the use of teams for empowerment, teams will form both laterally and vertically throughout the organization. As Figure 4-3 indicates, a permanent process improvement team (here, a business improvement team) that is directed by the quality council may address overall cross-functional improvements for the organization. By direction of the quality council, several cross-functional teams may be established to address specific improvement problems that span several functional areas. Within functional areas, one or more process improvement teams may be engaged. Finally, one or more functional areas may establish a work group or quality control circle to address overall improvements to the particular functional area.

Characteristics of Successful Teams

In order for a team to be effective, it should have certain characteristics, listed below.

1. *Sponsor.* In order to have effective liaison with the quality council, there should be a sponsor. Preferably the sponsor is a member of the quality council, thereby providing organizational support.

2. *Team charter.* A team charter is a document that defines the team's mission, boundaries, the background of the problem, the team's authority and duties, and resources. It also identifies the members and their assigned roles–leader, recorder, timekeeper, and facilitator (optional). Detailed information on roles is given in a later section. The sponsor and the team negotiate the charter.

---

[18] Dumaine, B., "The Trouble with Teams," *Fortune*, Vol. 130, No. 5 (1994): 86–87.

[19] Denton, Keith D., "How a Team Can Grow: Goal is to Become Self-Directed," *Quality Progress* (June 1999): 53–58.

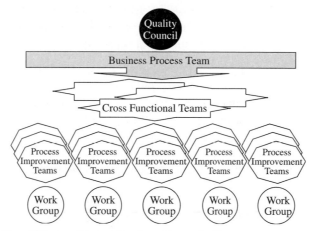

Figure 4-3 **The Use of Teams Throughout an Organization**

3. *Team composition*. The size of the team should rarely exceed ten people except in the case of natural work teams or self-directed teams. Larger teams have difficulty maintaining commitment, and interpersonal aspects become difficult to control. Teams should be diverse by having members with different skills, perspectives, and potential. Where appropriate, internal and external customers and suppliers should be included.

4. *Training*. As the need arises, members should be trained in problem-solving techniques, team dynamics, and communication skills. A later section discusses training in detail.

5. *Ground rules*. The team must develop its rules of operation and conduct. There should be open discussion on what will and will not be tolerated. Periodically the ground rules should be reviewed and revised when appropriate.

6. *Clear objectives*. Without clear objectives and goals, the team will have difficulty. In addition, the criteria for success should be agreed on with management. Detailed information on objectives and goals is given in Chapter 2.

7. *Accountability*. The team is accountable to perform. Periodic status reports should be given to the quality council. In addition, the team should review its performance to determine possible team process weaknesses and make improvements.

8. *Well-defined decision procedures*. Effective, acceptable, and timely decisions have to be made by the team. Detailed information on decisions is given later in the chapter.

9. *Resources*. Not only is funding and employee release time for the project important, but also important is access to information. The team cannot be expected to perform successfully without the necessary tools.

10. *Trust*. Management must trust the team to perform the task effectively. There must also be trust among the members and a belief in each other.

11. *Effective problem solving.* Decisions are based on the problem-solving method given in Chapter 5. They are not made on hunches or quick fixes.

12. *Open communication.* Members actively listen, without interruption, to other members, speak with clarity and directness, ask questions, and say what they mean.

13. *Appropriate leadership.* All teams need leadership—whether imposed by the quality council, or whether someone emerges as a leader figure as the life of the team progresses, or whether the leadership changes as the team matures. Detailed information on leadership is given in Chapter 2.

14. *Balanced participation.* All members must become involved in the team's activities by voicing their opinions, lending their knowledge, and encouraging other members to take part.

15. *Cohesiveness.* Members should be comfortable working with each other and act as a single unit, not as individuals or sub-groups.

Team Member Roles

Teams are usually selected or authorized by the quality council. A team will consist of a team leader, facilitator, recorder, timekeeper, and members. All team members have clearly defined roles and responsibilities.

The *team leader*, who is selected by the quality council, sponsor, or the team itself, has the following roles.[20]

- Ensures the smooth and effective operation of the team, handling and assigning record keeping, orchestrating activities, and overseeing preparation of reports and presentations.
- Facilitates the team process, ensures that all members participate during the meetings, prevents other members from dominating, actively participates when appropriate, guides without domineering, and uses positive interpersonal behavior.
- Serves as a contact point between the team and the sponsor or quality council.
- Orchestrates the implementation of the changes recommended by the team within organizational constraints and team boundaries.
- Monitors the status and accomplishments of members, assuring timely completion of assignments.
- Prepares the meeting agenda, including time, date, and location; sticks to the agenda or modifies it where appropriate; and ensures the necessary resources are available for the meeting.

---

[20]Jane E. Henry, "Lessons From Team Leaders," *Quality Progress* (March 1998): 57–59.

- Ensures that team decisions are made by consensus where appropriate, rather than by unilateral decision, handclasp decision, majority-rule decision, or minority-rule decision.

The *facilitator* is not a member of the team; he/she is a neutral assistant and may not be needed with a mature team. This person does not get involved in the meeting content or evaluation of the team's ideas. Roles are as follows:

- Supports the leader in facilitating the team during the initial stages of the team.
- Focuses on the team process; is concerned more with how decisions are made rather than the decision itself.
- Acts as resource to the team by intervening when necessary to keep the team on track.
- Does not perform activities that the team can do.
- Provides feedback to the team concerning the effectiveness of the team process.

The team *recorder*, who is selected by the leader or by the team and may be rotated on a periodic basis, has the following roles:

- Documents the main ideas of the team's discussion, the issues raised, decisions made, action items, and future agenda items.
- Presents the documents for the team to review during the meeting and distributes them as minutes after the meeting in a timely manner.
- Participates as a team member.

The *timekeeper*, who is selected by the leader or by the team and may be rotated on a periodic basis, has the following roles:

- Monitors the time to ensure that the team maintains the schedule as determined by the agenda.
- Participates as a team member.

The *team member*, who is selected by the leader, sponsor, or quality council or is a member of a natural work team, has the following responsibilities:[21]

- Contributes best, without reservation, by actively participating in meetings and sharing knowledge, expertise, ideas, and information.
- Respects other people's contributions—doesn't criticize, complain, or condemn.

---

[21] Karen A. Eichelberger, "Leading Change Through Projects," *Quality Progress* (January 1994): 87–90.

- Listens carefully and asks questions.
- Is enthusiastic—it's contagious and helps galvanize the entire team.
- Works for consensus on decisions and is prepared to negotiate important points.
- Supports the decisions of the team—badmouthing a decision or a member reduces the effectiveness of the team.
- Trusts, supports, and has genuine concern for other team members.
- Understands and is committed to team objectives.
- Respects and is tolerant of individual differences.
- Encourages feedback on own behavior.
- Acknowledges and works through conflict openly.
- Carries out assignments between meetings such as collecting data, observing processes, charting data, and writing reports.
- Gives honest, sincere appreciation.

Decision-Making Method[22]

Since the decision-making process is critical to the success of the team, it is essential to understand the different methods. Five types of decisions, as well as no decision, occur during the team process.

1. *Nondecision.* Occasionally a team will discuss a subject extensively and not arrive at a decision. This is unfortunate because time was wasted and the team ends up feeling poorly.

2. *Unilateral decision.* This type of decision is made by one person, usually the leader. Assuming that the problem-solving process was followed, the advantage of this type is that it saves time. However, it presumes that the leader has all the necessary information and the team will not react negatively to the decision. If the team reacts negatively, it can imperil team success.

3. *Handclasp decision.* When one person proposes a decision and another agrees, we have the handclasp decision. If the two parties are the most knowledgeable concerning this particular matter, then this decision can be effective. Otherwise, it will adversely affect team success.

4. *Minority-rule decision.* When a few team members dominate the discussion and impose their will on the majority, this type of decision occurs. This happens when members abdicate their responsibility and go along with the decision in order to be coopera-

---

[22] Adapted from M. Frohman, "Improve Group Problem Solving," Reprinted with permission from *Hydrocarbon Processing* (July 1989): 77–86. © 1989 by Gulf Publishing Co., all rights reserved.

tive and avoid conflict. Naturally, the results produce low enthusiasm for implementation and future involvement.

5. *Majority-rule decision.* This method is widely used when most of the team agree on the best alternative. It may stifle creativity and the search for compromises that lead to better solutions. In addition, the commitment for implementation may be compromised.

6. *Consensus.* This method requires sufficient discussion for all members to feel they can support the decision. Unanimous agreement is not required; it does mean that all members are willing to implement it. Consensus decisions usually take more time than other methods; however, the probability of successful implementation is enhanced. The key to the consensus method is to give everyone an opportunity to have input. As long as there is effective listening by team members, the method fosters creativity and produces more acceptable solutions. Consensus decision making requires use of the problem solving method. Further, team members should possess several problem solving qualities and traits to include: creativity, analytical thinking, intuitiveness, criticality, and the ability to synthesize.[23]

Ultimately, it is up to the team leader to select the appropriate method. If the leader has the trust of the team and the team understands the circumstances, whatever method is selected will be accepted.

Effective Team Meetings

If the participants know their roles and utilize the characteristics of successful teams, the probability of effective team meetings is enhanced. There are, however, a few items that can help improve the process:

- Meetings should be regularly scheduled; have a fixed time limit, and start on time. Participants should be notified ahead of time with the location, time, and objective. Avoid unnecessary meetings through e-mail, voice mail and telephone calls; however, also avoid accumulated issues.[24]

- An agenda should be developed, either at the end of the previous meeting or prior to the beginning of the next meeting. It should be sent to the participants prior to the meeting. Each agenda item includes a process, such as brainstorming, affinity diagram, discussion, and so forth; the presenters; and time guidelines.

- Agendas usually list: opening focus, previous meeting feedback, agenda review, agenda items, summary, and action items.

- Periodically, the meetings should be evaluated by the participants.

---

[23] Chaudhry, Abdul M., "To Be a Problem Solver, Be a Classicist," *Quality Progress* (June 1999): 47–51.

[24] Eckberg, John, "Fewer Meetings Can Reduce Inefficiency," *Business Monday* (July 31, 2000): 3.

	Agree	Disagree
1. The purpose of our meeting was well-defined.	0	0
2. We decided what we wanted to achieve by the end of the meeting.	0	0
3. We were sufficiently prepared for the meeting.	0	0
4. We reviewed our progress during the meeting.	0	0
5. We allocated the meeting time well.	0	0
6. We captured and developed spontaneous ideas.	0	0
7. We listened to all views for understanding.	0	0
8. We kept on track.	0	0
9. We kept our attention and concentration focused.	0	0
10. The meeting did not break up into small group discussions.	0	0
11. We reviewed and confirmed what had been agreed upon and how those decisions would be activated.	0	0
12. We had fun.	0	0

Figure 4-4 Example Meeting Evaluation Survey

A simple evaluation survey can be developed and completed by team members, such as the example provided in Figure 4-4.[25] Once the team has completed their evaluations individually, specific areas of improvement can be readily identified and addressed.

Successful team meetings require planning, training, and evaluation, as well as excellent leadership. Meetings should give workers direction and allow them to take action. Meetings should not be used to learn what action they should take.[26] Once at the meeting, stick to the agenda. Agendas keep the discussion moving and allow the meeting to run on time.

Stages of Team Development[27]

Organizations can dramatically improve team performance by understanding and recognizing the stages in the life cycle of teams. Knowing a team's location in the life cycle helps management understand team performance and avoid setting unrealistic objectives that limit a team's success. Bruce Tuckerman found that there were

---

[25] *Coaching and Teambuilding Skills for Managers and Supervisors*, SkillPath, Inc. 1992.

[26] Eckberg.

[27] Adapted, with permission, from Peter R. Scholtes, *The Team Handbook* (Madison, WI: Jointer Associates Inc., 1988).

four stages to a team's development. These stages are forming, storming, norming, and performing.[28]

Forming is the beginning stage where members become aware of the boundaries of acceptable behavior. Members are often not familiar with each other's skills, and each prefers to do the work on their own as there is a lack of trust. Members are cautious with their communication and tend to be formal. In general, the mission and goals of the team are still questionable, and the problems seem too large to solve.[29] It is a stage of transition from individual to member status and of testing the leader's guidance. Considerable time is spent in organizing and training. The team accomplishes little in regard to its objectives. To expedite the forming stage, an individual should be tasked with chartering the team.[30] In chartering a team, a facilitator commonly meets with the upper management to discuss the specific problem; he/she then develops a macro flowchart of the major processes associated with the product, service or process. From this information, the facilitator can better determine the team members that should be selected based on their skills and knowledge. The facilitator can then have the team meet to evaluate the problem posed by management, determine the type of training team members may need, and identify the appropriate team leader.

Storming is the most difficult stage as members start to realize the amount of work that lies ahead. There is a tendency to panic. Members rely almost solely on their personal and professional experience and resist working with other team members. There is a great deal of conflict, and the leader needs to be patient and flexible in working with the team. However, not all conflict is bad. If a team does not have any conflict, chances are the level of organizational performance is low.[31] Such teams adapt slowly to change, show apathy, or are stagnant. On the other hand, when conflict becomes disruptive, interferes with activities and makes coordination difficult, the team is dysfunctional. Owen indicates that good teams fight more than bad teams, at least at first.[32] Each individual, particularly those on cross-functional teams, brings with them both hierarchical and functional baggage, differences in goals, differences in perceptions, as well as different levels of work ethics, sense of time, career-family priorities, and attitudes toward authority. Team leaders and facilitators need to know how to manage team conflict so that it is productive and not destructive. Below are tips to help team members handle conflict.

- Ask those who disagree to paraphrase one another's comments. This may help them learn if they really understand one another.
- Work out a compromise. Agree on the underlying source of conflict, engage in a give and take, and finally agree on a solution.

---

[28] "Development Sequence in Small Groups," *Psychological Bulletin* (1965).

[29] Hoye, J. and T. Tupper, "Empowering Self-Managing Work Teams," *Quality Digest* (March 1994): 34–51.

[30] Cupello, James M., "The Gentle Art of Chartering a Team," *Quality Progress* (September 1995): 83–87.

[31] Chester, Raymond, "When Teams Go to War—Against Each Other," *Quality Progress* (June 1999): 25–28.

[32] Owen, Jean V., "Why Teams Fail," *Manufacturing Engineering* (September 1995): 63–69.

- Ask each member to list what the other side should do. Exchange lists, select compromises all are willing to accept, and test the compromise to see if it meshes with team goals.

- Have the sides each write ten questions for their 'opponents.' This will allow them to signal their major concerns about the other side's position. The answers often lead to compromise.

- Convince team members they sometimes may have to admit they are wrong. Help them save face by convincing them that changing a position shows strength.

- Respect the experts on the team. Give their opinions more weight when the conflict involves their expertise, but don't rule out conflicting opinions.

If managed properly, functional conflict leads to positive movement toward goals, innovation and creativity, and solutions to problems.

Norming is the stage where members begin to work together. Emotional conflict is reduced as cooperation, cohesion, and constructive criticism start to become the normal behavior. Because there is more time and energy to focus on the objectives, significant progress begins to occur.

Performing is the stage where the team members have settled their relationships and expectations. They better understand the project and begin performing by diagnosing and solving problems and choosing and implementing changes. Members understand their roles and work in concert to achieve their objective(s) effectively and efficiently.

Adjourning is a stage that is reserved for temporary teams. The team needs to evaluate its performance and determine lessons learned. This information can be transferred by members when they participate on future teams. There also needs to be a celebration to recognize the team's contribution to the organization.

As a result of proper training and effective leadership, some teams arrive at the performing stage so quickly that it may be difficult for an organization to observe the first three stages.

Ten Common People Problems and Their Solutions[33]

One way to deal with group problems is to talk about them as soon as they occur. Most problems require a more structured approach. Common team problems and their solutions are given below.

1. *Floundering* occurs when the team has trouble starting or ending a project or different stages of the project. Solutions to this state are to look critically at the improvement plan, review the mission statement, determine the cause of the holdup, and have each member write down reasons and discuss them at the next meeting.

---

[33] Adapted, with permission, from Peter R. Scholtes, *The Team Handbook*, (Madison, WI: Jointer Associates Inc., 1988).

2. *Overbearing participants* have an unusual amount of influence in the team. They usually have a position of authority or a particular expertise. Teams need these abilities; however, it becomes detrimental when they discourage discussion on their expertise and discount other members' ideas. Solutions are to reinforce the ground rules, talk to the person off-line and ask for cooperation, and enforce the importance of data and the problem-solving method.

3. *Dominating participants* like to hear themselves talk, use overlong anecdotes, and dominate the meeting. Members get discouraged and find excuses for missing meetings. Solutions are to structure discussion on key issues for equal participation, talk to the offending person off-line, and have the team agree on the need for limits and a balanced participation. In addition, the leader may act as a gatekeeper by asking questions such as "Joe, we heard from you; what do the others think?"

4. *Reluctant participants* feel shy or unsure of themselves and must be encouraged to contribute. Problems develop when there are no built-in activities that encourage introverts to participate and extroverts to listen. In addition to structured activities, solutions include dividing the task into individual assignments and acting as a gatekeeper by asking questions such as, "John, what is your experience in this area?"

5. *Unquestioned acceptance of opinions as facts* occurs when members assert personal beliefs with such confidence that other members think they are facts. Solutions are to request data and to follow the problem-solving method.

6. *Rush to accomplish* is common to teams being pushed by one or more members who are impatient for results. Teams must realize that improvements do not come easily and rarely overnight. Solutions are to remind members that the ground rules call for the problem-solving method or to confront the rusher off-line and explain the effects of impatience.

7. *Attribution* is the activity of guessing at a person's motives when we disagree or don't understand his or her opinion or behavior. Solutions are to reaffirm the importance of the problem-solving method, question whether this opinion is based on data, and find out the real meaning of the problem.

8. *Discounts and "plops"* arise when members fail to give credit to another's opinions or no one responds to a statement that "plops." Every member deserves the respect and attention from the team. Solutions are to reinforce active listening as a team behavior, support the discounted member, or talk off-line with members who frequently discount, put down, or ignore.

9. *Wanderlust: digression and tangents* happen when members lose track of the meeting's purpose or want to avoid a sensitive topic. Discussions then wander off in many directions at once. Solutions are to use a written agenda with time estimates, write meeting topics on flip charts, or redirect the conversation back to the agenda.

10. *Feuding team members* can disrupt an entire team with their disagreements. Usually these feuds predate the team and are best dealt with outside the team meetings. Solutions are to get the adversaries to discuss the issues off-line, offer to facilitate the discussion, and encourage them to form some contract about their behavior.

When people work together on a team, some of their energies are expended on "people issues." Mastery of these "people issues" leads to team success.

Common Barriers to Team Progress[34]

Evidence shows that the barriers given below are due primarily to the system rather than to the team.

- *Insufficient training.* Teams cannot be expected to perform unless they are trained in problem-solving techniques, group dynamics, and communication skills.

- *Incompatible rewards and compensation.* In general, organizations make little effort to reward team performance. Because of a strong focus on individual rewards it is difficult for individuals to buy into the team concept. Similarly, performance appraisals do not accept input from peers or team members.

- *First-line supervisor resistance.* Supervisors are reluctant to give up power, confident that they can do the work better and faster, are concerned about job security, and are ultimately held responsible.

- *Lack of planning.* A lack of common direction or alignment on the use of collaborative efforts, internal competition, redundancy, and fragmented work processes all prevent team progress.

- *Lack of management support.* Management must provide the resources and "buy into" the quality council/sponsor system.

- *Access to information systems.* Teams need access to organizational information such as business performance, competitive performance, financial data, and so forth.

- *Lack of union support.* Organizations need union support for the team to be successful.

- *Project scope too large.* The team and organization are not clear on what is reasonable, or management is abdicating its responsibility to guide the team.

- *Project objectives are not significant.* Management has not defined what role the team will play in the organization.

- *No clear measures of success.* The team is not clear about its charter and goals.

- *No time to do improvement work.* Values and beliefs of the organization are not compatible with the team's work. Individual departmental politics interfere with the team's progress. Management has not given the team proper resources.

---

[34] Information for this section comes from two surveys: Association for Quality and Participation, "Self-Directed Teams: A Study of Current Practice," Development Dimensions International and *Industry Week*, 1990, as reported in *Quality Digest* (October 1993): 42; and Wilson Learning Corporation, "Meeting the Collaborative Challenge: A Study of Supports and Barriers to Team Effectiveness," as reported in *Quality Digest* (April 1994): 8. And from two articles: Snee, Ronald D., K. H. Kelleher, J. G. Myers, and S. Reynard, "Improving Team Effectiveness," *Quality Progress* (May 1998): 43–48; and Beck, John D. W., and Neil M. Yeager, "How to Prevent Teams from Failing," *Quality Progress* (March 1996): 27–31.

- *Team is too large.* The organization lacks methods for involving people in ways other than team membership.
- *Trapped in groupthink.* Team members all have a mind-set that no actions are taken until everyone agrees with every decision.

With a knowledge of these barriers, management can evaluate their own performance and take the necessary corrective action to support team progress.

Training

Training is essential for an effective team. The quality council must take an active role in establishing training programs. Large organizations spend thousands of dollars in team training. For instance, the Tennessee plants of Saturn and Nissan spent large sums of money in training before they ever produced a vehicle. This large investment has its payoffs. Motorola, Inc. estimates that it earns $30 for every dollar invested in employee training. A recent study of small to mid-sized manufacturing firms found a significant positive relationship between company performance, as measured by profitability, and quality management training.[35]

The training must be experimental, because the trainees will retain 20% of what they hear and about 90% of what they do. Training should be practical and given on an as-needed basis. When possible, role-playing and case studies should be used. Trainers should be carefully selected for their knowledge, enthusiasm, and respect from the trainees.

Credibility must be established early. The team members should feel comfortable with the trainer and the program that has been developed. A clear picture of the objectives and how each member will benefit must be in place. The trainees should be encouraged to express their thoughts about the training program. Team leaders should be receptive to suggestions and make changes where warranted. Employees are much more likely to support a program that they helped develop.

The first step in the training process is to make everyone aware of what the training is all about. Thoughts, suggestions, and feedback should be gathered. The second step is to get acceptance. Trainees must feel that the training will be of value to them. The third step is to adapt the program. Is everyone ready to buy into it? Does everyone feel they are a part of what is going to take place? The fourth step is to adapt to what has been agreed upon. What changes must be made in behavior and attitudes?

In addition to team training covering group dynamics and communication skills, all members must receive training in quality awareness (TQM), specific problem solving techniques such as SPC, safety, and technical aspects of the job. The only difference among the types of training is that some may be required more often and for greater

---

[35] Ryan, Chuck, Richard H. Deane, and Ned P. Ellington, "Quality Management Training in Small to Midsized Manufacturing Firms," *Quality Management Journal*, Vol. 8, No. 2 (2001): 44–52.

TABLE 4-2
Who Needs to Receive Quality Training

Subject Matter	Top Management	Quality Managers	Other Middle Managers	Specialists	Facilitators	Work Force
Quality Awareness	X		X	X	X	X
Basic Concepts	X	X	X	X	X	X
Strategic quality management	X	X				
Personal Roles	X	X	X	X	X	X
Quality Processes	X	X	X	X	X	X
Problem Solving Methods		X	X	X	X	X
Basic Statistics	X	X	X	X	X	X
Advanced Statistics		X		X		
Quality in Functional Areas		X	X	X		
Motivation for Quality	X	X	X		X	

Reproduced, with permission, from J. M. Juran ed., *Quality Control Handbook*, 4th ed., (New York: McGraw-Hill, 1988).

lengths of time than others. Training programs fail for many different reasons, but they primarily fail because the focus is usually on the training itself and not on helping the organization improve in a real and measurable way.[36] To be efficient for the team members and the organization, training should be action oriented so that results can be obtained right away. Depending on an individual's position in the organization, Juran suggests different types of training in quality, as Table 4-2 suggests.

Team leaders play an important role in team building. There is a difference between being a supervisor and a team leader. Supervisors who become team leaders will experience a different situation than what they were accustomed to as supervisors. Team leaders share their responsibilities with other team members. They give team members a chance to succeed on their own. The team leader must be aware of the 85/15 rule, which means that 85% of the problems are part of the system. To be a good team leader requires specific training. Courses from local colleges in human relations, motivation, conflict resolution, communications, and related matters are recommended. Some organizations provide on-site training in these areas. Consultants are also available for this type of training. A well-trained team leader can help ineffective team members improve, but team members usually cannot help an ineffective team leader.

---

[36] Snee, Ronald D., "Make the View Worth the Climb," *Quality Progress* (November 2001): 58–61.

Suggestion System[37]

Suggestion systems are designed to provide the individual with the opportunity to be involved by contributing to the organization. Most of the ideas for continuous improvement will come from the team approach. However, once the foundation for a TQM organization has been established, a suggestion system can operate effectively and in parallel to the team approach. The key to an effective system is management commitment. Management must make it easy for employees to suggest improvements. Management should then review them promptly and if feasible, implement them.

Stimulating and encouraging employee participation starts the creative process. There are five ground rules:

1. *Be progressive* by regularly asking your employees for suggestions. Merely putting up a suggestion box will not create the necessary motivation.

2. *Remove fear* by focusing on the process and not on the person. When employees know that punitive actions will not occur, they are more likely to respond.

3. *Simplify the process* so it is easy to participate. Stamp out superfluous paperwork, review, and procedures.

4. *Respond quickly* to suggestions and within a specific period of time. The evaluation process must be simple and effective. The response, in writing, has three possible responses—acceptance, rejection, or referral to a committee for further evaluation. If accepted, a time frame for implementation should be given; if rejected, the reason for the rejection should be stated; and if referred to a committee, the evaluation time should be stated.

5. *Reward the idea* with published recognition so that everyone knows the value of the contribution.

Individual ideas are a vast untapped resource. The five-step approach helps to create an environment that opens communication between employees and managers. Idea generation is a skill that requires practice. It supplements the team process.

Recognition and Reward

Recognition is a form of employee motivation in which the organization publicly acknowledges the positive contributions an individual or team has made to the success of the organization. This acknowledgment is delivered using verbal and written praise and may include symbolic items such as certificates and plaques. Reward is something tangible such as theater tickets, dinner for two, or a cash award to promote desirable

---

[37] James A. Heath, "A Few Good Ideas for a Good Idea Program," *Quality Progress* (January 1994): 35–38.

behavior. Recognition and reward go together to form a system for letting people know they are valuable members of the organization.

Employees should be involved in the planning and implementation of the recognition and reward program. This activity should be performed by a cross-functional team that represents all areas of the organization. Systems that are developed with employee involvement will most likely succeed. It should be fully understood by the employees and reviewed periodically in order to continuously improve the system and because priorities—either the employee's or the organization's—may change. In addition, the system should be simple. Employees should be involved with the manager and sometimes the customer and supplier in the nomination and selection of the individuals and teams to be recognized and rewarded. Criteria for selection can utilize some of the information discussed in the section on appraisal.

The system that is developed by the team must have clear recognition criteria. Policies and procedures must be consistently and fairly applied throughout the organization. The system should be structured to avoid ranking individuals, because ranking fosters the counterproductive notion that there are winners and losers. Recognition should be valid, genuine, and meaningful for the giver and the recipient; it should not be used to manipulate people. The organization should recognize effort as well as easy-to-measure results. Recognition should not be based primarily on chance, which frequently occurs in employee-of-the-month programs.

The system should be so developed that monetary reward is not a substitute for compensation. While the reward may be delayed until an appropriate time, the recognition should be on a timely basis. Rewards should be appropriate to the improvement level—the greater the improvement, the greater the reward. They should be of value—a coffee cup does not provide much incentive to improve performance, especially when this is the third cup awarded to the employee and everyone else has two. It is also desirable for the employee to select the form of the reward from various alternatives.[38]

People like to be recognized, either as a team or individually. A person's feeling of achievement, value to the organization, knowing the organization cares, and having peer recognition may be more important than any reward. In addition to the plaque or framed certificate given at a formal banquet or informal pizza party, there are other forms of individual and team recognition. Other forms of recognition include pictures on the bulletin board, articles in newsletters or newspapers, letters to families, making a presentation to management, passing along compliments from others, personal phone calls or notes, placing positive notes in folders, and increased responsibility. Supervisors can also informally use the power of recognition by giving on-the-spot praise for a job well done whenever it is earned.

There are many different forms of individual and team rewards. Individual rewards include a better parking space, dinner out, gift certificates, gift to charity in the name of the recipient, washing an employee's car during the lunch hour, trips, and event tickets,

---

[38] Gene H. Milas, "How to Develop a Meaningful Employee Recognition Program," *Quality Digest* (May 1995): 139–141.

TABLE 4-3
Effective Reward Practices

Intrinsic Rewards	Extrinsic Rewards
• Non-monetary forms of recognition to acknowledge achievement of quality improvement goals	• Profit sharing
	• Gainsharing
• Celebrations to acknowledge achievement of quality improvement goals	• Employment security
	• Compensation time
• Regular expressions of appreciation by managers and leaders to employees to acknowledge achievement of quality improvement goals	• Individual based performance systems
	• Quality based performance appraisals
• 360 degree performance appraisals— feedback from co-workers (other than the immediate supervisor), subordinates or customers is incorporated into performance appraisals	
• Formal suggestion system available for individuals to make quality improvement suggestions	
• Developmental based performance appraisals	
• Quality based promotions	

Reproduced, with permission, from Richard S. Allen and Ralph H. Kilmann, "How Well Does Your Reward System Support TQM?" *Quality Progress* (December 1998): 47–51.

to name a few. Group rewards are similar and can also include an outing such as a ball game, bowling, and movies; group lunch or dinner; allowing the team to make some decisions affecting their work or allowing the team to spend their reward "earnings" to improve their work environment. Cash awards are also effective motivators for individual and team awards. Gainsharing is discussed next in this chapter. A survey of 100 organizations found the following intrinsic (those related to feelings of accomplishment or self-worth) and extrinsic (those related to pay or compensation issues) reward practices to be effective in their companies in supporting their TQM practices, as described in Table 4-3. Many organizations have periodic celebration banquets where awards are presented to individuals or teams.[39]

To summarize, an effective recognition and reward system:

1. Serves as a continual reminder that the organization regards quality and productivity as important.

---

[39] *1001 Ways to Reward Employees* (New York: Workman Publishing Co. Inc., 1994).

2. Offers the organization a visible technique to thank high achievers for outstanding performance.

3. Provides employees a specific goal to work toward. It motivates them to improve the process.

4. Boosts morale in the work environment by creating a healthy sense of competition among individuals and teams seeking recognition.

Gainsharing

Gainsharing is a financial reward and recognition system that results from improved organizational performance. It is different than profitsharing, in which the stockholders share a portion of the year-end profits with salaried and occasionally hourly employees. Gainsharing is based on the philosophy that people and teamwork are the keys to success. Because organizational success is dependent on team effort, the team shares in the rewards of success. Thus, gainsharing is a measurement of organizational productivity and a method to share productivity gains.

There are many different variations to the technique. We will illustrate the basic approach. This particular method utilizes labor costs and potential sales income for the calculations and is based on four-week periods; however, calculations are made on a weekly basis. At the end of the week, the team performance is calculated based on potential sales income from the week's production less rejections and outsourcing costs. Financial data shows that labor costs are a certain percentage of sales income, and this value multiplied by the income gives the *team goal*. *Team cost* is the sum of all labor costs for the week including fringe benefits. The *gain* or loss is the difference between the team cost and the team goal. For example:

Potential income = $535,000

Labor cost as a percent of sales = 27%

Team goal = $535,000 × 0.27 = $144,450

Actual team cost = $138,365

Gain = $144,450 − 138,365 = $6,085

Payments are usually made every four weeks, thereby providing motivational reinforcement. They are separate from the regular paycheck. Every four weeks gainsharing meetings are held to review the calculations, evaluate the performance, and discuss ways to make additional gains. Distribution of the gain can be to hourly personnel or to both salary and hourly personnel. It should be prorated by the employees' regular weekly earnings for four weeks. In other words, the gainsharing amount for an employee is the ratio of his four weeks earnings divided by the four weeks earnings of all employees in the plan. This ratio is multiplied by the gain. There are two types of performance strategies—

financial performance measure as illustrated by the example or physical performance measure such as pieces, weight, or volume.

One of the key issues is the amount of the gains. Organizations distribute between 30% and 100%, with 50% appearing to be equitable.

Another issue is the baseline determination, which in the example was 27%. The baseline can be based on historical information or, if unavailable, targeted information. It should be changed several times a year, using a weighted average, so that gains are for recent improvements rather than old ones. The baseline may also need to be adjusted for capital improvements or changes in mix.

Varian X-Ray Tube uses a simple gainsharing system to improve their yield. A pool is established by adding $125 for each good tube produced, subtracting $500 for each bad tube produced, and subtracting each bad tube returned from the customer. At the end of each quarter the money is divided equally among everyone in the production cycle who influenced quality.[40] Texas Nameplate Company started a gainsharing plan around 1997 when their defect rate was 3.7% (excellent compared to the industry average of 10%). Regardless of position or years with the company, all employees get the same share of the quarterly gain-sharing payout. By the end of 1997, employees reduced non-conformances to 1%.[41]

Gainsharing is an excellent motivational tool that improves quality, productivity, and, of course, the bottom line.

Performance Appraisal

The purpose of performance appraisals is to let employees know how they are doing, and provide a basis for promotions, salary increases, counseling, and other purposes related to an employee's future. There should be a good relationship between the employee and the appraiser. Employees should be made aware of the appraisal process, what is evaluated, and how often. Employees should be told how they are doing on a continuous basis, not just at appraisal time. The appraisal should point out strengths and weaknesses as well as how performance can be improved. Common appraisal formats are shown in Table 4-4.

Performance appraisals may be for the team or individuals. Regardless of the system, a key factor in a successful performance appraisal is employee involvement. An employee should always be given the opportunity to comment on the evaluation, to include protesting, if desired. Performance must be based on standards that are developed and agreed upon by the appraisor and employee. Standards normally contain an ideal level

---

[40] Robert H. Kluge, "An Incentive Compensation Plan With an Eye on Quality," *Quality Progress* (December 1996): 65–68.

[41] Stratton, Brad, "Texas Nameplate Company: All You Need is Trust," *Quality Progress* (October 1998): 29–32.

TABLE 4-4
Appraisal Formats

Type	Description
Ranking	Compares employees by ranking from highest to lowest.
Narrative	Gives a written description of employee's strengths and weaknesses.
Graphic	Indicates the major duties performed by the employee and rates each duty with a scale, which is usually from 1 (poor) to 5 (excellent).
Forced choice	Places each employee in a category with a predetermined percentage—for example, excellent (10%), very good (25%), good (30%), fair (25%), and poor (10%).

and an acceptable level. Standards should change when the situation changes, such as when equipment changes or new production techniques are developed.

Performance appraisals should be viewed as a positive way to get employees involved. Many supervisors look at appraisals as one of the unpleasant duties they must perform. Yet, if employees have been adequately interviewed as a part of the hiring process, properly trained, given help when needed, and counseled, then their performance will be a reflection on how well those tasks were performed. Performance appraisals also can be a pleasant duty for supervisors and can reveal how effective the employee is in contributing to the success of the organization.

Every effort should be made to avoid errors in performance evaluations. Culture, ethics, education level, and predetermined opinions can affect evaluations. It would be unfair indeed to render a poor rating based on bias or anything except how the employee has performed based on established standards. An unfair evaluation could cost the organization a valuable employee.

The traditional performance appraisal system has been criticized as being counterproductive and unnecessary by such quality experts as Deming and Scholtes. There are a number of arguments to support their opinion.

Appraisals nourish short-term performance and destroy long-term planning. Frequently, long-term gains are sacrificed by making the individual look good in the short term. This outlook is especially prevalent when we look at the emphasis on the quarterly profit and loss statement. Another criticism states that individual appraisal destroys teamwork. If teams are to become a cohesive unit of "all for one and one for all," then individual ranking would undermine the entire concept. The end result would be a team that performs poorer, not better. A third concern is the assumption that an individual is responsible for all results. In reality, the results are frequently beyond an individual's control, such as processes and equipment. Deming has stated that 85% of the problems are the result of the system. Last, there is a concern that appraisals are frequently based on subjectivity and immeasurables. They should be based on objectivity;

however, it is difficult to measure some attributes such as customer satisfaction and leadership.[42]

Rather than scrap performance appraisals, a number of practitioners have suggested that the performance appraisal system be improved. Some improvement suggestions are:

1. *Use rating scales that have few rating categories.* It is difficult to differentiate the middle range of performers (approximately 67%), whereas it is relatively easy to rate the 10 to 20% at each end. Therefore, scales should be limited to between 3 and 5.

2. *Require work team or group evaluations that are at least equal in emphasis to individual-focused evaluations.* The increased interdependence of tasks associated with TQM in the workplace dictates that team performance be utilized. This action will encourage team members to help, support, and cooperate with each other.

3. *Require more frequent performance reviews where such reviews will have a dominant emphasis on future performance planning.* Work team and individual performance data should be collected and reviewed with an evaluation of results and lessons learned. It may be necessary to have two reviews—one immediately after completion of the task and one when the performance cycle of the task allows evaluation of results. More frequent reviews with emphasis on improvement is much less threatening than the annual appraisal.

4. *Promotion decisions should be made by an independent administrative process that draws on current-job information and potential for the new job.* Placing too much weight on current performance in the selection process can force well-intentioned appraisers to make a poor decision. For example, the highest performing teller in a bank may not be the best person to be promoted to loan officer.[43]

5. *Include indexes of external customer satisfaction in the appraisal process.* In order to accomplish this process, the customers and their requirements will need to be identified, performance metrics determined using a rating scale, and the improvement process initiated. Evaluation will be based on the change in the metrics once the baseline has been established.

6. *Use peer and subordinate feedback as an index of internal customer satisfaction.* Initiation of this activity would be similar to the previous item.

7. *Include evaluation for process improvement in addition to results.* Process behavior tends to be more within the person's control. One of the basic concepts of TQM is continuous process improvement; therefore, if this concept is to be achieved, it must be

---

[42] George Eckes, "Practical Alternatives to Performance Alternatives," *Quality Progress* (November 1994): 57–60.

[43] J. Bruce Prince, "Performance Appraisal and Reward Practices for Total Quality Organizations," *Quality Management Journal* (January 1994): 36–46.

appraised. There is frequently a lag between process improvement and the results from that improvement.[44]

Despite Deming's reservations, performance appraisals can reinforce TQM concepts provided these suggestions are implemented where appropriate.

Unions and Employee Involvement

In general, unions support quality improvement programs but express concern regarding management exercising too much control over employees. Union representatives must be involved in any program involving employees. Although employee involvement has been widely accepted, it could be a problem if not properly addressed. In some instances where management takes too much control over employee involvement, it could be a violation of the National Labor Relations Act (NLRA) of 1935. Some have argued that a law passed to serve a good purpose in 1935 may not be appropriate for today's problems. However, unless the NLRA is amended, it is in the best interest of management to be sure actions taken will not violate the NLRA.

Teams should not discuss wages, rates of pay, hours of employment, or conditions of work. In some cases, these limitations will adversely effect the team's objective.[45]

Both management and unions must examine long-held views of what constitutes proper union-management relationships. Desire for unilateral power must be changed to shared power for the benefit of employees and the organization. A joint process of determining how best to proceed to effectively meet the competition, especially from foreign organizations, is the only sensible solution. Management must recognize and respect the unique role unions play in employee involvement. A feeling of trust must be established and a partnership developed between management and the union.

There are two ways in which unions and management have chosen to deal with the implementation of employee involvement in an organization. Some have chosen to work cooperatively, giving unions membership on quality councils and having them participate fully in planning, implementation, and evaluation of the entire effort. Others have adopted the more "traditional" mode of bargaining the impact and implementation actions affecting those in the improvement team. Each approach presents benefits and potential risks. Union involvement improves the continuous improvement process; however, union leadership runs the risk of criticism from other members if it is perceived as working too closely with management. The nature of the relationship will be determined by the back-

---

[44] Allan J. Weber, "Making Performance Appraisals Consistent With a Quality Environment," *Quality Digest* (June 1995): 65–69.

[45] Donald L. Dewar, "National Labor vs. Teams: What You Should Know," *Quality Digest* (May 1993): 60–62.

ground and history or the labor-management relations in the organization and the willingness of the union to participate. Ideally, the leadership of the organization will seek early involvement of the union and make the nature of the involvement as specific as possible.[46]

An example of union-management cooperation is illustrated by the collective bargaining agreement between the United Auto Workers and Ford Motor Company. It provides for joint leadership in the quality improvement effort by joint committees at the corporate, division, and facility levels. These committees have the authority of the contract to plan, implement, evaluate, and expand quality systems as needed. Many organizations can provide evidence that their successful quality systems can be attributed to the unions. Unions will grow if they are seen as a superior way to support democracy in the workplace and improve the performance of the organization.[47]

Benefits of Employee Involvement

Involving employees, empowering them, and bringing them into the decision-making process provides the opportunity for continuous process improvement. The untapped ideas, innovations, and creative thoughts of employees can make the difference between success and failure. Competition is so fierce that it would be unwise not to use every available tool.

Employee involvement improves quality and increases productivity, because

- Employees make better decisions using their expert knowledge of the process.
- Employees are more likely to implement and support decisions they had a part in making.
- Employees are better able to spot and pinpoint areas for improvement.
- Employees are better able to take immediate corrective action.
- Employee involvement reduces labor/management friction by encouraging more effective communication and cooperation.
- Employee involvement increases morale by creating a feeling of belonging to the organization.
- Employees are better able to accept change because they control the work environment.
- Employees have an increased commitment to unit goals because they are involved.

---

[46] Federal Quality Institute, *Employee Involvement and Quality Management in the Federal Government*, July 1993.

[47] Sidney P. Rubinstein, "Democracy and Quality as an Integrated System," *Quality Progress* (September 1993): 51–55.

Additional Comments

Employee involvement should not be looked at as a fad that will go away soon. It is a way of life, crucial to TQM, and it can mean the difference between being competitive and going out of business. Employees, not senior management, hold the future in their hands. The sign over the plant entrance that says, "Through these doors pass our most important asset, our employees" does not ring true when employees have a feeling that no one really cares. More involvement might be encouraged by the sign "No one of us knows as much as all of us."

As the organizational culture begins the process of change, resistance to this change will certainly be present. Keeping people informed will reduce resistance, especially when they see the benefits. Change is an ongoing process that must occur if an organization is to continue to exist in the competitive world. People do not necessarily resist change; they resist being changed, and problems arise when a person's comfort zone is disturbed.

Much of the information in this chapter has related to the role of management. However, we must not overlook the role of the work force. Workers must become knowledgeable about the needs of the customer and nominate quality problems for solution. In addition, workers must know what they are supposed to do and how they are doing and have a commitment to improving their job.

TQM Exemplary Organization[48]

Headquartered in San Antonio, TX, Clarke American provides a wide range of products and services to financial services partners across the United States. Products include personalized checks, checkbooks, checking account and bill-paying accessories, and financial forms. Services include customer contact call centers and e-commerce and direct response marketing solutions on behalf of their partners. The company has about 3,200 associates in its headquarters and at 17 manufacturing facilities and six customer contact call centers located in 15 states.

Clarke American's Key Leadership Team utilizes a goal deployment process to communicate and deploy values, directions, and performance expectations throughout the company. All associates receive company updates through weekly, monthly, quarterly, and annual meetings. Clarke American's eight values are: Customer First, Integrity and Mutual Respect, Knowledge Sharing, Measurement, Quality Workplace, Recognition, Responsiveness, and Teamwork. Customer satisfaction of its business products has consistently been above 96% since 1999 and reached 98% for September 2001, outperforming the banking industry average of 90%. Since 1995, revenue per associate has increased to $148,600, an 84% improvement.

---

[48] Malcolm Baldrige National Quality Award, 2001 Manufacturing Category Recipient, NIST/Baldrige Homepage.

The S.T.A.R. (Suggestions, Teams, Actions, Results) Program, initiated in 1995, allows associates to capture, implement, and share process improvements made to their work areas. Clarke American has implemented six S.T.A.R. ideas per associate for 2001 year-to-date, which exceeds both the average level reported by the Employee Involvement Association and the performance of a recent Baldrige winner. S.T.A.R. ideas implementation rates have increased from below 20% in 1995 to 70%, or over 20,000 ideas implemented for 2001 year-to-date.

Clarke American's overall associate satisfaction has improved from 72% in 1994 to 84% in 2000 and exceeds outside industry comparisons with two Baldrige Award recipients. Associate survey participation reached 96% in 2000, comparable to the world-class benchmark.

Clarke American uses a variety of methods to deliver training and education to its associates, including classroom teaching, individual coaching, and web- and computer-based training. Clarke American's 76.1 training hours per associate in 2000 exceeded the American Society for Training and Development Best in Class level of 60. The company's Team Excellence program (an award program for high performing teams) is responsible for over $15 million in cost reductions and $103 million in revenue growth from 1996 to 2000.

Manufacturing Cycle Time (in-plant production time) has improved by over 44% since 1995 and is under 18 hours for 2001 year-to-date. Manufacturing units per hour has improved over 150% since 1991, increasing from 10 to 26. Manufacturing cost per unit has improved 15% since 1995. Levels of internal errors have decreased 55% since 1995 and meet *Industry Week* magazine's average for best plants.

Exercises

1. As a supervisor, list ways to improve morale.

2. List the five levels in Maslow's hierarchy of needs and describe each level.

3. How do recognition and reward affect motivation?

4. List at least five reasons given by supervisors when resisting change.

5. Discuss the advantages of an empowered team.

6. You recently completed a performance appraisal for one of your employees. The employee is not happy with the evaluation and has asked for an appointment to discuss the evaluation process. Discuss the following:

   (a) The purpose of the performance evaluation.
   (b) The evaluation criteria.
   (c) The employee's options regarding the evaluation.

7. You have been asked to develop an employee involvement policy for your organization. Respond to the following:

   (a) Why do you need union involvement?
   (b) How will you get the union involved?
   (c) What resistance should you expect?

8. Describe the role of employees' involvement in TQM by responding to the following:

   (a) Why is employee involvement important to TQM?
   (b) Why do we need involved employees? We haven't before.
   (c) Employee time is valuable. How will it pay reasonable dividends?

9. Define the following:

   (a) teams
   (b) performance
   (c) reward
   (d) motivation
   (e) recognition
   (f) empowerment
   (g) gainsharing

10. Describe and analyze an incident where you wished you had the authority (empowerment) to make a decision but had a concern about whether or not you should make the decision on your own.

11. Conduct an employee opinion survey for a work unit and analyze the results. This may be done as an individual assignment or as a team effort.

12. Describe Herzberg's dissatisfiers and motivators.

13. What conditions are necessary for empowerment?

14. What are the different types of teams?

15. Why do teams work?

16. List five common barriers to team progress.

17. Evaluate an organization's

   (a) suggestion system
   (b) performance appraisal system
   (c) recognition and reward system
   (d) decision-making methods

This may be done as an individual assignment or as a team effort.

5

Continuous Process Improvement

Introduction

Quality-based organizations should strive to achieve perfection by continuously improving the business and production processes. Of course, perfection is impossible because the race is never over; however, we must continually strive for its attainment. Improvement is made by

- Viewing all work as a process, whether it is associated with production or business activities.
- Making all processes effective, efficient, and adaptable.
- Anticipating changing customer needs.
- Controlling in-process performance using measures such as scrap reduction, cycle time, control charts, and so forth.
- Maintaining constructive dissatisfaction with the present level of performance.
- Eliminating waste and rework wherever it occurs.
- Investigating activities that do not add value to the product or service, with the aim of eliminating those activities.
- Eliminating nonconformities in all phases of everyone's work, even if the increment of improvement is small.
- Using benchmarking to improve competitive advantage.
- Innovating to achieve breakthroughs.
- Incorporating lessons learned into future activities.
- Using technical tools such as statistical process control (SPC), experimental design, benchmarking, quality function deployment (QFD), and so forth.

Continuous process improvement is designed to utilize the resources of the organization to achieve a quality-driven culture. Individuals must think, act, and speak quality. An organization attempts to reach a single-minded link between quality and work execution by educating its constituents to "continuously" analyze and improve their own work, the processes, and their work group.[1]

Process

Process refers to business and production activities of an organization. Business processes such as purchasing, engineering, accounting, and marketing are areas where nonconformance can represent an opportunity for substantial improvement. Figure 5-1 shows a process model.

Inputs may be materials, money, information, data, etc. *Outputs* may be information, data, products, service, etc. The output of one process also can be the input to another process. Outputs usually require performance measures. They are designed to achieve certain desirable *outcomes* such as customer satisfaction. *Feedback* is provided in order to improve the process.

The *process* is the interaction of some combination of people, materials, equipment, method, measurement, and the environment to produce an outcome such as a product, a service, or an input to another process. In addition to having measurable input and output, a process must have value-added activities and repeatability. It must be effective, efficient, under control, and adaptable. In addition, it must adhere to certain *conditions* imposed by policies and constraints or regulations. Examples of such conditions may include constraints related to union-based job descriptions of employees, state and federal regulations related to storage of environmental waste, or bio-ethical policies related to patient care.

Process definition begins with defining the internal and/or external customers. The customer defines the purpose of the organization and every process within it. Because the organization exists to serve the customer, process improvements must be defined in terms of increased customer satisfaction as a result of higher quality products and services.

All processes have at least one owner. In some cases, the owner is obvious, because there is only one person performing the activity. However, frequently the process will cross multiple organizational boundaries, and supporting sub-processes will be owned by individuals within each of the organizations. Thus, ownership should be part of the process improvement initiatives.

At this point it is important to define an improvement. There are five basic ways to improve: (1) reduce resources, (2) reduce errors, (3) meet or exceed expectations of downstream customers, (4) make the process safer, and (5) make the process more satisfying to the person doing it.

---

[1] Danny G. Langdon, "A New Language of Work," *Quality Digest* (October 1994): 44–48.

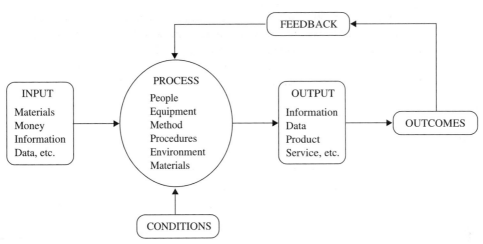

Figure 5-1 Input/Output Process Model

First, a process that uses more resources than necessary is wasteful. Reports that are distributed to more people than necessary wastes copying and distribution time, material, user read time, and, eventually, file space.

Second, for the most part, errors are a sign of poor workmanship and require rework. Typing errors that are detected after the computer printout require opening the file, making the correction, and printing the revised document.

Third, by meeting or exceeding expectations of downstream customers, the process is improved. For example, the better the weld, the less grinding required, making the appearance of a finish paint more pleasing.

The fourth way a process can be improved is by making it safer. A safer workplace is a more productive one with fewer lost-time accidents and less workers' compensation claims.

The fifth way to improve a process is to increase the satisfaction of the individual performing the process. Sometimes a little change, such as an ergonomically correct chair, can make a substantial change in a person's attitude toward their work.

This chapter presents several different approaches towards continuous process improvement. The first, Juran's Trilogy, approaches quality improvement from a cost-oriented perspective. The second is Shewhart's Plan-Do-Study-Act cycle. This approach is basically the engineering scientific method applied to continuous improvement and quality. A more in-depth description of the problem solving method is provided to further explain how to carry out the approach. The third is Kaizen, the Japanese approach to improvement. The Kaizen approach focuses on making small incremental improvements to the individual and the organization. It is actually more behavioral in nature than the other two approaches describe, as it often focuses on improving the individual and their individual job; thus, improvements to the organization as a whole are realized. The chapter concludes with a short discussion of reengineering and six-sigma concepts. These two approaches are becoming more popular in business, and they provide many of the basic concepts presented in the chapter.

The Juran Trilogy[2]

Process improvement involves planning. One of the best approaches is the one developed by Dr. Joseph Juran. It has three components: planning, control, and improvement, and is referred to as the Juran Trilogy. It is based loosely on financial processes such as budgeting (planning), expense measurement (control), and cost reduction (improvement).

Planning

The planning component begins with external customers. Once quality goals are established, marketing determines the external customers, and all organizational personnel (managers, members of multifunctional teams, or work groups) determine the internal customers. External customers may be quite numerous, as is the case of a bank supply organization, where they include tellers, financial planners, loan officers, auditors, managers, and the bank's customers. Where there are numerous customers, a Pareto diagram (see Chapter 18) might be useful to determine the vital few.

Once the customers are determined, their needs are discovered. This activity requires the customers to state needs in their own words and from their own viewpoint; however, real needs may differ from stated needs. For example, a stated need may be an automobile, whereas the real need is transportation or a status symbol. In addition, internal customers may not wish to voice real needs out of fear of the consequences. One might discover these needs by (1) being a user of the product or service, (2) communicating with customers through product or service satisfaction and dissatisfaction information, or (3) simulation in the laboratory. Because customer needs are stated from their viewpoint, they should be translated to requirements that are understandable to the organization and its suppliers.

The next step in the planning process is to develop product and/or service features that respond to customer needs, meet the needs of the organization and its suppliers, are competitive, and optimize the costs of all stakeholders. This step typically is performed by a multifunctional team. Quality function deployment (Chapter 12), Taguchi's quality engineering (Chapter 20), and quality by design (Chapter 13) are some of the approaches that can be used. It is important that the design team, rather than a single department, approve the final design and that the team be composed of all functional areas within an organization as well as customers and suppliers.

---

[2] Adapted, with permission, from J. M. Juran, ed., *Quality Control Handbook*, 4th ed. (New York: McGraw-Hill, 1988).

The fourth step is to develop the processes able to produce the product and/or service features. Some of this planning would have occurred during the previous step. This step is also performed by a multifunctional team with a liaison to the design team. Activities include determining the necessary facilities, training, and operation, control, and maintenance of the facilities. Of particular concern will be the "scaling up" from the laboratory or prototype environment to the real process environment. Additional activities include process capability evaluation and process control type and location.

Transferring plans to operations is the final step of the planning process. Once again, a multifunctional team with a liaison to the other teams is used. When training is necessary, it should be performed by members of the process planning team. Process validation is necessary to ensure, with a high degree of assurance, that a process will consistently produce a product or service meeting requirements. Positrol and process certification, discussed later in the chapter, are excellent techniques to use to help validate the process.

Control

Control is used by operating forces to help meet the product, process, and service requirements. It uses the feedback loop and consists of the following steps:

1. Determine items/subjects to be controlled and their units of measure.
2. Set goals for the controls and determine what sensors need to be put in place to measure the product, process, or service.
3. Measure actual performance.
4. Compare actual performance to goals.
5. Act on the difference.

Statistical process control (see Chapter 18) is the primary technique for achieving control. The basic statistical process control (SPC) tools are Pareto diagrams, flow diagrams, cause-and-effect diagrams, check sheets, histograms, control charts, and scatter diagrams. In addition, process capability information such as C_p and C_{pk} are used to determine if the process is capable and is centered.

Improvement

The third part of the trilogy aims to attain levels of performance that are significantly higher than current levels. Process improvements begin with the establishment of an effective infrastructure such as the quality council (see Chapter 2). Two of the duties of the council are to identify the improvement projects and establish the project teams with a project owner. In addition, the quality council needs to provide the teams with the resources to determine the causes, create solutions, and establish controls to hold the gains (see Chapter 4). The problem-solving method described in a later section may be applied to improve the process, while the quality council is the driver that ensures

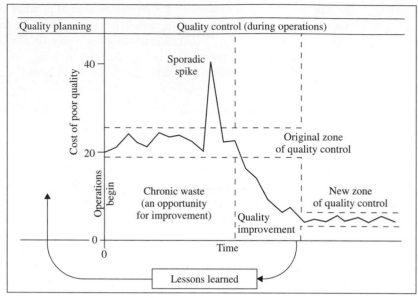

Figure 5-2 The Juran Trilogy Diagram
Adapted, with permission, from J. M. Juran, ed., *Quality Control Handbook,* 4th ed. (New York: McGraw-Hill, 1988).

that improvement is continuous and neverending. Process improvement can be incremental or breakthrough.

Figure 5-2 provides an example of how the three continuous improvement processes interrelate.[3] In the figure, Juran provides a distinction between sporadic waste and chronic waste. The sporadic waste can be identified and corrected through quality control. The chronic waste requires an improvement process. As a solution is found through the improvement process, lessons learned are brought back to the quality planning process so that new goals for the organization may be established.

Improvement Strategies[4]

There are four primary improvement strategies—repair, refinement, renovation, and reinvention. Choosing the right strategy for the right situation is critical. It is also true that proper integration of the strategies will produce never-ending improvement.

---

[3] Juran, J.M., "The Quality Trilogy," *Quality Progress* (August 1986): 19–24.

[4] This section adapted from Jack L. Huffman, "The Four R's of Total Improvement," *Quality Progress* (January 1997): 83–88. © American Society for Quality. Reprinted with permission.

Repair

This strategy is simple—anything broken must be fixed so that it functions as designed. There are two levels to this strategy. If a customer receives a damaged product, a quick fix is required. This level is a temporary or short-term measure. Although short-term measures shore up the problem, they should not become permanent. The second level occurs when an individual or team identifies and eliminates the root cause(s) of the problem and effects a permanent solution. It is important to note that the repair strategy does not make the process better than the original design.

Refinement

This strategy involves activities that continually improve a process that is not broken. Improvements to processes, products, and services are accomplished on an incremental basis. Refinement improves efficiency and effectiveness. It should become an integral part of every employee's job. Both individuals and teams can use this strategy. Typically it relies on doing things just a bit quicker, better, easier, or with less waste. This is the concept behind Kaizen to be discussed later in the chapter. The change may be so gradual that there is no appearance of change. The primary benefit of gradual change is that it produces little resistance from employees. However, because the change is so gradual, management may not recognize and reward the affected employees. Also, minor changes may not be documented or properly communicated.

Organizational programs—such as process improvement teams, suggestion systems, and empowerment—are combinations of repair and refinement. They provide the mechanisms for activities aimed at making these two strategies a part of the daily work life.

Renovation

This strategy results in major or breakthrough improvements. Although the resulting product, service, process, or activity might often appear to be different from the original, it is basically the same. Innovation and technological advancements are key factors in this approach. For example, the process of drilling a hole was originally done by hand with a cranking mechanism; however, with the advent of the electric motor, the electric drill was born. The electric drill has been continually refined by improved bits, chucks, and materials. More recently, another renovation occurred that was brought about by the development of rechargeable batteries. The rechargeable electric drill is basically the same as the old hand drill. Renovation is more costly than the previous strategies and is usually undertaken by teams rather than individuals.

Reinvention

Reinvention is the most demanding improvement strategy. It is preceded by the feeling that the current approach will never satisfy customer requirements. A new product, service, process, or activity is developed using teams based on a complete understanding of the customer's requirements and expectations. Reinvention or reengineering begins by imagining that the previous condition does not exist—in other words, a clean sheet of paper. Then the team uses in-depth knowledge of the customer's requirements and expectations and invents a new product, service, process, or activity. For example, the process of drilling holes using lasers or water jets was a reinvention.

Reinvention might also be desirable to maintain organization vitality or competitive advantage. An organization should use this strategy sparingly because of resistance to change and the fact that any new product, service, process, or activity will probably need to have the "bugs" removed by repair, refinement, and renovation.

Additional Comments

The repair and refinement strategies require that all employees have the freedom to solve problems and make incremental improvements in their jobs. Repair and refinement improvements are almost immediate with very little cost.

As previously stated, renovation and reinvention are effective in making breakthrough improvements; however, they usually are more costly, take longer to accomplish, and have a greater risk of failure.

Types of Problems[5]

There are five types of problems: compliance, unstructured, efficiency, process design, and product design. The first three are performance problems where an existing system is not performing satisfactorily, and the last two are design problems that require a new or improved design.

Compliance

Compliance problems occur when a structured system having standardized inputs, processes, and outputs is performing unacceptably from the user's viewpoint. These problems are identified by comparing with standards or by feedback from the internal or external customer. The major challenge is to determine the root cause of the nonconformity and then take corrective action. Diagnosis can be difficult, because products and processes are quite complex. Standards cannot address all of the potential problems due to the interaction of individually-acceptable characteristics.

Unstructured

Unstructured problems resemble compliance problems except that they are not specified by standards. The absence of standards may be due to system immaturity or to the need

---

[5] This section adapted from Gerald F. Smith, "Quality Problem Solving: Scope and Prospects," *Quality Management Journal* (Fall 1994): 25–40. © American Society for Quality. Reprinted with permission.

for flexibility in system performance. For example, an expert woodworker adjusts her activities to the grain and moisture content of the wood, and customer service workers adapt their behavior to individual customers. Identification of unstructured problems is usually brought about by negative customer feedback. The major challenges are to determine customer needs and to diagnose the causes of poor performance. Because of customer variability, it is difficult to determine why a product or service was unacceptable. Organizations need to treat each customer as an individual and maintain a database on acceptable and unacceptable behavior.

Efficiency

Efficiency problems occur when the system is performing unacceptably from the viewpoint of its owners or operators. In other words, the end user is satisfied; however, the process is more costly than desired, or working conditions are not acceptable. Problem solving is directed towards reducing cost and providing safe working conditions. Identification of such problems occurs from benchmarking and operator suggestions.

Process Design

Process-design problems involve the development of new processes and revision of existing processes. Many business and production processes have not been well designed or have become obsolete with advances in technology. Identification of problems is prompted by poor performance, the knowledge that we can do better (benchmarking), or the introduction of new products. It requires that user needs and relevant constraints be identified.

Product Design

Product-design problems involve the development of new products and the improvement of existing products. A major focus is to prevent process and end user problems by relying on customer needs. Although design work can be initiated as a result of poor product performance, problem solving usually occurs as a natural part of a competitive environment. A major challenge is translating, in a timely manner, user needs and constraints into product attributes and specifications, usually using quality function deployment (QFD).

The PDSA Cycle

The basic Plan-Do-Study-Act (PDSA) cycle was first developed by Shewhart and then modified by Deming.[6] It is an effective improvement technique. Figure 5-3 illustrates the cycle.

---

[6] Shewhart's cycle was called Plan-Do-Check-Act (PDCA).

Figure 5-3 The PDSA Cycle

The four steps in the cycle are exactly as stated. First, *plan* carefully what is to be done. Next, carry out the plan (*do* it). Third, *study* the results—did the plan work as intended, or were the results different? Finally, *act* on the results by identifying what worked as planned and what didn't. Using the knowledge learned, develop an improved plan and repeat the cycle. The PDSA cycle is a simple adaptation of the more elaborate problem-solving method discussed in the next section.

Problem-Solving Method

Process improvement achieves the greatest results when it operates within the framework of the problem-solving method. In the initial stages of a program, quick results are frequently obtained because the solutions are obvious or an individual has a brilliant idea. However, in the long term, a systematic approach will yield the greatest benefits.

The problem-solving method (also called the scientific method) has many variations depending, to some extent, on the use; however, they are all similar. There are seven phases, as shown in Figure 5-4. Also shown is the relationship to the PDSA cycle.

The phases are integrated because each phase is dependent upon the previous phase. Continuous process improvement is the objective, and these phases are the framework to achieve that objective.

Phase 1: Identify the Opportunity

The objective of this phase is to identify and prioritize opportunities for improvement. It consists of three parts: identify the problem, form the team (if one is not in existence) and define the scope.

Problem identification answers the question, "What are the problems?" The answer leads to those problems that have the greatest potential for improvement and have the greatest need for solution. Problems can be identified from a variety of inputs, such as the following:

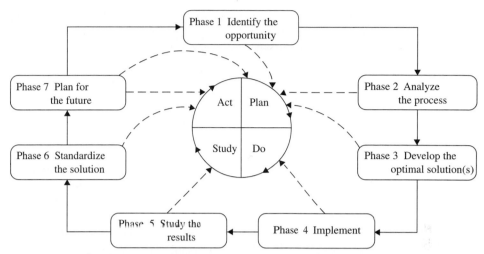

Figure 5-4 **Continuous Process Improvement Cycle**

- Pareto analysis of repetitive external alarm signals, such as field failures, complaints, returns, and others (see Chapter 18).
- Pareto analysis of repetitive internal alarm signals (for example, scrap, rework, sorting, and the 100% test).
- Proposals from key insiders (managers, supervisors, professionals, and union stewards).
- Proposals from suggestion schemes.
- Field study of users' needs.
- Data on performance of competitors (from users and from laboratory tests).
- Comments of key people outside the organization (customers, suppliers, journalists, and critics).
- Findings and comments of government regulators and independent laboratories.
- Customer surveys.
- Employee surveys.
- Brainstorming by work groups.

Problems identified provide opportunities for improvement. For a condition to qualify as a problem, it must meet the following three criteria:

- Performance varies from an established standard.
- Deviation from the perception and the facts.
- The cause is unknown; if we know the cause, there is no problem.

Identifying problems for improvement is not difficult, as there are many more problems than can be analyzed. The quality council or work group must prioritize problems using the following selection criteria:

1. Is the problem important and not superficial and why?
2. Will problem solution contribute to the attainment of goals?
3. Can the problem be defined clearly using objective measures?

In selecting its initial improvement opportunity, a work group should find a problem that, if solved, gives the maximum benefit for the minimum amount of effort.

The second part of Phase 1 is to form a team. If the team is a natural work group or one where members already work together, then this part is complete. If the problem is of a multifunctional nature, as most are, then the team should be selected and tasked by the quality council to address the improvement of a specific process. Goals and milestones are established. More information on teams is given in Chapter 4.

If the improvement strategy is repair or refinement, an individual, rather than a team, may be assigned to work on the problem.

The third part of Phase 1 is to define the scope. Failure in problem solving is frequently caused by poor definition of the problem. A problem well stated is half solved. Criteria for a good problem statement are as follows:

- It clearly describes the problem as it currently exists and is easily understood.
- It states the effect—what is wrong, when it happens, and where it is occurring, not why it is wrong or who is responsible.
- It focuses on what is known, what is unknown, and what needs to be done.
- It uses facts and is free of judgment.
- It emphasizes the impact on the customer.

An example of a well-written problem statement is:

As a result of a customer satisfaction survey, a sample of 150 billing invoices showed that 18 had errors that required one hour to correct.

The above statement describes the current state. We might also wish to describe the desired state, such as "Reduce billing errors by 75%."

In addition to the problem statement, this phase requires a comprehensive charter for the team. The charter specifies the following:

1. *Authority*. Who authorized the team?
2. *Objective and Scope*. What are the expected outputs and specific areas to be improved?

3. *Composition*. Who are the team members and process and sub-process owners?

4. *Direction and Control*. What are the guidelines for the internal operation of the team?

5. *General*. What are the methods to be used, the resources, and the specific milestones?

Phase 2: Analyze the Current Process

The objective of this phase is to understand the process and how it is currently performed. Key activities are to define process boundaries, outputs and customers, inputs and suppliers, and process flow; determine levels of customer satisfaction and measurements needed; gather data; and identify root causes.

The first step is for the team to develop a process flow diagram (see Chapter 18). A flow diagram translates complex work into an easily-understood graphic description. This activity is an "eye-opening" experience for the team, because it is rare that all members of the team understand the entire process.

Next, the target performance measures (see Chapter 7) are defined. Measurement is fundamental to meaningful process improvements. If something cannot be measured, it cannot be improved. There is an old saying that what gets measured gets done. The team will determine if the measurements needed to understand and improve the process are presently being used; if new ones are needed, the team will:

- Establish performance measures with respect to customer requirements.
- Determine data needed to manage the process.
- Establish regular feedback with customers and suppliers.
- Establish measures for quality/cost/timelines of inputs and outputs.

Once the target performance measures are established, the team can collect all available data and information. If these data are not enough, then additional new information is obtained. Gathering data (1) helps confirm that a problem exists, (2) enables the team to work with facts, (3) makes it possible to establish measurement criteria for baseline, and (4) enables the team to measure the effectiveness of an implemented solution. It is important to collect only needed data and to get the right data for the problem. The team should develop a plan that includes input from internal and external customers and ensures the plan answers the following questions:

1. What problem or operation do we want to learn about?
2. What are the data used for?
3. How many data are needed?
4. What conclusions can be drawn from the collected data?
5. What action should be taken as a result of the conclusion?

Data can be collected by a number of different methods, such as check sheets (see Chapter 18), computers with application software, data-collection devices like hand-held gauges, or an online system.

The team will identify the customers and their requirements and expectations as well as their inputs, outputs, and interfaces of the process. Also, they will systematically review the procedures currently being used.

Common items of data and information are:

- Customer information, such as complaints and surveys.
- Design information, such as specifications, drawings, function, bills of materials, costs design reviews, field data, service, and maintainability.
- Process information, such as routing, equipment, operators, raw material, and component parts and supplies.
- Statistical information, such as average, median, range, standard deviation, skewness, kurtosis, and frequency distribution.
- Quality information, such as Pareto diagrams, cause-and-effect diagrams, check sheets, scatter diagrams, control charts, histograms, process capability, acceptance sampling, run charts, life testing, inspection steps, and operator and equipment matrix analysis.
- Supplier information, such as process variation, on-time delivery, and technical competency.

The cause-and-effect diagram is particularly effective in this phase. Determining all of the causes requires experience, brainstorming, and a thorough knowledge of the process. It is an excellent starting point for the project team. One word of caution—the object is to seek causes, not solutions. Therefore, only possible causes, no matter how trivial, should be listed. Where data is not readily available for the process, many companies are turning to the use of simulation modeling to identify possible causes.[7,8]

It is important to identify the root cause. This activity can sometimes be determined by voting (see Chapter 18). It is a good idea to verify the most likely cause, because a mistake here can lead to the unnecessary waste of time and money by investigating possible solutions to the wrong cause. Some verification techniques are the following:

1. Examine the most likely cause against the problem statement.
2. Recheck all data that support the most likely cause.
3. Check the process when it is performing satisfactorily against when it is not by using the who, where, when, how, what, and why approach.

---

[7] Czarnecki, Hank, Bernard J. Schroer, Mel Adams, and Mary Spann, "Continuous Process Improvement Which It Counts Most: The Role of Simulation in Process Design," *Quality Progress* (May 2000): 74–80.

[8] Peterman, Mike, "Simulation Nation," *Quality Digest* (May 2001): 39–42.

4. Utilize an outside authority who plays "devil's advocate" with the data, information, and reasoning.

5. Use experimental design, Taguchi's quality engineering, and other advanced techniques to determine the critical factors and their levels.

6. Save a portion of the data used in the analysis to confirm during verification.

Once the root cause is determined, the next phase can begin.

Phase 3: Develop the Optimal Solution(s)

This phase has the objective of establishing potential and feasible solutions and recommending the best solution to improve the process. Once all the information is available, the project team begins its search for possible solutions. More than one solution is frequently required to remedy a situation. Sometimes the solutions are quite evident from a cursory analysis of the data.

In this phase, creativity plays the major role, and brainstorming (see Chapter 18) is the principal technique. Brainstorming on possible solutions requires not only a knowledge of the problem but also innovation and creativity.

There are three types of creativity: (1) create new processes, (2) combine different processes, or (3) modify the existing process. The first type is innovation in its highest form, such as the invention of the transistor. Combining two or more processes is a synthesis activity to create a better process. It is a unique combination of what already exists. This type of creativity relies heavily on benchmarking (see Chapter 8). Modification involves altering a process that already exists so that it does a better job. It succeeds when managers utilize the experience, education, and energy of empowered work groups or project teams. There is not a distinct line between the three types—they overlap.[9]

Creativity is the unique quality that separates mankind from the rest of the animal kingdom. Most of the problems that cause inefficiency and ineffectiveness in organizations are simple problems. There is a vast pool of creative potential available to solve these problems. Quality is greatly improved because of the finding and fixing of a large number of problems, and morale is greatly increased because it is enormously satisfying to be allowed to create.[10]

Areas for possible change are the number and length of delays, bottlenecks, equipment, timing and number of inspections, rework, cycle time, and materials handling. Consideration should be given to combining, eliminating, rearranging, and executing simultaneously the process steps. In particular, reducing cycle times, lowering inventory levels, and searching for non-value-added activities are excellent sources for change, as these typically have many hidden costs that, if minimized or eliminated, affect a

---

[9] Paul Mallette, "Improving Through Creativity," *Quality Digest* (May 1993): 81–85.

[10] George Box, "When Murphy Speaks—Listen," *Quality Progress* (October 1989): 79–84.

number of processes in the organization. For example, lowering inventory levels allows there to be less WIP to be transported, frees floor space, and lessens the management and accounting of the WIP, particularly if the inventory is time-dated material.

Once possible solutions have been determined, evaluation or testing of the solutions comes next. As mentioned, more than one solution can contribute to the situation. Evaluation and/or testing determines which of the possible solutions have the greatest potential for success and the advantages and disadvantages of these solutions. Criteria for judging the possible solutions include such things as cost, feasibility, effect, resistance to change, consequences, and training. Solutions also may be categorized as short range and long range. At a minimum, the solution must prevent recurrence.

One of the features of control charts is the ability to evaluate possible solutions. Whether the idea is good, poor, or has no effect is evident from the chart.

Phase 4: Implement Changes

Once the best solution is selected, it can be implemented. This phase has the objective of preparing the implementation plan, obtaining approval, and implementing the process improvements.

Although the project team usually has some authority to institute remedial action, more often than not the approval of the quality council or other appropriate authority is required. If such approval is needed, a written and/or oral report is given.

The contents of the implementation plan report must fully describe

- Why will it be done?
- How will it be done?
- When will it be done?
- Who will do it?
- Where will it be done?

Answers to these questions will designate required actions, assign responsibility, and establish implementation milestones. The length of the report is determined by the complexity of the change. Simple changes may require only an oral report, whereas other changes require a detailed, written report.

After approval by the quality council, it is desirable to obtain the advice and consent of departments, functional areas, teams, and individuals that may be affected by the change. A presentation to these groups will help gain support from those involved in the process and provide an opportunity for feedback with improvement suggestions.

The final element of the implementation plan is the monitoring activity that answers the following:

- What information will be monitored or observed, and what resources are required?
- Who will be responsible for taking the measurements?

- Where will the measurements be taken?
- How will the measurements be taken?
- When will the measurements be taken?

Measurement tools such as run charts, control charts, Pareto diagrams, histograms, check sheets, and questionnaires are used to monitor and evaluate the process change.

Pylipow provides a combination map to help formulate an action plan to help measure the results of an improvement. The map, shown in Table 5-1 provides the dimensions of: what is being inspected, the type of data, timing of data collection, by whom, how the results will be recorded, the necessary action that needs to be taken based on the results, and who is to take the action.

Phase 5: Study the Results

This phase has the objective of monitoring and evaluating the change by tracking and studying the effectiveness of the improvement efforts through data collection and review

TABLE 5-1
Combination Map of Dimensions for Process Control

What's Inspected	Type of Data	Timing	By Whom?	Type of Record	Action	By Whom?
Process variable: continuous	Variable	During run: on-line	Device	Electronic control chart	Process Improved	Automated equipment
Process variable: sample				Paper control chart		
		During run: off-line	Process Operator	Electronic trend chart	Process adjusted	Operator
Product Sample	Attribute			Paper trend chart	Lot sorted	
		After lot: complete	Inspector	Electronic list	Sample repaired or discarded	Inspector or mechanic
100% of product				Paper list		
				None		

Reproduced, with permission, from Peter E. Pylipow, "Understanding the Hierarchy of Process Control: Using a Combination Map to Formulate an Action Plan," *Quality Progress* (October 2000): 63–66.

of progress. It is vital to institutionalize meaningful change and ensure ongoing measurement and evaluation efforts to achieve continuous improvement.

The team should meet periodically during this phase to evaluate the results to see that the problem has been solved or if fine-tuning is required. In addition, the team will want to see if any unforeseen problems have developed as a result of the changes. If the team is not satisfied, then some of the phases will need to be repeated.

Phase 6: Standardize the Solution

Once the team is satisfied with the change, it must be institutionalized by positive control of the process, process certification, and operator certification. Positrol (positive control) assures that important variables are kept under control. It specifies the what, who, how, where, and when of the process and is an updating of the monitoring activity. Standardizing the solution prevents "backsliding." Table 5-2 gives an illustration of a few variables of a wave soldering process.

In addition, the quality peripherals—the system, environment, and supervision—must be certified. The partial checklist in Table 5-3 provides the means to initially evaluate the peripherals and periodically audit them to ensure the process will meet or exceed customer requirements for the product or service.

Finally, operators must be certified to know what to do and how to do it for a particular process. Also needed is cross-training in other jobs within the process to ensure next-customer knowledge and job rotation. Total product knowledge is also desirable. Operator certification is an ongoing process that must occur periodically.

Phase 7: Plan for the Future

This phase has the objective of achieving improved levels of process performance. Regardless of how successful initial improvement efforts are, the improvement process

TABLE 5-2
Positrol of a Wave Soldering Process

What	Specs.	Who	How	Where	When
An 880 flux	0.864 g ± 0.008	Lab technician	Sp. gravity meter	Lab	Daily
Belt speed	ft/min ± 10%	Process technician	Counter	Board feed	Each change
Preheat temperature	220° ± 5°	Automatic	Thermo- couple	Chamber entrance	Continuous

TABLE 5-3

Checklist for Process Certification

Quality System	Environment	Supervision
Authority to shut down line	Water/air purity	Coach, not boss
Preventive maintenance	Dust/chemical control	Clear instructions
Visible, audible alarm signals	Temp/humidity control	Combe tasks
Foolproof inspection	Electrostatic discharge	Encourage suggestions
Neighbor and self-inspection	Storage/inventory control	Feedback of results

continues. It is important to remember that TQM addresses the quality of management as well as the management of quality. Everyone in the organization is involved in a systematic, long-term endeavor to constantly improve quality by developing processes that are customer oriented, flexible, and responsive.

A key activity is to conduct regularly scheduled reviews of progress by the quality council and/or work group. Management must establish the systems to identify areas for future improvement and to track performance with respect to internal and external customers. They must also track changing customer requirements.

Continuous improvement means not only being satisfied with doing a good job or process but also striving to improve that job or process. It is accomplished by incorporating process measurement and team problem solving in all work activities. TQM tools and techniques are used to improve quality, delivery, and cost. Organizations must continuously strive for excellence by reducing complexity, variation, and out-of-control processes.

Lessons learned in problem solving, communications, and group dynamics, as well as technical know-how, must be transferred to appropriate activities within the organization.

Although the problem-solving method is no guarantee of success, experience has indicated that an orderly approach will yield the highest probability of success. Problem solving concentrates on improvement rather than control.

Note that there are many similar approaches to problem solving that deviate slightly from the one presented here; however, all such approaches provide similar features. A similar problem-solving approach was used by the Federal Communications Commission (FCC) when it began its quality effort in 1990. Their seven-step approach to continuous improvement included identifying improvement opportunities, prioritizing and selecting potential improvements, analyzing root causes, developing alternatives and selecting choice solutions, testing of solutions, implementing them, and tracking the effectiveness of the solutions. When it began its quality effort in 1991, the FCC was receiving roughly 900 license applications per year and had a nine-month backlog of

600 applications. During the first step, the quality improvement team brainstormed on 20 possible improvement ideas, which were then narrowed to five. Next, they prioritized the opportunities based on an estimate of the cost of poor quality. Upon collection of data, it was found that over half of the licensing applications received contained errors that doubled the processing time. Once the team identified this information, they developed an "opportunity statement" to "increase the percentage of error-free license applications from 40% to 70%." To analyze the root causes, the team flow-charted the licensing process and constructed a cause-and-effect diagram. Through a data collection effort, it was found that 50% of the errors were due to unqualified persons completing the license application, and that the license form and instructions were unclear. As a result, the team redesigned the application process so that the instructions were clearer and processing guidelines were understandable by the applicants. Before implementing the final solution, the form was pilot tested to a sample group. A little over a year, the team implemented the new form. Nine months after implementing their new solution, the percentage of applications received without errors increased from 40% to 80%, the backlog was reduced to 16 applications without staff increases, the speed of service improved 47%, and the cost of poor quality was reduced by 67%.[11]

Technology is also playing an important part in the management of continuous improvement. Many problem-solving approaches have been incorporated into software to help facilitate the continuous improvement process for organizations. According to a recent *Quality Progress* survey, 88% of the respondents indicated that their organization used software or similar technology to aid in the improvement process.[12]

Kaizen

Kaizen is a Japanese word for the philosophy that defines management's role in continuously encouraging and implementing small improvements involving everyone. It is the process of continuous improvement in small increments that make the process more efficient, effective, under control, and adaptable. Improvements are usually accomplished at little or no expense, without sophisticated techniques or expensive equipment. It focuses on simplification by breaking down complex processes into their sub-processes and then improving them.

The Kaizen improvement focuses on the use of:[13]

[11]Fontaine, Daniel J. and Diane B. Robinette, "FCC Makes Dramatic Quality Improvements," *Quality Progress* (November 1994): 87–91.

[12]Brown, Paula, "Technology and Performance Improvement: Intellectual Partners?" *Quality Progress* (April 1998): 69–71.

[13]Glenn Gee, Phil McGrath, and Mahyar Izadi, "A Team Approach to Kaizen," *Journal of Industrial Technology* (Fall 1996): 45–48.

1. Value-added and non-value-added work activities.

2. *Muda*, which refers to the seven classes of waste—over-production, delay, transportation, processing, inventory, wasted motion, and defective parts.

3. Principles of motion study and the use of cell technology.

4. Principles of materials handling and use of one-piece flow.

5. Documentation of standard operating procedures.

6. The five S's for workplace organization, which are five Japanese words that mean proper arrangement (*seiko*), orderliness (*seiton*), personal cleanliness (*seiketso*), cleanup (*seiso*), and discipline (*shitsuke*).

7. Visual management by means of visual displays that everyone in the plant can use for better communications.

8. Just-in-time principles to produce only the units in the right quantities, at the right time, and with the right resources.

9. *Poka-yoke* to prevent or detect errors.

10. Team dynamics, which include problem solving, communication skills, and conflict resolution.

Kaizen relies heavily on a culture that encourages suggestions by operators who continually try to incrementally improve their job or process. An example of a Kaizen-type improvement would be the change in color of a welding booth from black to white to improve operator visibility. This change results in a small improvement in weld quality and a substantial improvement in operator satisfaction. The PDSA cycle described earlier may be used to help implement Kaizen concepts.

Kaizen traditionally involves slow incremental improvements; however, with the influence of Toyota and the now-infamous Toyota Production System that incorporates lean manufacturing principles, many of the concepts of Kaizen can be implemented in a more rapid fashion. An example of such concepts being implemented is Fleetwood, a manufacturer of recreational vehicles. Since implementing Kaizen in one of their plants in 1998, there has been a 65% overall reduction in work in progress and a 22% overall reduction in cycle times.[14] Copeland Corporation, a manufacturer of air conditioning and refrigeration reciprocating compressors, began adopting an adaptation of Kaizen and lean manufacturing in the early 1990's. Since then, productivity has doubled, and there has been a 33% reduction in manufacturing floor space. In addition, time per unit has been reduced by 35%.[15] Kaizen has even been applied to determining capital cost projects.[16]

---

[14] Franco, Vanessa R., and Robert Green, "Kaizen at Fleetwood," *Quality Digest* (March 2000): 24–28.

[15] Schroer, Bernard J., Mel Adams, Steve Stewart, and Paul J. Componation, "Continuous Process Improvement the Quick Step Way," *Quality Progress* (February 1998): 85–89.

[16] Cheser, Raymond, "Financial Kaizen: Lowering Hurdles to Long-Term Investments," *Quality Progress* (April 1995): 57–61.

Reengineering

According to Hammer and Champy, reengineering is the fundamental rethinking and radical redesign of business processes to achieve dramatic improvements in critical measures of performance.[17] Many practitioners believe that TQM is associated with only incremental improvements. Nothing could be further from the truth—for many years, the Malcolm Baldrige National Quality Award has defined continuous improvement as referring to both incremental and "breakthrough" improvement. The Japanese have not only relied on *kaizen* but have developed policy management (*hoshin kanri*) and policy deployment (*hoshin tenkai*) in large part to produce the kind of large-scale breakthroughs that Hammer and Champy promote. Nor is this concept uniquely Japanese. Joseph Juran has had a long-standing emphasis on breakthrough efforts aimed at achieving unprecedented levels of performance.[18]

In 1997, EM Jorgensen Company applied reengineering using a five-phased problem solving approach that ultimately reduced operating costs by 12%. The focus of the project was to identify and eliminate non-value-added work and reduce corresponding costs while maintaining quality.[19]

Six-Sigma

In 1999, M. Harry and R. Schroeder published *Six Sigma: The Breakthrough Management Strategy Revolutionizing the World's Top Corporations*. Since that time, there has been considerable interest in the subject; therefore, the authors have devoted much space to a review of the concept.

Statistical Aspects

According to James Harrington, "Six sigma was simply a TQM process that uses process capability analysis (see Chapter 18) as a way of measuring progress."[20] Sigma, σ, is the Greek symbol for the statistical measurement of dispersion called standard deviation. It is the best measurement of process variability, because the smaller the deviation value, the less variability in the process. Figure 5-5 shows a process that is normally distributed and centered with the upper and lower specification limits (USL and LSL) estab-

---

[17] Michael Hammer and James Champy, *Reengineering the Corporation, A Manifesto for Business Revolution* (New York, NY: HarperCollins, 1993).

[18] Robert E. Cole, "Reengineering the Corporation: A Review Essay," *Quality Management Journal* (July 1994): 77–85.

[19] Dagestino, Kathryn, Wendy L. Moore, and Jorn Teutloff, "Hustle, That's All," *Quality Progress* (September 2000): 73–79.

[20] H. James Harrington, "Six Sigma's Long-Term Impact," *Quality Digest* (June 2001): 16.

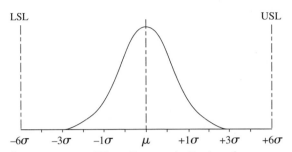

Figure 5-5 Nonconformance Rate When Process is Centered

lished at ± 6 σ. For this situation, 99.9999998% of the product or service will be between specifications, and the nonconformance rate will be 0.002 parts per million, or 2.0
per billion. The situation diagrammed represents a process capability index (C_p) of 2.0.
A C_p of 1.33 has been a defacto standard. Table 5-4 shows the percent between specifications, the nonconformance rate, and process capability for different specification limit
locations.

According to the six-sigma philosophy, processes rarely stay centered—the center tends to "shift" above and below the target, μ. Figure 5-6 shows a process that is
normally distributed, but has shifted within a range of 1.5σ above and 1.5σ below the
target. For the diagrammed situation, 99.9996600% of the product or service will be
between specifications and the nonconformance rate will be 3.4 ppm. This off-center
situation gives a process capability index (C_{pk}) of 1.5 with 1.0 being the defacto standard. Note that the index is calculated differently and, therefore, has a different symbol (C_p vs. C_{pk}). See Chapter 18 for a detailed analysis of the differences. Table 5-5
shows the percent between specifications, the nonconformance rate, and process capability for different specification limit locations. The magnitude and type of shift is

TABLE 5-4

**Nonconformance Rate and Process Capability
When the Process is Centered**

Specification Limit	Percent Conformance	Nonconformance Rate (ppm)	Process Capability (C_p)
±1σ	68.7	317300	0.33
±2σ	95.45	485500	0.67
±3σ	99.73	2700	1.00
±4σ	99.9937	63	1.33
±5σ	99.999943	0.57	1.67
±6σ	99.9999998	0.002	2.00

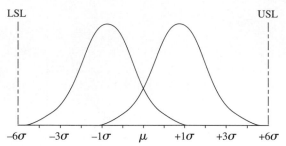

LSL   USL

-6σ -3σ -1σ μ $+1\sigma$ $+3\sigma$ $+6\sigma$

Figure 5-6 Nonconformance Rate When Process is Off-Center $\pm$ 1.5σ.

TABLE 5-5

Nonconformance Rate and Process Capability When the Process is Off-Center $\pm$1.5σ.

Specification Limit	Percent Conformance	Nonconformance Rate (ppm)	Process Capability (C_{pk})
$\pm1\sigma$	30.23	697700	-0.167
$\pm2\sigma$	69.13	308700	0.167
$\pm3\sigma$	93.32	66810	0.500
$\pm4\sigma$	99.3790	6210	0.834
$\pm5\sigma$	99.97670	2330	1.167
$\pm6\sigma$	99.9996600	3.4	1.500

a matter of discovery and should not be assumed ahead of time. None of the case studies in the literature have indicated a shift as great as 1.5σ. The automotive industry recognized the concept in the mid-1980's, evaluated it and deemed it unacceptable.[21] In fact, the original work of six sigma was based on only a few empirical studies of a single process.[22]

The statistical aspects of six-sigma tell us that we should reduce the process variability, σ, and try to keep the process centered on the target, μ;. These concepts are not new. They have been long advocated by Shewhart, Deming, and Taguchi and are covered in Chapter 18.

---

[21] D.H. Stamatis, "Who Needs Six Sigma, Anyway?" *Quality Digest* (May 2000): 33–38.

[22] Bender, Arthur, "6 × 2.5 = 9, Benderizing Tolerances—A Simple Practical Probability Method for Handling Tolerances for Limit-Stack-Ups," *Graphic Science* (December 1962): 17–21.

Other Aspects

Harry and Schroeder use a methodology called DMAIC, which stands for define, measure, analyze, improve, and control. This approach is somewhat similar but not as comprehensive as the seven phases of the problem-solving method discussed in this chapter. Their methodology features a breakthrough strategy using the project approach, which is similar to the same strategy advocated by Juran. Projects are identified by the amount of savings they can generate, which is simply good business sense and is one of the duties of the quality council as given in Chapter 2. The body of knowledge is not as comprehensive as that for a Certified Quality Engineer or the information in this textbook. Harry and Schroeder and others emphasized the need for management commitment and involvement, but these factors are necessary for any successful program and have been emphasized in this textbook. Except for the information in the next paragraph, six sigma has little to offer that isn't already available through other approaches.[23]

The Harry and Schroeder approach, however, does introduce an infrastructure of trained personnel to ensure that projects have the necessary resources to make improvements. A small group of individuals in the organization have the full-time job of making improvements. Competency levels of these individuals use the Karate designations of Green Belts, Black Belts, and Master Black Belts. Green Belts are the project leaders and have five days of classroom training. Black Belts help Green Belts define their projects, attend training with their Green Belts, and assist them with their projects after the training. Black Belts receive 160 hours of classroom instruction and one-on-one project coaching from Master Belts. Master Black Belts provide the technical leadership and much of the training for the program.[24]

Problems

There are a number of problems associated with the six-sigma methodology. It would be very difficult and not very cost effective for a small business to develop the required infrastructure. Even a medium-sized business would have difficulty paying for the high cost of the training. General Electric has spent over two billion dollars to develop their infrastructure.

In large companies, there is a great danger that the infrastructure will become a bureaucracy. At one flagship six-sigma company, a technical employee was admonished by a Black Belt for fixing several processes rather than turn them into six-sigma projects.[25] It is possible that operating personnel who know the most about the process will be outside the improvement loop. Certainly the concept of Kaizen is not compatible with having projects that average $175,000 in savings.

---

[23] Stamatis.

[24] Thomas Pyzdek, "The Six Sigma Infrastructure," *Quality Digest* (August 2001): 54.

[25] Anonymous, "The Emperor's New Woes, Revisited," *Quality Digest* (August 2001): 80.

According to Stamatis, "Six sigma presents absolutely nothing new to the quality field of defect prevention. It's little more than an old appraisal methodology that focuses on problems after they've already occurred."

Iomega, maker of Zip drives, began the implementation of its six-sigma program in 1998. The infrastructure of over 400 Master Black Belts, Black Belts, and Green Belts out of 3400 employees made impressive improvements. However, by May, 2001 the company was losing money, the share price went from $4.00 to $1.75 and the CEO, a former General Electric manager, was fired along with many employees.[26] It should also be pointed out that Motorola, where the six-sigma concept originated, has lost a considerable amount of market share of its wireless business and did not show a profit in 2001 for the first time in many years.

TQM Exemplary Organization[27]

Located 20 miles north of New York City, the Pearl River School District (PRSD) has five schools: three elementary schools (kindergarten through grade four), one middle school (grades 5 through 7), and one high school (grades 8 through 12). The district has about 330 employees and approximately 2,460 students. Ninety-four percent of the students beginning their schooling in Pearl River complete their high school education in the district.

The percentage of students graduating with a Regents diploma, a key objective of Pearl River School District, has increased from 63% in 1996 to 86% in 2001, while the percentage of students in schools with similar socio-economic profiles has decreased from 61% in 1996 to 58% in 2000. In comparison, the highest reporting district in New York had a 90% passing rate in 2001. In 2001, PRSD exceeded their benchmark on three of the eight State Regents content exams and was within three percentage points of the highest reporting district on the other five content exams.

Helping students to prepare for college, PRSD has improved Advanced Placement course performance from 34% of the students achieving a "3" or better in 1997 to 76% in 2001, while dramatically increasing the percentage of students taking the AP courses.

PRSD has reduced per-pupil expenditures (PPE) 9% over the last 11 years (from $14,563 in 1990/1991 to $13,180 in 2000/2001.

Overall PRSD student satisfaction, as measured using a recognized national survey, has increased from 70% in 1998 to 92% in 2001 and surpasses the highest score in the survey's databank (86% in 2001). Overall PRSD parent satisfaction, as measured with

---

[26] Louis F. Hannigan, "Letters," *Quality Digest* (October 2001): 8–9.

[27] Malcolm Baldrige National Quality Award, 2001 Education Category Recipient, NIST/Baldrige Homepage, Internet.

the same survey instrument, has increased from 62% in 1996 to 96% in 2001 and exceeds the highest score in the survey's databank (89% in 2001).

PRSD's overall staff and faculty satisfaction rate, as measured using a recognized national survey, has increased over the past four years from 89% to 98% for staff and 86% to 96% for faculty. These results exceed the survey databank's highest reported score for overall faculty and staff satisfaction combined (the composite faculty/staff satisfaction benchmark is 89%).

PRSD uses curriculum maps, developed by teams of teachers and senior leaders, to align its entire K-12 curriculum to state and national standards and to align instruction within and across all grade levels. These maps, which detail the content area covered as well as the method of instruction and assessment techniques used, are adjusted quarterly based on data analyses and through benchmarking the best practices of other school districts.

PRSD has a systematic nine-step process for strategy development at the district level, executed by the Board of Education and the Administrative Council. PRSD's educational design and delivery process uses a PDSA cycle to systematically plan, prioritize, design, and pilot new educational programs before they are introduced widely.

Exercises

1. List various techniques to sustain continuous improvement.

2. Working as an individual or in a team of three or more people, evaluate one or more of the following organizations concerning their use of the Juran Trilogy.

   (a) Large bank
   (b) Health-care facility
   (c) University academic department
   (d) University nonacademic department
   (e) Large department store
   (f) Grade school
   (g) Manufacturing facility
   (h) Large grocery store

3. Using a product such as a house, machine, or car, give an example of the four improvement strategies.

4. Give an example of the use of the PDSA cycle in your personal life and in your work experiences.

5. Select a problem in one of the processes of your daily life and use the seven phases to solve it.

6. Working as an individual or in a team of six or more people, implement the seven phases of the problem-solving method in one or more of the organizations listed in Exercise 2.

7. Describe how empowerment, work groups, and multifunctional teams would or would not affect the five types of problems.

6

Supplier Partnership

Introduction

An organization spends a substantial portion of every sales dollar on the purchase of raw materials, components, and services. In fact, 60% of the cost of goods sold in 2000 consisted of purchased goods. This is an increase from 20% in 1970.[1] Therefore, supplier quality can substantially affect the overall cost of a product or service. One of the keys to obtaining high-quality products and services is for the customer to work with suppliers in a partnering atmosphere to achieve the same quality level as attained within the organization.

Customers and suppliers have the same goal—to satisfy the end user. The better the supplier's quality, the better the supplier's long-term position, because the customer will have better quality. Because both the customer and the supplier have limited resources, they must work together as partners to maximize their return on investment.

There have been a number of forces that have changed supplier relations. Prior to the 1980s, procurement decisions were typically based on price, thereby awarding contracts to the lowest bidder. As a result, quality and timely delivery were sacrificed. One force, Deming's fourth point, addressed this problem. He stated that customers must stop awarding business based on the low bidder because price has no basis without quality. In addition, he advocated single suppliers for each item to help develop a long-term relationship of loyalty and trust. These actions will lead to improved products and services.

Another force changing supplier relations was the introduction of the just-in-time (JIT) concept. It calls for raw materials and components to reach the production operation in small quantities when they are needed and not before. The benefit of JIT is that inventory-related costs are kept to a minimum. Procurement lots are small and delivery is frequent. As a result, the supplier will have many more process setups, thus becoming

---

[1] Michael J. Abriatis, "Strategic Sourcing and Its Impact on Your Supplier Management Activities," SupplierInsight, LLC, 2001, Presentation at St. Louis. ASQ Chapter, December 2001.

a JIT organization itself. The supplier must drastically reduce setup time or its costs will increase. Because there is little or no inventory, the quality of incoming materials must be very good or the production line will be shut down. To be successful, JIT requires exceptional quality and reduced setup times.

The practice of continuous process improvement has also caused many suppliers to develop partnerships with their customers. Citing the company's effective use of Kaizen, the CEO of Freudenber-NOK approached Chrysler to implement a Kaizen project for every part it supplied to the automaker to reduce "controllable/variable" costs. The company freed 30% of its floor-space and increased revenues by 300% resulting in a strong alliance with its customer.[2]

Because approximately half of all revenues currently generated in the U.S. economy are derived from products and services developed in the last five years, many original equipment manufacturers (OEMs) are developing strategic partnerships with their suppliers. Suppliers are now taking on increased product-development responsibilities. In the development of new products, many suppliers are becoming involved in product design and complexity, formation of specifications, and component testing.[3]

A final force is ISO 9000, and in particular QS 9000 (ISO/TS 16949), which is mandated by the major automotive assembly firms. Specifically, first tier and tiers subsequent to the OEMs must maintain supply chain development through three key factors: zero defects, 100% on-time delivery, and a process for continuous improvement.[4]

These forces have changed adversarial customer-supplier relationships into mutually-beneficial partnerships. Joint efforts improve quality, reduce costs, and increase market share for both parties.

Principles of Customer/Supplier Relations[5]

Dr. Kaoru Ishikawa has suggested ten principles to ensure quality products and services and eliminate unsatisfactory conditions between the customer and the supplier:

1. Both the customer and the supplier are fully responsible for the control of quality.

2. Both the customer and the supplier should be independent of each other and respect each other's independence.

3. The customer is responsible for providing the supplier with clear and sufficient requirements so that the supplier can know precisely what to produce.

---

[2] Merrill, Ted, "The Shrinking Supply Base," *Actionline* (January/February 1995): 38–40.

[3] Merrill.

[4] Armstrong, Frank E., "QS 9000 Drives Automotive Supplier Development," *Quality Digest* (November 2000): 42–45.

[5] This section adapted, with permission, from *What Is Total Quality Control? The Japanese Way* by Kaoru Ishikawa, translated by David I. Lu (Upper Saddle River, NJ: Prentice Hall, 1985).

4. Both the customer and the supplier should enter into a nonadversarial contract with respect to quality, quantity, price, delivery method, and terms of payments.

5. The supplier is responsible for providing the quality that will satisfy the customer and submitting necessary data upon the customer's request.

6. Both the customer and the supplier should decide the method to evaluate the quality of the product or service to the satisfaction of both parties.

7. Both the customer and the supplier should establish in the contract the method by which they can reach an amicable settlement of any disputes that may arise.

8. Both the customer and the supplier should continually exchange information, sometimes using multifunctional teams, in order to improve the product or service quality.

9. Both the customer and the supplier should perform business activities such as procurement, production and inventory planning, clerical work, and systems so that an amicable and satisfactory relationship is maintained.

10. When dealing with business transactions, both the customer and the supplier should always have the best interest of the end user in mind.

Although most of these principles are common sense, a close scrutiny shows that a true partnering relationship exists with long-term commitment, trust, and shared vision. Ishikawa, like Deming, preaches a family-type relationship, where each party preserves their identity and independence.

Partnering[6]

Partnering is a long-term commitment between two or more organizations for the purpose of achieving specific business goals and objectives by maximizing the effectiveness of each participant's resources. The relationship is based upon trust, dedication to common goals and objectives, and an understanding of each participant's expectations and values. Benefits include improved quality, increased efficiency, lower cost, increased opportunity for innovation, and the continuous improvement of products and services. Partnering is a multifaceted relationship requiring constant nurturing to achieve continuous improvement and maximum benefit.

There are three key elements to a partnering relationship: long-term commitment, trust, and shared vision.

1. *Long-Term Commitment*. Experience has shown that the benefits of partnering are not achieved quickly. Problems require time to solve or processes need constant improvement. Long-term commitment provides the needed environment for both parties to

---

[6] This section adapted from Rusty Haggard, ed. *In Search of Partnering Excellence* (Austin, Texas: Construction Industry Institute, July 1991).

work toward continuous improvement. There must be total organizational involvement from the CEO to the workers.

Each party contributes its unique strengths to the processes. When these strengths are not sufficient, investment in new equipment, systems, or personnel may be required. The parties take risks that are commensurate with their rewards and the degree of the relationship. A supplier might not take these risks, such as acquiring new equipment or systems, without a long-term commitment.

Chrysler requires about 70 percent of the manufacturing tools it uses to be used by its suppliers as well.[7] Chrysler works early in the supplier relationship to expose and train the supplier to use CAE, CAD, and CAM software tools. Without supplier involvement, the use of advanced technologies within Chrysler would have had only marginal impact on the competition.

2. *Trust.* Trust enables the resources and knowledge of each partner to be combined to eliminate an adversarial relationship. Partners are then able to share information and accept reduced control. Mutual trust forms the basis for a strong working relationship. It should be viewed as a business paradigm shift and begins with the purchase contract that is nonadversarial. The purchasing function of the organization must be subordinate to the overall relationship goals and objectives. Open and frequent communication avoids misdirection and disputes while strengthening the relationship.

The parties should have access to each other's business plans and technical information, such as product and process parameters. In addition, they may share or integrate resources such as training activities, administrative systems, and equipment.

The strength of partnering is based on fairness and parity. Both parties become mutually motivated when "win-win" solutions are sought rather than "win-lose" solutions.

3. *Shared Vision.* Each of the partnering organizations must understand the need to satisfy the final customer. To achieve this vision, there should be an open and candid exchange of needs and expectations. Shared goals and objectives ensure a common direction and must be aligned with each party's mission. Employees of both parties should think and act for their common good. Each partner must understand the other partner's business so that equitable decisions are made. These decisions must be formulated and implemented as a team. Thus, the sharing of business plans aids in mutual strategic planning.

Sourcing

There are three types of sourcing: sole, multiple, and single. A *sole* source of supply implies that the organization is forced to use only one supplier. This situation is due to factors such as patents, technical specifications, raw material location, only one or-

---

[7] Ewasyshyn, Frank J., "Standard Warfare," *Actionline* (June 1995): 30–31.

ganization producing the item, or the item being produced by another plant or division of the organization. Partnering is a natural consequence of this type of sourcing, provided the supplier is willing to work together to satisfy the end user.

Multiple sourcing is the use of two or more suppliers for an item. Usually three suppliers are chosen, and their portion of the business is a function of their performance in terms of price, quality, and delivery. The theory of multiple sourcing is that competition will result in better quality, lower costs, and better service. However, in practice, an adversarial relationship may result without the claimed advantages. Multiple sourcing also eliminates disruption of supply due to strikes and other problems.

Single sourcing is a planned decision by the organization to select one supplier for an item when several sources are available. It results in large, long-term contracts and a partnering relationship. With a guaranteed future volume, the supplier can direct its resources to improve the processes. For the organization, the advantages are reduced business and production cost, complete accountability, supplier loyalty, and a better end product with less variability. Delivery disruption is always a problem and is even more so with JIT implementation. For the supplier, the advantages are new business from the customer and reduced cost of business and production processes because of economies of scale. Single sourcing has allowed organizations to reduce their supplier base. For example, Xerox eliminated 90% of its suppliers and improved supplier quality from 92% to 99.97% in six years. Through supplier consolidation, Merck cut its supplier base 75% in eight years; and Whirlpool reduced its suppliers 50% in four years.[8]

Supplier Selection

Before discussing supplier activities, it must be decided whether to produce or outsource a particular item. This decision is a strategic one that must be made during the design stage. The following three questions need to be answered:

1. How critical is the item to the design of the product or service?
2. Does the organization have the technical knowledge to produce the items internally? If not, should that knowledge be developed?
3. Are there suppliers who specialize in producing the item? If not, is the organization willing to develop such a specialized supplier?

These questions must be answered in terms of cost, delivery, quality, safety, and the acquisition of technical knowledge. One organization outsourced their trucking operation, warehousing, and accounts payable because it could be done better and cheaper.[9]

---

[8] Abriatis.

[9] A. Aswad, *TQM: A Unified Systems Approach* (Dearborn, Mich.: Unpublished manuscript, 1993).

Once the decision has been made to outsource, then the supplier must be selected. Following are ten conditions for selection and evaluation of suppliers.[10]

1. The supplier understands and appreciates the management philosophy of the organization.

2. The supplier has a stable management system. In determining this condition, several questions should be asked: Is there a quality policy statement that includes objectives for quality and its commitment to quality? Is the policy implemented and understood at all levels of the organization? Is there documentation that indicates who is in charge and responsible for quality in the organization? Is there a member of top management with the authority to execute a quality system? Does the management have scheduled reviews of its quality system to determine its effectiveness?

3. The supplier maintains high technical standards and has the capability of dealing with future technological innovations.

4. The supplier can provide those raw materials and parts required by the purchaser, and those supplied meet the quality specifications.

5. The supplier has the capability to produce the amount of production needed or can attain that capability.

6. There is no danger of the supplier breaching corporate secrets.

7. The price is right and the delivery dates can be met. In addition, the supplier is easily accessible in terms of transportation and communication. There must also be a system to trace the product or lot from receipt and all changes of production delivery.

8. The supplier is sincere in implementing the contract provisions. Does the supplier have a system for contract review, and does that system include a contract review of requirements and how differences between the contract and/or accepted order requirements should be resolved? Further, does the system allow the inclusion of amendments? Also, does the system include maintaining records of reviewed contracts?

9. The supplier has an effective quality system and improvement program such as ISO/QS 9000.

10. The supplier has a track record of customer satisfaction and organization credibility. A recent study by Andersen, the University of Cambridge, and Cardiff Business School found Japan to be the leader in the number of world class automotive supplier plants, but the U.S. held the top three supplier positions. Of the 13 supplier plants identified as "world class," five were from Japan.[11]

---

[10] Ishikawa.

[11] Smale, Daniel T., "Chain of Excellence," *Actionline* (March 1995): 24–26.

The preceding conditions go beyond evaluating a supplier on the basis of quality, price, and delivery. It is recommended that a large organization send a multifunctional team to assess these supplier conditions. The team may wish to score each condition on a scale of 1 to 5. Small organizations may wish to use a written questionnaire and survey potential suppliers by mail.

Supplier Certification

After supplier selection and approval, the next step is the certification process, which starts after the supplier begins shipment of the product. This process has been described by the Customer/Supplier Technical Committee of ASQ, which developed the following eight certification criteria:[12]

1. The customer and supplier shall have agreed upon specifications that are mutually developed, justifiable, and not ambiguous. Rarely do specifications contain all the information needed for manufacturing a product. With new products, the design team can significantly impact lead times and quality by working with the customer. However, for those products traditionally manufactured by the company and which are now being transferred to the supplier, several considerations should be made. In addition to design specifications, manufacturing, assembly, and packaging instructions should also be considered.[13]

2. The supplier shall have no product-related lot rejection for a significant period of time, say, one year, or significant number of lots, say, 20.

3. The supplier shall have no nonproduct-related rejections for a stated period of time, say, three months, or number of lots, say, five. Nonproduct-related nonconformities such as the wrong count or a billing error are not as serious as product-related ones and are usually correctable in a short period of time.

4. The supplier shall have no negative nonproduct-related incidents for a stated period, say, six months, or number of lots, say, ten. This criterion covers incidents or problems that occur even though inspection and tests showed conformance to specifications. Most likely the supplier would have been notified of the incident by memorandum or other written communication.

5. The supplier shall have a fully-documented quality system. ISO 9000 (see Chapter 10) is an excellent model to build a system even if registration is not the goal.

6. The supplier shall have successfully passed an on-site system evaluation. This evaluation could be by third party such as an ISO 9000 registrar or by a second party— the customer. Details on system audits are covered in Chapter 10.

---

[12] Adapted, with permission, from ASQ, "Supplier Certification—A Positive Response to Just-In-Time," *42nd Annual Quality Congress Transactions* (May 1988): 302–312. ©The American Society for Quality, 1988.

[13] Peterson, Yule S., "Outsourcing: Opportunity or Burden?" *Quality Progress* (June 1998): 63–64.

7. The supplier must conduct inspections and tests. Laboratory results are used for batch processes, and statistical process control (SPC) is used for piece part production.

8. The suppliers shall have the ability to provide timely inspection and test data. Because this documentation is necessary when the product arrives, it must be sent by computer or courier.

Occasionally it may be necessary to decertify a supplier as a result of a major problem. It is suggested that a supplier is allowed one failure before decertification.

Some organizations have gone beyond simple certification to a preferred supplier program. This achievement requires outstanding product and service performance by some of the suppliers. The main benefit of a preferred position is in new part development and subsequent purchases.

There are a number of benefits to certification. First, it eliminates receiving inspection, which allows the supplier to ship directly to stock. Second, a customer/supplier partnership is created, with each partner being responsible for its own appropriate quality. Finally, the number of suppliers is reduced to a manageable level, thus further reducing overhead costs.

Supplier Rating

The customer rates suppliers to:[14]

- Obtain an overall rating of supplier performance.
- Ensure complete communications with suppliers concerning their performance in the areas of quality, service, delivery, and any other measure the customer desires.
- Provide each supplier with a detailed and factual record of problems for corrective action.
- Enhance the relationship between the customer and the supplier.

A successful supplier rating system requires three key factors: (1) an internal structure to implement and sustain the rating program, (2) a regular and formal review process, and (3) a standard measurement system for all the suppliers.[15] A supplier rating system (often referred to as a scorecard system) is usually based on quality, delivery, and service: however some customers have added other categories, such as machineability and cost. These categories may also have subcategories. These basic categories are weighted, with quality usually given the greatest weight. A score is given to each category by means of a numer-

---

[14] R. J. Dekock, "Supplier Report Cards—A Route to Total Performance," *Tappi Journal* (October 1988): 109–115.

[15] Desai, Mahesh P. "Implementing a Supplier Scorecard Program," *Quality Progress* (February 1996): 73–75.

TABLE 6-1
An Example Supplier Scorecard

Item: Head stack assembly

Period: 4Q94		*Supplier A*	*Supplier B*	*Supplier C*	*Supplier D*	*Supplier E*
QUALITY PERFORMANCE	**MAXIMUM POINTS**	**ACTUAL POINTS**	**ACTUAL POINTS**	**ACTUAL POINTS**	**ACTUAL POINTS**	**ACTUAL POINTS**
Line returns	30	27.66	29.61	28.11	28.71	28.65
PPM deduction (Maximum−10)		− 10	− 10	− 10	− 10	− 10
Certified yield multiplier		0.9	0.94	0.87	0.85	0.72
Penalty: Field issues (Maximum−15)						
Stop shipment (Maximum−15)						
Line purge (−5 each time)						
Subtotal (0–30)	30	15.894	18.433	15.756	15.904	13.428
Process control	8	6.5	6.5	5.5	5	6
Process technology	6	5.2	4	5.2	4.8	4.6
Sustaining technical support	6	2.3	1.6	3.5	4	2.8
On-time delivery	20	20	18	19	19	18
Product technology	10	9.7	6.7	9.1	7.4	8.2
Lead time	15	13	13	13	13	13
Purchasing and material support	5	5	3	2	5	2
Performance matrix total	100	77.594	71.233	73.056	74.204	68.028
Price index = target price/actual price	1	0.878	0.947	1	0.905	0.967
SCORE = performance matrix × price index	100	68.127	67.457	73.056	67.154	65.783
Total Cost of Supply = ((100 − SCORE)/100) + 1	**1**	**1.3187**	**1.3254**	**1.2694**	**1.3285**	**1.3422**

1.0 = perfect
2.0 = worst possible

Reproduced, with permission, from Richard S. Allen and Ralph H. Kilmann, "How Well Does Your Reward System Support TQM?" *Quality Progress* (December 1998): 47–51.

ical value or a letter grade, which can then be converted to a numerical value. Table 6-1 shows a supplier scorecard for a head stack assembly developed by Conner Peripherals, a manufacturer and marketer of storage solutions for the computer industry. Objective criteria and weights were established for each of the categories of quality, process control and technology, support, delivery, product technology, lead time and purchasing. The table illustrates a comparative analysis of its suppliers.

Reports are prepared and issued quarterly, and grades should be provided to each supplier. To make reading the scorecards more effective, GM has initiated the use of a traffic light standard for its supplier quality scorecard. Supplier quality performance metric and ratings are categorized into one of the three colors of the traffic light. Red, yellow, and green colors are used to report performance metrics. Problem (red) and potential problem (yellow) metrics can be identified at a quick glance.[16] Federal Express (FedEx) and John Deere have web-based systems for their supplier scorecards—further enhancing the effectiveness of the scorecards.[17]

Relationship Development

The previous information on partnering, supplier selection, principles of customer/supplier relations, certification, and periodic rating contribute to the establishment of the relationship. Additional topics of inspection, training, teams, and recognition and reward contribute to the maintainability and growth of the relationship.

Inspection

The goal of inspection is to eliminate, substantially reduce, or automate the inspection activity. There are four phases of inspection: (1) 100% inspection, (2) sampling, (3) audit, and (4) identity check.

In the initial phase, 100% inspection of the *critical* quality characteristics by both the customer and the supplier is recommended. As the customer gains confidence in the supplier's quality performance, a change to sampling is initiated.

As the supplier gains confidence in its quality performance, a change to sampling is recommended, provided there is statistical control of the process using control charts and process capability (see Chapter 18). At this point, the customer changes to auditing the supplier's performance using a ship-lot scheme or some type of random sampling of the submitted lots.

In the third phase, the supplier continues statistical control of the process and initiates its own auditing. The customer now has complete confidence in the supplier and initiates identity checks, which verify the item number and quality for accounting and inventory control.

The fourth and final phase occurs when both the customer and supplier perform only identity checks. There is statistical control of the process and continuous improvement of the process. Experience in Japan and in the U.S. has shown that it takes about five years to achieve this final level of quality.

---

[16] Palady, Paul, "Exploiting the World's Most Recognized Standard," *Quality Progress* (February 2001): 54–61.

[17] Abriatis.

Training

In small organizations, the senior managers perform many different functions. Frequently no one has expertise in quality or the ability to train the work force. Therefore, the customer or a consultant must start the training process. Larger organizations may invite the supplier to attend their courses or present the course at the supplier's plant. Such training and the types of courses may be a requirement for partnership. Training should be viewed as an investment, not an expense.

Team Approach

Customer/supplier teams are established in a number of areas, such as product design, process design, and the quality system. It is a good idea to involve suppliers when the team is first assembled rather than at the end of its activities. Team meetings should occur at both parties' plants so they obtain a greater understanding of the processes.

Recognition

Creating incentives for suppliers is one way to ensure that they remain committed to a quality improvement strategy. Incentives may be in the form of a preferred supplier category with its rewards. Usually the supplier is interested in recognition such as publication of outstanding contributions in the customer's newsletter; a letter of commendation that can be posted on the TQM bulletin board; or a plaque that can be mounted in the supplier's reception area.

TQM Exemplary Organization[18]

Boeing Airlift and Tanker (A&T) designs, develops, and produces the C-17 Globemaster 111 airlifter. Capable of carrying a 170,000-pound load, these aircraft are used by the U.S. Air Force, the company's primary customer, to transport large, heavy cargo to sites around the world. A&T also supplies parts and services for transport aircraft and inflight refueling tankers.

In 1993, A&T overhauled its business, aiming to become "process-focused and customer-driven." It initiated partnerships with customers, unions, and suppliers. It replaced manager-controlled teams with empowered teams that now function like small businesses motivated by common, systematically-developed goals.

To help it "perform to plan," A&T has developed a seven-step approach for defining, managing, stabilizing, and improving processes. This process-based management, or

---

[18] Malcolm Baldrige National Quality Award, 1998 Manufacturing Category Recipient, NIST/Baldrige Homepage.

PBM, methodology also is used to set performance metrics that are not only indicators of efficiency but are also the chief drivers of customer satisfaction: quality, timeliness, and cycle time.

A&T's share of the U.S. military airlift market is 84%, almost eight times larger than its nearest competitor. The company credits its team structure with a better than 60% improvement in productivity, measured as revenue generated per employee. Productivity has increased from $200,000 per employee in 1994 to a projected $327,000 in 1998. For three of the last four years, A&T's productivity levels have topped those of its best competitor.

Partnering with suppliers also has paid off. Rejection rates have dropped from 0.9% in 1994 to 0.08% during 1998, and supplier on-time delivery has jumped to 99.8%, up from 75.9%. With its PBM methodology, A&T has improved the performance of its 50 major processes. From 1994 to 1998, performance on key quality measures has improved by 50%. Over the same span, A&T cut cycle time by more than 80%.

Since 1992, time spent on rework and repair of the C-17 has been reduced by 54%, a solid indicator of quality gains. Mean time between corrective maintenance has increased eightfold since 1993; the C-17's current level of performance is nearly four times better than that of the next best competitor's aircraft.

Trends in key measures of financial performance parallel gains in quality and operational performance. A&T's return on net assets was nearly seven times better than the next best competitor in 1997. Net asset turnover has improved by a factor of seven since 1994, while return on sales has improved nearly threefold.

Exercises

1. Working as an individual or in a team of two or three people, develop the steps to building a better supplier relationship with one of the following organizations:

   (a) Large bank
   (b) Health-care facility
   (c) University academic department
   (d) University nonacademic department
   (e) Large department store
   (f) Grade school
   (g) Manufacturing facility
   (h) Large grocery store

2. Working as an individual or in a team of two or three people, evaluate one or more of the organizations in Exercise 1 to determine if they are using Dr. Ishikawa's ten principles.

3. You have been employed as a quality assurance manager for a small metal fabrication firm (100 people). Your first assignment is to certify the suppliers and schedule a visit to each. Make a checklist with scoring criteria for your visit.

4. Working as an individual or in a team of two or three people, develop a supplier selection plan for one of the organizations listed in Exercise 1.

5. Working as an individual or in a team of two or three people, evaluate the customer/supplier relationship in terms of inspection, training, team approach, and recognition for one of the organizations listed in Exercise 1.

7

Performance Measures

Introduction

The sixth and final concept of Total Quality Measurement (TQM) is performance measures. One of the Malcolm Baldrige National Quality Award core values is managing by fact rather than by gut feeling. Managing an organization without performance measures is like a captain of a ship navigating without instrumentation. The ship would most likely end up traveling in circles, as would an organization. Measures play a vital part in the success or failure of an organization.

Basic Concepts[1]

Objectives

Performance measures are used to achieve one or more of the following seven objectives:

1. Establish baseline measures and reveal trends.
2. Determine which processes need to be improved.
3. Indicate process gains and losses.
4. Compare goals with actual performance.
5. Provide information for individual and team evaluation.
6. Provide information to make informed decisions.
7. Determine the overall performance of the organization.

---

[1] This section adapted, with permission, from Ray F. Boedecker, *Eleven Conditions for Excellence: The IBM Total Quality Improvement Process* (Quincy, Mass.: American Institute of Management, 1987).

Typical Measurements

What should be measured is frequently asked by managers and teams. The information below suggests some items that can be measured.

Human Resources:
Lost time due to accidents, absenteeism, turnover, employee satisfaction index, number of suggestions for improvement, number of suggestions implemented, number of training hours per employee, training cost per employee, number of active teams, number of grievances.

Customers:
Number of complaints, number of on-time deliveries, warranty data such as parts replacement, customer satisfaction index, time to resolve complaints, telephone data such as response time, mean time to repair, dealer satisfaction, report cards.

Production:
Inventory turns, SPC charts, C_p/C_{pk}, amount of scrap/rework, nonconformities per million units, software errors per 1000 lines of code, percent of flights that arrive on time, process yield, machine downtime, actual performance to goal, number of products returned, cost per unit.

Research and Development:
New product time to market, design change orders, R & D spending to sales, average time to process proposal, recall data, cost estimating errors.

Suppliers:
SPC charts, C_p/C_{pk}, on-time delivery, service rating, quality performance, billing accuracy, average lead time, percent of suppliers that are error free, just-in-time delivery target.

Marketing/Sales:
Sales expense to revenue, order accuracy, introduction cost to development cost, new product sales to total sales, new customers, gained or lost accounts, sales income to number of salespeople, number of successful calls per week.

Administration:
Revenue per employee, expense to revenue, cost of poor quality, percent of payroll distributed on time, number of days accounts receivable past due, number of accounts payable past due, office equipment up-time, purchase order errors, vehicle fleet data, order entry/billing accuracy.

A good metric compares the measurement of interest to the total possible outcomes, such as rework hours to total hours.

Criteria

All organizations have some measurements in place that can be adapted for TQM. However, some measurements may need to be added. In order to evaluate the existing measures or add new ones, the following ten criteria are recommended:

1. *Simple*: Measures should be understandable by those who will use them.

2. *Few in number*: The important measures must be distinguished from the unimportant ones so that users can concentrate on just a few. Two or three measures should be sufficient for any work group, with the number increasing for departments, functional areas, plants, and corporations. Quality councils may wish to use composite measures such as a customer satisfaction index. It is composed of several weighted metrics such as on-time delivery, cost, product or service quality, and complaints.

3. *Developed by users*: In order to ensure ownership of the measures, they must be developed by the user. Measures dictated by a higher authority will usually not receive support from downstream units. However, in some cases, measures are mandated by the customer.

4. *Relevance to customer*: Measures must be relevant to the needs of internal or external customers. Control over important changes should be vested in the people who are held responsible for the performance measure. They also decide what measures to use and set target goals.

5. *Improvement*: Although correcting nonconformances and making current decisions are important, the focus should be on improvement, prevention, and strategic long-term planning and goal setting. Measures are used to promote improvement, not to identify poor performance and penalize the low performers. They should be sensitive to the improvements made.

6. *Cost*: Of course, the bottom line is that cost and profit must reflect an improved financial picture, as shown by the cost of poor quality system and other financial data. In addition, the cost of measurement should be considered.

7. *Visible*: Facility-wide measures should be posted in a central location, such as the lunch or break room, where everyone can see them. Likewise, unit measures should be posted at the machine or work center.

8. *Timely*: Financial and accounting data are often presented too late to be actionable. This may require that measurements are taken hourly, daily, or weekly rather than monthly or quarterly as in traditional accounting systems. A significant portion of measurements need to be operational rather than financial.[2] Data needs to be measured, analyzed, and evaluated with respect to the desired goals so that the information can be used effectively in decision making.

---

[2] James W. Cortada, "Balancing Performance Measurements and Quality," *Quality Digest* (December 1994): 48–54.

9. *Aligned*: A comprehensive set of measures and indicators tied to customer and organizational performance requirements provides a way to align all activities with organizational goals.

10. *Results*: Key result measures need to be guided and balanced by the interests of all stakeholders—customers, employees, stockholders, suppliers, the public, and the community.

Use of these criteria will improve the suitability of the selected measures.

Strategy

The quality council has the overall responsibility for the performance measures. It ensures that all the measures are integrated into a total system of measures. To develop the system, the quality council will obtain appropriate information from all of the stakeholders. They will utilize the core values, goals, mission, and vision statements (see Chapter 2) as well as the objectives and criteria given above. With this information, the strategic measurement system is created.

An example of a system that emphasizes percent improvement might contain the functions and metrics as given below:

Quality

- Percent reduction in cost of poor quality
- Percent reduction in nonconformities
- Percent of certified suppliers
- Percent reduction in supplier base
- Percent reduction in corrective action cycle time

Cost

- Percent increase in inventory turnover
- Percent reduction in data transactions
- Percent increase in materials shipped direct to work-in-process by the supplier
- Percent increase in output dollars per employee
- Percent reduction in floor space utilization

Flexibility

- Percent reduction in cycle time
- Percent reduction in setup time
- Percent reduction in lot/batch size
- Percent increase in number of jobs mastered per employee
- Percent increase in common materials used per product

Reliability

- Percent of processes capable of $C_p = 2.0$
- Percent reduction in down time
- Percent reduction in warranty costs
- Percent reduction in design changes
- Percent increase in on-time delivery

Innovation

- Percent reduction in new product introduction time
- Percent increase in new product sales revenue as a percent of total sales revenue
- Percent increase in new patents granted
- Customer perception as a leader in innovation
- Percent of management time spent on or leading innovation

The above metrics are tracked monthly to show trends, identify problem areas, and allocate resources.[3]

Once the strategic measurement system is developed, the functional areas can develop their systems by involving their departments and work groups. The first step is to determine which processes or sub-processes are critical to providing input for the strategic system. Next, the critical metric(s) are determined using the information given above under Basic Concepts. This activity is followed by assigning responsibility for the collection, analysis, and dissemination of the data. The last step is the development of improvement procedures.

Each month the quality council should meet to monitor current activities and plan future ones. To assist them, a report package is prepared consisting of (1) performance measures; (2) narrative reports on competition, opportunities, and pertinent events; and (3) system audits.

Performance Measure Presentation

There are six basic techniques for presenting performance measures. The simplest and most common is the time series graph shown in Figure 7-1. Time as measured by days, weeks, months, and so forth, is shown on the horizontal axis, and the performance measure is shown on the vertical axis. This type of graph benchmarks the process and shows favorable and unfavorable trends in the measure.

A second form of presentation is the control chart (see Chapter 18). A control chart for percent nonconforming is shown in Figure 7-2.

A third presentation technique is the capability index, which is the ratio of the tolerance to the capability. There are two measures: one indicates the ability of the process

---

[3] Michael G. Tincher and Michael J. Stickler, "Measuring Continuous Improvement," *Actionline* (November 1994): 36–39.

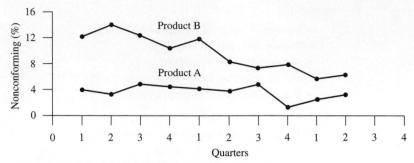

Figure 7-1 Time Series Graph for Percent Nonconforming

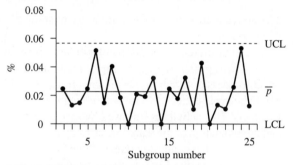

Figure 7-2 Control Chart for Percent Nonconforming

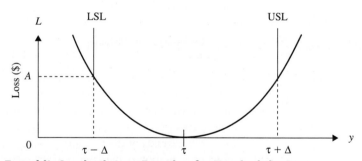

Figure 7-3 Taguchi's Quadratic Loss Function for Nominal-the-Best

to meet specifications, and the other indicates the centering of the process on the target (see Chapter 18).

Another way of measuring quality is Taguchi's loss function. This technique combines target, cost, and specifications into one measurement. Figure 7-3 illustrates the concept (see Chapter 20).

The fifth method of presenting performance measures is the cost of poor quality. Money attracts the attention of senior management; quality costs are described in the next section of this chapter.

The last method is the Malcolm Baldrige National Quality Award. Criteria for this award quite effectively measure the performance of the TQM effort on an annual basis. It is described in the last section of this chapter.

Quality Costs[4]

The value of quality must be based on its ability to contribute to profits. The goal of most organizations is to make money; therefore, decisions are made based on evaluating alternatives and the effect each alternative will have on the expense and income of the entity.

The efficiency of a business is measured in terms of dollars. The cost of poor quality can add to the other costs used in decision making, such as maintenance, production, design, inspection, sales, and other activities. This cost is no different than other costs. It can be programmed, budgeted, measured, and analyzed to help in attaining the objectives for better quality and customer satisfaction at less cost. A reduction in quality costs leads to increased profit.

Quality costs cross department lines by involving all activities of the organization— marketing, purchasing, design, manufacturing, and service, to name a few. Some costs, such as inspector salaries and rework, are readily identifiable; other costs, such as prevention costs associated with marketing, design, and purchasing, are more difficult to identify and allocate. There are failure costs associated with lost sales and customer goodwill, which may be impossible to measure and must be estimated.

Quality costs are defined as those costs associated with the nonachievement of product or service quality as defined by the requirements established by the organization and its contracts with customers and society. Simply stated, quality cost is the cost of poor products or services.

Management Technique

Quality costs are used by management in its pursuit of quality improvement, customer satisfaction, market share, and profit enhancement. It is the economic common denominator that forms the basic data for TQM. When quality costs are too high, it is a sign of management ineffectiveness, which can affect the organization's competitive position. A quality cost program provides warnings against oncoming, dangerous financial situations.

---

[4] This section is adapted from *Guide for Reducing Quality Costs*, 2 ed., 1987 and *Principles of Quality Costs*, 1986, by the Quality Cost Committee, with the permission of the American Society for Quality.

A quality cost program quantifies the magnitude of the quality problem in the language that management knows best—dollars. The cost of poor quality can exceed 20% of the sales dollar in manufacturing companies and 35% of the sales dollar in service organizations. In addition, the program may show quality problem areas that were previously unknown.

Quality costs identify opportunities for quality improvement and establish funding priorities by means of Pareto analysis. This analysis allows the quality improvement program to concentrate on the vital few quality problem areas. Once corrective action has been completed, the quality costs will measure the effectiveness of that action in terms of dollars.

A quality cost program lends credence to management's commitment to quality. Arguments for quality improvement are stronger when the quality costs show a need. The program also provides cost justification for corrective action. All costs associated with poor quality and its correction are integrated into one system to enhance the quality management function. Quality improvement is synonymous with a reduction in the cost of poor quality. Every dollar saved on quality cost has a positive effect on profits.

One of the principal advantages of the quality cost program is the identification of hidden and buried costs in all functional areas. Quality costs in marketing, purchasing, and design are brought to the forefront by the system. When senior management has all the facts on hidden and buried costs, they will demand a quality cost program.

A cost program is a comprehensive system and should not be perceived as merely a "fire-fighting" technique. For example, one response to a customer's problem could be to increase inspection. Although this action might eliminate the problem, the quality costs would increase. Real quality improvement occurs when the root cause of the problem is found and corrected.

Categories and Elements

For the convenience of future reference and use, detailed quality costs are identified in this section. There are four primary quality cost categories: prevention, appraisal, internal failure, and external failure. The list is not meant to contain every element of quality cost applicable to every organization. It is intended to give a general idea of what types of elements are contained within each category to help in deciding individual classifications. If a significant cost exists that fits any part of the general description of the quality cost element, it should be used. Sub-elements are identified; however, detailed descriptions are not included.

1.0 PREVENTIVE COST CATEGORY

The experience gained from the identification and elimination of specific causes of failure and their costs is utilized to prevent the recurrence of the same or similar failures in other products or services. Prevention is achieved by examining the total of such experience and developing specific activities for incorporation into the basic management system that will make it difficult or impossible for the same errors or failures to occur again. The prevention costs of poor quality have been defined to include the cost of all activities specifically designed for this purpose. Each activity may involve personnel from one or many departments. No attempt is made to define appropriate departments, because each organization is structured differently.

1.1 Marketing/Customer/User. Costs are incurred in the accumulation and continued evaluation of customer and user quality needs and perceptions (including feedback on reliability and performance) affecting user satisfaction with the organization's product or service. Sub-elements are marketing research, customer and user-perception surveys or focus groups, and contract and document review.

1.2 Product/Service/Design Development. Costs are incurred to translate customer and user needs into reliable quality standards and requirements and to manage the quality of new product or service developments prior to the release of authorized documentation for initial production. These costs are normally planned and budgeted and are applied to major design changes as well. Sub-elements are design quality progress reviews, design support activities, product design qualification tests, service design qualification, and field trials.

1.3 Purchasing. Costs are incurred to assure conformance to requirements of supplier parts, materials, or processes and to minimize the impact of supplier nonconformances on the quality of delivered product or services. This area involves activities prior to and after finalization of purchase order commitments. Sub-elements are supplier reviews, supplier rating, purchase order technical data reviews, and supplier quality planning.

1.4 Operations (Manufacturing or Service). Costs are incurred in assuring the capability and readiness of operations to meet quality standards and requirements, quality control planning for all production activities, and the quality education of operating personnel. Sub-elements are operations process validation, operations quality planning, design and development of quality measurement and control equipment, collecting quality costs, operations support quality planning, and operator quality education.

1.5 Quality Administration. Costs are incurred in the overall administration of the quality management function. Sub-elements are administrative salaries, administrative expenses, quality program planning, quality performance reporting, quality education, quality improvement, documenting and evaluating quality costs, and quality audits.

2.0 APPRAISAL COST CATEGORY

The first responsibility of a quality management system is assurance of the acceptability of product or service as delivered to customers. This category has the responsibility for evaluating a product or service at sequential stages, from design to first delivery and throughout the production process, to determine its acceptability for continuation in the production or life cycle. The frequency and spacing of these evaluations are based on a trade-off between the cost benefits of early discovery of nonconformities and the cost of the evaluations (inspections and tests) themselves. Unless perfect control can be achieved, some appraisal cost will always exist. An organization would never want the customer to be the only inspector. Thus, the appraisal costs of poor quality have been defined to include all costs incurred in the planned conduct of product or service appraisals to determine compliance to requirements.

2.1 Purchasing Appraisal Costs. Purchasing appraisal costs can generally be considered the costs incurred for the inspection and/or test of purchased supplies or service to determine acceptability for use. These activities can be performed as part of a receiving inspection function or as source inspection at the supplier's facility. Sub-elements are receiving or incoming inspections and tests, measurement equipment, qualification of supplier product, and source inspection and control programs.

2.2 Operations (Manufacturing or Service) Appraisal Costs. Operations appraisal costs can generally be considered the costs incurred for the inspections, tests, or audits required to determine and assure the acceptability of product or service to continue into each discrete step in the operations plan from start of production to delivery. In each case where material losses are an integral part of the appraisal operation, such as machine setup pieces or destructive testing, the cost of the losses is to be included. Sub-elements are planned operations, inspections, tests, audit, setup inspections and tests, special tests (manufacturing), process control measurements, laboratory support, measurement (inspection and test) equipment, and outside endorsements and certifications.

2.3 External Appraisal Costs. External appraisal costs are incurred any time there is need for field setup or installation and checkout prior to official acceptance by the customer and also when there is need for field trials of new products or services. Sub-elements are field performance evaluations, special product evaluations, and evaluations of field stock and spare parts.

2.4 Review of Test and Inspection Data. Costs are incurred for regular reviewing inspection and test data prior to release of the product for shipment, to determine whether product requirements have been met.

2.5 Miscellaneous Quality Evaluations. This area involves the cost of all support area quality evaluations (audits) to assure continued ability to provide acceptable support to the production process. Examples of areas included are mail rooms, storerooms, and packaging and shipping.

3.0 INTERNAL FAILURE COST CATEGORY

Whenever quality appraisals are performed, the possibility exists for discovery of a failure to meet requirements. When this happens, unscheduled and possibly unbudgeted expenses are automatically incurred. For example, when a complete lot of metal parts is rejected for being oversize, the possibility for rework must be evaluated first. Then the cost of rework may be compared to the cost of scrapping the parts and completely replacing them. Finally, a disposition is made, and the action is carried out. The total cost of this evaluation, disposition, and subsequent action is an integral part of internal failure costs.

In attempting to cover all possibilities for failure to meet requirements within the internal product or service life cycle, failure costs have been defined to include basically all costs required to evaluate, dispose of, and either correct or replace nonconforming products or services prior to delivery to the customer, as well as the cost to correct or replace incorrect or incomplete product or service description (documentation). In general, this includes all the material and labor expenses that are lost or wasted due to nonconforming or otherwise unacceptable work affecting the quality of end products or service. Corrective action that is directed toward elimination of the problem in the future may be classified as prevention.

3.1 Product or Service Design Failure Costs (Internal). Design failure costs can generally be considered the unplanned costs that are incurred because of inherent design inadequacies in released documentation for production operations. They do not include billable costs associated with customer-directed changes (product improvements) or major redesign efforts (product upgrading) that are part of an organization-sponsored marketing plan. Sub-elements are design corrective action, rework due to design changes, scrap due to design changes, and production liaison costs.

3.2 Purchasing Failure Costs. Costs are incurred due to purchased item rejects. Sub-elements are purchased material reject disposition costs, purchased material replacement costs, supplier corrective action, rework of supplier rejects, and uncontrolled material losses.

3.3 Operations (Product or Service) Failure Costs. Operations failure costs almost always represent a significant portion of overall quality costs and can generally be viewed as the costs associated with nonconforming product or service discovered during the operations process. They are categorized into three distinct areas: material review and corrective action, rework or repair costs, and scrap costs. Sub-elements are material review and corrective action costs, operations rework and repair costs, and internal failure labor losses.

4.0 EXTERNAL FAILURE COST CATEGORY

This category includes all costs incurred due to actual or suspected nonconforming product or service after delivery to the customer. These costs consist primarily of costs associated with the product or service not meeting customer or user requirements. The responsibility for these losses may lie in marketing or sales, design development, or operations. Determination of responsibility is not part of the system. Determination of responsibility can come about only through investigation and analysis of external failure cost inputs.

4.1 Complaint Investigations of Customer or User Service. This category includes the total cost of investigating, resolving, and responding to individual customer or user complaints or inquiries, including necessary field service.

4.2 Returned Goods. This category includes the total cost of evaluating and repairing or replacing goods not meeting acceptance by the customer or user due to quality problems. It does not include repairs accomplished as part of a maintenance or modification contract.

4.3 Retrofit and Recall Costs. Retrofit and recall costs are those costs required to modify or update products or field service facilities to a new design change level, based on major redesign due to design deficiencies. They include only the portion of retrofits that are due to quality problems.

4.4 Warranty Claims. Warranty costs include the total cost of claims paid to the customer or user after acceptance to cover expenses, including repair costs, such as removing defective hardware from a system, or cleaning costs, due to a food or chemical service accident. In cases where a price reduction is negotiated in lieu of a warranty, the value of this reduction should be counted.

4.5 Liability Costs. Liability costs are organization-paid costs due to liability claims, including the cost of product or service liability insurance.

4.6 Penalties. Penalty costs are those costs incurred because less than full product or service performance is achieved as required by contracts with customers or by government rules and regulations.

4.7 Customer or User Goodwill. This category involves costs incurred, over and above normal selling costs, to customers or users who are not completely satisfied with the quality of delivered product or service because the customers' quality expectations were greater than the quality they received.

4.8 Lost Sales. Lost sales comprise the value of the contribution to profit that is lost due to sales reduction because of quality problems.

Collection and Reporting

COLLECTION SYSTEM DESIGN

The development of the collection system requires the close interaction of the quality and accounting departments. Because accounting cost data are established by departmental cost codes, a significant amount of quality cost can be obtained from this source. In fact, the system should be designed using the organization's present system and modifying it where appropriate. Some existing sources for reporting quality costs are time sheets, schedules, minutes of meetings, expense reports, credit and debit memos, and so forth. Be aware that not all accounting data are accurate.

Some quality cost data cross departmental lines, and these types of costs are the most difficult to collect. Special forms may be required to report some quality costs. For example, scrap and rework costs may require analysis by quality control personnel to determine the cause and the departments responsible.

In some cases, estimates are used to allocate the proportion of an activity that must be charged to a particular element. For example, when the marketing department engages in research, it is necessary for the department supervisor to estimate the proportion of the activity that pertains to customer quality needs and should be charged as a quality cost. Work-sampling techniques can be a valuable tool for assisting the supervisor in making the estimate.

Insignificant costs of poor quality, such as a secretary retyping a letter, may be difficult to determine and may be overlooked. However, significant ones are frequently hidden or buried because the accounting system is not designed to handle them. Quality cost is a tool that can determine opportunities for quality improvement, justify the corrective action, and measure its effectiveness. Including insignificant activities is not essential to use the tool effectively. However, all significant activities or major elements must be captured, even if they are only estimated.

The comptroller's office must be directly involved in the design of the quality cost collection system. This office has the ability to create a new system that will integrate quality costs into the existing accounting system. An ideal system would be one where the quality cost is the difference between actual cost and the cost if everyone did a perfect job or the difference between actual revenues and revenues if there were no unhappy customers. This ideal is most likely impossible to obtain.

Allocating the costs to the proper element is difficult. Some example situations are

1. Incoming inspection would be appraisal, whereas supplier certification would be prevention.
2. An 800 number would be prorated between the cost of doing business and customer complaints.
3. Cost of a team meeting might be due to failure, but cost of the solution might be appraisal or prevention.

Quality costs should be collected by product line, projects, departments, operators, nonconformity classification, and work centers. This manner of collection is sufficient for subsequent quality cost analysis. Procedures are developed to ensure that the system functions correctly. Micro reports are prepared for functional areas and departments, and macro reports are done for the TQM function.

QUALITY COST BASES

Quality costs by themselves present insufficient information for analysis. A baseline is required that will relate quality costs to some aspect of the business that is sensitive to change. Typical bases are labor, production, sales, and unit. When these baselines are compared with quality costs, an index is obtained.

Labor. Quality cost per hour of direct labor is a common index. Direct labor information is readily available, because it is used for other indexes. Automation affects the base over an extended period of time; therefore, the value of a labor base is limited to comparisons within a short period of time. Sometimes direct labor dollars are used rather than direct labor hours. This technique eliminates the inflation factor because dollars are divided by dollars.

Production. Quality costs per dollar of production cost is another common index. Production cost is composed of direct labor, direct material, and overhead. Production cost information is readily available, because it is used for other indexes. Because there are three costs involved, this index is not significantly affected by material price fluctuations or by automation. Design cost, marketing cost, or purchasing cost might be appropriate in some situations as a substitute for production cost.

Sales. Quality cost per dollar of net sales is the most common type of index. This information is a valuable tool for higher management decision making. Because sales lag behind production and are frequently subject to seasonal variations, this index is sometimes a poor one for short-term analysis. It is also affected by changes in selling price and shifts in available markets. However, in the eyes of senior management, there may be no better common denominator than net sales for year-to-year planning and measurement.

Unit. Quality cost per unit, such as number of boxes, kilograms of aluminum, or meters of cloth, is an excellent index where product lines are similar. However, where product lines are dissimilar, comparisons are difficult to make and interpret.

Because each of the various indexes has disadvantages, it is the normal practice to use three indexes. From experience, the most useful indexes are used to compare trends in quality costs.

For current, ongoing applications, various ratios can be used. These ratios will reflect management emphasis on areas that are undergoing quality improvement. Typical ratios that may be considered are

- Operations failure costs as a percent of production costs.
- Purchasing quality costs as a percent of materials costs.
- Design quality costs as a percent of design costs.

There is no limit to the number of ratios that can be used. Since there is no single perfect ratio, use of more than one ratio is recommended.

QUALITY COST REPORT

The basic quality cost control instrument is the quality cost report, which is usually issued by the accounting department. An example of this type of report is shown in Figure 7-4. Provision is made to report the quality costs for the current month for each cost element as well as the current and prior year-to-date values. Applicable indexes and ratios are shown at the bottom of the report.

Prevention Costs	$ (000)	Current Month	Year-to-Date Current	Year-to-Date Prior Yr.
Marketing/Customer				
Product/Service Development				
Purchasing				
Operations				
Quality Administration				
Total				

Appraisal Costs	$ (000)	Current Month	Year-to-Date Current	Year-to-Date Prior Yr.
Product/Service Development				
Purchasing				
Operations				
External Appraisal Costs				
Total				

Internal Failure Costs	$ (000)	Current Month	Year-to-Date Current	Year-to-Date Prior Yr.
Product/Service Design				
Purchasing				
Operations (Subtotal)				
Material Review				
Rework				
Repair				
Reappraisal				
Extra Operations				
Scrap				
Total				

External Failure Costs	$ (000)	Current Month	Year-to-Date Current	Year-to-Date Prior Yr.
Customer Complaints				
Returned Goods				
Retrofit Costs				
Warranty Claims				
Liability Costs				
Penalties				
Customer Goodwill				
Total				

Baseline Data	$ (000)	Current Month	Year-to-Date Current	Year-to-Date Prior Yr.
Net Sales				
Direct Labor				
Production				
Design				

Quality Cost Ratios	$ (000)	Current Month	Year-to-Date Current	Year-to-Date Prior Yr.
External Failure Cost/Net Sales				
Operations Failure Costs/Production Costs				
Operations Appraisal Costs/Production Costs				
Purchasing Quality Costs/Material Costs				
Design Quality Costs/Design Costs				

Figure 7-4 Quality Cost Summary Report

181

By comparing current costs with historical ones, a certain amount of control can be exercised. It is also possible to establish a budget for each cost element. By comparing actual quality costs with budgeted costs, favorable and unfavorable variances can be determined.

Analysis

Analysis techniques for quality costs are quite varied. The most common techniques are trend and Pareto analysis. The objective of these techniques is to determine opportunities for quality improvement.

TREND ANALYSIS

Trend analysis involves simply comparing present cost levels to past levels. It is suggested that at least one year elapse before drawing any conclusions from the data. Trend analysis provides information for long-range planning. It also provides information for the instigation and assessment of quality improvement programs. Data for trend analysis come from the monthly report and the detailed transactions that make up the elements. Trend analysis can be accomplished by cost category, by sub-category, by product, by measurement base, by plants within a corporation, by department, by work center, and by combinations thereof. The graphs of some of these trend types are shown in Figure 7-5. Times scales for these time-series graphs may be by month, quarter, or year, depending on the purpose of the analysis.

Figure 7-5(a) shows a graph of the four cost categories by quarter. It is the cumulative type, where the second line from the bottom includes the prevention and the appraisal costs; the third line from the bottom includes the internal failure, appraisal, and prevention costs; and the top line includes all four cost categories. Figure 7-5(a) shows that prevention and internal failure costs are increasing, but appraisal costs remain unchanged and external failure costs are decreasing.

Figure 7-5(b) shows the trend analysis for three different measurement bases. The differences in the trends of the three bases point to the need for more than one base. A decrease in the percent of net sales during the fourth quarter is due to a seasonal variation, whereas the variation in production costs for the third quarter is due to excessive overtime costs.

Figure 7-5(c) shows the trend analysis for two different products. The figure shows that the costs for product B are better than those for product A. In fact, product B is showing a nice improvement, whereas product A's costs are increasing. An increase in prevention and appraisal costs will, it is hoped, improve the external and internal failure costs of product A. It is important to note that comparisons between products and plants should be made with extreme caution.

A trend graph for the external failure category is shown in Figure 7-5(d). Returned costs and lost sales costs have increased, whereas costs for the other sub-categories have remained unchanged. In this figure, the index is by production costs and the time period is by quarters.

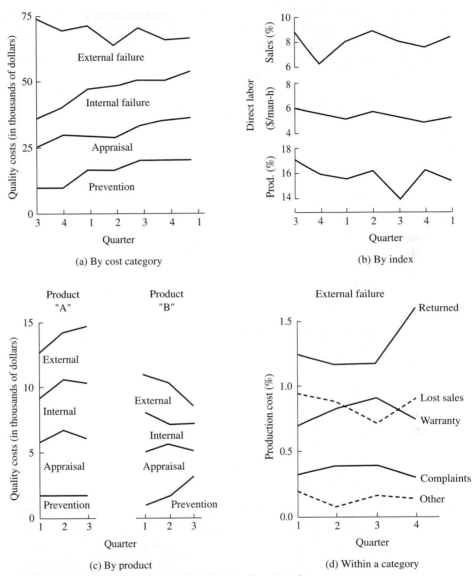

(a) By cost category

(b) By index

(c) By product

(d) Within a category

Figure 7-5 Typical Long-Range Trend Time-Series Graphs

Figure 7-6 shows a short-run trend analysis chart for the assembly area. The ratio of rework costs to total assembly costs in percent is plotted by months. This ratio is compared to the quality measure, percent nonconforming. Both curves show a decrease, which supports the basic concept that quality improvement is synonymous with reduced costs.

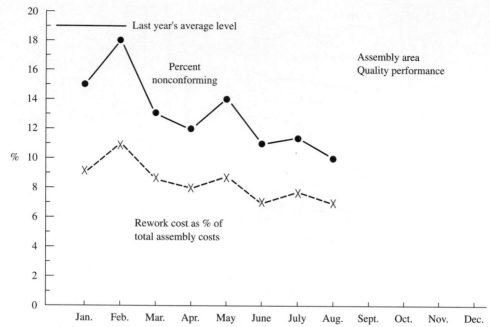

Figure 7-6 Typical Short-Run Trend Analysis Graph

Trend analysis is an effective tool, provided it is recognized that some period-to-period fluctuations are chance variations. These variations are similar to those that occur on control charts. The important factor to observe is the trend. It is also important to note that there may be a time lag between the occurrence of a cost and the actual reporting of that cost.

PARETO ANALYSIS

One of the most effective cost-analysis tools is the Pareto analysis, which is discussed in Chapter 18. A typical Pareto diagram for internal failures is shown in Figure 7-7(a). Items are located in descending order, beginning with the largest one on the left. A Pareto diagram has a few items that represent a substantial amount of the total. These items are located on the left of the diagram and are referred to as the vital few. A Pareto diagram has many items that represent a small amount of the total. These items are located on the right and are referred to as the useful many. Pareto diagrams can be established for quality costs by operator, by machine, by department, by product line, by nonconformity, by category, by element, and so forth.

Once the vital few are known, projects can be developed to reduce their quality costs. In other words, money is spent to reduce the vital few quality costs; little or no money is spent on the useful many.

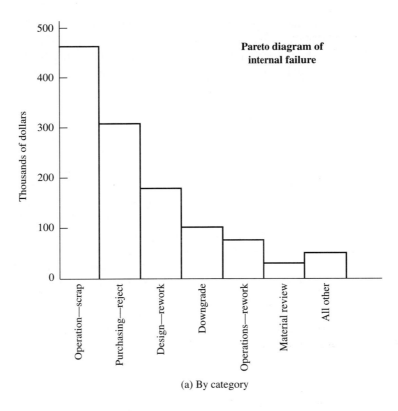

(a) By category

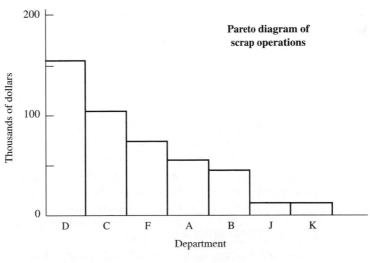

(b) By element

Figure 7-7 Pareto Analysis

Figure 7-7(b) shows a Pareto diagram by department. This Pareto diagram is actually an analysis of one of the vital few elements (operations—scrap) in the Pareto diagram for the internal failure category, as shown in Figure 7-7(a). Based on the diagram, department D would be an excellent candidate for a quality improvement program.

Optimizing Costs

In analyzing quality costs, management wants to know the optimum costs. This information is difficult to specify.

One technique is to make comparisons with other organizations. More and more organizations use net sales as an index, which makes comparison somewhat easier. Difficulties arise, however, because many organizations keep their costs secret. Also, accounting systems treat the collection of costs differently. For example, overhead costs may or may not be included in a particular cost element. There are many variations in types of manufacturing and service organizations that cause quality costs to vary appreciably. Where complex, highly reliable products are involved, quality costs may be as high as 20% of sales; in industries that produce simple products with low tolerance requirements, quality costs may be less than 5% of sales.

Another technique is to optimize the individual categories. Failure costs are optimized when there are no identifiable and profitable projects for reducing them. Appraisal costs are also optimized when there are no identifiable and profitable projects for reducing them. Prevention costs are optimized when most of the dollar cost is used for improvement projects, when the prevention work itself has been analyzed for improvement, and when nonproject prevention work is controlled by sound budgeting.

A third technique for determining the optimum is to analyze the relationships among the cost categories. Figure 7-8 shows an economic model for quality costs provided by Juran. As the quality of conformance improves and approaches 100%, failure costs are reduced until they theoretically approach zero. In other words, if the product or service is perfect, there are no failure costs. To achieve a reduction in failure costs, it is necessary to increase appraisal and prevention costs. Combining the two curves gives the total quality cost curve. The model shows that as quality increases, quality costs decrease; however, there is a school of thought that it is uneconomical to achieve 100% conformance. In this model, the upper two curves turn upward, and their costs go to infinity rather than converge, as shown by the dashed lines.

Note that the model of Figure 7-8 is for an entire system of quality. When analyzing an individual quality characteristic, it should be noted that it is possible to make the quality so high that it would be uneconomical.

Quality Improvement Strategy

The idea of a quality improvement strategy is that each failure has a root cause, causes are preventable, and prevention is cheaper. Based on this concept, the following strategy is used:

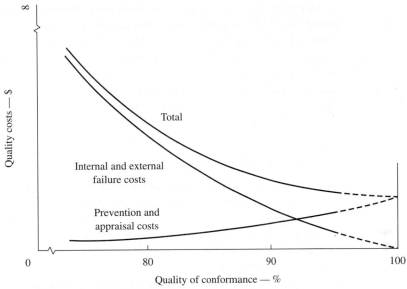

Figure 7-8 Optimum Quality Costs Concept
Reproduced, with permission, from J. M. Juran and Frank M. Gryna, *Juran's Quality Control Handbook*, 4 ed. McGraw-Hill Book Co., New York, 1988.

1. Reduce failure costs by problem solving.
2. Invest in the "right" prevention activities.
3. Reduce appraisal costs where appropriate and in a statistically sound manner.
4. Continuously evaluate and redirect the prevention effort to gain further quality improvement.

PROJECT TEAM

Once the problem area has been determined using the analysis techniques, a project team can be established. There are two types of problems: those that a department can correct with little or no outside help and those that require coordinated action from several functional areas in the organization.

Problems of the first type do not require an elaborate system. The project team could be composed of the operating supervisor, operator, quality engineer, maintenance supervisor, and other appropriate personnel, such as an internal customer or internal supplier. Usually the team has sufficient authority and resources to enact corrective action without approval of their superiors. Problems of this type usually account for about 15% of the total.

Unfortunately, according to Deming, about 85% of quality problems cross departmental and functional area lines. Because these problems are usually more costly and more difficult to solve, a more elaborate and structured project team is established. Members of the team would most likely be composed of personnel from operations, quality, design, marketing, purchasing, and any other area of the entity. The team receives written authority from the quality council or a similar body. Resources are allocated and a schedule of activities is prepared. Periodic reports are given to the council. A member of the quality council should act as a sponsor to the team.

REDUCING FAILURE COSTS

Most of the quality improvement projects will be directed toward reducing failure costs. It is a fact that failures detected at the beginning of operations are less costly than failures detected at the end of operations or by the customer, and such failures are cheaper to correct. Therefore, external failures are frequently targeted for improvement because they can give the greatest return on investment: increased customer satisfaction and reduced production costs.

The project team must concentrate on finding the root cause of the problem. In this regard, it may be necessary to trace the potential cause to purchasing, design, or marketing. Care must be exercised to ensure that the basic cause has been found rather than some pseudo-cause. Once the cause has been determined, the project team can concentrate on developing the corrective action to control or, preferably, eliminate the problem.

Follow-up activities are conducted to ensure that the corrective action was effective in solving the problem. The team should also review similar problems to determine if a similar solution might be effective. Finally, the cost saving is calculated and a final report is presented to the quality council.

PREVENTION OF QUALITY COSTS

Rather than solve problems that are costing money, it would be better if problems could be prevented. Prevention activities are related to employee attitudes and to formal techniques to eliminate problems in the product cycle before the problems become costly.

Employee attitudes toward quality are determined by top management's commitment to quality and the involvement of both in the quality improvement program. Suggestions for achieving this commitment and involvement are as follows:

1. Include both groups as members of project teams.
2. Establish a quality council with the CEO as the chair and functional area managers as members.

3. Involve employees in the annual quality improvement program.

4. Provide a system whereby employees can present quality improvement ideas.

5. Communicate quality expectations to employees.

6. Publish an organization newsletter.

7. Hold a quarterly meeting of all employees.

Using formal techniques for preventing quality problems before they occur is a more desirable activity than problem solving. The following are some examples of these techniques:

1. New-product verification programs that require a comprehensive review before release for quantity production.

2. Design-review programs of new or changed designs that require involvement of appropriate functional areas at the beginning of the design process (concurrent engineering).

3. Supplier selection programs that concentrate on quality rather than price.

4. Reliability testing to prevent high field-failure costs.

5. Thorough training and testing of employees so that their jobs are done right the first time and every time.

6. Voice of the customer, such as quality function deployment.

Effective management of prevention costs will provide the greatest quality improvement potential.

REDUCING APPRAISAL COSTS

As failure costs are reduced, most likely the need for appraisal activities will be reduced. Programs for cost improvement can have a significant impact on total costs. Periodically, a project team should review the entire appraisal activity to determine its effectiveness. Typical questions that the project team might investigate are these:

1. Is 100% inspection necessary or would statistical process control work more efficiently and effectively?

2. Can inspection stations be combined, relocated, or eliminated?

3. Are inspection methods the most efficient?

4. Could the inspection and test activity be automated?

5. Could data be more efficiently collected, reported, and analyzed using the computer?

6. Should operating personnel be responsible for inspection, thus decreasing costs?

7. Is appraisal being used as a substitute for prevention?

Program Implementation

The first step in the implementation of a quality cost program is to determine if the program can be beneficial to the organization. Small organizations with limited resources are cautioned that implementation time and expense are extensive. It might be better to concentrate on one metric, such as scrap or easily measured external failures. A simple system using one metric will provide very conservative numbers.

For larger organizations, a review and analysis of the cost data, when made in sufficient detail, will usually indicate that the costs are quite large. Before proceeding, it is necessary to determine that top management is receptive to new ideas.

A presentation is prepared and given to top management to convince them of the need for the program. The presentation should describe the results to expect, the implementation plan, and the return on investment. Emphasis is placed on the organization-wide aspects of quality costs and not just the operational aspects. It should be pointed out to management that they will need to take an active role in the program.

The program will have a greater chance of success if a single product line or department is used on a trial basis. Selection of the trial area should be strongly influenced by its potential to produce quick and significant results. A full-time leader who has the confidence of senior management will be needed. The steps of the trial program are measurement of quality costs, determination of the appropriate indexes and ratios, establishment of trend-analysis charts, identification of improvement opportunities, assignment of project teams, and reporting of results.

All personnel who will be involved with the system should be educated and trained. This initial training will be limited to those involved with the trial program and key members of each functional area. Education will concentrate on the purpose of quality costs: identification of opportunities for quality improvement, justification of corrective action, and measurement of results.

Concurrent with the progress of the trial program, basic accounting procedures are revised to accommodate the quality cost system. Each cost element is described, as well as how the data will be collected or estimated. Also, the methods for treating fringe benefits, overhead, and other accounting adjustments are determined. To ensure the integrity and acceptance of the data, the comptroller approves the procedures.

After the trial program is complete, the quality cost program is expanded to include the entire organization. Because of better reporting, quality costs may actually increase while the system is in the development period. Data are collected onto appropriate spreadsheets by department, product, project, and so forth. Trend and Pareto analyses are conducted to determine opportunities for improvement. Projects are assigned, and an ongoing system is in operation.

Malcolm Baldrige National Quality Award[5]

The Malcolm Baldrige National Quality Award (MBNQA) is an annual award to recognize U.S. organizations for performance excellence. It was created by Public Law 100–107 on August 20, 1987. The award promotes: understanding of the requirements for performance excellence and competitiveness improvement, sharing of information on successful performance strategies, and the benefits derived from using these strategies. There are five categories: manufacturing, service, small business, health care, and education. Three awards may be given each year in each category. Competition for the awards is intense, and interestingly, many organizations who are not interested in the award are, nevertheless, using the categories as a technique to measure their TQM effort on an annual assessment basis.

Criteria for Performance Excellence

The criteria for performance excellence are the basis for making awards and for giving feedback to applicants. In addition, they (1) help improve performance practices and capabilities, (2) facilitate communication and sharing of best practices information among U.S. organizations of all types, and (3) serve as a working tool for understanding and managing performance, planning, training, and assessment. The results-oriented goals are designed to deliver ever-improving value to customers, resulting in marketplace success, and to improve overall organization performance and capability. The criteria are derived from the set of core values and concepts described in Chapter 2, Leadership.

The core values and concepts are embodied in seven categories, as shown in Figure 7-9.

The seven categories shown in the figure are subdivided into 20 examination items. Each examination item consists of sets of areas to address. Information is submitted by applicants in response to specific requirements of these areas.

Key Characteristics of the Criteria

1. The criteria are directed toward results. They focus principally on seven key areas of business performance. Results are a composite of

- Customer satisfaction/retention.
- Market share, new market development.
- Product and service quality.
- Productivity, operational effectiveness, and responsiveness.
- Human resource performance/development.
- Supplier performance/development.
- Public responsibility/corporate citizenship.

---

[5] Adapted from U.S. Department of Commerce, *Malcolm Baldrige National Quality Award 1998 Criteria*, 1997.

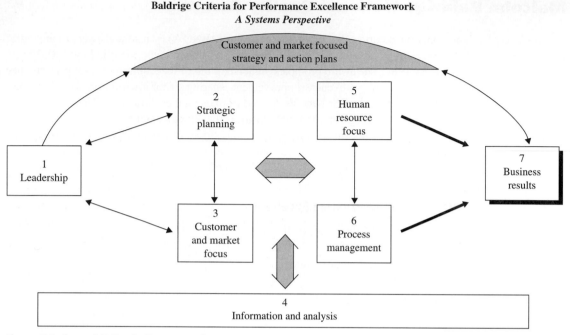

Baldrige Criteria for Performance Excellence Framework
A Systems Perspective

Figure 7-9 Award Criteria Framework

Improvements in these seven areas contribute significantly to organization perform-ance, including financial performance. The results also recognize the importance of sup-pliers, the needs of communities, and the needs of the nation.

2. The criteria are nonprescriptive and adaptable because

    • The focus is on results, not on procedures or tools. Organizations are encouraged to develop and demonstrate creative, adaptive, and flexible approaches, for meeting basic requirements. Nonprescriptive requirements are intended to fos-ter incremental and major "breakthrough" improvement.

    • Selection of tools, techniques, and systems usually depends upon factors such as business type and size, the organization's stage of development, and em-ployee capabilities and responsibilities.

    • The focus is on common requirements within an organization rather than on spe-cific procedures, which fosters better understanding, communication, sharing, and alignment while supporting diversity and creativity in approaches.

3. The criteria support a systems approach to maintaining organization-wide goal alignment. A systems approach to goal alignment, particularly when strategy and goals change over time, requires dynamic linkages among criteria items. In the criteria, action-

oriented learning takes place using feedback between processes and results through cycles of learning.

The learning cycles have four clearly defined stages, similar to Shewhart's P-D-S-A.

1. Planning, including design of processes, selection of measures, and deployment of requirements.

2. Execution of plans.

3. Assessment of progress, taking into account internal and external results.

4. Revision of plans based upon assessment findings, learning, new inputs, and new requirements.

4. The criteria support goal-based diagnosis. The criteria and the scoring guidelines make up a two-part diagnostic (assessment) system. The criteria are a set of 20 performance-oriented requirements. The scoring guidelines indicate the assessment dimensions—approach, deployment, and results—and the key factors used to assess against each dimension. An assessment thus provides a profile of strengths and opportunities for improvement relative to the 20 basic requirements. In this way, assessment leads to actions, which contribute to the results composite previously described. This diagnostic assessment is thus a useful management tool that goes beyond most performance reviews and is applicable to a wide range of strategies and management systems.

Criteria for Performance Excellence

Table 7-1 shows the seven award categories and the 20 items with their point values. It is important to note that almost half of the total score is based on results.

The *Leadership* category examines the company's leadership system and senior leaders' personal leadership. It examines how senior leaders and the leadership system address values, company directions, performance expectations, a focus on customers and other stakeholders, learning, and innovation. Also examined is how the company addresses its societal responsibilities and provides support to key communities.

The *Strategic Planning* category examines how the company sets strategic directions and how it develops the critical strategies and action plans to support the directions. Also examined are how plans are deployed and how performance is tracked.

The *Customer and Market Focus* category examines how the company determines requirements, expectations, and preferences of customers and markets. Also examined is how the company builds relationships with customers and determines their satisfaction.

The *Information and Analysis* category examines the selection, management, and effectiveness of use of information and data to support key company processes and action plans, and the company's performance management system.

The *Human Resource Focus* category examines how the company enables employees to develop and utilize their full potential, aligned with the company's objectives. Also examined are the company's efforts to build and maintain a work environment and work climate conducive to performance excellence, full participation, and personal and organizational growth.

TABLE 7-1
Award Categories and Item Listing with Point Values

1	**Leadership**		**110**
	1.1	Leadership System 80	
	1.2	Company Responsibility and Citizenship 30	
2	**Strategic Planning**		**80**
	2.1	Strategy Development Process 40	
	2.2	Company Strategy 40	
3	**Customer and Market Focus**		**80**
	3.1	Customer and Market Knowledge 40	
	3.2	Customer Satisfaction and Relationship Enhancement 40	
4	**Information and Analysis**		**80**
	4.1	Selection and Use of Information and Data 25	
	4.2	Selection and Use of Comparative Information and Data 15	
	4.3	Analysis and Review of Company Performance 40	
5	**Human Resource Focus**		**100**
	5.1	Work Systems 40	
	5.2	Employee Education, Training, and Development 30	
	5.3	Employee Well-Being and Satisfaction .30	
6	**Process Management**		**100**
	6.1	Management of Product and Service Processes 60	
	6.2	Management of Support Processes 20	
	6.3	Management of Supplier and Partnering Processes 20	
7	**Business Results**		**450**
	7.1	Customer Satisfaction Results 125	
	7.2	Financial and Market Results 125	
	7.3	Human Resource Results 50	
	7.4	Supplier and Partner Results 25	
	7.5	Company-Specific Results 125	
		TOTAL POINTS	**1000**

The ***Process Management*** category examines the key aspects of process management, including customer-focused design, product and service delivery, support, and supplier and partnering processes involving all work units. The category examines how key processes are designed, implemented, managed, and improved to achieve better performance.

The ***Business Results*** category examines the company's performance and improvement in key business areas: customer satisfaction, financial and marketplace performance, human resource results, supplier and partner performance, and operational performance. Also examined are performance levels relative to competitors.

Scoring System

The system for scoring applicant responses is based on three evaluation dimensions: (1) approach, (2) deployment, and (3) results.

Approach refers to how the applicant addresses the item requirements. The factors used to evaluate approaches include:

- Appropriateness of the methods to the requirements.
- Effective use of the methods.
- Degree to which the approach is systematic, integrated, and consistently applied; embodies effective evaluation/improvement/learning cycles; and is based on reliable information and data.
- Evidence of innovative and/or significant and effective adaptations of approaches used in other applications or types of businesses.

Deployment refers to the extent to which the applicant's approach is applied to all requirements of the item. The factors used to evaluate deployment include:

- Use of the approach in addressing business and item requirements.
- Use of the approach by all appropriate work units.

Results refer to outcomes in achieving the purposes given in the item. The factors used to evaluate results include:

- Current performance.
- Performance relative to appropriate comparisons and/or benchmarks.
- Rate, breadth, and importance of performance improvements.
- Demonstration of sustained improvement and/or sustained high-level performance.
- Linkage of results measures to key performance measures identified in the business overview and in approach/deployment items.

Use of the scoring system requires considerable training. Examiners receive more than three days of training, with most of the time devoted to the scoring system. A simpler system is given by the sample self-evaluation, which is shown in the next section. This approach would be more appropriate for small and medium-sized organizations.

Sample Self-Evaluation[6]

The following self-evaluation consists of a series of statements, organized into the major categories of the Baldrige Award criteria. Use subjective judgment to grade how well your organization conforms to the criteria by assigning a numerical rating from 1 to 10 to each statement, with 10 being high and 1 being low. Add the scores in each category and normalize. For example, the five leadership items total to 32; therefore the category score is $32/50 \times 110 = 70$. Use the individual and total scores to monitor the status of the quality management program. Use the first score as a baseline and subsequent scores to monitor progress.

1. Leadership

_____ Senior executives are actively and personally involved in developing the quality goals and standards for the organization, communicating these goals, planning for quality, and supervising its implementation and progress.

_____ All levels of management demonstrate through their words and actions that quality is the first priority within the organization.

_____ There is a willingness to assist departments and individual employees to improve.

_____ We operate in a matter consistent with a high sense of ethics, concern for public health, and concern for the environment.

_____ We have a system to evaluate the effectiveness of its leadership.

2. Strategic Planning

_____ We have an effective short-range (one to two years) plan for implementing TQM.

_____ We have an effective long-range (three years or more) plan for leadership in quality and customer satisfaction.

---

[6] Adapted, with permission, from G. W. Chase, *Implementing TQM in a Construction Company* (Washington, D.C.: Associated General Contractors of America, 1993).

_____ The information in the plans is adequately disseminated within the organization.

_____ We evaluate and improve our planning process.

_____ We constantly determine future requirements of the customer.

3. Customer and Market Focus

_____ We have developed strategies to maintain and build customer relationships.

_____ We have effective means to determine client expectations.

_____ We effectively communicate those expectations to the work force.

_____ We have established standards to meet those expectations.

_____ We have developed effective means (surveys, visits, etc.) to measure the level of client satisfaction with all processes that affect client expectations.

_____ We have a good client-contractor communications system.

_____ We conduct a post-project follow-up with customers.

_____ Employees visit customer sites, as appropriate, to help promote understanding.

_____ We openly share information with the customer.

_____ We are responsive to customer inquiries.

_____ We are responsive to customer complaints.

_____ Employees at all levels are alerted to report possible customer dissatisfaction with any product or service.

_____ Those who interface with the customer receive special training (listening, complaint resolution, negotiation, and the like).

4. Information and Analysis

_____ We have an accurate and timely database that provides information on customers, internal operations, organization performance, and costs and finances.

_____ We benchmark ourselves against others who are leaders in particular areas and use the data to help improve quality.

_____ Information collected is pertinent to the improvement effort.

_____ Information collected is analyzed and actually used to support improvement.

_____ We evaluate and improve our information and analysis system.

5. Human Resource Focus

_____ Human resource and management plans support quality.

_____ We have an effective training program on quality awareness, teamwork, and structured problem solving.

_____ We provide effective training in technical skills.

_____ The training program is open to all employees.

_____ All employees are involved in process improvement and customer satisfaction.

_____ Employees are encouraged to make recommendations for improvement.

_____ Employees, individually and in teams, are recognized for improvement.

_____ A positive work environment is maintained for the well-being, growth, and positive attitude of employees.

_____ Personnel practices such as recruitment, hiring, training, and other services are evaluated to determine their effectiveness.

_____ Job site conditions are evaluated for possible improvement.

6. Process Management

(These statements refer to all processes performed by the organization, including administrative, logistical, engineering, and construction.)

_____ All processes performed by this organization have been identified, and the ownership of each process has been established.

_____ All areas of duplication have been identified.

_____ An effective system exists within the organization to prioritize processes for improvement.

_____ Performance standards for processes have been established.

_____ A system to measure process performance against the standards has been developed.

_____ We have an effective system for improving those processes identified as needing improvement.

_____ There is an effective means of disseminating "lessons learned" information from project to project and throughout the organization.

_____ Quality requirements are effectively communicated to subcontractors and suppliers.

_____ Subcontractor and supplier quality are effectively monitored and the results are furnished to them.

_____ We have an effective method for evaluating the process improvement system itself.

7. Business Results

We can show quantifiable improvement in the following areas (rate each one):

_____ Safety/number of worker compensation claims.

_____ Employee satisfaction/absenteeism/turnover.

_____ Grievances/strikes.

_____ Satisfaction with our performance on the part of other parties with whom we deal—i.e., architects/engineers, subcontractors, suppliers, government agencies.

_____ Punch (defect) lists.

_____ On-time performance.

_____ Reduced delivery times.

_____ Financial return.

_____ Rework.

_____ Subcontractor quality.

_____ Supplier quality.

_____ Engineering processes.

_____ Logistical processes.

_____ Administrative processes.

_____ Construction processes.

_____ Customer (client) satisfaction.

_____ Repeat business.

_____ Market share.

Comments

The MBNQA provides a plan to keep improving all operations continuously and a system to measure these improvements accurately. Benchmarks are used to compare the organization's performance with the world's best and to establish stretch goals. A close partnership with suppliers and customers that feeds improvements back into the operation is required. There is a long-lasting relationship with customers, so that their wants are translated into products and services that go beyond delivery. Management from top to bottom is committed to improving quality. Preventing mistakes and looking for improvement opportunities is built into the culture. There is a major investment in human resources by means of training, motivation, and empowerment.

According to Dr. J. M. Juran, who studied the winners of the award, the gains have been stunning. The gains can be accomplished by large and small U.S. organizations and by U.S. workers. The gains include quality, productivity, and cycle time.

TQM Exemplary Organization[7]

Spicer Driveshaft, part of the Dana Corporation, is North America's largest independent manufacturer of automotive driveshafts and related components, supplying customers in the United States and around the world. Headquartered in Toledo, Ohio, Spicer Driveshaft has 17 plants and offices in the United States. More than two-thirds of its 3,300 employees work in five manufacturing and sub-assembly plants.

The company's quality policy—"Dedicated to total quality and continuous improvement"—guides the entire business. Its Quality Council sits at the pinnacle of Spicer Driveshaft's pyramid-like leadership system, where it is positioned to commit quality policy to organizational practice. Balancing present and future is a top concern of management, as reflected in the company's philosophy that "to have a future we must perform today, but to build a better future we must plan for it today." All of Spicer Driveshaft's senior leaders are involved in a two-phase strategic planning process that sets the company's five-year strategic business goals along with its annual business and performance objectives. Expectations for the coming year are set during the annual Hell-week, a Dana Corporation process that results in measurable performance objectives, detailed plans for resource allocation and capital investment, customer-focus strategies, and other key elements. As a result of this systematic process, detailed 12-month plans—along with long-range performance goals and resource needs—are developed for each Spicer Driveshaft facility and department.

The organization's Total Quality Management Control Plan is its chief vehicle for aligning key business drivers, long-term strategies, annual plans, and specific performance objectives. At the heart of this plan are 17 measurable TQM indicators that provide a common focus on quality and convey the relationship between today's performance and the company's targets for improvement. For example, indicators for customer satisfaction—one of five key business drivers—are on-time delivery, customer performance ratings, aftermarket order fill, and results of the company's comprehensive annual customer survey.

The vertically-integrated measurement system enables data to be aggregated and consolidated for analyses of trends or to be broken out for a fine-grained analysis of operational performance. Considerable effort is devoted to ensuring that Spicer Driveshaft's measurement system corresponds with the company's strategic directions and that the data collected and analyzed are causally connected to performance. A cross-functional team holds quarterly measurement summits to evaluate the system, make adjustments, and decide what improvements are needed to respond to current and future business needs.

Aided by an information technology system that supports real-time communication and data exchanges with customers, dedicated teams of sales, engineering, quality, and warranty personnel are assigned to each Spicer Driveshaft customer. These Customer

---

[7] Malcolm Baldrige National Quality Award, 2000 Manufacturing Category Recipient, NIST/Baldrige Home-page, Internet.

Platform Teams are charged with building and maintaining long-term relationships. They are responsible for capturing current customer requirements, anticipating new ones, meeting with customer personnel that install Spicer Driveshaft products, ensuring quick and effective access to key points of contact in the company, and tracking complaints and concerns. Most teams hold monthly meetings with their customers to review designs, resolve pending issues, and plan future programs.

Employees are encouraged to suggest and implement changes. On average, each employee submits three suggestions for improvement each month. In 1999, almost 80% of these ideas were implemented. Many ideas are advanced during continuous improvement "blitzes" that management encourages at all facilities—for both production and support operations. During blitzes, teams gather to brainstorm, identify opportunities for improvement, and then proceed immediately to implement their ideas. At some facilities, blitzes are held as often as every three or four weeks.

Results of the annual, 57-question Quality Culture Survey and other indicators of employee well-being indicate consistently high levels of employee morale. For example, Spicer Driveshaft's employee turnover rate is below 1%, which is better than the best competitor; and the attendance rate has topped 98% for the last six years.

The company's return on net assets has improved to more than 25% in 2000, as compared with less than 20% in 1997. Internal defect rates have decreased over 75% from 1996 to 2000 and are approaching best-in-class levels, while defect rates for key suppliers have decreased to less than one-fifth the level for the best-known competitor. From 1998 to 2000, overall customer satisfaction, as measured in a third-party survey, has averaged 80% or better, topping all competitors. Customer complaints have dropped steadily, from 6.8 per million units shipped in 1995 to about 2.8 per million units shipped in 2000, and since 1996, Spicer Driveshaft has not lost a single customer.

Exercises

1. Working in a team of three or more people, what performance measures would you recommend for the following organizations?

    (a) Large bank
    (b) Health-care facility
    (c) University academic department
    (d) University nonacademic department
    (e) Large department store
    (f) Grade school
    (g) Manufacturing facility
    (h) Large grocery store

2. Working as an individual or in a team of three or more people, evaluate the strategy used by one of the organizations listed in Exercise 1.

3. Construct a Pareto diagram[8] for the analysis of internal failures for the following data (the numbers in parentheses refer to cost elements):

Type of Cost	Dollars (Thousands)
Purchasing—rejects (3.2)	205
Design—scrap (3.1)	120
Operations—rework (3.3)	355
Purchasing—rework (3.2)	25
All other	65

4. Construct a Pareto diagram for the analysis of the external failure costs for a cellular telephone manufacturer using the following data:

Type of Cost	Dollars (Thousands)
Customer complaints (4.1)	20
Returned goods (4.2)	30
Retrofit costs (4.3)	50
Warranty claims (4.4)	90
Liability costs (4.5)	10
Penalties (4.6)	5
Customer goodwill (4.7)	25

5. A building construction organization needs a Pareto diagram for the analysis of the following design department quality costs:

Elements	Dollars (Thousands)
Progress reviews (1.2)	5
Support activities (1.2)	3
Qualification tests (1.2)	2
Corrective action (3.1)	15
Rework (3.1)	50
Scrap (3.1)	25
Liaison (3.1)	2

---

[8] Detailed information on the Pareto diagram is given in Chapter 18.

6. Construct a Pareto diagram for the analysis of the following purchasing department quality costs of a major airline:

Element	Dollars (Thousands)
Supplier review (1.3)	10
Supplier rating (1.3)	5
Specification review (1.3)	2
Supplier quality planning (1.3)	5
Receiving inspection (2.1)	95
Measuring equipment (2.1)	60
Qualification of supplier product (2.1)	5
Source inspection (2.1)	15
Material reject (3.2)	120
Material replacement (3.2)	180
Supplier corrective action (3.2)	53
Rework of supplier (3.2)	5

7. Construct a trend analysis graph for the quality cost categories and the total. Quality cost data for a wheelbarrow manufacturer as a percent of net sales are as follows:

Year	Prevention	Appraisal	Internal Failure	External Failure	Total
1	0.2	2.6	3.7	4.7	11.2
2	0.6	2.5	3.3	3.6	10.0
3	1.2	2.8	4.0	1.8	9.8
4	1.2	1.7	3.4	1.2	7.5
5	1.0	1.3	1.8	0.9	5.0

8. For a homeowners' insurance organization, prepare graphs and analyze the internal failure costs for the past eight months using the labor index.

Month	Cost	Direct Labor (Worker-hours)
June	$74,000	18,000
July	$69,000	16,600
Aug.	$71,000	17,300
Sept.	$74,000	17,800
Oct.	$72,000	17,600
Nov.	$74,000	17,500
Dec.	$73,000	16,800
Jan.	$81,000	18,200

9. Prepare graphs and analyze the appraisal costs of a leading bank for the past eight months using the net sales index.

Month	Cost	Net Sales (Thousands)
Feb.	$45,000	$2,500
Mar.	$43,500	$2,290
April	$46,100	$2,560
May	$45,800	$2,540
June	$47,000	$2,470
July	$48,600	$2,550
Aug.	$49,900	$2,500
Sept.	$49,300	$2,580

10. For a hardware manufacturer, prepare graphs and analyze the internal failure costs for the past six months using the net sales index.

Month	Cost	Net Sales (Thousands)
Mar.	$45,300	$ 755
April	$45,800	$ 790
May	$46,100	$ 840
June	$47,000	$ 925
July	$48,600	$1,050
Aug.	$49,300	$1,232

11. For a microwave manufacturer, prepare and analyze the graph of the procurement appraisal costs as a percent of total purchased material costs using the following data:

Month	Procurement Appraisal Costs (Thousands)	Purchased Material Costs (Thousands)
June	8.5	102
July	7.9	127
Aug.	9.9	116
Sept.	7.2	115
Oct.	7.7	108
Nov.	6.2	112

12. Prepare a short-range trend chart of the operations appraisal cost/production cost ratio using the following data.

Month	Operation Appraisal Costs (Thousands)	Production Costs (Thousands)
Jan.	$10	$100
Feb.	$13	$120
Mar.	$ 9	$115
April	$11	$145
May	$ 9	$125
June	$ 8	$ 95
July	$ 8	$105

What information does the chart give? Suggest additional information that could be valuable.

13. Using the sample self-evaluation for the construction industry, design a similar instrument for one of the organizations listed in Exercise 1.

14. Working in a team of three or more people, visit one of the organizations listed in Exercise 1 and conduct an assessment of their TQM performance using the self-evaluation developed in Exercise 13.

8

Benchmarking

Introduction

Benchmarking is a systematic method by which organizations can measure themselves against the best industry practices. It promotes superior performance by providing an organized framework through which organizations learn how the "best in
class" do things, understand how these best practices differ from their own, and implement change to close the gap. The essence of benchmarking is the process of
borrowing ideas and adapting them to gain competitive advantage. It is a tool for continuous improvement.

Benchmarking is an increasingly popular tool. It is used extensively by both manufacturing and service organizations, including Xerox, AT&T, Motorola, Ford, and
Toyota. Benchmarking is a common element of quality standards, such as the
Chrysler, Ford, and General Motors Quality System Requirements. These standards
stipulate that quality goals and objectives be based on competitive products and
benchmarking, both inside and outside the automotive industry. The Malcolm
Baldrige National Quality Award similarly requires that applicants benchmark external organizations.

Benchmarking Defined

Benchmarking is the systematic search for best practices, innovative ideas, and highly effective operating procedures. Benchmarking considers the experience of others and uses
it. Indeed, it is the common-sense proposition to learn from others what they do right and
then imitate it to avoid reinventing the wheel. Benchmarking is not new and indeed has
been around for a long time. In fact, in the 1800s, Francis Lowell, a New England

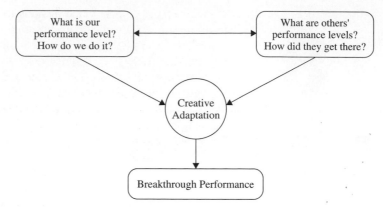

CHAPTER 8

Figure 8-1 Benchmarking Concept
Reprinted with the permission of the Institute of Industrial Engineers, 3577 Parkway Lane, Suite 200, Norcross, GA 30092, 770-449-0461. Copyright © 1995.

colonist, studied British textile mills and imported many ideas along with improvements he made for the burgeoning American textile mills.

As shown in Figure 8-1, benchmarking measures performance against that of best-in-class organizations, determines how the best in class achieve those performance levels, and uses the information as the basis for adaptive creativity and breakthrough performance.[1]

Implicit in the definition of benchmarking are two key elements. First, measuring performance requires some sort of units of measure. These are called metrics and are usually expressed numerically. The numbers achieved by the best-in-class benchmark are the target. An organization seeking improvement then plots its own performance against the target. Second, benchmarking requires that managers understand *why* their performance differs. Benchmarkers must develop a thorough and in-depth knowledge of both their own processes and the processes of the best-in-class organization. An understanding of the differences allows managers to organize their improvement efforts to meet the goal. Benchmarking is about setting goals and objectives and about meeting them by improving processes.

Reasons to Benchmark

Benchmarking is a tool to achieve business and competitive objectives. It is powerful and extremely effective when used for the right reasons and aligned with organization strategy. It is not a panacea that can replace all other quality efforts or management

---

[1] Christopher E. Bogan and Michael J. English, "Benchmarking for Best Practices: Winning Through Innovative Adaptations," *Quality Digest* (August 1994): 52–62.

processes. Organizations must still decide which markets to serve and determine the strengths that will enable them to gain competitive advantage. Benchmarking is one tool to help organizations develop those strengths and reduce weaknesses.

By definition, benchmarking requires an external orientation, which is critical in a world where the competitor can easily be on the other side of the globe. An external outlook greatly reduces the chance of being caught unaware by competition. Benchmarking can notify the organization if it has fallen behind the competition or failed to take advantage of important operating improvements developed elsewhere. In short, benchmarking can inspire managers (and organizations) to compete.

In contrast to the traditional method of extrapolating next year's goal from last year's performance, benchmarking allows goals to be set objectively, based on external information. When personnel are aware of the external information, they are usually much more motivated to attain the goals and objectives. Also, it is hard to argue that an objective is impossible when it can be shown that another organization has already achieved it.

Benchmarking is time and cost efficient because the process involves imitation and adaptation rather than pure invention. Benchmarking partners provide a working model of an improved process, which reduces some of the planning, testing, and prototyping effort. As the old saying goes, Why reinvent the wheel?

The primary weakness of benchmarking, however, is the fact that best-in-class performance is a moving target. For example, new technology can create quantum leap performance improvements, such as the use of electronic data interchange (EDI). Automobile makers no longer use paper to purchase parts from suppliers. A computer tracks inventory and transmits orders directly to a supplier's computers. The supplier delivers the goods, and payment is electronically transmitted to the supplier's bank. Wal-Mart uses bar-code scanners and satellite data transmission to restock its stores, often in a matter of hours. These applications of EDI save tens of thousands of worker hours and whole forests of trees, as well as helping to meet customer requirements.

For functions that are critical to the business mission, organizations must continue to innovate as well as imitate. Benchmarking enhances innovation by requiring organizations to constantly scan the external environment and to use the information obtained to improve the process. Potentially useful technological breakthroughs can be located and adopted early.

Process

Organizations that benchmark, adapt the process to best fit their own needs and culture. Although the number of steps in the process may vary from organization to organization, the following six steps contain the core techniques.

1. Decide what to benchmark.
2. Understand current performance.
3. Plan.

TABLE 8-1

Approaches to Benchmarking

AT&T's 12-Step Process	Xerox's 10-Step Process
1. Determine who the clients are—who will use the information to improve their processes.	1. Identify what is to be benchmarked.
2. Advance the clients from the literacy stage to the champion stage.	2. Identify comparative organizations.
3. Test the environment. Make sure the clients can and will follow through with benchmarking findings.	3. Determine data-collection method and collect data.
4. Determine urgency. Panic or disinterest indicate little chance for success.	4. Determine current performance gap.
5. Determine scope and type of benchmarking needed.	5. Project future performance levels.
6. Select and prepare the team.	6. Communicate benchmark findings and gain acceptance.
7. Overlay the benchmarking process onto the business planning process.	7. Establish functional goals.
8. Develop the benchmarking plan.	8. Develop action plans.
9. Analyze the data.	9. Implement specific actions and monitor progress.
10. Integrate the recommended actions.	10. Recalibrate benchmarks.
11. Take action.	
12. Continue improvement.	

4. Study others.
5. Learn from the data.
6. Use the findings.

Table 8-1 illustrates how AT&T and Xerox have adapted benchmarking to their own needs. AT&T, in its first six steps, explicitly incorporates training and makes sure that personnel using benchmarking results to improve their processes buy into the program. The assumption is that if the process owners are not committed, they will ignore the results and the effort will have been wasted. Steps 7 through 12 represent the core benchmarking process.

Xerox, in Steps 5 through 8, devotes extra effort to integrating benchmarking results into its formal planning process. This involves justification to senior management and gaining agreement from senior management. Again, steps are added to fit the process to the organizational need, but the core activities are consistent.

Deciding What to Benchmark

Benchmarking can be applied to virtually any business or production process. Improvement to best-in-class levels in some areas will contribute greatly to market and financial success, whereas improvement in other areas will have no significant impact. Most organizations have a strategy that defines how the firm wants to position itself and compete in the marketplace. This strategy is usually expressed in terms of mission and vision statements. Supporting these statements is a set of critical activities, which the organization must do successfully to realize its vision. They are often referred to as *critical success factors.* Critical processes are usually made of a number of sub-processes. In general, when deciding what to benchmark, it is best to begin by thinking about the mission and critical success factors.

For example, take the case of two insurance organizations. The chairperson of the first expresses the organization's vision as becoming the "easiest in the industry to do business with." He wants to sell customers all their insurance needs by emphasizing speed of writing policies and an outstanding level of customer service. Critical success factors in this case could include a 24-hour, 800-number service, fast payment of claims, database systems that can relate information on all policies held by each customer, and reduced cycle time. Benchmarking customer service processes would have a substantial impact on the vision.

The chairperson of the second organization admits that his organization is only an average performer in terms of customer service but intends to reduce the cost of insurance through excellent investment performance. Because today's premiums are invested to pay tomorrow's claims, higher earnings from investments would allow the organization to charge less. The critical success factors for this firm could include hiring and training good financial managers, using telecommunications to track and act on developments in global money markets, development of on-line, real-time information systems, and expert forecasting. Benchmarking investment processes would be appropriate in this case.[2]

Some other questions that can be raised to decide high impact areas to benchmark are:

1. Which processes are causing the most trouble?
2. Which processes contribute most to customer satisfaction and which are not performing up to expectations?
3. What are the competitive pressures impacting the organization the most?
4. What processes or functions have the most potential for differentiating our organization from the competition?[3]

---

[2] Peter G. W. Keen, *Shaping the Future: Business Design Through Information Technology* (Boston: Harvard Business School Press, 1991).

[3] Paul Adam and Richard Vandewater, "Benchmarking and the Bottom Line: Translating Business Reengineering into Bottom-line Results," *Industrial Engineering* (February 1995): 24–26.

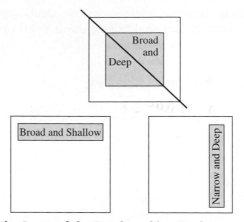

Figure 8-2 Choosing the Scope of the Benchmarking Study
Source: Sarah Lincoln and Art Price, "What Benchmarking Books Don't Tell You," *Quality Progress* (March 1996): 33–36.

In deciding what to benchmark, it is best not to choose too large a scope. A benchmarking study should be done quickly, or it may not get done at all. Teams can get very bogged down in the technicalities of benchmarking and take a year or longer to complete a study. Many circumstances can change in an organization over a year. Team members or management may change in a year's time, and that may compromise the study or even force a study to be abandoned. In order to limit the scope of a study and thereby limit the time it takes to conduct the study, it is best to choose a broad and shallow scope or a narrow and deep scope as shown in Figure 8-2. Broad and shallow studies ask, "What is done?" and span many functions and people and do not go into detail in any one area. Broad and shallow studies are useful in developing strategies, setting goals, and reorganizing functions to be more effective. Narrow and deep studies ask, "How is it done?" and delve into a few aspects of a process or function. Narrow and deep studies are useful in changing how people perform their jobs. Some benchmarking teams start with a broad-and-shallow scope and identify a few areas of particular interest to do a narrow and deep study. Other benchmarking teams identify the narrow and deep target immediately, based on existing data or experience.

Pareto analysis can be a helpful technique for deciding what processes to investigate. It is often effective to start with the process output and trace back to the inputs, asking what, how, where, when, and why questions along the way. Cause-and-effect diagrams and flow diagrams are excellent tools for tracing outputs back to inputs and for examining factors that influence the process. The bottlenecks identified become benchmarking candidates.

At this point, it is appropriate to begin thinking about metrics (measurements). Numerical measures illustrate the effects of improvement and thereby aid in deciding where to direct benchmarking activities. One quick and meaningful metric is the value added per employee. Measuring labor productivity is a fundamental indicator of efficiency that strongly correlates with profitability.

Understanding Current Performance

To compare practices to outside benchmarks, it is first necessary to thoroughly understand and document the current process. It is essential that the organization's performance is well understood. Several techniques, such as flow diagrams and cause-and-effect diagrams, and understanding. Attention must be paid to inputs and outputs. Careful questioning is necessary to identify circumstances that result in exceptions to the normal routine. Exceptions commonly consume a good deal of the process resources; however, process participants may not think to mention them during interviews.

Those working in the process know the most about it and are the most capable of identifying and correcting problems. The benchmarking team should be comprised of those who own or work in the process to ensure suggested changes are actually implemented.

When documenting the process, it is important to quantify it. Units of measure must be determined. These are the key metrics that will be compared during the benchmarking investigation. Common examples include unit costs, hourly rates, asset measures, and quality measures. In some cases, important measures are not available or are unclear. Decisions will have to be made as to whether the information can be estimated or if additional data-collection efforts are necessary. Data form the baseline for benchmark comparisons.

Special care should be taken when using accounting information. Most accounting systems were developed to satisfy external reporting requirements to the IRS and the SEC. As a result, costs may be aggregated in a way that the activities under study are misrepresented. Benchmarkers should take the time to determine what is and what is not included in accounting information.

Planning

Once internal processes are understood and documented, it is possible to make decisions about how to conduct the study. If not already selected, a benchmarking team should be chosen. The team should decide what type of benchmarking to perform, what type of data are to be collected, and the method of collection. Organizations that are candidates to serve as the benchmark need to be identified. Finally, timetables should be agreed upon for each of the benchmarking tasks and the desired output from the study.

Benchmark planning is a learning process. In fact, the entire purpose of benchmarking is to learn. There is a tendency to want to call several organizations immediately and schedule visits. This activity is usually a waste of time. It is better first to use information in the public domain to focus the inquiry and to find appropriate benchmark partners.

There are three main types of benchmarking: internal, competitive, and process. In most large firms, similar activities are performed in different operating divisions. For example, Bell Labs trained engineers to copy the work and social habits of the best performers. Some of these habits were as simple as managing work in-baskets, accepting constructive criticism, and seeking help instead of wasting time. Engineers who went through the Bell Labs program boosted their productivity by ten percent in eight months.[4] Internal comparisons have several advantages. Data are easy to obtain because problems of confidentiality don't exist. Often, dialog with internal groups generates immediate improvement ideas or defines common problems that help to focus external inquiries.

Product competitors are an obvious choice to benchmark. Any organization's survival depends on its performance relative to the competition. In most cases, products and processes are directly comparable. Some competitors do share information. For instance, mortgage bankers compare their product types, service fees, and interest rates on a weekly basis. On the other hand, some organizations would never knowingly share proprietary information. However, there are several ways to obtain data. Particularly good sources are information in the public domain and third parties. For instance, *Consumer Reports* evaluates the features of various products, *Morningstar* evaluates the financial performance of various stocks, and J.D. Powers evaluates automobile customer-satisfaction levels. Buying a competitor's product to take apart and test is another common practice. Exxon partners with its customers to obtain information about competitors. The organization observes both its products and its competitor's products in use at the customer's location and collects comparative data.[5]

Process benchmarking is sometimes known as functional or generic benchmarking. The idea is that many processes are common across industry boundaries, and innovations from other types of organizations can be applied across industries. For example, every industry has payroll and accounts receivable functions. All kinds of organizations design new products and have logistics functions. A classic example of this type of benchmarking is the case of Southwest Airlines. When Southwest was unhappy with the airplane turnaround time, it benchmarked auto-racing pit crews and implemented many new ideas. Likewise, Motorola looked to Domino's Pizza and Federal Express for the best ways to speed up delivery systems. Another example of process benchmarking is when Remington Rifle Co. used Maybelline cosmetics' shiny lipstick cartridge production process techniques to produce shinier rifle shells.[6]

---

[4] Bogan.

[5] "Beyond Benchmarking," *European Quality* (October 1993).

[6] Bogan.

Process benchmarking has several advantages. Compared with competitive benchmarking, it is much easier to get organizations to share information. It is relatively easy to find organizations with world-class operations through published information and through discussions with suppliers and consultants who specialize in the field. However, care must be taken to pick firms that are comparable. Often data must be adjusted to arrive at a meaningful metric.

Many excellent techniques are available to assist in setting project timetables. These range from simple Gant charts to project evaluation and review technique (PERT). Excellent discussions of these methods can be found in management texts. Relatively inexpensive personal computer software that automates these techniques is also widely available.

Identifying the best firms to find a benchmark is a research project. There is no preexisting magic list of best-in-class companies. In fact, "best-in-class" depends on the organization's needs. Find organizations that are the best performers relative to the defined measures established by using the critical success factors. Identify a large number of possible candidates and reduce the list to come up with a short list for further research. Best practices can be found internally, in a competitor, in the industry, in another U.S. organization, or in a global organization. A hierarchy of sources is given in Figure 8-3.

The search starts with publicly-available information, such as that in trade journals and on the Internet. Magazines are published for industries, occupations, and functions, from accounting to zookeeping. These feature success story articles, technical information, and regular lists of top-performing organizations. Often they are published by associations whose members and officers are additional sources. There are also numerous benchmarking databases, such as The Industry Week Survey of Manufacturers Benchmarking Database, which contains information from 1,757 North American manufacturing firms. There is a nominal fee for searches, and data can be sorted by industry type or question.

Using public sources of information requires a grasp of key process metrics. Researchers should look for numbers and ratios to find industry best practices. Many sources of financial information are available in the public domain. Annual reports and Securities and Exchange Commission filings can be accessed through business libraries and online services. Standard ratios are available for all publicly-traded organizations in the United States and for many foreign firms. If the benchmarking team includes a skilled financial person, he or she should be able to derive additional measures from published information.

World Class
Any Organization, USA
Industry-wide
Competitor
Internally

Figure 8-3 **Hierarchy of Best Practices**

Government agencies also compile large quantities of industry information. This data can be acquired through government publications and by talking directly to government experts. Finally, business contacts, including suppliers, consultants, customers, and people within the organization, can be a gold mine of information. Often a benchmarker is referred to someone else for additional information. It is frequently worth the effort to follow these leads.

The planning process should result in a "short list" of possible benchmark partners. The scope of the study and the type of benchmarking may require examination of several outside organizations. When a process is broken into sub-processes, it is common to discover that a single organization is not best-in-class for all sub-processes. In these cases, studying multiple organizations ensures that the best practices are discovered.

Studying Others

Benchmarking studies look for two types of information: a description of how best-in-class processes are practiced and the measurable results of these practices. In seeking this information, benchmarkers can use internal sources, data in the public domain, original research, or—most likely—a combination of sources. Considerations include the cost and time involved in gathering data and the need for appropriate data quality and accuracy.

When most people think of benchmarking, they generally think of conducting original research through site visits and interviews. This is not always necessary, and some organizations find industrial tourism a waste of time. Needed information that is easier and faster to obtain may be available internally or publicly. In any case, internal and public sources should have been examined during the planning process, so benchmarkers will have a good idea as to what additional information should be collected.

Three techniques for conducting original research are questionnaires, site visits, and focus groups. Questionnaires are particularly useful to ensure respondent anonymity and confidentiality, when data are desired from many external organizations, and when using a third party to collect information. Respondents can be surveyed by mail, by telephone, or in person. Additionally, questionnaires can be developed as preparation for a site visit, as a checklist during a site visit, or as a follow-up device. As with any survey, careful design and interpretation are essential, especially when questionnaires are administered by mail or phone.

Site visits provide the opportunity to see processes in action and for face-to-face contact with best-in-class operators. Site visits usually involve a tour of the operation or plant followed by a discussion period. Because personnel of both the visiting and the host organizations devote time, it is important to prepare properly for the visit. Laying the groundwork starts with the initial contact, which should establish a basis of mutual learning and information sharing as well as rapport. The initial contact can be made through marketing representatives if a supplier/customer relationship exists, through occupational or trade groups, or simply by one professional calling another. Before visiting, the parties should agree on an itinerary so that needed staff and information will be available. As mentioned previously, internal operations should be fully understood before the visit, and relevant publicly-available information should have been acquired. As soon as possible following the trip, the visiting team should hold a debriefing to document the findings and determine follow-up activities.

Focus groups are simply panels of benchmarking partners brought together to discuss areas of mutual interest. Most often the panels are comprised of people who have some previous joint benchmarking activity. Alternatively, panels can be comprised of customers, suppliers, or members of a professional organization such as the American Society for Quality (ASQ).

Learning from the Data

Learning from the data collected in a benchmarking study involves answering a series of questions:

Is there a gap between the organization's performance and the performance of the best-in-class organizations?

What is the gap? How much is it?

Why is there a gap? What does the best-in-class do differently that is better?

If best-in-class practices were adopted, what would be the resulting improvement?

Benchmarking studies can reveal three different outcomes. External processes may be significantly better than internal processes (a negative gap). Process performance may be approximately equal (parity). Or the internal process may be better than that found in external organizations (positive gap). Negative gaps call for a major improvement effort. Parity requires further investigation to determine if improvement opportunities exist. It may be that when the process is broken down into sub-processes, some aspects are superior and represent significant improvement opportunities. Finally, the finding of a positive gap should result in recognition for the internal process.

There are at least two ways to prove that one practice is superior to another. If the processes being compared are clearly understood and adequate performance measures are available, the practices can be analyzed quantitatively. Summary measures and ratios, such as activity costs, return on assets, defect rates, or customer satisfaction levels, can be calculated and compared. It is fairly simple to determine superior practices, as the numbers speak for themselves, provided relevant measures are used.

A second way to prove superiority is through market analysis. Consumers of products and services vote with their checkbooks. Does the market prefer one process over others? If so, it can be judged superior. How many more customers would we have if we delivered in 24 hours instead of five days? Another way to use market analysis is to price outside services. If we had excess capacity, could we sell this service to others? For how much? What do suppliers charge for this process?

Identifiable benchmark gaps must be described and quantified. By definition, processes have inputs, activities, and outputs. Processes determined to be superior should be described using words and graphics to the level of detail necessary so that each step can be understood and emulated. The level of detail must be sufficient to allow eventual quantification. Describing best-in-class processes in appropriate detail is the primary way to determine why there is a gap and how to close it.

Once best-in-class practices are described and understood, key process measures should be quantified. The objective is to determine in summary form the overall effect on the internal operation of adapting the best-in-class practices. In other words, what is the size of the gap and what are the appropriate benchmark metrics and objectives?

Any summary measures are likely to be synthetic or derived rather than directly measured from external processes. One reason is that when a process is broken down to its component steps, a single external operation may not be the best in all sub-processes. Numbers may come from several organizations and then be combined to arrive at a combined best-in-class projection. Second, even if a single best-in-class benchmark exists, there will almost certainly be enough situational differences to require adjustments in the measures. These include differences in industry, operation size and scale, geographic reach, and required outputs. In many cases, it is appropriate that metrics be expressed as ranges rather than single point numbers.

When best-in-class processes have been described and quantified, additional analysis is necessary to determine the root causes of the gaps. Gaps are a result of process practices themselves, general business practices, and the organizational and operational structure. Given enough time, anything can be changed. However, some judgment is needed to determine what can be done in the relevant planning period to arrive at an appropriate benchmark goal or objective.

Process practices are the methods that make up the process itself. An example is a customer-fulfillment process that consists of receiving an order, selecting it from the warehouse, packing the order, shipping it, billing it, collecting payment, and updating the customer record for each transaction. Of course, each of these sub-processes may consist of multiple steps. Business practices are more general in nature and may apply to many or all of the organization's processes. These include personnel policy and procedures, accounting practices, and measurement and reward systems. Organizational and operational structure has to do with the location of activities, the organization chart, separation of responsibilities, and information system capabilities. Process practices are generally the easiest to change. Changing general business practices and organizational and operational structure will often be long-term projects and will almost certainly affect other processes. However, objective information developed through benchmarking studies can offer compelling reasons to make changes.

Using the Findings

When a benchmarking study reveals a negative gap in performance, the objective is to change the process to close the gap. Benchmarking is a waste of time if change does not occur as a result. To effect change, the findings must be communicated to the people within the organization who can enable improvement. The findings must translate to goals and objectives, and action plans must be developed to implement new processes.

Two groups must agree on the change. The first group consists of the people who will run the process, the process owners. The second group consists of the people, usually upper management, who can enable the process by incorporating changes into the planning process and providing the necessary resources. Process owners may be inclined to disbelieve or discount the findings, particularly if the gap is large. Therefore, it is important to completely describe how the results were obtained from the external organizations studied. Of course, current practices can't generate best-in-class results, but changing the process can.

Process changes are likely to affect upstream and downstream operations as well as suppliers and customers. Therefore, senior management has to know the basis for and payoff of new goals and objectives in order to support the change. As discussed in the previous section, changes in business practices and in organizational and operational structure may be indicated. These changes have to be considered and incorporated into the strategic planning process.

Because findings are objective, the benchmarking process helps make the case to both groups. The effect of change can be predicted quantitatively and the process fully described.

When acceptance is gained, new goals and objectives are set based on the benchmark findings. Exactly how this happens depends on the individual organization's planning process. The generic steps for the development and execution of action plans are:

1. Specify tasks.
2. Sequence tasks.
3. Determine resource needs.
4. Establish task schedule.
5. Assign responsibility for each task.
6. Describe expected results.
7. Specify methods for monitoring results.

Goals and objectives should be consistent with the execution of the action plan so that the end result is process superiority. The best results are obtained when process owners fully participate in the design and execution of the plan.

The next step is to repeat the benchmarking process. Benchmarking is a continuous improvement tool. It is not to be done once to create one permanent improvement and thereby miss the opportunity for future improvements. In order to avoid complacency, benchmarking must be used continuously to pursue emerging new ideas.

Pitfalls and Criticisms of Benchmarking

The basic idea of benchmarking can be summed up quite simply. Find someone who executes a process better than you do and imitate what he or she does. The most persistent criticism of benchmarking comes from the idea of copying others. How can an organization be truly superior if it does not innovate to get ahead of competitors? It is a good question, but one can also ask the reverse: How can an organization even survive if it loses track of its external environment?

Benchmarking is not a panacea. It is not a strategy, nor is it intended to be a business philosophy. It is an improvement tool. To be effective, it must be used properly. Benchmarking isn't very helpful if it is used for processes that don't offer much opportunity for improvement. It breaks down if process owners and managers feel threatened or do not accept and act on the findings. Over time, things change, and what was state-of-the-art yesterday may not be today. Some processes may have to be benchmarked repeatedly.

Benchmarking is also not a substitute for innovation; however, it is a source of ideas from outside the organization. Business success depends on setting and achieving goals and objectives. Benchmarking forces an organization to set goals and objectives based on external reality. Consumers don't care if a process achieved a 20% year-to-year productivity gain. They care about quality, cost, and delivery, and they vote with their checkbooks for the superior organization.

TQM Exemplary Organization[7]

Located in Garland, Texas, KARLEE is a contract manufacturer of precision sheet metal and machined components for customers in the telecommunications, semiconductor, and medical-equipment industries. Since beginning in 1974 as a one-man, garage-based machine shop, the company, which employs 550 people, has developed into a one-stop supplier of manufacturing services. Its work ranges from initial design and prototyping to painting and assembly to integration of cabling and power elements.

To guide improvements in manufacturing and service performance, the company makes extensive use of benchmarking studies. Among other things, these comparisons

---

[7] Malcolm Baldrige National Quality Award, 2000 Manufacturing Category Award Recipient, NIST/Baldrige Homepage, Internet.

help to eliminate potential blind spots resulting from difficulties in gathering information on competitor performance and capabilities.

Annual goals are aligned with the company's five key business drivers: customer satisfaction; operational performance; financial performance; community service; and team member safety, satisfaction, and development. Members of the Steering Committee work with functional and cross-functional teams to translate the goals into improvement projects with measurable objectives.

Manufacturing teams use statistical process control methods to monitor process performance. In addition, teams in all areas conduct monthly self-audits, and the Quality Assurance Department performs a monthly assessment of team performance, yielding a weighted quality rating for each team and each department. Results of these evaluations are posted on team, department, and corporate bulletin boards. This permits all team members to check progress toward accomplishing company objectives.

Manufacturing cell teams are empowered to schedule work, manage inventory, and design the layout of their work areas. Every team has a budget for recognition and celebration, which complements the company's broader program of rewards and recognition. These range from free movie passes to monthly and quarterly awards for outstanding performance by team members and leaders. In the area of supplier/customer communication, KARLEE representatives participate on customers' design and production-planning teams.

Between 1996 and 2000, production volumes tripled. Still, assembly lead times were trimmed from weeks to two or three days and, in some instances, to a few hours. Over the same period, KARLEE's surveys indicated that its customer satisfaction had improved by nearly a third. Since 1995, labor productivity (measured in terms of sales per hour of labor) has nearly doubled, and waste has been reduced to less than 0.5% of sales, down from nearly 1.5%. The number of inventory turns, a measure of organizational efficiency, has improved from an average of 9.2 in 1995 to 15.7 in fiscal year 2000.

Exercises

1. Efficiency has been defined as "doing things better" and effectiveness as "doing better things." Describe how benchmarking can be used to improve both efficiency and effectiveness.

2. Explain how an organization might benefit from benchmarking organizations in a completely different industry.

3. Identify and explain the three main types of benchmarking. In what circumstances would each type be most appropriate?

4. What difficulties are typically encountered when benchmarking direct competitors? Describe several ways to work around these problems.

5. What are the advantages to using benchmarking as an improvement tool? What are the disadvantages?

6. What is a critical success factor? How is it important in benchmarking?

7. What is a metric? How are metrics used?

8. What three different outcomes can benchmarking studies reveal? What course of action is appropriate for each outcome?

9. Benchmarking studies are a search for two types of information—an understanding of best-in-class processes and the metrics that result. In your opinion, which piece of information is more important? Why?

10. Describe two ways to determine a superior process.

11. Describe several methods for conducting a benchmarking study. What are some of the considerations in choosing the method(s)?

12. Why is it important to understand internal processes before studying those of other organizations? What tools are useful in examining internal processes?

9

Information Technology

Introduction

Information Technology (IT) is a tool like the other tools presented in this textbook. And like the other tools, it helps the TQM organization achieve its goals. Over the past few decades, computers and quality management practices have evolved together and have supported each other. This interdependence will continue in the near future.

Information Technology is defined as computer technology (either hardware or software) for processing and storing information, as well as communications technology for transmitting information.[1] There are three levels of information technology:[2]

Data are alphanumeric and can be moved about without regard to meaning.

Information is the meaningful arrangement of data that creates patterns and activates meanings in a person's mind. It exists at the point of human perception.

Knowledge is the value-added content of human thought, derived from perception and intelligent manipulation of information. Therefore, it is the basis for intelligent action.

Organizations need to become proficient in converting information to knowledge.

History

The first computer was the ENIAC (Electronic Numerical Integrator and Computer), which was completed in 1946. The first use was by the government to manage the national census and for research on nuclear weapons. Table 9-1 shows the history of information technology. These dates are guides, since hardware and software developed over several years.

---

[1] E. Wainright Martin, et. al., *Managing Information Technology* 4th ed (Upper Saddle River, NJ: Prentice Hall, 2001).

[2] Kurt Albrecht, "Information: The Next Quality Revolution," *Quality Digest* (June 1999): 30–32.

TABLE 9-1
History of Information Technology

Timeline	Machine	Applications
1946–1963	Vacuum tube with input by punch cards or magnetic tape.	Scientific and engineering.
1964–1976	Distributed access to mainframe. Compatible models.	Accounting, inventory, and business transactions.
1977–1984	Mid-range computers with user-friendly interfaces.	Users involved in system development.
1985–1996	Personal Computers, local area networks	Desktop systems with spreadsheets and word processors.
1997–Future	Wireless technology. Internet as primary platform.	E-mail. Electronic commerce systems.

Adapted from: Gary W. Dickson and Gerardine DeSanctis, *Information Technology and the Future Enterprise*, Prentice Hall, Upper Saddle River, NJ, 2001

There has been a phenomenal growth in capacity, speed, and miniaturization (reduced size) in the last 50 years. This growth will continue to accelerate with a doubling of performance every 18 months.

Computers and the Quality Function[3]

Computers play an essential role in the quality function. They perform very simple operations at fast speeds with an exceptionally high degree of accuracy. A computer must be programmed to execute these simple operations in the correct sequence in order to accomplish a given task. Computers can be programmed to perform complex calculations, to control a process or test, to analyze data, to write reports, and to recall information on command. The quality function needs served by the computer are: (1) data collection, (2) data analysis and reporting, (3) statistical analysis, (4) process control, (5) test and inspection, and (6) system design. In addition, the computer serves as the platform for Intranet and Internet utilization.

Data Collection

The collection, utilization, and dissemination of quality control information is best accomplished when the information is incorporated into an information technology (IT) system. IT maintains relationships with other activities, such as inventory control, pur-

---

[3] Adapted, with permission, from Dale H. Besterfield, *Quality Control*, 5th ed. (Upper Saddle River, NJ: Pearson Education, Inc. 1998).

chasing, design, marketing, accounting, and production control. It is essential for all the quality needs described in this chapter. Linkages are developed between the stored data records of the various activities in order to obtain additional information with a minimum of programming and to improve the storage utilization.

Computers are well suited for the collection of data. Principal benefits are faster data transmission, fewer errors, and lower collection costs. Data are transmitted to the computer by paper or magnetic tape, optical character recognition, touch telephone, wireless transmission, keyboard, voice, pointer, bar-code scan, and direct interface with a process.

The type and amount of data are the principal problems of data collection. Sources of data are process inspection stations, scrap and waste reports, product audits, testing laboratories, customer complaints, service information, process control, and incoming material inspection. From these sources a vast amount of data can be collected. The decision as to how much data to collect and analyze is based on the reports to be issued, the processes to be controlled, the records to be retained, and the nature of the quality improvement program.

Sometimes information is stored in the computer in order for it to be transmitted efficiently to remote terminals. For example, the operating instructions, specifications, drawings, tools, inspection gages, and inspection requirements for a particular job are stored in the computer. This information is then provided to the employee at the same time the work assignment is given. One of the principal advantages of this type of system is the ability to quickly update or change the information. Another advantage is the likelihood of fewer errors, since the operator is using current information rather than obsolete or hard-to-read instructions.

However, a computer does not have an unlimited amount of storage capacity; therefore, quality control data are periodically analyzed to determine what data to retain in the computer, what data to store by another method, and what data to destroy. Data can be stored on magnetic tape, CD, or a diskette and reentered into the computer if needed. Product liability requirements determine the amount and type of data to retain as well as the retention period.

Pacific Bell used handheld computers, which could be operated with one hand, and bar codes to almost flawlessly inventory 27,000 different small metal circuit boards. The system, developed by a multifunction team, resulted in a reduction in spares from 7.5 to 2.5 per 100 in use and a savings of almost $100 million.[4]

Data Analysis, Reduction, and Reporting

While some of the quality information is merely stored in the computer for retrieval at a future time, most of the information is analyzed, reduced to a meaningful amount, and disseminated in the form of a report. These activities of analysis, reduction, and reporting are programmed to occur automatically as the data are collected or to occur on command by the computer operator.

---

[4] 1997 RIT/USA Today Quality Cup for service.

SCRAP AND REWORK COST REPORT FOR THE WEEK ENDING 11/26

PART#	CODE	TICKET	QTY	MATERIAL	LABOR	OVERHEAD	TOTAL
1194	E	2387	40000	800.00	.00	24.80	824.80
1276	E	1880	15	31.50	2.28	5.59	39.37
1276	D	2021	7	11.76	.94	2.30	15.00
1276	E	2442	10	16.80	1.34	3.28	21.42
9020	D	808	1	30.79	6.01	14.72	51.52
9600	D	2411	3	48.03	19.00	46.55	113.38
9862	D	2424	1	23.73	4.92	12.05	40.70
TOTAL				$13,627.35	2,103.65	5,153.98	21,307.41

(a) Scrap and Rework Report

RECAP OF FAILURE CODES SHOWING AMOUNT AND PERCENT OF TOTAL

CODE	EXPLANATION	AMOUNT	%
A	#OPERATION MISSED	5.36	
B	#BROKEN PARTS	.00	
C	#MISSING PARTS	.00	
D	#IMPROPER MACHINING	11,882.72	56
E	#FOUNDRY OR PURCHASING	8,841.79	41
F	#MECHANICAL FAILURE	.00	
G	#IMPROPER HANDLING	533.10	3
H	#OTHER	44.44	
		$21,307.41	100

(b) Summary by Failure Code

DEPARTMENT 4   MONTH OF OCTOBER

RANK	CODE	CODE DESCR.	$ SCRAP	$ RWK	TOTAL	%
01	D-T2	TURN	7,500	4,105	11,605	28.5
02	D-H1	HOB	5,810	681	6,491	16.0
03	D-G6	GRIND	4,152	1,363	5,515	13.8
04	D-D4	DRILL	793	3,178	3,971	9.8
05	D-L1	LAP	314	2,831	3,145	7.8

(c) Pareto Analysis

Figure 9-1 Typical scrap and rework reports: weekly cost report, weekly summary by failure code, and Pareto analysis by nonconformity code and department

Typical reports for scrap and rework as produced by a computer are shown in Figure 9-1. The weekly scrap and rework cost report of Figure 9-1(a) is a listing by part number of the information transmitted to the computer from the internal failure deficiency report. Identifiers reported for each transaction are a function of the report and the space available. For this report the identifiers are part number, operation code, and deficiency ticket number.

The basic data can be summarized in a number of different ways. Figure 9-1(b) shows a summary by failure code. Summaries are also compiled by operator, department, work center, defect, product line, part number, subassembly, vendor, and material.

P CHART
MACHINING DEPARTMENT

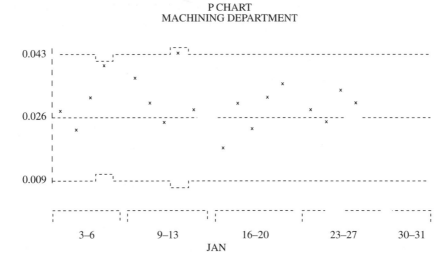

Figure 9-2 Computer-generated *p* chart

A monthly Pareto analysis of the data by defect for Department 4 is shown in Figure 9-1(c). This Pareto analysis is in tabular form; however, the computer could have been programmed to present the information in graphical form, as illustrated by the Pareto analysis in Chapter 18. Pareto analyses could also have been computed for operators, work centers, departments, part numbers, and so on.

The previous paragraphs have described the reports associated with scrap and rework. Reports for inspection results, product audits, service information, customer complaints, vendor evaluation, and laboratory testing are all similar. Information of a graphical nature, such as for a *p* chart, can be programmed, displayed at a terminal, and reproduced as shown in Figure 9-2. This particular *p*-chart program uses control limits based on an average subgroup size and then computes individual control limits based on the performance for that day. The chart is current as of January 24. Data for the rest of the month will be posted as they occur.

Data can also be analyzed while being accumulated, rather than on a weekly or monthly basis. When this technique is practiced, decision rules can be employed in the program which will automatically signal the likelihood of a quality problem. In this manner, information concerning a potential problem is provided and corrective action taken in real time. For example, an operator could have a display monitor at the workstation which would automatically post data to an $\overline{X}$ and R chart. The data could have been collected automatically by the equipment or by an electronic gauge that would transfer the data to the monitor.

A New York Telephone multifunctional team developed a state-of-the-art fraud-detection system and saved the company $5 to $8 million per year. The team reduced the time to detect fraud from between two to four weeks to three days. International calls that exceeded a certain amount were printed out monthly and sent through interoffice mail to a supervisor who examined it for fraud and then requested a service representative to take action. Rather than wait for the monthly printout, the team changed the program so the computer alerted the service representative for action whenever a telephone number accumulated $200 in international calls in any three-day period.[5]

Statistical Analysis

The first and still an important use of the computer in quality control is for statistical analysis. Most of the statistical techniques discussed in this book can be easily programmed. Once programmed, considerable calculation time is saved, and the calculations are error-free.

Many statistical computer programs have been published in the *Journal of Quality Technology* and can easily be adapted to any computer or programming language. In addition, information on statistical analysis techniques has been published in *Applied Statistics*. Most of these programs have been incorporated into software packages. Some major software programs such as EXCEL have very sophisticated analysis techniques, such as ANOVA.

The advantages of programmed statistical software packages are

1. Time-consuming manual calculations are eliminated.
2. Timely and accurate analyses may be performed to diagnose one-time problems or to maintain process control.
3. Many practitioners with limited knowledge in advanced statistics can perform their own statistical analyses.

Once a statistical package of computer programs is developed or purchased, the quality engineer can specify a particular sequence of statistical calculations to use for a given set of conditions. The results of these calculations can provide conclusive evidence or suggest additional statistical calculations for the computer to perform. Many of these tests are too tedious to perform without the use of a computer.

Using statistical process control, the U.S. Postal Service, in Royal Oak, MI found ways to reroute more mail to the automatic sorting machine. This improvement resulted in an annual savings of $700,000 for the facility.[6]

Process Control

The first application of computers in process control was with numerically controlled (N/C) machines. Numerically controlled machines used punched paper to transmit instructions to the computer, which then controlled the sequence of operations. Paper tape is no longer used to provide instructions to a machine. Computer Numerically Con-

---

[5] 1993 RIT/USA Today Quality Cup for service.

[6] 1999 RIT/USA Today Quality Cup for government.

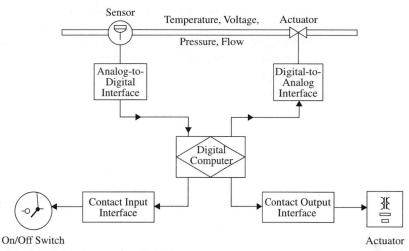

Figure 9-3 Automated process control system

trolled (CNC) machines, robots, and Automatic Storage and Retrieval Systems (ASRS) provide the basic equipment for an automated factory. The measurement and control of critical variables to keep them on target with minimum variation and within acceptable control limits requires sophisticated equipment.

An automated process control system is illustrated by the flow diagram of Figure 9-3. While the computer is a key part of automated process control, it is not the only part. There are two major interfacing subsystems between the computer and the process.

One subsystem has a sensor that measures a process variable such as temperature, pressure, voltage, length, weight, moisture content, and so on, and sends an analog signal to the digital computer. However, the digital computer can receive information only in digital form, so the signal is converted by an analog-to-digital interface. The variable value in digital form is evaluated by the computer to determine if the value is within the prescribed limits. If such is the case, no further action is necessary; however, if the digital value is outside the limits, corrective action is required. A corrected digital value is sent to the digital-to-analog interface, which converts it to an analog signal that is acceptable to an actuator mechanism, such as a valve. Then the actuator mechanism increases or decreases the variable.

The other subsystem is essentially an attribute type, which either determines if a contact is on/off or controls an on/off function. Through the contact input interface, the computer continuously scans the actual on/off status of switches, motors, pumps, and so on, and compares these to the desired contact status. The computer program controls the sequence of events performed during the process cycle. Operating instructions are initiated by specific process conditions or as a function of time and are sent to the contact output interface. This interface activates a solenoid, sounds an alarm, starts a pump, stops a conveyor, and so on.

The four interfaces in Figure 9-3 are capable of handling a number of signals at the same time. Also, the two subsystems can operate independently or in conjunction with each other. Since the computer operates in microseconds and the subsystems operate in milliseconds, a timing problem can occur unless the feedback loops are as tight as possible so that corrective action is immediate.[7] The benefits that are obtained from automatic process control are:

1. Constant product quality, due to a reduction in process variation.
2. More uniform startup and shutdown, since the process can be monitored and controlled during these critical periods.
3. Increased productivity, because fewer people are needed to monitor the controls.
4. Safer operation for personnel and equipment, by either stopping the process or failing to start the process when an unsafe condition occurs.

One of the first automated process-controlled installations occurred at Western Electric's North Carolina plant in 1960. The product variables were controlled by the computer using $\overline{X}$ and R control chart techniques. For example, the resistance value of deposited carbon resistors coming out of the furnace was controlled by the amount of methane in the furnace and by the speed through the furnace. Since the inspection and packaging operations were also under computer control, the entire production facility was completely automated.[8]

A nuclear generating station is another example of a fully-automated system where the only human interaction occurs at the computer console.

An example of an automated process control for a business operation is given by the Naval Aviation Depot Operations Center at Patuxent River, MD. A multifunctional team automated the travel process of request, reservations, and reimbursement. The computer program holds profiles on individual travelers so that two-thirds of the information on the travel form is in the computer and the traveler only needs to input the itinerary. The computer makes all of the calculations for the cash advance and the reimbursement. Each week the commanding officer receives for his review and signature a one-page summary of all planned trips. The travel department can determine the year-to-date history of any traveler and whether there are any outstanding transactions. Results of the automated system are: (1) travel changes have dropped from 100 to five per month, (2) virtually 100% of travel plans are for real trips that are taken rather than 56% in the past, (3) 95% of reimbursement claims are error-free rather than 67% in the past, (4) The department has saved $42,000 in typist salaries and administrative staff has fallen from 50 to 22, and (5) a survey of travelers showed a satisfaction rating of 3.87 out of 4.00.[9]

---

[7] N. A. Poisson, "Interfaces for Process Control," *Textile Industries*, 134, No. 3 (March 1970): 61–65.

[8] J. H. Boatwright, "Using a Computer for Quality Control of Automated Production," *Computers and Automation*, 13, No. 2 (February 1964): 10–17.

[9] 1992 RIT/USA Today Quality Cup for government.

Automated Test and Inspection

If test and inspection are considered a process in itself or part of a production process, then automated test and inspection is similar to the previous section on automated process control. Computer-controlled test and inspection systems offer the following advantages: improved test quality, lower operating cost, better report preparation, improved accuracy, automated calibration, and malfunction diagnostics. Their primary disadvantage is the high cost of the equipment.

Computer-controlled, automated inspection can be used for go/no-go inspection decisions or for sorting and classifying parts in selective assembly. Artificial vision is sometimes used in these processes. Automated inspection systems have the capacity and speed to be used on high-volume production lines.

Automated test systems can be programmed to perform a complete quality audit of a product. Testing can be sequenced through the various product components and subassemblies. Parameters such as temperature, voltage, and force can be varied to simulate environmental and wear conditions. Reports are automatically prepared to reflect the performance of the product.

When automated test and inspection is applied to automated or semiautomated production, the computer can generate the inspection instructions at the same time the product is designed.

System Design

Software applications adapted to the quality function are becoming more sophisticated and comprehensive. There are numerous packages that combine many of the quality functions. Figure 9-4 illustrates a typical quality software package menu. Execution of

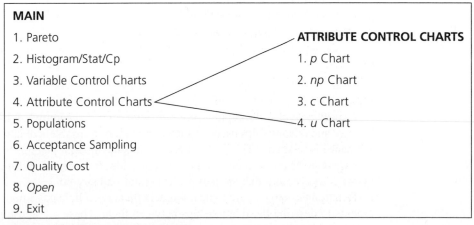

Figure 9-4 Quality software menu

the menu is by function key, cursor and entry key, voice, mouse, or linkage from another program. For example, one sequence of events creates a file, collects data, and analyzes it. These activities involve

File creation

Data collection

Analysis

All these activities involve submenus. Thus, for the attribute control chart menu, there is a submenu for the types of attribute charts.

These software packages are user-friendly with a help provision and tutorials. Packaged software is much cheaper than custom software. It usually has the benefit of proven usage and technical support. Annually, *Quality Progress* publishes an updated directory of applications software particular to the quality function.

The integration of the various quality functions with other activities requires an extremely sophisticated system design. Components of a total system are available in:

CADD: Computer-Aided Drafting and Design

CAM: Computer-Aided Manufacturing

CAE: Computer-Aided Engineering

MRP: Materials Requirements Planning

MRP II: Manufacturing Resource Planning

CAPP: Computer-Aided Process Planning

CIM: Computer-Integrated Manufacturing

MIS: Management Information System

MES: Manufacturing Execution Systems

ERP: Enterprise Resource Planning

HRIS: Human Resource Information Systems

TQM: Total Quality Management

Integration of these components into a total system will become commonplace in the near future. It will require the use of expert systems, relational databases, and adaptive systems.

Expert systems are computer programs that capture the knowledge of experts as a set of rules and relationships used for such applications as problem diagnosis or system performance assessment. This technology permits the thought patterns and lessons learned by experts to be consolidated and used. It provides the foundation for many of the smart systems for learning that are part of the crystal-ball system.

Relational databases are logical pointers that create linkages among different data elements to describe the relationships between them. These relationships preserve information within the system for consistent application across the entire organization.

Adaptive systems permit a system to learn from data patterns or repetitive situations. Data flow is monitored to detect, characterize, and record events that describe the actions to be taken in similar situations.[10]

When the computer is used effectively, it becomes a powerful tool to aid in the improvement of quality. However, the computer is not a device that can correct a poorly-designed system. In other words, the use of computers in quality is as effective as the people who create the total system. Bill Gates has observed: "The computer is just a tool to help in solving identified problems. It isn't, as people sometimes seem to expect, a magical panacea. The first rule of any technology used in a business is that automation applied to an efficient operation will magnify the efficiency. The second is that automation applied to an inefficient operation will magnify the inefficiency."[11]

The Internet and Other Electronic Communication

The Internet is a worldwide network of computer networks. It began in 1969 as a means of exchanging data between universities and the U.S. military. In 1991, the National Science Foundation, which was responsible for the Internet, released the ban on commercial use of it. In 1994, the first commercial web browser, Netscape Navigator, was released. Since that time, the number of computers connected to the Internet has grown exponentially. No single group is in charge of the Internet. Anyone with a computer connected to the Internet has the ability to give other users access to the data stored on that computer, if the owner so chooses.[12]

The Internet contains an incredible amount of information and knowledge on subjects that range from abbey to zebra. Autonomous agents or search engines are used to determine all those locations that contain a particular requested subject. Website information on broad topics such as art, entertainment, health, investment, news, sports, and weather are available from a server without using a search engine.

Intranet

Within organizations, local-area networks (LANs) efficiently share data among users by keeping large amounts of transaction data on large central computers, while connecting personal computers (PCs) to them. LANs facilitate data sharing such as e-mail messages, transactions, decisions and searches, calendars, scheduling, teamwork and authorship, and access to the Internet. The most recent data are stored on the central computer, and authorized individuals have access to it. Messages sent through e-mail

---

[10] Gregory Watson, "Bringing Quality to the Masses: The Miracle of Loaves and Fishes," *Quality Progress* (June 1998): 29–32.

[11] Bill Gates, *The Road Ahead*, (New York, NY: Viking Penguin Books, 1995).

[12] David Anderson, *Managing Information Systems*, (Upper Saddle River, NJ: Prentice Hall, 2000).

provide efficient organizational information to co-workers. Bill Gates recently sent an e-mail to all Microsoft employees informing them that security would have the highest priority in the development of new programs. Employees can use chat rooms for suggestions, questions, and comments. To improve scheduling, networks are linked to employee calendars to make sure everyone is available for a meeting at a particular date and time. Groupware, a software program, uses the network to share data for teamwork and authorship.[13] The Boeing 777 was the first "paperless airplane" designed using shared data and a sophisticated CADD program.

Instant Messaging

Organizations are finding that e-mail clogs computer networks and increasingly takes up employees' time. IBM is using instant messaging rather than e-mail because it is faster. It also dodges the frustration of phone tag because users who put colleagues on a "buddy list" know when they are accessible online. Unlike e-mail that can languish unnoticed for hours, instant messages pop up on the recipient's screen. Most organization instant-messaging services encrypt messages for security.[14]

Video Conferencing[15]

Video conferencing is a technique where people at remote locations participate in a conference whereby they not only hear but see each other. Kinko's has 19 locations throughout the country offering video conferencing. Video conferencing allows more employees to participate in a meeting that otherwise would have been limited to a few people. Documents, photos, and graphics can be used to convey a difficult concept.

The standard video conferencing setting consists of a dedicated room equipped with desks, chairs, two large screen monitors, camera, and network connection. The vast majority of customers use a dedicated digital circuit such as DSL. Equipment and digital service costs have declined considerably in recent years. Organizations that use video conferencing save participant time and travel cost.

People often fail to recognize that it takes longer to communicate in a video conference than face-to-face. It slows down the kind of spontaneity that you might experience in a setting where everyone is together. Participants need to work harder to be sure that the conference is successful.

Many organizations such as Cisco are using the technique to make one-to-many broadcasts for internal communication with its employees.

---

[13] Anderson.

[14] Jon Swartz, "E-mail Overload Taxes Workers and Companies." *USA Today* (June 26, 2001): A1, and Paul Davidson, "More Businesses Turn to Instant Messaging," *USA Today* (October 23, 2000): B1.

[15] Peter Shinkle, "Video Conferencing Lets Businesses Be in Two Places at Once," *St. Louis Post Dispatch*, (October 1, 2001) BP8 and Chris Cobbs, "Video Conferencing is More Than a Flash on the Screen," *St. Louis Post Dispatch*, (October 1, 2001) BP9.

Virtual Teaming[16]

A virtual team can be defined as a group of individuals largely dependent on electronic techniques to jointly complete a project, regardless of differences in members' geographic location, time zone, or organizational border. Software, known as groupware, is used to help teams communicate in cyberspace. Virtual teams use a combination of Internet, e-mail, instant messaging, PC-to-PC connections, shared computer screens, and linked databases. Members are usually given a distinct website for posting progress, charts, meeting minutes, statistics, meeting agenda, and other shared documents. Team members also rely on telephone, facsimile, and teleconferencing including one-on-one.

Virtual teams reduce costs by hiring members without paying relocation costs. New members, specialists, and consultants can be quickly and inexpensively added to the team on an as-needed basis. Large organizations can put their best people on a particular project regardless of their location. Members can be located in countries where the organization wishes to do business. Individuals who are not effective with face-to-face teams may thrive in virtual teams as would foreign members who have oral (but not written) language difficulties. Handicapped people, retired individuals, and those with elder- or child-care responsibilities are excellent sources for members.

Start-up with a virtual team is similar to a traditional team. One important difference is that the members do not meet face to face. This situation can be rectified by a video conference at start-up and as needed during the team's duration. Additionally, one-on-one video conferences will provide the vehicle for the team members to become better acquainted.

Document Management[17]

Globally integrated, paperless documentation is being used by forward-thinking organizations. Applicable groupware software such as QSET makes remote and paperless assessments possible. The software must be capable of:

- Ensuring that audit trails track the history of all documents and actions and enable remote auditing.

- Supporting multiple organization, customer and supplier sites and mobile users in multiple countries.

- Reliably managing organizational knowledge by means of workflow between individuals and groups or teams.

- Providing powerful security and access control features.

---

[16] Mark R. Hagen, "Teams Expand into Cyberspace," *Quality Progress* (June 1999): 90–93.

[17] Adapted from Stanley H. Salot Jr. and Anne Downey, "Tomorrow's Document Management," *Quality Digest* (February 2001): 43–46.

- Integrating many kinds of information in mixed media such as text documents, spreadsheets, flow charts, photographs, CAD drawings, embedded objects, and attachments.
- Offering schedule management, with alarms set to trigger when target dates approach.
- Linking to other software, such as gauge management packages.

These characteristics address all of the elements required to provide evidence of compliance to internal organization as well as international standards and policies.

Remote auditing is particularly attractive because a single individual can interpret standards and guidelines in a uniform way for all of an organization's sites. For example, Sydney Network Operations used QSET groupware and had a successful audit performed at its Sidney, Australia site from its London office. Waterford Crystal links its paperless documentation for ISO 9000 and ISO 14000 within national intranet sites and among international Internet sites in the U.S., Ireland, Europe, and Australia.

E-Learning

E-learning is offered in a variety of formats such as CD-ROM-based, LAN-based and web-based. It has a number of advantages over the traditional classroom.[18]

- Individuals or groups can access the instruction when it's needed at a convenient time and location such as home, work, or road.
- Only a computer is necessary and it is most likely already on hand. Classroom learning requires an instructor, room, equipment, and enough participants to make it economical.
- Learners can immediately apply what they learn, because the topics are taken when they are needed rather than when it's convenient for the organization.
- It takes less time. Some studies have shown that it takes about 50% less time to learn a particular topic.
- It can be customized to meet the individual's needs. Some people are fast learners while others take a longer time. Slow learners are not embarrassed to spend more time on more difficult topics. Programs can adapt to the individual's performance by changing the learning sequence and media.
- Interactive exercises can be provided to test knowledge, apply skills, and experiment in a nonjudgmental environment.
- Retention and on-the-job effectiveness is increased because the instruction is customized.

---

[18] Robin McDermott, "Are You Ready for Computer-based Training?" *Quality Digest* (August 2001): 35–38.

- Materials can be reviewed at a later date.
- Participants do not need to travel to obtain specialized training such as experimental design that only a few in the organization need.

Advances in computer hardware and software make e-learning the best way for organizations to achieve their education and training needs.

Graybar Electric Co. of St. Louis, MO, an electrical distributor, provides one example of e-learning success. Over 9,000 employees at 240 locations have access to more than 50,000 courses. Topics include product training, safety issues, skills enhancements, technical training, and employee development courseware. With training at a single source, the organization optimizes its educational offerings while minimizing the cost.[19]

The following guidelines will help to evaluate an e-learning program and its courseware.[20]

- Supplier selection should be based on criteria given in Chapter 6 (Supplier Partnership).
- Licensing and computer requirements should be clearly stated.
- Instructional content must be accurate, effectively sequenced, and motivating to maintain student interest and enhance bottom-line performance.
- Graphics, audio, interactivity, links, and browsing must reinforce the learning experience rather than serve as a distraction.
- Prior knowledge must be assessed to ensure efficient learning.
- Web-based programs must have provision for e-mail or instant messaging with a mentor or instructor and a chat room for people taking the same course.
- Students must be able to revisit the program to review the material.
- Tracking tools should be used to measure a student's progress and performance.

E-learning will only be successful if its planning and implementation is well-thought out to ensure it meets the needs of the organization.

E-Government

Government is increasing its use of the Internet to simplify processing of information. Examples are as follows:

The U.S. Patent and Trademark Office developed an interactive Web-based system that anyone can use to file a trademark application. The system has improved the quality of initial applications and helps maintain the quality of application processing.

---

[19] Teresa Sininger Cochran, "Electronic Education," *Quality Digest* (October 2000): 41–44.

[20] Cochran.

For many years the IRS has processed income tax returns electronically and made refunds via direct deposit to the taxpayer's bank account. More recently, the IRS has developed a secure system for paying taxes, which includes scheduled payments via bank transfer, confirmation of payment, and review of tax payment history.

Unemployed workers complete their applications for unemployment payments without assistance from counselors using computers in the unemployment office. This information is transferred to a central computer, which evaluates the data and approves the issuing of the check.

E-Commerce

The linking of every kind of machine and computer with telecommunications has changed what tasks are done by whom and where. Processes can reside across multiple organizations—from suppliers to customers—and still be effectively managed. Supply chains have been reengineered; employees are free of geographical limitations, and products are manufactured around the globe. Processes do not begin or end within one facility, team, or organization.

For example, using the Internet, you can order a lapel pin from a contact in the U.S., who will design it on his personal computer, obtain your approval for the design, search for competitive bids, and send the design to, say, Hong Kong for manufacturing. The design will be downloaded to a machine that will automatically produce the lapel pin, inspect for quality, and package and label the contents. It will be shipped by next day air with the entire process, excluding air travel time, taking less than a few hours.[21]

Business-to-Business[22]

E-commerce applications between businesses have existed since the early 1980's. These early business-to-business (B2B) applications were proprietary systems using private networks, but they were not economically feasible for small businesses.

Wal-Mart and Kmart are excellent examples of B2B using the electronic data interchange (EDI) standard. When a customer purchases a product at the checkout counter, the computer stores this information for later transmission to the supplier. This process would continue until a particular inventory level was reached. At this point the supplier would manufacture and ship sufficient items to replace those that had been sold. There is no shuffling of paperwork—all transactions are between the organization's and the supplier's computers.

One of the best-known B2B examples prior to the Internet was American Airlines, SABRE system. In the late 1960's, the system allowed the largest travel agencies to access its order-entry and transaction processing system.

---

[21] James W. Cortada, "At Crossroads of Computing and Quality," *Quality Progress* (July 1998): 53–55.

[22] Adapted from E. Wainwright Martin, et. al., *Managing Information Technology*, (Upper Saddle River, NJ: Prentice Hall 2001).

Business-to-business e-commerce via the Internet is expected to grow rapidly because of (1) low-cost entry and operational costs, (2) global reach with its large number of trading partners, and (3) the benefits of reduced cycle time, product cost savings, and improved B2B coordination. Online B2B intermediaries host online marketplace exchanges that bring together relevant buyers and sellers. Tradeout.com is one of these auction intermediaries that is open to multiple industries. Registered sellers post product category description, location, quantity, price, payment terms, and delivery date; registered buyers submit bids; and the low bidder is sent an e-mail giving the seller's contact information.

There are industry-specific intermediaries such as e-steel.com, which facilitates for steel suppliers the entire procurement process: soliciting, accepting, evaluating response, and negotiating price. Major industries such as auto and aerospace have established industry consortia to magnify their buying power.

Business-to-Customer[23]

Broadly defined business-to-customer (B2C) is the electronic transmission of buyer-seller transactions and related information between individual end customers and one or more businesses. The buyer benefits from easy access to product information, agents to help find things and compare costs, sales and service 24/7 (24 hours a day, seven days a week) anywhere, and online distribution of a digitized product or service. The seller benefits from lower costs, global outreach, multimedia marketing channel and market research opportunities, 24/7 sales and customer support channel, and distribution channel for a digitized product or service.

Business-to-customer systems enable firms to compete on both cost and differentiation. For example, Dell Computer Corporation's website allows customers to use point-and-click technology to select computer specifications, components, and delivery options. Customers can experiment with different configurations to obtain the design they want for the price they want, at any time of the day or week, without waiting to speak to a person. With this self-service website, Dell has improved its ability to compete on both cost and service differentiation. This direct market strategy is valued by its targeted customers and improves their sales and customer service efficiencies.

E-commerce B2C can be divided up into three categories: product retailers, service retailers, and retailing intermediaries. Amazon.com is one of the leading product retailers, which started out selling books and music but later expanded to other consumer products. Its success forced other book retailers to expand their operations to include the Internet.

Organizations that provide services have also been early users of B2C. One of the first pioneers, and still one of the leaders, is E*Trade for the brokerage services industry. Other service industries that extensively use the Internet are the real estate and travel industries.

---

[23] Martin.

Retailing intermediaries such as Priceline.com and eBay obtain revenue by charging fees for transactions. Purchase agent intermediaries are provided by agent technology embedded in portals such as Yahoo, America Online (AOL), and Microsoft Network (MSN).

Website Design[24]

Designing a good website is no different than designing a good product or service. It begins with stating the objectives such as increasing sales, gaining more customers, providing information to stakeholders, selling products directly, or reducing costs.

Next, define the customer segments that will use the website. Different segments will most likely have widely varying needs. Most important is to discover the main reasons potential customers will come to the site. Also helpful is knowing the potential customers' equipment, computer literacy, and demographics.

The third step is the website design. Priority should be given to addressing the reasons people come to the site. Content should be written according to the requirements of online readers: very short and with liberal use of bulleted lists and keywords. The local navigation system to move the users around the site should be very simple with few global navigation features. Users should be able to obtain the desired information with a few clicks of a mouse. If pages are to be accessed or downloaded, access and downloads should occur quickly.

The fourth step is the selection of the software and hardware. A critical issue is maintainability. It should be easy to manage the site; update it; and respond to questions, orders, complaints, and other inquires.

The next step is to test the website as though it were a product. Intensive interactions with focus groups of intended customers are used to ensure that the website is meeting their needs.

The last step is implementation and quality control. Performance measures will be needed to determine the effectiveness of the site and if any changes are necessary. Typical measures are: number of hits, transactions, length of stay, navigation sequences, dead ends, and failed links. In addition, a third party organization, such as Clicksure, could evaluate the website and determine that there are quality programs in place for security, order filling, customer complaint management, and more.[25]

For example, the multifunctional Web Innovation Team of Electric Insurance used traditional quality tools to make an existing web page better. Quoting speed went 50% faster; e-mail response time improved 72%; and database response time improved 90%. Improvements made by the team were: (1) placing disqualifying questions at the beginning, so denied clients could exit to a partner that takes high-risk clients, (2) adding help buttons, so potential clients wouldn't exit, (3) simplifying and streamlining the

---

[24] A. Blanton Godfrey, "Web Site Quality," *Quality Digest* (October 2000): 20.

[25] Robert Green, "New Standard Aims to Improve E-Quality," *Quality Digest* (October 2000): 8.

presentation, so it would download faster, (4) adding simple graphics, so customers know where they are in the process, (5) highlighting missing information in red, and (6) handling potential clients at night and weekends because one-third of the inquiries were after hours.[26]

Information Quality Issues

Information quality issues encompass sufficiency, accuracy, timeliness, intellectual property, security, cybercrime, privacy, pollution, creativity, and control and prevention.

Sufficiency

To make an intelligent decision, it is important to know when enough information has been obtained. Data and information will be easy to obtain, and it is tempting to analyze and use it rather than seek and find the appropriate information. Conversely, there may not be the luxury of waiting until all the data is present to make that perfect decision. There is a fine line between too much and too little information. In either case, the information needs to be simple.

For example, if taken correctly, oral contraceptives are 99.9 percent effective—one user out of 1,000 will become pregnant. Evidently, the information given to women is not sufficient, because one in every 20 U.S. users conceive.[26]

A magazine recently requested real-life Dilbert quotes from organizations. An employee of Electric Boat sent in the following: "E-mail is not to be used to pass on information or data. It should be used only for company business." In order for the quote to be sufficient, it should have stated 'personal information or data.'

Accuracy

If the information in the system is not accurate, its efficiency won't make any difference. When one puts garbage in, one can only expect to get garbage out.

The following three examples emphasize the need for accuracy in information technology:

- The AMA estimates that 90,000 Americans die each year because of mistakes in diagnosis, treatment, or medication. VA hospitals are now setting up a system for reporting errors anonymously, and NASA will run it.[27]

---

[26] Rita Robin, "Millions Pay Price for Pill Misuse," *USA Today*, (August 14, 2000): 6D. 2000 RIT/USA Today Quality Cup for service.

[27] The Associated Press, "VA Hospital Set Up System for Reporting Errors Anonymously," *St. Louis Post Dispatch* (May 31, 2000): A3.

- Twenty-five percent of the calls to the IRS receive incorrect information. Then they are held responsible.[28]
- Recently a university acknowledged that it falsified data in a three-year cancer study.[29]

Timeliness

It is critical to product and service design time that information be received in a timely manner so that the organization can compete in world markets. AOL's instant messaging software is a good example of timeliness. Another example is video conferencing. It eliminates travel and speeds up the creative and decision making process. Standardized CADD/CAM systems can instantly span the globe and be interactive with suppliers and customers creating virtual teams.

Systems crash, and people must rely on photocopiers, facsimile, and overnight carriers. Or, there is a wait time because of an overloaded system.

The winning quote of the Dilbert contest mentioned earlier comes from Microsoft: "As of tomorrow, employees will only be able to access the building using individual security cards. Pictures will be taken next Wednesday and employees will receive their cards in two weeks."

Intellectual Property

When most people think of intellectual property, they think of patents; however, intellectual property also includes copyrighted material such as books, movies, music, and videos. Some organizations are obtaining patents for ideas that aren't really new and are collecting licensing fees from others that prefer to pay rather than fight in court.

Large organizations are filing patent infringement lawsuits against entrepreneurs with new ideas. It is costly and time consuming to fight big organizations, and potential investors are scared away.

The U.S. Patent Office is swamped with a record 500 applications per day, which amounts to over 200,000 per year. This number is an increase of 61% from three years ago. The Patent Office developed a website to make applying for a patent much easier. As a result, Internet-related applications will exceed 5,000 in 2000.[30]

Examples of three high-profile cases follow:

- British Telecom seeks to collect from U.S. service providers for an Internet hyperlink patent issued in 1986.[31]

---

[28] Albrecht.

[29] Edward T. Pound, "University Acknowledges Violations in 3-Year Cancer Study," *USA Today* (July 12, 2000): 4A.

[30] Del Jones, "Surge in Ideas, Turnover Swamp Patent Office," *USA Today* (September 11, 2000): IA.

[31] Robert Barr, "British Telecom Seeks to Collect in U.S. on Internet Hyperlink Patent," *St. Louis Post Dispatch* (June 22, 2000) C7.

- Amazon.com has patented its one click for their products and two clicks for Barnesnoble.com.[32]
- In a recent ruling, MP3 [song sharing service] was ordered to pay $250 million for copyright violation.[33]

Cybersquatters (using a famous person's or company's name) are losing intellectual property rulings. Since it began hearing cases in December, 2000, the World Intellectual Property Organization is siding for the plaintiff about 80% of the time.[34]

The developers of ISO 9000:2000 recognized the importance of intellectual property by including in the latest revision a sub-subclause that states: "The organization shall have policies that protect the privacy of customer information including intellectual property."

Security

There are two major security issues—access security, which is the control of access to a computer that is physically connected to the Internet; and transaction security, which is the control of a given communication such as a business transaction to ensure that it is not violated. Safeguarding information from loss, destruction, theft, tampering, or sabotage is a high priority.

The primary technique of access security to a computer is by using firewalls, which are devices that block unauthorized users from remote sites. Considering the number of viruses and compromises of commercial and government systems, it appears that considerable improvement is needed in firewalls. Even wireless telephones with text capability are not immune to viruses.[35]

Of particular concern are the 2.5 million computers of the U.S. military. The U.S. military is developing countermeasures against computer virus attacks from other countries or terrorists that would close communication networks, financial systems, power grids, and military activities. Information warfare may be the next battlefield.[36]

At the time of their creation, programs should be written with security in mind; security should not be an afterthought. In fact, Bill Gates, via e-mail, has instructed all Microsoft employees to give security the highest priority when developing programs.

The other type of security is transaction security, and there has been considerable improvement in that regard. E-signatures are now legal.[37] Encryption makes sending personal information more secure. Using existing encryption methods, it would take three

---

[32] Del Jones, "Businesses Battle Over Intellectual Property," *USA Today* (August 2, 2000): 1B.

[33] Keith L. Alexander, "MP3 Ordered to Pay $250M for Copyright Violation," *USA Today* (September 6, 2000): 1B.

[34] Jon Swartz, "Profiteers Get Squat for Web Names," *USA Today* (August 25, 2000): 1B.

[35] The Associated Press, "Experts Say New Virus That Targets Cell Phones also Threatens Handheld Computers," *St. Louis Post Dispatch* (June 7, 2000): A7.

[36] Andrea Stone, "Cyberspace the Next Battlefield," *USA Today* (June 19, 2000): 1A.

[37] Elan Ruskin, "Financial Firms Brace for Brave New E-world," *St. Louis Post Dispatch* (July 23, 2000): E1.

years for the fastest computers to crack the code. Therefore, giving your charge card over the Internet carries very little risk.

The Army has developed a biometrics system to replace the password. It identifies body parts, voice patterns, and even body odors.[38] In addition, research on written signatures shows certain patterns that can be digitized. These developments hold great promise.

Cybercrime

The Internet Fraud Complaint Center receives more than 200,000 consumer complaints per year. A Pareto analysis of the complaints is as follows:[39]

Description	Percent
Auction fraud	48.8
Products not delivered	19.2
Securities/commodities fraud	16.9
Credit card fraud	4.8
Identity theft	2.9
Business Opportunity Fraud	2.5
Professional Services Fraud	1.2
Travel scams	0.3
Pyramid marketing scams	0.3
Check fraud	0.1
Other	3.0

Auction fraud includes failure to deliver, misrepresentation, and shill bidding. eBay claims that the problem is minuscule with only 1 out of 40,000 listings resulting in a confirmed case of fraud.[40]

Because credit card theft is becoming common, credit card fraud is common on the Internet. The use of stolen credit cards resulted in an e-tailer write off of $230 million, which is 10 times the amount written off by brick and mortar stores. According to Meriden Research, online fraud may be as high as 10% of sales. E-tailers are installing software that flags suspicious activity on an account.[41]

Another cybercrime that affects business is the stealing of a domain name. It is very easy to register a domain name with the 40 or more registrars, and it is also very easy to change the domain name. The hijacked name is transferred to another registrar and the information stolen. Also, the organization affected is out of business until the thief is dis-

---

[38] Richard Willing, "Army's New Password: Biometrics," *USA Today* (June 22, 2000): 3A.

[39] Alison Gerber, "Police Perplexed in Dealing with Cybercrime," *USA Today* (August 29, 2000): 5A.

[40] Deborah Kong, "Internet Auction Fraud Increases," *USA Today* (June 23, 2000): 3B.

[41] Paul Davidson, "Credit Card Fraud Takes Swipe at Retailers on Internet," *USA Today* (July 17, 2000): 1B.

covered. A registrar may handle as many as 40,000 transactions per day, and it is expected that there will be 160 million domain names in existence by 2004.[42]

Local police departments are struggling to deal with cybercrime because: few officers are trained in cybercrime; they have jurisdictional concerns when the parties are in different towns, states, or countries; and there are not enough personnel.[43]

Online legal sites have recently been established to mediate disputes. Litigation is also possible using the Anti-Cybersquatting Consumer Protection Act.

Privacy

Despite growing concerns about privacy, more Americans than ever are sharing intimate details of their lives in online support groups, seeking health information, and conducting financial transactions on the web.

According to the Federal Trade Commission, only 8% of website companies carry a seal indicating their commitment to protect consumer privacy. Companies can change their policy. Recently, Amazon.com announced that it was changing its privacy policy by sharing its customer information with other businesses and marketing organizations.[44] As online firms go bankrupt, their customer information, which is considered an asset, goes to the highest bidder. Once a person's social security number is known, it is a relatively easy task to find on the Internet information on private details such as bank account, creditors, investments, mortgage, and creditors.[45]

"Cookies"—which are small files placed on a user's hard drive to help track online movements—are often unfamiliar to Internet users. Also 'web bugs' which are a 1 pixel by 1 pixel dot on a web page, can also collect user information. Organizations say tracking users' movements helps them serve customers better. Richard Smith of the privacy Foundation wants these web bugs to be visible and when clicked on, they would pop up with an explanation.

To compound the privacy problem, Internet startups called "aggregators" combine, with the customer's permission, a great deal of customer information on one page. Information includes investments, credit cards, banking, bills, e-mail boxes, and frequent flier miles.[46]

The FBI has a software program that is attached to the hardware of some Internet service providers. It is designed to access a suspected criminal's e-mail but can be used on anyone's e-mail. A court order is required for its use. It has been used in 25 investigations.[47]

---

[42] Deborah Radcliff, "Domain Name Game," *Computer World* (June 12, 2000): 71.

[43] Gerber.

[44] Alcestis Oberg, "Why Does Amazon Think It Owns My Privacy?" *USA Today* (September 12, 2000): 29A.

[45] William G. Phillips, "Combing the Web to Find Myself," *St. Louis Post Dispatch* (November 26, 2000): EV1.

[46] Paul Davidson, "Pouring Web Favorites onto One Site," *USA Today* (August 1, 2000): B1.

[47] Kevin Johnson, "FBI Defends E-Mail Surveillance Tool," *USA Today* (July 24, 2000): 16A.

The Federal Trade Commission has endorsed a plan by the Network Advertising Initiative to self-regulate information they gather about customers. About 90% of Internet advertisers belong to this organization. The plan requires firms: [1] not to use personal identifiable information of a sensitive medical, financial, or sexual nature or social security numbers; [2] to protect consumer data from loss, misuse, or improper access; [3] to notify customers of profiling activities; and [4] to give customers an opportunity to approve the merger of information with identifying information.[48]

New software [P3P] has been developed which controls many of the privacy abuses. It will be incorporated into windows operating systems and browsers and has the backing of AOL, Microsoft, and IBM.

Pollution

There is too much outdated information, especially on the Internet. Two million web pages are added per day. It seems that everyone who has a PC has a web page. Search engines have become catalogs for useless information; however, because of competition, they will become faster and better. Just like the automobile, the more PCs added to a system, the greater the pollution and the slower the entire system.

The "paperless society" that the experts forecasted years ago is a myth. Annual paper consumption between 1990 and 1998 increased from 87 million tons to 99 million tons.[49] Offices will use e-mail for interoffice mail and then put a memo in each person's in box. Suppliers send bills with a return envelope, even when the payment is by electronic transfer.

The U.S. House recently passed legislation to stem the junk e-mail flood. Internet service providers are given new legal weapons to combat junk e-mail that clog their systems.

Creativity

Creativity is drawing insights and conclusions from existing information to invent, innovate, or conceptualize new systems, products, or services. In other words, it is new knowledge, which is the highest form of information technology.

On October 19, 1999, the Encyclopedia Britannica went online. There were 10 million or more hits per day, which caused tremendous software and hardware problems. Only 100,000 people reached the first page. Britannica should have used existing information to anticipate the volume of visitors. After all, America Online has had similar problems.[50] Many children were disappointed on Halloween because Hershey chocolate introduced a new computerized ordering system that didn't work. Maytag had a similar problem. These four instances all happened in 1999.

---

[48] Michael McCarthy, "Net Advertisers, FTC Agree on Privacy Policy," *USA Today*.

[49] Blair A. Robertson and Matthew Barrows, "Paperless Society is Buried Under Tons of Printouts," *St. Louis Post Dispatch* (June 8, 2000): C8.

[50] The Associated Press, "Encyclopedia Britannica Free Web Site Gets Swamped," *St. Louis Post Dispatch* (October 28, 1999): A8.

Two positive examples follow. A pager is used to notify the operator or supervisor when a process has gone out of control. After an accident, General Motor's On Star system dials 911 and reports the location of the accident.

This is only the beginning of information technology applications. Some of the technologies of the future are given later in this chapter.

Control and Prevention

The control and prevention of quality problems associated with information technology will be similar to any product or service. A number of solutions have already been mentioned in this chapter. Like any product or service, many errors or glitches will go unnoticed for years.

Many of the TQM principles and practices, and tools and techniques in this textbook will provide additional solutions. In particular, ISO 9000, Quality by Design, FMEA, and SPC will be most effective.

Standards bodies like the World Wide Web Consortium (W3C) decide which basic technologies the industry will have in common.

Technologies of the Future

Given below is a brief description of the advances in information technology that are in various stages of development. Topics are wireless, artificial intelligence, virtual e-commerce, e-paper, wallet PC, and e-book.

The first generation of the *wireless* revolution was the analog cellphone; the second generation is the digital variety in common use today. Work is in process to develop the third generation, called 3G. The goal is to build the same high-speed data transmission speeds and "always on" services that are present in current broadband and cable modems.[51]

Using the power of the computer, *artificial intelligence* (AI) recreates, using software, the portions of the human brain that make decisions. An example of primitive AI in use today occurs when a commercial airplane lands in foggy conditions. Information programmed into the computer accesses data from the airplane's instruments and decides, much as a pilot would, how to adjust the flaps, throttle, and other controls in order to safely land the airplane. Researchers are driven by the pursuit of understanding human intelligence in order to create more advanced AI. Considering that the world's fastest computer has about one thousandths the computational power of a human brain, their task will take decades.[52]

---

[51] Edward C. Baig, "The Era of Living Wirelessly," *USA Today* (June 26, 2001): 1E, 2E.

[52] Kevin Maney, "Artificial Intelligence Isn't Just a Movie," *USA Today* (June 20, 2001): 1A, 2A.

Virtual e-commerce is a technique to let a prospective customer experience an item before it's purchased. For example, suppose you wish to purchase a sofa for your living room. If you don't have the living room in 3D in your computer, then a digital camera or camcorder is used to download that information. You then access the furniture store, select a sofa style with a particular fabric, and see if it fits the decor of your living room. You can change your selection as many times as necessary and even modify the design. In addition, you will be able to rearrange the furniture in your living room to optimize the sofa's location. Once you are satisfied with the sofa, the item is purchased and sent to the factory, where it is produced and shipped to your home.

The E Ink Corporation of Cambridge, MA has developed the first prototype of *e-paper*. Like paper, it is light and bendable. It also reflects outside light, which makes it easy to read, and, like a computer screen, it can be constantly refreshed. The final product is still years away, but e-paper could revolutionize computer screens, books, and other print media.[53]

The *wallet PC* will be about the same size as the wallet you carry in your pocket or purse. It will have all the power and features of a present-day computer and will include GPS, biometric security system, and keyless access to facilities and vehicles. In addition, it will be able to send and receive digital funds, making present forms of money obsolete.[54]

Ultimately, incremental improvements in computer and screen technology will give us a lightweight *e-book*, which will be about the size and weight of today's paperback books. The display will show high-resolution text, pictures, and video. Any document on the Internet will be accessible and pages will be turned or located by voice command.[55]

Conclusion

According to Alan Greenspan, Chairman of the Federal Reserve, "Our economy is benefiting from structural gains in productivity that have been driven by a remarkable wave of technological innovation. What differentiates this period from other periods in our history is the extraordinary role played by information and communication technologies."[56]

No country is making the transition to a knowledge-based economy better than the U.S. Nine of the ten largest organizations in the world are U.S. organizations, compared with two in 1990; nine of the top 15 banks are based in the U.S., whereas none were in

---

[53] Justin Pope, "Companies Compete to Develop Viable Electronic Paper," *St. Louis Post Dispatch* (January 1, 2001): BP2.

[54] Gates.

[55] Gates.

[56] The Associated Press, "Information Technology Raises Productivity, Greenspan Says," *St. Louis Post Dispatch* (June 14, 2000): C2.

1990. For the first time, the richest person in the world, Bill Gates, doesn't own any assets such as factories, railroads, gold or oil. He only owns knowledge.[57]

Perhaps Winston Churchill said it best: "The empires of the future are the empires of the mind."

TQM Exemplary Organization[58]

Headquartered in Carrollton, Texas, STMicroelectronics, Inc.—Region Americas (ST) ranks among the world's top manufacturers of semiconductor integrated circuits, supplying consumer-electronics, automotive, medical, telecommunications, and computer-equipment markets. Examples are integrated circuits for smart cards, digital set-top boxes for TVs, disk drives, compact disks, and specialized automotive applications.

The company's nine-step planning process also gathers complementary information on market and technology trends as well as competitor performance. At the operational level, continuous improvement goals are set to meet or exceed "best in class" benchmarks. The corporate Worldwide Standard System, for example, benchmarks key processing parameters at 14 semiconductor-manufacturing plants worldwide to establish best-known levels of industry performance in service, quality, and manufacturing. The president devotes 30 to 35 weeks a year to visiting customers.

ST views its suppliers as "seamless extensions" of the company. It develops an annual "Supplier Quality & Service Plan," which not only sets goals for suppliers, but which also specifies how ST will review performance, share data, and carry out other responsibilities in the relationship. A key tool is a five-year technology roadmap that is updated every six months. The roadmap effectively integrates anticipated customer requirements, ST's long-term innovation goals, and expectations for suppliers. The supplier-management program earned "best in class" rating in an independent evaluation of performance in 19 benchmark areas.

In 1998, ST initiated a "gung ho" program to promote teaming and employee empowerment, resulting in the redesign of manufacturing work systems and jobs—all with the aim of encouraging and enabling employees to take control of their work. Backed up by extensive training in teaming and problem-solving methods for manufacturing workers and "supervisor as coach" training for managers, the program was implemented rapidly, and the transformation is nearly complete at all manufacturing sites.

Teams determine workflow, assignments, and break and vacation schedules. They also set up and monitor their training and development plans, and they conduct peer reviews that are factored into formal performance reviews and merit increases. Compensation

---

[57] Teresa McUsic, "Economist Declares U.S. on Top of the World," *St. Louis Post Dispatch* (July 26, 1999): BP17.

[58] Malcolm Baldrige National Quality Award, 1999 Manufacturing Category Recipient, NIST/Baldrige Homepage, Internet.

systems are designed to reward cross-training and achievement of skill development objectives, while a variable incentive plan provides monthly bonuses to teams and individuals who meet production goals. More than 72% of direct manufacturing workers are certified to perform four job functions. Employee satisfaction levels in 1999 exceeded the industry composite in 8 of 10 categories; "lost day injuries" have declined from 1.01 injuries per 100 workers in 1996 to 0.65—74% below the industry average.

ST's performance measurement system is supported by a state-of-the-art information and communication network, which permits team-level analysis of progress toward operational targets and helps to ensure fact-based, decision-making at all levels of the organization. Between 1993 and 1998, ST's annual investment in expanding and increasing the utility of its information technology—from enterprise resource planning software to document control systems—has increased more than 200%.

The company believes that setting demanding environmental standards helps it improve operational and financial performance. This is illustrated by the nearly 20% decline since 1997 in energy used to manufacture silicon wafers, helping the company meet its goal of continuous cost reduction.

Exercises

1. Using the Internet or other sources, find examples of the role computers play in each of the six quality functions.

2. Why are companies encrypting instant messages and e-mail? What are the advantages of using instant messaging instead of e-mail?

3. What are the advantages and disadvantages of virtual teams?

4. What are the advantages and disadvantages of document management on the Internet?

5. What effect will e-learning have on public education from Kindergarten through the 12th grade?

6. Why has e-commerce grown so quickly?

7. Compare the websites of three B2B and three B2C organizations. What are the similarities and differences within a particular industry?

8. Describe the different types of websites.

9. Design your own website.

10. Using the Internet or other sources, find examples of the quality issues of information technology.

11. Describe some of the ways the Internet has had an impact on your activities.

12. What are the advantages and disadvantages of wireless communication?

13. Does AI have any ethical conditions, and if so, what are they?

10

Quality Management Systems

Introduction

The International Organization for Standardization (ISO) was founded in 1946 in Geneva, Switzerland, where it is still based. Its mandate is to promote the development of international standards to facilitate the exchange of goods and services worldwide. ISO is composed of more than 90 member countries. The United States representative is the American National Standards Institute (ANSI).

The ISO Technical Committee (TC) 176 developed a series of international standards for quality systems, which were first published in 1987. The standards (ISO 9000, 9001, and 9004) were intended to be advisory and were developed for use in two-party contractual situations and internal auditing. However, with their adoption by the European Community (EC) and a worldwide emphasis on quality and economic competitiveness, the standards have become universally accepted.

Most countries have adopted the ISO 9000 series as their national standards. Likewise, thousands of organizations throughout the world have quality systems registered to the standard. In the United States, the national standards are published by the American National Institute/American Society for Quality (ANSI/ASQ) as the ANSI/ASQ Q9000 series. Government bodies throughout the world, including the United States, are also using the standards. U.S. government agencies using the series are the Department of Defense (DOD) and the Food and Drug Administration (FDA).

In a two-party system, the supplier of a product or service would develop a quality system that conformed to the standards. The customers would then audit the system for acceptability. This two-party system results in both the supplier and customer having to participate in multiple audits, which can be extremely costly. This practice is replaced by a third-party registration system.

A quality system registration involves the assessment and periodic surveillance audit of the adequacy of a supplier's quality system by a third party, who is a registrar. When a system conforms to the registrar's interpretation of the standard, the registrar issues a certificate of registration to the supplier. This registration ensures customers or potential customers that a supplier has a quality system in place and it is being monitored.

Benefits of ISO Registration

There are various reasons for implementing a quality system that conforms to an ISO standard. The primary reason is that customers or marketing are suggesting or demanding compliance to a quality system. Other reasons are needed improvement in processes or systems and a desire for global deployment of products and services.[1] As more and more organizations become registered, they are requiring their subcontractors or suppliers to be registered, creating a snowball effect. Consequently, in order to maintain or increase market share, many organizations are finding they must be in conformance with an ISO standard. Internal benefits that can be received from developing and implementing a well-documented quality system can far outweigh the external pressures.

A study of 100 Italian manufacturing firms was undertaken to determine if there was any improvement in performance after registration. Significant improvement was noted in:

Internal quality as measured by the percent of scrap, rework, and nonconformities at final inspection.

Production reliability as measured by the number of breakdowns per month, percent of time dedicated to emergencies, and percent of downtime per shift.

External quality as measured by product accepted by customers without inspection, claims of nonconforming product, and returned product.

Time performance as measured by time to market, on-time delivery, and throughput time.

Cost of poor quality as measured by external nonconformities, scrap, and rework.

On the negative side, prevention and appraisal costs increased.[2]

Additional examples of benefits after registration are:

---

[1] F. C. Weston, Jr., "What Do Managers Really Think of the ISO 9000 Registration Process?" *Quality Progress* (October 1995): 67–73.

[2] Pietro Romano, "ISO 9000: What Is Its Impact On Performance?" *Quality Management Journal* (Vol. 7, No. 3, 2000): 38–55.

The American Institute of Certified Public Accountants (AICPA) now has a quality system that works, and there was a 4% improvement in gross margins, which was the largest improvement in their history.[3]

Northtown Ford automobile dealership in Toronto, Ontario raised customer satisfaction and loyalty by 20%, and it had a 55% increase in customers who would recommend the dealership.[4]

United Airlines reduced the average engine overhaul cycle time from 120 days to 60 days.[5]

Cleveland Center for Joint Reconstruction has experienced lower costs and more control and consistency in the care it provides.[6]

ISO 9000 Series of Standards

The ISO 9000 Series of Standards is generic in scope. By design, the series can be tailored to fit any organization's needs, whether it is large or small, a manufacturer or a service organization. It can be applied to construction, engineering, health care, legal, and other professional services as well as the manufacturing of anything from nuts and bolts to spacecraft. Its purpose is to unify quality terms and definitions used by industrialized nations and use those terms to demonstrate a supplier's capability of controlling its processes. In very simplified terms, the standards require an organization to say what it is doing to ensure quality, then do what it says, and, finally, document or prove that it has done what it said.

The three standards of the series are described briefly in the following paragraphs:

ISO 9000:2000—Quality Management Systems (QMS)—fundamentals and vocabulary discusses the fundamental concepts related to the QMS and provides the terminology used in the other two standards.

ISO 9001:2000—Quality Management Systems (QMS)—requirements is the standard used for registration by demonstrating conformity of the QMS to customers, regulatory, and the organization's own requirements.

ISO 9004:2000—Quality Management Systems (QMS)—guidelines for performance improvement provides guidelines that an organization can use to establish a QMS focused on improving performance.

---

[3] Norman Ho, "ISO 9000: No Longer a Stranger to Service," *Quality Digest* (June 1999): 33–36.

[4] *Quality Digest* news item.

[5] James P. O'Neil, "Using ISO 9000 to Go Beyond Industry Norms," *Quality Progress* (December 1998): 43–44.

[6] Laura M. Fox, "Enhancing Health Care: An ISO 9000 Case Study," *Quality Digest* (November 1998): 37–39.

Sector-specific Standards

The ISO 9000 system is designed as a simple system that could be used by any industry. Other systems have been developed that are specific to a particular industry such as automotive or aerospace. These systems use the ISO 9001 as the basic framework and modify it to their needs. There are currently three other quality systems: AS9100, ISO/TS 16949, and TL 9000.

One of the problems with sector-specific standards is the need for suppliers with customers in different industries to set up quality systems to meet each sector's requirements. For example, a packaging supplier that services the aerospace, automobile, and telecommunications industries would need to set up its system to accommodate not only ISO 9001 but three other standards. In addition, the Registration Accreditation Board (RAB) points out that sector-specific standards have created a need for specialized auditors and training courses. On the positive side, the standardization of requirements beyond ISO 9001 makes compliance by key suppliers and implementation by major customers much easier.[7]

AS9100

This aerospace industry quality system was officially released by the Society of Automotive Engineers in May 1997. Its development and release represents the first attempt to unify the requirements of NASA, DOD, and FAA, while satisfying the aerospace industry's business needs. In March 2001, the International Aerospace Quality Group (IAQG) aligned AS9100 with ISO 9001:2000. Industry-specific interpretations and methodologies are identified in italics and bold type. These additions are accepted aerospace approaches to quality practices and general requirements. Aerospace organizations in Europe, Japan, and the U.S. will certify registrars and auditors.[8]

ISO/TS 16949

This standard is entitled *Quality Systems Automotive Suppliers—Particular Requirements for the Application of ISO 9001*. It harmonizes the supplier quality requirements of the U.S. big three as provided in QS 9000 Third Edition[9] with the French, German and Italian automakers. The standard has been approved by Asian automakers. The goal of this technical specification is the development of fundamental quality systems that provide for continuous improvement, emphasizing defect prevention, and the reduction of variation and waste in the supply chain. There are three basic levels: (1) ISO 9001, (2) sector-specific requirements, and (3) company-specific requirements, and if appro-

---

[7] Leslie Norris, "The Pros and Cons of Sector-Specific Standards," *Quality Progress* (April 1999): 92–3.

[8] Dale K. Gordon, "What the Aerospace Sector is Doing," *Quality Progress* (August 2001): 80.

[9] This standard, which was developed in 1994 by Chrysler, Ford, and General Motors, was not updated to reflect the ISO 9001:2000 standard and, therefore, is obsolete.

ISO 9001 Requirements		
Common TL 9000 Requirements (QSR)—Book 1		
Hardware Specific Requirements	Software Specific Requirements	Services Specific Requirements
Common TL 9000 Measurements (QSM)—Book 2		
Hardware Specific Measurements	Software Specific Measurements	Services Specific Measurements

Figure 10-1 Structure of the TL 9000 Requirements

priate levels for division-specific, commodity-specific, and part-specific requirements. Registrars will need to be certified to the standard and their number will be limited.

It is assumed that this standard will show the same rate of improvement as QS 9000. GM reported that supplier parts-per-million defect rate improved about 85% for the first five years of the use of QS 9000.[10]

TL 9000

The Quality Excellence for Suppliers of Telecommunications Forum (QuEST) wrote TL 9000 to consolidate the various quality system requirements within the telecommunications industry. This forum was created to develop the standard wherein suppliers such as Motorola and Lucent, and telecom service providers such as Verizon, Southwestern Bell, and AT&T would have an equal vote in developing the new strategy. It is a specific set of requirements based on ISO 9001 that defines the design, development, production, delivery, installation, and maintenance of telecommunications products and services. Customers and suppliers receive a number of benefits including continuous improvement, enhanced customer/supplier relationships, efficient management of external audits, worldwide standards, increased competitiveness which results in overall cost reduction, industry benchmarks for performance metrics, and a platform for improvement initiatives.

Figure 10-1 shows the structure of the TL 9000 standard and its five layers. The first layer is the ISO 9000 requirements. It is followed by Book 1, called *TL9000 Quality System Requirements (QSR)*, which establishes a common set of requirements applicable to hardware, software, and services. The second layer of Book 1 provides specific requirements for hardware, software, and services. In the first layer of Book 2, called *Quality System Measurements (QSM)*, the common industry measurements such as billing errors are specified. In the last layer the specific measurements for hardware, software, and services are defined.

---

[10] Susan E. Daniels, "Management System Standards Poised for Momentum Boost," *Quality Progress* (March 2000): 31–39.

The unique feature of the standard is the use of the metrics specified in the QSM book to communicate and monitor actual results. Cost and performance-based metrics provides information to enable the industry to measure progress and evaluate results of quality system implementation. The University of Texas at Dallas (UTD) will administer the QSM. Participants will report specially coded metrics information to UTD, which stores and analyzes the data. Descriptive statistics such as mean, range, median, standard deviation, and best in industry is calculated. This information is available to the over 200 forum members on the forum's website. A supplier's identity remains anonymous at all times. Each organization can benchmark its performance against the industry standard and determine which of their processes need improvement—thereby improving customer-supplier relations.[11]

ISO 9001 Requirements[12]

The standard has eight clauses: Scope, Normative References, Definitions, Quality Management Systems, Management Responsibility, Resource Management, Product and/or Service Realization, and Measurement, Analysis, and Improvement. The first three clauses are for information while the last five are requirements that an organization must meet. The numbering system used in the standard is followed in this section.

The application of a system of processes within an organization, together with their identification and interactions and the managing of these processes, is referred to as the process approach. This approach emphasizes the importance of:

- Understanding and fulfilling the requirements.
- The need to consider processes in terms of value added.
- Obtaining results of process performance and effectiveness.
- Continual improvement of processes based on objective measure.

For the five required clauses, the system is shown in Figure 10-2.

1. Scope

The purpose of the standard is for the organization to demonstrate its ability to provide a product[13] that meets customer and regulatory requirements and achieves customer sat-

---

[11] Eugene E. Hutchison, "The Road to TL 9000: From the Bell Breakup to Today," *Quality Progress* (June 2001): 33–37.

[12] Adapted, with permission, from *Quality Management Systems—Requirements,* ANSI/ISO/ASQ Q9001: 2000, © 2000 ASQ Quality Press. (Milwaukee, WI: ASQ 2000).

[13] The standard defines product as including both product and service.

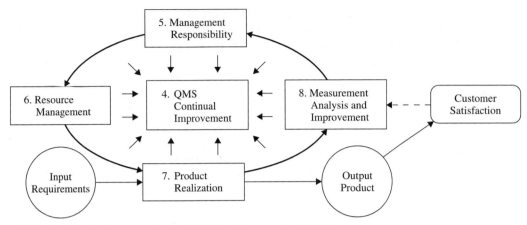

Figure 10-2 Model of a Process-Based Quality Management System

isfaction. This purpose is accomplished by evaluating and continually improving the system, rather than the product. The requirements of the standard are intended to be applicable to all types and sizes of organizations. Requirements in Clause 7, Product Realization, that are not appropriate to the organization, can be excluded.

2. Normative Reference

ISO 9000:2000 *Quality Management Systems—Fundamentals and vocabulary* are a normative reference that provides applicable concepts and definitions.

3. Terms and Definitions

For the purposes of this standard, the terms and definitions given in ISO 9000:2000 apply. In addition the supply chain is defined as:

Supplier → Organization → Customer

4. Quality Management System (QMS)

4.1 GENERAL REQUIREMENTS

The organization shall establish, document, implement, and maintain a QMS and continually improve its effectiveness. The organization shall (a) identify needed processes such as management activities, provision of resources, product realization, and measurement, (b) determine their sequence and interaction, (c) determine criteria and methods for effective operation and control of these processes, (d) ensure the availability of resources and information necessary to support and monitor these processes, (e) monitor, measure, and analyze these processes, and (f) implement actions to achieve planned results and continual improvement of these processes. Outsourced processes that affect the quality of the product shall be identified and included in the system.

4.2 DOCUMENTATION

4.2.1 General   Documentation shall include (a) statements of a quality policy and quality objectives, (b) a quality manual, (c) required documented procedures, (d) needed documents to ensure effective planning, operation, and control of processes, and (e) required records. A procedure or work instruction is needed if its absence could adversely affect the product quality. The extent of the documentation will depend on the organization's size and type of activities; the complexity of the processes and their interactions; and the competency of the employees. For example: a small organization may verbally notify a manager of an upcoming meeting, whereas a large organization would need written notification. The standard should satisfy the contractual, statutory, and regulatory requirements and the needs and expectations of customers and other interested parties. Documentation may be in any form or type of medium.

4.2.2 Quality Manual   A quality manual shall be established and maintained that includes (a) the scope of the QMS with details and justification for any exclusions, (b) the documented procedures or reference to them, and (c) a description of the interaction among the QMS processes.

4.2.3 Control of Documents   Documents required by the QMS shall be controlled. A documented procedure shall be in place to define the controls needed to (a) approve documents prior to use, (b) review, update, and re-approve as necessary, (c) identify the current revision status, (d) ensure that current versions are available at the point of use, (e) ensure that documents are legible and readily identified, (f) identify and distribute documents of external origin, and (g) provide for the prompt removal of obsolete documents and suitably identify any that may be retained. Documented procedure means that the procedure is established, documented, implemented, and maintained. They are required in elements 4.2.3, 4.2.4, 8.2.2, 8.3, 8.5.2, and 8.5.3.

4.2.4 Control of Records   Records shall be established and maintained to provide evidence of conformity to requirements and the effective operation of the QMS. They shall be legible, readily identifiable, and retrievable. A documented procedure shall be established to define the controls needed for the identification, storage, protection, retrieval, retention time, and disposition of records. Records can be used to document traceability and to provide evidence of verification, preventive action, and corrective action. They are required in elements 5.5.6, 5.6.3, 6.2.2, 7.2.2, 7.3.4, 7.3.6, 7.3.7, 7.4.1, 7.5.2, 7.6, and 8.2.4.

5. Management Responsibility

5.1 MANAGEMENT COMMITMENT

Top management shall provide evidence of its commitment to the development, implementation, and continual improvement of the QMS by (a) communicating the need to meet customer, legal, and regulatory expectations, (b) establishing a quality policy, (c) ensuring that quality objectives are established, (d) conducting management reviews, and (e) ensuring the availability of resources. Top management is defined as the person or group of people who directs and controls an organization.

5.2 CUSTOMER FOCUS

Top management shall ensure that customer requirements are determined and met with the aim of enhancing customer satisfaction.

5.3 QUALITY POLICY

Top management shall insure that the quality policy (a) is appropriate to the organization's purpose or mission, (b) includes a commitment to comply with requirements and continually improve the effectiveness of the QMS, (c) provides a framework for establishing and reviewing the quality objectives, (d) is communicated and understood within the organization, and (e) is reviewed for continuing stability. The quality policy gives the overall intention and direction of the organization related to quality.

5.4 PLANNING

5.4.1 Quality Objectives Top management shall ensure that quality objectives are established at relevant functions and levels within the organization and include product requirements. They shall be measurable and consistent with the quality policy. In addition, they should ensure that customer expectations are met. Quality objectives are something sought or aimed for related to quality. For example, finishing department scrap will be reduced from 5.0% to 4.3% and the first line supervisor is the person responsible.

5.4.2 Quality Management System Planning Top management shall ensure that the planning of the QMS is accomplished in order to meet the requirements of the QMS as stated in the General Requirements, Element 4.1, as well as the Quality Objectives, 5.4.1. In addition, the integrity of the QMS is maintained when changes are planned and implemented.

5.5 RESPONSIBILITY, AUTHORITY, AND COMMUNICATION

5.5.1 Responsibility and Authority Top management shall ensure that responsibilities and authorities are defined and communicated within the organization. Responsibilities can be defined in job descriptions, procedures, and work instructions. Authorities and interrelationships can be defined in an organization chart.

5.5.2 Management Representative Top management shall appoint a member of management, regardless of his/her other duties, that shall have the responsibility and authority that includes (a) ensuring that processes needed for the QMS system are established, implemented, and maintained, (b) reporting to top management on the performance of the QMS and any need for improvement, and (c) ensuring the promotion of awareness of customer requirements throughout the organization. Appointment of a member of top management as the representative can contribute to the effectiveness of the QMS.

5.5.3 Internal Communication Top management shall ensure that appropriate communication channels are established within the organization and that communication takes place regarding the QMS. Typical communication techniques are management workplace briefing, recognition of achievement, bulletin boards, e-mail, and in-house news brochures.

5.6 MANAGEMENT REVIEW

5.6.1 General Top management shall review the QMS at planned intervals to ensure its continuing suitability, adequacy, and effectiveness. This review shall include assessing opportunities for improvement and the need for changes to the QMS including the quality policy and quality objectives. Records from the reviews shall be maintained.

5.6.2 Review Input The input to the review shall include information on (a) results of audits, (b) customer feedback, (c) process performance and product conformity, (d) status of corrective and preventative performance, (e) follow-up actions from previous management reviews, (f) changes that could affect the QMS, and (g) recommendations for improvement.

5.6.3 Review Output The output from the review shall include any decisions and actions related to (a) improvement of the effectiveness of the QMS and its processes, (b) improvement of the product related to customer requirements, and (c) resource needs. Top management can use the outputs as inputs to improvement opportunities.

6. Resource Management

6.1 PROVISION OF RESOURCES

The organization shall determine and provide the resources needed (a) to implement and maintain the QMS and continually improve its effectiveness, and (b) to enhance customer satisfaction by meeting customer requirements. Resources may be people, infrastructure, work environment, information, suppliers, natural resources, and financial resources. Resources can be aligned with quality objectives.

6.2 HUMAN RESOURCES

6.2.1 General Personnel performing work that affects product quality shall be competent on the basis of appropriate education, training, skills, and experience.

6.2.2 Competence, Awareness and Training The organization shall (a) determine the necessary competence for personnel performing work affecting product quality, (b) provide training or take other actions to satisfy these needs, (c) evaluate the effectiveness of the actions taken, (d) ensure that its personnel are aware of the relevance and importance of their activities and how they contribute to the achievement of the quality objectives, and (e) maintain appropriate records of education, training, skills, and experience. Competency is defined as the demonstrated ability to apply knowledge and skills. It can be contained in the job description by function, group, or specific position. Training effectiveness can be determined by before and after tests, performance, or turnover.[14] *ISO 10015 Guidelines for Training* will help organizations comply with this standard.

6.3 INFRASTRUCTURE

The organization shall determine, provide, and maintain the infrastructure needed to achieve conformity to product requirements. Infrastructure includes, as applicable (a) buildings, workspace, and associated utilities, (b) process equipment (both hardware and software), and (c) supporting services (such as transport or communication).

6.4 WORK ENVIRONMENT

The organization shall determine and manage the work environment needed to achieve conformity to product requirements. Creation of a suitable work environment can have a positive influence on employee motivation, satisfaction, and performance.

7. Product Realization

7.1 PLANNING OF PRODUCT REALIZATION

The organization shall plan and develop the processes needed for product realization. Planning of product realization shall be consistent with the requirements of the other processes of QMS. In planning product realization, the organization shall determine the following, as appropriate: (a) quality objectives and requirements for the product; (b) the need to establish processes, documents, and provide resources specific to the product; (c) required verification, validation, monitoring, inspection, and test activities specific to the product and the criteria for product acceptance; and (d) records

---

[14] Jeanne Ketola and Kathy Roberts, "Demystify ISO 9001:2000," *Quality Progress* (September 2001): 65–70.

needed to provide evidence that the realization processes and resulting product or service meet requirements. The output of this planning shall be in a form suitable for the organization's method of operations. A document specifying the processes of the QMS (including the product realization processes) and the resources to be applied to a specific product, project or contract, can be referred to as a quality plan. The organization may also apply the requirements given in 7.3 to the development of the product realization processes.

7.2 CUSTOMER-RELATED PROCESSES

7.2.1 Determination of Requirements Related to the Product   The organization shall determine (a) requirements specified by the customer, including the requirements for delivery and post-delivery activities, (b) requirements not stated by the customer but necessary for specified or intended use, where known, (c) statutory and regulatory requirements related to the product, and (d) any additional requirements determined by the organization.

7.2.2 Review of Requirements Related to the Product   The organization shall review the requirements related to the product. This review shall be conducted prior to the organization's commitment to supply a product to the customer (for example, submission of tenders, acceptance of contracts or orders, acceptance of changes to contracts or orders) and shall ensure that (a) product requirements are defined, (b) contract or order requirements differing from those previously expressed are resolved, and (c) the organization has the ability to meet the defined requirements. Records of the results of the review and actions arising from the review shall be maintained. Where the customer provides no documented statement of requirement, the customer requirements shall be confirmed by the organization before acceptance. Where product requirements are changed, the organization shall ensure that relevant documents are amended and that relevant personnel are made aware of the changed requirements. In some situations, such as Internet sales, a formal review is impractical for each order. Instead, the review can cover relevant product information such as catalogs or advertising material.

7.2.3 Customer Communication   The organization shall determine and implement effective arrangements for communicating with customers in relation to (a) product information, (b) inquiries, contracts, or order handling, including amendments, and (c) customer feedback, including customer complaints.

7.3 DESIGN AND DEVELOPMENT

7.3.1 Design and Development Planning   The organization shall plan and control the design and development of the product. During the design and development planning, the organization shall determine (a) the design and development stages, (b) the review, verification and validation that are appropriate to each design and development stage, and (c) the responsibilities and authorities for design and development. The organization shall manage the interfaces between different groups involved in design and development to ensure effective communication and clear assignment of responsibility. Planning output shall be updated, as appropriate, as the design and development progresses.

7.3.2 Design and Development Inputs   Inputs relating to product requirements shall be determined and records maintained. These shall include (a) functional and performance requirements, (b) applicable statutory and regulatory requirements, (c) where applicable, information derived from previous similar designs, and (d) other requirements essential for design and development. These inputs shall be reviewed for adequacy. Requirements shall be complete, unambiguous and not in conflict with each other.

7.3.3 Design and Development Outputs   The outputs of design and development shall be provided in a form that enables verification against the design and development input and shall be approved prior to release. Design and development outputs shall (a) meet the input requirements for design and development, (b) provide appropriate information for purchasing, production, and for service provision, (c) contain or reference product acceptance criteria, and (d) specify the characteristics of the product that are essential for its safe and proper use.

7.3.4 Design and Development Review   At suitable stages, systematic reviews of design and development shall be performed in accordance with planned arrangements (a) to evaluate the ability of the results of design and development to meet requirements, and (b) to identify any problems and propose necessary actions. Participants in such reviews shall include representatives of functions concerned with the design and development stage(s) being reviewed. Records of the results of the reviews and any necessary actions shall be maintained. Risk assessment such as FMEA, reliability prediction, and simulation techniques can be undertaken to determine potential failures in products or processes.

7.3.5 Design and Development Verification   Verification shall be performed in accordance with planned arrangements to ensure that the design and development outputs have met the design and development input requirements. Records of the results of the verification and any necessary actions shall be maintained. Verification confirms, through objective evidence, that the specified requirements have been fulfilled. Confirmation can comprise activities such as performing alternate calculations, comparing the new design specification to a similar proven design specification, undertaking tests and demonstrations, and reviewing documents prior to issue.

7.3.6 Design and Development Validation   Design and development validation shall be performed in accordance with planned arrangements to ensure that the resulting product is capable of meeting the requirements for the specified application or intended use, when known. Wherever practicable, validation shall be completed prior to the delivery or implementation of the product. Records of the results of validation and any necessary actions shall be maintained. Validation confirms, through objective evidence, that the requirements for a specific intended use have been fulfilled.

7.3.7 Control of Design and Development Changes   Design and development changes shall be identified and records maintained. The changes shall be reviewed, verified and validated, as appropriate, and approved before implementation. The review of design and development changes shall include evaluation of the effect of the changes on constituent parts and product already delivered. Records of the results of the review of changes and any necessary actions shall be maintained.

7.4 PURCHASING

7.4.1 Purchasing Process   The organization shall ensure that purchased product conforms to specified purchase requirements. The type and extent of control applied to the supplier and the purchased product shall be dependent upon the effect of the purchased product on subsequent product realization or the final product. The organization shall evaluate and select suppliers based on their ability to supply product in accordance with the organization's requirements. Criteria for selection, evaluation, and re-evaluation shall be established. Records of the results of evaluations and any necessary actions arising from the evaluation shall be maintained. This standard does not apply to items such as office and maintenance supplies, unless they are a product.

7.4.2 Purchasing Information   Purchasing information shall describe the product to be purchased, including where appropriate (a) requirements for approval of product, procedures, processes, and equipment, (b) requirements for qualification of personnel, and (c) QMS requirements. The organization shall ensure the adequacy of specified requirements prior to their communication to the supplier.

7.4.3 Verification of Purchased Product   The organization shall establish and implement the inspection or other activities necessary for ensuring that purchased product meets specified purchase requirements. Where the organization or its customer intends to perform verification at the supplier's premises, the organization shall state the intended verification arrangements and method of product release in the purchasing information.

7.5 PRODUCTION AND SERVICE PROVISION

7.5.1 Control of Production and Service Provision   The organization shall plan and carry out production and service provision under controlled conditions. Controlled conditions shall include, as applicable (a) the availability of information that describes the characteristics of the product, (b) the availability of work instructions, as necessary, (c) the use of suitable equipment, (d) the availability and use of monitoring and measuring devices, (e) the implementation of monitoring and measurement, and (f) the implementation of release, delivery, and post-delivery activities.

7.5.2 Validation of Processes for Production and Service Provision   The organization shall validate any processes for production and service provision where the resulting output cannot be verified by subsequent monitoring or measurement. This includes any processes where deficiencies become apparent only after the product is in use or the service has been delivered. Validation shall demonstrate the ability of these processes to achieve planned results. The organization shall establish arrangements for these processes including, as applicable (a) defined criteria for review and approval of the processes, (b) approval of equipment and qualification of personnel, (c) use of specific methods and procedures, (d) requirements for records, and (e) revalidation.

7.5.3 Identification and Traceability   Where appropriate, the organization shall identify the product by suitable means throughout product realization. The organization shall identify the product status with respect to monitoring and measurement requirements. Where traceability is a requirement, the organization shall control and record the unique identification of the product. In some industry sectors, configuration management is a means by which identification and traceability are maintained. Identification can frequently be accomplished with a production router or traveller.

7.5.4 Customer Property   The organization shall exercise care with customer property while it is under the organization's control or being used by the organization. The organization shall identify, verify, protect and safeguard customer property provided for use or incorporation into the product. If any customer property is lost, damaged, or otherwise found to be unsuitable for use, this shall be reported to the customer and records maintained. Customer property can include intellectual property.

7.5.5 Preservation of Product   The organization shall preserve the conformity of product during internal processing and delivery to the intended destination. This preservation shall include identification, handling, packaging, storage, and protection. Preservation shall also apply to the constituent parts of a product.

7.6 CONTROL OF MONITORING AND MEASURING DEVICES

The organization shall determine the monitoring and measurement to be undertaken and the monitoring and measuring devices needed to provide evidence of conformity of product to determined requirements. The organization shall establish processes to ensure that monitoring and measurement can be carried out and are carried out in a manner that is consistent with the monitoring and measurement requirements. Where necessary to ensure valid results, measuring equipment shall (a) be calibrated or verified at specified intervals or prior to use, against measurement standards; where no such standards exist, the basis used for calibration or verification shall be recorded, (b) be adjusted or readjusted as necessary, (c) be identified to enable calibration status to be determined, (d) be safeguarded from adjustments that would invalidate the measurement result, and (e) be protected from damage and deterioration during handling, maintenance and storage. In addition, the organization shall assess and record the validity of the previous measuring results when the equipment is found not to conform to requirements. The organization shall take appropriate action on the equipment and any product affected. Records of the results of calibration and verification shall be maintained. When used in the monitoring and measurement of specified requirements, the ability of computer software to satisfy the intended application shall be confirmed. This shall be undertaken prior to initial use and reconfirmed as necessary. *ISO 10012-1:1992 Quality assurance requirements for measuring equipment—Part 1, ISO 10012-2:1997 Quality assurance for measuring equipment—Part 2*, and *ISO 17025-1999 General requirements for the competence of testing and calibration laboratories* can be used for guidance.

8. Measurement, Analysis, and Improvement

8.1 GENERAL

The organization shall plan and implement the monitoring, measurement, analysis, and improvement processes needed (a) to demonstrate conformity of the product, (b) to ensure conformity of the QMS, and (c) to continually improve the effectiveness of the QMS. This shall include determination of applicable methods, including statistical techniques, and the extent of their use.

8.2 MONITORING AND MEASUREMENT

8.2.1 Customer Satisfaction   As one of the measurements of the performance of the QMS, the organization shall monitor information relating to customer perception as to whether the organization has met customer requirements. The methods for obtaining and using this information shall be determined.

8.2.2 Internal Audit   The organization shall conduct internal audits at planned intervals to determine whether the QMS (a) conforms to the planned arrangements (see 7.1), to the requirements of this standard, and to the requirements established by the organization, and (b) is effectively implemented and maintained. An audit program shall be planned, taking into consideration the status and importance of the processes and areas to be audited, as well as the results of previous audits. The audit criteria, scope, frequency, and methods shall be defined. Selection of auditors and conduct of audits shall ensure objectivity and impartiality of the audit process. Auditors shall not audit their own work. The responsibilities and requirements for planning and conducting audits and for reporting results and maintaining records shall be defined in a documented procedure. The management responsible for the area being audited shall ensure that actions are taken without undue delay to eliminate detected nonconformities and their causes. Follow-up activities shall include the verification of the actions taken and the reporting of verification results. *ISO 19011 Guidelines on quality and/or environmental management auditing* can be used for guidance.

8.2.3 Monitoring and Measurement of Processes   The organization shall apply suitable methods for monitoring and, where applicable, measurement of the QMS processes. These methods shall demonstrate the ability of the processes to achieve planned results.

When planned results are not achieved, correction and corrective action shall be taken, as appropriate, to ensure conformity of the product.

8.2.4 Monitoring and Measurement of Product and Service   The organization shall monitor and measure the characteristics of the product to verify that product requirements have been met. This shall be carried out at appropriate stages of the product realization process in accordance with the planned arrangements. Evidence of conformity with the acceptance criteria shall be maintained. Records shall indicate the person(s) authorizing release of product. Product release and service delivery shall not proceed until the planned arrangements have been satisfactorily completed, unless otherwise approved by a relevant authority and, where applicable, by the customer.

8.3 CONTROL OF NONCONFORMING PRODUCT

The organization shall ensure that product which does not conform to product requirements is identified and controlled to prevent its unintended use or delivery. The controls and related responsibilities and authorities for dealing with nonconforming product shall be defined in a document procedure. The organization shall deal with nonconforming product in one or more of the following ways: (a) by taking action to eliminate the detected nonconformity; (b) by authorizing its use, release or acceptance under concession by a relevant authority and, where applicable, by the customer; and (c) by taking action to preclude its original intended use or application. Records of the nature of nonconformities and any subsequent actions taken, including concessions obtained, shall be maintained. When nonconforming product is corrected, it shall be subject to re-verification to demonstrate conformity to the requirements. When nonconforming product or service is detected after delivery or use has started, the organization shall take action appropriate to the effects, or potential effects, of the nonconformity.

8.4 ANALYSIS OF DATA

The organization shall determine, collect, and analyze appropriate data to demonstrate the suitability and effectiveness of the QMS and to evaluate where continual improvement of the effectiveness of the QMS can be made. This shall include data generated as a result of monitoring and measurement and from other relevant sources. The analysis of data shall provide information relating to (a) customer satisfaction, (b) conformity to product requirements, (c) characteristics and trends of processes and products, including opportunities for preventive action, and (d) suppliers.

8.5 IMPROVEMENT

8.5.1 Continual Improvement   The organization shall continually improve the effectiveness of the QMS through the use of the quality policy, quality objectives, audit results, analysis of data, corrective and preventive actions, and management review.

8.5.2 Corrective Action   The organization shall take action to eliminate the cause of non-conformities in order to prevent recurrence. Corrective actions shall be appropriate to the effects of the nonconformities encountered. A documented procedure shall be established to define requirements for (a) reviewing nonconformities (including customer complaints), (b) determining the causes of nonconformities, (c) evaluating the need for action to ensure that nonconformities do not recur, (d) determining and implementing action needed, (e) records of the results of action taken, and (f) reviewing corrective action taken.

8.5.3 Preventive Action   The organization shall determine action to eliminate the causes of potential nonconformities in order to prevent their occurrence. Preventive actions shall be appropriate to the effects of the potential problems. A documented procedure shall be established to define requirements for (a) determining potential nonconformities and their causes, (b) evaluating the need for action to prevent occurrence of nonconformities, (c) determining and implementing action needed, (d) records of results of action taken, and (e) reviewing preventive action taken. Preventive action is taken to prevent occurrence while corrective action is taken to prevent reoccurrence.

Eight total quality management principles form the basis for the QMS standards. They are customer focus, leadership, employee involvement, process approach, system approach to management, continual improvement, factual approach to decision making, and mutually-beneficial supplier relationships. These principles are similar to the core values of the Malcolm Baldrige National Quality Award.

Implementation

There are a number of steps that are necessary to implement a quality management system.

1. Top Management Commitment

The most important step in implementing a quality system that will meet or exceed an ISO 9000 standard is to acquire the full support of upper management. The chief executive officer (CEO) must be willing to commit the resources necessary to achieve certification. This is critical to the success of the project. Without the CEO's support, the process may continuously run into unnecessary roadblocks or even be doomed to failure. Because top management is assigned specific responsibilities in the standard, it is necessary that they be involved in its implementation.

2. Appoint the Management Representative

Once the commitment has been made, the process can proceed by adopting a project team approach and treating it the same as any other business undertaking. The next step is the appointment of a management representative. This person is responsible for coordinating the implementation and maintenance of the quality system and is the contact person for all parties involved in the process, both internal and external. The representative can be a member of the top management group who is able to ensure that the quality system is effectively implemented, documented, and maintained. The implementation of the quality system should involve everyone in the organization.

3. Awareness

This step requires an awareness program. Because the process is going to affect every member of the organization as well as require their input, it stands to reason that everyone should understand the quality system. They should know how it will affect day-to-day operations and the potential benefits. This information can be relayed through short, one-hour awareness training sessions. Be sure everyone knows the intent of the standard. At the Cleveland Center for Joint Reconstruction, staff buy-in didn't happen until they realized that the new system would allow them to make a difference in their day-to-day activities.[15]

4. Appoint an Implementation Team

After everyone has been informed of the organization's intentions to develop the quality system, an implementation team should be assembled. This team should be drawn from all levels and areas of the organization so that it is representative. Committees for each of the five clauses may be used. The team should identify the QMS processes and their sequence and interaction. It is important to keep the project visible for all employees.

5. Training

The implementation team, supervisors, and internal audit team should be trained. This activity can be accomplished by sending team leaders for training and having them train the other team members or by bringing the training in-house for all team members through a one- or two-day seminar.

6. Time Schedule

This activity develops a time schedule for the implementation and registration of the system. This time frame will vary, depending on the size and type of organization and the extent of its existing quality system. Most organizations can complete the entire process in less than 1.5 years. Divide the implementation process into manageable units. Be sure to provide for the celebration of small victories.

---

[15] Laura M. Fox, "Enhancing Health Care: An ISO 9000 Case Study," *Quality Digest* (November 1998): 37–39.

7. Select Element Owners

The implementation team selects owners for each of the system elements. Many of these owners will be members of the implementation team. Owners may be assigned more than one element. Each owner has the option of selecting a team to assist in the process. The more people involved, the more effective the system.

8. Review the Present System

Perform a review of the present quality system. Copies of all the quality manuals, procedures, work instructions, and forms presently in use are obtained. These documents are sorted into the system elements to determine what is available and what is needed to complete the system. This activity is a gap analysis and can be performed by the element owners and their teams or by an external consultant.

9. Write the Documents

Prepare written quality policy and procedure manuals—they can be combined into one document. Write appropriate work instructions to maintain the quality of specific functions. This process should involve every employee, because the best person to write a work instruction is the one who performs the job on a regular basis. Stream International of Crawfordsville, IN encouraged employees to expose the flaws in existing processes and document new processes that would work correctly. However, it is important to be prudent when creating documentation. Too much documentation or complicated documentation will destroy the system.

10. Install the New System

Integrate the policies, procedures, and work instructions into the day-to-day workings of the organization, and document what is being done. It is not necessary for all elements to be implemented at the same time. Be sure all people are trained.

11. Internal Audit

Conduct an internal audit of the quality system. This step is necessary to ensure that the system is working effectively and to provide management with information for the comprehensive management review. Minor corrections to the system are made as they occur. A cross-section of trained people should be used for the audit team.

12. Management Review

Conduct a management review. The management review is used to determine the effectiveness of the system in achieving the stated quality goals. The system is revised as needed.

13. Preassessment

This step is optional. If a good job has been done on the previous steps, preassessment is not necessary.

14. Registration

This step has three parts: choosing a registrar, submitting an application, and conducting the registrar's system audit. Considerations in choosing a registrar include cost, lead time, your customer's acceptance of the registrar, the registrar's accreditation, and familiarity with your industry. The application for registration should also include supplying the registrar with the policy and procedure manuals for their review. The time involved in the registrar's system audit will vary depending on the size and complexity of the organization and the number of auditors involved. A registrar's audit usually lasts one to three days and will consist of an opening meeting to describe the process the auditors will follow, the audit itself, and a closing meeting to discuss the findings of the audit.

Some of these steps, such as documentation, internal auditing, and registration are described in greater detail in the sections that follow. Some pitfalls to successful implementation are:

Using a generic documentation program or another organization's documentation program.

Overdocumentation or documentation that is too complex.

Using external consultants without internal ownership and involvement.

Limiting documentation to text rather than other types of media.

Neglecting to obtain top management's involvement.

Developing a system that does not represent what actually occurs.

Documentation

A quality system is the method used to ensure that the quality level of a product or service is maintained. The system documentation can be viewed as a hierarchy containing four tiers, as shown in Figure 10-3. All documentation moves from one level to the next in a descending order. If the system is properly structured, changes at one level will seldom affect the levels above it, but may affect those below.

Policy

The first tier of documentation is the policy manual. This is the document that defines what will be done and why. A quality policy manual should be written so it is clear,

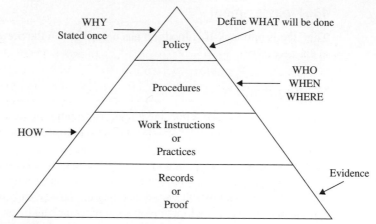

Figure 10-3 The Documentation Pyramid

precise, practical, and easy to understand. The why can be stated just once as a quality policy statement. This statement should be a short, simple definition of the organization's quality intentions. For example:

> Quality is the responsibility of each Tempset employee. We pledge to continuously provide products and services that meet or exceed customer expectations.
>
> TEMPSET INC., ST. LOUIS, MO.

The remainder of the policy manual addresses what will be done to comply with the standard being used. Another way of looking at the policy manual is to think of it as the commandments of the system. Each element of the standard is addressed individually and usually requires one page or less.

Procedure

The second tier of documentation is the quality procedures. These procedures describe the methods that will be used to implement and perform the stated policies. The procedures define who should perform specific tasks, when the task should be done, and where documentation will be made showing that the task was performed. Procedures should be oriented so that they apply to all areas within the organization. They dictate the strategies that will be used to ensure the quality of the system. Procedures are more detailed than the policies; however, they, too, should be written in a manner that will allow for easy understanding. It should be noted that procedures are not required for all elements. Many organizations combine the policy and procedures into one document. A procedure is needed if its absence would adversely affect the activity.

Work Instructions

Work instructions are usually department, machine, task, or product oriented and spell out how a job will be done. These instructions are the most detailed of the documentation hierarchy. A work instruction may be in the form of a detailed drawing, recipe, routing sheet, specific job function (for example, turn nut four turns clockwise), photograph, video, or simply a sample for comparison of conformity. The writing of a work instruction is best carried out by the employee who performs the task. This person knows the process and the problems encountered in that process. However, a documentation specialist may be needed to do the actual writing. This method also creates a pride of ownership in the document, making it more likely to be carried out. Additionally, employee participation helps to ensure that future improvements will be suggested. Not every task requires a work instruction. For example, you don't need to tell a computer specialist to turn on the PC.

Records

Records are a way of documenting that the policies, procedures, and work instructions have been followed. Records may be forms that are filled out, a stamp of approval on a product, or a signature and date on some type of document, such as a routing sheet. Records are used to provide traceability of actions taken on a specific product or batch of products. They provide data for corrective action and a way of recalling products, if necessary.

Document Development

Although documentation is required by the system, its most important purpose is to provide guidelines for internal quality management. In this respect it can be considered one approach to the road of continuing quality improvement and business success. Where does this road start? The answer is with the quality system that is already in place. If an organization has been in business for any length of time, with some degree of success, it has already established procedures for supplying its product or service to customers. This preexisting documentation is the starting point for developing the documents necessary for registration.

To begin creating the documentation system, the implementation team should gather all the existing policies, procedures, work instructions, and forms that are presently in use. Each document should be reviewed and an attempt should be made to fit it into one of the elements. If a document does not appear to pertain to any element, it should be set aside. Where it belongs may become evident at a later time. In addition, the team should decide if the document is currently accurate and up to date. If it is not, it should be updated or discarded.

Now it is time to involve as many employees as possible. Remember, writing the documents will probably be the easy part of the implementation process. Putting the policies and procedures to work will be the most difficult. The more people involved in the creation of the system, the greater the likelihood the system will perform satisfactorily. Involved people are more likely to implement the procedures and ensure that they remain current than people who have had no input. If the organization is large enough, a team of three or more members should be appointed for each element. The team members should come from all areas of the organization, not just from the management or quality areas. Each team is assigned an owner and charged with the responsibility of writing the policy and procedures for that element. They can also be given the responsibility of interviewing personnel and writing the necessary work instructions and applicable documentation forms. A consultant may be needed during this phase to facilitate the team's activities.

As the documents are produced, the implementation team becomes the review committee. If changes appear necessary, suggestions are made and reviewed with the team. The initiating team then either clarifies what has been written or revises the documents as required. When the documents have been completed, they should be formatted in a manner that will allow for simple and effective document control.

Writing the Documents

The basic thought to keep in mind when writing the documents is to create simplicity out of complexity. To accomplish this objective, the documents must be simple and concise.

Simplicity can be obtained by having one idea addressed per paragraph, short subject-verb-object type sentences, and a simple paragraph-numbering system as shown in Figure 10-4. Write to an eighth grade reading level—most newspapers write to the sixth- or seventh-grade level. In addition, use 13- or 14-point type, because it is easier to read and have plenty of white space. Unfortunately, a simple document is not easy to develop—it takes time and a commitment to excellence.

Being concise requires that you write only what's needed. Remove all irrelevant material and avoid the use of special jargon that is common to only one industry or organization. Consider the who, what, when, where, why, and how of the concept being addressed. Write what you are doing. If you need to write "what you ought to be doing" for compliance to an element, then underline it and take the necessary action to achieve compliance. Avoid writing procedures on how to fill out forms. They become records and should be designed to be self-explanatory. Use flow diagrams and check sheets wherever possible rather than lengthy verbiage. The revision process should be as painless as possible. In fact, employees should be encouraged to initiate changes and improvements in procedures and work instructions.[16]

The first step in writing the documents is to create a format that can be used throughout the documentation hierarchy. Although it is not required by ISO, it is helpful to auditors if documents follow the numbering system "QPol" in ISO 9001. Justification for

---

[16] C. W. Russ Russo, "12 Rules to Make Your ISO 9000 Documentation Simple and Easy to Use," *Quality Progress* (March 1997): 51–53.

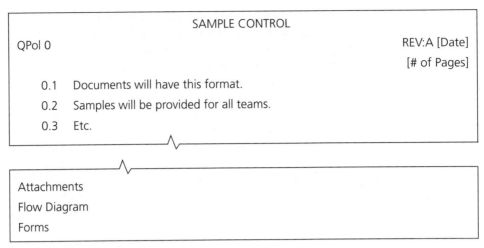

Figure 10-4 Format Example

the exclusion of any elements must be stated in Element 4.2.2, Quality Manual. Each document should have a title, a number that is unique to only one document, a date, revision number or letter for control purposes, and the number of pages it contains. In the case of the policy and procedure manuals, the title can be the same as the ISO element they reference. Work instructions and records should have titles that identify their purpose. All policy documents may start with "QPol" to denote a quality policy and be followed by their element number (4.1, 4.2.1, and so forth). Procedures can follow the same system by changing "QPol" to "QPro" followed by the title and element number, and so on, through work instructions, flow diagrams, and records. Figure 10-4 shows a simple and effective method for the formatting of documents.

When designing the manuals, simplicity and ease of use should determine the structure to be used. A cover page will list the organization name and location as well as the title of the document. The table of contents can list the revision letter or number of each document within the manual, as well as the location. The policy manual, being the first tier of the hierarchy, should have a copy of the organization's quality policy and statement of the purpose of the quality system. These statements are usually signed by the CEO of the organization. Examples of purpose statements are:

> This quality policy manual has been prepared to provide assistance to all employees in understanding and implementing the quality assurance activities associated with their jobs.

> In recognizing the responsibilities as a manufacturer (service organization) to comply fully with all contractual provisions and statutory requirements of society, we have developed this comprehensive quality system to assure customers that products (services) supplied will be in conformance to requirements and without nonconformities. The program described is in conformance to the requirements of ISO 9001.

A distribution page should be included in the master copy of the manual as a record of who has received a controlled copy. Controlled copies are those that must be updated each time a revision or change is made to the manual. The distribution page provides a method for control of the document, which is required by Element 4.2.3, Control of Documents. Uncontrolled copies may be distributed to customers upon their request and should contain a statement that they will not be automatically updated.

Each of the elements of ISO 9001 should be addressed in the policy manual. Elements that do not pertain to the standard can contain a statement such as, "Not applicable—see Element 4.2.2 for justification." The elements of the standard contain many statements that use the word *shall*, which is a key word in that any statement using it must be addressed by the quality system. An example of the policy statement of a small cast iron foundry that employs 85 people is given below for Element 7.2.2, Review of Requirements Related to the Product.

> Prior to the acceptance of a customer's order, their requirements will be reviewed to determine that:
>
> 1. They are clearly defined and do not differ from the original proposal or sales offer.
>
> 2. Any differences are resolved and any changes are appropriately recorded and affected people notified.
>
> 3. Wirco Castings Inc. has the ability to meet them.
>
> Where the customer does not provide requirements, Wirco Castings' standard requirements will be used and the customer so notified.
>
> Record of the review will be recorded in the Part History File.

Analysis of the policy shows that all of the information in the standard has been included. The policy is simply a rewording of the standard. Note that the statement does not include the scope or the purpose, because they are obvious.

The second tier of documentation is the procedures manual. Unless the procedure contains proprietary information, it can be included with the policy. Otherwise, the procedures manual, like the policy manual, should use a cover sheet, distribution page, and table of contents that reflects a current revision letter or number. Procedures are the methods used to carry out the requirements of the policy and are more detailed. Procedure writing can be simplified by using a flow diagram of the required actions. Figure 10-5 is an example of a flow diagram for Element 7.2.2.

The flow diagram shows who does the work, what they do, and the where is obviously in the organization's office. It is short and to the point, simple to audit, contains no unnecessary information, and illustrates the process very effectively.[17] Examples of documents used to show compliance of a procedure can be attached to the procedure or referenced and placed in an appendix. In this case, the policy and the procedure can be on the same page.

---

[17] Tony Wright, "ISO 9001 without Tears," *Quality Progress* (August 2001): 57–61.

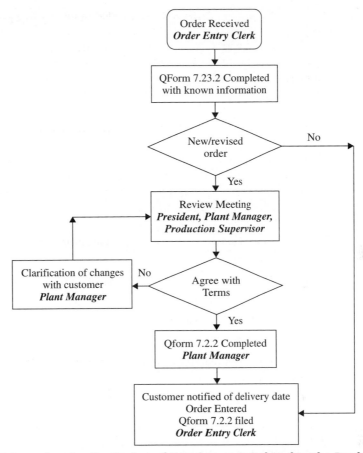

Figure 10-5 Procedure for the Review of Requirements Related to the Product

The third tier of the document pyramid is for work instructions which are specialized and used only as required for quality considerations. They must fit the organization's requirements. As much as possible, however, they should follow the same type of format and numbering system as the policy and procedure manual in order to maintain consistency. Work instructions come in many forms, such as drawings, recipes, routing sheets, operation sheets, samples, photographs, and videos.

The last tier of the pyramid is for records or proof that the policies and procedures have been followed. Most of the records will be readily available and no writing will be necessary. Like work instructions, records use many types of media, such as forms that are filled out, stamp of approval on a product, or a signature and date on a routing sheet. Figure 10-6 shows a check sheet that was used in the procedure for Element 7.2.2. It was filed as evidence that the procedure was followed. The check sheet was designed so that it not only aided the process but so that it also served as the record.

REVIEW OF CUSTOMERS' REQUIREMENTS

QFD m 7.2.2

REV:A[01 Jan 99]

[1 Page]

Customer Name: _____ Date: _____

Contact Number: _____ Reviewed By: _____

Compare With

Description	OK	Comments
Name		
Address		
Telephone Number		
Contact Person		
Casting Price		
Tooling Price		
Quantity		
Engr. Change/Revision		
Material Specification		
Shipping Containers		
Freight Carrier		
F.O.B. Point		
Delivery Date		

Additional Comments: _____

_____

_____

_____

_____

_____

_____

Figure 10-6 Check Sheet Used with Procedure for the Review of Requirements Related to the Product

An electronic document control system is an excellent way to manage change and ease collaboration. Such a system allows an organization to store documents in an access-controlled database that can route documents to appropriate personnel for developing, revising, or editing. Collaborated documents can then be routed to the appropriate personnel for electronic signature. An electronic database allows the system to always be current without obsolete policies and procedures available for misuse.

Establishing the database on the Internet or on an intranet provides remote users with the capability to access documents and to participate in development, review, collaboration, and approval processes. This capability allows travelling or offsite employees to stay involved and keep the document control and change management process moving effectively. A web-based system will also provide for external auditing without auditor travel.[18]

Internal Audits

After the policies, procedures, and work instructions have been developed and implemented, checks must be made to ensure that the system is being followed and the expected results are being obtained. This activity is accomplished through the internal audit, which is one of the key elements of the ISO 9000 standard. All elements should be audited at least once per year and some more frequently, depending on need.

Objectives

There are five objectives of the internal audit. They are to:

- Determine that actual performance conforms to the documented QMS.
- Initiate corrective action activities in response to deficiencies.
- Follow up on noncompliance items from previous audits.
- Provide continued improvement in the system through feedback to management.
- Cause the auditee to think about the process, thereby encouraging possible improvements.

Auditor

Audits should be performed by qualified individuals who have received training in auditing principles and procedures. Training programs are available from ASQ and RAB. Training should include classroom information as well as practical demonstration by the

---

[18] Roger Crist, "E-Documenting for Better Control," *Quality Digest* (March 2001): 41–45.

trainer and a critiqued audit by the trainee. To be able to audit efficiently, an individual should possess good written and oral communication skills, be a good listener, and be good at taking notes. Other skills should include the ability to concentrate on the task at hand and not be distracted by other activities that are taking place at the same time, be observant and questioning, and be able to separate relevant facts from other information.

The auditor should be objective, honest, and impartial. Of course, the auditor should be prepared by being knowledgeable about the standards.

Techniques

During the actual audit, there are a number of techniques that the auditor should employ. The objective is to collect evidence, and there are three methods: examination of documents, observation of activities, and interviews.

The easiest method is to examine the documents. The auditor should start with the quality manual to determine that the policies cover the QMS standards, and that they are controlled and assessable. Next, the documents are examined in a systematic manner. For example, the auditor would check the purchase orders to determine whether they were accurate and followed the procedures; all appropriate attachments were present; all orders were numbered, signed, and dated; only approved suppliers were used; and so forth. Document control ensures that (1) documents are identified with a title, revision date, and responsible owner; (2) documents are readily available to users; (3) a master list by department or function for procedures, work instructions, and records is appropriately located; (4) there are no obsolete documents at workstations; and (5) changes follow a prescribed procedure.[19]

Observation of activities is also an easy method that requires an aptitude for detail. For example, to evaluate the reservation of product element the auditor would observe the identification, handling, packaging, storage, and protection of the product.

The most difficult method of collecting evidence is by interviewing the employee or auditee. However, there are ways to make the process easier. First, place the auditee in a nonthreatening environment by starting with introductions and an explanation of the purpose of the audit. This initial conversation can be followed by easy questions such as, "How long have you been working for the organization?" Humor is also very effective in placing one at ease. In addition, use basic human behavior techniques such as giving compliments, using a person's first name, encouraging suggestions, and so forth.

Second, spend as much time listening and as little time as possible talking. Encourage employees to talk about the process. Then paraphrase your interpretations of their statements so there are no misunderstandings.

Third, if and when you find deficiencies in processes and systems, separate the significant from the trivial. Reserve the major issues for your report and the minor ones for the auditee. Focus on the system and not on the auditee.

---

[19] William A. Stimson, "Internal Quality Auditing," *Quality Progress* (November 2001): 39–43.

Fourth, discuss the major issues informally with the auditee first. The auditor's job is to identify problems and allow the organization to determine solutions. Be sure that the auditee understands the problem, agrees that it is a problem, and agrees that corrective action is necessary. If the auditee does not agree, there will be little or no cooperation. Sometimes the auditor, based on his experience, will have an idea that might solve the problem. It should be discussed in such a manner that the auditee believes it is his/her idea.[20]

Fifth, use the appropriate type of question. There are open questions, closed questions, clarifying questions, leading questions, and aggressive questions. Each type is discussed in the paragraphs that follow.

Examples of open questions are:

"When are supplier reviews performed?"

"How is the inspection status identified on this item?"

"Where does this document come from?"

This type of question is designed to get a wide range of answers rather than a simple "yes" or "no." They are used to obtain an opinion, an explanation of a process, a person's attitudes, or the reasoning behind an action. The disadvantage of open questions is that the auditor can receive more information than desired.

Examples of closed questions are:

"Do you have a work instruction for this operation?"

"Does this instrument require calibration?"

"Is this die supplied by the customer?"

This type of question can be answered with yes or no and provides evidence or facts quickly. Closed questions are used to gather specific evidence and reduce any misunderstanding. The disadvantage of closed questions is that the interview can appear to be an interrogation.

Examples of clarifying questions are:

"Tell me more about this operation."

"Please give me some examples."

"What do you mean by parting line mismatch?"

This type of question is used to obtain further information. It helps to prevent misunderstanding and encourages the auditee to relax and be more open. The disadvantages are that these questions can give the impression that the auditor is not listening or that the auditor is stupid. Also, when used too often, they are time consuming.

---

[20] Peter Hawkins, ed., "Five Steps to 'Win-Win' Audits," *Quality Management* (Issue 1915, August 10, 1996): 1–4.

An example of a leading question is:

"Don't you agree that the nonconformity was caused by not understanding the purchase order?"

This type of question should be avoided, because it encourages the auditee to provide a particular answer and will bias the audit findings.

An example of an aggressive question is:

"You don't mean to tell me that this test is the only one you perform?"

This type of question should be avoided because it is offensive and argumentative.

The auditor should primarily use open questions with an occasional closed and clarifying question, as the interview may necessitate. For effective communication, there must be mutual trust between auditor and auditee.

Procedure

Before the audit takes place, an audit plan and checklist should be prepared by the lead auditor. As much time is spent planning as doing. The contents of an audit plan should identify the activity or department to be audited; list the procedures, documents, and regulatory requirements involved; name the audit team; and list who is to be notified of the audit and who will receive audit reports. The plan should also contain a schedule similar to Figure 10-7. This schedule includes audit notification, audit conducted, corrective action required, if any, and follow-up, if any.

In addition, an audit matrix, as illustrated in Figure 10-8, can be very helpful. It determines the most-affected areas and elements.

Checklists ensure that the audit is efficient and give the auditor control of the process. It can take the form of questions to ask, the sequence in which they should be asked, and space for writing the results. Checklist questions should be based on the procedures, records, and work instructions to be audited, referencing the specific paragraphs being addressed.

The audit itself has three parts, the preaudit meeting, the audit, and a closing meeting. During the preaudit meeting, the audit process and timetable are discussed and prior audits are reviewed. Minutes of the meeting should be recorded and included with the audit documentation. A list of those attending the meeting is recorded in the minutes.

The purpose of the audit is to determine how well the quality system has been implemented and maintained. In large organizations, an escort should be provided by the area being audited. Escorts become witnesses who can provide backup to an event should a finding be challenged at a later time. The escort is usually a supervisor or key person of the audited area. The audit includes interviewing people working in the area and checking various records that back up the interviews. Often what surfaces from records of one area will lead to further questions that will have to be answered in other

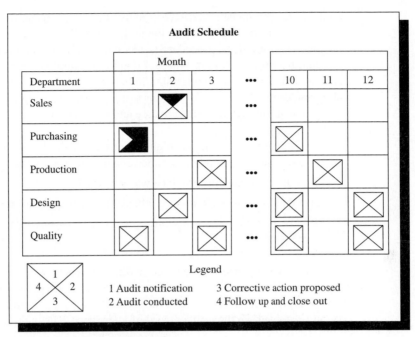

Figure 10-7 Audit Schedule Example

Element	Sales	Purch.	Prod.	Design	QC
4.1	X	X	X	X	X
4.2.1	X	X	X	X	X
⋮	⋮	⋮	⋮	⋮	⋮
7.3.1				X	
7.3.2	X	X	X	X	X
⋮	⋮	⋮	⋮	⋮	⋮
7.4.1		X			
7.4.2		X			
⋮	⋮	⋮	⋮	⋮	⋮
8.5.1	X	X	X	X	X
8.5.2	X	X	X	X	X
8.5.3	X	X	X	X	X

Figure 10-8 Audit Matrix Example

areas. Notes should be made to be sure that there is adequate follow-up. The audit is not only a measure of conformity to the system, it is also a measure of the system itself. It should determine if the procedure is adequate or if it is time for a change. The object of the auditing process is to provide for continuous improvement and increased customer satisfaction. The audit findings should be written out in detail from the auditors' notes and should include the conforming as well as the nonconforming items. Separate reports are prepared for each nonconformance and should include:

1. The element title and a unique identification number such as NC 7.2.3, where the NC stands for nonconformance and the other numbers give the element number.
2. Where the nonconformance was observed.
3. Objective evidence used as a basis for the nonconformance.
4. The nonconformance worded as closely as possible to the language of the requirement.

At the closing meeting, the lead auditor presents a summary of the audit findings along with the evidence that supports them. An estimate is made of when the final report will be issued. The distribution of the report is agreed upon. Again, minutes of the meeting are recorded, along with a record of attendance. The audit report will:

1. Have a cover sheet that includes the audit date, names of the audit team, areas audited, distribution list, a statement that the audit is only a sample, and a unique reference number, and it will be signed by the lead auditor.
2. List the nonconformances and copies of all nonconformance reports.
3. Outline procedures for corrective action and subsequent follow-up.

Additional Comments

Until 1987, when ISO 9000 was adopted, internal auditing was confined to the control of financial processes. In addition to quality and financial auditing, there are now other assurance functions, such as security, safety, and environment that need to be audited as part of a total risk management package. Top management and other stakeholders are interested in obtaining audit information that is current, reliable, and accurate. They want to know that processes are stable and safe, and that risks are identified and mitigated. It is expected that all of the different audits will be integrated into a generic, value-added model of partnering, assessment, and business process improvement.[21]

---

[21] Greg Hutchins, "The State of Quality Auditing," *Quality Progress* (March 2001): 25–29.

Registration

Quality system registration is the assessment and audit of a quality system by a third party, known as a registrar. There are two parts: selecting a registrar and the registration process.

Selecting a Registrar[22]

In the United States, a Registrar Accreditation Board (RAB) was established in 1989 as an affiliate of the American Society of Quality (ASQ) to develop a program to evaluate the quality of the services offered by registrars. The RAB maintains a list of approved registrars. Registrar selection can be based on the following criteria.

1. QUALIFICATIONS AND EXPERIENCE

Of particular importance is the number of companies that have been registered, their experience in particular industry sectors, and their customers' structure, such as size and location. *Quality Digest's* annual customer satisfaction survey in the July issue, rates registrars in five categories—interpersonal relations, value added, consistent interpretations, administration, and communications. It is also helpful to know the registrar's financial condition to be assured that it will stay in business. The registrar should remain current by participating in the Independent Association of Accredited Registrars.

2. CERTIFICATE RECOGNITION

The registrar must be approved by a regulatory agency such as RAB. It must be recognized by existing and potential customers. For example, an organization might sell to a particular country or a specific industry such as the medical industry. Are there international cooperative agreements? The registrar should provide references and prior customer feedback. It may be helpful to interview prior customers. A database of all registered organizations in North America is maintained at www.qualitydigest.com.

3. THE REGISTRATION PROCESS

The registrar should have a structured registration procedure that is tailored to the organization's needs. They should be responsive to requests. A significant factor in the registration process is the objective of improving quality and productivity. The registrar should not only evaluate the system but also identify opportunities for more efficient

---

[22] Adapted from Stefan Heinloth, "Selecting a Registrar," *Quality Digest* (September 1996): 33–38.

practices. Of future importance is the ability of the registrar to perform multiple types of audits: environmental, quality, security, and workplace safety.

4. TIME AND COST CONSTRAINTS

The evaluation should include the lead time necessary prior to the audit. In addition, the evaluation should include the time and cost required for the initial audit and the surveillance audits. Be wary of additional fees such as the use of a subcontractor that has expert knowledge or language skills.

5. AUDITOR QUALIFICATIONS

Of particular importance is the auditor's qualifications. The ISO 19011 auditing standard requires that auditors: (1) know the standard, (2) know the types of processes, the organization, and the customers, and (3) have the knowledge, temperament, and experience to be credible. Because the auditor and registrar are exposed to sensitive information about the organization, it is vital that a nondisclosure policy be maintained. It is also vital that the auditor has no conflict of interest with the organization. The registrar should provide proof of qualifications, knowledge, and experience. The organization should be able to refuse a particular auditor and have a suitable replacement found.[23]

It is wise to take time to select the best registrar for an organization's needs in order to avoid dissatisfaction. The vice president of Engineered Systems Inc. in Deleware, OH comments about his direct experience with a registrar: "I was frustrated with their level of unresponsiveness. We were never given a 'point person' as a contact, and they did not return phone calls." Other areas of dissatisfaction by other organizations are: constantly rescheduling audits, billing undisclosed expenses, arrogant and argumentative auditors, and reporting findings in an untimely fashion.[24]

Registration Process

The registration process has six basic steps: application for registration, document review, preassessment, assessment, registration, and follow-up surveillance. Registrars require a completed application to begin the registration process. The application contains the rights and obligations of both parties, determines which standard the applicant will use for the registration, and leads to the formalized contract for services.

After accepting the application and setting a timeframe for registration, the registrar will review the quality system documentation. Some registrars want only the policy manual, whereas others require the policy and procedure manuals. The registrar then compares the organization's documentation with the appropriate standard to determine if the intent of the standard has been met.

---

[23] Nigel Withey, "How to Select an Auditor," *Quality Digest* (October 1998): 31–34.

[24] Phillip C. Dobyns and Jill C. Smolnik, "Tough Choices!" *Quality Digest* (November 1999): 28–32.

Not all registrars require a preassessment; however, most recommend one be conducted. The preassessment is a broad overview of the organization's operations to determine an initial preparedness for a full assessment or audit. A preassessment could identify a major deficiency or lack of documentation that can be corrected before the audit takes place, thus enhancing the possibility of approval on the first audit attempt. In other cases, the preassessment is an option that the organization may not need.

After determining that the organization's documents conform to the selected standard, a full audit or assessment is performed. Typically an audit will take two to four days and will involve two or more auditors at the organization's facility. The audit will follow the same procedure as that outlined in the internal audit procedures and cover all areas and all procedures of the organization in one audit. The client of the audit should be in charge. They should demand capable, honest, and meaningful examinations in return for the money invested. The organization's internal audits should lead to continual improvement; the third-party audit process should verify that the organization's quality management system is performing effectively.[25]

The lead auditor will conduct a closing meeting, which will consist of a verbal summary of the audit findings and a recommendation concerning registration. If the applicant has only minor noncompliances, the recommendation would be for registration. If one or more major noncompliances are registered but appear to be easily corrected, the recommendation may be for a conditional approval pending corrective action. The recommendation for disapproval will be made if it is determined that procedures have not been implemented or at least one element of the standard has not been addressed.

After registration is approved, the registrar will conduct surveillance audits at intervals of six months to a year. These audits will not be full audits but random checks of some elements to ensure that the system continues to function. Registration is good for three years, at which time the organization must be recertified.

Closing Comments

Remember, third-party audits and registration are not a requirement of the ISO 9000 standards. The standards are written for contractual situations between a customer and a supplier. Registration is one way to demonstrate compliance to the standard. The requirements specified in the standards are aimed at preventing nonconformities during all stages of the business functions. Before entering into a contract for registration, management must be able to justify the cost versus the potential gains in continued or increased business.

No single standard has had more universal or worldwide results in increasing the awareness of quality than the ISO 9000 series. As of December 31, 2001, there were over

---

[25] Dale K. Gordon, "Caveat Emptor," *Quality Progress* (August 2001): 80–81.

510,000 organizations registered from 158 countries. It must be pointed out that a quality system is only *one* of the many tools of total quality management. Many organizations have used registration as an end in itself and senior management has abrogated its responsibility and leadership for TQM. The ISO 9000 quality system is an excellent first step towards TQM.[26]

TQM Exemplary Organization[27]

With customers in 86 countries, Solar Turbines Inc. is the world's largest supplier of mid-range industrial gas turbine systems. The San Diego-based company's turbine engines and compressors are used in the production and transmission of oil and gas, for industrial power generation, and in the propulsion systems of high-speed ferries. Eighty percent of Solar's 6,200 employees are distributed among 15 locations in the United States; 20% are deployed among sites in 23 foreign nations.

Hallmarks of Solar's approach include a dynamic strategic planning process, which is an extensive teamwork system that is aligned and coordinated throughout the entire company, and an "authority delegation process" that enables employees who are closest to the work to design, manage, and improve work systems and processes. Devised with knowledge gained from benchmarking other organizations, Solar believes its authority delegation process is unique. It has reduced non-value-added steps in decision-making and helped the company to respond quickly to changing customer needs and competitive conditions.

Training and education needs are formally addressed during strategic planning. Solar estimates that total expenditures for training are equivalent to about 15% of its payroll. Awards and bonuses reinforce the workforce's commitment to achieving business goals. Incentive payouts have helped Solar to meet or exceed goals for increasing its return on assets. Payouts increased 7.6% of salary in 1994 to 10.4% of salary in 1997.

Sources of information on customer requirements and competitors' capabilities include competitive business reports by field service representatives, regular visits to customer facilities by Solar executives, annual satisfaction surveys, end-of-project surveys, complaints, and reviews of won and lost bids for business. This and other intelligence gleaned from listening posts around the world is analyzed for emerging business opportunities.

Using a four-phase new product introduction process, the company has been quick to seize opportunities. The process integrates the efforts of 30 or more teams and sub-teams that involve all stakeholders, including customers and suppliers. Since 1994, the new product development cycle has been trimmed from 39 months to 22 months, and qual-

---

[26] Kenneth S. Stephens, "ISO 9000 and Total Quality," *Quality Management Journal* (Fall 1994): 57–69.

[27] Malcolm Baldrige National Quality Award, 1998 Manufacturing Category Recipient, NIST/Baldrige Homepage, Internet.

ity has improved. The number of warranty claims has decreased significantly since 1995, and non-recoverable commissioning costs have been cut.

For customers, benefits resulting from gains in quality include lower maintenance costs. Industry-sponsored studies show that maintenance costs for Solar-made industrial turbines are 42% lower than the average for all suppliers.

Solar's share of the global market for new turbine engines has risen from less than 20% in 1970 to a position of global market leadership. Since 1988, the company has tripled its annual revenues and increased its profits by a factor of 11. Improvements in productivity have fueled these gains in business performance. Revenues generated per employee increased by 61% between 1993 and 1997.

Exercises

1. Briefly describe the purpose of an ISO 9000 quality system.

2. What is a quality policy statement?

3. Describe the four tiers of quality documentation.

4. Determine which element of ISO 9001 is referenced in each of the following situations:

    (a) An audit found that no supplier reviews were being performed.
    (b) There were no inspection records.
    (c) During an audit, it was found that a punch press operator had not received the technical instructions necessary for running the punch press.
    (d) During an audit, it was discovered that no manager had been given the responsibility of ensuring that the quality system was being maintained.

5. What are the basic differences among the quality systems discussed in the text?

6. Why is it important to have element owners?

7. Why is documentation the most common reason for noncompliance?

8. Prepare a list of internal audit questions for three elements.

9. Working as an individual or in a team of three or more people, perform an internal audit and write a report on three elements at a local organization.

10. Describe how a two-party audit system works.

11. What can be accomplished by the addition of a third party registering a quality system?

12. List five benefits that could be realized by implementing an ISO 9000 quality system.

13. How would you determine the registrar to select?

11

Environmental Management System

Introduction

The International Organization for Standards (ISO) completed the Quality Management System (ISO 9000) in 1987. Its worldwide success, along with increased emphasis on environmental issues, were instrumental in ISO's decision to develop environmental management standards. In 1991, ISO formed the Strategic Advisory Group on the Environment (SAGE), which led to the formation of Technical Committee (TC) 207 in 1992.

The mission of TC 207 is to develop standards for an environmental management system (EMS) which was identified as ISO 14000. Like the ISO 9000 standards, which do not address the performance of the product or service, the committee used the concept that the standards addressed the process rather than the end goal. Thus, they are process standards rather than performance standards. TC 207 has established six sub-committees: environmental management systems, environmental auditing, environmental labeling, environmental performance evaluation, life-cycle assessment, and terms and definitions. In addition, a working group on environmental aspects in product standards was formed. Each country has a member body of ISO, which for the United States is the American National Standards Institute (ANSI). They have designated the American Society of Testing and Materials (ASTM) and the American Society for Quality (ASQ) to administer the work of the Technical Advisory Group (TAG) and its sub-groups. Members include industry, associations, environmental groups, consultants, academicians, and government (EPA, DOE, and Department of Commerce). The chairperson of each sub-group represents the U.S. position in the respective TC 207 sub-group.

Experience with ISO 9000 made it easier to develop ISO 14000, and a subsequent revision of ISO 9000 capitalized on many of the improvements in ISO 14000. The EMS is part of a comprehensive management system that addresses how the overall business activities, including its products and services, impact the environment. The EMS maximizes company participation in environmental performance now and in the future. Processes for obtaining registration closely resemble those involved with ISO 9000 and related quality standards. The differences lie mainly in what the standard requires rather than the registration process.[1]

ISO 14000 Series Standards

The series is divided into two separate areas—the organization evaluation standards and the product evaluation standards. In addition, ISO 14050 covers terms and definitions that are common to both areas.

Organizational Evaluation Standards

These standards are shown in Figure 11-1 and consist of three categories: Environmental Management System (EMS), Environmental Auditing (EA), and Environmental Performance Evaluation (EPE).

ISO 14001, entitled, "Environmental Management Systems—Specifications with Guidance for Use," gives the elements that organizations are required to conform to if they seek registration. This standard is the heart of the standards and will be discussed in greater detail later in the chapter. The standards given below support the EMS.

ISO 14004, entitled, "Environmental Management Systems—Guidelines on Principles, Systems, and Supporting Techniques," provides supplementary material. It is for information only and is not to be used for registration.

ISO 14010, entitled, "Guidelines for Environmental Auditing—General Principles on Environmental Auditing," provides information for internal or external auditing. The audit is a systematic documented verification process of objectively obtaining and evaluating evidence to determine whether activities, events, conditions, systems, etc., conform to criteria and communicate the information to the organization.

ISO 14011, entitled, "Guidelines for Environmental Auditing—Audit Procedures—Auditing of Environmental Management Systems," provides information on how to plan and conduct an audit. Some topics are audit team, audit plan, implementation, and report.

ISO 14012, entitled, "Qualification Criteria for Environmental Auditors Performing Environmental Management System Audits," covers information on auditor qualifications, training, and personal attributes and skills.

ISO 14031, entitled, "Guidelines on Environmental Performance Evaluation," presents information on recording information to track performance. It helps the organization meet the requirements of ISO 14001, Section 4.5.1, Monitoring and Measuring. This standard is being drafted.

---

[1] Joe Lissenden, "ISO 9000 Eases ISO 14001 Registration," *Quality Digest* (May 1999): 41–44.

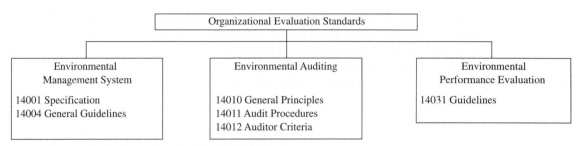

Figure 11-1 Organizational Evaluation Standards

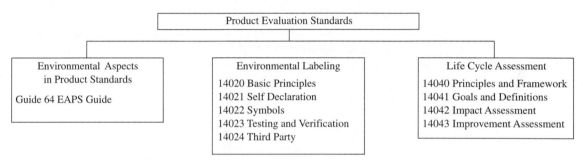

Figure 11-2 Product Evaluation Standards

Product Evaluation Standards

These standards are under development and are shown in Figure 11-2. They consist of three categories: Environmental Aspects in Product Standards (EAPS), Environmental Labeling (EL), and Life-Cycle Assessment (LCA).

Guide 64, entitled, "Environmental Aspects in Product Standards," is designed to help writers develop product standards. Writers should carefully consider the environmental consequences when developing criteria, elements, and characteristics that go into the standard.

ISO 14020, entitled, "Environmental Labeling—Basic Principles for All Environmental Labeling," provides guidance on the goals and principles that should be used in all labeling programs. Product improvement is a desirable benefit but not the objective of the standard.

ISO 14021, entitled, "Environmental Labeling—Self-Declaration of Environmental Claims: Terms and Definitions," applies to organizations that are declaring that their product has an environmental attribute such as being recyclable or energy efficient. The standard ensures that this type of labeling is accurate, verifiable, and not deceptive.

ISO 14022, entitled, "Environmental Labeling—Symbols," provides a standard set of symbols for use by organizations.

ISO 14023, entitled, "Environmental Labeling—Testing and Verification Methodologies," provides information on the appropriate methods to use to confirm the genuineness of the product as stated by the environmental label.

ISO 14024, entitled, "Environmental Labeling—Practitioner Programs: Guiding Principles, Practices, and Certification Procedures for Multiple Criteria Programs," establishes criteria for third-party labeling or seal programs. These programs determine which products have overall environmental superiority as compared to other products.

ISO 14040, entitled, "Life-Cycle Assessment—Principles and Framework," provides an overview of the practice, applications, and limitations of LCA. Life-cycle assessment attempts to determine the long-range environmental effect of a product. This assessment is an enormously difficult task because of the unforeseen and frequently controversial nature of a product's life cycle.

ISO 14041, entitled, "Life-Cycle Assessment—Goals and Definition/Scope and Inventory Analysis," is intended to provide guidelines for the preparation, conduct, and critical review of the life-cycle inventory analysis. This analysis involves the compilation and quantification of relevant inputs and outputs of a product system.

ISO 14042, entitled, "Life-Cycle Assessment—Impact Assessment," is intended to use the results of the inventory analysis to evaluate the significance of potential environmental impacts. Currently, the body of knowledge in this area is mostly subjective.

ISO 14043, entitled, "Life-Cycle Assessment—Improvement Assessment," is intended to provide information to improve the total environmental performance of a product system. The development of this standard will be extremely difficult until the impact assessment standard is developed because you can't improve the product until you know the environmental impact.

The organizational evaluation standards are operational and effective because, like ISO 9000, the focus was on the process rather than the product. The development and acceptance of the product evaluation standards will be much more difficult. In particular, scientific knowledge concerning life-cycle assessment is limited.

Concepts of ISO 14001

This standard provides organizations with the elements for an environmental management system (EMS), which can be integrated into other management systems to help achieve environmental and economic goals. It describes the requirements for registration and/or self-declaration of the organization's EMS. Demonstration of successful implementation of the system can be used to assure other parties that an appropriate EMS is in place. It was written to be applicable to all types and sizes of organizations and to accommodate diverse geographical, cultural, and social conditions. As previously mentioned, the requirements are based on the process and not on the product. It does, however, require commitment to the organization's EMS policy, applicable regulations, and continual improvement.

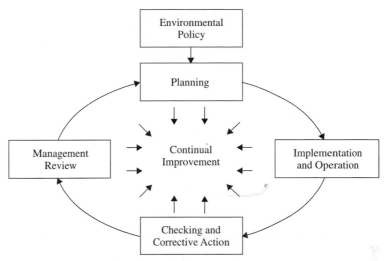

Figure 11-3 Environmental Management System Model

The basic approach to EMS is shown in Figure 11-3. It begins with the environmental policy, which is followed by planning, implementation and operation, checking and corrective action, and management review. The approach follows the PDSA cycle. There is a logical sequence of events to achieve continual improvement. Many of the requirements may be developed concurrently or revisited at any time. The overall aim is to support environmental protection and prevention of pollution in balance with socioeconomic needs.

The standard is not intended to create nontariff barriers or to change an organization's legal obligations. In addition, it does not include aspects of occupational health and safety management, although an organization may include these aspects in the documentation.

In order to understand the requirements, a few definitions are necessary. *Environment* is defined as the global surroundings in which an organization operates and includes air, water, land, natural resources, flora, fauna, humans, and their interaction. *Environmental aspect* is defined as an element of an organization's activities, products, or services that can interact with the environment. Examples are wastewater discharge, air emissions, and energy usage. *Environmental impact* is defined as any change, whether adverse or beneficial, wholly or partially resulting from an organization's activities, products, or services. Examples are impacts on habitat, water supply, and soil erosion. *Environmental objective* is an overall environmental goal, arising from the policy statement, that an organization sets for itself and which is quantified when practical. They define how the policy will be achieved. For example, an objective could be to control the temperature of the wastewater effluent. *Environmental target* is a detailed performance requirement and should be quantified when practical. It needs to be met in order to achieve the objective. For example the wastewater temperature should be controlled between 10° C and 14° C.

There are four sections to the standard—scope, normative references, definitions, and EMS requirements—and an informative annex. The EMS requirements are given in Section 4 of the standard and are covered next.

Requirements of ISO 14001[2]

The standard is divided into six parts or clauses and has a total of 18 requirements. The numbering system used is identical to the standard.

4.1 General Requirements

The organization shall establish and maintain an environmental management system that includes policy, planning, implementation and operation, checking and corrective action, and management review. These requirements are given in the rest of the standard.

Because the document is available to the public and other stakeholders, the organization may wish to include in this narrative a brief description of the company. In addition, this clause is a good place to include manual control and distribution.

In developing the EMS, keep it as simple as possible. It will work better when it is easy to follow and easy to understand. It can always be expanded at a later time, making certain that the registrar is informed of the change. It is not necessary to start over—use existing procedures such as ISO 9000 where applicable. Existing information may need to be reformatted, but this action is easier than starting from scratch.

4.2 Environmental Policy

The organization's policy statement should be based on its mission and values. It should show management commitment, leadership, and direction for the environmental activities. Management will ensure that the policy is implemented and carried out. An initial environmental review is suggested which includes the following:

Identification of legislative and regulatory requirements.

Identification of environmental aspects of its activities, products, or services that can have significant impact and liabilities.

Identification of existing activities with suppliers.

Identification of existing management policies and procedures.

Evaluation of past performance with regard to the above.

Feedback from investigation of previous incidents of noncompliance.

---

[2] This section adapted from ANSI/ISO 14001-1996, *Environmental Management Systems—Specification with Guidance for Use* (Milwaukee, WI: ASQ, 1996) and from David L. Goetsch & Stanley B. Davis, *ISO 14000 Environmental Management* (Upper Saddle River, NJ: Prentice Hall, 2001).

Identification of opportunities for competitive advantage.

Identification of benchmarking opportunities.

Having this information will help the organization develop its environmental policy.

The policy must be relevant to the organization's nature, scale, and environmental impact of its activities, products, and services.

The policy must ensure that management is committed to continual improvement and prevention of pollution. Total Quality Management practitioners were disappointed that earlier versions of ISO 9000 did not include this requirement. Refer to Chapter 5 (continual process improvement) for information. Management's commitment must be apparent to all the employees because employees tend to do what is important to management.

The policy includes a commitment to comply with relevant legislation and regulations, and with any other requirements applicable to the organization, industry, and locale. Other requirements may include items such as permits, licenses, and voluntary program activities.

The policy provides a framework for setting and reviewing environmental objectives and targets. Their setting should aim to comply with legislative and regulatory requirements. Provision must be made for periodic review of progress in meeting the objectives and targets.

The policy must be documented, implemented, and maintained; it also must be communicated to all employees. Documenting the policy means that it must be in written or electronic format. Implementing it means that it must be put into practice by everyone involved in the EMS. Maintaining it means that the policy is dynamic and provision for updating must be provided. Communicating the policy to the employees is a never-ending job; it requires repetition and the use of different forms of media.

The policy must be available to the public. Seldom do organizations make internal policies available to the public; however, where the environment is concerned, the public is a major stakeholder. Suggested approaches are to distribute the policy to libraries, chambers of commerce, environmental organizations, or other public access organizations. Of course copies should be made available in the organization's reception area and to anyone that asks for one. Each year AmerenUE publishes its average amount of emissions of carbon dioxide, nitrogen oxides, and sulfur dioxide as well as the amount of nuclear waste.

4.3 Planning

This area contains four elements: environmental aspects, legal and other requirements, objectives and targets, and environmental management program(s).

4.3.1 ENVIRONMENTAL ASPECTS

The relationship among the environmental aspects, environmental impacts, and the standard is necessary for successful implementation of the standard. It requires that environmental aspects of an organization's activities, products, and services that it can control and influence be identified in order to determine the environmental impact.

ISO 14004 lists nine issues that can be considered in an organization's procedures for the identification of aspects and their impacts.

1. What are the environmental aspects of the organizations activities, products, and services?
2. Do the organization's activities, products, or services create any significant adverse environmental impacts?
3. Does the organization have a procedure for evaluating the environmental consideration, for example, sensitive environmental areas?
4. Does the location of the organization require special environmental consideration, for example, sensitive environmental aspects and their associated impacts?
5. How will any intended changes or additions to activities, products, or services affect the environmental aspects and their associated impacts?
6. How significant or severe are the potential environmental impacts if a process failure occurs?
7. How frequently will the situation arise that could lead to the impact?
8. What are the significant environmental aspects, considering impacts, likelihood, severity, and frequency?
9. Are the significant environmental impacts local, regional, or global in scope?

The process is somewhat similar to a FMEA analysis that is discussed in Chapter 14. Consideration should be given to abnormal and emergency situations, startup and shutdown, and normal operations. It is worth noting that there is a cause-and-effect relationship between the environmental aspect and its impact.

Those aspects that relate to significant impacts shall be considered in setting objectives. It is not necessary for every aspect to have an objective—only that it be considered. This information must be kept current.

4.3.2 LEGAL AND OTHER REQUIREMENTS

The standard requires the organization to have a procedure to identify and have access to all legal and other requirements to which it subscribes. In general, legal environmental requirements are those attributed to governmental legislative and regulatory action. Other requirements usually include industry codes of practice, contracts, agreements with public authorities, and nonregulatory guidelines. Even if some of these requirements are voluntary, the organization is accountable to those with which it agreed to comply.

According to ISO 14004, issues to be considered in the procedure should include how the organization:

Accesses and identifies legal and other requirements.

Keeps track of legal and other requirements.

Keeps track of changes to legal and other requirements.

Communicates relevant information about legal and other requirements to employees.

The number and complexity of legal and other requirements throughout the world can make the procedure quite complex; however, the organization need only identify those requirements that are applicable to the environmental aspects of its activities, products, and services. Examples of laws that might apply are Clean Air Act (U.S.), Public Health Act (U.K.), and Chemical Products Act (Sweden).

Resources that can help include: (1) local, state and federal governments, (2) industry trade associations, (3) consulting services, and (4) external databases.

4.3.3 OBJECTIVES AND TARGETS

The organization shall establish and maintain these objectives and targets at each relevant function and level. They shall be consistent with the policy statement, especially in regard to the prevention of pollution. An example of an objective for a paper manufacturer would be "Reduce tree cutting," and some targets would be "Increase chipper yield to 90% by 1999" and "Increase recycled material to 25% by 2001."

In addition to the environmental aspects, and the legal and other requirements which were previously discussed, this clause also requires that the organization consider:

The best technological option to mitigate an aspect.

Economic viability of the option.

Cost-effectiveness of the option.

Appropriateness of the option to the situation.

Affordability of the option, given the organization's financial, operational, and business situation.

Views of interested parties such as: employees, regulatory agencies, and any other stakeholders.

Objectives may apply to one person, group, function, or to the entire organization. They should be developed by those who are involved in their attainment. ISO 14004 lists different forms of objectives, such as:

Reduce waste and the depletion of resources.

Reduce or eliminate the release of pollutants in the environment.

Design products to minimize their environmental impact in production, use, and disposal.

Control the environmental impact of sources of raw material.

Minimize any significant adverse environmental impact of new developments.

Promote environmental awareness among employees and the community.

4.3.4 ENVIRONMENTAL MANAGEMENT PROGRAM(S)

The organization shall establish and maintain a program(s) for achieving the objectives and targets. It shall include designation of the responsible function, team, or individual and a timeframe for achievement.

This requirement can be achieved with a simple form. It will require completion of the following items:

1. State the objective/target.
2. State the purpose (How the objective/target will support the policy).
3. Describe how the objective/target will be achieved.
4. State the program (team) leader.
5. Designate departments and individuals responsible for specific tasks.
6. Establish the schedule for completion of the tasks.
7. Establish the program review, which will include format, content, and review schedule.

Refer to the information on teams in Chapter 4 (employee involvement) and the problem-solving method in Chapter 5 (continuous process improvement).

4.4 Implementation and Operation

This area contains seven elements: structure and responsibility; training, awareness, and competency; communication; EMS documentation; document control; operational control; and emergency preparedness and response.

4.4.1 STRUCTURE AND RESPONSIBILITY

Roles, responsibilities, and authorities shall be defined, documented, and communicated for all personnel affecting the EMS. They must be given the freedom and authority to take the necessary actions. An organization chart is one method to show the flow of authority. A management representative must be appointed and given the authority to ensure that this standard is being met and to periodically report to senior management the status of EMS with the aim of improvement. This appointment must not be viewed by top management as a way to avoid their involvement in the EMS. The management representative can only be as effective as their involvement.

Senior management must provide the resources in terms of people, technology, and money to implement and maintain an effective system that achieves its objectives.

4.4.2 TRAINING, AWARENESS, AND COMPETENCY

Training needs should be evaluated on a regular basis, usually annually, to ensure their effectiveness. There are two types of training: general awareness and job competency. General awareness includes the importance of conformance to the EMS, the relationship of significant environmental impacts to the employees' work activities, employee roles and responsibilities, and potential consequences of failing to follow specific operating procedures. Personnel performing tasks that can cause significant environmental impacts shall be competent based on education, training, or experience. Records must be maintained to document that the training requirements have been met.

At a minimum, this training should include:

Record of training needs assessments.

Task competency requirements.

Training procedures.

Training plans.

Records of training delivered to specific employees.

Registrar's audits will require these documented records, and they will be valuable for internal operations and litigation defense if needed.

4.4.3 COMMUNICATION

A key aspect of any management program is communication with all stakeholders. The standard requires that procedures shall be established and maintained for internal communication among all employees.

Effective communication up, down, and laterally should ensure that questions are answered and that understanding is complete and accurate. Internal environmental communication procedures should address reporting on environmental activities to:

Demonstrate management's commitment to the environment and EMS.

Handle concerns and questions about environmental aspects of the organization's activities, products, and services.

Inform appropriate employees of all legal and regulatory changes and all changes to the EMS.

Raise awareness of the organization's environmental activities.

Ensure that all employees are aware of objectives, targets, programs, and achievements.

Publish results of internal and external audits as well as management reviews.

Maintain a high level of employee focus on environmental issues.

In addition, procedures shall be established for receiving, documenting, and responding to relevant external communication from interested parties. It is up to the organization to decide what is or is not relevant. However, from a practical matter, it is best to respond to all external inquiries.

Furthermore, the organization shall consider processes for external communication of its environmental aspects and record its decision to implement or to not implement those processes. Many organizations take a proactive approach and externally communicate their environmental aspects. Some organizations such as the O'Fallon, Illinois Water Department communicate not only their environmental aspects, but their objectives, targets, and achievements periodically to their constituents. Organizations that do not take a proactive approach should record that fact and present reasons for their actions.

Additional information on communication is given in Chapter 2 (leadership) and Chapter 9 (information technology).

4.4.4 ENVIRONMENTAL MANAGEMENT SYSTEM DOCUMENTATION

The organization shall establish and maintain information, in paper or electronic form, to describe the core elements of the system and their interaction and provide direction to applicable related documents. ISO 14000 requires a documentation system very similar to ISO 9000, which makes integration of the two systems very easy. The organization must show that it is actually practicing what the documentation states. In other words, "Say what you do and do what you say."

4.4.5 DOCUMENT CONTROL

This element requires that procedures be established and maintained to control all EMS documents. Examples are blueprints, test procedures, work instructions, and, of course, the EMS manual. Provisions must be made for the review and approval of documents for adequacy before they are issued and after any changes. The purpose of document control is to ensure that appropriate and current issues of documents are in place at all locations. Obsolete documents must be removed and destroyed or stored in a safe place if retention for legal purposes is necessary. Documents shall be legible, dated, readily identifiable, and easily located.

The best document control system is the simplest one that meets the needs of the organization and ISO 14000. If the organization has an existing system such as ISO 9000, it can be used as a model.

ISO documentation can be viewed as four levels as shown in Figure 11-4. Level 1, the policy level, is the EMS manual that includes the environmental policy with policies responding to each clause. Organizational charts and other forms of documentation can be used to clearly define core elements of the system and how they relate to Level 2 procedures. The organization may wish to list environmental aspects; objectives; targets; and legal, regulatory, and other requirements at this level.

Level 2, the procedure level, describes what the organization does to meet Level 1 policies. There are 17 procedures and while only three are explicitly required to be documented, it is best from an effectiveness standpoint to document all 17.

Level 3, the practice level, describes the work instructions by which operating personnel perform their tasks. They are step-by-step instructions dealing with activities re-

Figure 11-4 Documentation Hierarchy

quired by the standard. Organizations involved with TQM or ISO 9000 will already have these activities documented.

Level 4, the proof level, is the location of all forms, records, drawings, and so forth that represent the objective evidence or proof of the performance of the EMS.

It is important to note that the system should be an efficient one and not a bureaucratic one—keep it simple. In addition, the documentation must show the interaction of the elements and provide direction to related documents such as flow charts, check sheets, and drawings.

4.4.6 OPERATIONAL CONTROL

This element aligns operations and activities with the identified significant environmental aspects, environmental policy, and environmental objectives and targets. The organization shall plan these activities to ensure that the procedures:

Cover situations where their absence could lead to deviations from the policy and the objectives and targets.

Stipulate operating criteria which are the details and instructions that would normally be included in any process, procedure, or step-by-step work instruction. They include equipment to be used, materials required, process settings, maintenance program, and so forth.

Cover the identification of environmental aspects of goods and services and communicate relevant procedures and requirements to suppliers and contractors. Ford Motor Co., which has registered all 140 facilities in 26 countries, requires its suppliers to be certified to ISO 14001. Other major companies such as IBM, General Motors, Zerox, and Honda of America also have made the same stipulation.[3]

---

[3] Stanley Fielding, "ISO 14001 Brings Change and Delivers Profits," *Quality Digest* (November 2000): 32–35.

4.4.7 EMERGENCY PREPAREDNESS AND RESPONSE

Procedures are required to identify and respond to potential accidents and emergency situations. In addition, the procedures should prevent or mitigate the environmental impact of these accidents and emergency situations. If plans and procedures are required by law, they will usually suffice for the standard. Emergency plans should include at a minimum:

Emergency organization and responsibilities of key personnel.

Details of emergency services such as fire department and spill cleanup services.

Internal and external communication plans.

Actions to be taken for the different types of emergencies.

Information on hazardous materials and their impact, including information about equipment and protective clothing.

Training plans and testing for effectiveness.

These procedures shall be reviewed and revised, if necessary, especially after an emergency. A checklist for lessons learned could include:

Did we follow procedures?

If not, why and how did we deviate?

What did we do that was right?

What did we do that was wrong?

What procedural changes would result in a more effective response?

These questions can also be asked after any emergency drill or simulation which would test the procedures for their effectiveness.

4.5 Checking and Corrective Action

This area contains four elements: monitoring and measuring, nonconformance and corrective and preventative action, records, and EMS audit.

4.5.1 MONITORING AND MEASURING

Effective decisions usually require quantifiable data. The organization is required to monitor and measure the key characteristics of its objectives and activities in order to assess its performance in meeting environmental operations and targets. An example of a key characteristic is energy consumed, and the measurement method is kilowatts and gas/therms. Measuring equipment is of little value if it is not accurate or functioning properly. Procedures must be in place to control, regularly calibrate, maintain, and record all EMS equipment, whether it belongs to the organization, employee, or an outside agency. In addition, procedures are required to periodically evaluate compliance to relevant regulations.

4.5.2 NONCONFORMANCE AND CORRECTIVE AND PREVENTATIVE ACTION

Procedures are required to define responsibility and authority for (1) handling and investigating nonconformance, (2) taking action to mitigate any impacts, and (3) initiating corrective and preventative action. Refer to Chapter 5 (continuous process improvement) for information on corrective and preventive action. Briefly, the process should include:

Identifying the root cause of the nonconformance.

Identifying and implementing the necessary corrective action.

Implementing or modifying controls necessary to prevent a recurrence.

Recording any changes in the written procedures.

Since operating personnel are usually the most knowledgeable people concerning the process, they should be involved in the corrective and preventative action activity. Any action taken to eliminate the causes should be appropriate to the magnitude of the problem and commensurate with the environmental impact. In addition, any changes to the procedures resulting from corrective and preventative action should be implemented and recorded.

4.5.3 RECORDS

Procedures are required for the identification, maintenance, and disposition of environmental records such as training, audits, equipment calibration, and reviews. Records shall be legible, identifiable, and traceable to the activity, product, or service. They should be readily retrievable; protected against damage, deterioration, and loss; and provided with retention times. Most organizations use some type of system for storage and retrieval of documents and records that can readily be adapted to ISO 14000.

4.5.4 EMS AUDIT

The purpose of this audit is to ensure that the EMS conforms to plans and is being properly implemented and maintained. Internal or self audit and external audit information should be distributed to senior management to assist in the management review process. Audit procedures should cover the scope, frequency and methodologies, and responsibilities and requirements for conducting audits and reporting results. The audit schedule should be based on the importance of the element and the results of previous audits. Additional information on audits is given in Chapter 10 (quality systems).

4.6 Management Review

Management review and revision, if applicable, is required to ensure the continuing suitability, adequacy, and effectiveness of the EMS. The intent of this clause is to involve top management in the EMS continuous improvement process. Management must evaluate the feedback data and make improvements to the system.

Reviews will most likely occur on a monthly basis and cover some of the elements at each review. A fixed schedule of reviews is required to cover all the elements. ISO 14004 recommends that the review include:

Review of environmental objectives and targets.

Review of environmental performance against legal and other requirements.

Evaluation of the effectiveness of the EMS's elements.

Evaluation of the continued suitability of the policy in light of changing legislation; changing expectations; changing requirements of interested parties; changes in activities, products, and services; new technology; lessons learned; market preferences and expectations; and effectiveness of reporting and communication.

Reviews should make use of information from audit reviews, performance information, changing circumstances, and the commitment to continuous improvement.

Benefits of EMS

EMS benefits can be categorized as global and organizational.

Global[4]

There are three global benefits: (1) facilitate trade and remove trade barriers, (2) improve environmental performance of planet earth, and (3) build consensus that there is a need for environmental management and a common terminology for EMS.

The proliferation of national and regional standards has led to confusion and to trade barriers. This international standard will serve to unify countries in their approach to labeling, environmental management, and life-cycle assessment. This approach also will help to remove trade barriers and facilitate trade. The drafters of the standard have been careful to avoid creating a document that will hamper trade. ISO 14000 provides the framework whereby its successful promotion within countries can lead to progress that will reassure the worldwide community. As the EMS is implemented worldwide, it will increasingly satisfy concerns for environmental protection in trade discussions and agreements.

Although the standard does not specify performance, it is reasonable to expect that ISO 14000 will play a significant role in environmental improvement worldwide. Be-

---

[4] This section adapted from Joseph Cascio, Gayle Woodside, and Philip Mitchell, *ISO 14000 Guide* (New York: McGraw-Hill, 1996).

cause of the success of ISO 9000 in improving quality, we can reasonably expect that a significant improvement will occur in the environment. Based on data collected during registration audits, many ISO 14001 EMS lead auditors are convinced that an EMS does improve regulatory compliance.[5]

As the environmental standards are developed and implemented worldwide, it will build worldwide consensus that there is a need to use ISO 14000. In addition, a common terminology allows people in different countries to speak to each other, thereby sharing improvement ideas, prevention information, and system problems.

Organizational

According to ISO 14004, an organization benefits from an EMS in a number of ways as given below:

- Assuring customers of a commitment to environmental management.
- Meeting customer requirements, the primary reason for organizations to become certified.
- Maintaining a good public/community relations image.
- Satisfying investor criteria and improving access to capital.
- Obtaining insurance at reasonable cost.
- Increasing market share that results from a competitive advantage. After certification, Acushnet Rubber obtained more business from European customers.[6]
- Reducing incidents that result in liability. United Chem-Con Inc.'s plant in Lancing, NC is seeing a reduced potential for accidental releases of hazardous materials.[7]
- Improving defense posture in litigation.
- Conserving input materials and energy. Ford's Michigan truck facility reduced water consumption by almost one million gallons per day and also reduced energy consumption by replacing fluorescent bulbs with metal halide bulbs at a savings of $66,000 per year.[8]
- Facilitating the attainment of permits and authorization.
- Improving industry/government relations.

---

[5] Marilyn Block, "ISO 14001 and Regulatory Compliance," *Quality Progress* (February 2001): 84–85.

[6] Joe Lissenden.

[7] Ibid.

[8] Ibid.

Many companies such as 3M, Ping, Ford, and Xerox have found that there are other organizational benefits than those given above. These are:

Cost effective. Between 1975, when their "Pollution Prevention Pays" program began, and 2000, 3M saved over $810 million in reduced air emissions, water discharge, and solid waste.[9]

Enhanced internal communications. Ping's design and production groups work with the environmental people prior to implementing any changes in order to evaluate the impact on employees, facilities, and the community.[10]

Effective decision-making. With useful data, management is better able to achieve goals and objectives.

Improved teamwork. By sharing responsibilities, employees feel that they are part of an organization that is doing the right thing.

Focus on prevention. Organizations become more proactive on improving the internal (workplace) and external environment.

Integrating ISO 14000 with ISO 9000

EMS implementation can seem like a time-consuming and costly undertaking. However, organizations that have implemented ISO 9000 have a distinct advantage over those that are unfamiliar with the process. Depending on the company, 25 to 50% of the requirements may already be in place. Most registrars encourage organizations to integrate their EMS with their other management systems such as ISO 9000. By integrating the two systems, there will be less documentation and lower implementation cost.[11] Presently, ISO has a committee studying the two standards for the purpose of minimizing differences.

Ping, a golf equipment manufacturer, recently was certified to both ISO 9000 and ISO 14000. The audit took place in September 2000 with two quality auditors and two environmental auditors conducting a week-long assessment at Ping's headquarters in Phoenix and their golf bag manufacturer in Mexico. It is rare for a company the size of Ping (1000+ employees) to achieve certification with no nonconformity reports on the first assessment.[12]

Relationship to Health and Safety

The ISO 14001 standard assumes that cultural transformation occurs through employee involvement and responsibility from the bottom up, not through dictates from the top.

---

[9] Ibid.

[10] Robert T. Driescher, "A Quality Swing With Ping," *Quality Progress* (August 2001): 37–41.

[11] Joe Lissenden.

[12] Robert T. Driescher.

That assumption and other concepts present in the standard are applicable to health and safety. Therefore, it is reasonable to consider the use of the standard in an integrated approach that can bring about improvement for all three. For example, we can measure pollutants in employee's work environments to determine if it meets OSHA's permissible exposure level. Then we can monitor the occurrence of illnesses as recorded at the medical clinic and correlate those illnesses to measured airborne concentrations. In effect, we can measure progress in all three areas with a built-in efficiency and cost savings.[13]

Plasticolor Inc., which produces high-technology colorants, has integrated its quality, health and safety, and environmental management systems. This integration has saved the organization $100,000 in workers' compensation premiums.[14]

Additional Comments

Many aspects of ISO 14000 are basically the same as ISO 9000; therefore, they are not repeated in this chapter. Refer to Chapter 10 for information on (1) implementation, (2) writing the documents, (3) internal audits, and (4) registration. For the most part, the word *environment* can be substituted for the word *quality*.

Currently, the standard is in the process of being revised. This effort will be guided by three precepts:

- Revisions should clarify the intent of existing language.
- Language should be modified to improve compatibility with ISO 9000.
- Revisions should not be substantive.[15]

On December 31, 2001 there were about 36,000 organizations registered to ISO 14000 in 85 countries. Since its inception, the rate of growth has been increasing.

TQM Exemplary Organization[16]

Founded in 1946, Texas Nameplate Company, Inc. manufactures and sells identification and information labels that are affixed to refrigerators, oil-field equipment, high-pressure valves, trucks, computer equipment, and other products made by its

---

[13] Joe Cascio and Kent T. Baughn, "Health, Safety, and ISO 14001," *Manufacturing Engineering* (May 2000): 126–135.

[14] Annette Dennis McCully, "Unlikely Partners: How QS 9000 and ISO 14000 work together," *Quality Digest* (June 1998): 31–34.

[15] Marilyn R. Block, "ISO 14000 Revisions Likely to be Minor," *Quality Progress* (September 2001) 100–101.

[16] Malcolm Baldrige National Quality Award, 1992 Small Business Category Recipient, NIST/Baldrige Homepage, Internet.

1,000 customers. Located in Dallas, the family-owned business's manufacturing techniques include chemical etching, photo engraving, and screen printing. In 1996, TNC also won the Texas Quality Award.

"Closely knit" describes TNC's external relationships. Long-term partnerships with customers and suppliers are the rule. Sixty-two percent of customers have been purchasing TNC nameplates for 10 or more years. Of TNC's 140 suppliers, nearly two-thirds have been shipping materials to TNC for more than a decade. Sustained relationships with quality-minded suppliers have enabled TNC to nearly eliminate inspections of incoming materials.

Profit-sharing and gain-sharing incentives, along with higher-than-industry-average pay scales, serve to reinforce the workforce's commitment to quality and foster company loyalty. In TNC's 1997 employee survey, employee satisfaction rates ranged from 72% to almost 88% in the five areas that employees say are most important: fair pay, job content satisfaction, recognition, fairness/respect, and career development. A comparable national average shows rates of 50% to 57% on these same areas.

TNC is making good on its pledge to delight its customers. An independent, third-party survey shows TNC's customers consistently give the company an "excellent" rating (5 to 6 on a scale of 6) in 12 key business areas, including quality product, reliable performance, on-time delivery, and overall satisfaction. Since 1995, the number of orders shipped has increased 16%, while TNC raised its on-time delivery record to 98%, up from 95%.

One of TNC's key business drivers is environmental consciousness. The company already exceeds regulatory requirements, and it is working toward eliminating all hazardous waste from its chemical etching process. Notable improvements since 1994 include a 14% reduction in chemical waste generated and a 30% reduction in emissions of volatile organic compounds. In key areas of financial performance, TNC has made significant gains.

Gross profit as a percentage of sales increased from 50.5% in 1994 to 59% in 1998. Net profit (measured as a percent of net sales) more than doubled during the same time period. TNC has reduced its non-conformances from 3.65% to about 1.0% of billings in the last four years. This is attributed to the company's process improvements and gain-sharing program, which rewards employees for reducing non-conformances. Through this program, over $145,000 was distributed to employees in one year as profit savings, which equates to a $1.26 per hour raise for each employee. Nationally, its share of the nameplate market has grown from almost 3% in 1994 to 5% in 1997.

Exercises

1. Why are the product evaluation standards in the development stage?

2. How does the conceptual approach to ISO 14001 differ from ISO 9001?

3. What is the overall aim of the EMS standard?

4. How is the aim achieved?

5. Which of the elements in ISO 9001 are similar to ISO 14001?

6. Individually or with a team of three or more people, develop a self-assessment questionnaire for ISO 14001.

7. Individually or with a team of three or more people, determine which three EMS benefits would be most important for a hospital, oil company, pharmaceutical company, university, food processor, paint manufacturer, and paper manufacturer.

8. Using the building where you live, determine the environmental aspects and impacts. Establish hypothetical objectives and targets.

9. Visit an organization in your community and determine if their accident and emergency preparedness plan meets the ISO 14001 criteria.

10. You have been appointed the EMS management representative for your organization. Develop a plan to become registered.

12

Quality Function Deployment

Introduction

Dr. Mizuno, professor emeritus of the Tokyo Institute of Technology, is credited with initiating the quality function deployment (QFD) system. The first application of QFD was at Mitsubishi, Heavy Industries, Ltd., in the Kobe Shipyard, Japan, in 1972. After four years of case study development, refinement, and training. QFD was successfully implemented in the production of mini-vans by Toyota. Using 1977 as a base, a 20% reduction in startup costs was reported in the launch of the new van in October 1979, a 38% reduction by November 1982, and a cumulative 61% reduction by April 1984. Quality function deployment was first introduced in the United States in 1984 by Dr. Clausing of Xerox. QFD can be applied to practically any manufacturing or service industry. It has become a standard practice by most leading organizations, who also require it of their suppliers.

Quality function deployment (QFD) is a planning tool used to fulfill customer expectations. It is a disciplined approach to product design, engineering, and production and provides in-depth evaluation of a product. An organization that correctly implements QFD can improve engineering knowledge, productivity, and quality and reduce costs, product development time, and engineering changes.

Quality function deployment focuses on customer expectations or requirements, often referred to as the voice of the customer. It is employed to translate customer expectations, in terms of specific requirements, into directions and actions, in terms of engineering or technical characteristics, that can be deployed through:

Product planning

Part development

Process planning

Production planning

Service industries

Quality function deployment is a team-based management tool in which customer expectations are used to drive the product development process. Conflicting characteristics or requirements are identified early in the QFD process and can be resolved before production.

Organizations today use market research to decide what to produce to satisfy customer requirements. Some customer requirements adversely affect others, and customers often cannot explain their expectations. Confusion and misinterpretation are also a problem while a product moves from marketing to design to engineering to manufacturing. This activity is where the voice of the customer becomes lost and the voice of the organization adversely enters the product design. Instead of working on what the customer expects, work is concentrated on fixing what the customer does not want. In other words, it is not productive to improve something the customer did not want initially. By implementing QFD, an organization is guaranteed to implement the voice of the customer in the final product or service.

Quality function deployment helps identify new quality technology and job functions to carry out operations. This tool provides a historic reference to enhance future technology and prevent design errors. QFD is primarily a set of graphically oriented planning matrices that are used as the basis for decisions affecting any phase of the product development cycle. Results of QFD are measured based on the number of design and engineering changes, time to market, cost, and quality. It is considered by many experts to be a perfect blueprint for quality by design.

Quality function deployment enables the design phase to concentrate on the customer requirements, thereby spending less time on redesign and modifications. The saved time has been estimated at one-third to one-half of the time taken for redesign and modification using traditional means. This saving means reduced development cost and also additional income because the product enters the market sooner.

The QFD Team

When an organization decides to implement QFD, the project manager and team members need to be able to commit a significant amount of time to it, especially in the early stages. The priorities of the projects need to be defined and told to all departments within the organization so team members can budget their time accordingly. Also, the scope of the project must be clearly defined so questions about why the team was formed do not arise. One of the most important tools in the QFD process is communication.

There are two types of teams—designing a new product or improving an existing product. Teams are composed of members from marketing, design, quality, finance, and production. The existing product team usually has fewer members, because the QFD process will only need to be modified. Time and inter-team communication are two very important things that each team must utilize to their fullest potential. Using time effectively is the essential resource in getting the project done on schedule. Using inter-team communication to its fullest extent will alleviate unforeseen problems and make the project run smoothly.

Team meetings are very important in the QFD process. The team leader needs to ensure that the meetings are run in the most efficient manner and that the members are kept informed. The meeting format should have some way of measuring how well the QFD process is working at each meeting and should be flexible, depending on certain situations. The duration of the meeting will rely on where the team's members are coming from and what needs to be accomplished. These workshops may have to last for days if people are coming from around the world or for only hours if everyone is local. There are advantages to shorter meetings, and sometimes much more can be accomplished in a shorter meeting. Shorter meetings allow information to be collected between times that will ensure that the right information is being entered into the QFD matrix. Also, they help keep the team focused on a quality improvement goal.

Benefits of QFD

Quality function deployment was originally implemented to reduce start-up costs. Organizations using QFD have reported a reduced product development time. For example, U.S. car manufacturers of the late 1980s and early 1990s needed an average of five years to put a product on the market, from drawing board to showroom, whereas Honda put a new product on the market in two and a half years and Toyota did it in three years. Both organizations credit this reduced time to the use of QFD. Product quality and, consequently, customer satisfaction improve with QFD due to numerous factors depicted in Figure 12-1.

Improves Customer Satisfaction

Quality function deployment looks past the usual customer response and attempts to define the requirements in a set of basic needs, which are compared to all competitive information. All competitors are evaluated equally from customer and technical perspectives. This information can then be prioritized using a Pareto diagram. Management can then place resources where they will be the most beneficial in improving quality. Also, QFD takes the experience and information that are available within an organization and puts them together as a structured format that is easy to assimilate. This is important when an organization's employee leaves a particular project and a new employee is hired.

Reduces Implementation Time

Fewer engineering changes are needed when using QFD, and, when used properly, all conflicting design requirements can be identified and addressed prior to production. This results in a reduction in retooling, operator training, and changes in traditional quality

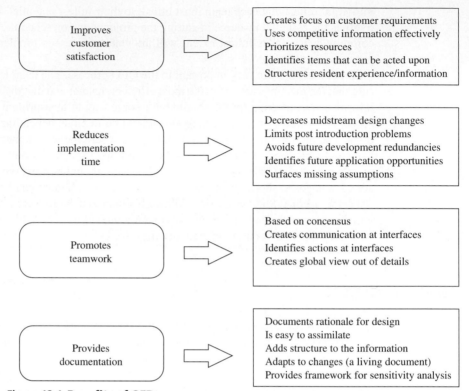

Figure 12-1 Benefits of QFD
Reproduced with permission from James L. Brossert, *Quality Function Deployment—A Practitioner's Approach* (Milwaukee, WI: ASQC Quality Press, 1991).

control measures. By using QFD, critical items are identified and can be monitored from product inception to production. Toyota reports that the quality of their product has improved by one-third since the implementation of QFD.

Promotes Teamwork

Quality function deployment forces a horizontal deployment of communication channels. Inputs are required from all facets of an organization, from marketing to production to sales, thus ensuring that the voice of the customer is being heard and that each department knows what the other is doing. This activity avoids misinterpretation, opinions, and miscues. In other words, the left hand always knows what the right hand is doing. Efficiency and productivity always increase with enhanced teamwork.

Provides Documentation

A database for future design or process improvements is created. Data that are historically scattered within operations, frequently lost and often referenced out of context, are now saved in an orderly manner to serve future needs. This database also serves as a training tool for new engineers. Quality function deployment is also very flexible when new information is introduced or things have to be changed on the QFD matrix.

The Voice of the Customer

Because QFD concentrates on customer expectations and needs, a considerable amount of effort is put into research to determine customer expectations. This process increases the initial planning stage of the project definition phase in the development cycle. But the result is a total reduction of the overall cycle time in bringing to the market a product that satisfies the customer.

The driving force behind QFD is that the customer dictates the attributes of a product. Customer satisfaction, like quality, is defined as meeting or exceeding customer expectations. Words used by the customers to describe their expectations are often referred to as the voice of the customer. Sources for determining customer expectations are focus groups, surveys, complaints, consultants, standards, and federal regulations. Frequently, customer expectations are vague and general in nature. It is the job of the QFD team to analyze these customer expectations into more specific customer requirements. Customer requirements must be taken literally and not incorrectly translated into what organization officials desire.

Quality function deployment begins with marketing to determine what exactly the customer desires from a product. During the collection of information, the QFD team must continually ask and answer numerous questions, such as

What does the customer really want?

What are the customer's expectations?

Are the customer's expectations used to drive the design process?

What can the design team do to achieve customer satisfaction?

There are many different types of customer information and ways that an organization can collect data, as shown in Figure 12-2. The organization can search (solicited) for the information, or the information can be volunteered (unsolicited) to the organization. Solicited and unsolicited information can be further categorized into measurable (quantitative) or subjective (qualitative) data. Furthermore, qualitative information can be found in a routine (structured) manner or haphazard (random) manner.

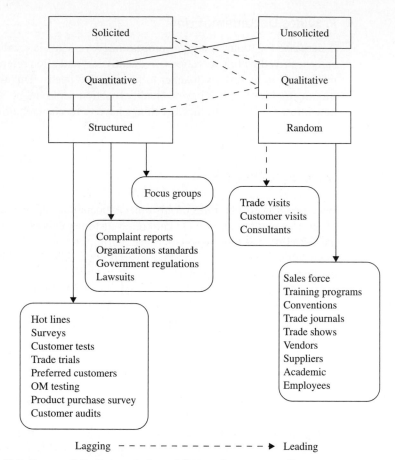

Figure 12-2 Types of Customer Information and How to Collect It
Reproduced with permission from James L. Brossert, *Quality Function Deployment—A Practitioner's Approach* (Milwaukee, WI: ASQC Quality Press, 1991).

Customer information, sources, and ways an organization can collect data can be described as follows:

Solicited, measurable, and routine data are typically found by customer surveys, market surveys, and trade trials; working with preferred customers; analyzing products from other manufacturers; and buying back products from the field. This information tells an organization how it is performing in the current market.

Unsolicited, measurable, and routine data tend to take the form of customer complaints or lawsuits. This information is generally disliked; however, it provides valuable learning information.

Solicited, subjective, and routine data are usually gathered from focus groups. The object of these focus groups is to find out the likes, dislikes, trends, and opinions about current and future products.

Solicited, subjective, and haphazard data are usually gathered from trade visits, customer visits, and independent consultants. These types of data can be very useful; however, they can also be misleading, depending on the quantity and frequency of information.

Unsolicited, subjective, and haphazard data are typically obtained from conventions, vendors, suppliers, and employees. This information is very valuable and often relates the true voice of the customer.

The goal of QFD is not only to meet as many customer expectations and needs as possible, but also to exceed customer expectations. Each QFD team must make its product either more appealing than the existing product or more appealing than the product of a competitor. This situation implies that the team has to introduce an expectation or need in its product that the customer is not expecting but would appreciate. For example, cup holders were put into automobiles as an extra bonus, but customers liked them so well that they are now expected in all new automobiles.

Organization of Information

Now that the customer expectations and needs have been identified and researched, the QFD team needs to process the information. Numerous methods include affinity diagrams, interrelationship diagrams, tree diagrams, and cause-and-effect diagrams. These methods are ideal for sorting large amounts of information. The affinity diagram, which is ideally suited for most QFD applications, is discussed next.

Affinity Diagram

The affinity diagram (see Chapter 17) is a tool that gathers a large amount of data and subsequently organizes the data into groupings based on their natural interrelationships. An affinity diagram should be implemented when

Thoughts are too widely dispersed or numerous to organize.

New solutions are needed to circumvent the more traditional ways of problem solving.

Support for a solution is essential for successful implementation.

This method should not be used when the problem is simple or if a quick solution is needed. The team needed to accomplish this goal effectively should be a multidisciplinary one that has the needed knowledge to delve into the various areas of the problem.

A team of six to eight members should be adequate to assimilate all of the thoughts. Constructing an affinity diagram requires four simple steps:

1. Phrase the objective.
2. Record all responses.
3. Group the responses.
4. Organize groups in an affinity diagram.

The first step is to phrase the objective in a short and concise statement. It is imperative that the statement be as generalized and vague as possible.

The second step is to organize a brainstorming session in which responses to this statement are individually recorded on cards and listed on a pad. It is sometimes helpful to write down a summary of the discussion on the back of the cards so that, in the future when the cards are reviewed, the session can be briefly explained.

Next, all the cards should be sorted by placing the cards that seem to be related into groups. Then, a card or word is chosen that best describes each related group, which becomes the heading for each group of responses. Finally, lines are placed around each group of responses, and related clusters are placed near each other with a connecting line.

House of Quality

The primary planning tool used in QFD is the house of quality. The house of quality translates the voice of the customer into design requirements that meet specific target values and matches those against how an organization will meet those requirements. Many managers and engineers consider the house of quality to be the primary chart in quality planning.

The structure of QFD can be thought of as a framework of a house, as shown in Figure 12-3.

The parts of the house of quality are described as follows:

The exterior walls of the house are the customer requirements. On the left side is a listing of the voice of the customer, or what the customer expects in the product. On the right side are the prioritized customer requirements, or planning matrix. Listed are items such as customer benchmarking, customer importance rating, target value, scale-up factor, and sales point.

The ceiling, or second floor, of the house contains the technical descriptors. Consistency of the product is provided through engineering characteristics, design constraints, and parameters.

The interior walls of the house are the relationships between customer requirements and technical descriptors. Customer expectations (customer requirements) are translated into engineering characteristics (technical descriptors).

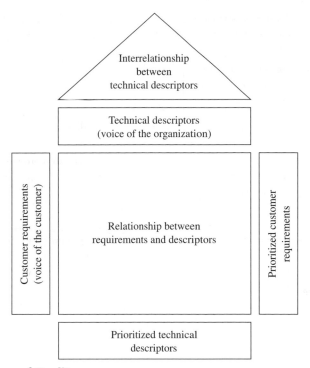

Figure 12-3 House of Quality
Reproduced with permission from James L. Brossert, *Quality Function Deployment—A Practitioner's Approach* (Milwaukee, WI: ASQC Quality Press, 1991).

The roof of the house is the interrelationship between technical descriptors. Trade-offs between similar and/or conflicting technical descriptors are identified.

The foundation of the house is the prioritized technical descriptors. Items such as the technical benchmarking, degree of technical difficulty, and target value are listed.

This is the basic structure for the house of quality; once this format is understood, any other QFD matrices are fairly straightforward.

Building a House of Quality

The matrix that has been mentioned may appear to be confusing at first, but when one examines each part individually, the matrix is significantly simplified. A basic house of quality matrix is shown in Figure 12-4. There is a considerable amount of information contained within this matrix. It is easier to understand once each part of the matrix is discussed in detail.

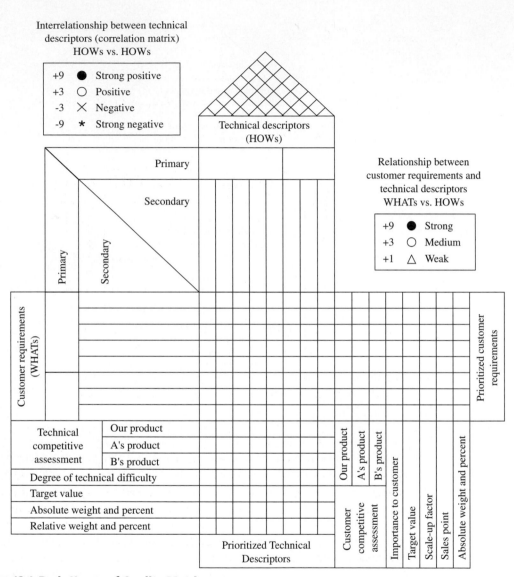

Figure 12-4 Basic House of Quality Matrix

	Primary		Secondary		Tertiary
Customer requirements (WHATs)		Aesthetics	Reasonable cost		
			Aerodynamic look		
			Nice finish		
			Corrosion resistant		
		Performance	Lightweight		
			Strength		
			Durable		

Figure 12-5 Refinement of Customer Requirements

Step 1—List Customer Requirements (WHATs)

Quality function deployment starts with a list of goals/objectives. This list is often referred as the WHATs that a customer needs or expects in a particular product. This list of primary customer requirements is usually vague and very general in nature. Further definition is accomplished by defining a new, more detailed list of secondary customer requirements needed to support the primary customer requirements. In other words, a primary customer requirement may encompass numerous secondary customer requirements. Although the items on the list of secondary customer requirements represent greater detail than those on the list of primary customer requirements, they are often not directly actionable by the engineering staff and require yet further definition. Finally, the list of customer requirements is divided into a hierarchy of primary, secondary, and tertiary customer requirements, as shown in Figure 12-5. For example, a primary customer requirement might be dependability and the corresponding secondary customer requirements could include reliability, longevity, and maintainability.

EXAMPLE PROBLEM

A company that manufactures bicycle components such as cranks, hubs, rims, and so forth wants to expand their product line by also producing handlebar stems for mountain bikes. Begin the development process of designing a handlebar stem for a mountain bike by first listing the customer requirements or WHAT the customer needs or expects in a handlebar stem.

Two primary customer requirements might be aesthetics and performance. Secondary customer requirements under aesthetics might be reasonable cost, aerodynamic look, nice finish, and corrosion resistance. Although reasonable cost is not considered aesthetics, it will be placed under that category for the sake of this example. Secondary customer requirements under performance might be light weight, strength, and durability. Many other customer requirements could be listed; however, for simplicity, only the aforementioned ones will be used. Furthermore, it is not necessary to break down the customer requirements to the tertiary level. These primary and secondary customer requirements are shown in Figure 12-5.

Step 2—List Technical Descriptors (HOWs)

The goal of the house of quality is to design or change the design of a product in a way that meets or exceeds the customer expectations. Now that the customer needs and expectations have been expressed in terms of customer requirements, the QFD team must come up with engineering characteristics or technical descriptors (HOWs) that will affect one or more of the customer requirements. These technical descriptors make up the ceiling, or second floor, of the house of quality. Each engineering characteristic must directly affect a customer perception and be expressed in measurable terms.

Implementation of the customer requirements is difficult until they are translated into counterpart characteristics. Counterpart characteristics are an expression of the voice of the customer in technical language. Each of the customer requirements is broken down into the next level of detail by listing one or more primary technical descriptors for each of the tertiary customer requirements. This process is similar to refining marketing specifications into system-level engineering specifications. Further definition of the primary technical descriptors is accomplished by defining a list of secondary technical descriptors that represent greater detail than those on the list of primary technical descriptors. This is similar to the process of translating system-level engineering specifications into part-level specifications. These secondary technical descriptors can include part specifications and manufacturing parameters that an engineer can act upon. Often the secondary technical descriptors are still not directly actionable, requiring yet further definition. This process of refinement is continued until every item on the list is actionable. Finally, the list of technical descriptors is divided into a hierarchy of primary, secondary, and tertiary technical descriptors, as shown in Figure 12-6.

This level of detail is necessary because there is no way of ensuring successful realization of a technical descriptor that the engineering staff does not know how to accomplish. The process of refinement is further complicated by the fact that through each level of refinement, some technical descriptors affect more than one customer requirement and can even adversely affect one another. For example, a customer requirement for an automobile might be a smooth ride. This is a rather vague statement; however, it is important in the selling of an automobile. Counterpart characteristics for a smooth ride

	Primary	Secondary	Tertiary
Technical descriptors (HOWs)	Material selection	Steel	
		Aluminum	
		Titanium	
	Manufacturing process	Welding	
		Die casting	
		Sand casting	
		Forging	
		Powder metallurgy	

Figure 12-6 Refinement of Technical Descriptors

could be dampening, anti-roll, and stability requirements, which are the primary technical descriptors. Brainstorming among the engineering staff is a suggested method for determining the technical descriptors.

EXAMPLE PROBLEM

Continue the development process of designing a handlebar stem for a mountain bike (see previous Example) by listing the technical descriptors or HOW the company will design a handlebar stem.

Two primary technical descriptors might be material selection and manufacturing process. Secondary technical descriptors under material selection might be steel, aluminum, and titanium. Secondary technical descriptors under manufacturing process might be welding, die casting, sand casting, forging, and powder metallurgy. Numerous other technical descriptors could be listed, such as finishing process and type of bolt, to name a few; however, for simplicity, only the aforementioned ones will be used. Furthermore, it is not necessary to break down the technical descriptors to the tertiary level. These primary and secondary technical descriptors are shown in Figure 12-6.

Step 3—Develop a Relationship Matrix Between WHATs and HOWs

The next step in building a house of quality is to compare the customer requirements and technical descriptors and determine their respective relationships. Tracing the relationships between the customer requirements and the technical descriptors can become very

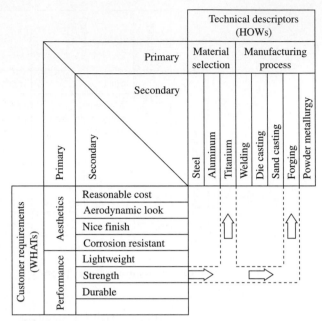

Figure 12-7 Structuring an L-Shaped Diagram

confusing, because each customer requirement may affect more than one technical descriptor, and vice versa.

STRUCTURING AN L-SHAPED DIAGRAM

One way to reduce the confusion associated with determining the relationships between customer requirements and technical descriptors is to use an L-shaped matrix, as shown in Figure 12-7. The L shape, which is a two-dimensional relationship that shows the intersection of related pairs of items, is constructed by turning the list of technical descriptors perpendicular to the list of customer requirements. The L-shaped matrix makes interpreting the complex relations very easy and does not require a significant amount of experience.

EXAMPLE PROBLEM

Continue the development process of designing a handlebar stem for a mountain bike (see previous Examples) by structuring an L-shaped diagram.

The L shape is constructed by turning the list of technical descriptors (see Figure 12-6) perpendicular to the list of customer requirements (see Figure 12-5). The L-shaped diagram for designing a handlebar stem for a mountain bike is shown in Figure 12-7.

RELATIONSHIP MATRIX

The inside of the house of quality, called the relationship matrix, is now filled in by the QFD team. The relationship matrix is used to represent graphically the degree of influence between each technical descriptor and each customer requirement. This step may take a long time, because the number of evaluations is the product of the number of customer requirements and the number of technical descriptors. Doing this early in the development process will shorten the development cycle and lessen the need for future changes.

It is common to use symbols to represent the degree of relationship between the customer requirements and technical descriptors. For example,

A solid circle represents a strong relationship.

A single circle represents a medium relationship.

A triangle represents a weak relationship.

The box is left blank if no relationship exists.

It can become difficult to comprehend and interpret the matrix if too many symbols are used. Each degree of relationship between a customer requirement and a technical descriptor is defined by placing the respective symbol at the intersection of the customer requirement and technical descriptor, as shown in Figure 12-8. This method allows very complex relationships to be depicted and interpreted with very little experience.

The symbols that are used to define the relationships are now replaced with numbers; for example,

$$\bullet = 9$$
$$\circ = 3$$
$$\triangle = 1$$

These weights will be used later in determining trade-off situations for conflicting characteristics and determining an absolute weight at the bottom of the matrix.

After the relationship matrix has been completed, it is evaluated for empty rows or columns. An empty row indicates that a customer requirement is not being addressed by any of the technical descriptors. Thus, the customer expectation is not being met. Additional technical descriptors must be considered in order to satisfy that particular customer requirement. An empty column indicates that a particular technical descriptor does not affect any of the customer requirements and, after careful scrutiny, may be removed from the house of quality.

EXAMPLE PROBLEM

Continue the development process of designing a handlebar stem for a mountain bike (see previous Examples) by adding the relationship matrix to the house of quality.

Customer requirements (WHATs)			Technical descriptors (HOWs)							
			Material selection			Manufacturing process				
Primary	Secondary		Steel	Aluminum	Titanium	Welding	Die casting	Sand casting	Forging	Powder metallurgy
Aesthetics		Reasonable cost	●	●	△	●	○	●	○	△
		Aerodynamic look		△	△	△	●	○	○	●
		Nice finish	○	●	●	△	●	△	○	●
		Corrosion resistant	△	●	●	△	○	○	○	○
Performance		Lightweight	△	●	●					△
		Strength	●	○	●	△	○	○	●	△
		Durable	●	○	○	△	●	○	●	○

Relationship between customer requirements and technical descriptors WHATs vs. HOWs

+ 9 ● Strong
+ 3 ○ Medium
+ 1 △ Weak

Figure 12-8 Adding Relationship Matrix to the House of Quality

The relationship matrix is constructed by assigning symbols or numbers to represent the degree of influence between each technical descriptor and each customer requirement. For instance, the relationship between the customer requirement of lightweight and the technical descriptor of steel would be weak (+ 1) because steel is heavier than aluminum and titanium. Conversely, the relationship between the customer requirement of reasonable cost and the technical descriptor of steel would be strong (+ 9) because steel is cheaper than aluminum and titanium. The relationship matrix for designing a handlebar stem for a mountain bike is shown in Figure 12-8. Empty spaces indicate that no relationship exists.

Step 4—Develop an Interrelationship Matrix Between HOWs

The roof of the house of quality, called the correlation matrix, is used to identify any interrelationships between each of the technical descriptors. The correlation matrix is a triangular table attached to the technical descriptors, as shown in Figure 12-9. Symbols are used to describe the strength of the interrelationships; for example,

A solid circle represents a strong positive relationship.

A circle represents a positive relationship.

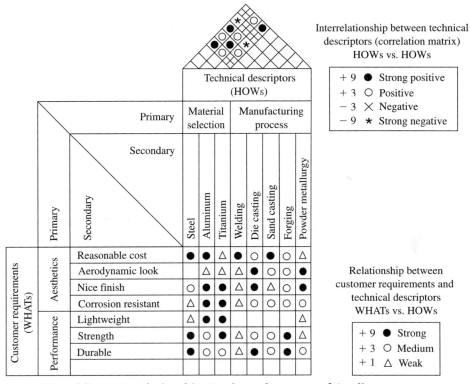

Interrelationship between technical
descriptors (correlation matrix)
HOWs vs. HOWs

+ 9	●	Strong positive
+ 3	○	Positive
− 3	✕	Negative
− 9	★	Strong negative

Relationship between
customer requirements and
technical descriptors
WHATs vs. HOWs

+ 9	●	Strong
+ 3	○	Medium
+ 1	△	Weak

Figure 12-9 Adding Interrelationship Matrix to the House of Quality

An X represents a negative relationship.

An asterisk represents a strong negative relationship.

The symbols describe the direction of the correlation. In other words, a strong positive interrelationship would be a nearly perfectly positive correlation. A strong negative interrelationship would be a nearly perfectly negative correlation. This diagram allows the user to identify which technical descriptors support one another and which are in conflict. Conflicting technical descriptors are extremely important because they are frequently the result of conflicting customer requirements and, consequently, represent points at which tradeoffs must be made. Tradeoffs that are not identified and resolved will often lead to unfulfilled requirements, engineering changes, increased costs, and poorer quality. Some of the tradeoffs may require high-level managerial decisions, because they cross functional area boundaries. Even though difficult, early resolution of tradeoffs is essential to shorten product development time.

An example of tradeoffs is in the design of a car, where the customer requirements of high fuel economy and safety yield technical descriptors that conflict. The added weight of stronger bumpers, air bags, antilock brakes, and the soon-to-come federal side-impact standards will ultimately reduce the fuel efficiency of the car. In the case of conflicting technical descriptors, Taguchi methods (see Chapter 20) can be implemented, or pure common sense dictates.

EXAMPLE PROBLEM

Continue the development process of designing a handlebar stem for a mountain bike (see previous Examples) by adding the interrelationship matrix to the house of quality.

The interrelationship matrix is constructed by assigning symbols or numbers to represent the degree of correlation (positive or negative) between each of the technical descriptors. For instance, the interrelationship between the technical descriptors of titanium and sand casting would be a strong negative ($-$ 9) correlation because a titanium part would never be sand cast. Conversely, the interrelationship between the technical descriptors of aluminum and die casting would be a strong positive (+ 9) correlation because aluminum is usually die cast. The interrelationship matrix for designing a handlebar stem for a mountain bike is shown in Figure 12-9. Empty spaces indicate that no correlation exists, either positive or negative.

Step 5—Competitive Assessments

The competitive assessments are a pair of weighted tables (or graphs) that depict item for item how competitive products compare with current organization products. The competitive assessment tables are separated into two categories, customer assessment and technical assessment, as shown in Figures 12-10 and 12-11, respectively.

CUSTOMER COMPETITIVE ASSESSMENT

The customer competitive assessment is the block of columns corresponding to each customer requirement in the house of quality on the right side of the relationship matrix, as shown in Figure 12-10. The numbers 1 through 5 are listed in the competitive evaluation column to indicate a rating of 1 for worst and 5 for best. These rankings can also be plotted across from each customer requirement, using different symbols for each product.

The customer competitive assessment is a good way to determine if the customer requirements have been met and identify areas to concentrate on in the next design. The customer competitive assessment also contains an appraisal of where an organization stands relative to its major competitors in terms of each customer requirement. Both assessments are very important, because they give the organization an understanding on where its product stands in relationship to the market.

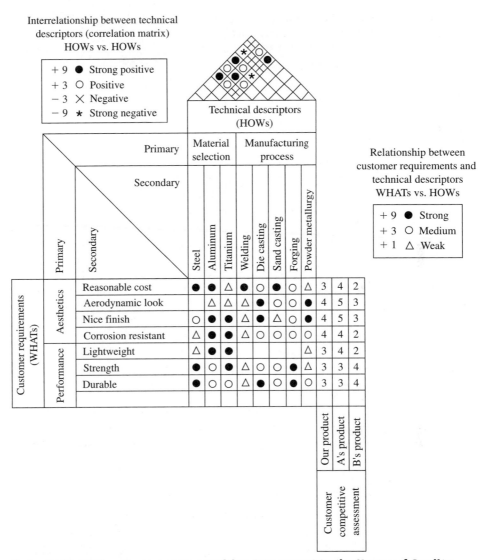

Figure 12-10 Adding Customer Competitive Assessment to the House of Quality

EXAMPLE PROBLEM

Continue the development process of designing a handlebar stem for a mountain bike (see previous Examples) by adding the customer competitive assessment to the house of quality.

The customer competitive assessment is constructed by assigning ratings for each customer requirement from 1 (worst) to 5 (best) for the new handlebar stem and major

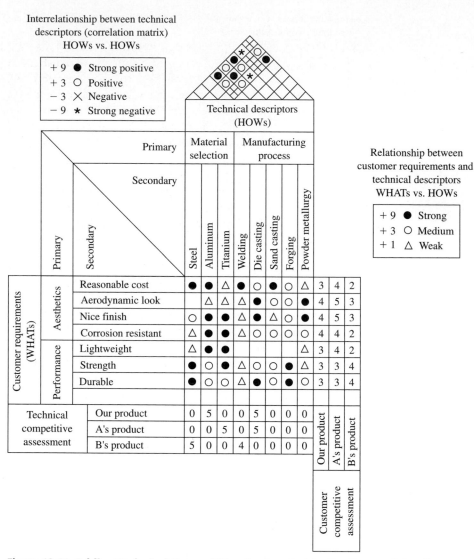

Figure 12-11 Adding Technical Competitive Assessment to the House of Quality

competitor A's and B's handlebar stem. The customer competitive assessment for designing a handlebar stem for a mountain bike is shown in Figure 12-10.

TECHNICAL COMPETITIVE ASSESSMENT

The technical competitive assessment makes up a block of rows corresponding to each technical descriptor in the house of quality beneath the relationship matrix, as shown in

Figure 12-11. After respective units have been established, the products are evaluated for each technical descriptor.

Similar to the customer competitive assessment, the test data are converted to the numbers 1 through 5, which are listed in the competitive evaluation row to indicate a rating, 1 for worst and 5 for best. These rankings can then be entered below each technical descriptor using the same numbers as used in the customer competitive assessment.

The technical competitive assessment is often useful in uncovering gaps in engineering judgment. When a technical descriptor directly relates to a customer requirement, a comparison is made between the customer's competitive evaluation and the objective measure ranking.

Customer requirements and technical descriptors that are strongly related should also exhibit a strong relationship in their competitive assessments. If an organization's technical assessment shows its product to be superior to the competition, then the customer assessment should show a superior assessment. If the customer disagrees, then a mistake in engineering judgment has occurred and should be corrected.

EXAMPLE PROBLEM

Continue the development process of designing a handlebar stem for a mountain bike (see previous Examples) by adding the technical competitive assessment to the house of quality.

The technical competitive assessment is constructed by assigning ratings for each technical descriptor from 1 (worst) to 5 (best) for the new handlebar stem and major competitor A's and B's handlebar stem. The technical competitive assessment for designing a handlebar stem for a mountain bike is shown in Figure 12-11.

Step 6—Develop Prioritized Customer Requirements

The prioritized customer requirements make up a block of columns corresponding to each customer requirement in the house of quality on the right side of the customer competitive assessment as shown in Figure 12-12. These prioritized customer requirements contain columns for importance to customer, target value, scale-up factor, sales point, and an absolute weight.

IMPORTANCE TO CUSTOMER

The QFD team—or, preferably, the focus group—ranks each customer requirement by assigning it a rating. Numbers 1 through 10 are listed in the importance to customer column to indicate a rating of 1 for least important and 10 for very important. In other words, the more important the customer requirement, the higher the rating.

Importance ratings represent the relative importance of each customer requirement in terms of each other. Assigning ratings to customer requirements is sometimes difficult, because each member of the QFD team might believe different requirements should be ranked higher. The importance rating is useful for prioritizing efforts and making trade-off decisions.

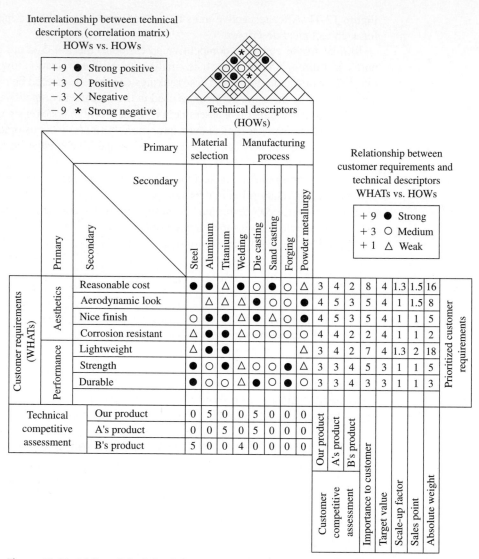

Figure 12-12 Adding Prioritized Customer Requirements to the House of Quality

EXAMPLE PROBLEM

Continue the development process of designing a handlebar stem for a mountain bike (see previous Examples) by determining the importance to customer of each customer requirement.

The importance to customer is determined by rating each customer requirement from 1 (least important) to 10 (very important). For instance, if light weight is important to the customer, then it could be assigned a value of 7. Conversely, if durability is not very important to the customer, then it could be assigned a value of 3. The importance to customer for designing a handlebar stem for a mountain bike is shown in Figure 12-12.

TARGET VALUE

The target-value column is on the same scale as the customer competitive assessment (1 for worst, 5 for best can be used). This column is where the QFD team decides whether they want to keep their product unchanged, improve the product, or make the product better than the competition.

EXAMPLE PROBLEM

Continue the development process of designing a handlebar stem for a mountain bike (see previous Examples) by determining the target value for each customer requirement.

The target value is determined by evaluating the assessment of each customer requirement and setting a new assessment value that either keeps the product as is, improves the product, or exceeds the competition. For instance, if lightweight has a product rating of 3 and the QFD team wishes to improve their product, then the target value could be assigned a value of 4. The target value for designing a handlebar stem for a mountain bike is shown in Figure 12-12.

SCALE-UP FACTOR

The scale-up factor is the ratio of the target value to the product rating given in the customer competitive assessment. The higher the number, the more effort is needed. Here, the important consideration is the level where the product is now and what the target rating is and deciding whether the difference is within reason. Sometimes there is not a choice because of difficulties in accomplishing the target. Consequently, the target ratings often need to be reduced to more realistic values.

EXAMPLE PROBLEM

Continue the development process of designing a handlebar stem for a mountain bike (see previous Examples) by determining the scale-up factor for each customer requirement.

The scale-up factor is determined by dividing the target value by the product rating given in the customer competitive assessment. For instance, if lightweight has a product rating of 3 and the target value is 4, then the scale-up factor is 1.3. The scale-up factor for designing a handlebar stem for a mountain bike is shown in Figure 12-12. Note that the numbers for scale-up factor are rounded off in Figure 12-12.

SALES POINT

The sales point tells the QFD team how well a customer requirement will sell. The objective here is to promote the best customer requirement and any remaining customer requirements that will help in the sale of the product. For example, the sales point is a value between 1.0 and 2.0, with 2.0 being the highest.

EXAMPLE PROBLEM

Continue the development process of designing a handlebar stem for a mountain bike (see previous Examples) by determining the sales point for each customer requirement.

The sales point is determined by identifying the customer requirements that will help the sale of the product. For instance, an aerodynamic look could help the sale of the handlebar stem, so the sales point is given a value of 1.5. If a customer requirement will not help the sale of the product, the sales point is given a value of 1. The sales point for designing a handlebar stem for a mountain bike is shown in Figure 12-12.

ABSOLUTE WEIGHT

Finally, the absolute weight is calculated by multiplying the importance to customer, scale-up factor, and sales point:

Absolute Weight = (Importance to Customer)(Scale-up Factor)(Sales Point)

A sample calculation is included in Figure 12-12. After summing all the absolute weights, a percent and rank for each customer requirement can be determined. The weight can then be used as a guide for the planning phase of the product development.

EXAMPLE PROBLEM

Continue the development process of designing a handlebar stem for a mountain bike (see previous Examples) by determining the absolute weight for each customer requirement.

The absolute weight is determined by multiplying the importance to customer, scale-up factor, and sales point for each customer requirement. For instance, for reasonable cost the absolute weight is $8 \times 1.3 \times 1.5 = 16$. The absolute weight for designing a handlebar stem for a mountain bike is shown in Figure 12-12. Note that the numbers for absolute weight are rounded off in Figure 12-12.

Step 7—Develop Prioritized Technical Descriptors

The prioritized technical descriptors make up a block of rows corresponding to each technical descriptor in the house of quality below the technical competitive assessment,

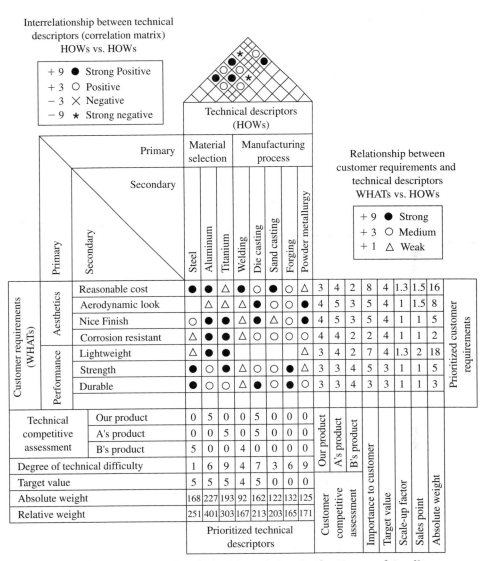

Figure 12-13 Adding Prioritized Technical Descriptors to the House of Quality

as shown in Figure 12-13. These prioritized technical descriptors contain degree of technical difficulty, target value, and absolute and relative weights. The QFD team identifies technical descriptors that are most needed to fulfill customer requirements and need improvement. These measures provide specific objectives that guide the subsequent design and provide a means of objectively assessing progress and minimizing subjective opinions.

DEGREE OF DIFFICULTY

Many users of the house of quality add the degree of technical difficulty for implementing each technical descriptor, which is expressed in the first row of the prioritized technical descriptors. The degree of technical difficulty, when used, helps to evaluate the ability to implement certain quality improvements.

EXAMPLE PROBLEM

Continue the development process of designing a handlebar stem for a mountain bike (see previous Examples) by determining the degree of difficulty for each technical descriptor.

The degree of difficulty is determined by rating each technical descriptor from 1 (least difficult) to 10 (very difficult). For instance, the degree of difficulty for die casting is 7, whereas the degree of difficulty for sand casting is 3 because it is a much easier manufacturing process. The degree of difficulty for designing a handlebar stem for a mountain bike is shown in Figure 12-13.

TARGET VALUE

A target value for each technical descriptor is also included below the degree of technical difficulty. This is an objective measure that defines values that must be obtained to achieve the technical descriptor. How much it takes to meet or exceed the customer's expectations is answered by evaluating all the information entered into the house of quality and selecting target values.

EXAMPLE PROBLEM

Continue the development process of designing a handlebar stem for a mountain bike (see previous Examples) by determining the target value for each technical descriptor.

The target value for each technical descriptor is determined in the same way that the target value was determined for each customer requirement (see appropriate Example). The target value for designing a handlebar stem for a mountain bike is shown in Figure 12-13.

ABSOLUTE WEIGHT

The last two rows of the prioritized technical descriptors are the absolute weight and relative weight. A popular and easy method for determining the weights is to assign numerical values to symbols in the relationship matrix symbols, as shown previously in Figure 12-8. The absolute weight for the jth technical descriptor is then given by

$$a_j = \sum_{i=1}^{n} R_{ij}c_i$$

where a_j = row vector of absolute weights for the technical descriptors
$\qquad (i = 1,\dots, m)$
$\qquad$ R_{ij} = weights assigned to the relationship matrix $(i = 1,\dots, n, j = 1,\dots, m)$
$\qquad$ c_i = column vector of importance to customer for the customer requirements
$\qquad (i = 1,\dots, n)$
$\qquad$ m = number of technical descriptors
$\qquad$ n = number of customer requirements

EXAMPLE PROBLEM

Continue the development process of designing a handlebar stem for a mountain bike (see previous Examples) by determining the absolute weight for each technical descriptor.

The absolute weight for each technical descriptor is determined by taking the dot product of the column in the relationship matrix and the column for importance to customer. For instance, for aluminum the absolute weight is

$$9 \times 8 + 1 \times 5 + 9 \times 5 + 9 \times 2 + 9 \times 7 + 3 \times 5 + 3 \times 3 = 227.$$

The absolute weight for designing a handlebar stem for a mountain bike is shown in Figure 12-13. The greater values of absolute weight indicate that the handlebar stem should be an aluminum die casting.

RELATIVE WEIGHT

In a similar manner, the relative weight for the jth technical descriptor is then given by replacing the degree of importance for the customer requirements with the absolute weight for customer requirements. It is

$$b_j = \sum_{i=1}^{n} R_{ij} d_i$$

where b = row vector of relative weights for the technical descriptors $(j = 1,\dots, m)$
$\qquad$ d_i = column vector of absolute weights for the customer requirements
$\qquad (i = 1,\dots, n)$

Higher absolute and relative ratings identify areas where engineering efforts need to be concentrated. The primary difference between these weights is that the relative weight also includes information on customer scale-up factor and sales point.

These weights show the impact of the technical characteristics on the customer requirements. They can be organized into a Pareto diagram to show which technical characteristics are important in meeting customer requirements. Along with the degree of technical difficulty, decisions can be made concerning where to allocate resources for quality improvement.

Each QFD team can customize the house of quality to suit their particular needs. For example, columns for the number of service complaints may be added.

EXAMPLE PROBLEM

Continue the development process of designing a handlebar stem for a mountain bike (see previous Examples) by determining the relative weight for each technical descriptor.

The relative weight for each technical descriptor is determined by taking the dot product of the column in the relationship matrix and the column for absolute weight in the prioritized customer requirements. For instance, for die casting the relative weight is

$$3 \times 16 + 9 \times 8 + 9 \times 5 + 3 \times 2 + 0 \times 18 + 3 \times 5 + 9 \times 3 = 213.$$

The relative weight for designing a handlebar stem for a mountain bike is shown in Figure 12-13. The greater values of relative weight also indicate that the handlebar stem should be an aluminum die casting.

QFD Process

The QFD matrix (house of quality) is the basis for all future matrices needed for the QFD method. Although each house of quality chart now contains a large amount of information, it is still necessary to refine the technical descriptors further until an actionable level of detail is achieved. Often, more than one matrix will be needed, depending on the complexity of the project. The process is accomplished by creating a new chart in which the HOWs (technical descriptors) of the previous chart became the WHATs (customer requirements) of the new chart, as shown in Figure 12-14. This process continues until each objective is refined to an actionable level. The HOW MUCH (prioritized technical descriptors) values are usually carried along to the next chart to facilitate communication. This action ensures that the target values are not lost during the QFD process. If the target values are changed, then the product is not meeting the customer requirements and not listening to the voice of the customer, which defeats the purpose of QFD.

An example of the complete QFD process from the beginning to the end is shown in the flow diagram in Figure 12-15. The first chart in the flow diagram is for the product-planning phase. For each of the customer requirements, a set of design requirements is determined, which, if satisfied, will result in achieving customer requirements. The next chart in the flow diagram is for part development. Design requirements from the first chart are carried to the next chart to establish part-quality characteristics. The term *part-quality characteristics* is applied to any elements that can aid in measuring the evolution of quality. This chart translates the design requirements into specific part details. Once the part-quality characteristics have been defined, key process operations can be defined

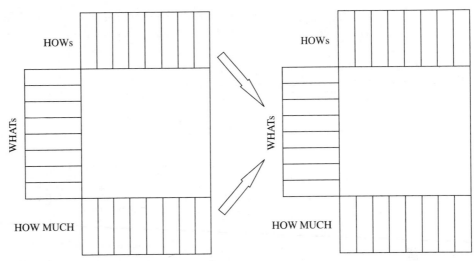

Figure 12-14 Refinement of the QFD Chart

in the process-planning phase. The next step is process planning, where key process operations are determined from part-quality characteristics. Finally, production requirements are determined from the key process operation.

Numerous other house of quality planning charts can be used to improve quality and customer satisfaction. Some of these are the following:

The demanded quality chart uses analysis of competitors to establish selling points.

The quality control process chart shows the nature of measurement and corrective actions when a problem arises.

The reliability deployment chart is done to ensure a product will perform as desired. Tests are done, such as failure mode and effect analysis (FMEA), to determine the failure modes for each part.

The technology deployment chart searches for the advanced or, more importantly, the proper technologies for the operations.

The use of these charts is dependent upon the type of product and scope of the project.

An example of the QFD approach can be found in the corrosion problems with Japanese cars of the 1960s and 1970s that resulted in large warranty expenses. The Toyota Rust QFD Study resulted in a virtual elimination of corrosion warranty expenses. The customer requirement of years of durability was achieved, in part, by the design requirement of no visible rust in three years. It was determined that this could be obtained by ensuring part-quality characteristics, which include a minimum paint film build and maximum surface-treatment crystal size. The key process operation that provides these part-quality characteristics consists of a three-coat process, which includes a dip tank.

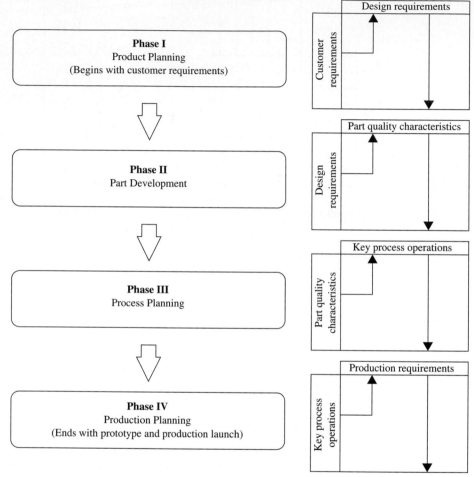

Figure 12-15 The QFD Process

The production requirements are the process parameters within the key process operations, which must be controlled in order to achieve the required part-quality characteristics and customer requirements.

Examples

There are hundreds of examples of organizations employing quality function deployment techniques in new product development and improvement of existing products, however, examples of the use of quality function deployment in the service industries is very limited. The following examples concentrate on the application of quality function deployment in the service industry, namely higher education.

1. In 1997, Rainstar University, a science-based, holistic health institution in Scottsdale, AZ, adopted quality function deployment to ensure meeting customer (graduates) and accreditation needs.[1] Quality function deployment was used to not only design the course content and curriculum based on customer needs, but also to ensure that each academic unit focused on the graduate.

2. Tennessee Technological University's College of Business Administration used quality function deployment to redesign their internal research resources center (RRC).[2] The RRC serves faculty and students in the areas of computer applications, research, test preparation, manuscript preparation, and so forth at the university. Customer requirements included reliability, responsiveness, assurance, empathy, and tangibles such as appearance of the physical facility, equipment, personnel, and materials. Numerous recommendations resulted from the study, such as: a better document handling procedure, a formal training procedure, and a new layout of the facility.

Conclusion

Quality function deployment—specifically, the house of quality—is an effective management tool in which customer expectations are used to drive the design process or to drive improvement in the service industries. Some of the advantages and benefits of implementing QFD are:

An orderly way of obtaining information and presenting it.

Shorter product development cycle.

Considerably reduced start-up costs.

Fewer engineering changes.

Reduced chance of oversights during the design process.

An environment of teamwork.

Consensus decisions.

Everything is preserved in writing.

---

[1] Ian D. Bier and Robert Cornesky, "Using QFD to Construct a Higher Education Curriculum," *Quality Progress* (April 2001): 64–68.

[2] R. Nat Natarajan, Ralph E. Martz and Kyosuke Kurosaka, "Applying QFD to Internal Service System Design," *Quality Progress* (February 1999): 65–70.

QFD forces the entire organization to constantly be aware of the customer requirements. Every QFD chart is a result of the original customer requirements that are not lost through misinterpretation or lack of communication. Marketing benefits because specific sales points that have been identified by the customer can be stressed. Most importantly, implementing QFD results in a satisfied customer.

TQM Exemplary Organization[3]

Established in 1963, today Los Alamos National Bank (LANB) is the largest independent bank in New Mexico. LANB provides a full range of financial services to consumer, commercial, and government markets in northern New Mexico. LANB was created originally to address the banking needs of its unique namesake community. LANB is owned and operated by Trinity Capital Corp., a one-bank holding company. With assets of $700 million, LANB has 184 employees and branches in Los Alamos, White Rock, and Santa Fe.

Senior leaders set the bank's long-term strategic direction and annual corporate objectives, following detailed analyses of leading and lagging indicators of trends in the economy, markets, customer behavior, technology, employee skills, supplier capabilities, and other key factors. At the departmental level, planning becomes an organization-wide activity involving all personnel. Corporate objectives are accomplished through action plans that often span several departments. Totaling about 90 in the year 2000, action plans are converted into individual work goals for all employees, about a third of whom participate on long- or short-term teams.

Under the leadership of LANB's Quality Council, which has members from every area and level of the company, the performance appraisal system was redesigned to magnify the direct link between job performance and corporate performance. Once employees complete the annual appraisal process, they have a complete snapshot of what they must do to perform at a high level and to earn the attendant incentives and rewards, which includes profit sharing and employee stock ownership. Such incentive payouts average over 21% of an employee's annual salary.

Employees are expected to create value for customers, and they are given the authority and resources to act proactively and decisively. For example, all workers have the authority to resolve complaints on the spot.

LANB was quick to embrace the Internet and to provide online banking services, which have been received enthusiastically by customers. Introduced in March 1999, the service was being used by more than 6,000 LANB customers as of the end of 2000.

In its most recent survey, 80% of LANB customers said they were "very satisfied" with the service they received—considerably better than the levels received by its pri-

---

[3] Malcolm Baldrige National Quality Award, 2000 Service Category Recipient, NIST/Baldrige Homepage, Internet.

mary competitors and the national average of 55% for all banks. Returns on key financial indicators exceed local competitors and the national average. For example, the bank's net income has increased by more than 60% over the last five years, and earnings per share increased from $1.20 to nearly $2.00. For the past three years, employee satisfaction results have been well above those of banks its size in five of eight key indicators of employee satisfaction.

In 1999, LANB received New Mexico's highest quality award, the Zia. In 1996, *Inc.* magazine named LANB one of the 26 "Banks We Love."

Exercises

1. Working individually or in a team, list four or more primary customer requirements for one or more of the following production items or service industries. Also, refine the primary customer requirements to a second level.

   (a) Mountain bike
   (b) Racing bike
   (c) Pizza
   (d) Textbook
   (e) Automatic teller machine
   (f) Automobile cruise control
   (g) Coffee maker
   (h) Computer mouse
   (i) Rechargeable drill/driver
   (j) University academic department
   (k) Call center
   (l) Restaurant
   (m) Hospital or medical center
   (n) Department store
   (o) Website for computer sales
   (p) Hair salon
   (q) Grocery store

2. Working individually or in a team, list six or more primary technical descriptors for one or more of the selections used in Exercise 1. Make an attempt to address all the customer requirements from Exercise 1 and refine the secondary technical descriptors to a second level.

3. Working individually or in a team, form an L-shaped matrix and complete the relationship matrix, including weights, for one or more of the selections used in Exercises 1 and 2.

4. Working individually or in a team, complete the interrelationship matrix for one or more of the selections used in Exercise 2.

5. Working individually or in a team, compare two similar products or service industries based on the customer assessment of the customer requirements used in Exercise 1. Choose one of the products to be your organization's product.

6. Working individually or in a team, compare two similar products or service industries based on technical assessment of the technical descriptors used in Exercise 2. Choose one of the products to be your organization's product.

7. Working individually or in a team, complete the house of quality and comment on the results for one or more of the selections used in Exercises 1 through 6.

13

Quality by Design

Introduction

Quality by design principles are changing the way U.S. managers think and conduct business. Loosely defined, quality by design is the practice of using a multidisciplinary team to conduct conceptual thinking, product design, and production planning all at one time. It is also known as concurrent engineering, simultaneous engineering, or parallel engineering. The team is composed of specialists from business, engineering, production, and the customer base. Suppliers of process equipment, purchased parts, and services are also included on the team at appropriate times. Quality by design has recently encouraged changes in management structures. Some managers claim to have used it informally before it became popular.

In the past, the major functions within an organization would complete their task by "throwing it over the wall" to the next department in the sequence and would not be concerned with any internal customer problems that might arise. Hence, the term *sequential engineering* was used to describe the process. Quality by design, or concurrent engineering, requires the major functions to be performed at the same time. This system provides immediate feedback, which prevents problems with quality and productivity from occurring.

A broad definition of quality by design is a team of specialists who simultaneously design and develop a product to ensure ease of producibility and customer satisfaction. Figure 13-1 shows flow diagrams for both sequential (or traditional) engineering on the left and quality by design or concurrent engineering on the right. In quality by design, engineering (such as mechanical, electrical, structural, quality, material), production, and business (such as purchasing, marketing, finance) as well as suppliers and customers brainstorm together to develop a product that considers all facets of its functionality as well as its costs. When each of the specialists has early input to the product definition and specifications, cost is minimized and performance is maximized. Thus, better-quality products are manufactured for less cost with shorter time to market.

349

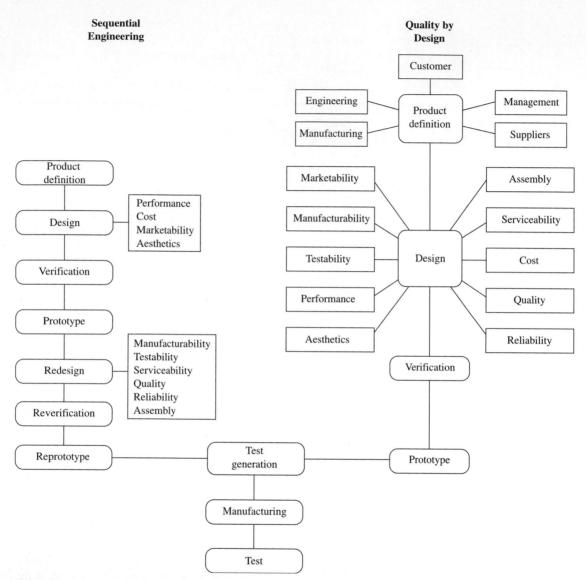

Figure 13-1 Product Development Flow Diagram

Getting input at the beginning from all areas eliminates engineering changes later in the project. Communication flows better and people are more apt to compromise to assure better manufacturability instead of unknowingly creating more work for the next discipline. As mentioned previously, designs would be thrown over the wall to the next area. For instance, it would be difficult for the electrical engineers to know why the structural engineers designed sections in a component that would require special processes in order to run wires through the product. These simple problems, which arise from ignorance of other specialization areas, are eliminated from projects, and thus, lead times to market are shortened.

As shown in Figure 13-1, sequential engineering requires repeated steps of redesign, reverification, and reprototype in order to compile all previous design stages. For example, during the first design phase in sequential engineering, only performance, cost, marketability, and aesthetics might be considered. After verifying the design and building the first prototype, it is determined that the product needs to be redesigned for producibility, testability, serviceability, quality, and reliability. In the quality by design (or concurrent) engineering model, however, the initial design phase encompasses all of the aforementioned attributes, thus eliminating the need for redesign.

There is obviously a longer lead time involved in the traditional method, because each step is performed independently and sequentially, one after another. As problems arise, the project is sent back to the appropriate area and the process starts over. Because there is a high level of technical specialization at each step, numerous cycles are common. The quality by design (or concurrent) engineering method combines all these steps into one. The product is designed to be successful at each stage of its life cycle. It is designed correctly the first time, considering all attributes and facets of its life, such as marketability, assembly, and serviceability, before release to testing and, finally, to production.

Rationale for Implementation

Project budgets for all industries are becoming more crucial to any product's marketability. In the 1970s, accounting methods and budgets were not as critical as they are today. U.S. producers were able to pass unaccounted costs to the consumer through price increases. In the past, consumers had only a few brands to choose from, so the price was dictated by the cost of production plus a reasonable profit. Imported products helped balance the demand for quality products at reasonable prices and allowed consumers to set the market price. Often, there was little to no markup on goods, forcing inefficient suppliers to close their doors or produce specialized products that had higher contribution margins.

Design changes that occur late in the product development cycle cause increased lead times and, thus, higher costs. Quality by design helps control design changes by shifting all the design to the beginning of the project rather than throughout its whole life cycle, as shown in Figure 13-2. The shifting of all design to the beginning of the project increases the time required for initial design; however, the future benefits outweigh this increase. For example, a change made during the design stage could cost up to ten times as much as one made during the testing stage. Spending ten times as much to change features that could have been designed into the product at the beginning justifies the purchase of high-powered product development software. The amount of time required in the quality by design model for product definition and specifications can be significantly

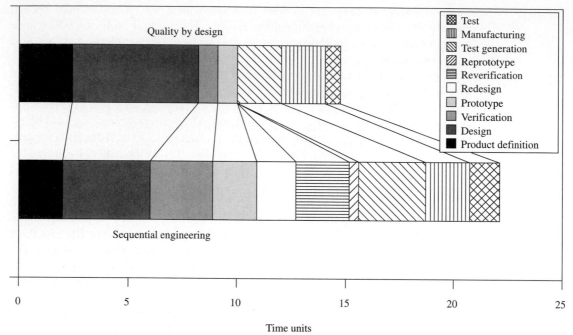

Figure 13-2 **Hypothetical Product Development Time Line**

greater than that required in the sequential engineering model. However, the increased time is warranted because the brainstorming sessions among specialists result in a more complete final product definition.

Fewer design changes and shorter product lead times both equate to a quicker response to customer needs; however, there are even better reasons for using quality by design. Lower reject and scrap rates on the shop floor quickly improve profits.

Cash flow is crucial to an organization's operating budget. Sales dollars pay the present period expenses, which keeps the facility producing the products that will be sold tomorrow. Customer returns can take a large bite out of an organization's operating budget and can hinder product scheduling in order to perform rework.

By using quality by design, the product is designed within production capabilities in order for statistical process control to be effective. Producing products well within process capabilities will cause a chain reaction of customer satisfaction. Customer returns will decrease, and rework costs will also decrease. As a result, profit margins become larger, because the time that was previously used to rework in-house nonconformities and customer returns can now be used to produce new products. Thus, organizations are taking two steps forward and one giant step back every day they continuously inspect products that could have been designed within process capabilities rather than at or below process capabilities.

Benefits

Because consumer trends drive market demands, an organization's ability to react six months before the competition can significantly improve profits. Obviously, timing is important, but consumers will switch brands if they can get a similar product of the same quality for less money. Furthermore, if a product is not designed with costs in mind, inefficiencies will soon erode the profits gained from short lead times. Quality by design provides manufacturers with the tools and communication and management techniques required to develop products in a timely and cost-efficient manner from the beginning and throughout a product's life.

The primary benefit of implementing quality by design techniques is a significant decrease in time to market. Other benefits of quality by design techniques are:

Faster product development.

Better quality.

Less work in progress.

Fewer engineering change orders.

Increased productivity.

The above benefits are also the underlying reason for a decrease in a product's time to market.

According to the National Institute of Standards and Technology, implementation of quality by design methods can reduce engineering changes by 65% to 90%. This decrease in engineering changes can cut product development times by 30% to 70%, reduce time to market by 90%, and increase quality by as much as 200% to 600%. Furthermore, due to the improvements in quality, less rework significantly reduces direct labor costs.

Teams

Quality by design utilizes teams to take advantage of prior experience, emphasize early high-quality decisions, and support the fulfillment of customer requirements, feedback constraints, and the efficient management of risk and change as the product moves from conceptual design to sales. These teams include product developers from marketing, research and development, design, production, test, and logistics, to name a few, along with project and program management. Suppliers and customers should also be included as part of the team when appropriate. To work concurrently, everyone must share ideas and work toward a common goal.

In order for quality by design to work, a change in the way business is done must occur. Quality by design techniques require a change in the "business as usual" philosophy by removing the walls that stand in the way of faster product development and, consequently, lower costs. People can no longer be concerned with only their own function—an exchange of ideas must travel upstream as well as downstream. The input from production, quality, and service departments, in addition to supplier and customer input, are invaluable to the design and development of a product.

Implementing the quality by design philosophy requires a top-down commitment. Bringing together team members from business, engineering, and production requires either that they be co-located or that a system to share information be installed. Team members must be committed to the project, not to their functional departments. The right people need to be put into management roles, and it is vital to know the strengths and weaknesses of all team members. The job needs to be done right the first time by statistically validating every process to assure produceability.

More produceable designs will be achieved through better interaction between design team members. This process begins when design, testing, production, and other members provide input during the final revisions of the product proposal from marketing instead of after the product has already been designed.

Studies have shown that somewhere between 60% and 95% of the overall product cost is determined during the design phase. A product's parts, assembly, test, and service costs are dictated far more often in the product's design than in the actual production, testing, or servicing. The earlier these design decisions are made, the larger their impact.

To avoid problems with teams, reward team members for extra work, level the playing field, and compensate team members more or less equally. Suppliers must have the trust of the team to keep highly engineered parts confidential. Team members should treat other team members as internal customers. These are just a few examples of how to increase the benefits of quality by design.

Today, with reduced travel budgets, time constraints, and joint ventures throughout the world, more and more companies are relying on virtual project teams or distance management to conduct business. There are numerous potential difficulties associated with participating in or leading a virtual team. Some of the effective leadership skills needed to manage a virtual team are very similar to those needed in any leadership role:[1]

Use technology that fits the situation.

Communicate effectively.

Build a community based on high-quality values among members.

Establish goals, expectations, purpose, and vision.

Lead by example with focus on results.

Coordinate across organizational boundaries.

Whenever working in or leading a virtual team, it is of utmost importance to allow the dynamics of the team to evolve and react quickly to changes.

---

[1] Joyce Thompson, "Leading Virtual Teams," *Quality Digest* (September 2000): 42–46.

Examples of Teams

There are numerous examples of organizations, from manufacturing to service, employing teams to save money and improve quality. The following examples give a wide range of successful organizations that applied teams.

1. A 15-member quality-improvement team at Pacific Bell won the 1994 RIT/USA Today Quality Cup in the service category by reducing damage to buried cables by 24% the previous year.[2] The team accomplished the reduction by first determining that the majority of cable cuts was the result of construction. They then persuaded contractors to work in better harmony with Pacific Bell to drastically reduce construction problems.

2. In 1995, Sun Microsystems launched its SunTeams program to implement a team-improvement process as part of its quality initiative.[3] The program focuses on employees taking ownership of a process and improving it, such as increasing customer satisfaction or loyalty. Since its inception, some SunTeams have reduced product failures by 80% and cut workstation-manufacturing time from ten days to two days.

3. Lear's auto supplier plant in Strasburg, Virginia won the 1999 RIT/USA Today Quality Cup in the manufacturing category by reducing paint spots on auto parts.[4] A nine-member multi-disciplinary team decided to replace a waterfall with a vacuum filter made of cardboard. The problem fix resulted in a reduction of 16% in the scrap rate and a reduction of 25% in defects, a 33% increase in productivity, and a savings of $112,000 per year.

4. A multi-disciplinary virtual team of workers from American Airlines, Federal Express, Airbus Industries, General Electric, and primarily Allied Signal won the 1998 RIT/USA Today Quality Cup in the manufacturing category by reducing the repair rate on an airflow valve in jet engines.[5] The team increased the time between valve repairs by 75% and produced a possible savings of over $5,000 per plane per year.

5. In 1995, prior to Chrysler launching its new minivan, a serious flaw was found in the wiper system, which was made by a subcontractor, ITT. A six-member team from ITT quickly found the problem in the dimensional tolerance of the motor assembly and fixed the problem without seriously delaying the launch of the new minivan.[6] As a result of their quick, team-oriented solution to the problem, they won the 1997 RIT/USA Today Quality Cup in the manufacturing category and received nearly $75 million in new business from other automakers.

6. Rayovac formed a quality by design team composed of people from design, engineering, sales, quality, manufacturing, purchasing, customer service, finance, and the

---

[2] 1994 RIT/USA Today Quality Cup.

[3] Elizabeth Larson, "Teams Shine at Sun Microsystems," *Quality Digest* (May 1999): 10.

[4] 1999 RIT/USA Today Quality Cup.

[5] 1998 RIT/USA Today Quality Cup.

[6] 1997 RIT/USA Today Quality Cup.

plastic parts supplier to design their new fluorescent camping light. Using this quality by design team, they were able to reduce the usual product development time from three years to one year.

Communication Models

The communication flow for sequential engineering is in series, compared with quality by design (or concurrent) engineering, which has a parallel communication flow. The traditional model for communication in organizations across the United States uses a hierarchy of units, as shown in Figure 13-3. For simplicity, not all departments are included within each discipline (for example, design and finance could have also been included in engineering and business, respectively). Although needed for the effective management of resources, this hierarchy does not foster communications across the organization, but rather only up the chain of command. The traditional model allows for a great many structured communication paths among similar functional units in the organization. For example, all the various engineering groups in the organization can usually easily communicate with any other engineering group. However, this model is structured to impede communication between product engineering and marketing, for instance.

In the traditional organizational structure, each level in the hierarchy should only perform duties that are assigned from the level above. Thus, if the system is designed well, cross communications need not be necessary. This system worked well in the face of no

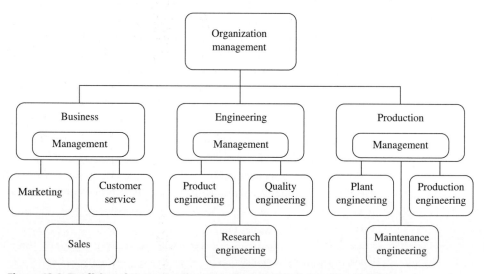

Figure 13-3 Traditional Organization Structure and Information Paths

competition. However, as can be seen by U.S. industry in the 1970s and 1980s, this system had difficulty surviving against the more advanced organizational systems of other countries. In order to circumvent the lack of flexibility in the traditional organizational structure, a quality by design organization structure should be adopted, as shown in Figure 13-4.

In the quality by design organizational structure, information paths are opened up between departments in different disciplines. In other words, a field service employee can talk directly with a production engineer about a common service problem that could be easily remedied in the production phase of product development. Similarly, design engineers can consult with production workers about difficulties in assembling their designs. The primary advantage of the quality by design organizational structure is the opening of communication paths between employees and their subsequent empowerment in the decision-making process.

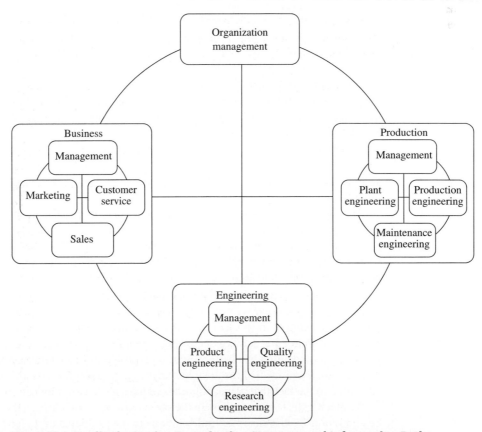

Figure 13-4 Quality by Design Organization Structure and Information Paths

Implementation

The implementation of quality by design is no easy task for any organization. A great deal of time, effort, and money needs to be expended in order for the culture of the organization to accept the various basic concepts that make quality by design work. These concepts, which include looking at the whole product life cycle, agreeing that there are indeed both internal customers and suppliers as well as outside ones, and having a commitment to quality for the entire process of making the product and not just the product itself, are key to the success of quality by design.

The easiest way for an organization to progress toward a quality by design environment is simply to gather together everyone who will be involved in a project at its beginning and allow the communication channels to open. This meeting of all project members can reap great rewards. The first of such benefits is that project members can meet face to face all their internal and external customers and suppliers, which has the effect of personalizing the project for each member. It also opens personal channels of communication, because there are now people, not just faceless names, associated with each phase of the project. Another important feature of the initial meeting is that the members of the project come to understand the overall goals of the project. The meeting can also be used to quickly clear up any misconceptions project members may have about the project.

Once this initial meeting has taken place, there should be regular meetings at set intervals to allow the project members to renew communication paths and to exchange ideas and complaints about various phases of the project. The intervals between project meetings must be long enough to allow for meaningful questions to develop but short enough so that important design decisions can be discussed by the group. With this in mind, the project leader must schedule the meetings while also considering the constraints on the schedules of each member of the group. Unfortunately, this scheduling quickly becomes a logistical nightmare.

By using dedicated project teams, the hindrance of regular meetings can be eliminated. This is a system in which members of each functional unit are either recruited or assigned to a project team that stays together from project to project. By implementing such a system, the organization can establish project teams that have a sense of togetherness, whose paths of communication are already in place, and where each member fully knows everyone's capabilities. This approach is a very elegant solution to implementing quality by design; however, it is only a partial one. The reason that the system is flawed is due to the aging of the project team. As the team does more and more projects together, a sense of stability and settling occurs in communication between the members. They no longer try to find better and better solutions to problems that the project faces, but instead they rely on solutions that the team has arrived at in past projects. This limitation can be attributed to the fact that newer solutions require more communication.

By placing the team members in the same location (co-locating), the project team can be continuously stimulated to find solutions to the problems of the project. Co-location dramatically increases communication between project members and, thus, stimulates continuous improvements. However, there are a number of disadvantages associated with co-location. The first is the high cost of moving and providing for the project members. Second, by moving individual members out of their functional unit environment, the organization takes away the paths of communication that previously existed within the respective units. For example, in moving a die designer out of his department, the designer can no longer effectively communicate with other designers, which can result in a sub-optimal die design.

Computer network technology allows the organization to have the advantages of a co-located team but still retain all advantages of a functional organization. By networking the team together, the project is turned into a managed set of resources and applications through which the team communicates. This technology has a threefold advantage. First, it eliminates the cost of co-location. Second, it allows for maximum communication between project members and outside consultants. Finally, it records the progress of the project for management and accounting uses.

Although each of the aforementioned steps toward implementing quality by design adds advantages, it also increases costs. These costs, both in time and in money, must be considered before any model is applied to an organization. Each solution also requires progressively more difficult culture changes in the organization for the solution to be effective. By first establishing project meetings, management can slowly begin to change the culture of the organization. After these cultural changes have become ingrained, the organization may add a project facilitator or go directly into dedicated project teams. Once these teams have been established, the organization may wish to co-locate each project team or even try to network all the projects.

The implementation of quality by design can be viewed as a path of stepping-stones on the way to true quality by design. The pace of the travel on the stepping-stones should be dictated only by how far the organization wants to step and how much they want to risk falling off the path.

The Chrysler Corporation is an example of a successful organization that has implemented co-location of teams and workspace restructuring.

Chrysler Corporation used a quality by design approach to bring the Viper model from an auto-show concept car to full production in less than three years with a budget of $50 million. This was accomplished by co-locating the team and knocking down barriers between design and production in order to maximize communication and working relationships. Chrysler flattened the vertical hierarchy of the organization into three levels, consisting of team members, team leaders, and a project manager. Experts and outside suppliers were brought in on an as-needed basis to help resolve problems before they occurred.

Tools

Computer-aided drafting (CAD) and computer-aided manufacturing (CAM) have bridged the gap between design and rapid prototypes. Computer-aided drafting files can be converted to tool path geometry and then downloaded directly to a computer numerically controlled (CNC) machine. A model can then be cut for the design team to evaluate and discuss in terms of design options. The following sections describe many of the tools needed to make quality by design work. Without these tools, quality by design is not as effective. It is only when the proper mix of tools is judiciously implemented that quality by design will radically reduce lead times.

Chronology of Quality by Design Tools

Many quality by design tools were not readily available to the business, engineering, and production departments of organizations until the late 1980s and early 1990s. The prime mover for the explosion of quality by design tools has been the exponential growth of desktop computer processing power with advanced computer graphics capabilities. To realize the phenomenal growth in quality by design tools resulting from the personal computer revolution, one need only look at the advances in word processing, drafting, and engineering analysis.

Until the early 1980s, secretaries throughout the world relied on typewriters for the word processing of all documents. Editing of these documents and bulk mailings required substantial amounts of time and organization resources in addition to the original effort. Often, organizations employed more secretaries and support staff than employees directly related to product development and production. Since the late 1980s, almost every office assistant has had access to a personal computer with word processing software. These software programs make bulk mailings as simple as writing a single letter, and editing a document can take a fraction of the time required for the original manuscript.

Major aircraft manufacturers have used CAD software since the late 1970s. However, it is only since the late 1980s that small to medium-sized organizations have utilized the power of personal computer-based CAD. Computer-aided drafting software now allows engineers at organizations of all sizes to draw designs and make changes in a fraction of the time required by the old pencil-and-paper techniques.

An even more dramatic example is the explosion of personal computer-based engineering analysis software packages such as finite element analysis. The theoretical background for finite element analysis was first developed in the 1950s and 1960s and coincides with the early advances in digital computers. Until the late 1980s, only aircraft organizations, automobile manufacturers, and government laboratories utilized the advantages of engineering analysis software because of their access to high-powered supercomputers. In the 1990s, even the smallest of organizations could purchase a personal computer-based finite element software package.

Organizational Tools

Many of the tools implemented by an organization need to be understood by all employees. The primary organizational tools for a quality by design environment are:

Total Quality Management philosophies.

Computer networks.

ISO 9000.

ISO 14000.

Total productive maintenance.

Quality function deployment.

Information technology.

Electronic meeting software.

Enterprise resource planning software.

Total Quality Management (TQM) is a new way of doing business. (It was defined in Chapter 1.) All employees must understand these principles so they can also understand the organization goals and help achieve them.

Computer networks consist of both local area networks and global information networks. Local area networks allow users to share information between interconnected personal computers within an organization. Global information networks allow users to share information between different computer systems separated by thousands of miles.

ISO stands for International Organization for Standards. The ISO 9000 (QMS) series is a standardized quality system that was discussed in Chapter 10. The ISO 14000 (EMS) series is a standardized environmental management system that is discussed in Chapter 11.

Total productive maintenance is a system for keeping a plant and its equipment at their highest productive levels through the cooperation of all levels of production and maintenance. It is defined in Chapter 16.

Quality function deployment (QFD) relates customer requirements or expectations with engineering characteristics and production processes. QFD was discussed in Chapter 12. QFD is a means to translate the voice of the customer into design parameters that can be deployed horizontally through product planning, design, engineering, production, assembly, and field service. Results of QFD are measured based on the number of design and engineering changes, time to market, cost, and quality. Thus, QFD is considered by many experts to be a perfect blueprint for quality by design.

Electronic meeting software (EMS) provides a means for individuals to communicate their opinions within a group in a structured and creative manner.[7] By using EMS, companies can nurture individuals without the inhibitions and distractions associated with face-to-face contact. EMS works by first posing a question or problem to a user group. Then, the users all respond anonymously at the same time. Once everyone has responded, every user can see all of the answers. This creates an environment where

---

[7] Elizabeth Scott Anderson and Jill Smith Slater, "Electronic Meeting Software Makes Communicating Easier," *Quality Progress* (April 1995): 83–86.

people respond to a question, not a person, and are guaranteed no reprisals. In this manner, better outcomes (solutions) can be achieved, compared to the typical (face-to-face) meeting style.

Enterprise resource planning (ERP) software unites numerous applications and/or separate systems (financials, human resources, sales, distribution, manufacturing, materials procurement, manufacturing, and so forth) within the management of a company under the umbrella of one software database.[8] For instance, ERP allows product-scanning software to interface with financials, materials procurement, sales, and distribution databases or software. Product data management (PDM) software is a subset of ERP and is used by companies to perform many time-intensive tasks, such as design reviews and approvals, transforming conceptual designs into end products.[9] Both ERP and PDM are used extensively by companies successful in e-commerce via the Internet. Furthermore, these tools are now being developed using the XML language (successor to HTML), so they are compliant with future Internet innovations, such as the semantic web.

Product Development Tools

Quality by design tools that decrease total product development time utilize high-powered software and the latest in desktop computers. The primary quality by design tools for product development are:

Computer-aided drafting software.

Solid modeling software.

Finite element analysis software.

Parametric analysis software.

Rapid prototyping techniques.

Design for manufacture and assembly (and service and environment) techniques.

Failure mode and effect analysis.

Computer-aided drafting (CAD) software is used by organizations to produce engineering production drawings. These drawings can be done in planar view, isometric, and/or three-dimensional perspectives, with complete dimensioning and tolerancing. The power of CAD allows engineering changes to be easily incorporated into the drawings in a fraction of the time required by the old pencil-and-paper techniques. Another major advantage of CAD is its compatibility with downstream engineering and produc-

---

[8] Patrick Waurzyniak, "ERP Embraces the Web," www.sme.org/manufacturingengineering (October 2000): 42–52.

[9] Steve Shoaf, "PDM or ERP: Making the Connection," www.sme.org/manufacturingengineering (May 1999): 144–147.

tion software and hardware. Drawings from CAD software can be easily incorporated into software packages such as finite element analysis, computer-aided manufacturing, design for manufacture, and CNC machines.

Geometric modeling software is used to create a visual verification of a component or a system of components. By viewing a three-dimensional solid model, problems between part interactions can be easily identified prior to analysis and production. Geometric modeling is often referred to as solid modeling. Numerous geometric modeling software packages are available; however, the major computer-aided drafting packages are equipped to handle add-on modeling software. Today, advanced solid modeling software (sometimes call CAD for computer aided design versus computer aided drafting) packages are capable of doing die and mold tooling design from solid part models, sheet metal forming, and other advanced features.[10] They have also evolved to work seamlessly with computer aided manufacturing software by using solid models instead of wire-frame and surface models.[11]

Finite element analysis (FEA) software packages are widely regarded as the most powerful tool available for a design engineer. The scope of finite element techniques encompasses all engineering fields, such as solid mechanics, fluid mechanics, heat transfer, vibrations, and electromagnetics, to name the broadest categories. The advantage of a finite element analysis software package lies in its power to analyze and optimize the response of a system prior to prototype development and testing. This tool can help detect problems early, allowing the quality by design team to implement alternative changes together and quickly test the product changes to see the effects on quality and performance.

Parametric analysis software is an extension on the concept of a combination between geometric or solid modeling software and finite element software. Typically, an analysis using the finite element method involves defining the part geometry and material properties and its loading; determining the solution for stress, temperature, flow, and so forth; and interpreting the solution results. When the results indicate that a design change is necessary, the part geometry must be changed and the solution process repeated. Repeating this procedure numerous times can be very costly and time consuming. The procedure is especially laborious if the model is complex or if many changes must be made. Parametric analysis software gives the user the ability to automate any changes by programming the software to make decisions based on specified functions, variables, and selected analysis criteria. The software can be programmed to give the user control over virtually any variable such as dimensions, materials, loadings, constraint locations, and mesh refinement. Parametric analysis software expands the capabilities of geometric or solid modeling software and FEA software to include parametric modeling from parts libraries and design optimization.

---

[10] Patrick Waurzyniak, "CAD/CAM Tools Raise the Bar," www.sme.org/manufacturingengineering (January 2001): 52–60.

[11] Jean Owen, "CAM Embraces Solids," *Manufacturing Engineering* (February 1999): 80–90.

Rapid prototyping techniques are used to quickly produce a physical "one-piece" model of a component or product. There are six rapid prototyping techniques commercially available. These are: stereolithography (STL), solid ground curing (SGC), selective laser sintering (SLS), fused deposition modeling (FDM), direct shell production casting (DSPC), and laminated object method (LOM). These techniques utilize information from CAD and geometric modeling software to produce exact geometric replicas of an engineering design in significantly less time than traditional machining processes. In stereolithography, in one of the most popular techniques, a three-dimensional plastic model of a part is produced by curing a liquid photomonomer with a laser. Similarly, solid ground curing produces a plastic model by curing a liquid resin with a UV light source. In the selective laser sintering process, plastic powders and waxes are sintered with an infrared laser to produce a model. Plastic or wax wire is melted and delivered by means of an extrusion head to produce a model in a process called fused deposition modeling. The aforementioned processes produce a solid part, whereas in the direct shell production casting method an ink jet nozzle applies a liquid binder to a ceramic powder to produce a shell mold of the part. In the laminated object method, a sheet of paper is rolled onto a platform and then a laser is used to cut away the excess paper to form a model. It should be noted that rapid prototyping techniques do not produce a model with realistic mechanical characteristics. However, recently, a new form of rapid prototyping, called rapid toolmaking, can actually make a metal mold for a short production run. Rapid toolmaking bridges the gap between the need for a small number of prototypes and full production by using special materials or post-processes, such as copper polyamide, heat sintered stainless steel powders, and epoxy/steel blends, to name a few.[12]

Design for manufacture and assembly (DFMA) is a design philosophy that identifies production and assembly problems. Software programs alert engineers of design problems prior to production. Potential problems, such as excessive costs due to part complexity, number of parts, difficult assembly procedures, increased assembly times, and unreasonable or unwarranted tolerances, can be identified, and changes in a design can be made before design effort continues or, more importantly, before full production commences. Recently, DFMA has evolved to also include design for service and design for environment. In design for service, a product or process is designed for efficient repair and maintenance by establishing assembly and disassembly sequences, generating a degree of difficulty and time estimate for service, and identifying the service life of particular parts. In design for environment, a product or process is designed such that its disposal presents no adverse environmental impact while being cost-effective.

Failure mode and effect analysis (FMEA) is an analytical technique to identify foreseeable failure modes of a product or process and plan for their elimination. In other words, FMEA can be explained as a group of activities intended to: recognize and evaluate the potential failure of a product or process and its effects; identify actions that

---

[12] Robert Aronson, "Toolmaking Through Rapid Prototyping," *Manufacturing Engineering* (November 1998): 52–56.

could eliminate or reduce the chance of the potential failure occurring; and document the process. FMEA requires a team effort to most easily and inexpensively alleviate changes in design and production. There are two primary types of FMEA: design and process (covered in Chapter 14).

Production Tools

Improving the quality of manufactured parts and decreasing the production cycle time requires the use of high-powered software programs integrated with computer-controlled machine tools and modern facilities. The primary quality by design tools for production are:

Robotics.

Computer-aided manufacturing.

Computer numerical controlled tools.

Continuous process improvement.

Just-in-time production.

Virtual manufacturing software.

Agile (or lean) manufacturing.

Advanced measurement and verification.

Since the 1960s and 1970s robots have steadily become more advanced and more prevalent in manufacturing. From what began as simple automation processes evolved into robots performing advanced welding operations, tolerance verification, material handling and precision painting on automobile assembly lines. The advantages of robotics is obvious (reduced overhead and labor costs, significantly faster throughput, and a potential for zero defects, scrap and rework, to name a few), however, the capital investment can at times be prohibitive. Robots have become faster and have better controllers for very sophisticated operations, and have increased load capacity compared to their predecessors.[13] They are capable of operating within the open-architecture personal computers, and they interact seamlessly with most major CAD/CAM software packages.[14] Today, an engineer can design a product in any major CAD package and then transfer the design to robot simulation software to consider manufacturing options. At this point in their development, the only limitation to their future advancement is the human interface. Robots are now being developed as autonomous systems, and robots, of the marsupial type, were even used in the search and rescue operation at the World Trade Center after the events of September 11, 2001.

[13] Russ Olexa, "More Brawn and Brains," www.sme.org/manufacturingengineering (September 2001): 90–120.

[14] Patrick Waurzyniak, "Robotics Revolution," *Manufacturing Engineering* (February 1999): 40–50.

Computer-aided manufacturing (CAM) software is used to identify machine tool paths and other production parameters to optimize the machining of a part. After a part has been completely drawn using a CAD or geometric modeling program, CAM software identifies critical machining parameters based primarily on the part geometry, size, dimensions and tolerances, and material. Critical machining parameters include machine tool feed rates, stock required, bit size, and optimum tool path, to name a few. Today, CAM systems work almost seamlessly with most computer aided design software. They have achieved a high level of intelligence with full associativity between the solid model and tool path, standardized feature recognition, higher speeds, and knowledge- (or history-) based machining.[15]

Machine tools, such as mills, lathes, and presses, that are completely controlled by a microprocessor are called computer numerical control (CNC) machine tools. Advanced CNC machines and modern facilities also can automate material handling. Specialized computer languages, such as G and M codes, and coordinate locations are used for programming CNC machines. Once a part has been completely drawn using a CAD or geometric modeling program, it can be easily transferred to a CAM program and then machined through an interface between the CAM program and CNC machine. Typically, the operator needs little knowledge of the actual programming languages involved because of user-friendly interfaces between the software packages.

Continuous process improvement (CPI), as it applies to quality by design, is a systematic year-after-year study to improve the production processes involved in production. Production processes are continuously improved by making them effective, efficient, and adaptable to changes. This process involves eliminating waste and rework, reducing scrap and cycle time, eliminating activities that do not increase product value, and eliminating nonconformities wherever they occur.

Just-in-time (JIT) production is a process-control method and production philosophy that provides parts, components, and assemblies to production at the exact time they are needed. The result of JIT production is less inventory of raw materials, smaller inventories of parts, less work in process, and shorter lead times. Benefits of JIT production are a significant reduction in floor space, less overhead, and, most importantly, a reduction in cost. A possible pitfall of JIT production is a reduction of inventories to critically low levels. Consequently, care must be taken to choose suppliers with excellent quality products and services as well as a knowledge of production lead and process times.

With virtual manufacturing software, production engineers are able to create a factory on their desktop computer. They can simulate a production facility with mechanical handling robots, automated arc and spot welding systems, drilling and riveting machinery, automated painting and coating, numerically-controlled machining, coordinated measuring, and assembly processes showing the complete manufacturing and production operations in a virtual setting. Virtual manufacturing software allows production engineers to analyze and debug production facilities prior to the capital equipment investment.

---

[15] Patrick Waurzyniak, "CAM Gets Smarter," www.sme.org/manufacturingengineering (July 2000): 56–69.

Agile manufacturing helps organizations thrive in a rapidly changing, competitive marketplace by incorporating versatility into the manufacturing environment. An agile manufacturing environment responds quickly to marketplace demands by quickly incorporating new technologies into products and easily adapting to many different customer needs. Recently, flexible manufacturing systems, also called manufacturing cells and centers, have become commonplace. These cells or centers are capable of doing multiple machining operations, materials handling, and so forth while also being modular in design and easily adaptable to new configurations.[16] Although similar in nature to agile manufacturing, because the focus is on bringing a cost-effective product to market quicker, lean manufacturing strives to do more with less. That is, less human effort, less factory space, less capital investment and less engineering to produce the product in half the time.[17] To accomplish lean manufacturing, many technological changes must take place with the organization: production should be a continuous flow or at least a supermarket flow; the cyclic nature of the supply and demand on the production system should be smoothed out; agile (flexible) manufacturing systems should be implemented; total productive maintenance should be practiced by empowering employees; waste should be eliminated; and the organization should strive for 100% quality prior to inspection.[14,18]

Recently, advances in measurement and verification have brought together the worlds of computer-oriented product development tools and computer-oriented manufacturing tools. Coordinate (also called computer) measuring machines (CMMs) can automatically measure a three-dimensional object and transfer the information back and forth to computer aided design software for measurement, alignment, dimensioning, and verification.[19] What started from a two-dimensional physical probe system has evolved into three-dimensional probe systems,[20] hand-held probes, photogrammetry dots, laser trackers, and more recently, laser radar,[21] laser stripe illumination, and line-scan camera technology.[22] The newest systems are capable of defining part shapes automatically with extremely high precision. For instance, the latest technology is capable of measuring the complex curvature of an airfoil for a turbine engine.[23] Today, CMMs can also be used in an automated process to verify a machined part in real-time to make necessary adjustments.

[16] Robert Aronson, "Cells and Centers," *Manufacturing Engineering* (February 1999): 52–60.

[17] Drew Lathin and Ron Mitchell, "Learning from Mistakes," *Quality Progress* (June 2001): 39–45.

[18] John Allen, "Make Lean Manufacturing Work for You," www.sme.org/manufacturingengineering (June 2000): 34–40.

[19] Simon Raab, "CAD's Final Frontier," *Manufacturing Engineering* (April 1999): 84–90.

[20] Marco Manganelli, "Measuring the Real World with High-Performance Scanning Systems," *Quality Digest* (September 2000): 37–41.

[21] David A. White, "Coherent Laser Radar," *Quality Digest* (August 1999): 35–38.

[22] Robert Green, "Measuring Complex Curves with a New Twist," *Quality Digest* (September 1999): 35–38.

[23] Ibid.

Statistical Tools

Quality engineers are the primary users of statistical tools associated with a quality by design environment; however, all employees should be able to use statistical tools where appropriate. The primary statistical tools that cover all facets of design, testing, and production are:

Design of experiments.

Statistical process control.

Design of experiments (DOE) or experimental design, which is discussed in Chapter 19, is a numerical study that identifies the variables in a process or product that are the critical parameters or cause significant variation in the process. By using formal experimental techniques, the effect of many variables can be studied at one time. Changes to the process or product are introduced in a random fashion or by carefully planned, highly structured experiments. There are three approaches to DOE: classical, Taguchi (see Chapter 20) and Shainin. The wise practitioner will become familiar with all three approaches and develop his own methodology.

Statistical process control (SPC) is the primary TQM tool (see Chapter 18). It is a charting technique used to monitor process variations and correct problems before producing scrap. Because DOE identifies the critical parameters and their target values, its use should actually precede SPC in most circumstances. It is not unusual to find after an experiment that SPC was controlling the wrong variable or that the target was incorrect.

Pitfalls of Quality by Design Tools

Note that, by the title of this section, there are no negatives to implementing quality by design tools. Keep in mind that before any of the aforementioned tools will help in the quality by design process, employees must have experience—and often expertise—with them. In fact, due to inexperience, these tools will initially lengthen lead times. For example, when a design engineer/drafter is first introduced to computer-aided drafting software, his/her first production drawing could take triple the previous time. However, after proper training and even limited experience, the same drawing could take one-third less time and significantly reduce the time allocated towards future modifications.

Without proper training, many of these tools can be dangerous in the wrong hands. Therefore, it is important to have technical people in the quality by design group who are proficient with the tools. An organization intending to implement a quality by design philosophy needs to allocate significant resources toward employee professional development and education. Because of the initial capital investment, the rewards of a quality by design environment are very rarely realized in the short term. On the positive side, an investment in the quality by design tools often results in an increase in employee retention and satisfaction.

Examples of Tools

There are numerous examples of organizations, from manufacturing to service, employing quality by design tools in product development and production to reduce their time to market, to reduce costs, and to improve quality. The following examples give a wide range of organizations, albeit primarily larger organizations, that have successfully applied quality by design. However, there are also small organizations throughout the world benefiting from quality by design.

1. Possibly one of the greatest examples of quality by design is the design and construction of the Boeing 777 that was nearly 100% designed, analyzed, and tested using multi-disciplinary teams, design for manufacture and assembly, computer-aided-design and analysis software, computer numerical control machines, and a vast array of computer networking with their suppliers. More recently, a team from Boeing and Boeing won the 2000 RIT/USA Today Quality Cup for manufacturing when it increased the wear-out rate on an ozone converter from one year to three years.[24] Using quality by design, the team saved $20 million and created another $10 million in business from additional sales.

2. Another example of quality by design in the aircraft industry is the design and construction of the F-22 joint strike fighter produced by Lockheed Martin and X-32 joint strike fighter produced by Boeing.

    a. A team of individuals from primarily TRW and Lockheed, and also Motorola, Rockwell, Texas Instruments, ITT, and GEC won the 1994 RIT/USA Today Quality Cup for manufacturing by using quality by design approaches adapted from the automobile industry and relying on constant teleconferencing.[25] As a result of the team's effort, the team cut the cost of F-22 communication and navigation systems from $2.1 million to $1.6 million per jet. The team convinced the Department of Defense that commercial parts (versus rigid military specification) could be used for many of the components. The team also reduced the number of semiconductor-driven boxes from 12 to 1.

    b. Lockheed Martin used extensive simulations and numerous software programs in its F-22 program to address manufacturing, fixtures, maintenance, ergonomics, cutting time, and costs.[26] They used digital manufacturing software and other solutions to improve quality and reduce labor costs. For instance, some jobs that took 96 man-hours were reduced to one and one-half man-hours.

---

[24] 2000 RIT/USA Today Quality Cup.

[25] 1994 RIT/USA Today Quality Cup.

[26] "Simulation Aids Manufacturability for the Joint Strike Fighter." www.sme.org/manufacturingengineering (October 2001): 30–32.

c. Likewise, Boeing used virtual numerical control software and simulation and verification software to automate tool paths before metal cutting.[27]

3. Iomega Corp. was the co-winner of the 2001 RIT/USA Today Quality Cup in the manufacturing category by using various principles of quality by design in the design of their new HipZip that plays digital music files.[28] Because of a very quick time to market deadline, team members at Iomega used a multi-fold strategy: the design was based on what the customer (not the engineer) wanted; aluminum molds for evaluation were made in several days compared to three months; product testing was performed in sequence with the design process; and the product was designed for easy manufacturability (for example one type of screw was used in the whole design).

4. Starting in the early 1980s with the purchase of The Harley-Davidson Motor Company from AMF, the company rebounded from extremely poor performance (and products) in the previous decade(s) by using many of the facets of quality by design. Throughout the late 1980s and 1990s they implemented many programs to enhance their company performance, such as: materials as needed (part of JIT), a successful TPM program, computer-aided manufacturing, design for manufacturing and assembly, and agile (or lean) manufacturing. As a result of their efforts, they are one of the most stable and successful companies in the world, in not only motorcycle production and sales, but also in all facets of the global economy.

5. BMW's X5 SUV was the first BMW automobile to be 100% digitally designed using 3-D computer-aided design programs.[29] Using CAD, they reduced vehicle development time, achieved tighter manufacturing tolerances, performed design tests and structural evaluation, including simulations, and verified safety issues (rollover), allowing BMW to respond faster to customer needs (changes) in future versions of the vehicle.

6. For the big three U.S. automakers, implementing quality by design techniques has increased their profits and helped regain their market share and dominance. For instance, General Motors eliminated 900 parts from the 1995 Chevrolet Lumina compared to the 1994 model and reduced assembly time by 33%. At Ford Motor Company, the 1994 Mustang was redesigned in just 35 months using quality by design. In the new Plymouth Neon, only 300 kinds of fasteners are used, compared to 650 for most vehicles, making the Neon one of the big three's first profitable small cars.

7. General Electric Aerospace applied quality by design to a ground-based radar system. What normally would have taken six to nine months to design and put into production only took three months, equating to a 60% reduction in engineering and testing time.

8. Ingersoll-Rand Corporation incorporated quality by design in a recent product development project. They designed a hand-held, air-powered grinder that normally would

---

[27] Patrick Waurzyniak, "Simulations Speed Production," www.sme.org/manufacturingengineering (April 2001): 36–40.

[28] Matt Krantz, "Engineers Get in Tune to Save Time," *USA Today* (May 10, 2001): 3B.

[29] Robert A. Green, "BMW Drives Safety with Quality," *Quality Digest* (August 2001): 26–28.

have taken four years, total development. Development took only one year using quality by design.

9. Lamb Technicon, a subsidiary of Litton Industries, used virtual manufacturing software for Chrysler Corporation's Cirrus and Stratus vehicle assembly. By simulating the operation of 40 spot welding and mechanical handling robots with virtual manufacturing software, the amount of time required to program the robots was reduced from an estimated 1600 engineering manhours to 300.

10. Ford Motor Company has started a new advanced computer technology called C3P that will improve efficiencies throughout the process of developing a vehicle from concept to production. C3P is designed to provide a seamless transition from computer-aided engineering to computer-aided drafting to computer-aided manufacturing. The new C3P initiative will be used in all stages of vehicle development to improve quality, time to market, and cost.

These are success stories of organizations that implemented quality by design tools properly, but one must keep in mind that many of these organizations had not only mastered the technical tools needed. They also maximized the use of the technical tools by improving communication within the team(s) at the beginning of the project.

Misconceptions and Pitfalls

Some organizations claim to have been using quality by design for quite some time. This may be so, but it is also possible that they have redefined quality by design to fit their methods rather than changing their present management styles. The following is a list of some of the common misconceptions that should be understood by those claiming to have used quality by design.

1. Quality by design is not simultaneous design and production; it encourages just the opposite. Nothing is produced until all designs are agreed upon between all the producers required to fabricate the product.

2. Quality by design is not a quick fix or magical formula for success; it is a way of thinking. The people involved in the quality by design group must be specialists before they are incorporated in the group. If this technical expertise is not present, little will be gained with quality by design principles.

3. Quality by design does not require multiple tests of the product to be conducted until the optimum design is achieved. Quality by design applies a one-pass design, where the product passes testing the first time.

4. Quality by design is often confused with inspection techniques used in TQM. Quality by design is highly dependent upon a TQM environment, but the same inspection methods are not required. Quality by design incorporates repeatability into its

products, either automatically or manually. Quality by design considers and applies what was learned about process capabilities in the TQM setting. Thus, products are stringently designed well within process capabilities to facilitate SPC.

With the promise of huge savings, many organizations may see the benefit of quality by design and invest in massive amounts of technology, hire consultants, tear down walls between departments, and purchase software and hardware, only to be disappointed with the return on their investment. The following is a list of some of the common pitfalls to avoid if an organization is considering implementing quality by design.

1. Team members should be assigned to functional departments, as in sequential engineering; however, their primary loyalty lies with the quality by design team. Do not eliminate the sequential engineering process; instead, perform all design up front as a group with improved communication. For instance, do not plan for ten man-years to optimize component designs after a system has been fully prototyped or plan for multiple design iterations of a new product before manufacturing.

2. Avoid promising to meet an unobtainable schedule, because missing an unobtainable schedule carries a more severe penalty than meeting a longer one. For instance, do not inflate a fabrication lead time to allow for anticipated or uncontrolled design changes.

3. Avoid using tight tolerances and stringent requirements to obtain a one-pass design.

4. Avoid changing product definition and specifications during the design phase. Costs increase exponentially when features are added through the development cycle that cause design, tooling, and production systems to change.

5. Avoid "business as usual" parts vendoring by using the low bidder.

6. Avoid automating the product development phase before it is simplified.

Of course, these are only some of the possible pitfalls, and the manner in which an organization implements quality by design depends on its size, structure, and product line.

TQM Exemplary Organization[30]

Founded in 1979, privately-held Trident manufactures precision sheet metal components, electromechanical assemblies, and custom products, mostly in the office-equipment, medical-supply, computer, and defense industries. It has grown from a three-person operation to an employer of 167 people, occupying a modern, 83,000-square-foot facility.

---

[30] Malcolm Baldrige National Quality Award, 1996 Manufacturing Category Recipient, NIST/Baldrige Homepage, Internet.

Trident has established "quality as its basic business plan" to accomplish short- and long-term goals for each of its five key business drivers: customer satisfaction, employee satisfaction, shareholder value, operational performance, and supplier partnerships. All goals, however, contribute to achieving Trident's overarching aim of total customer satisfaction. Each improvement project begins with a thorough analysis of how to meet or exceed customer requirements in four critical areas: quality, cost, delivery, and service. Metrics are designed to ensure that progress toward the customer-targeted improvements can be evaluated. The company's data-collection system provides all personnel with a current record of the company's progress toward its goals. Performance data also are reviewed daily in each department and weekly by the Senior Executive Team. Once each month, this team aggregates the data for the entire company and reports on progress toward goals set for each of the five key business drivers.

Regular contact with customers and suppliers is an essential element of Trident's quality strategy. Senior executives meet twice a year with representatives of each customer company for in-depth discussions on Trident's performance as a supplier, while 41 customer-contact personnel interact with these firms on a daily basis. Customers, as well as key suppliers, also participate in Continuous Involvement Meetings, initiated by Trident, to gain full understanding of a customer's new or modified product design.

Trident also uses technology to strengthen links to customers and suppliers. Electronic data interchange capabilities, for example, permit paperless transactions, while file-exchange capabilities enable customers to send their designs electronically to Trident's computer-aided design and manufacturing equipment.

Organized into functional departmental teams, employees "own" specific processes and are given responsibility for identifying problems and opportunities for improvement. To foster innovation, employees have the authority to modify their process, using the company's documented process improvement procedure, which focuses attention on non-value-added activities that can be eliminated.

The company also relies heavily on the contributions of cross-functional teams, and it encourages employees to diversify their work skills and abilities. Eighty percent of Trident workers are trained in at least two job functions, well on the way to the 1998 goal of 100 percent.

To reinforce worker commitment to continuous improvement, the company regularly acknowledges exemplary performance. Reward and recognition of employees have climbed steadily, from just nine incidents in 1988 to 1,201 in 1995.

Improvements set in motion by Trident's total quality strategy has catalyzed performance gains that have cascaded throughout the organization and generated benefits reaped by customers. Employee turnover has declined dramatically, from 41% in 1988 to 5% in 1994 and 1995. The company correlates these positive workforce trends with increasing productivity and rising levels of customer satisfaction. Sales per employee rose from $67,000 in 1988 to $116,000 in 1995.

Nonconformance rates have fallen consistently, so much so that Trident now offers a full guarantee against nonconformances in its custom products. Customer complaints have fallen 80%, and time spent on rework has decreased 90%. On the service side, the company has greatly improved its on-time delivery performance from 87% in 1990 to 99.94% in 1995. Machines made for one of Trident's major customers go directly to that company's distribution center for shipping. For the past two years, no nonconformances have been reported in these Trident-built machines.

Employees have submitted over 125 process improvement ideas per month and 97% have been implemented. These and other improvements have enabled Trident to maintain its status as key supplier to major customers, even after those organizations trimmed suppliers by 65 to 75%.

Exercises

1. Briefly describe the difference between sequential engineering and quality by design (or concurrent) engineering.

2. List 15 general attributes that a quality by design team should consider during the product design phase of product development.

3. Select members of a quality by design team for the development and production of two or more of the following products. If possible, the team should be limited to ten members of different disciplines.

   (a) Ballpoint pen
   (b) Car windshield sunscreen
   (c) Manual can opener
   (d) Computer keyboard
   (e) Clothes iron

4. Design the workspace for two or more of the items you used in Exercise 3.

5. Using trade journals and professional society magazines, list three or more commercially-available software packages for two of the following quality by design tools. Also, try to compare the software packages on the basis of cost, attributes, and performance.

   (a) Computer networks
   (b) Computer-aided drafting
   (c) Solid modeling
   (d) Finite element analysis
   (e) Parametric analysis
   (f) Rapid prototyping
   (g) Computer-aided manufacturing

(h) Virtual manufacturing
(i) Statistical process control
(j) Experimental design
(k) Other quality by design software

6. Using trade journals, professional society magazines, periodicals, and your networking ability, identify three examples of quality by design success stories and discuss their results.

7. Individually or with a team, identify an organization in your local area with which you are associated or have familiarity that practices quality by design and discuss the effectiveness of the practices.

8. Individually or with a team, identify an organization in your local area with which you are associated or have familiarity that does not practice quality by design and describe facets of the organization that you would change to improve time to market and lower costs.

14

Failure Mode and Effect Analysis

Introduction

Failure Mode and Effect Analysis (FMEA) is an analytical technique (a paper test) that combines the technology and experience of people in identifying foreseeable failure modes of a product or process and planning for its elimination. In other words, FMEA can be explained as a group of activities intended to

Recognize and evaluate the potential failure of a product or process and its effects.

Identify actions that could eliminate or reduce the chance of potential failures.

Document the process.

FMEA is a "before-the-event" action requiring a team effort to easily and inexpensively alleviate changes in design and production.

There are several types of FMEA: design FMEA, process FMEA, equipment FMEA, maintenance FMEA, concept FMEA, service FMEA, system FMEA, environmental FMEA, and others. However, for all intents and purposes, all of the types can be broadly categorized under either design FMEA or process FMEA. For instance, equipment, service, and environmental FMEA are just slightly modified versions of process FMEA, and system FMEA is a combination of design and process FMEA. For this reason, the remainder of this chapter will concentrate primarily on design FMEA and process FMEA.

Design FMEA aids in the design process by identifying known and foreseeable failure modes and then ranking failures according to relative impact on the product. Implementing Design FMEA helps establish priorities based on expected failures and severity of those failures and helps uncover oversights, misjudgments, and errors that may have been made. Furthermore, design FMEA reduces development time and cost of manufacturing processes by eliminating many potential failure modes prior to operation of the process and by specifying the appropriate tests to prove the designed product.

Process FMEA is used to identify potential process failure modes by ranking failures and helping to establish priorities according to the relative impact on the internal or external customer. Implementing process FMEA helps to identify potential manufacturing or assembly causes in order to establish controls for occurrence reduction and detection. Furthermore, design and process FMEA document the results of the design and production processes, respectively.

Reliability

Reliability is one of the most important characteristics of any product, no matter what its application. Reliability is also an important aspect when dealing with customer satisfaction, whether the customer is internal or external. Customers want a product that will have a relatively long service life, with long times between failures. However, as products become more complex in nature, traditional design methods are not adequate for ensuring low rates of failure. This problem gave rise to the concept of designing reliability into the product itself.

Reliability may be defined as the probability of the product to perform as expected for a certain period of time, under the given operating conditions, and at a given set of product performance characteristics. One important consideration when performing reliability studies is the safety of the product or the process. The criticality of a product or process changes drastically when human safety considerations are involved. Reliability tests and studies can form the basis for safety studies.

Reliability Requirements

In all cases, the acceptance of a certain product or process is subject to meeting a certain set of given requirements for reliability of the product or process. It is, however, important to realize that although the definition for reliability is relatively simple, the customer and the supplier may have different definitions of what constitutes failure. This common agreement on what constitutes reliability should be defined in terms of influence on other related systems, the reliability of past similar systems, the complexity of the failure, and finally the relative criticality of the failure.

It is the engineer's task to define all of the previously-stated items, and in many instances, the engineer has only past experience and personal knowledge of like systems to define these different aspects of failure accurately. A simple example of this task is comparing a certain nonconformity that causes the product to become inoperable to another type of nonconformity that causes only slight inconvenience to the consumer. There is no great analysis needed to determine that the first failure has a greater criticality than the second failure, which only slightly inconveniences the customer.

Based on the definition of the part, assembly, or process under consideration, the reliability of each sub-system and the factors involved in the reliability must be found, and the appropriate relationships for each part, class, or module of the product must be computed. This will help to develop an approved parts list, parts application study, critical components list, and an organized method for changing parameters as needed. This information then leads to a formal system for managing FMEA based on probability of the nonconformity occurring, probability of the customer noticing the nonconformity (defect), and the probability of the nonconformity actually being undetected and being shipped to the customer.

Failure Rate

A vast majority of products follow a very familiar pattern of failure. When no information is known about the reliability (probability of survival) or, conversely, failure of a product, component, system or process, except the failure rate which is a constant, periods of failure can conveniently be modeled by an exponential distribution. The probability of survival of this type of product using an exponential distribution may be expressed as

$$R_t = e^{-t\lambda} = e^{-\frac{t}{\theta}}$$

where R_t = the reliability or probability of survival
t = the time specified for operation without failure
λ = the failure rate
θ = the mean time to failure

EXAMPLE PROBLEM

Assume that a product has a constant failure rate of $\lambda = 0.002$ per hour. What is the probability that it will survive or be reliable during the first 100 hours of operation?

$$R_t = e^{-t\lambda} = e^{-(100)(0.002)} = e^{-0.2} = 0.980$$

Thus, there is a 98% chance that the product will survive during the first 100 hours of operation.

The failures of most products can be classified into three main categories: debug, chance, and wear out. The first of these (debug) includes a high failure rate at the initial stages because of inappropriate use or flaws in the design or manufacturing. The next category (chance) is the failure of the product due to accidents, poor maintenance, or limitations on the design. The final category (wear out) covers failure after the product or process has performed as expected for at least the amount of time given by the manufacturer as the product or process life. A successful design or process should ideally fail only in this last method.

Intent of FMEA

Continually measuring the reliability of a machine, product, or process is an essential part of Total Quality Management. When acquiring new machines, creating a new product, or even modifying an existing product, it is always necessary to determine the reliability of the product or process. One of the most powerful methods available for measuring the reliability of the process or product is FMEA. As previously stated, FMEA is an analytical technique that combines the technology and experience of people in identifying foreseeable failure modes of a product or process and planning for its elimination. This method can be implemented in both the design and the process areas and basically involves the identification of the potential failure modes and the effect of those on both the internal and the external customer.

FMEA attempts to detect the potential product-related failure modes. The technique is used to anticipate causes of failure and prevent them from happening. FMEA uses occurrence and detection probability criteria in conjunction with severity criteria to develop risk prioritization numbers for prioritization of corrective action considerations. This method is an important step in debugging and preventing problems that may occur in the manufacturing process. It should be noted that for FMEA to be successful, it is extremely important to treat the FMEA as a living document, continually changing as new problems are found and being updated to ensure that the most critical problems are identified and addressed quickly.

The FMEA evaluation should be conducted immediately following the design phase of product production and, definitely in most cases, before purchasing and setting up any machinery. One purpose of FMEA is to compare the design characteristics relative to the planned manufacturing or assembly methods to make certain that the product meets the customers' requirements. Corrective actions should begin as soon as a failure mode is identified. Another purpose of FMEA is to provide justification for setting up a process in a certain manner. FMEA may be viewed as the formal manner in which engineers will analyze all possible nonconformities and problems that may arise in a given process or with a certain product. This will, in a sense, encourage all the engineers' analyses and findings to be in an organized, user-friendly format.

The use of FMEA in both the product and process areas of manufacturing is more important today than it has ever been. Current products are more complicated than ever, and this requires more organization and precaution than ever. It will take far more planning to produce current products with the same reliability as prior products. Consumers today also are far more particular than they have been in the past, demanding products of the highest quality for the lowest possible cost. FMEA also allows the engineer to keep a record of all thoughts and actions taken to ensure a safe and reliable product. This becomes extremely important with the customers' current mode of thinking—needing to assign blame whenever something is not exactly as expected. In addition, the judicial system has become increasingly strict and more unforgiving than ever before. The most important aspect of this discussion is to follow up on any and all concerns that seem critical and to document the concerns and changes made, continuously updating the FMEA. All changes and concerns between the design stage and the delivery of the product to the consumer should be noted in a thorough, precise, and organized manner.

Design (product) FMEA or process FMEA can provide the following benefits:

1. Having a systematic review of component failure modes to ensure that any failure produces minimal damage to the product or process.

2. Determining the effects that any failure will have on other items in the product or process and their functions.

3. Determining those parts of the product or the process whose failure will have critical effects on product or process operation (those producing the greatest damage), and which failure modes will generate these damaging effects.

4. Calculating the probabilities of failures in assemblies, sub-assemblies, products, and processes from the individual failure probabilities of their components and the arrangements in which they have been designed. Since components have more than one failure mode, the probability that one will fail at all is the sum of the total probability of the failure modes.

5. Establishing test program requirements to determine failure mode and rate data not available from other sources.

6. Establishing test program requirements to verify empirical reliability predictions.

7. Providing input data for trade-off studies to establish the effectiveness of changes in a proposed product or process or to determine the probable effect of modifications to an existing product or process.

8. Determining how the high-failure-rate components of a product or process can be adapted for higher-reliability components, redundancies, or both.

9. Eliminating or minimizing the adverse effects that assembly failures could generate and indicating safeguards to be incorporated if the product or the process cannot be made fail-safe or brought within acceptable failure limits.

10. Helping uncover oversights, misjudgments, and errors that may have been made.

11. Helping reduce development time and cost of manufacturing processes by eliminating many potential modes prior to operation of the process and by specifying the appropriate tests to prove the designed product.

12. Providing training for new employees.

13. Tracking the progress of a project.

14. Communicating to other professionals who may have similar problems.

The FMEA document, however, cannot solve all design and manufacturing problems and failures. The document, by itself, will not fix the identified problems or define the action that needs to be taken. Another misconception is that FMEA will replace the basic problem-solving process (see Chapter 5).

FMEA Team

The FMEA methodology is a team effort where the responsible engineer involves assembly, manufacturing, materials, quality, service, supplier, and the next customer (whether internal or external). The team leader has certain responsibilities, which include determining the meeting time and place, communicating with the rest of the team, coordinating corrective action assignments and follow-up, keeping files and records of FMEA forms, leading the team through completion of the forms, keeping the process moving, and finally, drawing everyone into participation. There also should be a recorder who records the results on the form and distributes results to participants in a timely manner.

FMEA Documentation

As stated before, the concept of FMEA is nothing new to engineers. Engineers, or anyone designing and building a product, have always incorporated the concepts of FMEA in their thinking process. However, FMEA does help keep those ideas available for future use and for the use of others. One engineer may find a potential problem elementary and not worth extra attention; a second engineer may not realize the problem altogether. The purpose of the FMEA document is to allow all involved engineers to have access to others' thoughts and to design and manufacture using this collective group of thoughts, thus promoting a team approach. It cannot be stressed enough that in order for the document to be effective, representatives from *all* affected areas must be consulted and their input always included. Also, for the document to be effective, it *must* be continually updated as changes occur throughout the design and manufacturing process.

Block Diagram

Design FMEA should always begin with a block diagram. The block diagram can be used to show different flows (information, energy, force, fluid, and so forth) involved with the component being analyzed. The primary purpose of the block diagram is to understand the input to the block, the function of the block, and the output of the design. Another purpose is to establish a logical order to the analysis. Any and all block diagrams used in developing the FMEA document should be included with the document throughout all phases of development.

A block diagram is started by first listing all of the components of the system, their functions, and the means of connection or attachment between components. Then, the components of the system are placed in blocks, and their functional relationships are represented by lines connecting the blocks. For example, the system components for a low-cost child's remote-control car could be:

Chassis.

Body.

Steering servo.

Motor.

Steering linkage.

Battery holder.

Drive shaft.

Front and rear wheels.

Batteries.

Remote sending and receiving units.

These system components would be attached to one another using the following connection methods:

Screws.

Snap fit.

Press fit.

Compressive fit.

Cotter pins.

Wires.

Bushings.

Shaft couplings.

In order to construct the block diagram, as shown in Figure 14-1, of a low-cost child's remote-control car, each of the system components represents a block, and certain blocks are connected to one another. For example, the motor is connected to the chassis with screws, to the drive shift with a shaft coupling, to the battery holder with wires, and to the remote receiving unit with wires.

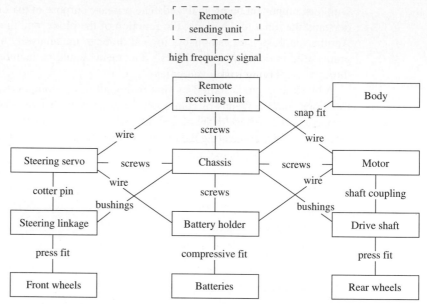

Figure 14-1 Functional Block Diagram of a Child's Low-Cost Remote Control Car

For a more complicated system of components, a hierarchical representation can be used to aid in determining the interconnection between components. Of course, each component of the system can be further decomposed into its individual components (for example, a wheel could be decomposed into a hub and a tire). Furthermore, if certain components are not to be included in the FMEA, dotted lines can be used for the blocks, as illustrated by the remote sending unit in Figure 14-1.

Other Documentation

The other three documents needed are the design or process intent, the customer needs and wants, and the FMEA form, which is explained in detail in the remainder of this chapter.

Stages of FMEA

The four stages of FMEA are given below:

1. Specifying Possibilities
   a. Functions
   b. Possible Failure Modes

     c. Root Causes

     d. Effects

     e. Detection/Prevention

  2. Quantifying Risk

     a. Probability of Cause

     b. Severity of Effect

     c. Effectiveness of Control to Prevent Cause

     d. Risk Priority Number

  3. Correcting High Risk Causes

     a. Prioritizing Work

     b. Detailing Action

     c. Assigning Action Responsibility

     d. Check Points on Completion

  4. Re-evaluation of Risk

     a. Recalculation of Risk Priority Number

General forms for design FMEA and process FMEA are shown in Figures 14-2 and 14-3, respectively.

The Design FMEA Document

The top section in the form (see Figure 14-2) is used mainly for document tracking and organization.

FMEA Number

On the top left corner of the document is the FMEA Number, which is only needed for tracking.

Item

The Item space is used only to clarify which exact component or process is being analyzed. The appropriate level of analysis should be included here, along with the name and number of the system or sub-system being analyzed.

FAILURE MODE AND EFFECT ANALYSIS
(DESIGN FMEA)

FMEA Number _____

Page _____ of _____

Item _____ Design Responsibility _____ Prepared By _____

Model Number/Year _____ Key Date _____ FMEA Date (Orig.) _____ (Rev.) _____

Core Team _____

Item/ Function	Potential Failure Mode	Potential Effect(s) of Failure	S	C L A S S	Potential Cause(s)/ Mechanism(s) of Failure	O	Current Design Controls	D	R P N	Recommended Actions	Responsibility and Target Completion Dates	Actions Taken	Action Results			
													S E V	O C C	D E T	R P N

Figure 14-2 Design FMEA Form
Reprinted, with permission, from the *FMEA Manual* (Chrysler, Ford, General Motors Supplier Quality Requirements Task Force).

386

Design Responsibility

The team in charge of the design or process should be identified in the space designated Design Responsibility. The name and company (or department) of the person or group responsible for preparing the document should also be included.

Prepared By

The name, telephone number, and address should be included in the Prepared By space for use when parts of the document need explanation.

Model Number/Year

Both the name and identification number of the system, sub-system, or component should be included in the Model Number/Year space to avoid confusion between similar components.

Key Date

The date the initial FMEA is due should be placed in the Key Date space.

FMEA Date

The date the original FMEA was compiled and the latest revision date should be placed in the FMEA Date space.

Core Team

In the space reserved for Core Team, the names of the responsible individuals and departments that have authority to perform tasks should be listed. If the different people or departments involved are not working closely or are not familiar with each other, team members' names, departments, and phone numbers should be distributed.

Item/Function

In this section, the name and number of the item being analyzed is recorded. This information should be as precise as possible to avoid confusion involving similar items. Next, the function of the item is to be entered below the description of the item. No specifics should be left out in giving the function of the item. If the item has more than one function, they should be listed and analyzed separately. The function of the item should be completely given, including the environment in which the system operates (including temperature, pressure, humidity, and so forth); it should also be as concise as possible.

Potential Failure Mode

The Potential Failure Mode information may be one of two things. First, it may be the method in which the item being analyzed may fail to meet the design criteria. Second, it may be a method that may cause potential failure in a higher-level system or may be the result of failure of a lower-level system. It is important to consider and list each potential failure mode. All potential failure modes must be considered, including those that may occur under particular operating conditions and under certain usage conditions, even if these conditions are outside the range given for normal usage. A good starting point when listing potential failure modes is to consider past failures, concern reports, and group "brainstorming." Also, potential failure modes must be described in technical terms, not terms describing what the customer will see as the failure. Some typical failure modes may include cracked, deformed, loosened, leaking, sticking, short circuited, oxidized, and fractured.[1]

Potential Effect(s) of Failure

The potential effects of failure are the effects of the failure as perceived by the customer. Recall that the customer may be internal or may be the end user of the product. The effects of failure must be described in terms of what the customer will notice or experience, so if conditions are given by the customer there will be no dispute as to which mode caused the particular failure effect. It must also be stated whether the failure will impact personal safety or break any product regulations. This section of the document must also forecast what effects the particular failure may have on other systems or sub-systems in immediate contact with the system failure. For example, a part may fracture, which may cause vibration of the sub-system in contact with the fractured part, resulting in an intermittent system operation. The intermittent system operation could cause performance to degrade and then ultimately lead to customer dissatisfaction. Some typical effects of failure may include noise, erratic operation, poor appearance, lack of stability, intermittent operation, and impaired operation.[2]

Severity (S)

Severity is the assessment of the seriousness of the effect of the potential failure mode to the next component, sub-system, system, or customer if it occurs. It is important to realize that the severity applies only to the effect of the failure, not the potential failure mode. Reduction in severity ranking must not come from any reasoning except for a direct change in the design. It should be stressed that no single list of severity criteria is applicable to all designs; the team should agree on evaluation criteria and on a ranking

---

[1,2]Reprinted, with permission, from the *FMEA Manual* (Chrysler, Ford, General Motors Supplier Quality Requirements Task Force).

TABLE 14-1
Rankings of Severity of Effect for Design FMEA

EFFECT	CRITERIA: SEVERITY OF EFFECT	RANKING
Hazardous Without Warning	Very high ranking when potential failure mode affects safe operation and/or regulation noncompliance. Failure occurs without warning.	10
Hazardous With Warning	Very high ranking when potential failure mode affects safe operation and/or regulation noncompliance. Failure occurs with warning.	9
Very High	Item or product is inoperable, with loss of function. Customer very dissatisfied.	8
High	Item or product is operable, but with loss of performance. Customer dissatisfied.	7
Moderate	Item or product is operable, but with loss to comfort/ convenience items inoperable. Customer experiences discomfort.	6
Low	Item or product is operable, but with loss of performance of comfort/convenience items. Customer has some dissatisfaction.	5
Very Low	Certain item characteristics do not conform. Noticed by most customers.	4
Minor	Certain item characteristics do not conform. Noticed by average customer.	3
Very Minor	Certain item characteristics do not conform. Noticed by discriminating customers.	2
None	No effect.	1

Reprinted, with permission, from the *FMEA Manual* (Chrysler, Ford, General Motors Supplier Quality Requirements Task Force).

system that are consistent throughout the life of the document. Severity should be rated on a 1-to-10 scale, with a 1 being none and a 10 being the most severe. The example of evaluation criteria given in Table 14-1 is just that, *an example*; the actual evaluation criteria will be diverse for a variety of systems or sub-systems evaluated.

Classification (CLASS)

This column is used to classify any special product characteristics for components, sub-systems, or systems that may require additional process controls. There should be a special method to designate any item that may require special process controls on the form.

Potential Cause(s)/Mechanism(s) of Failure

Every potential failure cause and/or mechanism must be listed completely and concisely. Some failure modes may have more than one cause and/or mechanism of failure; each of these must be examined and listed separately. Then, each of these causes and/or mechanisms must be reviewed with equal weight. Typical failure causes may include incorrect material specified, inadequate design, inadequate life assumption, over-stressing, insufficient lubrication capability, poor environment protection, and incorrect algorithm. Typical failure mechanisms may include yield, creep, fatigue, wear, material instability, and corrosion.

Occurrence (O)

Occurrence is the chance that one of the specific causes/mechanisms will occur. This must be done for every cause and mechanism listed. Reduction or removal in occurrence ranking must not come from any reasoning except for a direct change in the design. Design change is the only way a reduction in the occurrence ranking can be effected. Like severity criteria, the likelihood of occurrence is based on a 1-to-10 scale, with 1 being the least chance of occurrence and 10 being the highest chance of occurrence. Some evaluation questions are:

What is the service history/field experience with similar systems or sub-systems?

Is the component similar to a previous system or sub-system?

How significant are the changes if the component is a "new" model?

Is the component completely new?

Is the component application any different than before?

Is the component environment any different than before?[3]

The example of occurrence criteria given in Table 14-2 is just that, *an example*; the actual occurrence criteria will be diverse for a variety of systems or sub-systems evaluated. The team should agree on an evaluation criteria and ranking system that remains consistent throughout the life of the design FMEA.

Current Design Controls

In this portion of the form, the activities that assure the design sufficiency for the failure mode or mechanism are listed. These activities may include, but are not limited to, prevention measures, design validation, and design verification. These controls may be supported through tests, which may include physical testing, mathematical studies,

---

[3] Reprinted, with permission, from the *FMEA Manual* (Chrysler, Ford, General Motors Supplier Quality Requirements Task Force).

TABLE 14-2
Rankings of Possible Failure Rates (Occurrence (O)) for Design FMEA

PROBABILITY OF FAILURE	POSSIBLE FAILURE RATES	RANKING
Very High: Failure is almost inevitable.	> 1 in 2	10
	1 in 3	9
High: Repeated failures.	1 in 8	8
	1 in 20	7
Moderate: Occasional failures.	1 in 80	6
	1 in 400	5
	1 in 2000	4
Low: Relatively few failures.	1 in 15,000	3
	1 in 150,000	2
Remote: Failure is unlikely.	< 1 in 1,500,000	1

Reprinted, with permission, from the *FMEA Manual* (Chrysler, Ford, General Motors Supplier Quality Requirements Task Force).

feasibility reviews, and prototype testing. In general, there are three types of design controls that

1. Prevent the cause/mechanism or failure mode effect from occurring or reduce the rate of occurrence.
2. Detect the cause/mechanism and lead to corrective actions.
3. Detect only the failure mode.

Obviously, the preferred method is to use the first type of design control when possible. If this first method is employed, the occurrence ranking may be changed on the following version of the document. But in order to accurately improve the occurrence rating for the particular failure mode or mechanism, the design control must be employed as an intricate part of the design. If it is not possible to procure the first control listed, the second and third controls may have to be used, preferably using the second control listed over the third design control. The third type listed can in no manner be used to improve the occurrence rate of the failure mode.

Detection (D)

This section of the document is a relative measure of the assessment of the ability of the design control to detect either a potential cause/mechanism or the subsequent failure mode before the component, sub-system, or system is completed for production. Most typically, in order to achieve a lower detection ranking in subsequent versions of the document, the planned design control must be improved. As with the occurrence criteria

TABLE 14-3
Rankings of Likelihood of Detection by Design Control for Design FMEA

DETECTION	CRITERIA: LIKELIHOOD OF DETECTION BY DESIGN CONTROL	RANKING
Absolute Uncertainty	Design control will not and/or cannot detect a potential cause/mechanism and subsequent failure mode: or there is no design control.	10
Very Remote	Very remote chance the design control will detect a potential cause/mechanism and subsequent failure mode.	9
Remote	Remote chance the design control will detect a potential cause/mechanism and subsequent failure mode.	8
Very Low	Very low chance the design control will detect a potential cause/mechanism and subsequent failure mode.	7
Low	Low chance the design control will detect a potential cause/mechanism and subsequent failure mode.	6
Moderate	Moderate chance the design control will detect a potential cause/mechanism and subsequent failure mode.	5
Moderately High	Moderately high chance the design control will detect a potential cause/mechanism and subsequent failure mode.	4
High	High chance the design control will detect a potential cause/mechanism and subsequent failure mode.	3
Very High	Very high chance the design control will detect a potential cause/mechanism and subsequent failure mode.	2
Almost Certain	Design control will almost certainly detect a potential cause/mechanism and subsequent failure mode.	1

Reprinted, with permission, from the *FMEA Manual* (Chrysler, Ford, General Motors Supplier Quality Requirements Task Force).

given earlier, the example of detection criteria given in Table 14-3 is just that, *an example*; the actual detection criteria will be diverse for a variety of systems or sub-systems evaluated. The team should agree on an evaluation criteria and ranking system that remains consistent throughout the life of the design FMEA.

Risk Priority Number (RPN)

By definition, the Risk Priority Number is the product of the severity (*S*), occurrence (*O*), and detection (*D*) rankings, as shown below:

$$RPN = (S) \times (O) \times (D)$$

This product may be viewed as a relative measure of the design risk. Values for the *RPN* can range from 1 to 1000, with 1 being the smallest design risk possible. This value is then used to rank order the various concerns in the design. For concerns with a relatively high *RPN*, the engineering team must make efforts to take corrective action to reduce the *RPN*. Likewise, because a certain concern has a relatively low *RPN*, the engineering team should not overlook the concern and neglect an effort to reduce the *RPN*. This is especially true when the severity of a concern is high. In this case, a low *RPN* may be extremely misleading, not placing enough importance on a concern where the level of severity may be disastrous. In general, the purpose of the *RPN* is to rank the various concerns on the document. However, every concern should be given the full attention of the team, and every method available to reduce the *RPN* should be exhausted.

Recommended Actions

After every concern has been examined and given a risk priority number, the team should begin to examine the corrective action(s) that may be employed, beginning with the concern with the greatest *RPN* and working in descending order according to *RPN*. Also, concerns with high severity criteria should be examined with the lead group of concerns.

The purpose of the recommended actions is to reduce one or more of the criteria that constitute the risk priority number. An increase in design validation actions will result in a reduction in only the detection ranking. Only removing or controlling one or more of the causes/mechanisms of the failure mode through design revision can effect a reduction in the occurrence ranking. And only a design revision can bring about a reduction in the severity ranking. Some actions that should be considered when attempting to reduce the three rankings include, but are not limited to: design of experiments, revised test plan, revised design, and revised material selection/specification.

It is important to enter "None" if there are no recommended actions available to reduce any of the ranking criteria. This is done so future users of the document will know the concern has been considered.

Responsibility and Target Completion Dates

Here the individual or group responsible for the recommended actions and the target completion date should be entered as reference for future document users.

Actions Taken

After an action has been implemented, a brief description of the actual action and its effective date should be entered. This is done after the action has been implemented so future document users may track the progress of the plan.

RESULTING *RPN*

After the corrective actions have been identified, the resulting severity, occurrence, and detection rankings should be re-estimated. Then the resulting *RPN* should be recalculated and recorded. If no actions are taken, this section should be left blank. If no actions are taken and the prior rankings and *RPN* are simply repeated, future document users may reason that there were recommended actions taken, but that they had no effect. After this section is completed, the resulting *RPN*s should be evaluated, and if further action is deemed necessary, steps from the Recommended Actions section should be repeated.

The Process FMEA Document

The basic philosophy concerning the process FMEA document (see Figure 14-3) is almost identical to that of the design FMEA document examined earlier. Process FMEA is an analytical technique utilized by a Manufacturing Responsible Engineering Team as a means to assure that, to the extent possible, potential failure modes and their associated causes/mechanisms have been considered and addressed. Like design FMEA, the concept of the process FMEA document is nothing new to engineers. However, as with design FMEA, the concepts in creating and maintaining the document previously were kept only as thoughts of the engineer. Process FMEA is only documentation of the opinions of the responsible engineering team as a whole. Process FMEA is just as important as design FMEA and for the same reasons. Notable similarities between the design and process FMEA include:

Actively involving representatives from all affected areas.

Including all the concerns from all the involved departments.

Treating the document as a living document that is being revised constantly and updated over time.

A process FMEA is required for all new parts/processes, changed parts/processes, and carryover parts/processes in new applications or environments. The process FMEA document should be initiated before or at the feasibility stage, prior to tooling for production, and take into account all manufacturing operations, from individual components to assemblies. Early review and analysis of new or revised processes is promoted to anticipate, resolve, or monitor potential process concerns during the manufacturing planning stages of a new model or component program.

When creating and/or revising the process FMEA document, it may be assumed that the product will meet the design intent as designed. However, knowledge of potential failures due to a design weakness can be included in process FMEA, if desired. Process

FAILURE MODE AND EFFECT ANALYSIS
(PROCESS FMEA)

FMEA Number _____

Page _____ of _____

Item _____ Process Responsibility _____ Prepared By _____

Model Number/Year _____ Key Date _____ FMEA Date (Orig.) _____ (Rev.) _____

Core Team _____

Process Function Requirements	Potential Failure Mode	Potential Effect(s) of Failure	S E V	C L A S S	Potential Cause(s)/ Mechanism(s) of Failure	O C C	Current Process Controls	D E T	R P N	Recommended Actions	Responsibility and Target Completion Dates	Action Results				
												Actions Taken	S E V	O C C	D E T	R P N

Figure 14-3 Process FMEA Document
Reprinted, with permission, from the *FMEA Manual* (Chrysler, Ford, General Motors Supplier Quality Requirements Task Force).

395

FMEA does not rely on product design changes to overcome weaknesses in the process, but it does take into consideration a product's design characteristics relative to the planned manufacturing or assembly process to assure that, to the extent possible, the resulting product meets customer needs and expectations.

Just as the philosophies of design FMEA and process FMEA are similar, so are the corresponding documents. For this reason, instead of reviewing the entire process FMEA document, as was done for the design FMEA document, only the differences in the two documents will be given. All other aspects in the two documents may be assumed to be identical, for their respective purposes. The top section of the document has the same form and purpose as the design FMEA document, except Design Responsibility becomes Process Responsibility.

Process Function/Requirements

Instead of entering the item being analyzed and its function, as in the design FMEA, a description of the process being analyzed is given here. Examples of this process include, but are not limited to, turning, drilling, tapping, welding, and assembling. The purpose of the process should be given as completely and concisely as possible. If the process being analyzed involves more than one operation, each operation should be listed separately along with its description.

Potential Failure Mode

In process FMEA, one of three types of failures should be listed here. The first and most prevalent is the manner in which the process could potentially fail to meet the process requirements. The two remaining modes include potential failure mode in a subsequent (downstream) operation and an effect associated with a potential failure in a previous (upstream) operation. It should, for the most part, be assumed that the incoming parts and/or material are correct according to the general definition of nonconformity. Each potential failure mode for the particular operation must be listed in terms of a component, sub-system, system, or process characteristic. The assumption is made that the failure could but may not necessarily occur. Another aspect of viewing what is and what is not acceptable must come from the side of the customer, whether internal or external. Some knowledge of design FMEA is needed in this aspect of process FMEA.

Potential Effect(s) of Failure

Like design FMEA, the potential effects of failure are the effects as perceived by the customer, whether internal or external (the end-user). The effects of failure must be described in terms of what the customer will notice or experience, so if conditions are given by the customer there will be no dispute as to which mode caused the particular failure effect. It must also be stated whether the failure will impact personal safety or break any product regulations.

Severity (*S*)

Severity has the same role as it does in design FMEA. If need be, the severity section for a design FMEA should be reviewed. It is worth mentioning that severity applies only to effect. Also, a different type of severity criteria than for design FMEA is used. If the customer affected by a failure mode is the assembly plant or product user, assessing the severity may lie outside the immediate process engineer's field of experience. And like the severity for design FMEA, the severity for process FMEA is estimated on a scale from 1 to 10. The following example of evaluation criteria given in Table 14-4 is just that, *an example*; the actual evaluation criteria will be diverse for a variety of processes evaluated.

Classification (CLASS)

This column is used to classify any special product characteristics for components, sub-systems, or systems that may require additional process controls. There should be some special method to designate any item that may require special process controls on the form.

Potential Cause(s)/Mechanism(s) of Failure

Potential cause of failure is defined as how the failure could occur, described in terms of something that can be corrected or controlled. Every possible failure cause for each failure mode should be listed as completely and concisely as possible. Many causes are not mutually exclusive, and to correct or control the cause, design of experiments may be considered to determine which root causes are major contributors and which can be controlled. Only specific errors and malfunctions should be listed; ambiguous phrases should not be used.

Occurrence (*O*)

The occurrence section of process FMEA is the same as in design FMEA. Recall, occurrence is how frequently the specific failure cause/mechanism is projected to occur. Also note that the occurrence ranking number has a meaning rather than just a relative value. Table 14-5 contains only an example of occurrence criteria; criteria specific to a specific application should be used.

Current Process Controls

Like those for the design FMEA document, current process controls are descriptions of the controls that either prevent, to the extent possible, the failure mode from occurring or detect the failure mode if it should occur. The current design controls section should be reviewed at this time.

TABLE 14-4

Rankings of Severity of Effect for Process FMEA

EFFECT	CRITERIA: SEVERITY OF EFFECT	RANKING
Hazardous Without Warning	May endanger machine or assembly operator. Very high severity ranking when a potential failure mode affects safe operation and/or involves noncompliance with regulation. Failure will occur without warning.	10
Hazardous With Warning	May endanger machine or assembly operator. Very high severity ranking when a potential failure mode affects safe operation and/or involves noncompliance with regulation. Failure will occur with warning.	9
Very High	Major disruption to production line. 100% of product may have to be scrapped. Item inoperable, loss of primary function. Customer very dissatisfied.	8
High	Minor disruption to production line. A portion of product may have to be sorted and scrapped. Item operable, but at reduced level. Customer dissatisfied.	7
Moderate	Minor disruption to production line. A portion of product may have to be scrapped (no sorting). Item operable, but some comfort items inoperable. Customer experiences discomfort.	6
Low	Minor disruption to production line. 100% of product may have to be reworked. Item operable, but some comfort items operable at reduced level of performance. Customer experiences some dissatisfaction.	5
Very Low	Minor disruption to production line. Product may have to be sorted and a portion reworked. Minor adjustments do not conform. Defect noticed by customer.	4
Minor	Minor disruption to production line. A portion of product may have to be reworked on-line, but out of station. Minor adjustments do not conform. Defect noticed by average customer.	3
Very Minor	Minor disruption to production line. A portion of product may have to be reworked on-line, but out of station. Minor adjustments do not conform. Defect noticed by discriminating customer.	2
None	No effect.	1

Reprinted, with permission, from the *FMEA Manual* (Chrysler, Ford, General Motors Supplier Quality Requirements Task Force).

TABLE 14-5
Rankings of Possible Failure Rates (Occurrence (O)) for Process FMEA

PROBABILITY OF FAILURE	POSSIBLE FAILURE RATES	RANKING
Very High: Failure is almost inevitable.	> 1 in 2	10
	1 in 3	9
High: Generally associated with processes similar to previous processes that have often failed.	1 in 8	8
	1 in 20	7
Moderate: Generally associated with processes similar to previous processes that have experienced occasional failures.	1 in 80	6
	1 in 400	5
	1 in 2000	4
Low: Isolated failures associated with similar processes.	1 in 15,000	3
Very Low: Only isolated failures associated with almost identical processes.	1 in 150,000	2
Remote: Failure is unlikely. No failures ever associated with almost identical processes.	< 1 in 1,500,000	1

Reprinted, with permission, from the *FMEA Manual* (Chrysler, Ford, General Motors Supplier Quality Requirements Task Force).

Detection (*D*)

Detection is an assessment of the probability that the proposed current process control will detect a potential weakness or subsequent failure mode before the part or component leaves the manufacturing operation or assembly location. Assume the failure has occurred and then assess the capabilities of the current process control to prevent shipment of the part having this nonconformity (defect) or failure mode. Never automatically assume that detection ranking is low because occurrence is low, but do assess the ability of the process controls to detect low frequency failure modes or prevent them from going further in the process. The evaluation criteria and ranking system (see Table 14-6) should be agreed on by the entire team and should remain consistent throughout the FMEA process.

The remaining sections of process FMEA do not differ from the sections of design FMEA. The design-responsible engineer is responsible for assuring that all actions recommended have been implemented or adequately addressed. FMEA is a living document and should always reflect the latest design level and the latest relevant actions, including those occurring after start of production. The last portion of this chapter contains a simple example of how to prepare the FMEA document.

TABLE 14-6
Rankings of Likelihood of Detection by Process Control for Process FMEA

DETECTION	CRITERIA: LIKELIHOOD OF DETECTION BY PROCESS CONTROL	RANKING
Absolutely Impossible	No known controls available to detect failure mode.	10
Very Remote	Very remote likelihood current controls will detect failure mode.	9
Remote	Remote likelihood current controls will detect failure mode.	8
Very Low	Very low likelihood current controls will detect failure mode.	7
Low	Low likelihood current controls will detect failure mode.	6
Moderate	Moderate likelihood current controls will detect failure mode.	5
Moderately High	Moderately high likelihood current controls will detect failure mode.	4
High	High likelihood current controls will detect failure mode.	3
Very High	Very high likelihood current controls will detect failure mode.	2
Almost Certain	Current controls almost certain to detect the failure mode. Reliable detection controls are known with similar processes.	1

Reprinted, with permission, from the *FMEA Manual* (Chrysler, Ford, General Motors Supplier Quality Requirements Task Force).

Other Types of FMEA

As stated at the beginning of this chapter, there are numerous types of FMEA other than design FMEA and process FMEA. Some of the other types are described below.

By making some simple modifications to process FMEA, it can be used for maintenance (or equipment) FMEA. In maintenance FMEA two column headings from process FMEA are modified as follows:[4] Process Function Requirements becomes Equipment/ Process Function; Current Process Controls becomes Predictive Methods/Current Controls; and the Class column is eliminated. Maintenance (or equipment) FMEA could be used to diagnose a problem on an assembly line or test the potential failure of prospective equipment prior to making a final purchase.

Similar to maintenance FMEA, environmental FMEA is also only a slight modification of process FMEA. In environmental FMEA, the columns of process FMEA are

---

[4] Teodor Cotnareanu, "Old Tools—New Uses: Equipment FMEA," *Quality Progress* (December 1999): 48–52.

modified as follows:[5] Process Function Requirements becomes Sub Process/Function; Potential Failure Mode becomes Environmental Aspect; Potential Effect(s) of Failure becomes Environmental Impact; Potential Cause(s)/Mechanism(s) of Failure becomes Condition/Situation; Current Process Controls becomes Present Detection Systems; and the Class column is eliminated. Environmental FMEA could be used to evaluate the environmental impact or correct the impact of manufacturing. For example, the effect of chemicals used in the semiconductor industry could be evaluated.

Another type of FMEA, service FMEA, is a modification to the standard process FMEA, because most types of services can be considered processes. For example, a moving van company performs a service that involves the following functions as part of the service to the customer: receive request, schedule van, go to client, pack client material, store material, deliver to new address, unpack material, and collect for services. During any one of these functions, there are possible failure modes, such as: while receiving the request, the customer can't find the number, the phone is busy, customer loses number, or customer changes mind. So, essentially, a process FMEA document can be used for service FMEA.

Processes within the service industry can be analyzed prior to customers seeing them, thereby preventing any initial loss of business. For example, service FMEA can be used to analyze a new web-based youth sports registration system prior to debut to prevent the loss of participants. Some of the major airlines have used service FMEA to completely analyze the way they are servicing their customers. Service FMEA has also been used as a prevention tool in the services offered by a medical clinic cafeteria, resulting in effective prevention of errors.[6]

Example of FMEA Document Preparation

The example shown in Figure 14-4 goes through the process of preparing an FMEA document—in this case, a design FMEA document. As stated earlier, the top portion of the document requires no explanation. It is used strictly for tracking and information about the FMEA item, team, and important dates. Next is the Item/Function section of the document. Notice that both a brief but complete description of the item (front door of car) and all functions of the item are given in this section. Care should be taken not to leave out any function the item might have. The Potential Failure Mode (corroded interior lower door panels) is then shown. The description in this section should be as specific as possible so that there is no ambiguity as to which mode is being analyzed.

---

[5] Willy W. Vandenbrande, "How to Use FMEA to Reduce the Size of Your Quality Toolbox," *Quality Progress* (November 1998): 97–100.

[6] Roberto G. Rotondaro and Claudia L. deOliveira, "Using Failure Mode Effect Analysis (FMEA) to Improve Service Quality," Proceedings of the 12th Annual Conference of the Production and Operations Management Society, (2001).

FAILURE MODE AND EFFECT ANALYSIS
(DESIGN FMEA)

FMEA Number __1234__

Page __4__ of __5__

Item __Body Closures__   Design Responsibility __Body Engineering__   Prepared By __John Doe, Senior Body Supervisor__

Model Number/Year __1999 4 dr/Sedan__   Key Date __12/28/98__   FMEA Date (Orig.) __9/12/98__   (Rev.) __10/24/98__

Core Team __T. Fender - Car Product Div.; Childers - Manufacturing; J. Ford - Assy. Oop (Smith, Harris, Black, Doe)__

Item/ Function	Potential Failure Mode	Potential Effect(s) of Failure	S	C L A S S	Potential Cause(s)/ Mechanism(s) of Failure	O	Current Design Controls	D	R P N	Recommended Actions	Responsibility and Target Completion Dates	Action Results			
												Actions Taken	S E V	O C C	D E T	R P N
Front Door L.H. H8HX-000-Z	Corroded interior lower door panels	Deteriorated life of door leads to: Unsatisfactory appearance due to rust	7		Upper edge of protective wax application is too low on door panel	6	Vehicle general test T-118 T-109 T-301	7	294	Add lab accelerated corrosion testing	A Tate Body Engrg 8X 09 03	Based on results, No. 1481, upper edge spec. raised 125 mm	7	2	2	24
Ingress to and egress from vehicle																
Occupant protection from weather, noise, side impact		Impaired function of interior door hardware			Wax application plugs door drain holes	3	Lab test using "worst case" wax application and hole size	1	21	None		Based on test, 3 more vent holes provided				
Support anchor for door hardware including mirror, hinges, latch, and window																
Provide proper surface for appearance items																

Figure 14-4 Example of Design FMEA Form
Reprinted, with permission, from the *FMEA Manual* (Chrysler, Ford, General Motors Supplier Quality Requirements Task Force).

Remember that the remainder of the sections should be completed for only one item and potential failure mode at a time.

Though there is only one item and potential failure mode, it can be seen that there may be multiple Potential Effect(s) of Failure associated with each item and potential failure mode. It is necessary for all the potential effects of failure (unsatisfactory appearance due to rust and impaired function of interior door hardware) to be given here. Even one potential effect missing could cause confusion throughout the engineering team. A consensus should be used when determining the Severity (S) of each potential failure mode. No matter how many potential effects of failure are present, only one value of severity should be used for each potential failure mode. After this, all possible Potential Cause(s)/Mechanism(s) of Failure (upper edge of protective wax application is too low on door and wax application plugs door drain holes) should be listed. Care should be taken to include all possible causes and mechanisms of failure, no matter how trivial some may seem. In this portion of the document, it is imperative that all team members are involved in the brainstorming process. For each of these potential causes/mechanisms of failure, there needs to be a separate Occurrence (O), Current Design Controls, and Detection (D) ranking. These rankings should also be given a value agreed upon by the entire group, using criteria supported by the entire group. Once these portions of the document are filled, the RPN can be found, and the different causes and effects of failure can be compared.

If there are any Recommended Actions (Add lab accelerated corrosion test) agreed upon by the team, they should be listed next. These include any actions that may help to bring the RPN to a lower level. However, in many instances there may not be any recommended actions to list. Instead of leaving the portion empty, it is advisable to enter "None" in the area. This is done so future readers of the document will realize that thought was given to recommended actions, but the group could find none. It is important to realize that if there are no recommended actions for a particular cause and effect of failure, there is no method in which to improve the RPN. Also, the Responsibility and Target Completion Date section of the document will be left blank. If there is a recommended action, however, this section cannot be left blank, and a new RPN should be calculated using new rankings. This example proves how orderly and concisely a group of engineers' thoughts can be recorded not only for their own future use but also for the use of others.

TQM Exemplary Organization[7]

Employee-owned Operations Management International, Inc. (OMI) runs more than 170 wastewater and drinking water treatment facilities in 29 states and eight other nations. Between 1998 and 2000, OMI's public customers realized first-year savings that

---

[7] Malcolm Baldrige National Quality Award, 2000 Service Category Recipient, NIST/Baldrige Homepage, Internet.

averaged $325,000, their operating costs decreased more than 20%, and facility compliance with environmental requirements improved substantially.

Annual average revenue per associate improved from $92,600 in 1997 to almost $108,000 in 2000—an increase of more than 15%. Associate turnover decreased from 25.5% in 1994 to 15.5% in 1999, better than the national average of 18.6% and the service industry average of 27.1%.

Market share in its core business segment has increased to 60%, up from 50% in 1996. Over this span, total revenue grew at an average annual rate of 15%, as compared with 4.5% for OMI's top competitor.

OMI's *Obsessed With Quality* process which corresponds with the principles and criteria of the Malcolm Baldrige National Quality Award, spans the entire company, links all personnel levels, and creates a common foundation and focus for OMI's far-flung operations.

OMI uses a variety of approaches and tools to initiate and then drive progress toward the organization's short-term objectives and five-year improvement goals. For example, long-standing focus teams provide continuity of effort and sustain organization-wide commitment in five key areas: leadership, information and analysis, human resources, process management, and customer satisfaction. Like many other teams at OMI, membership spans the entire organization in terms of function and personnel, including top management and hourly employees. Other techniques to foster alignment and to ensure that important information flows to all OMI offices and facilities include newsletters, regional meetings, e-mail, and the organization's annual project management summit. Information among OMI operated facilities on best practices, emerging technologies, and training results is exchanged at these summits.

The company uses surveys, interviews, focus groups, and market research to learn customers' current and long-term requirements. A contract renewal rate of almost 95% in 1999 and the industry's top rank in the average length of customer retention indicates that OMI is well versed in the requirements of its customers. For all six components of customer satisfaction, scores show an eight-year improvement trend, all rising above 5 on a 7-point scale for which 1 means "very poor" and 7 means "excellent."

For OMI, protecting the environment is part of its contractual obligation. However, many OMI-managed facilities are model performers. The company has won more than 100 federal and state awards for excellence in the past five years; more than half of these were earned in the last two years.

Exercises

1. A major manufacturer of computers has determined that their new machines will have a constant failure rate of 0.2 per year under normal operating conditions. How long should the warranty be if no more than 5% of the computers are returned to the manufacturer for repair?

2. A company in the service industry gives a one-year, money-back guarantee on their service assuming that only 10% of the time will they have to return money due to an unsatisfied customer. Assuming a constant value, what is the company's failure rate?

3. Working individually or in a team, construct a block diagram for one or more of the following products.

    (a) Flashlight
    (b) Computer mouse
    (c) Home hot-water heater
    (d) Toaster
    (e) Rechargeable drill/driver
    (f) Toddler's toy, such as a walking chair
    (g) Sub-system of your automobile
    (h) Bicycle
    (i) 3-1/2″ floppy disk
    (j) Automobile roof-top rack

4. Working individually or in a team, perform design FMEA on one or more of the following products listed in Exercise 3. Start the design FMEA process by identifying a common failure mode for that product or a potential failure mode. Then, complete the design FMEA form by addressing all categories listed in the form.

5. Perform process FMEA to anticipate what you could do to eliminate any problems while changing a tire. Assume that you have just pulled off to the side of the road and have opened the trunk to remove the jack. Think of the process of replacing the tire and what you can put in place to avoid problems the next time you change a tire. Complete the process FMEA form.

6. Working individually or in a team, perform process FMEA to anticipate what you could do to eliminate any problems in one or more of the following processes.

    (a) Making a pizza
    (b) Sorting and washing five loads of laundry
    (c) Following a recipe for cookies
    (d) Mowing your lawn
    (e) Waking up in the morning and going to work or school

15

Products Liability

Introduction

The marvels of technology have provided needed and useful new products. Competition among manufacturers is a significant motivating factor for providing new and modified products. However, competition sometimes forces the marketing of products before they have been adequately tested. Indeed, unproved technology creates hazards that are unknown prior to product use. Highly diverse and technically-complicated product design has also increased the severity and frequency of injuries. The number of product accidents is roughly estimated at 50 million per year, at an annual cost to the nation of $50 billion.[1] Thus, there is a need to reduce the risk of injuries and to compensate injured consumers.

Consumers are initiating lawsuits in record numbers as a result of injury, death, and property damage from faulty product design or faulty product workmanship. The number of product liability lawsuits has skyrocketed since 1965. Jury verdicts in favor of the injured party have continued to rise in recent years. The size of the judgment or settlement has also increased significantly, which has caused an increase in product liability insurance. Although the larger manufacturers have been able to absorb the judgment or settlement cost and pass the cost on to the consumer, smaller manufacturers have occasionally been forced into bankruptcy. Although injured consumers must be compensated, it is also necessary to maintain viable manufacturing entities.

The reasons for product injuries fall generally into three areas—the behavior or knowledge of a product user, the environment where the product is used, and whether the factory has designed and constructed the product carefully using safety analysis and quality control. Due to the varying environments and product users' capacities and habits, it is difficult to devise an adequate safety program to reduce injury. Changing human behavior and environments, although not impossible, is more difficult than changing manufacturing design and improving quality control. Reducing the risk of injury is best

---

[1] See the CPSC's Annual Reports and the National Safety Council's annual editions of *Accident Facts* (these estimates include injuries from toxic substances).

accomplished by stimulating manufacturing creativity. As a result, the law has placed great responsibility upon manufacturers for injuries attributable to defective products.

There are reasons why the manufacturers' liability for product injury has increased. Manufacturers are in the best position to know what are the safest designs, materials, construction methods, and modes of use. Because of the complex designs of products, consumers often lack the information to decide rationally among the risks inherent in them. Consumers expect manufacturers to design products with safety as a priority. Consumers can choose stereos for their cars, but they depend on the manufacturer to select the appropriate tire design and pressure so that an automobile is reasonably stable. Indeed, manufacturers promulgate the risk of product injury by placing products on the market and have the means to spread the cost of injury by appropriately pricing products to include all the costs, even the costs of injury.

The safety and quality of products has been steadily improving. Manufacturers have met the challenge admirably: for instance, using safety glass where previously glass shards caused many severe injuries, placing safety guards around lawn mower blades to prevent lacerations and amputations, redesigning hot water vaporizers to reduce the risk of burns to children, and removing sharp edges on car dashboards to minimize secondary collision injuries.

History

Historical records indicate that in ancient times, the producers of grain were liable for the quality of their product. This liability was based on a sample, since it was physically impossible to inspect each and every grain. If the sample was of good quality, the entire shipment was considered to be good; if the sample was of poor quality, the entire shipment was considered to be poor.

By the fourteenth century, sampling inspection of textiles was commonplace. Seals and official stamps were used by producers, wholesalers, and government inspectors to attest to the quality of the goods. Sampling was used rather than 100% inspection because it was not economically feasible to inspect every yard of cloth. Economic damages were awarded to plaintiffs for defective[2] products and, in some cases, damages were awarded for injuries sustained. However, lawsuits were infrequent, because manufactured products were of simple design, handcrafted, and relatively safe to use.

By the middle of the eighteenth century, two concepts had developed that affected products liability for about two centuries. *Caveat emptor* (let the buyer beware) is a concept that resulted from Adam Smith's "invisible hand" theory of commercial regulation. The concept that the purchaser was to take care of his or her own interests has appeal to Americans, who prize individualism and free enterprise. The other legal doctrine is privity of contract, which required that the manufacturer and the injured party have a con-

---

[2] In this chapter, the term *defective* is used instead of the term *nonconforming*, because it is the legal term.

tractual relationship. The customer, under the privity of contract doctrine, could not directly sue the manufacturer for a defective product. Thus, the manufacturer was liable only to the wholesaler, the wholesaler to the retailer, and the retailer to the customer. If the retailer went out of business, the customer had no suit. If the injured party had used the product but was not the purchaser of the product, there could be no suit. For instance, if a husband was injured by a product purchased by his wife, there could be no suit because the husband had not purchased the product, so he did not have privity of contract. Both the *caveat emptor* principle and the privity of contract doctrine fostered the industrial revolution by limiting manufacturers' liability.

Initially, an exception was made to the privity of contract doctrine for inherently or imminently dangerous products such as food, drugs, and firearms. Then in 1916, the *MacPherson v. Buick Motor Company* case marked the beginning of the end of the privity of contract doctrine in other areas of products liability. The court held that the Buick Motor Company was negligent because it failed to inspect a defective wheel purchased from a component part manufacturer before incorporating the wheel in the finished product. The court further held that Buick owed a duty of care and vigilance to those ultimately expected to use the product, the consumer, and not just to the immediate purchaser, the retail dealer. It is now a standard practice in the automotive industry that tires are the only part of the vehicle not warranted by the vehicle manufacturer. It is interesting that the landmark *MacPherson v. Buick Motor Company* case has a similar fact pattern to the Bridgestone/Firestone tire problem that caused accidents, particularly in Ford Explorers.

Product Safety Law

Local, state, and federal laws regulate many products. For instance, many municipalities have adopted building codes that require safety standards for building products. Also, states have enacted various laws to regulate such items as fireworks, toys, life preservers, and mattresses to enhance safety in order to protect their citizenry. Generally, these laws are in response to a local tragedy and have mild administrative sanctions or are not enforced. However, in 1972, a significant federal consumer safety law, the Consumer Product Safety Act (CPSA), was passed.

The purposes of this act are:

1. To protect the public against unreasonable risks of injury associated with consumer products.
2. To assist consumers in evaluating the comparative safety of consumer products.
3. To develop uniform safety standards for consumer products and to minimize conflicting state and local regulations.
4. To promote research and investigation into the causes and prevention of product-related deaths, illnesses, and injuries.

A five-member commission, appointed by the President with the advice and consent of the Senate, administers this act and other similar acts, such as the Refrigerator Safety Act and the Flammable Fabrics Act. The commission is authorized to establish product safety standards relating to performance, composition, design, construction, finishing, labeling, or packaging of products. All consumer products used in and around a household or school or for recreation are covered by the CPSA, except for products administered by other agencies. Exempted products covered by other agencies include cars, boats, airplanes, food, drugs, cosmetics, tobacco, and poisons.

The commission is required to maintain an injury information clearinghouse to collect, investigate, analyze, and disseminate injury data. It may conduct research and investigations on the safety of consumer products. The commission is relying principally on the development of voluntary safety standards; however, conditions may warrant civil or criminal penalties. The act does not provide for any compensation to the injured consumer. Compliance with a consumer product safety rule does not relieve any manufacturer from liability under common law or state legislative law. However, compliance with an applicable federal standard can sometimes be useful evidence that the manufacturer was not negligent in its duties.

Products Liability Law

Products liability law controls the private litigation of product accidents, which provides compensation to the injured party. Products liability law involves the tort law of negligence or strict liability and the contract law of sales or warranty. The liability may arise as a result of a defect in design or manufacturing, improper service, breach of warranty, or negligence in marketing due to improper directions, warnings, or advertising.

In all products liability suits, the plaintiff must prove causation. The plaintiff must prove that the product was substantially responsible for her injury. This can be done by proving that it is more probable than not—or 51% likely—that the product caused the injury.

Negligence is often considered the "classic" theory of products liability. In essence, the manufacturer owes a duty of care to the consumer when constructing and designing products. In order to be compensated, the injured consumer must prove that the manufacturer was careless or lax in its duty and thus produced a defective product that caused injury to the consumer. The negligence case focuses on the manufacturer's conduct.

The doctrine of strict liability provides that one who sells a product in a defective condition that is unreasonably dangerous to a consumer is liable for harm caused to the user or the user's property. The focus in a strict liability suit is whether the product is defective and not whether the manufacturer's conduct was careless. Under the doctrine of strict liability, the injured party must prove that the product was defective and unreasonably dangerous, the defect was present at the time of manufacture, and the defect caused the injury. In addition, almost all courts require the injured party to prove that a safer alternative design was available at the time of manufacture.

Whether the product is considered "defective" is one of the central issues in any products liability case. A manufacturing defect can easily be proved merely by comparing a defective product to a nondefective one by the same manufacturer. However, proving a design defect can be difficult. Some of the factors used by the jury to assess whether a product design is defective and unreasonably dangerous are:

1. The utility of the product.
2. The feasibility and approximate cost of safety improvements.
3. The public's common knowledge of the product's inherent danger.
4. The frequency and severity of injuries that result from the product.
5. The adequacy of instructions and warnings.
6. The environment where the product was used.
7. The consumer's reasonable care in using the product.
8. The age and the condition of the product.

Generally, the agreement between parties to a contract concerning the quality or the safety of a product takes the form of warranties, which are controlled by the Uniform Commercial Code or the law of sales. There are two types of warranties—an express warranty and an implied warranty. An express warranty is a material statement made voluntarily by a manufacturer or merchant in sales brochures or sales talk to induce sales. A consumer who relies upon a false material statement that results in injury can bring an express warranty suit because the product is not what it was expressly stated to be. An implied warranty provides that the product is reasonably fit for the general purpose for which the product was designed. The duty to provide a reasonably fit product is implied by law; thus it is automatically a part of every sales contract made by a merchant and cannot be waived by a private contract agreement.

Defenses

A substantial portion of the trial is spent determining the cause of the accident. The defendant makes every effort to prove that the product was not responsible for the injury. The defendant will attempt to prove that the plaintiff's bad judgment, the plaintiff's failure to maintain the product properly, or the plaintiff's improper use of the product are the causes of the injury. It is also possible that the accident was caused by an alteration or change in the product after it left the manufacturer. The legal theories that can be used to defend a products liability suit are comparative negligence, assumption of risk, misuse, and Statutes of Repose.

Comparative negligence is gaining acceptance even in the strict liability cause of action. Comparative negligence apportions fault and thus a corresponding amount of damages to the injured consumer who has been negligent in the use of a product. For instance, if the jury determined that the cause of the accident was 30% the fault of the consumer due to improper use of the product and 70% the fault of the manufacturer due to unsafe design, then the manufacturer will have to pay only 70% of the damage award. The award is apportioned based upon the degree of negligence or fault of the parties.

Sometimes an organization can defend a products liability suit by proving that the injured consumer assumed the risk of injury. Some courts will not allow an injured consumer to recover if the consumer knew and understood the specific risk and voluntarily exposed herself to the danger, thus taking a calculated risk. Other courts merge the assumption of risk doctrine into comparative negligence and hold that if the product could have been designed to avoid the known danger, then the organization is also held apportionately liable.

Misuse can be another defense. Some courts may completely bar recovery to an injured plaintiff who has misused a product, whereas other courts will consider the misuse as a factor in assessing comparative negligence. Generally, the degree of misuse determines whether it is a factor in assessing comparative negligence or whether it negates recovery.

Some states have enacted Statutes of Repose or allow the "useful life defense." Statutes of Repose provide that if a product does not injure a person within an 8-, 10-, or 12-year period or within the useful life of the product from the date of manufacture, it is presumed to be free from defect unless the injured party can prove otherwise. Sometimes these statutes provide for a complete bar to all products liability actions or a bar just to strict liability actions. The statutes can provide relief to defendants, who are vulnerable to lawsuits decades after manufacture of the product.

Proof and the Expert Witness

Proof that the product was defective at the time of manufacture is frequently difficult, because the product may be entirely or partly destroyed by the accident. Expert testimony may be needed to ascertain when the defect occurred. This testimony will usually follow the line of reasoning that a microscopic flaw, which was present during the manufacturing operation, caused the product to fail at a future date—for instance, the use of "dirty steel" in the manufacturing process.

Expert witnesses are engaged by both sides of the litigation to prove their arguments. The defendant uses the services of expert technical witnesses within the manufacturing organization as well as outside or independent technical experts. Although organization experts are usually more knowledgeable about the product, the independent expert is considered to be less biased.

The first requirement of an expert technical witness is to be technically competent in the area of testimony. Technical competency can be substantiated by impressive credentials, such as education, registration, and technical publications. In addition, the technical witness's personal character must be above reproach. Perhaps the most important requirement of an acceptable technical witness is the ability to communicate with the judge and the jury. The technical expert must be able to explain and teach nontechnical people the technical aspects of the case. Testimony concerning science, product design, and quality control must be given in a simple and truthful manner.

The technical expert and the lawyer will work together to develop an effective case. It is the duty of the expert to apprise the lawyer of the favorable and unfavorable technical aspects of the case. The lawyer has the primary responsibility for litigation strategy, but the litigation strategy should be developed in cooperation with the technical expert.

Other methods of proof include records pertaining to product design, test and inspection results, customer complaints, sales history, and sales literature. Also, the use of quality concepts and systems based on government and industry standards helps to build an effective case.

Financial Loss

Perhaps the largest financial loss is the court judgment. When a judge or a jury reaches a verdict for the plaintiff, the amount of the monetary award is also specified. The award compensates the injured consumer for past and future medical expenses, loss of earning capacity, and past and future physical and mental pain as a result of any permanent disability or disfigurement. If the defendant organization has knowingly or recklessly placed an unsafe product on the market that injures a consumer, punitive damages are awarded. Punitive damages are used to punish a defendant organization for its reckless or knowing disregard for human life and to deter organizations from producing dangerous products for profit. Punitive damages are not available in a strict liability suit or a suit based on contract law. Punitive awards are rare, but they can be quite high. For example, many of the awards Ford Motor Company paid for the Ford Pinto fires were due to punitive damages. Also, the public believes that corporate enterprises have unlimited funds, which tends to make awards generous.

If the defendant loses the case, the effect can be much greater than the loss of one lawsuit. The loss of a lawsuit increases the probability of future successful lawsuits against the same product and the bad publicity decreases consumer sales. The larger enterprises can either absorb the financial loss or pass it on to the customer. However, smaller enterprises may have insufficient assets and/or liability insurance to cover the award and may thus be forced into bankruptcy. This result is unfortunate, because it may adversely affect the competitive nature of a particular product or industry.

Regardless of who wins the lawsuit, the defendant has certain legal expenses. These expenses include the attorneys' fees, technical expert fees, and investigation fees. In addition, at least one organization representative will be present at all times during the trial, which indirectly adds to the expense.

Other financial considerations that may result directly or indirectly from a products liability lawsuit are

1. The cost of increased product liability insurance premiums, especially in high-risk areas such as industrial chemicals and medical devices.
2. The cost of recall, replacement, or repair of a product.
3. The cost of damage to an organization's reputation and customer base.
4. The cost of a hold or delay in production due to a potential defect.
5. The cost of increased quality efforts for prevention or appraisal.

The Future of Products Liability

The Department of Commerce has published a Model Uniform Products Liability Act. The model law provides uniformity, which is likely to stabilize product liability insurance rates, which are set on a country-wide basis. Although the act was never passed by the U.S. Congress, it is offered for voluntary use by the states. Many states have adopted the essence of the act in their case law.

Presently, the growth in products liability cases can be attributed to only a few products—asbestos, the Dalkon shield, and bendectin. The annual average growth in cases since 1981 is 4% per year if those three products are removed. The 4% increase in products liability case filings is commensurate with other civil filings and personal injury cases.[3]

The future challenge in products liability cases is in the area of toxic products, such as asbestos and agent orange. Toxic products present different obstacles than other products. Toxic products often produce chronic diseases with a long latency period, as opposed to an immediate accident injury. Generally, many people have been exposed to toxic products, and the amount of total liability threatens the solvency of a significant number of chemical or drug manufacturers using similar product formulas. The remote risk that a product defect will cause injury in the second or third generation is difficult for a manufacturer to evaluate. The manufacturer has difficulty in estimating the future liability in order to spread the cost when one product causes damage to many people over an extended period of time. Toxic product cases are particularly burdensome on the state and federal judicial system and may be the impetus for a national toxic tort compensation system.

Recently, European legislatures and courts are following U.S. trends in products liability law. U.S. organizations that export to Europe should be aware that strict products liability law is now being adopted in many European states.

---

[3] *Product Liability—Extent of "Litigation Explosion" in Federal Courts Questioned*, Briefing Report to the Subcommittee on Commerce, Consumer Protection and Competitiveness, Committee on Energy and Commerce, House of Representatives. United States General Accounting Office, January 1988.

Prevention[4]

Insurance companies make the initial payments from products liability losses; however, the organization ultimately pays the price. The manufacturer of a consumer product must protect itself against the risk of products liability litigation or at least reduce the risk to a level that will allow a reasonable profit and continued growth. To accomplish this goal, a products liability prevention program is required. Although these programs will vary from corporation to corporation, certain common elements are essential for an effective program.

Organization

To have an effective products liability prevention program, an organizational structure must be established. This structure will be a function of the size of the organization and the talents of available employees. The organizational structure must specify responsibilities and have the necessary authority to achieve those responsibilities. Corporate policies should reflect the prevention concepts that are covered in the remaining pages of this chapter.

A formal product-safety committee should be established, with either a safety engineer or an outside consultant as a member. The function of the committee is to review and coordinate the various activities. Members of the committee should be from the legal, design, manufacturing, marketing, and quality areas, with the safety engineer or other knowledgeable person as the chair. In addition, the chair will (1) maintain liaison with insurance organizations and government regulators, (2) participate in injury cases, (3) maintain the education program, (4) conduct program audits, (5) act as a consultant to functional areas, and (6) keep informed of trends.

If the organization does not have a safety engineer, then one should be selected from within the organization or externally. The selected individual must:

- Have thorough technical knowledge of the products being produced.
- Have a manufacturing background.
- Demonstrate professionalism and diplomacy, both internally and externally.
- Have direct access to senior management.
- Be respected by all.
- Be able to take charge of a project.
- Be a team player.

Once this individual is selected, everyone must be made aware of his or her role. Potential problems such as letters or calls from clients, notification by insurance

---

[4] This section is adapted, with permission, from W. H. Koch, *Products Liability Risk Control*, Technical Paper IQ75-538 (Dearborn, Mich.: Society of Manufacturing Engineers).

companies, or notifications from law firms should be directed to the product safety engineer.[5]

Education

Education is the cornerstone of an effective program. All employees should be made aware of the importance of product safety. An initial effort using available purchased materials, training sessions, and printed materials can educate personnel about the products liability prevention program. As new or transferred employees become part of the organization, they should be exposed to the same educational effort. Employees need to know how to handle first notifications of product-related incidents and curious phone calls regarding possible incidents.

Some form of continuing education is part of the plan of action. Information such as changes in state and national law, results of relevant lawsuits, and feedback on product audits is especially important to disseminate to employees.

New-Product Review

New products are more likely to be involved in products liability litigation than well-established products; therefore, a special review is required before the product can be released to manufacturing. This review is the organization's first and least expensive chance to identify and correct problems. The safety of the consumer is the paramount consideration in the review process, with function, cost, and sales appeal being of secondary importance. In other words, product safety is one of the design parameters. Quality and engineering personnel need to learn how their products perform under conditions that (1) are adverse, (2) have previously been considered abusive, and (3) a plaintiff's attorney will consider reasonably foreseeable.

Product-safety design techniques should be adopted. Some of these techniques are (1) Failure Mode and Effect Analysis (FMEA), (2) fault-free analysis, (3) fail-safe concepts, (4) Weibull and other test data analysis, (5) safety symbol for safety-oriented product characteristics, and (6) coded identification for traceability.

A written description of the product by the designer is the starting point for the review process. This description includes the intended use of the product, expected life, probable failure, limiting design parameters, service environment, development tests, and final acceptance criteria. The design and development of the product are thoroughly documented.

A product review team is established that has no preconceived notions about the product. The review team evaluates the product's compliance with present and foreseeable industry and government standards, as well as applicable codes, laws, and regulations.

---

[5] Randall Goodden, "Reduce the Potential Impact of Product Liability on Your Organization," *Quality Progress* (January 1995): 85–88.

Customer requirements and a customer's known or anticipated end use of the item are also reviewed. In addition, the team reviews any past injury data of related products. A general list of possible hazards to look for by the product review team is:

Crushing hazards.

Shearing hazards.

Cutting hazards.

Entanglement hazards.

Drawing-in or trapping hazards.

Impact hazards.

Puncture hazards.

Abrasion hazards.

Exposed live part—electrical hazards.

Electrostatic exposure.

Thermo hazards (exposed high temperature parts).

Noise hazards (exposed to high sound frequencies).

Exposure to gases or fumes hazards.

Fire or explosion hazards.

Unexpected start-up hazards.[6]

If the above list had been consulted, the following products liability case against a company that manufactures range hoods for above the stove may not have been filed. In this products liability case, two young brothers were fighting in the kitchen when one suddenly pushed the other into the sharp edge of the range hood, causing a massive head injury.

The attorney acknowledged that his client was involved in horseplay at the time of the accident, but stated that the mother could have been walking around in the kitchen, lost her balance and hit her own head on the sharp projecting corner of the range hood, and suffered the same massive head injury. It isn't the actions that are to be blamed, but the hazard the range hood poses. In cross-examination of the manufacturer's design, the engineers' counsel for the plaintiff asked, "Would it have cost any more for you to have manufactured a rounded edge on the range hood, versus the sharp pointed edge shown on the product in question?" The designer replied, "No." The attorney asked, "Would a rounded edge on the product have affected the performance of the range hood in any manner?" Once again the designer answered, "No." Counsel for the plaintiff won the case based on defective design, and reasonably foreseeable risk of harm.[7]

---

[6] Adapted from *Product Liability Prevention—A Strategic Guide,* Randall L. Goodden, © 2000 by American Society for Quality 99.

[7] Ibid., 100.

It is frequently impossible to design a product economically with zero safety incidents. In these situations, the unsafe area is guarded or protected from injury exposure. Product defects can, in some situations, be designed to occur in such a manner that a disabling injury does not occur. If it is not possible or practical to design and/or guard against an injury exposure, then adequate warnings by word, color, or illustration should be permanently attached to the product.

Customer-oriented tests are performed to predict the misuse of the product. Designers test a product to determine if it performs as intended when correctly used. A customer-oriented test tries to determine what happens when the product is misused. Consideration is given to the wide variance in the physical and mental ability of *all* potential customers. Documentation of tests should be accomplished in such a manner that additional legal risks are not created.

Because minor design and material changes to an existing product can cause disabling injury, the same type of review is necessary for any and all changes. Design control is a requirement of ISO 9000.

Initial Production Review

The new product review is usually based on hand-built prototypes. Therefore, a subsequent review is necessary on the first production items to determine if any defects are encountered that did not materialize in the prototypes. For an inherently hazardous product, a limited production run and controlled distribution are recommended. From this limited sample, meaningful information can be obtained from customers while the liability risk exposure is minimal.

The production review evaluates the manufacturing plan to determine the adequacy of:

Failure Mode and Effect Analysis (FMEA).

Tooling and work-holding devices.

Production machinery.

Materials handling.

Test equipment.

Inspection system.

Sampling plan.

Packaging and shipping.

Operating instructions.

Safety warnings.

Advanced service information for distributors and dealers.

All personnel who are active in the initial production-review process can informally evaluate the product design for safety. The more people evaluating a product for safety, the greater the likelihood that a potential liability exposure will be detected before the product is sold in the marketplace. Process control is a requirement of ISO 9000.

Periodic Production Audits

Most manufacturing organizations periodically perform production audits to verify or validate the effectiveness of the quality control system. Production audits are a requirement of ISO 9000. These audits can be extended to evaluate the safety parameters. The audit should be performed on recently manufactured products, or products that have been through the distribution system, and products that have been in customer use for a substantial period of time. Inspection and testing of the product is based on a simulation of the customer's activities. Feedback from the audit is sent to the product safety committee.

Control of Warranties, Advertisements, Agreements, and the Like

The products liability prevention program must continually review the warranty, advertising literature, dealer agreements, catalogs, and technical publications. The review should include

1. A check to determine that the terms and conditions of sale are limited to a statement of merchantability, which means that the product is of good material and workmanship. The use of such phrases as *safe* and *ensures the safety of the operator* are to be avoided. If the product is referred to as "safe" and a person is injured, that action establishes that the product is defective.

2. An analysis by legal counsel of all advertising copy, sales brochures, promotional literature, and technical reports and presentations.

3. An examination of purchase orders to determine the acceptability of any special warranty provisions.

4. An analysis of dealer distributorship and franchise agreements to determine the handling of "defective" items. These agreements are allowed in court and can constitute an admission that the organization manufactures "defective" products.

5. A check to determine that the words *nonconformity* and *nonconforming unit* have been used where appropriate.

6. An evaluation of the cost problems of warranties, such as:

    -   Identifying and measuring significant variables affecting warranty costs.
    -   Measuring costs of warranting product reliability.
    -   Determining the different product characteristics.
    -   Determining the type of warranty service to be provided.[8]

---

[8] Richard L. Patterson, "Product Warranties," *Quality Progress* (August 1987): 43–45.

Warning Labels and Instructions[9]

A major insurance company conducted a study of random product liability cases and determined that the largest cause of manufacturer's negligence was inadequate or nonexistent warnings. See Figure 15-1 for a breakdown of product liability causes.

It seems that much time and effort is put into the engineering of a new product, and such things as warnings and operating instructions are given to a lesser-ranked individual to supervise. Engineers may in fact not be the best individuals to write the warnings and instructions. Engineers can become so familiar with the product that they feel the dangers are common knowledge among end users and do not need to be expressly stated. Many products now being used by the general public were once only being used by professionals with much training. The language engineers use to write the warnings and instructions may be too technical. It may be helpful to have someone with no technical knowledge write the warnings and instructions along with someone who has expertise with the product. It would be unwise to overlook the level of knowledge the average user possesses. These warnings and instructions should be well thought out and written and presented with care.

Many courts presume that if an adequate warning had been given, the user would have read and heeded the warning. A product is not defective when it has a warning, that if followed, makes the product safe to use. Warnings need to be placed in an area where they will be noticed and understood by the end user. The American National Standards Institute has issued guidelines for the design of product safety signs and labels. The guidelines use specific colors, design, and content. According to the American National

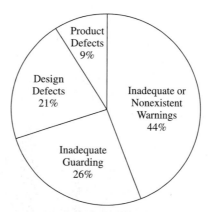

Figure 15-1 **Breakdown of Product Liability Causes**

[9] Adapted from *Product Liability Prevention—A Strategic Guide,* Randall L. Goodden, © 2000 by American Society for Quality 103–119.

Standards Institute, a product safety sign must alert persons to the type of hazard, the degree of hazard seriousness, the consequence of involvement with the hazard, and how to avoid the hazard. The use of a picture or symbol is not required by the guidelines but is highly recommended. A picture or symbol can be helpful to users who are illiterate or do not speak English. See Figure 15-2 for an example of a pictorial warning.

Warnings and instructions are not necessarily the same. Manufacturers must understand how to separate warnings from instructions. A warning calls attention to danger, whereas an instruction prescribes procedures for efficient use of the product and also for avoiding danger. A manufacturer may provide an instruction but fail to provide a warning that alerts the user to the danger. A manufacturer may provide a warning but fail to provide an instruction that will enable the user to avoid the danger. Both a warning and instruction must be provided. The warnings and instructions should be individual to each product and not generically written for many products in a product line. Lastly, warnings should not be overdone, because overuse of warnings would dilute the importance of the message. For instance, a warning label is not needed on every step on a ladder. See Figure 15-3 for the difference between a warning and an instruction.

Complaints and Claims

A complaint or a claim is a communication between the marketplace and the organization concerning the performance of the product. This information serves to alert the

Figure 15-2 Pictorials and Symbols
Reprinted, with permission, from *Product Liability Prevention—A Strategic Guide,* Randall Goodden, © 2000 by ASQ Quality Press 114.

Figure 15-3 Warning and Safety Instructions
Reprinted, with permission, from *Product Liability Prevention—A Strategic Guide,* Randall Goodden,
© 2000 by ASQ Quality Press 115.

manufacturer to the need for corrective action. A Pareto analysis of complaints can lead to a change in product design or manufacturing that will reduce the exposure to disabling injuries.

The investigation of bodily injury or property damage claims or product-safety complaints should be acted upon quickly. Usually, the notice of a claim or complaint is given to a dealer, distributor, or employee. This initial notice is sent to the proper department for action. The product safety engineer, as well as the insurance company, reviews the situation and determines:

The cause of the claim or complaint.

The nature and seriousness of the injury, if one has occurred.

The failure mode that caused the situation, if there was one.

The age of the defect and whether it was present when the product was sold.

The negligence of the parties.

An early investigation can lead to quick settlement of reasonable claims or the preparation of defenses for those claims that may require litigation.

The complaint and claim procedure should make provision for notifying the appropriate departments, depending on the seriousness of the claim. It may even be necessary to implement the product-recall plan. Corrective action is a requirement of ISO 9000.

Retention of Records and Document Control

The defense of a products liability lawsuit necessitates the availability of design, production, and sales records. Particular types of records that should be retained are:

Product development and test records.

Results of process, product, and system inspection and audits.

Records of verbal and written communications with customers relative to requirements, product application, nonstandard materials, and claims.

Original design data.

Service-life data.

Acceptance and approvals by government agencies, customers, or independent testing organizations.

Critical raw material acceptance records.

Records are maintained in such a manner that the material or product can be traced to a given shipment, operator, machine, time, and so on.

Records must be protected from loss by storage in fireproof cabinets and by having duplicate sets. The question of how long records should be retained is based on a number of considerations. Often, records are maintained for the expected useful life of the product plus 18 years, in order to cover the time when an injured minor could bring a lawsuit upon reaching the legal age of majority. Other retention considerations are the inherent risk of the product, the need for records critical to the defense, and the method of storage. A record retention procedure is a requirement of ISO 9000. One sample retention period for records is shown in the following table:

TABLE 15-1
Sample Retention Periods[10]

Record Type	Retention Period
Audit records	3 years
Blueprints (obsolete)	10 years
Blueprint revision records	7 years
Correspondence (general)	1 year
Correspondence (general, customers, and suppliers)	1 year
Customer product complaints	3 years
Customer (supplied) product specifications	10 years
Design reliability verification lab test reports	10 years
Design review meeting minutes	3 years
Insurance policies (expired)	5 years
Internal reports	3 years
Inventory records	7 years
Invoices	7 years
New product introduction minutes	3 years
Procedures (obsolete)	5 years
Process instructions (obsolete)	5 years
Production inspection and audit reports	3 years
Product test reports (daily)	3 years
Purchase orders	7 years
Receiving records	1 year
Sales records	7 years
Scrap records	1 year
Shipping and distribution records	3 years
Supplier performance evaluations	1 year
Supplier rejected material reports	1 year

Documents should be centrally controlled instead of in individual files where one employee may keep a document for one year and another employee may keep a document for fifteen years. Also, documents should be worded properly to deal with delicate management issues and decisions. Memos should objectively state the issue and the resolution of

---

[10] Ibid., 124.

the issue. To avoid the "smoking gun" document, memos should not be written in haste or in anger. Another consideration of document control is to determine who has access to certain data. Sometimes data is restricted and does not get to the internal quality auditors. Efforts need to be made to get this information to those who can improve the quality system.[11]

ISO 9000 Documents

A product liability lawsuit represents the ultimate quality failure of a product. Plaintiff attorneys are increasingly using certified quality management programs to create the perception that any manufacturer not using certified quality management programs is negligent. A manufacturer without a formal quality program is viewed as negligent in its internal efforts to prevent product defects.[12] Again, the ISO 9000 documents should be prepared carefully. The Eastern District Court of Arkansas recently ordered Case Corp. to furnish its ISO 9000 materials to the lawyers of several plaintiffs in liability lawsuits against the farm machine manufacturer. The farmers' attorneys claim that if Case followed ISO procedures, all nonconformances should have been documented. ISO procedures require Case to conduct design validation and take corrective action for non-conformances that should be reviewed by management with executive responsibility. The plaintiffs want to show that Case failed to conform to the requirements of its own quality manual and was thereby negligent.

Product-Recall Plan

The cost of recalling a product varies significantly with the type of product and the quantities involved. The costs can be substantial and have forced more than one organization into bankruptcy. An effective recall contingency plan helps to minimize the recall costs and the products liability risk.

Once notification of a defective product is received, the organization must decide whether or not to recall all products suspected of having the defective condition. This decision is based on three factors:

1. The maximum exposure to personal injury or property damage if the product is not recalled. This determination will be based on the pattern of defect, the quantity involved, the severity of the risk, and the cost of the recall.

2. The form of communication (radio, TV, newspaper, telephone, and registered letter) used to contact the users of the product.

3. Determining if the product will be repaired or replaced or if the customer will be reimbursed.

---

[11] Randall Goodden, "How a Good Quality Management System Can Limit Lawsuits," *Quality Progress* (June 2001): 55–59.

[12] Ibid.

If the defective condition is classified as a substantial product hazard, the Consumer Product Safety Commission may order the manufacturer to take specific action. In such a case, the decision is made for the manufacturer.

When a recall is required, it is extremely important to identify those units with the defective condition and correlate this identification with the applicable manufacturing records. This type of identification is referred to as *traceability*. The traceability of a product can have a decided influence on whether 100 or 10,000 units are recalled. For some products, the expiration date is also important. Traceability is a requirement of ISO 9000.

Subrogation

Part of a products liability prevention program involves the raw material, component parts, and subassembly suppliers. The same elements of evaluation and safety criteria that are applicable to the buyer are applicable to the supplier. A visit to the supplier's plant and an audit of its prevention program is a necessity. The supplier should also visit the buyer's plant to evaluate product safety exposure of the raw material, component part, or subassembly.

All communication between supplier and buyer concerning defective raw materials, component parts, and subassembly are made in writing. The buyer advises the supplier of all relevant product safety information, such as complaints, audits, warranties, and product reviews. Purchasing oversight is a requirement of ISO 9000.

Risk Criteria

If an organization manufactures a broad range of products, it usually has a range of potential product liability loss. Some products, for inherent reasons, pose a much greater risk than others; therefore, products are evaluated based on certain individual risk criteria. The degree of prevention control is then based on the degree of potential liability loss. This technique enables an organization to exert its maximum preventive effort on those vital few products where it is most needed. Failure Mode and Effect Analysis is an excellent starting point from which dollar values can be estimated.

Standards

All prevention programs, especially those of large corporations, should involve employees in the development of design and manufacturing standards. Because manufacturers have the most to lose from stringent, unrealistic standards, their employees should be involved in professional groups that develop standards. Also, the organization's legal staff should be actively involved in the evolution of products liability law.

Audit

Periodic audits of the prevention program are absolutely essential to determine whether or not the program is operating satisfactorily. These audits are, for the most part, system audits, which operate in much the same manner as audits of the total quality system. Periodic audits are useful tools for measuring progress and for providing feedback to improve the prevention program. The audits are scheduled and performed by internal organization personnel or knowledgeable external people. Results of the audit are written and circulated within the organization. Audits are a requirement of ISO 9000.

Customer Service

The customer service activity can have a great deal of influence on the effectiveness of the prevention program. By making friends rather than enemies, the likelihood of a lawsuit is substantially reduced. Customer service should report observations on how the product is being used or misused and any near misses. Also, if a repair activity is involved, it must be subjected to the same requirements as the initial production.

Redress

Customers will usually accept failures if there is redress that requires:

A warranty policy that responds to customer needs.

The availability of information concerning the redress procedure.

Prompt handling of complaints, returns, and claims.

Repair facilities that give prompt, skilled, and fair-priced service.

Organizations can improve customer loyalty through an effective redress policy.

Resources are limited; therefore, the perfect product is, in many cases, an unattainable goal. In the long term, customers pay for the cost of regulations and lawsuits. It is appropriate to mention the old cliché, "An ounce of prevention is worth a pound of cure." An adequate prevention program can substantially reduce the risk of damaging litigation.

TQM Exemplary Organization[13]

Operating three manufacturing facilities with a total of 380 employees, Sunny Fresh Foods (SFF) of Monticello, MN manufactures and distributes more than 160 different types of egg-based food products to more than 1,200 U.S. foodservice operations, such as quick service restaurants, schools, hospitals, convenience stores, and food processors. Products include refrigerated and frozen liquid pasteurized eggs and scrambled egg mixes, zero-cholesterol and fat-free egg products, omelets and other pre-cooked frozen entrees, and peeled hard-cooked eggs.

---

[13] Malcolm Baldrige National Quality Award, 1999 Small Business Category Recipient, NIST/Baldrige Homepage, Internet.

SFF refers to its workers as "stakeholders," an acknowledgment of their integral role. And it makes sure that these stakeholders share in the benefits of continuous improvement. For example, the base pay level is set at slightly below the industry midpoint for salaried stakeholders, but incentives can increase earnings to above the 75th percentile. In addition, an extensive reward and recognition system—from monetary rewards for exemplary safety performance to an extra vacation day for quality achievements—also helps to motivate employees to contribute to the organization's progress toward its improvement goals. Production employees rotate workstations every 20 minutes to prevent repetitive stress injuries and boredom and to reinforce quality processes.

Action plans, along with performance measures for each, are aligned with SFF's six key business drivers: work process improvement, competitive advantage, positive work experience, customer focus and satisfaction, supplier relationships and performance, and support services. This serves as the basis for the annual operating plan, including key indicators for tracking progress toward each performance improvement target.

Key Indicator Reports assess short-term organizational performance, tying it to SFF's core values, key strategies, and long-term goals. These weekly reports display critical performance measures and are analyzed for trends to identify opportunities and areas requiring corrective actions. In monthly management-team reviews and quarterly business reviews, these indicators are summarized in a "balanced scorecard," a progress update viewed from the perspective of SFF's six key business drivers.

Innovations, a near perfect record for on-time delivery, and high levels of customer satisfaction have helped SFF to earn sole-supplier status from several major national restaurant chains. Many customers also have recognized SFF's superior performance with supplier awards.

In its 1999 customer survey, SFF earned scores of 100% on three of its five key indicators of satisfaction—on-time delivery, technical support, and customer service access. Scores on the other two indicators—product performance and product freshness—topped 90%. Not coincidentally, claims filed by customers have dropped precipitously from initially low levels to substantially better than six sigma levels of quality.

Return on gross investment has tripled over the last five years; annual increases in operating profits have averaged 25% over the last five years. Total waste was reduced 21% while production volume grew 10% from fiscal year 1996–1997 to fiscal year 1997–1998.

Exercises

1. Write a warning label or operating instructions for the following products:

    (a) Trampoline
    (b) In-line skates

(c) Cars
(d) Power saw
(e) Fireworks
(f) A book on diet or a diet drink
(g) Electric curlers
(h) Swimming pool

2. Should the products given in Exercise 1 be marketed, or are they unreasonably dangerous?

3. Do those who smoke cigarettes or drink alcohol assume the risk of getting lung or liver disease? Do those who jump on a trampoline assume the risk of falling off? Explain your answer.

4. How can the products given in Exercise 1 be designed either to prevent or to minimize customer misuse of the product? For example, a circuit breaker could be attached to the electrical cord of curlers to prevent electrical shock if the customer uses the curlers near a bathtub or sink. Is the cost of the safety improvement feasible?

5. Devise a products liability prevention program tailored to meet the needs of one of the products from Exercise 1. Organize the program to include education, new-product and production review, and a product-recall plan.

6. Devise a compensation plan for injured users where the product defect manifests itself in the second or third generation, such as when a man or woman takes a prescribed drug that injures their future children.

16

Total Productive Maintenance

Introduction

Good maintenance is fundamental to a productive manufacturing system; try running a production line with faulty equipment. Total Productive Maintenance (TPM) is keeping the current plant and equipment at its highest productive level through cooperation of all areas of the organization. Generally, the first task is to break down the traditional barriers between maintenance and production personnel so they are working together. Individuals working together without regard to organizational structure, using their skills and ingenuity, have a common objective—peak performance or total productivity.

This approach does not mean that such basic techniques as predictive and preventative maintenance are not used; they are essential to building a foundation for a successful TPM environment. Predictive maintenance is the process of using data and statistical tools to determine when a piece of equipment will fail, and preventative maintenance is the process of periodically performing activities such as lubrication on the equipment to keep it running.

The total maintenance function should be directed towards the elimination of unplanned equipment and plant maintenance. The objective is to create a system in which all maintenance activities can be planned and not interfere with the production process. Surprise equipment breakdowns should not occur. Before the advent of computer-aided manufacturing, operators in some organizations were responsible for their machines and took a certain pride of ownership. With the help of maintenance technicians, operators spent part of their work time keeping their equipment in good running order. Recent technical advances have given us more tools to perform the maintenance function.

Analyzing TPM into its three words, we have:

Total = All encompassing by maintenance and production individuals working together.

Productive = Production of goods and services that meet or exceed customers' expectations.

Maintenance = Keeping equipment and plant in as good as or better than the original condition at all times.

The overall goals of TPM are:

1. Maintaining and improving equipment capacity.
2. Maintaining equipment for life.
3. Using support from all areas of the operation.
4. Encouraging input from all employees.
5. Using teams for continuous improvement.

Organizations that apply principles (programs in) of total quality management, failure mode effect analysis, employee involvement, continuous improvement, just-in-time manufacturing, statistical process control, and experimental design, to name a few, cannot be successful without also paralleling the principles (program in) total quality management.[1] For example, when equipment downtime and equipment failures are not regular, how can a company implement just-in-time manufacturing? Or, how can organizations practice employee involvement when machine operators or people in the maintenance department are not part of the team and encouraged to report problems?

The Plan

The first activity in any assessment of performance is to determine the current operating parameters. Where are we today? What systems do we have in place, and how do they work? What is the current condition of the plant and equipment? Are we starting from scratch, or do we have workable systems that only need to be improved?

Total Productive Maintenance (TPM) is an extension of the Total Quality Management (TQM) philosophy to the maintenance function. Seven basic steps get an organization started toward TPM:

1. Management learns the new philosophy.
2. Management promotes the new philosophy.

---

[1] Eugene Sprow, "TPM—Good for Everyone," *Manufacturing Engineering* (April 1995): 12.

3. Training is funded and developed for everyone in the organization.

4. Areas of needed improvement are identified.

5. Performance goals are formulated.

6. An implementation plan is developed.

7. Autonomous work groups are established.

There is no single correct method for implementation; however, these steps will provide a good framework.

Learning the New Philosophy

One of the most difficult things for senior management to deal with is change. They need to learn about TPM and how it will affect their operations. There are many successful examples; there are also many organizations that have tried various techniques to improve performance and failed. Benchmarking with a successful organization will provide valuable information.

Any cultural change takes a special dedication, by management to provide long-term, top to bottom support for improvement. The easy approach is to accept today's good performance numbers and say, "Why change?" The answer is to gain a competitive edge and to increase profits. Many of an organization's competitors are most likely improving and will be far ahead of other non-changing organizations in the future. There also exists, in management, the concept that somehow because "I am the chief, I know more than those who work here."

TPM is merely trying to tap into an unused resource, the brain power and problem-solving ability of all the organization's employees. Thus, it is necessary to allow people to make decisions. This approach is not permissive management, because management is still responsible for the performance of the organization. It does, however, represent a different way of managing.

Many organizations have had the flavor-of-the-month approach to changing management techniques. This approach has led to credibility problems with employees. Management is changed and the new manager does not build on past accomplishments but develops a "new system" that will presumably solve all of the organization's problems. Lack of ownership seems to cause low morale and dissatisfaction with management. Ownership should be based on what is good for the customer and for the employees that serve the customer. A look at approaches at Southwest Airlines or Hewlett Packard helps to understand what needs to be done. These organizations, and others, emphasize employee well-being and empowerment. It is difficult to argue with their performance numbers.

Initially this change will require more work by management. Eventually, it will mean less work as all individuals start solving their own problems.

Promoting the Philosophy

Senior management must spend significant time in promoting the system. They must sell the idea and let the employees know that they are totally committed to its success. Like TQM or any other major change in an organization, there must be total commitment from the top. If the belief in the new philosophy and commitment are not there, then positive results will not happen. Too often lip service is given to a "new idea." This action is usually brought on by a belief that the new system will solve some immediate problems and lead to an immediate return on investment. A long-term commitment to the new philosophy is required. It has been proven by other organizations to be a better way of doing business.[2]

Management should lead the way by practicing the new philosophy. Organizations that are having difficulties owe it, in part, to insincere leadership. One of the best ways to implement the new philosophy is just to start doing it. In other words, start giving the maintenance and production personnel more autonomy. Once the employees realize that management is serious about taking the organization in a new, more positive direction, employees usually respond. Introducing TPM with a huge fanfare leads employees to shrug it off as the latest method for getting them to work harder. Management must first build credibility, and the best way to accomplish that task is to change first and lead the way.

Training

Teach the philosophy to managers at all levels. Begin with senior management, and work down to first-line supervisors.

Don't just teach the HOW: also teach the WHY. Senior management must spend time learning about and understanding the ramifications of applying this philosophy to their organization. Is senior management dedicated to the long-term commitment required to achieve positive results? Some managers may need to be replaced or take early retirement because they will not change their way of dealing with people. Those managers who readily respond to the new philosophy should also be identified.

Middle management must learn how to deal with the team approach and become familiar with how small autonomous work groups function. This organizational level seems to have the greatest difficulty with this type of change. In recent years, downsizing has come at the expense of middle managers. Of course, historically this has been an inflated area of management. The philosophies that are promoted within TPM and TQM do lead to flatter management structures. When you allow people to make their own

---

[2] Seiichi Nakajima, *Total Productive Maintenance* (Productivity Press Inc., 1988).

decisions, you do not need as many layers of managers making sure employees are doing their job correctly.

First-line supervisors need to learn their role in what most likely will be a new environment. Supervisors who have been used to guiding their groups will find this an easy transition. The day of the autocratic manager has disappeared. Those managers who have been telling employees everything to do will find this difficult. Supervisors will relinquish some of their power, although that power may be more perceived than actual. A highly-educated workforce does not tolerate that management style. In reality, a supervisor is only as good as their ability to coach their team.

Employees need to learn about the various tools used in performing their tasks as part of an autonomous work group. There needs to be some instruction in the area of jobs that maintenance people do and jobs that production people do. A great benefit of TPM is the cross-pollination of ideas between maintenance technicians and production operators.

Improvement Needs

There are usually some machines that seem to be on the verge of breaking down or require an excessive amount of maintenance. Employees who work with the equipment on a daily basis are better able to identify these conditions than anyone else in the organization. A good first step is to let the operators and maintenance technicians tell management which machines and systems need the most attention. An implementation team of operators and technicians to coordinate this process is essential. This action will build credibility and start the organization towards TPM.

One of the first steps for the team is to identify the current status. In other words, what is the baseline? The following measurements were developed by the Japanese and are accepted by most practitioners.

Six major loss areas need to be measured and tracked:

Downtime Losses

1. Planned

   a. Start-ups

   b. Shift changes

   c. Coffee and lunch breaks

   d. Planned maintenance shutdowns

2. Unplanned Downtime

   a. Equipment breakdown

   b. Changeovers

   c. Lack of material

Reduced Speed Losses

3. Idling and minor stoppages

4. Slow-downs

Poor Quality Losses

5. Process nonconformities

6. Scrap

These losses can be quantified into three metrics and can be summarized into one equipment effectiveness metric. Equations for these metrics follow.

Downtime losses are measured by equipment availability using the equation

$$A = \left(\frac{T}{P}\right) \times 100$$

where A = availability
T = operating time (P − D)
P = planned operating time
D = downtime

Reduced speed losses are measured by tracking performance efficiency using the equation

$$E = \left(\frac{C \times N}{T}\right) \times 100$$

where E = performance efficiency
C = theoretical cycle time
N = processed amount (quantity)

Poor quality losses are measured by tracking the rate of quality products produced using the equation

$$R = \left(\frac{N - Q}{N}\right) \times 100$$

where R = rate of quality products
N = processed amount (quantity)
Q = nonconformities

Equipment effectiveness is measured as the product of the decimal equivalent of the three previous metrics using the equation

$$EE = A \times E \times R$$

where EE = equipment effectiveness, or overall equipment effectiveness (OEE)

The target for improvement is 85% equipment effectiveness.

EXAMPLE PROBLEM

Last week's production numbers on machining center JL58 were as follows:

Scheduled operation = 10 hours/day; 5 days/week

Manufacturing downtime due to meetings, material outages, training, breaks, and so forth
 = 410 minutes/week

Maintenance downtime scheduled and equipment breakdown = 227 minutes/week

Theoretical (standard) cycle time = 0.5 minutes/unit

Production for the week = 4450 units

Defective parts made = 15 units

P = 10 hours/day $\times$ 5 days/week $\times$ 60 minutes/hour = 3000 minutes/week

D = 410 minutes/week + 227 minutes/week = 637 minutes/week

$T = (P - D) = 3000 - 637 = 2363$ minutes

$$A = \left(\frac{T}{P}\right) \times 100$$
$$= \left(\frac{2363}{3000}\right) \times 100$$
$$= 78.8\%$$

$$E = \left(\frac{C \times N}{T}\right) \times 100$$
$$= \left(\frac{0.5 \times 4450}{2363}\right) \times 100$$
$$= 94.2\%$$

$$R = \left(\frac{N - Q}{N}\right) \times 100$$
$$= \left(\frac{4450 - 15}{4450}\right) \times 100$$
$$= 99.7\%$$

$$EE = A \times E \times R$$
$$= 0.788 \times 0.942 \times 0.997$$
$$= 0.740 \text{ or } 74.0\%$$

Clearly the equipment availability should be improved to reach the goal of 85% equipment effectiveness.

Goal

Goals should be set after the improvement needs are identified. A good first goal is to establish the timeframe for fixing the first prioritized problem. Technicians and operators will probably want it done faster than management because it causes them more problems on a daily basis. Identifying needs and setting goals begins the process of getting the organization to work together as a team.

Developing Plans

First, develop and implement an overall plan of action for training all employees. Plans for developing the autonomous work groups should take place during the training phase.

Plan to use teams of maintenance technicians and operators to work on particularly troublesome problems. Priorities can be set and management can make a commitment with resources to correct some of the basic problems. Using the team approach will set the stage for the development of autonomous work groups, which are teams established for daily operations. At this point, employees should have input into how these autonomous teams are structured.

Part of the planning process should take into consideration that autonomous work groups will change over time. As processes and procedures are improved, the structure of the whole organization will change. It would be unreasonable not to expect autonomous work groups to change also.

Autonomous Work Groups

Autonomous work groups are established based on the natural flow of activity. First, make the operator responsible for the equipment and the level of maintenance that he is capable of performing. Next, identify the maintenance personnel who work in certain areas or have certain skill levels. Operators and maintenance personnel are brought together, resulting in an autonomous work group. These groups must have the authority to make decisions about keeping the equipment in first-class running order.

The structure of autonomous work groups will vary with different applications and types of industries. The team approach given in Chapter 4, Employee Involvement, provides the necessary information to determine the structure.

Maintenance technicians are also consultants to the operating personnel. They train operators in how to do certain tasks, such as oiling, minor troubleshooting, and set-ups.

The overall goal of the autonomous work group is to reduce the occasions for maintenance activity. A side benefit is freeing up highly skilled maintenance technicians from the more mundane routine tasks. Skilled technicians are utilized more effectively in doing major overhauls and assisting with troubleshooting problems that the autonomous work group cannot handle.

Summary

The seven-step plan outlined in this chapter provides a framework to establish TPM. It should be modified to meet different organizational needs. An effective total productive maintenance program will lead to improved quality and productivity and, of course, an improved bottom line.

Examples

There are numerous examples of organizations employing total productive maintenance to empower their production workers and to save time and money on maintenance. The following examples give a wide range of organizations that applied total productive maintenance.

1. The U.S. Postal Service of Albany, New York used total productive maintenance to save $86,000 annually by standardizing procedures and reducing the use of outside contractors for vehicle work.[3] Based on their revision of maintenance procedures, 11 other facilities in the Northeast are changing their practices, and $4.5 million could be saved if 179 sites nationwide also change their practices. Because of their efforts, the U.S. Postal Service of Albany, New York was a 2000 RIT/USA Today Quality Cup finalist.

2. Yamato Kogyo Corp. of Japan, a motorcycle control-cable maker, received a total productive maintenance award from Yamaha Corp. in the 1990s.[4] Using total productive maintenance, they improved productivity by 130%, cut accidents by 90%, reduced

---

[3] 2000 RIT/USA Today Quality Cup.

[4] David A. Turnbide, "Japan's New Advantage: Total Productive Maintenance," *Quality Progress* (March 1995): 121–123.

defects by 95%, and increased the employee suggestion rate by over 300% to 5 per employee per month.

3. A team of workers at Kadena Air Base in Japan won the 1995 RIT/USA Today Quality Cup for government by using total productive maintenance to reduce the failure rate of AIM-9 missiles from 102 per month to 15 or less per month.[5] After the multi-disciplinary team brainstormed the missile malfunctions and repairs, they focused on the argon gas used to cool the missile as the source of the problems. Results of the team's total productive maintenance program included: repair after a missile fails to launch the first time; technicians verify that the argon bottles seal properly; fit all argon bottles with new $0.13 O-ring seals; train pilots to describe malfunctions to technicians; and begin tracking repairs on the metal probes to which the argon bottle attaches.

4. Sonic Ishikawa Corp. of Japan, a suspension and steering components subcontractor for Japanese automakers, received an award from the Japan Institute for Plant Maintenance, for its total productive maintenance effort.[6] Their effort in total productive maintenance involved four phases: (1) organizing teams to reduce equipment failures and defects; (2) better design for manufacturability and better production management; (3) improving plant automation; and (4) improving office automation. The results of their effort on total productive maintenance were a 75% reduction in defects, 50% higher productivity, and a 95% reduction in equipment breakdowns.

5. An eight-person multi-disciplinary team of workers at the Tennessee Valley Authority's Brown Ferry nuclear plant won the 1997 RIT/USA Today Quality Cup for government and former Vice President Al Gore's Hammer award, by using total productive maintenance to save $12.7 million in maintenance costs over an 18-month period.[7] The team's primary focus was to reduce the hand-to-hand processing of paperwork by implementing several software programs. As a result of the team's work, change procedures were reduced from 25 hours to 8 hours, processing work orders were reduced from 37 hours to 22 hours, and reactor shutdown, for maintenance, was reduced from 32 days to 19 days.

There are numerous other success stories of organizations using total productive maintenance: Daihatsu Motors in 1988, Suzuki in 1992, Harley-Davidson in 1993, and others, such as, Eastman-Kodak, Du Pont, Texas Instruments, Proctor & Gamble, and AT&T.

---

[5] 1997 RIT/USA Today Quality Cup for government.

[6] David A. Turnbide, "Japan's New Advantage: Total Productive Maintenance," *Quality Progress* (March 1995): 121–123.

[7] 1997 RIT/USA Today Quality Cup for government.

TQM Exemplary Organization[8]

The Ritz-Carlton Hotel Company, an independent division of Marriott International, Inc., manages 36 luxury hotels in North America, Europe, Asia, Australia, the Middle East, Africa, and the Caribbean. All have received four- or five-star ratings from the Mobil Travel Guide and diamond ratings from the American Automobile Association.

More than 85% of the company's 17,000 employees—known as "The Ladies and Gentlemen of The Ritz-Carlton"—are front-line workers in hotels. Through extensive training programs and by offering opportunities for professional development, the company encourages personnel to advance in the organization. Ritz-Carlton President and Chief Operating Officer Horst Schulze began his career in the hospitality industry as a waiter's apprentice at a hotel in Europe.

The organization's mission is: "To be the premier worldwide provider of luxury travel and hospitality products and services." Everyone receives a wallet-sized copy of the "Gold Standards," which consist of the company's Motto, Credo, Employee Promise, Three Steps of Service, and The Ritz-Carlton Basics—essentially a listing of performance expectations and the protocol for interacting with customers and responding to their needs. These are reinforced in training (which totals 250 hours for first-year front-line employees), in the daily five- to 10-minute briefing at the start of every shift, and through the company's reward and recognition system.

At every level, The Ritz-Carlton is detail-oriented. Steps for all quality-improvement and problem-solving procedures are documented, methods of data collection and analysis are reviewed by third-party experts, and standards are established for all processes. Key processes also are dissected to identify points at which errors may occur.

To cultivate customer loyalty, The Ritz-Carlton has instituted an approach of "customer customization," which relies on extensive data gathering and capitalizes on the capabilities of advanced information technology. Information gathered during various types of customer contacts, such as responses to service requests by overnight guests or post-event reviews conducted with meeting planners, are systematically entered into a database, which holds almost one million files. Accessible to all Ritz-Carlton hotels worldwide, the database enables hotel staff to anticipate needs of returning guests and to initiate steps that will help to ensure a high-quality experience.

In an independent survey, 99% of guests said they were satisfied with their overall experience; more than 80% were "extremely satisfied." Any employee can spend up to $2,000 to immediately correct a problem or handle a complaint. First-year managers and employees receive 250 to 310 hours of training.

Financial performance also is trending upward. Total fees; earnings before income taxes, depreciation and amortization; and pre-tax return on investment have nearly

---

[8] Malcolm Baldrige National Quality Award, 1999 Service Category Recipient, NIST/Baldrige Homepage, Internet.

doubled since 1995, with return on investment increasing from 5.3% in 1995 to 9.8% in 1998. Revenue per available room (the industry's measure of market share) continues to grow, exceeding the industry average by more than 300%.

From a field of 3,528 nominees, Ritz-Carlton was selected "Overall Best Practices Champion"—1998 study by Cornell School of Hotel Administration and McGill University.

Exercises

1. The bearing department is planning their schedule for the following week. They need an understanding of last week's performance. The schedule called for two 8-hour shifts per day for five days. Downtime charged to production averaged 76 minutes per day. Downtime charged to maintenance averaged 135 minutes per day. Calculate the actual running time and the percentage of available time.

2. Refer to Exercise 1. The total products produced was 1,235. The standard called for a production run of 1500. Calculate the theoretical and actual cycle time per unit. Assume 10% planned downtime for theoretical cycle time. What was the performance efficiency?

3. What is the rate of quality products if 35 units out of the 1,235 completed in Exercise 2 are nonconforming?

4. What is the equipment effectiveness for the information given in Exercises 1, 2, and 3?

5. Find the equipment effectiveness percentage for an organization with the following data.

   Schedule is one ten-hour shift, five days per week.
   Total downtime allowed is 9% of schedule.
   Actual run time to theoretical has averaged 92% over the past six months.
   Quality acceptance rate has been running at 98%.

6. Working individually or in a team, brainstorm how total productive maintenance could be applied to some of the following service industries.

   (a) Photo printing business
   (b) Copy center
   (c) Transmission shop
   (d) Bagel shop
   (e) Quick oil change shop
   (f) Gas station

17

Management Tools

Introduction

While the statistical process control (SPC) tools discussed in Chapter 18 are excellent problem-solving tools, there are many situations where they are not appropriate. This chapter discusses some additional tools that can be very effective for teams and, in some cases, for individuals. They do not use hard data but rely on subjective information. Application of these tools has been proven useful in process improvement, cost reduction, policy deployment, and new-product development.

Why, Why

Although this tool is very simple, it is effective. It can be a key to finding the root cause of a problem by focusing on the process rather than on people. The procedure is to describe the problem in specific terms and then ask why. You may have to ask why three or more times to obtain the root cause. An example will help illustrate the concept.

Why did we miss the delivery date?

It wasn't scheduled in time.

Why?

There were a lot of engineering changes.

Why?

Customer requested them.

The team suggested changing the delivery date whenever engineering changes occurred.

This tool is very beneficial in developing critical thinking. It is frequently a quick method of solving a problem.

Forced Field Analysis

This analysis is used to identify the forces and factors that may influence the problem or goal. It helps an organization to better understand promoting or driving and restraining or inhibiting forces so that the positives can be reinforced and the negatives reduced or eliminated. The procedure is to define the objective, determine criteria for evaluating the effectiveness of the improvement action, brainstorm the forces that promote and inhibit achieving the goal, prioritize the forces from greatest to least, and take action to strengthen the promoting forces and weaken the inhibiting forces. An example will illustrate the tool.

Objective: Stop Smoking

Promoting Forces ———➔	◀——— *Inhibiting Forces*
Poor Health ———➔	◀——— Habit
Smelly Clothing ———➔	◀——— Addiction
Poor Example ———➔	◀——— Taste
Cost ———➔	◀——— Stress
Impact on Others ———➔	◀——— Advertisement

The benefits are the determination of the positives and negatives of a situation, encouraging people to agree and prioritize the competing forces, and identify the root causes.

Nominal Group Technique

This technique provides for issue/idea input from everyone on the team and for effective decisions. An example will illustrate the technique. Let's assume that the team wants to decide which problem to work on. Everyone writes on a piece of paper the problem they think is most important. The papers are collected, and all problems are listed on a flip chart. Then each member of the team uses another piece of paper to rank the problems from least important to most important. The rankings are given a numerical value starting at 1 for least important and continuing to the most important. Points for each problem are totaled, and the item with the highest number of points is considered to be the most important.

Affinity Diagram

This diagram allows the team to creatively generate a large number of issues/ideas and then logically group them for problem understanding and possible breakthrough solution. The procedure is to state the issue in a full sentence, brainstorm using short sentences on self-adhesive notes, post them for the team to see, sort ideas into logical groups, and create concise descriptive headings for each group. Figure 17-1 illustrates the technique.

Large groups should be divided into smaller groups with appropriate headings. Notes that stand alone could become headers or placed in a miscellaneous category. Affinity diagrams encourage team creativity, break down barriers, facilitate breakthroughs, and stimulate ownership of the process.

Interrelationship Digraph[1]

The Interrelationship Diagraph (ID) clarifies the interrelationship of many factors of a complex situation. It allows the team to classify the cause-and-effect relationships among all the factors so that the key drivers and outcomes can be used to solve the problem. The procedure is somewhat more complicated than the previous tools; thus, it will be itemized.

1. The team should agree on the issue or problem statement.

2. All of the ideas or issues from other techniques or from brainstorming should be laid out, preferably in a circle as shown in Figure 17-2(a).

3. Start with the first issue, "Lack of respect for others" (A), and evaluate the cause-and-effect relationship with "Lack of awareness of impact" (B). In this situation, Issue B is stronger than Issue A; therefore, the arrow is drawn from Issue B to Issue A as shown in Figure 17-2(c). Each issue in the circle is compared to Issue A as shown in Figure 17-2(c), (d), (e), and (f). Only Issues B and E have a relationship with Issue A. The first iteration is complete.

4. The second iteration is to compare Issue B with Issues C, D, E, and F. The third iteration is to compare Issue C with Issues D, E, and F. The fourth iteration is to compare Issue D with Issues E and F. The fifth iteration is to compare Issue E with Issue F.

5. The entire diagram should be reviewed and revised where necessary. It is a good idea to obtain information from other people on upstream and downstream processes.

6. The diagram is completed by tallying the incoming and outgoing arrows and placing this information below the box. Figure 17-3(d) shows a completed diagram.

Issue B is the "driver" because it has zero incoming arrows and five outgoing arrows. It is usually the root cause. The issue with the highest incoming arrows is Issue E. It is a meaningful measure of success.

---

[1] This section adapted, with permission, from Michael Brassard, *The Memory Jogger Plus+* (Methuen, Mass.: GOAL/QPC, 1989).

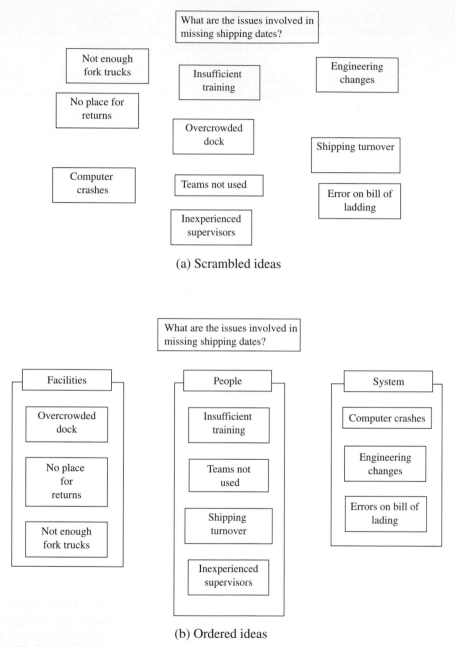

(a) Scrambled ideas

(b) Ordered ideas

Figure 17-1 Affinity Diagram

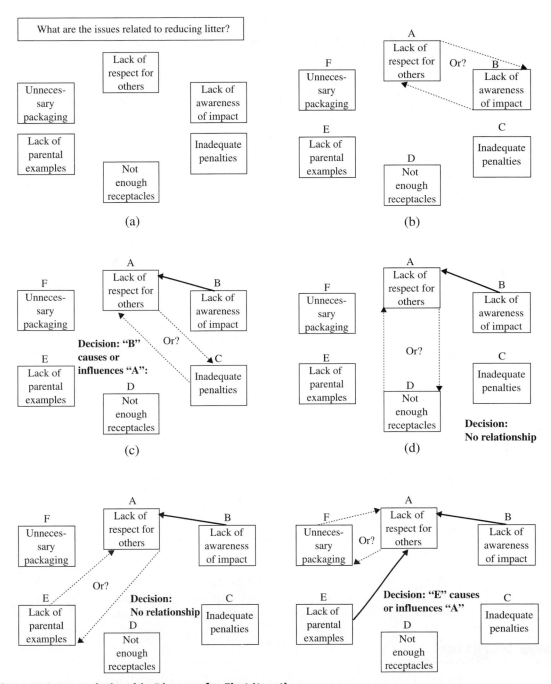

Figure 17-2 Interrelationship Diagram for First Iteration

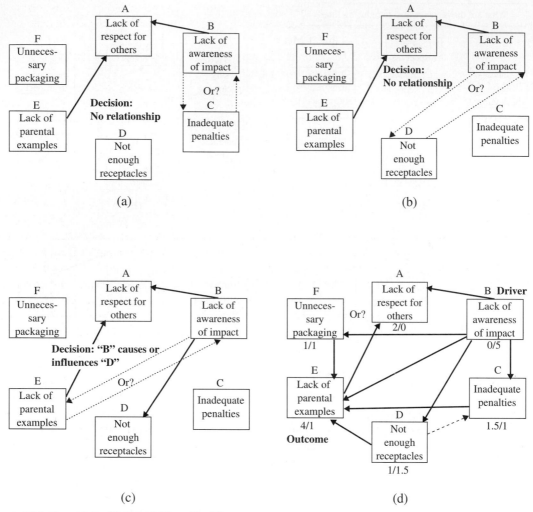

Figure 17-3 Completed Interrelationship Diagram

A relationship diagram allows a team to identify root causes from subjective data, systematically explores cause-and-effect relationships, encourages members to think multidirectionally, and develops team harmony and effectiveness.

Tree Diagram

This tool is used to reduce any broad objective into increasing levels of detail in order to achieve the objective. The procedure is to first choose an action-oriented objective statement from the interrelationship diagram, affinity diagram, brainstorming, team mission statement, and so forth. Second, using brainstorming, choose the major headings as shown in Figure 17-4 under Means.

The third step is to generate the next level by analyzing the major headings. Ask, "What needs to be addressed to achieve the objective?" Repeat this question at each level. Three levels below the objective are usually sufficient to complete the diagram and make appropriate assignments. The diagram should be reviewed to determine if these actions will give the results anticipated or if something has been missed.

The tree diagram encourages team members to think creatively, makes large projects manageable, and generates a problem-solving atmosphere.

Matrix Diagram

The matrix diagram allows individuals or teams to identify, analyze, and rate the relationship among two or more variables. Data are presented in table form and can be objective or subjective, which can be given symbols with or without numerical values. Quality function deployment (QFD), which was discussed in Chapter 12, is an outstanding example of the use of the matrix diagram. There are at least five standard formats: L-shaped (2 variables), T-shaped (3 variables), Y-shaped (3 variables), C-shaped (3 variables), and X-shaped (4 variables). Our discussion will be limited to the L-shaped format, which is the most common.[2]

Figure 17-5 illustrates a matrix diagram for using the seven management and planning tools. The procedure for the diagram is for the team to first select the factors affecting a successful plan. Next select the appropriate format, which in this case is the L-shaped diagram. That step is followed by determining the relationship symbols. Any symbols can be adopted, provided the diagram contains a legend as shown in the bottom of the figure. Numerical values are sometimes associated with the symbol as we previously did with QFD. The last step is to complete the matrix by analyzing each cell and inserting the appropriate symbol.

The matrix diagram clearly shows the relationship of the two variables. It encourages the team to think in terms of relationships, their strength, and any patterns.

Prioritization Matrices

These tools prioritize issues, tasks, characteristics, and so forth, based on weighted criteria using a combination of tree and matrix diagram techniques. Once prioritized, effective decisions can be made. Prioritization matrices are designed to reduce the team's

---

[2] Detailed information on the other formats is available from Michael Brassard, *The Memory Jogger Plus+* (Methuen, Mass.: GOAL/QPC, 1996).

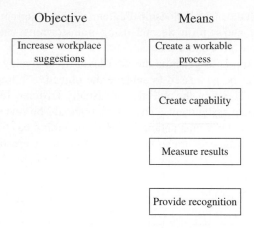

(a) Objective and means

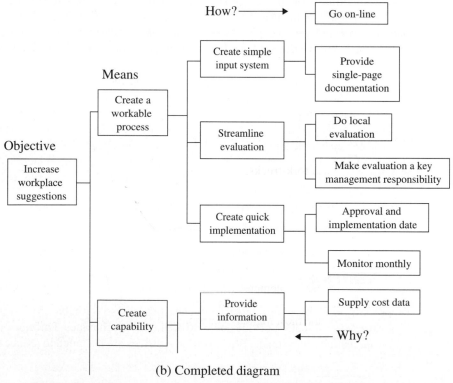

(b) Completed diagram

Figure 17-4 Tree Diagram

Use / Tool	Creativity	Analysis	Consensus	Action
Affinity diagram	○		○	△
Interrelationship digraph		○	◎	
Tree diagram		◎		◎
Prioritization matrix			○	
Matrix diagram		○	◎	○
PDPC	◎	◎	◎	○
Activity network diagram			◎	○

Legend: Always ○   Frequently ◎   Occasionally △

Figure 17-5 Matrix Diagram for Uses of the Seven Management Tools
Reproduced, with permission, from Ellen R. Domb, "7 New Tools: The Ingredients for Successful Problem Solving," *Quality Digest* (December 1994).

options rationally before detailed implementation planning occurs. It utilizes a combination of tree and matrix diagrams as shown in Figure 17-6. There are 15 implementation options; however, only the first three, beginning at "train supervisors," and the last one "purchase fork-trucks," are shown in the tree diagram. There are four implementation criteria, however, as shown at the top of the matrix. Prioritization matrices are the most difficult of the tools in this chapter; therefore, we will list the steps for creating one.

1. Construct an L-shaped matrix combining the options, which are the lowest level of detail of the tree diagram with the criteria. This information is given in Table 17-1.

2. Determine the implementation criteria using the nominal group technique (NGT) or any other technique that will satisfactorily weight the criteria. Using NGT, each team member submits the most important criteria on a piece of paper. They are listed on a flip chart, and the team members submit another piece of paper rank ordering those listed on the flip chart. Those criteria with the greatest value are the most important. The team decides how many of the criteria to use. In this situation, the team decides to use the four criteria shown at the top of the matrix.

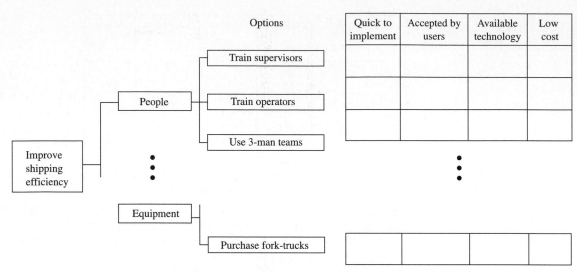

Figure 17-6 **Prioritization Matrix for Improving Shipping Efficiency**

3. Prioritize the criteria using the NGT. Each team member weights the criteria so the total weight equals 1.00, and the results are totaled for the entire team as shown below:

Criteria	Member #1	Member #2		Total
Accepted by users	.30	.25		1.50
Low cost	.15	.20	•••	0.35
Quick to implement	.40	.30		2.10
Available technology	.15	.25		0.45
	1.00	1.00		

4. Using NDT, rank order the options in terms of importance by each criterion, average the results, and round to the nearest whole number. Thus, this ranking should be from one to the number of options for each criterion. For example, train operators is ranked 13 for quick to implement.

5. Compute the option importance score under each criterion by multiplying the rank by the criteria weight as shown in Table 17-1. The options with the highest total are those that should be implemented first.

There are two other techniques that are more complicated. (For information on these techniques, see *The Memory Jogger Plus+*).

TABLE 17-1
Improve Shipping Efficiency Using the Consensus Criteria Method

	CRITERIA				
Options	Quick to Implement	Accepted by Users	Available Technology	Low Cost	Total
Train Operators	13(2.10) = 27.3	15(1.50) = 22.5	11(0.45) = 5.0	13(0.35) = 4.6	59.4
Train Supervisors	12(2.10) = 25.2	11(1.50) = 16.5	12(0.45) = 5.4	8(0.35) = 2.8	49.9
Use 3-person Teams	8(2.10) = 16.8	3(1.50) = 4.5	13(0.45) = 5.9	14(0.35) = 4.9	32.1
⋮	⋮	⋮	⋮	⋮	⋮
Purchase Fork-trucks	6(2.10) = 12.6	12(1.50) = 18	10(0.45) = 4.5	1(0.35) = 0.4	35.5

Process Decision Program Chart

Programs to achieve particular objectives do not always go according to plan, and unexpected developments may have serious consequences. The process decision program chart (PDPC) avoids surprises and identifies possible countermeasures. Figure 17-7 illustrates the PDPC.

The procedure starts with the team stating the objective, which is to plan a successful conference. That activity is followed by the first level, which is the conference activities of registration, presentations, and facilities. Only the presentation activity is illustrated. In some cases a second level of detailed activities may be used. Next, the team brainstorms to determine what could go wrong with the conference, and these are shown as the "what-if" level. Countermeasures are brainstormed and placed in a balloon in the last level. The last step is to evaluate the countermeasures and select the optimal ones by placing an O underneath. Place an X under those that are rejected.

The example has used a graphical format. PDPC can also use an outline format with the activities listed. The probability, in percent, that a "what-if" will occur can be included in the box. Countermeasures should be plausible. PDPC should be used when the task is new or unique, complex, or potential failure has great risks. This tool encourages team members to think about what can happen to a process and how countermeasures can be taken. It provides the mechanism to effectively minimize uncertainty in an implementation plan.

Activity Network Diagram

This tool goes by a number of different names and deviations, such as program evaluation and review technique (PERT), critical path method (CPM), arrow diagram, and

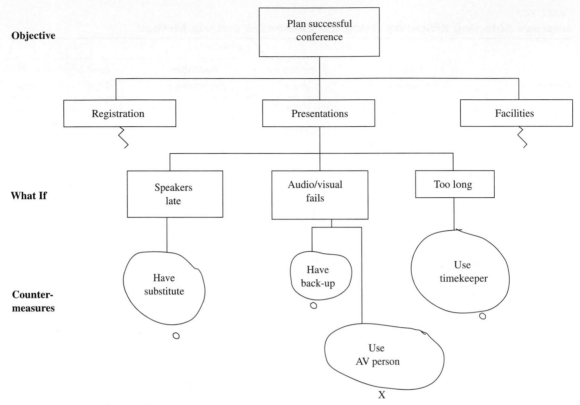

Objective

What If

Counter-measures

Figure 17-7 PDPC for Conference Presentation

activity on node (AON). It allows the team to schedule a project efficiently. The diagram shows completion times, simultaneous tasks, and critical activity path. Given below is the procedure to follow:

1. The team brainstorms or documents all the tasks to complete a project. These tasks are recorded on self-adhesive notes so all members can see them.

2. The first task is located and placed on the extreme left of a large view work surface, as shown in Figure 17-8(a).

3. Any tasks that can be done simultaneously are placed below, as shown in Figure 17-8(b).

4. Repeat Steps 2 and 3 until all tasks are placed in their correct sequence, as illustrated in Figure 17-8(c). Note: Because of space limitations, not all of the tasks are shown.

5. Number each task and draw connecting arrows. Determine the task completion time and post it in the lower left box. Completion times are recorded in hours, days, or weeks.

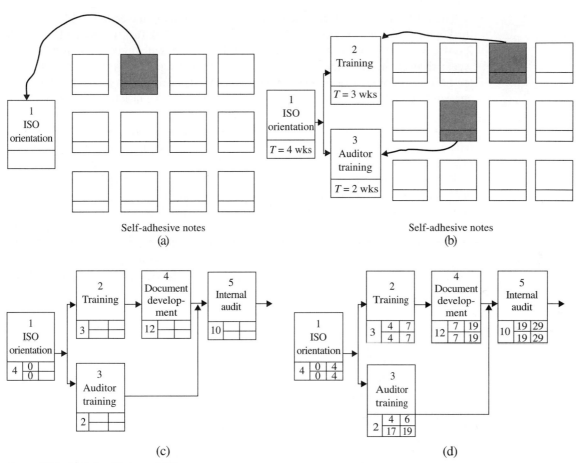

Figure 17-8 Activity Network Diagram

6. Determine the critical path by completing the four remaining boxes in each task. As shown below, these boxes are used for the earliest start time (ES), earliest finish (EF), latest start (LS), and latest finish (LF).

Activity time [T]	Earliest Start [ES]	Earliest Finish [EF]
	Latest Start [LS]	Latest Finish [LF]

The ES for Task 1 is 0, and the EF is 4 weeks later using the equation EF = ES + T; the ES for Task 2 is 4 weeks, which is the same as the EF of Task 1, and the EF of Task 2 is 4 + 3 = 7. This process is repeated for Tasks 4 and 5, which gives a total time of 29 weeks through the completion of the internal audit. If the project is to stay on schedule, the LS and LF for each of these tasks must equal the ES and EF, respectively. These values can be calculated by working backwards—subtracting the task time. They are shown in Figure 17-8(d).

Task 3, auditor training, does not have to be in sequence with the other tasks. It does have to be completed during the 19th week, because the ES for Task 5 is 19. Therefore, the LF for Task 3 is also 19 and the LS is 17. Auditor training could start after Task 1, which would give an ES of 4 and an EF of 6. The slack for Task 3 equals LS − ES [17 − 4 = 13]. The critical path is the longest cumulative time of connecting activities and occurs when the slack of each task is zero; thus, it is 1, 2, 4, and 5.

The benefits of an activity network diagram are (1) a realistic timetable determined by the users, (2) team members understand their role in the overall plan, (3) bottlenecks can be discovered and corrective action taken, and (4) members focus on the critical tasks. For this tool to work, the task times must be correct or reasonably close.

Summary

The first three tools can be used in a wide variety of situations. They are simple to use by individuals and/or teams.

The last seven tools in the chapter are called the seven management and planning tools. Although these tools can be used individually, they are most effective when used as a system to implement an improvement plan. Figure 17-9 shows a suggested flow diagram for this integration.

The team may wish to follow this sequence or modify it to meet their needs.

TQM Exemplary Organization[3]

The Chugach School District Office is based in Anchorage, Alaska. Chugach's 214 students are scattered throughout 22,000 square miles of mostly isolated and remote areas of south central Alaska. With 30 faculty and staff, it is the smallest organization to ever win a Baldrige Award. Education is delivered in the workplace, in the community, in the home, and in school to students from preschool up to age 21 using a comprehensive, standards-based system. With heavy use of technology, education for Chugach students can occur 24-hours a day, seven days a week. Half of the students in the district are Alaska Natives.

---

[3] Malcolm Baldrige National Quality Award, 2001 Education Category Recipient, NIST/Baldrige Homepage, Internet.

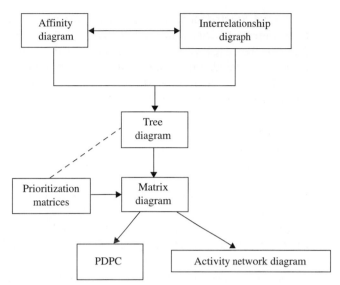

Figure 17-9 System Flow Diagram

Chugach School District (CSD) involves all stakeholders in its strategic planning process—including students, parents, community members, and businesses—to develop a shared vision, organizational performance goals, a five-year timeline of activities, and one-year targets. The goals address student learning and development in basic skills, individual needs of students, character development, transition skills, and technology. In 2001, stakeholders gave high satisfaction ratings to CSD in these five outcome areas with basic skills at 96%, individual needs of students at 89%, character development education at 84%, transition skills at 89%, and technology at 89%.

The superintendent and senior leaders use a community-wide, highly participatory consensus approach, called Onward to Excellence, to set organizational values, short and long-term directions, and performance expectations. Twice-a-month teleconference calls with stakeholders at remote sites and in-service programs provide opportunities for senior leaders to reinforce organizational values, directions, and expectations and to promote ethical values, faculty and staff empowerment, innovation, and organizational learning.

Results on the California Achievement Tests improved in all content areas from 1995 to 1999. Average national percentile scores increased in reading from 28th to 71st, in language arts from 26th to 72nd, in math from 54th to 78th, and in spelling from 22nd to 65th. The percentage of CSD students who take college entrance exams has increased from 0 to 70% since 1998.

Chugach has the highest percentage of its budget directed to instruction, compared with all other rural Alaskan districts. CSD administrative and support service expenses fell from 25% in 1994 to the current level of 10%.

Every CSD student has an Individual Learning Plan (ILP). ILPs are developed jointly with students, teachers, and parents. ILPs enable students to learn at their own pace. To move to the next level in the curriculum, students are required to demonstrate proficiency with the identified skills and knowledge at that particular level.

CSD reduced the faculty turnover rate from an average of 55% during 1975–1994 to an average of 12% during 1995–2000. It has a performance-based pay component and provides flexible working conditions, job rotation, job share contracts, and a high degree of empowerment to counter the effects of working in remote isolated areas. CSD provides 30 days of training annually for faculty, twice the number offered by any other school district in the state. Training facilitates alignment in action plans, organizational performance goals, and legal requirements. Training addresses how to assess student needs, instruct and support students, use ILPs, monitor learning, analyze results, and determine opportunities to improve student learning.

Technology is used to enhance student learning, to improve student technology skills, and to improve the efficiency of its academic and administrative operations. Through aggressive pursuit of grant funding, the district increased the number of computers from two per 27 students in 1994 to 21 per 27 students in 2001. In addition, when students reach Level IV in all content standards, they receive a personal wireless laptop computer, a vital means of communication for students living in remote sites. Overall student use of the Internet increased from 5% in 1998 to 93% in 2001.

Exercises

1. Determine why you did poorly on a recent examination by using the why, why tool.

2. Use the forced field analysis to

    (a) Lose weight.
    (b) Improve your GPA.
    (c) Increase your athletic ability in some sport.

3. Prepare an affinity diagram, using a team of three or more people, to plan

    (a) An improvement in the cafeteria.
    (b) A spring-break vacation.
    (c) A field trip to a local organization.

4. Using a team of three or more people, prepare an interrelationship digraph for the

    (a) Computer networking of nine locations in the organization's facility.
    (b) Implementation of a recognition and reward system.
    (c) Performance improvement of the accounting department or any other work group.

5. Develop a tree diagram, using a team of three or more people, for

   (a) The customer requirements for a product or service.
   (b) Planning a charity walk-a-thon.

6. The church council is planning the activities for a successful carnival. Using a team of three or more people, design a tree diagram to determine detailed assignments.

7. Develop a matrix diagram to design an organization-wide training or employee involvement program. Use a team of three or more people.

8. Using a team of three or more people, construct a matrix diagram to

   (a) Determine customer requirements for a new product or service.
   (b) Allocate team assignments to implement a project such as new student week.
   (c) Compare teacher characteristics with potential student performance.

9. Develop a prioritization matrix, using the tree diagram developed in Exercise 6.

10. Construct a PDPC for

    (a) A charity walk-a-thon (see Exercise 5).
    (b) The church carnival of Exercise 6.
    (c) The matrix diagram developed in Exercise 7.

11. Using a team of three or more people, construct an activity network diagram for

    (a) Constructing a cardboard boat.
    (b) An implementation schedule for a university event such as a graduation.
    (c) Developing a new instructional laboratory.

12. Select a problem or situation and, with a team of three or more people, use the seven management and planning tools to implement an action plan. If one of the tools doesn't fit, justify its exclusion.

18

Statistical Process Control[1]

Introduction

One of the best technical tools for improving product and service quality is *statistical process control* (SPC). There are seven basic techniques. Since the first four techniques are not really statistical, the word *statistical* is somewhat of a misnomer. Furthermore, this technical tool not only *controls* the process but has the capability to improve it as well.

Pareto Diagram

Alfredo Pareto (1848–1923) conducted extensive studies of the distribution of wealth in Europe. He found that there were a few people with a lot of money and many people with little money. This unequal distribution of wealth became an integral part of economic theory. Dr. Joseph Juran recognized this concept as a universal that could be applied to many fields. He coined the phrases *vital few* and *useful many*.

A Pareto diagram is a graph that ranks data classifications in descending order from left to right, as shown in Figure 18-1. In this case, the data classifications are types of coating machines. Other possible data classifications are problems, complaints, causes, types of nonconformities, and so forth. The vital few are on the left, and the useful many are on the right. It is sometimes necessary to combine some of the useful many into one classification called "other". When this category is used, it is placed on the far right.

The vertical scale is dollars (or frequency), and the percent of each category can be placed above the column. In this case, Pareto diagrams were constructed for both frequency and dollars. As can be seen from the figure, machine 35 has the greatest number of nonconformities, but machine 51 has the greatest dollar value. Pareto diagrams can

---

[1] Adapted, with permission, from Dale H. Besterfield, *Quality Control*, 6th ed. (Upper Saddle River, NJ: Prentice Hall, 2001).

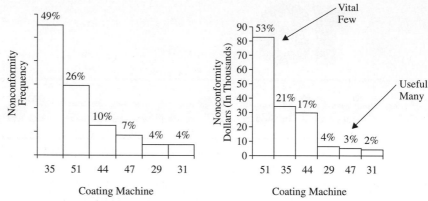

Figure 18-1 Pareto Diagram

be distinguished from histograms (to be discussed) by the fact that the horizontal scale of a Pareto diagram is categorical, whereas the scale for the histogram is numerical.

Pareto diagrams are used to identify the most important problems. Usually, 75% of the total results from 25% of the items. This fact is shown in the figure, where coating machines 35 and 51 account for about 75% of the total.

Actually, the most important items could be identified by listing them in descending order. However, the graph has the advantage of providing a visual impact, showing those vital few characteristics that need attention. Resources are then directed to take the necessary corrective action.

Examples of the vital few are:

A few customers account for the majority of sales.

A few processes account for the bulk of the scrap or rework cost.

A few nonconformities account for the majority of customer complaints.

A few suppliers account for the majority of rejected parts.

A few problems account for the bulk of the process downtime.

A few products account for the majority of the profit.

A few items account for the bulk of the inventory cost.

Construction of a Pareto diagram is very simple. There are five steps:

1. Determine the method of classifying the data: by problem, cause, nonconformity, and so forth.
2. Decide if dollars (best), frequency, or both are to be used to rank the characteristics.
3. Collect data for an appropriate time interval or use historical data.

4. Summarize the data and rank order categories from largest to smallest.

5. Construct the diagram and find the vital few.

Note that a quality improvement of the vital few, say, 50%, is a much greater return on investment than a 50% improvement of the useful many. Also, experience has shown that it is easier to make a 50% improvement in the vital few. The use of a Pareto diagram is a never-ending process. For example, let's assume that coating machine 51 is the target for correction in the improvement program. A project team is assigned to investigate and make improvements. The next time a Pareto analysis is made, another machine, say, 35 becomes the target for correction, and the improvement process continues until coating machine nonconformities become an insignificant quality problem.

The Pareto diagram is a powerful quality improvement tool. It is applicable to problem identification and the measurement of progress.

Process Flow Diagram

For many products and services, it may be useful to construct a process flow diagram. Figure 18-2 shows a flow diagram for the order entry activity of a make-to-order company that manufactures gasoline filling station hose nozzles. These diagrams show the flow of the product or service as it moves through the various processing operations. The diagram makes it easy to visualize the entire system, identify potential trouble spots, and locate control activities. It answers the question, "Who is the next

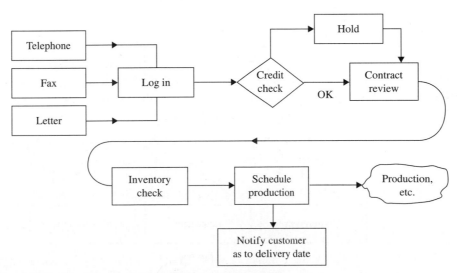

Figure 18-2 Flow Diagram for an Order Entry Activity

customer?" Improvements can be accomplished by changing, reducing, combining, or eliminating steps.

Standardized symbols are used by industrial engineers; however, they are not necessary for problem solving. The symbols used in the figure should be sufficient.

Cause-and-Effect Diagram

A cause-and-effect (C&E) diagram is a picture composed of lines and symbols designed to represent a meaningful relationship between an effect and its causes. It was developed by Dr. Kaoru Ishikawa in 1943 and is sometimes referred to as an Ishikawa diagram or a fishbone diagram because of its shape.

C&E diagrams are used to investigate either a "bad" effect and to take action to correct the causes or a "good" effect and to learn those causes that are responsible. For every effect, there are likely to be numerous causes. Figure 18-3 illustrates a C&E diagram with the effect on the right and causes on the left. The effect is the quality characteristic that needs improvement. Causes are sometimes broken down into the major causes of work methods, materials, measurement, people, equipment, and the environment. Other major causes could be used for service-type problems, as indicated in the chapter on customer satisfaction.

Each major cause is further subdivided into numerous minor causes. For example, under work methods, we might have training, knowledge, ability, physical characteristics, and so forth. C&E diagrams are the means of picturing all these major and minor causes. Figure 18-4 shows a C&E diagram for house paint peeling using four major causes.

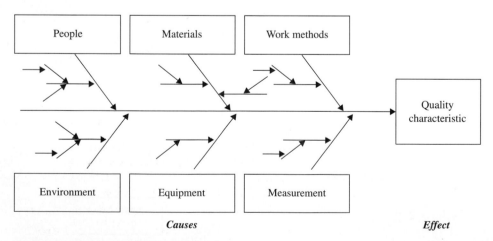

Figure 18-3 Cause-and-Effect Diagram

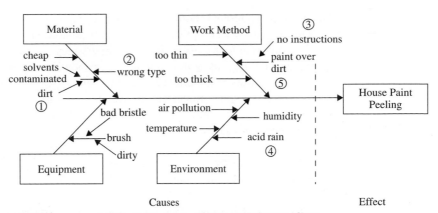

Causes   Effect

Figure 18-4 Cause-and-Effect Diagram of House Paint Peeling

The first step in the construction of a C&E diagram is for the project team to identify the effect or quality problem. It is placed on the right side of a large piece of paper by the team leader. Next, the major causes are identified and placed on the diagram.

Determining all the minor causes requires brainstorming by the project team. Brainstorming is an idea-generating technique that is well suited to the C&E diagram. It uses the creative thinking capacity of the team.

Attention to a few essentials will provide a more accurate and usable result:

1. Participation by every member of the team is facilitated by each member taking a turn giving one idea at a time. If a member cannot think of a minor cause, he or she passes for that round. Another idea may occur at a later round. Following this procedure prevents one or two individuals from dominating the brainstorming session.

2. Quantity of ideas, rather than quality, is encouraged. One person's idea will trigger someone else's idea, and a chain reaction occurs. Frequently, a trivial, or "dumb," idea will lead to the best solution.

3. Criticism of an idea is not allowed. There should be a freewheeling exchange of information that liberates the imagination. All ideas are placed on the diagram. Evaluation of ideas occurs at a later time.

4. Visibility of the diagram is a primary factor of participation. In order to have space for all the minor causes, a 2-foot by 3-foot piece of paper is recommended. It should be taped to a wall for maximum visibility.

5. Create a solution-oriented atmosphere and not a gripe session. Focus on solving a problem rather than discussing how it began. The team leader should ask questions using the why, what, where, when, who, and how techniques.

6. Let the ideas incubate for a period of time (at least overnight) and then have another brainstorming session. Provide team members with a copy of the ideas after the first session. When no more ideas are generated, the brainstorming activity is terminated.

Once the C&E diagram is complete, it must be evaluated to determine the most likely causes. This activity is accomplished in a separate session. The procedure is to have each person vote on the minor causes. Team members may vote on more than one cause. Those causes with the most votes are circled, as shown in Figure 18-4, and the four or five most likely causes of the effect are determined.

Solutions are developed to correct the causes and improve the process. Criteria for judging the possible solutions include cost, feasibility, resistance to change, consequences, training, and so forth. Once the team agrees on solutions, testing and implementation follow.

Diagrams are posted in key locations to stimulate continued reference as similar or new problems arise. The diagrams are revised as solutions are found and improvements are made.

The C&E diagram has nearly unlimited application in research, manufacturing, marketing, office operations, service, and so forth. One of its strongest assets is the participation and contribution of everyone involved in the brainstorming process. The diagrams are useful to

1. Analyze actual conditions for the purpose of product or service quality improvement, more efficient use of resources, and reduced costs.
2. Eliminate conditions causing nonconformities and customer complaints.
3. Standardize existing and proposed operations.
4. Educate and train personnel in decision-making and corrective-action activities.

Check Sheets

The main purpose of check sheets is to ensure that the data is collected carefully and accurately by operating personnel. Data should be collected in such a manner that it can be quickly and easily used and analyzed. The form of the check sheet is individualized for each situation and is designed by the project team. Figure 18-5 shows a check sheet for paint nonconformities for bicycles.

Figure 18-6 shows a check sheet for temperature. The scale on the left represents the midpoint and boundaries for each temperature range. Data for this type of check sheet is frequently recorded by placing an "X" in the appropriate square. In this case, the time has been recorded in order to provide additional information for problem solving.

Whenever possible, check sheets are also designed to show location. For example, the check sheet for bicycle paint nonconformities could show an outline of a bicycle, with X's indicating the location of the nonconformities. Creativity plays a major role in the design of a check sheet. It should be user-friendly and, whenever possible, include information on time and location.

CHECK SHEET

Product: Bicycle 32   Number inspected: 2217

Nonconformity type	Check	Total
Blister	𝍸𝍸 𝍸𝍸 𝍸𝍸 𝍸𝍸 I	21
Light spray	𝍸𝍸 𝍸𝍸 𝍸𝍸 𝍸𝍸 𝍸𝍸 𝍸𝍸 𝍸𝍸 III	38
Drips	𝍸𝍸 𝍸𝍸 𝍸𝍸 𝍸𝍸 II	22
Overspray	𝍸𝍸 𝍸𝍸 I	11
Runs	𝍸𝍸 𝍸𝍸 𝍸𝍸 𝍸𝍸 𝍸𝍸 𝍸𝍸 𝍸𝍸 𝍸𝍸 𝍸𝍸 II	47
Others	𝍸𝍸	5
	Total	144
Number Nonconforming	𝍸𝍸 III	113

Figure 18-5 Check Sheet for Paint Nonconformities

387.4 385 382.5						
382.4 380 377.5						
377.4 375 372.5	10.0					
372.4 370 367.5						
367.4 365 362.5	7.0	7.5	9.0			
362.4 360 357.5	8.0	8.5				
357.4 355 352.5	9.5					

Figure 18-6 Check Sheet for Temperature

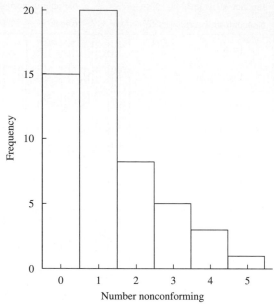

Figure 18-7 Frequency Histogram

Histogram

The first "statistical" SPC technique is the histogram. It describes the variation in the process, as illustrated by Figure 18-7. The histogram graphically estimates the process capability and, if desired, the relationship to the specifications and the nominal (target). It also suggests the shape of the population and indicates if there are any gaps in the data.

In industry, business, and government the mass of data that have been collected is voluminous. Even one item, such as the number of daily billing errors of a large bank, can represent such a mass of data that it can be more confusing than helpful. For example, consider the data shown in Table 18-1. Clearly these data, in this form, are difficult to use and are not effective in describing the data's characteristics. Some means of summarizing the data are needed to show what value the data tend to cluster about and how the data are dispersed or spread out. Two techniques are needed to accomplish this summarization of data—graphical and analytical.

Ungrouped Data

The graphical technique is a plot or picture of a frequency distribution, which is a summarization of how the data points (observations) occur within each subdivision of observed values or groups of observed values. Analytical techniques summarize data by

TABLE 18-1
Number of Daily Accounting Errors

0	1	3	0	1	0	1	0
1	5	4	1	2	1	2	0
1	0	2	0	0	2	0	1
2	1	1	1	2	1	1	
0	4	1	3	1	1	1	
1	3	4	0	0	0	0	
1	3	0	1	2	2	3	

TABLE 18-2
Tally of Number of Daily Accounting Errors

Number Nonconforming	Tabulation	Frequency
0	ⅢⅢ ⅢⅢ ⅢⅢ	15
1	ⅢⅢ ⅢⅢ ⅢⅢ ⅢⅢ	20
2	ⅢⅢ |||	8
3	ⅢⅢ	5
4					3
5			1

computing a measure of the central tendency (average, median, and mode) and a measure of the dispersion (range and standard deviation). Sometimes both the graphical and analytical techniques are used.

Because unorganized data are virtually meaningless, a method of processing the data is necessary. Table 18-1 will be used to illustrate the concept. An analyst reviewing the information as given in this table would have difficulty comprehending the meaning of the data. A much better understanding can be obtained by tallying the frequency of each value, as shown in Table 18-2.

The first step is to establish an *array*, which is an arrangement of raw numerical data in ascending or descending order of magnitude. An array of ascending order from 0 to 5 is shown in the first column of the table. The next step is to tabulate the frequency of each value by placing a tally mark under the tabulation column and in the appropriate row. Start with the numbers 0, 1, 1, 2, . . . of Table 18-1 and continue placing tally marks until all the data have been tabulated. The last column of the table is the numerical value for the number of tallies and is called the *frequency*.

Analysis of Table 18-2 shows that one can visualize the distribution of the data. If the "Tabulation" column is eliminated, the resulting table is classified as a frequency distribution, which is an arrangement of data to show the frequency of values in each category. The frequency distribution is a useful method of visualizing data and is a basic statistical concept. To think of a set of numbers as having some type of distribution is fundamental to solving quality control problems. There are different types of frequency distributions, and the type of distribution can indicate the problem-solving approach.

When greater visual clarity is desired, frequency distributions are presented in graphical form called histograms. A *histogram* consists of a set of rectangles that represent the frequency of the observed values in each category. Figure 18-7 is a histogram for the data in Table 18-2. Because this is a discrete variable, a vertical line in place of a rectangle would have been theoretically correct. However, the rectangle is commonly used.

Grouped Data

When the number of categories becomes large, the data are grouped into cells. In general, the number of cells should be between 5 and 20. Broad guidelines are as follows: Use 5 to 9 cells when the number of observations is less than 100; use 8 to 17 cells when the number of observations is between 100 and 500; and use 15 to 20 cells when the number of observations is greater than 500. To provide flexibility, the number of cells in the guidelines are overlapping. Figure 18-8 shows a histogram for grouped data of the quality characteristic, temperature. The data were collected using the check sheet for temperature (see Figure 18-6). The *interval* is the distance between adjacent cell midpoints. Cell *boundaries* are halfway between the cell midpoints. If an odd cell interval is chosen, which in this case is five degrees, the midpoint value will be to the same degree of accuracy as the ungrouped data. This situation is desirable, because all values in the cell take on the midpoint value when any additional calculations are made.

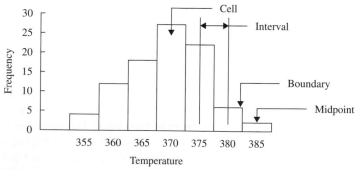

Figure 18-8 Histogram for Grouped Data

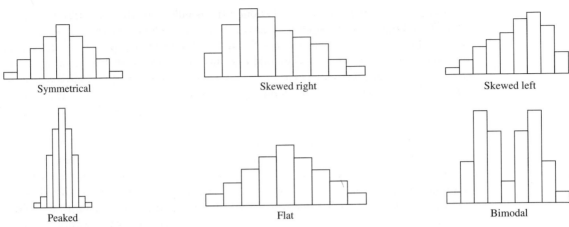

Symmetrical   Skewed right   Skewed left

Peaked   Flat   Bimodal

Figure 18-9 Different Histogram Shapes

Histogram Shapes

Histograms have certain identifiable characteristics, as shown in Figure 18-9. One characteristic of the distribution concerns the symmetry or lack of symmetry of the data. Are the data equally distributed on each side of the center, or are the data skewed to the right or to the left? Another characteristic concerns the peakedness, or *kurtosis*, of the data.

A final characteristic concerns the number of modes, or peaks, in the data. There can be one mode, two modes (bi-modal), or multiple modes.

Histograms can give sufficient information about a quality problem to provide a basis for decision making without further analysis. They can also be compared in regard to location, spread, and shape. A histogram is like a snapshot of the process showing the variation. Histograms can determine the process capability, compare with specifications, suggest the shape of the population, and indicate discrepancies in the data, such as gaps.

Statistical Fundamentals

Before a description of the next SPC tool, it is necessary to have a background in statistical fundamentals. *Statistics* is defined as the science that deals with the collection, tabulation, analysis, interpretation, and presentation of quantitative data. Each division is dependent on the accuracy and completeness of the preceding one. Data may be collected by a technician measuring the tensile strength of a plastic part or by an operator using a check sheet. It may be tabulated by simple paper-and-pencil techniques or by the use of a computer. Analysis may involve a cursory visual examination or exhaustive calculations. The final results are interpreted and presented to assist in the making of decisions concerning quality.

Data may be collected by direct observation or indirectly through written or verbal questions. The latter technique is used extensively by market research personnel and public opinion pollsters. Data that are collected for quality control purposes are obtained by direct observation and are classified as either variables or attributes. Variables are those quality characteristics that are measurable, such as a weight measured in grams. Attributes, on the other hand, are those quality characteristics that are classified as either conforming or not conforming to specifications, such as a "go–no go" gauge.

A histogram is sufficient for many quality control problems. However, with a broad range of problems a graphical technique is either undesirable or needs the additional information provided by analytical techniques. Analytical methods of describing a collection of data have the advantage of occupying less space than a graph. They also have the advantage of allowing for comparisons between collections of data. They also allow for additional calculations and inferences. There are two principal analytical methods of describing a collection of data: measures of central tendency and measures of dispersion.

Measures of Central Tendency

A measure of central tendency of a distribution is a numerical value that describes the central position of the data or how the data tend to build up in the center. There are three measures in common use in quality: (1) the average, (2) the median, and (3) the mode.

The average is the sum of the observations divided by the number of observations. It is the most common measure of central tendency and is represented by the equation[2]

$$\overline{X} = \frac{\sum_{i=1}^{n} X_i}{n}$$

where $\overline{X}$ = average and is read as "X bar"
n = number of observed values
X_i = observed value
Σ = sum of

Unless otherwise noted, $\overline{X}$ stands for the average of observed values, $\overline{X}_X$. The same equation is used to find

$$\overline{\overline{X}} \text{ or } \overline{X}_{\overline{x}} - \text{average of averages}$$
$$\overline{R} - \text{average of ranges}$$
$$\overline{p} - \text{average of proportions, etc.}$$

Another measure of central tendency is the median, Md, which is defined as the value that divides a series of ordered observations so that the number of items above it

---

[2] For data grouped into cells, the equation uses ΣfX, where f = cell frequency and X = cell midpoint.

is equal to the number below it. Two situations are possible—when the number in the series is odd and when the number in the series is even. When the number in the series is odd, the median is the midpoint of the values, provided the data are ordered. Thus, the ordered set of numbers 3, 4, 5, 6, 8, 8, and 10 has a median of 6. When the number in the series is even, the median is the average of the two middle numbers. Thus, the ordered set of numbers 3, 4, 5, 6, 8, and 8 has a median that is the average of 5 and 6, which is $(5 + 6)/2 = 5.5$.

The mode, Mo, of a set of numbers is the value that occurs with the greatest frequency. It is possible for the mode to be nonexistent in a series of numbers or to have more than one value. To illustrate, the series of numbers 3, 3, 4, 5, 5, 5, and 7 has a mode of 5; the series of numbers 22, 23, 25, 30, 32, and 36 does not have a mode; and the series of numbers 105, 105, 105, 107, 108, 109, 109, 109, 110, and 112 has two modes, 105 and 109. A series of numbers is referred to as unimodal if it has one mode, bimodal if it has two modes, and multimodal if there are more than two modes. When data are grouped into a frequency distribution, the midpoint of the cell with the highest frequency is the mode, because this point represents the highest point (greatest frequency) of the histogram.

The average is the most commonly-used measure of central tendency. It is used when the distribution is symmetrical or not appreciably skewed to the right or left; when additional statistics, such as measures of dispersion, control charts, and so on, are to be computed based on the average; and when a stable value is needed for inductive statistics. The median becomes an effective measure of the central tendency when the distribution is positively (to the right) or negatively (to the left) skewed. The median is used when an exact midpoint of a distribution is desired. When a distribution has extreme values, the average will be adversely affected, whereas the median will remain unchanged. Thus, in a series of numbers such as 12, 13, 14, 15, 16, the median and average are identical and are equal to 14. However, if the first value is changed to a 2, the median remains at 14, but the average becomes 12. A control chart based on the median is user-friendly and excellent for monitoring quality. The mode is used when a quick and approximate measure of the central tendency is desired. Thus, the mode of a histogram is easily found by a visual examination. In addition, the mode is used to describe the most typical value of a distribution, such as the modal age of a particular group.

Measures of Dispersion

A second tool of statistics is composed of the measures of dispersion, which describe how the data are spread out or scattered on each side of the central value. Measures of dispersion and measures of central tendency are both needed to describe a collection of data. To illustrate, the employees of the plating and the assembly departments of a factory have identical average weekly wages of $325.36; however, the plating department has a high of $330.72 and a low of $319.43, whereas the assembly department has a high of $380.79 and a low of $273.54. The data for the assembly department are spread out, or dispersed, farther from the average than are those of the plating department.

One of the measures of dispersion is the range, which for a series of numbers is the difference between the largest and smallest values of observations. Symbolically, it is represented by the equation

$$R = X_h - X_l$$

where R = range
        X_h = highest observation in a series
        X_l = lowest observation in a series

The other measure of the dispersion used in quality is the standard deviation. It is a numerical value in the units of the observed values that measures the spreading tendency of the data. A large standard deviation shows greater variability of the data than does a small standard deviation. In symbolic terms, it is represented by the equation

$$s = \sqrt{\frac{\sum\limits_{i=1}^{n}\left(X_i - \overline{X}\right)^2}{n-1}}$$

where s = sample standard deviation
        X_i = observed value
        $\overline{X}$ = average
        n = number of observed values

Unless otherwise noted, s stands for s_X, the sample standard deviation of observed values. The same equation is used to find

        $s_{\overline{X}}$ = sample standard deviation of averages
        s_p = sample standard deviation of proportions
        s_s = sample standard deviation of standard deviations, etc.

The standard deviation is a reference value that measures the dispersion in the data. It is best viewed as an index that is defined by the formula. The smaller the value of the standard deviation, the better the quality, because the distribution is more closely compacted around the central value. The standard deviation also helps to define populations, as discussed in the next section.

In quality control the range is a very common measure of the dispersion. It is used in one of the principal control charts. The primary advantage of the range is in providing a knowledge of the total spread of the data. It is also valuable when the amount of data is too small or too scattered to justify the calculation of a more precise measure of dispersion. As the number of observations increases, the accuracy of the range decreases, because it becomes easier for extremely high or low readings to occur. It is suggested that the use of the range be limited to a maximum of ten observations. The standard deviation is used when a more precise measure is desired.

The average and standard deviation are easily calculated with a hand calculator.

EXAMPLE PROBLEM

Determine the average, median, mode, range, and standard deviation for the height of seven people. Data are 1.83, 1.91, 1.78, 1.80, 1.83, 1.85, 1.87 meters.

$$\overline{X} = \Sigma X/n = (1.83 + 1.91 + \cdots + 1.87)/7 = 1.84$$

$$Md = \{1.91, \ 1.87, \ 1.85, \ 1.83, \ 1.83, \ 1.80, \ 1.78\} = 1.83$$

$$Mo = 1.83$$

$$R = X_h - X_l = 1.91 - 1.78 = 0.13$$

$$s = \sqrt{\frac{\sum_{i=1}^{n}\left(X_i - \overline{X}\right)^2}{n-1}} = \sqrt{\frac{(1.91 - 1.84)^2 + \cdots + (1.78 - 1.84)^2}{7-1}}$$

$$= 0.04$$

Population and Sample

At this point, it is desirable to examine the concept of a population and a sample. In order to construct a frequency distribution of the weight of steel shafts, a small portion, or sample, is selected to represent all the steel shafts. The population is the whole collection of steel shafts. When averages, standard deviations, and other measures are computed from samples, they are referred to as statistics. Because the composition of samples will fluctuate, the computed statistics will be larger or smaller than their true population values, or parameters. Parameters are considered to be fixed reference (standard) values or the best estimate of these values available at a particular time. The population may have a finite number of items, such as a day's production of steel shafts. It may be infinite or almost infinite, such as the number of rivets in a year's production of jet airplanes. The population may be defined differently, depending on the particular situation. Thus, a study of a product could involve the population of an hour's production, a week's production, 5,000 pieces, and so on.

Because it is rarely possible to measure all of the population, a sample is selected. Sampling is necessary when it may be impossible to measure the entire population; when the expense to observe all the data is prohibitive; when the required inspection destroys the product; or when a test of the entire population may be too dangerous, as would be the case with a new medical drug. Actually, an analysis of the entire population may not be as accurate as sampling. It has been shown that 100% manual inspection of low percent nonconforming product is not as accurate as sampling. This is probably due to the fact that boredom and fatigue cause inspectors to prejudge each inspected item as being acceptable.

When designating a population, the corresponding Greek letter is used. Thus, the sample average has the symbol $\overline{X}$ and the population mean the symbol μ (mu). Note that the word *average* changes to *mean* when used for the population. The symbol $\overline{X}_0$ is the standard or reference value. Mathematical concepts are based on μ, which is the true value—$\overline{X}_0$ represents a practical equivalent in order to use the concepts. The sample

TABLE 18-3
Comparison of Sample and Population

Sample	Population
Statistic X—average s—sample standard deviation	Parameter $\mu(X_0)$—mean $\sigma(s_0)$—standard deviation

standard deviation has the symbol s, and the population standard deviation the symbol σ (sigma). The symbol s_0 is the standard or reference value and has the same relationship to σ that $\overline{X}_0$ has to μ. The true population value may never be known; therefore, the symbol $\hat{\mu}$ and $\hat{\sigma}$ are sometimes used to indicate "estimate of." A comparison of sample and population is given in Table 18-3. A sample frequency distribution is represented by a histogram, whereas a population frequency distribution is represented by a smooth curve. To some extent, the sample represents the real world and the population represents the mathematical world. The equations and concepts are based on the population.

The primary objective in selecting a sample is to learn something about the population that will aid in making some type of decision. The sample selected must be of such a nature that it tends to resemble or represent the population. How successfully the sample represents the population is a function of the size of the sample, chance, the sampling method, and whether or not the conditions change.

Normal Curve

Although there are as many different populations as there are conditions, they can be described by a few general types. One type of population that is quite common is called the normal curve, or Gaussian distribution. The normal curve is a symmetrical, unimodal, bell-shaped distribution with the mean, median, and mode having the same value. A curve of the normal population for the resistance in ohms of an electrical device with population mean, μ, of 90 Ω and population standard deviation, σ, of 2 Ω is shown in Figure 18-10. The interval between dotted lines is equal to one standard deviation, σ.

Much of the variation in nature and in industry follows the frequency distribution of the normal curves. Thus, the variations in the weights of elephants, the speeds of antelopes, and the heights of human beings will follow a normal curve. Also, the variations found in industry, such as the weights of gray iron castings, the lives of 60-watt light bulbs, and the dimensions of steel piston rings, will be expected to follow the normal curve. When considering the heights of human beings, we can expect a small percent-

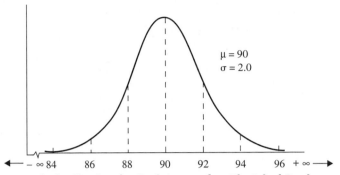

μ = 90
σ = 2.0

◄— – ∞ 84   86   88   90   92   94   96 + ∞ —►

Figure 18-10 Normal Distribution for Resistance of an Electrical Device

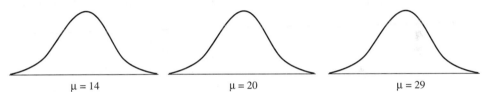

μ = 14   μ = 20   μ = 29

Figure 18-11 Normal Curves with Different Means but Identical Standard Deviations

age of them to be extremely tall and a small percentage to be extremely short, with the majority of human heights clustering about the average value. The normal curve is such a good description of the variations that occur to most quality characteristics in industry that it is the basis for many quality control techniques.

There is a definite relationship among the mean, the standard deviation, and the normal curve. Figure 18-11 shows three normal curves with different mean values; note that the only change is in the location. Figure 18-12 shows three normal curves with the same mean but different standard deviations. The figure illustrates the principle that the larger the standard deviation, the flatter the curve (data are widely dispersed), and the smaller the standard deviation, the more peaked the curve (data are narrowly dispersed). If the standard deviation is zero, all values are identical to the mean and there is no curve.

The normal distribution is fully defined by the population mean and population standard deviation. Also, as seen by Figures 18-11 and 18-12, these two parameters are independent. In other words, a change in one parameter has no effect on the other.

A relationship exists between the standard deviation and the area under the normal curve, as shown in Figure 18-13. The figure shows that in a normal distribution, 68.26% of the items are included between the limits of $\mu + 1\sigma$ and $\mu - 1\sigma$, 95.46% of the items are included between the limits $\mu + 2\sigma$ and $\mu - 2\sigma$, and 99.73% of the items are included between $\mu + 3\sigma$ and $\mu - 3\sigma$. One hundred percent of the items are included between the limits $+\infty$ and $-\infty$. These percentages hold true regardless of the shape of the normal curve. The fact that 99.73% of the items are included between $\pm 3\sigma$ is the basis for variable control charts.

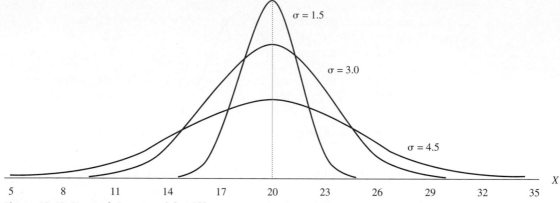

Figure 18-12 **Normal Curves with Different Standard Deviations but Identical Means**

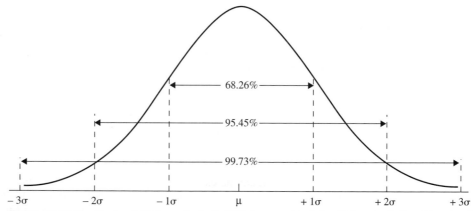

Figure 18-13 **Percent of Values Included Between Certain Values of the Standard Deviation**

Introduction to Control Charts

Variation

One of the axioms, or truisms, of production is that no two objects are ever made exactly alike. In fact, the variation concept is a law of nature because no two natural items in any category are the same. The variation may be quite large and easily noticeable, such as the height of human beings, or the variation may be very small, such as the weights of fiber-tipped pens or the shapes of snowflakes. When variations are very small, it may appear that items are identical; however, precision instruments will show differences. If two items appear to have the same measurement, it is due to the limits of our measuring instruments. As measuring instruments have become more refined, variation has continued to exist; only the increment of variation has changed. The ability to measure variation is necessary before it can be controlled.

There are three categories of variations in piece part production:

1. Within-piece variation is illustrated by the surface roughness of a piece, wherein one portion of the surface is rougher than another portion or the width of one end of a keyway varies from the other end.

2. Piece-to-piece variation occurs among pieces produced at the same time. Thus, the light intensity of four consecutive light bulbs produced from a machine will be different.

3. Time-to-time variation is illustrated by the difference in product produced at different times of the day. Thus, product produced in the early morning is different from that produced later in the day, or as a cutting tool wears, the cutting characteristics change.

Categories of variation for other types of processes such as a continuous and batch are not exactly the same; however, the concept is similar.

Variation is present in every process due to a combination of the equipment, materials, environment, and operator. The first source of variation is the equipment. This source includes tool wear, machine vibration, workholding-device positioning, and hydraulic and electrical fluctuations. When all these variations are put together, there is a certain capability or precision within which the equipment operates. Even supposedly identical machines will have different capabilities. This fact becomes a very important consideration when scheduling the manufacture of critical parts.

The second source of variation is the material. Because variation occurs in the finished product, it must also occur in the raw material (which was someone else's finished product). Such quality characteristics as tensile strength, ductility, thickness, porosity, and moisture content can be expected to contribute to the overall variation in the final product.

A third source of variation is the environment. Temperature, light, radiation, particle size, pressure, and humidity all can contribute to variation in the product. In order to control environmental variations, products are sometimes manufactured in white rooms. Experiments are conducted in outer space to learn more about the effect of the environment on product variation.

A fourth source is the operator. This source of variation includes the method by which the operator performs the operation. The operator's physical and emotional well-being also contribute to the variation. A cut finger, a twisted ankle, a personal problem, or a headache can make an operator's quality performance vary. An operator's lack of understanding of equipment and material variations due to lack of training may lead to frequent machine adjustments, thereby compounding the variability. As our equipment has become more automated, the operator's effect on variation has lessened.

The preceding four sources account for the true variation. There is also a reported variation, which is due to the inspection activity. Faulty inspection equipment, the incorrect application of a quality standard, or too heavy a pressure on a micrometer can be the cause of the incorrect reporting of variation. In general, variation due to inspection should be one-tenth of the four other sources of variations. Note that three of these sources are present in the inspection activity—an inspector or appraiser, inspection equipment, and the environment.

Run Chart

A run chart, which is shown in Figure 18-14, is a very simple technique for analyzing the process in the development stage or, for that matter, when other charting techniques are not applicable. The important point is to draw a picture of the process and let it "talk" to you. A picture is worth a thousand words, provided someone is listening. Plotting the data points is a very effective way of finding out about the process. This activity should be done as the first step in data analysis. Without a run chart, other data analysis tools— such as the average, sample standard deviation, and histogram—can lead to erroneous conclusions.

The particular run chart shown in Figure 18-14 is referred to as an $\overline{X}$ chart and is used to record the variation in the average value of samples. Other charts, such as the R chart (range) or p chart (proportion) would have also served for explanation purposes. The horizontal axis is labeled "Subgroup Number," which identifies a particular sample consisting of a fixed number of observations. These subgroups are plotted by order of production, with the first one inspected being 1 and the last one on this chart being 25. The vertical axis of the graph is the variable, which in this particular case is weight measured in kilograms.

Each small solid diamond represents the average value within a subgroup. Thus, subgroup number 5 consists of, say, four observations, 3.46, 3.49, 3.45, and 3.44, and their

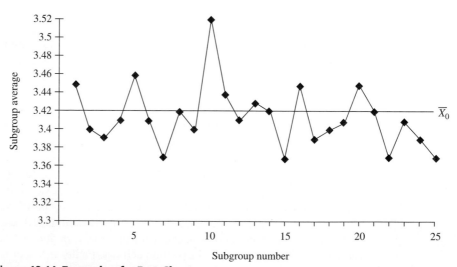

Figure 18-14 Example of a Run Chart

average is 3.46 kg. This value is the one posted on the chart for subgroup number 5. Averages are used on control charts rather than individual observations because average values will indicate a change in variation much faster. Also, with two or more observations in a sample, a measure of the dispersion can be obtained for a particular subgroup.

The solid line in the center of the chart can have three different interpretations, depending on the available data. First, it can be the average of the plotted points, which in the case of an $\overline{X}$ chart is the average of the averages or "X-double bar." Second, it can be a standard or reference value, $\overline{X}_0$, based on representative prior data, an economic value based on production costs or service needs, or an aimed-at value based on specifications. Third, it can be the population mean, μ, if that value is known.

Control Chart Example

One danger of using a run chart is its tendency to show every variation in data as being important. In order to indicate when observed variations in quality are greater than could be left to chance, the control chart method of analysis and presentation of data is used. The control chart method for variables is a means of visualizing the variations that occur in the central tendency and dispersion of a set of observations. It is a graphical record of the quality of a particular characteristic. It shows whether or not the process is in a stable state by adding statistically determined control limits to the run chart.

Figure 18-15, is the run chart of Figure 18-14 with the control limits added. They are the two dashed outer lines and are called the upper and lower control limits. These limits are established to assist in judging the significance of the variation in the quality of the product. Control limits are frequently confused with specification limits, which are the permissible limits of a quality characteristic of each individual unit of a product. However, control limits are used to evaluate the variations in quality from subgroup to

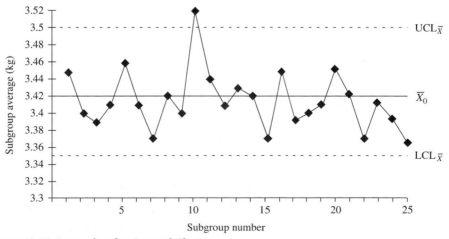

Figure 18-15 Example of a Control Chart

subgroup. Therefore, for the $\overline{X}$ chart, the control limits are a function of the subgroup averages. A frequency distribution of the subgroup averages can be determined with its corresponding average and standard deviation.

The control limits are then established at $\pm 3\sigma$ from the central line. Recall, from the discussion of the normal curve, that the number of items between $+ 3\sigma$ and $- 3\sigma$ equals 99.73%. Therefore, it is expected that more than 997 times out of 1,000, the subgroup values will fall between the upper and lower limits. When this situation occurs, the process is considered to be in control. When a subgroup value falls outside the limits, the process is considered to be out of control, and an assignable cause for the variation is present. Subgroup number 10 in Figure 18-15 is beyond the upper control limit; therefore, there has been a change in the stable nature of the process, causing the out-of-control point. As long as the sources of variation fluctuate in a natural or expected manner, a stable pattern of many chance causes (random causes) of variation develops. Chance causes of variation are inevitable. Because they are numerous and individually of relatively small importance, they are difficult to detect or identify. Those causes of variation that are large in magnitude, and therefore readily identified, are classified as assignable causes.[3] When only chance causes are present in a process, the process is considered to be in a state of statistical control. It is stable and predictable. However, when an assignable cause of variation is also present, the variation will be excessive, and the process is classified as out of control or beyond the expected natural variation of the process.

Unnatural variation is the result of assignable causes. Usually, but not always, it requires corrective action by people close to the process, such as operators, technicians, clerks, maintenance workers, and first-line supervisors. Natural variation is the result of chance causes—it requires management intervention to achieve quality improvement. In this regard, between 80% and 85% of the quality problems are due to management or the system and 15% to 20% are due to operations. Operating personnel are giving a quality performance as long as the plotted points are within the control limits. If this performance is not satisfactory, the solution is the responsibility of the system rather than of the operating personnel.

Variable Control Charts

In practice, control charts are posted at individual machines or work centers to control a particular quality characteristic. Usually, an $\overline{X}$ chart for the central tendency and an R chart for the dispersion are used together. An example of this dual charting is illustrated in Figure 18-16, which shows a method of charting and reporting inspection results for rubber durometer.

At work center number 365-2 at 8:30 A.M., the operator selects four items for testing and records the observations of 55, 52, 51, and 53 in the rows marked X_1, X_2, X_3, and X_4,

---

[3] Dr. W. Edwards Deming uses the words *common* and *special* for "chance" and "assignable."

$\bar{X}$ and R Charts

Work Center Number 365-2

QualityCharacteristic Durometer   Date 3/6/93

Time	8:30 AM	9:30 AM	10:40 AM	11:50 AM	1:30 PM								
Subgroup	1	2	3	4	5	6	7	8	9	10	11	12	13
X_1	55	51	48	45	53								
X_2	52	52	49	43	50								
X_3	51	51	50	45	48								
X_4	53	50	49	43	50								
Sum	211	210	196	176	201								
$\bar{X}$	52.8	52.5	49	44	50.2								
R	4	1	2	2	5								

$\bar{X}$ Chart

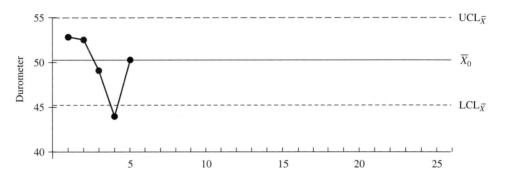

R Chart

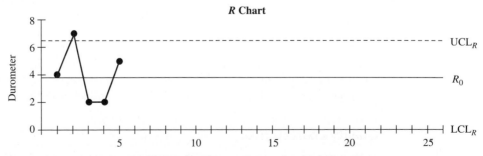

Figure 18-16 Example of a Method of Reporting Inspection Results

respectively. A subgroup average value of 52.8 is obtained by summing the observation and dividing by 4, and the range value of 4 is obtained by subtracting the low value, 51, from the high value, 55. The operator places a small solid circle at 52.8 on the $\overline{X}$ chart and a small solid circle at 4 on the R chart and then proceeds with his other duties.

The frequency with which the operator inspects a product at a particular machine or work center is determined by the quality of the product. When the process is in control and no difficulties are being encountered, fewer inspections may be required. Conversely, when the process is out of control or during start-up, more inspections may be needed. The inspection frequency at a machine or work center can also be determined by the amount of time that must be spent on noninspection activities. In the example problem, the inspection frequency appears to be every 60 or 65 minutes.

At 9:30 A.M. the operator performs the activities for subgroup 2 in the same manner as for subgroup 1. It is noted that the range value of 7 falls on the upper control limit. Whether to consider this in control or out of control would be a matter of organization policy. It is suggested that it be classified as in control and a cursory examination for an assignable cause be conducted by the operator. A plotted point that falls exactly on the control limit is a rare occurrence.

The inspection results for subgroup 2 show that the third observation, X_3, has a value of 57, which exceeds the upper control limit. It is important to remember the earlier discussion on control limits and specifications. In other words, the 57 value is an individual observation and does not relate to the control limits. Therefore, the fact that an individual observation is greater than or less than a control limit is meaningless.

Subgroup 4 has an average value of 44, which is less than the lower control limit of 45. Therefore, subgroup 4 is out of control, and the operator will report this fact to the departmental supervisor. The operator and supervisor will then look for an assignable cause and, if possible, take corrective action. Whatever corrective action is taken will be noted by the operator on the $\overline{X}$ and R charts or on a separate form. The control chart indicates when and where trouble has occurred. The identification and elimination of the difficulty is a production problem. Ideally, the control chart should be maintained by the operator, provided time is available and proper training has been given. When the operator cannot maintain the chart, then it is maintained by quality control.

The control chart is used to keep a continuing record of a particular quality characteristic. It is a picture of the process over time. When the chart is completed and stored in an office file, it is replaced by a fresh chart. The chart is used to improve the process quality, to determine the process capability, to determine when to leave the process alone and when to make adjustments, and to investigate causes of unacceptable or marginal quality. It is also used to make decisions on product or service specifications and decisions on the acceptability of a recently-produced product or service.

Quality Characteristic

The variable that is chosen for the $\overline{X}$ and R charts must be a quality characteristic that is measurable and can be expressed in numbers. Quality characteristics that can be expressed in terms of the seven basic units (length, mass, time, electrical current, temperature, substance, or luminous intensity), as well as any of the derived units, such as power, velocity, force, energy, density, and pressure, are appropriate.

Those quality characteristics affecting the performance of the product would normally be given first attention. These may be a function of the raw materials, component parts, subassemblies, or finished parts. In other words, high priority is given to the selection of those characteristics that are giving difficulty in terms of production problems and/or cost. An excellent opportunity for cost savings frequently involves situations where spoilage and rework costs are high. A Pareto analysis is also useful for establishing priorities. Another possibility occurs where destructive testing is used to inspect a product.

In any organization, a large number of variables make up a product or service. It is, therefore, impossible to place $\overline{X}$ and R charts on all variables. A judicious selection of those quality characteristics is required.

Subgroup Size and Method

As previously mentioned, the data that are plotted on the control chart consist of groups of items called rational subgroups. It is important to understand that data collected in a random manner do not qualify as rational. A rational subgroup is one in which the variation within the group is due only to chance causes. This within-subgroup variation is used to determine the control limits. Variation between subgroups is used to evaluate long-term stability. Subgroup samples are selected from product or a service produced at one instant of time or as close to that instant as possible, such as four consecutive parts from a machine or four documents from a tray. The next subgroup sample would be similar, but for product or a service produced at a later time—say, one hour later.

Decisions on the size of the sample or subgroup require a certain amount of empirical judgment; however, some helpful guidelines are:

1. As the subgroup size increases, the control limits become closer to the central value, which makes the control chart more sensitive to small variations in the process average.

2. As the subgroup size increases, the inspection cost per subgroup increases. Does the increased cost of larger subgroups justify the greater sensitivity?

3. When costly and/or destructive testing is used and the item is expensive, a small subgroup size of two or three is necessary, because it will minimize the destruction of expensive product.

4. Because of the ease of computation, a sample size of five is quite common in industry; however, when inexpensive electronic hand calculators are used, this reason is no longer valid.

5. From a statistical basis a distribution of subgroup averages, $\overline{X}$'s, is nearly normal for subgroups of four or more even when the samples are taken from a nonnormal population. This statement is proved by the central limit theorem.

There is no rule for the frequency of taking subgroups, but the frequency should be often enough to detect process changes. The inconveniences of the factory or office layout and the cost of taking subgroups must be balanced with the value of the data obtained. In general, it is best to sample quite often at the beginning and reduce the sampling frequency when the data permit.

The precontrol rule for the frequency of sampling could also be used. It is based on how often the process is adjusted. If the process is adjusted every hour, then sampling should occur every 10 minutes; if the process is adjusted every 2 hours, then sampling should occur every 20 minutes; if the process is adjusted every 3 hours, then sampling should occur every 30 minutes; and so forth.

Data Collection

Assuming that the quality characteristic and the plan for the rational subgroup have been selected, a team member such as a technician can be assigned the task of collecting the data as part of his normal duties. The first-line supervisor and the operator should be informed of the technician's activities; however, no charts or data are posted at the work center at this time.

Because of difficulty in the assembly of a gear hub to a shaft using a key and keyway, the project team recommends using $\overline{X}$ and R charts. The quality characteristic is the shaft keyway depth of 6.35 mm (0.250 in.). Using a rational subgroup of four, a technician obtains five subgroups per day for five days. The samples are measured, the subgroup average and range are calculated, and the results are recorded on the form as shown in Table 18-4. Additional recorded information includes the date, time, and any comments pertaining to the process. For simplicity, individual measurements are coded from 6.00 mm. Thus, the first measurement of 6.35 is recorded as 35.

It is necessary to collect a minimum of 25 subgroups of data. A fewer number of subgroups would not provide a sufficient amount of data for the accurate computation of the control limits, and a larger number of subgroups would delay the introduction of the control chart.

Trial Central Lines and Control Limits

The central lines for the $\overline{X}$ and R charts are obtained using the equations

$$\overline{\overline{X}} = \Sigma \, \overline{X}_i / g \qquad\qquad \overline{R} = \Sigma \, R_i / g$$

where $\overline{\overline{X}}$ = average of the subgroup averages (read "X double bar")
          $\overline{X}_i$ = average of the ith subgroup
          g = number of subgroups
          $\overline{R}$ = average of the subgroup ranges
          R_i = range of the ith subgroup

TABLE 18-4
Data on the Depth of the Keyway (millimeters)

Subgroup Number	Date	Time	MEASUREMENTS				Average $\overline{X}$	Range R	Comment
			X_1	X_2	X_3	X_4			
1	7/23	8:50	35	40	32	37	6.36	0.08	
2		11:30	46	37	36	41	6.40	0.10	
3		1:45	34	40	34	36	6.36	0.06	
4		3:45	69	64	68	59	6.65	0.10	New, temporary
5		4:20	38	34	44	40	6.39	0.10	operator
.	.	.	.	.	.	.	.	.	
.	.	.	.	.	.	.	.	.	
.	.	.	.	.	.	.	.	.	
17	7/29	9:25	41	40	29	34	6.36	0.12	
18		11:00	38	44	28	58	6.42	0.30	Damaged oil line
19		2:35	35	41	37	38	6.38	0.06	
20		3:15	56	55	45	48	6.51	0.11	Bad material
21	7/30	9:35	38	40	45	37	6.40	0.08	
22		10:20	39	42	35	40	6.39	0.07	
23		11:35	42	39	39	36	6.39	0.06	
24		2:00	43	36	35	38	6.38	0.08	
25		4:25	39	38	43	44	6.41	0.06	
Sum							160.25	2.19	

Trial control limits for the charts are established at $\pm\, 3\sigma$ from the central line, as shown by the equations

$$\text{UCL}_{\overline{x}} = \overline{\overline{X}} + 3\sigma_{\overline{x}} \qquad \text{UCL}_R = \overline{R} + 3\sigma_R$$
$$\text{LCL}_{\overline{x}} = \overline{\overline{X}} - 3\sigma_{\overline{x}} \qquad \text{LCL}_R = \overline{R} - 3\sigma_R$$

where   UCL = upper control limit
         LCL = lower control limit
         $\sigma_{\overline{x}}$ = population standard deviation of the subgroup averages
         σ_R = population standard deviation of the range

In practice, the calculations are simplified by using the product of the average of the range $(\overline{R})$ and a factor (A_2) to replace the three standard deviations $(A_2\overline{R} = 3\sigma_{\overline{x}})$ in the equation for the $\overline{X}$ chart. For the R chart, the range is used to estimate the standard deviation of the range. Therefore, the derived equations are

$$\mathrm{UCL}_{\overline{X}} = \overline{\overline{X}} + A_2\overline{R} \qquad\qquad \mathrm{UCL}_R = D_4\overline{R}$$
$$\mathrm{LCL}_{\overline{X}} = \overline{\overline{X}} - A_2\overline{R} \qquad\qquad \mathrm{LCL}_R = D_4\overline{R}$$

where A_2, D_3, and D_4 are factors that vary with the subgroup size and are found in Appendix A. For the $\overline{X}$ chart, the upper and lower control limits are symmetrical about the central line. Theoretically, the control limits for an R chart should also be symmetrical about the central line. But, for this situation to occur, with subgroup sizes of six or less, the lower control limit would need to have a negative value. Because a negative range is impossible, the lower control limit is located at zero by assigning to D_3 the value of zero for subgroups of six or less.

When the subgroup size is seven or more, the lower control limit is greater than zero and symmetrical about the central line. However, when the R chart is posted at the work center, it may be more practical to keep the lower control limit at zero. This practice eliminates the difficulty of explaining to the operator that points below the lower control limit on the R chart are the result of exceptionally good performance rather than poor performance. However, quality personnel should keep their own charts with the lower control limit in its proper location, and any out-of-control low points should be investigated to determine the reason for the exceptionally good performance. Because subgroup sizes of seven or more are uncommon, the situation occurs infrequently.

In order to illustrate the calculations necessary to obtain the trial control limits and the central line, the data concerning the depth of the shaft keyway will be used. From Table 18-4, $\Sigma\overline{X} = 160.25$, $\Sigma R = 2.19$, and $g = 25$; thus, the central lines are

$$\overline{\overline{X}} = \Sigma\,\overline{X}/g = 160.25/25 = 6.41 \text{ mm}$$
$$\overline{R} = \Sigma\,R/g = 2.19/25 = 0.0876 \text{ mm}$$

From Appendix Table A, the values for the factors for a subgroup size (n) of four are $A_2 = 0.729$, $D_3 = 0$, and $D_4 = 2.282$. Trial control limits for the $\overline{X}$ chart are

$$\mathrm{UCL}_{\overline{X}} = \overline{\overline{X}} + A_2\overline{R} \qquad\qquad \mathrm{LCL}_{\overline{X}} = \overline{\overline{X}} - A_2\overline{R}$$
$$= 6.41 + (0.729)(0.0876) \qquad\qquad = 6.41 - (0.729)(0.0876)$$
$$= 6.47 \text{ mm} \qquad\qquad\qquad = 6.35 \text{ mm}$$

Trial control limits for the R chart are

$$\mathrm{UCL}_R = D_4\overline{R} \qquad\qquad\qquad \mathrm{LCL}_R = D_3\overline{R}$$
$$= (2.282)(0.0876) \qquad\qquad = (0)(0.0876)$$
$$= 0.20 \text{ mm} \qquad\qquad\qquad = 0 \text{ mm}$$

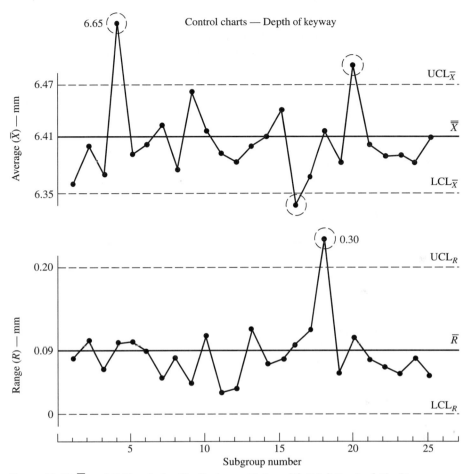

Figure 18-17 $\overline{X}$ and R Charts for Preliminary Data with Trial Control Limits

Figure 18-17 shows the central lines and the trial control limits for $\overline{X}$ and R charts for the preliminary data.

Revised Central Lines and Control Limits

Revised central lines and control limits are established by discarding out-of-control points with assignable causes and recalculating the central lines and control limits. The R chart is analyzed first to determine if it is stable. Because the out-of-control point at subgroup 18 on the R chart has an assignable cause (damaged oil line), it can be discarded from the data. The remaining plotted points indicate a stable process.

The $\overline{X}$ chart can now be analyzed. Subgroups 4 and 20 had an assignable cause, whereas the out-of-control condition for subgroup 16 did not. It is assumed that subgroup 16's out-of-control state is due to a chance cause and is part of the natural variation of the process.

The recalculated values are $\overline{X}_0 = 6.40$ mm and $R_0 = 0.079$. They are shown in Figure 18-18. For illustrative purposes, the trial values are also shown. The limits for both the $\overline{X}$ and R charts became narrower, as was expected. No change occurred in LCL_R because the subgroup size is less than 7. The figure also illustrates a simpler charting technique in that lines are not drawn between the points. Also, $\overline{X}_0$ and R_0, the standard or reference values, are used to designate the central lines.

The preliminary data for the initial 25 subgroups are not plotted with the revised control limits. These revised control limits are for reporting the results for future subgroups. To make effective use of the control chart during production, it should be displayed in a conspicuous place, where it can be seen by operators and supervisors.

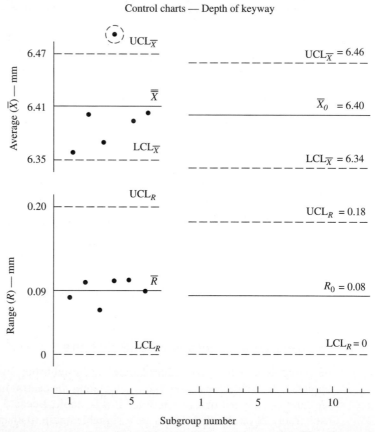

Control charts — Depth of keyway

Figure 18-18 Trial Control Limits and Revised Control Limits for $\overline{X}$ and R Charts

Before proceeding to the action step, some final comments are appropriate. First, many analysts eliminate this step in the procedure because it appears to be somewhat redundant. However, by discarding out-of-control points with assignable causes, the central line and control limits are more representative of the process. If this step is too complicated for operating personnel, its elimination would not affect the next step.

Second, the central line $\overline{X}_0$ for the $\overline{X}$ chart is frequently based on the specifications. In such a case, the procedure is used only to obtain R_0. If, in our example problem, the nominal value of the characteristic is 6.38 mm, then $\overline{X}_0$ is set to that value and the upper and lower control limits are

$$\text{UCL}_{\overline{X}} = \overline{X}_0 + A_2 R_0 \qquad\qquad \text{LCL}_{\overline{X}} = \overline{X}_0 - A_2 R_0$$
$$= 6.38 + (0.729)(0.079) \qquad\qquad = 6.38 - (0.729)(0.079)$$
$$= 6.44 \text{ mm} \qquad\qquad\qquad = 6.32 \text{ mm}$$

The central line and control limits for the R chart do not change. This modification can be taken only if the process is adjustable. If the process is not adjustable, then the original calculations must be used.

Third, it follows that adjustments to the process should be made while taking data. It is not necessary to run nonconforming material while collecting data, because we are primarily interested in obtaining R_0, which is not affected by the process setting. The independence of $\overline{X}_0$ and R_0 provides the rationale for this concept.

Fourth, the process determines the central line and control limits. They are not established by design, manufacturing, marketing, or any other department, except for $\overline{X}_0$ when the process is adjustable.

Achieving the Objective

When control charts are first introduced at a work center, an improvement in the process performance usually occurs. This initial improvement is especially noticeable when the process is dependent on the skill of the operator. Posting a quality control chart appears to be a psychological signal to the operator to improve performance. Most workers want to produce a quality product or service; therefore, when management shows an interest in the quality, the operator responds.

Figure 18-19 illustrates the initial improvement that occurred after the introduction of the $\overline{X}$ and R charts in January. Owing to space limitations, only a representative number of subgroups for each month are shown in the figure. During January the subgroup ranges had less variation and tended to be centered at a slightly lower point. A reduction in the range variation occurred also.

Not all the improved performance in January was the result of operator effort. The first-line supervisor initiated a program of tool-wear control, which was a contributing factor.

At the end of January new central lines and control limits were calculated using the data from subgroups obtained during the month. It is a good idea, especially when a chart

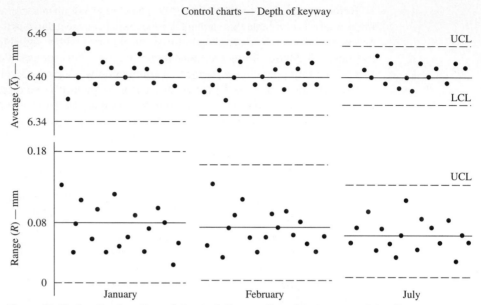

Figure 18-19 Continuing Use of Control Charts, Showing Improved Quality

is being initiated, to calculate standard values periodically to see if any changes have occurred. This reevaluation can be done for every 25 or more subgroups, and the results can be compared to the previous values.

New control limits for the $\overline{X}$ and R charts and central line for the R chart were established for the month of February. The central line for the $\overline{X}$ chart was not changed because it is the nominal value. During the ensuing months, the maintenance department replaced a pair of worn gears, purchasing changed the material supplier, and tooling modified a workholding device. All these improvements were the result of investigations that tracked down the causes for out-of-control conditions or were ideas developed by a project team. The generation of ideas by many different personnel is the most essential ingredient for continuous quality improvement. Ideas from the operator, first-line supervisor, quality assurance, maintenance, manufacturing engineering, and industrial engineering should be evaluated. This evaluation or testing of an idea requires 25 or more subgroups. The control chart will tell if the idea is good, is poor, or has no effect on the process. Quality improvement occurs when the plotted points of the $\overline{X}$ chart converge on the central line, when the plotted points of the R chart trend downward, or when both actions occur. If a poor idea is tested, then the reverse occurs. Of course, if the idea is neutral, it will have no effect on the plotted point pattern.

To speed up the testing of ideas, the taking of subgroups can be compressed in time as long as the data represent the process by accounting for any hourly or day-to-day fluctuations. Only one idea should be tested at a time; otherwise, the results will be confounded.

At the end of June, the periodic evaluation of the past performance showed the need to revise the central lines and the control limits. The performance for the month of July and subsequent months showed a natural pattern of variation and no quality improvement. At that point, no further quality improvement would be possible without a substantial investment in new equipment or equipment modification.

Dr. Deming has stated that if he were a banker, he would not lend money to an organization unless statistical methods were used to prove that the money was necessary. This is precisely what the control chart can achieve, provided that all personnel use the chart as a method of quality improvement rather than a monitoring function.

When the objective for initiating the charts has been achieved, their use should be discontinued or the frequency of inspection be substantially reduced to a monitoring action by the operator. The median chart is an excellent chart for the monitoring activity. Efforts should then be directed toward the improvement of some other quality characteristic. If a project team was involved, it should be recognized and rewarded for its performance and disbanded.

The U.S. Postal Service at Royal Oak, Michigan used a variables control chart to reduce nonconformance in a sorting operation from 32% to less than 6%. This activity resulted in an annual savings of $700,000 and earned the responsible team the 1999 RIT/USA Today Quality Cup for government.

State of Control

When the assignable causes have been eliminated from the process to the extent that the points plotted on the control chart remain within the control limits, the process is in a state of control. No higher degree of uniformity can be attained with the existing process. However, greater uniformity can be attained through a change in the basic process resulting from quality improvement ideas.

When a process is in control, there occurs a natural pattern of variation, which is illustrated by the control chart in Figure 18-20. This natural pattern of variation has

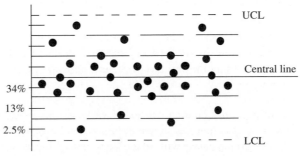

Figure 18-20 Natural Pattern of Variation of a Control Chart

(1) about 34% of the plotted points on an imaginary band between one standard deviation on both sides of the central line, (2) about 13.5% of the plotted points in an imaginary band between one and two standard deviations on both sides of the central line, and (3) about 2.5% of the plotted points in an imaginary band between two and three standard deviations on both sides of the central line. The points are located back and forth across the central line in a random manner, with no points beyond the control limits. The natural pattern of the points, or subgroup average values, forms its own frequency distribution. If all the points were stacked up at one end, they would form a normal curve.

When a process is in control, only chance causes of variation are present. Small variations in machine performance, operator performance, and material characteristics are expected and are considered to be part of a stable process.

When a process is in control, certain practical advantages accrue to the producer and consumer:

1. Individual units of the product will be more uniform, or, stated another way, there will be less variation.

2. Because the product is more uniform, fewer samples are needed to judge the quality. Therefore, the cost of inspection can be reduced to a minimum. This advantage is extremely important when 100% conformance to specifications is not essential.

3. The process capability, or spread of the process, is easily attained from 6σ. With a knowledge of the process capability, a number of reliable decisions relative to specifications can be made, such as the product specifications; the amount of rework or scrap when there is insufficient tolerance; and whether to produce the product to tight specifications and permit interchangeability of components or to produce the product to loose specifications and use selective matching of components.

4. The percentage of product that falls within any pair of values can be predicted with the highest degree of assurance. For example, this advantage can be very important when adjusting filling machines to obtain different percentage of items below, between, or above particular values.

5. It permits the customer to use the supplier's data and, therefore, to test only a few subgroups as a check on the supplier's records. The $\overline{X}$ and R charts are used as statistical evidence of process control.

6. The operator is performing satisfactorily from a quality viewpoint. Further improvement in the process can be achieved only by changing the input factors: materials, equipment, environment, and operators. These changes require action by management.

When only chance causes of variation are present, the process is stable and predictable over time, as shown in Figure 18-21(a). We know that future variation as shown by the dotted curve will be the same unless there has been a change in the process due to an assignable cause.

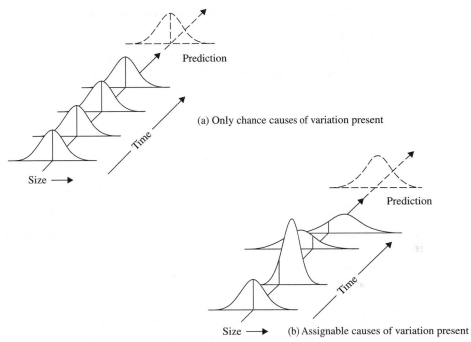

Figure 18-21 Stable and Unstable Variation

Out-of-Control Process

Figure 18-21(b) illustrates the effect of assignable causes of variation over time. The unnatural, unstable nature of the variation makes it impossible to predict future variation. The assignable causes must be found and corrected before a natural stable process can continue.

The term *out of control* is usually thought of as being undesirable; however, there are situations where this condition is desirable. It is best to think of the term *out of control* as a change in the process due to an assignable cause.

A process can also be considered out of control even when the points fall inside the 3σ limits. This situation, as shown in Figure 18-22, occurs when unnatural runs of variation are present in the process. It is not natural for seven or more consecutive points to be above or below the central line as shown at (a). Another unnatural run occurs at (b), where six points in a row are steadily increasing or decreasing. At (c), the space is divided into four equal bands of 1.5σ. The process is out of control when there are two successive points at 1.5σ beyond.[4]

---

[4] For more information, see A. M. Hurwitz and M. Mather, "A Very Simple Set of Process Control Rules," *Quality Engineering* 5, no. 1 (1992–1993): 21–29.

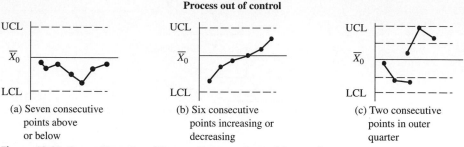

Process out of control

(a) Seven consecutive points above or below

(b) Six consecutive points increasing or decreasing

(c) Two consecutive points in outer quarter

Figure 18-22 Some Unnatural Runs—Process Out of Control

There are some common questions to ask when investigating an out-of-control process:

1. Are there differences in the measurement accuracy of the instruments used?
2. Are there differences in the methods used by different operators?
3. Is the process affected by the environment? If so, have there been any changes?
4. Is the process affected by tool wear?
5. Were any untrained workers involved in the process?
6. Has there been any change in the source of the raw materials?
7. Is the process affected by operator fatigue?
8. Has there been any change in maintenance procedures?
9. Is the equipment being adjusted too frequently?
10. Did samples come from different shifts, operators, or machines?

It is advisable to develop a checklist for each process using these common questions as a guide.

Process Capability

Control limits are established as a function of the averages—in other words, control limits are for averages. Specifications, on the other hand, are the permissible variation in the size of the part and are, therefore, for individual values. The specification or tolerance limits are established by design engineers to meet a particular function. Figure 18-23 shows that the location of the specifications is optional and is not related to any of the other features in the figure. The control limits, process spread (process capability), distribution of averages, and distribution of individual values are interdependent. They are determined by the process, whereas the specifications have an optional location. Control charts cannot determine if the process is meeting specifications.

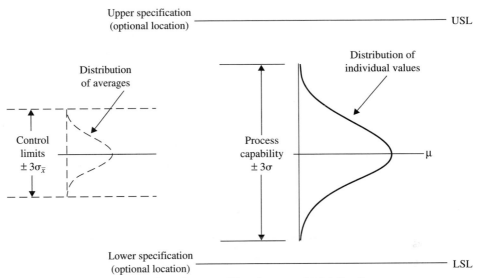

Figure 18-23 Relationship of Limits, Specifications, and Distributions

The true process capability cannot be determined until the X and R charts have achieved the optimal quality improvement without a substantial investment for new equipment or equipment modification. When the process is in statistical control, process capability is equal to 6σ, where $\sigma = R_0/d_2$ and d_2 is a factor from Appendix Table A. In the example problem, it is

$$6\sigma = 6(R_0/d_2) = 6(0.079/2.059) = 0.230$$

It is frequently necessary to obtain the process capability by a quick method rather than by using the $\overline{X}$ and R charts. This method assumes the process is stable or in statistical control, which may or may not be the case. The procedure is as follows:

1. Take 25 subgroups of size 4, for a total of 100 measurements.
2. Calculate the range, R, for each subgroup.
3. Calculate the average range: $\overline{R} = \Sigma R/g$.
4. Calculate the estimate of the population standard deviation:

$$\sigma = \overline{R}/d_2$$

where d_2 is obtained from Appendix Table A and is 2.059 for $n = 4$.

5. The process capability will equal 6σ.

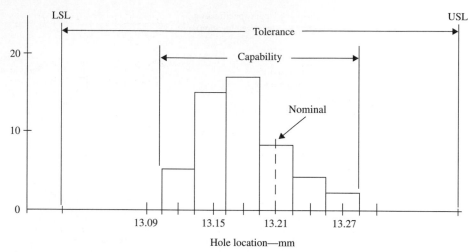

Figure 18-24 Relationship of Process Capability to Tolerance

Remember that this technique does not give the true process capability and should be used only if circumstances require its use. Also, more than 25 subgroups can be used to improve accuracy.

The relationship of process capability and specifications is shown in Figure 18-24. Tolerance is the difference between the upper specification limit (USL) and the lower specification limit (LSL). Process capability and the tolerance are combined to form a capability index, defined as

$$C_p = \frac{USL - LSL}{6\sigma}$$

where　USL − LSL = upper specification − lower specification, or tolerance
　　　　　C_p = capability index
　　　　　6σ = process capability

If the capability index is greater than 1.00, the process is capable of meeting the specifications; if the index is less than 1.00, the process is not capable of meeting the specifications. Because processes are continually shifting back and forth, a C_p value of 1.33 has become a de facto standard, and some organizations are using a 2.00 value. Using the capability index concept, we can measure quality, provided the process is centered. The larger the capability index, the better the quality. We should strive to make the capability index as large as possible. This result is accomplished by having realistic specifications and continual striving to improve the process capability.

The capability index does not measure process performance in terms of the nominal or target value. This measure is accomplished using C_{pk}, which is

$$C_{pk} = \frac{\text{Min}\left\{(\text{USL} - \overline{X}) \text{ or } (\overline{X} - \text{LSL})\right\}}{3\sigma}$$

A C_{pk} value of 1.00 is the de facto standard, with some organizations using a value of 1.33. Figure 18-25 illustrates C_p and C_{pk} values for processes that are centered and also off center by 1σ.

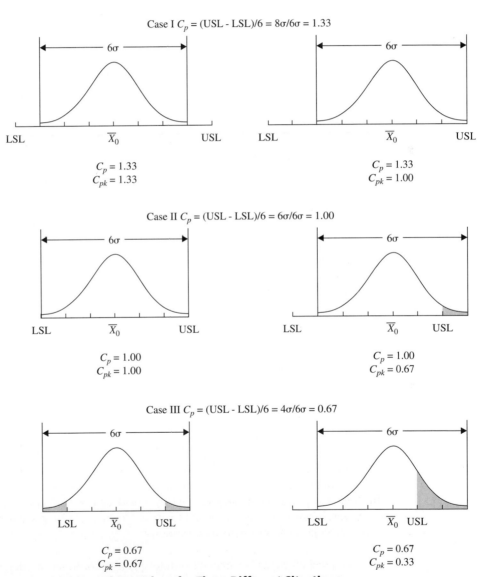

Figure 18-25 **C_p and C_{pk} Values for Three Different Situations**

Comments concerning C_p and C_{pk} are as follows:

1. The C_p value does not change as the process center changes.
2. $C_p = C_{pk}$ when the process is centered.
3. C_{pk} is always equal to or less than C_p.
4. A C_{pk} value greater than 1.00 indicates the process conforms to specifications.
5. A C_{pk} value less than 1.00 indicates that the process does not conform to specifications.
6. A C_p value less than 1.00 indicates that the process is not capable.
7. A C_{pk} value of zero indicates the average is equal to one of the specification limits.
8. A negative C_{pk} value indicates that the average is outside the specifications.

Quality professionals will use these eight items to improve the process. For example, if a C_p value is less than one, then corrective action must occur. Initially 100% inspection is necessary to eliminate noncomformities. One solution would be to increase the tolerance of the specifications. Another would be to work on the process to reduce the standard deviation or variability.

Different Control Charts for Variables

Although most of the quality control activity for variables is concerned with the $\overline{X}$ and R charts, there are other charts that find application in some situations. These charts are described in Table 18-5.

Control Charts for Attributes

An attribute, as defined in quality, refers to those quality characteristics that conform to specifications or do not conform to specifications. There are two types:

1. Where measurements are not possible, for example, visually inspected items such as color, missing parts, scratches, and damage.

2. Where measurements can be made but are not made because of time, cost, or need. In other words, although the diameter of a hole can be measured with an inside micrometer, it may be more convenient to use a "go–no go" gauge and determine if it conforms or does not conform to specifications.

Where an attribute does not conform to specifications, various descriptive terms are used. A *nonconformity* is a departure of a quality characteristic from its intended level

TABLE 18-5
Different Control Charts for Variables

Type	Central Line	Central Limits	Comments
$\overline{X}$ and s	$\overline{\overline{X}}$	$UCL_{\overline{x}} = \overline{\overline{X}} + A_3\overline{s}$ $LCL_{\overline{x}} = \overline{\overline{X}} - A_3\overline{s}$	Use when more sensitivity is desired than R; when
	$\overline{s}$	$UCL_s = B_4\,\overline{s}$ $LCL_s = B_3\,\overline{s}$	$n > 10$; and when data are collected automatically.
Moving average, $M\overline{X}$ and moving range, MR	$\overline{\overline{X}}$	$UCL_{\overline{x}} = \overline{\overline{X}} + A_2\overline{R}$ $LCL_{\overline{x}} = \overline{\overline{X}} - A_2\overline{R}$	Use when only one observation is possible at a time.
	$\overline{R}$	$UCL_R = D_4\overline{R}$ $LCL_R = D_3\overline{R}$	Data needn't be normal.
X and moving R	$\overline{X}$	$UCL_x = \overline{X} + 2.660\,\overline{R}$ $LCL_x = \overline{X} - 2.660\,\overline{R}$	Use when only one observation is possible at a time
	$\overline{R}$	$UCL_R = 3.276\,\overline{R}$ $LCL_R = (0)\,\overline{R}$	and the data are normal. Equations are based on a moving range of two.
Median and Range	Md_{md}	$UCL_{Md} = Md_{Md} + A_5\,R_{Md}$ $LCL_{Md} = Md_{Md} - A_5\,R_{Md}$	Use when process is in a maintenance mode. Benefits
	R_{md}	$UCL_R = D_6\,R_{Md}$ $LCL_R = D_5\,R_{Md}$	are less arithmetic and simplicity.

or state that occurs with a severity sufficient to cause an associated product or service not to meet a specification requirement. The definition of a defect is similar, except it is concerned with satisfying intended normal or reasonably foreseeable usage requirements. Defect is appropriate for use when evaluation is in terms of usage, and nonconformity is appropriate for conformance to specifications.

The term *nonconforming unit* is used to describe a unit of product or service containing at least one nonconformity. Defective is analogous to defect and is appropriate for use when a unit of product or service is evaluated in terms of usage rather than conformance to specifications.

In this section we are using the terms *nonconformity* and *nonconforming unit*. This practice avoids the confusion and misunderstanding that occurs with *defect* and *defective* in product-liability lawsuits.

Variable control charts are an excellent means for controlling quality and subsequently improving it; however, they do have limitations. One obvious limitation is that these charts cannot be used for quality characteristics that are attributes. The converse is not true, because a variable can be changed to an attribute by stating that it conforms or does not conform to specifications. In other words, nonconformities such as missing parts, incorrect color, and so on, are not measurable, and a variable control chart is not applicable.

Another limitation concerns the fact that there are many variables in a manufacturing entity. Even a small manufacturing plant could have as many as 1,000 variable quality characteristics. Because $\overline{X}$ and R charts are needed for each characteristic, 1,000 charts would be required. Clearly, this would be too expensive and impractical. A control chart for attributes can minimize this limitation by providing overall quality information at a fraction of the cost.

There are two different groups of control charts for attributes. One group of charts is for nonconforming units. A proportion, p, chart shows the proportion nonconforming in a sample or subgroup. The proportion is expressed as a fraction or a percent. Another chart in the group is for number nonconforming, np.

Another group of charts is for nonconformities. A c chart shows the count of nonconformities in an inspected unit such as an automobile, bolt of cloth, or roll of paper. Another closely-related chart is the u chart, which is for the count of nonconformities per unit.

Much of the information on control charts for attributes is similar to that already given in Variable Control Charts. Also see the information on State of Control.

Objectives of the Chart

The objectives of attribute charts are to

1. Determine the average quality level. Knowledge of the quality average is essential as a benchmark. This information provides the process capability in terms of attributes.

2. Bring to the attention of management any changes in the average. Changes, either increasing or decreasing, become significant once the average quality is known.

3. Improve the product quality. In this regard, an attribute chart can motivate operating and management personnel to initiate ideas for quality improvement. The chart will tell whether the idea is an appropriate or inappropriate one. A continual and relentless effort must be made to improve the quality.

4. Evaluate the quality performance of operating and management personnel. Supervisors should be evaluated by a chart for nonconforming units. One chart should be used to evaluate the chief executive officer (CEO). Other functional areas, such as engineering, sales, finance, etc., may find a chart for nonconformities more applicable for evaluation purposes.

5. Suggest places to use $\overline{X}$ and R charts. Even though the cost of computing and charting $\overline{X}$ and R charts is more than that of charts for attributes, they are much more sensitive to variations and are more helpful in diagnosing causes. In other words, the attribute chart suggests the source of difficulty, and $\overline{X}$ and R charts find the cause.

6. Determine acceptance criteria of a product before shipment to the customer. Knowledge of attributes provides management with information on whether or not to release an order.

Use of the Chart

The general procedures that apply to variable control charts also apply to the p chart. The first step in the procedure is to determine the use of the control chart. The p chart is used for data that consist of the proportion of the number of occurrences of an event to the total number of occurrences. It is used in quality control to report the proportion nonconforming in a product, quality characteristic, or group of quality characteristics. As such, the proportion nonconforming is the ratio of the number nonconforming in a sample or subgroup to the total number in the sample or subgroup. In symbolic terms, the equation is

$$p = \frac{np}{n}$$

where p = proportion (fraction or percent) nonconforming in the sample or subgroup
n = number in the sample or subgroup
np = number nonconforming in the sample or subgroup

The p chart is an extremely versatile control chart. It can be used to control one quality characteristic, as is done with $\overline{X}$ and R charts; to control a group of quality characteristics of the same type or of the same part; or to control the entire product. The p chart can be established to measure the quality produced by a work center, by a department, by a shift, or by an entire plant. It is frequently used to report the performance of an operator, group of operators, or management as a means of evaluating their quality performance. A hierarchy of utilization exists so that data collected for one chart can also be used on a more all-inclusive chart. The use for the chart or charts will be based on securing the greatest benefit for a minimum of cost.

Subgroup Size

The second step is to determine the size of the subgroup. The subgroup size of the p chart can be either variable or constant. A constant subgroup size is preferred; however, there may be many situations, such as changes in mix and 100% automated inspection, where the subgroup size changes.

If a part has a proportion nonconforming, p, of 0.001 and a subgroup size, n, of 1000, then the average number nonconforming, np, would be one per subgroup. This situation would not make a good chart, since a large number of values, posted to the chart, would be zero. If a part has a proportion nonconforming of 0.15 and a subgroup size of 50, the average number of nonconforming units would be 7.5, which would make a good chart.

Therefore, the selection of the subgroup size requires some preliminary observations to obtain a rough idea of the proportion nonconforming and some judgment as to the average number of nonconforming units that will make an adequate graphical chart. A minimum size of 50 is suggested as a starting point. Inspection can either be by audit

TABLE 18-6

Inspection Results of Hair Dryer Blower Motor, Motor Department, May

Subgroup Number	Number Inspected n	Number Nonconforming np	Proportion Nonconforming p
1	300	12	0.040
2	300	3	0.010
3	300	9	0.030
.	.	.	.
.	.	.	.
.	.	.	.
19	300	16	0.053
20	300	2	0.007
21	300	5	0.017
22	300	6	0.020
23	300	0	0.0
24	300	3	0.010
25	300	2	0.007
Total	7500	138	

or on-line. Audits are usually done in a laboratory under optimal conditions. On-line provides immediate feedback for corrective action.

Data Collection

The third step requires data to be collected for at least 25 subgroups, or the data may be obtained from historical records. Perhaps the best source is from a check sheet designed by a project team. Table 18-6 gives the inspection results from the motor department for the blower motor in an electric hair dryer. For each subgroup, the proportion nonconforming is calculated. The quality technician reported that subgroup 19 had an abnormally large number of nonconforming units, owing to faulty contacts.

Trial Central Lines and Control Limits

The fourth step is the calculation of the trial central line and control limits. The average proportion nonconforming, $\bar{p}$, is the central line and the control limits are established at 3σ. The equations are

$$\bar{p} = \Sigma np / \Sigma n$$

$$UCL = \bar{p} + 3\sqrt{\frac{\bar{p}(1 - \bar{p})}{n}} \qquad LCL = \bar{p} - 3\sqrt{\frac{\bar{p}(1 - \bar{p})}{n}}$$

where $\bar{p}$ = average proportion nonconforming for many subgroups
n = number inspected in a subgroup

Calculations for the central line and the trial control limits using the data on the electric hair dryer are as follows:

$$\bar{p} = \Sigma np / \Sigma n = 1.38/7500 = 0.018$$

$$UCL = \bar{p} + 3\sqrt{\frac{\bar{p}(1 - \bar{p})}{n}} \qquad LCL = \bar{p} - 3\sqrt{\frac{\bar{p}(1 - \bar{p})}{n}}$$

$$= 0.018 + 3\sqrt{\frac{0.018(1 - 0.018)}{300}} \qquad = 0.018 - 3\sqrt{\frac{0.018(1 - 0.018)}{300}}$$

$$= 0.041 \qquad\qquad\qquad = -0.005 \text{ or } 0.0$$

Calculations for the lower control limit resulted in a negative value, which is a theoretical result. In practice, a negative proportion nonconforming would be impossible. Therefore, the lower control limit value of -0.005 is changed to zero.

When the lower control limit is positive, it may in some cases be changed to zero. If the p chart is to be viewed by operating personnel, it would be difficult to explain why a proportion nonconforming that is below the lower control limit is out of control. In other words, performance of exceptionally good quality would be classified as out of control. To avoid the need to explain this situation to operating personnel, the lower control limit is left off the chart. When the p chart is to be used by quality control personnel and by management, a positive lower control limit is left unchanged. In this manner, exceptionally good performance (below the lower control limit) will be treated as an out-of-control situation and be investigated for an assignable cause. It is hoped that the assignable cause will indicate how the situation can be repeated.

The central line, $\bar{p}$, and the control limits are shown in Figure 18-26; the proportion nonconforming, p, from Table 18-6 is also posted to that chart. This chart is used to determine if the process is stable and is not posted. Like the $\overline{X}$ and R charts, the central line and control limits were determined from the data.

Revised Central Line and Control Limits

The fifth step is completed by discarding any out-of-control points that have assignable causes and recalculating the central line and control limits. The equations are the same except p_0, the standard or reference value, is substituted for $\bar{p}$.

Most industrial processes, however, are not in control when first analyzed, and this fact is illustrated in Figure 18-26 by subgroup 19, which is above the upper control limit and,

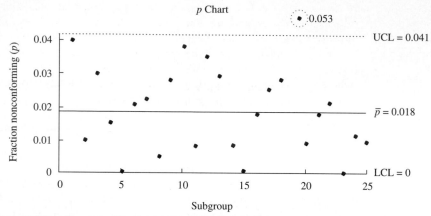

Figure 18-26 _p_ Chart to Illustrate the Trial Central Line and Control Limits Using the Data of Table 18-6

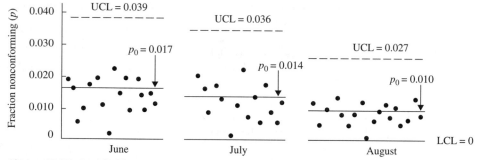

Figure 18-27 Continuing Use of the _p_ Chart for Representative Values of the Proportion Nonconforming, _p_

therefore, is out of control. Because subgroup 19 has an assignable cause, it can be discarded from the data, and a new $\bar{p}$ can be computed with all of the subgroups except 19. The value of p_0 is 0.017, which makes the UCL = 0.039 and the LCL = $-$ 0.005, or 0.0.

The revised control limits and the central line are shown in Figure 18-27. This chart, without the plotted points, is posted in an appropriate place and the proportion nonconforming, p, for each subgroup is plotted as it occurs.

Achieving the Objective

Whereas the first five steps are planning, the last step involves action and leads to the achievement of the objective. The revised control limits were based on data collected in May. Some representative values of inspection results for the month of June are shown in Figure 18-27. Analysis of the June results shows that the quality improved. This improvement is expected, because the posting of a quality control chart usually results in improved quality. Using the June data, a better estimate of the proportion nonconforming is obtained. The new value ($p_0 = 0.014$) is used to obtain the UCL of 0.036.

During the latter part of June and the entire month of July, various quality improvement ideas generated by a project team are tested. These ideas are new shellac, change in wire size, stronger spring, $\overline{X}$ and R charts on the armature, and so on. In testing ideas, there are three criteria: a minimum of 25 subgroups are required, the 25 subgroups can be compressed in time as long as no sampling bias occurs, and only one idea can be tested at a time. The control chart will tell whether the idea improves the quality, reduces the quality, or has no effect on the quality. The control chart should be located in a conspicuous place so operating personnel can view it.

Data from July are used to determine the central line and control limits for August. The pattern of variation for August indicates that no further improvement resulted. However, a 41% improvement occurred from June (0.017) to August (0.010). At this point, considerable improvement was obtained from testing the ideas of the project team. Although this improvement is very good, the relentless pursuit of quality improvement must continue—1 out of every 100 is still a nonconforming unit. Perhaps a detailed failure analysis or technical assistance from product engineering will lead to additional ideas that can be evaluated. A new project team may help.

Quality improvement is never finished. Efforts may be redirected to other areas based on need and/or resources available.

Like X and R charts, the p chart is most effective if it is posted where operating and quality control personnel can view it. Also, like $\overline{X}$ and R charts, the control limits are three standard deviations from the central value. Therefore, approximately 99% of the plotted points will fall between the upper and lower control limits.

A control chart for subgroup values of p will aid in disclosing the occasional presence of assignable causes of variation in the process. The elimination of these assignable causes will lower p_0 and, therefore, have a positive effect on spoilage, production efficiency, and cost per unit. A p chart will also indicate long-range trends in the quality, which will help to evaluate changes in personnel, methods, equipment, tooling, materials, and inspection techniques.

The process capability is the central line for all attribute charts. Management is responsible for the capability. If the value of the central line is not satisfactory, then management must initiate the procedures and provide the resources to take the necessary corrective action. As long as operating personnel (operators, first-line supervisors, and maintenance workers) are keeping the plotted points within the control limits, they are doing what the process is capable of doing. When the plotted point is outside the control limit, operating personnel are usually responsible.

A plotted point below the lower control limit is due to exceptionally good quality. It should be investigated to determine the assignable cause, so that if it is not due to an inspection error, it can be repeated.

Additional types of charts for attributes are shown in Table 18-7, with comments concerning their utilization.

TABLE 18-7
Different Types of Control Charts for Attributes*

Type	Central Line	Control Limits	Comments
p	$\bar{p}$	$UCL = \bar{p} + 3\sqrt{\dfrac{\bar{p}(1-\bar{p})}{n}}$ $LCL = \bar{p} - 3\sqrt{\dfrac{\bar{p}(1-\bar{p})}{n}}$	Use for nonconforming units with constant or variable sample size.
np	$\overline{np}$	$UCL = \overline{np} + 3\sqrt{\overline{np}(1-\bar{p})}$ $LCL = \overline{np} - 3\sqrt{\overline{np}(1-\bar{p})}$	Use for nonconforming units, where np is the number nonconforming. The sample size must be constant.
c	$\bar{c}$	$UCL = \bar{c} + 3\sqrt{\bar{c}}$ $LCL = \bar{c} - 3\sqrt{\bar{c}}$	Use for nonconformities within a unit where c is the count of nonconformities. The sample size is one inspected unit, i.e., a case of 24 cans.
u	$\bar{u}$	$UCL = \bar{u} + 3\sqrt{\dfrac{\bar{u}}{n}}$ $LCL = \bar{u} - 3\sqrt{\dfrac{\bar{u}}{n}}$	Use for nonconformities within a unit where u is the count of nonconformities per unit. The sample size can vary.

*For more information see *Quality Control*, 6th ed., by Dale H. Besterfield (Upper Saddle River, NJ: Prentice Hall, 2001).

Scatter Diagrams

The simplest way to determine if a cause-and-effect relationship exists between two variables is to plot a scatter diagram. Figure 18-28 shows the relationship between automotive speed and gas mileage. The figure shows that as speed increases, gas mileage decreases. Automotive speed is plotted on the *x*-axis and is the independent variable. The independent variable is usually controllable. Gas mileage is on the *y*-axis and is the dependent, or response, variable. Other examples of relationships are as follows:

Cutting speed and tool life.

Temperature and lipstick hardness.

Striking pressure and electrical current.

Temperature and percent foam in soft drinks.

Yield and concentration.

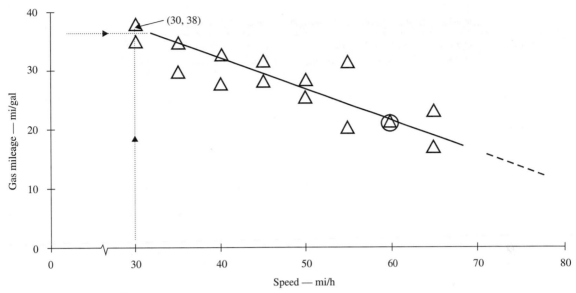

Figure 18-28 Scatter Diagram

Training and errors.

Breakdowns and equipment age.

Accidents and years with the organization.

There are a few simple steps for constructing a scatter diagram. Data are collected as ordered pairs (x, y). The automotive speed (cause) is controlled and the gas mileage (effect) is measured. Table 18-8 shows resulting x, y paired data. The horizontal and vertical scales are constructed with the higher values on the right for the x-axis and on the top for the y-axis. After the scales are labeled, the data are plotted. Using dotted lines, the technique of plotting sample number 1 (30, 38) is illustrated in Figure 18-28. The x-value is 30, and the y-value is 38. Sample numbers 2 through 16 are plotted, and the scatter diagram is complete. If two points are identical, the technique illustrated at 60 mi/h can be used.

Once the scatter diagram is complete, the relationship or correlation between the two variables can be evaluated. Figure 18-29 shows different patterns and their interpretation. At (a), there is a positive correlation between the two variables, because as x increases, y increases. At (b), there is a negative correlation between the two variables, because as x increases, y decreases. At (c), there is no correlation, and this pattern is sometimes referred to as a shotgun pattern. The patterns described in (a), (b), and (c) are easy to understand; however, those described in (d), (e), and (f) are more difficult. At (d), there may or may not be a relationship between the two variables. There appears to be a

TABLE 18-8
Data on Automotive Speed vs. Gas Mileage

Sample Number	Speed (mi/h)	Mileage (mi/gal)	Sample Number	Speed (mi/h)	Mileage (mi/gal)
1	30	38	9	50	26
2	30	35	10	50	29
3	35	35	11	55	32
4	35	30	12	55	21
5	40	33	13	60	22
6	40	28	14	60	22
7	45	32	15	65	18
8	45	29	16	65	24

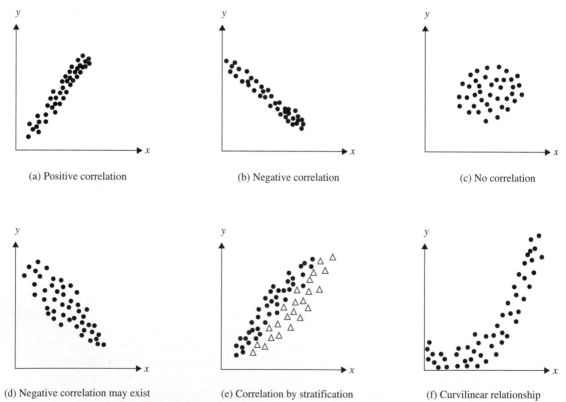

(a) Positive correlation

(b) Negative correlation

(c) No correlation

(d) Negative correlation may exist

(e) Correlation by stratification

(f) Curvilinear relationship

Figure 18-29 **Different Scatter Diagram Patterns**

negative relationship between x and y, but it is not too strong. Further statistical analysis is needed to evaluate this pattern. At (e), we have stratified the data to represent different causes for the same effect. Some examples are gas mileage with the wind versus against the wind, two different suppliers of material, and two different machines. One cause is plotted with a small solid circle, and the other cause is plotted with an open triangle. When the data are separated, we see that there is a strong correlation. At (f), we have a curvilinear relationship rather than a linear one.

When all the plotted points fall on a straight line, we have a perfect correlation. Because of variations in the experiment and measurement error, this perfect situation will rarely, if ever, occur.

It is sometimes desirable to fit a straight line to the data in order to write a prediction equation. For example, we may wish to estimate the gas mileage at 42 mi/h. A line can be placed on the scatter diagram by sight or mathematically using least squares analysis. In either approach, the idea is to make the deviation of the points on each side of the line equal. Where the line is extended beyond the data, a dashed line is used, because there are no data in that area.

Summary

The seven techniques of statistical process control (SPC) are powerful ones to improve the quality and hold the gains afterwards. SPC is applicable for any type organization—health care, education, manufacturing, government, banking, insurance, construction, etc.

TQM Exemplary Organization[5]

Founded in 1900, Granite Rock Company employs 400 people and produces rock, sand, and gravel aggregates; ready-mix concrete; asphalt; road treatments; and recycled road-base material. It also retails building materials made by other manufacturers and runs a highway-paving operation.

Since 1980, the regional supplier to commercial and residential builders and highway construction companies has increased its market share significantly. Productivity also has increased, with revenue earned per employee rising to about 30% above the national industry average. Most of the improvement has been realized since 1985, when Granite Rock started its Total Quality Program. The program stresses customer satisfaction with teams carrying out quality improvement projects. In 1991, nearly all workers took part in at least one of the company's 100-plus quality teams.

---

[5] Malcolm Baldrige National Quality Award, 1992 Small Business Category Recipient, NIST/Baldrige Homepage, Internet.

In 1991, Granite Rock employees averaged 37 hours of training at an average cost of $1,697 per employee, 13 times more than the construction-industry average. Many employees are trained in statistical process control, root-cause analysis, and other quality-assurance and problem-solving methods.

Applying statistical process control to all product lines has helped the company reduce variable costs and produce materials that exceed customer specifications and industry- and government-set standards. For example, Granite Rock's concrete products consistently exceed the industry performance specifications by 100 times. Granite Rock's record for delivering concrete on time has risen from less than 70% in 1988 to 93.5% in 1991. The reliability of several key processes has reached the six-sigma level which is a nonconforming rate of 3.4 per million.

Charts for each product line help executives assess Granite Rock's performance relative to competitors on key product and service attributes, ranked according to customer priorities. Ultimate customer satisfaction is assured through a system where customers can choose not to pay for a product or service that doesn't meet expectations; however, dissatisfaction is rare. Costs incurred in resolving complaints are equivalent to 0.2% of sales, as compared with the industry average of 2%.

Exercises

1. A major record-of-the-month club collected data on the reasons for returned shipments during a quarter. Results are: wrong selection, 50,000; refused, 195,000; wrong address, 68,000; order canceled, 5,000; and other, 15,000. Construct a Pareto diagram.

2. Form a project team of six or seven people, elect a leader, and construct a cause-and-effect diagram for bad coffee from a 22-cup coffee maker used in the office.

3. Design a check sheet for the maintenance of a piece of equipment such as a gas furnace, laboratory scale, or typewriter.

4. Construct a flow diagram for the manufacture of a product or the providing of a service.

5. An organization that fills bottles of shampoo tries to maintain a specific weight of the product. The table gives the weight of 110 bottles that were checked at random intervals. Make a tally of these weights and construct a frequency histogram. (Weight is in kilograms.)

6.00	5.98	6.01	6.01	5.97	5.99	5.98	6.01	5.99	5.98	5.96
5.98	5.99	5.99	6.03	5.99	6.01	5.98	5.99	5.97	6.01	5.98
5.97	6.01	6.00	5.96	6.00	5.97	5.95	5.99	5.99	6.01	5.98
6.01	6.03	6.01	5.99	5.99	6.02	6.00	5.98	6.01	5.98	5.99
6.00	5.98	6.05	6.00	6.00	5.98	5.99	6.00	5.97	6.00	6.00
6.00	5.98	6.00	5.94	5.99	6.02	6.00	5.98	6.02	6.01	6.00
5.97	6.01	6.04	6.02	6.01	5.97	5.99	6.02	5.99	6.02	5.99
6.02	5.99	6.01	5.98	5.99	6.00	6.02	5.99	6.02	5.95	6.02
5.96	5.99	6.00	6.00	6.01	5.99	5.96	6.01	6.00	6.01	5.98
6.00	5.99	5.98	5.99	6.03	5.99	6.02	5.98	6.02	6.02	5.97

6. Determine the average, median, mode, range, and standard deviation for each group of numbers.

(a) 50, 45, 55, 55, 45, 50, 55, 45, 55
(b) 89, 87, 88, 83, 86, 82, 84
(c) 11, 17, 14, 12, 12, 14, 14, 15, 17, 17
(d) 16, 25, 18, 17, 16, 21, 14
(e) 45, 39, 42, 42, 43

7. Control charts for $\overline{X}$ and R are to be established on a certain dimension part, measured in millimeters. Data were collected in subgroup sizes of 6 and are given below. Determine the trial central line and control limits. Assume assignable causes and revise the central line and limits.

Subgroup Number	$\overline{X}$	R	Subgroup Number	$\overline{X}$	R
1	20.35	0.34	14	20.41	0.36
2	20.40	0.36	15	20.45	0.34
3	20.36	0.32	16	20.34	0.36
4	20.65	0.36	17	20.36	0.37
5	20.20	0.36	18	20.42	0.73
6	20.40	0.35	19	20.50	0.38
7	20.43	0.31	20	20.31	0.35
8	20.37	0.34	21	20.39	0.38
9	20.48	0.30	22	20.39	0.33
10	20.42	0.37	23	20.40	0.32
11	20.39	0.29	24	20.41	0.34
12	20.38	0.30	25	20.40	0.30
13	20.40	0.33			

8. The following table gives the average and range in kilograms for tensile tests on an improved plastic cord. The subgroup size is 4. Determine the trial central line and control limits. If any points are out of control, assume assignable causes, and determine the revised limits and central line.

Subgroup Number	$\bar{X}$	R	Subgroup Number	$\bar{X}$	R
1	476	32	14	482	22
2	466	24	15	506	23
3	484	32	16	496	23
4	466	26	17	478	25
5	470	24	18	484	24
6	494	24	19	506	23
7	486	28	20	476	25
8	496	23	21	485	29
9	488	24	22	490	25
10	482	26	23	463	22
11	498	25	24	469	27
12	464	24	25	474	22
13	484	24			

9. Assume that the data in Exercise 7 are for a subgroup size of 4. Determine the process capability.

10. Determine the process capability for Exercise 8.

11. Determine the capability index before ($\sigma_0 = 0.038$) and after ($\sigma_0 = 0.030$) improvement for the chapter example problem using specifications of 6.40 ± 0.15 mm.

12. What is the C_{pk} value after improvement for Exercise 11 when the process center is 6.40? When the process center is 6.30? Explain.

13. The Get-Well Hospital has completed a quality improvement project on the time to admit a patient using $\overline{X}$ and R charts. They now wish to monitor the activity using median and range charts. Determine the central line and control limits with the latest data in minutes, as given here.

Subgroup Number	Observation			Subgroup Number	Observation		
	X_1	X_2	X_3		X_1	X_2	X_3
1	6.0	5.8	6.1	13	6.1	6.9	7.4
2	5.2	6.4	6.9	14	6.2	5.2	6.8
3	5.5	5.8	5.2	15	4.9	6.6	6.6
4	5.0	5.7	6.5	16	7.0	6.4	6.1
5	6.7	6.5	5.5	17	5.4	6.5	6.7
6	5.8	5.2	5.0	18	6.6	7.0	6.8
7	5.6	5.1	5.2	19	4.7	6.2	7.1
8	6.0	5.8	6.0	20	6.7	5.4	6.7
9	5.5	4.9	5.7	21	6.8	6.5	5.2
10	4.3	6.4	6.3	22	5.9	6.4	6.0
11	6.2	6.9	5.0	23	6.7	6.3	4.6
12	6.7	7.1	6.2	24	7.4	6.8	6.3

14. The viscosity of a liquid is checked every half hour during one three-shift day. What does the run chart indicate? Data are 39, 42, 38, 37, 41, 40, 36, 35, 37, 36, 39, 34, 38, 36, 32, 37, 35, 34, 33, 35, 32, 38, 34, 37, 35, 35, 34, 31, 33, 35, 32, 36, 31, 29, 33, 32, 31, 30, 32, and 29.

15. Determine the trial central line and control limits for a p chart using the following data, which are for the payment of dental insurance claims. Plot the values on graph paper and determine if the process is stable. If there are any out-of-control points, assume an assignable cause and determine the revised central line and control limits.

Subgroup Number	Number Inspected	Number Nonconforming	Subgroup Number	Number Inspected	Number Nonconforming
1	300	3	14	300	6
2	300	6	15	300	7
3	300	4	16	300	4
4	300	6	17	300	5
5	300	20	18	300	7
6	300	2	19	300	5
7	300	6	20	300	0
8	300	7	21	300	2
9	300	3	22	300	3
10	300	0	23	300	6
11	300	6	24	300	1
12	300	9	25	300	8
13	300	5			

16. Determine the trial limits and revised control limits for a *u* chart using the data in the table for the surface finish of rolls of white paper. Assume any out-of-control points have assignable causes.

Lot Number	Sample Size	Total Noncon-formities	Lot Number	Sample Size	Total Noncon-formities
1	10	45	15	10	48
2	10	51	16	11	35
3	10	36	17	10	39
4	9	48	18	10	29
5	10	42	19	10	37
6	10	5	20	10	33
7	10	33	21	10	15
8	8	27	22	10	33
9	8	31	23	11	27
10	8	22	24	10	23
11	12	25	25	10	25
12	12	35	26	10	41
13	12	32	27	9	37
14	10	43	28	10	28

17. An *np* chart is to be established on a painting process that is in statistical control. If 35 pieces are to be inspected every 4 hours, and the fraction nonconforming is 0.06, determine the central line and control limits.

18. A quality technician has collected data on the count of rivet nonconformities in four-meters travel trailers. After 30 trailers, the total count of nonconformities is 316. Trial control limits have been determined and a comparison with the data shows no out-of-control points. What is the recommendation for the central line and the revised control limits for a count of nonconformities chart?

19. By means of a scatter diagram, determine if a relationship exists between product temperatures and percent foam for a soft drink.

Day	Product Temperature °F	Foam %	Day	Product Temperature °F	Foam %
1	36	15	11	44	32
2	38	19	12	42	33
3	37	21	13	38	20
4	44	30	14	41	27
5	46	36	15	45	35
6	39	20	16	49	38
7	41	25	17	50	40
8	47	36	18	48	42
9	39	22	19	46	40
10	40	23	20	41	30

19

Experimental Design

Introduction

Industry has become increasingly aware of the importance of quality. It is being used as a business strategy to increase market share. Organizations are achieving world-class quality by using designed experiments. Experimental design is one of the most powerful techniques for improving quality and increasing productivity. Through experimentation, changes are intentionally introduced into the process or system in order to observe their effect on the performance characteristic or response of the system or process. A statistical approach is the most efficient method for optimizing these changes. An engineer can do investigation without statistics using ad hoc and heuristic approaches. However, an engineer can be much more efficient in his/her investigation if armed with statistical tools.

Any experiment that has the flexibility to make desired changes in the input variables of a process to observe the output response is known as experimental design. Experimental design is a systematic manipulation of a set of variables in which the effect of these manipulations is determined, conclusions are made, and results are implemented. The primary goals of a designed experiment are to:

Determine the variable(s) and their magnitude that influences the response.

Determine the levels for these variables.

Determine how to manipulate these variables to control the response.

A good experiment must be efficient. It is not an isolated test but a well-planned investigation that points the way toward understanding the process. Knowledge of the process is essential to obtain the required information and achieve the objective. Resources in the form of money, people, equipment, materials, and, most important, time, must be allocated. Efficiency does not mean producing only conforming units. Knowledge is also gained from nonconforming units.

Statistical process control (SPC) methods and experimental design techniques are powerful tools for the improvement and optimization of a process, system, design, and so forth. SPC assumes that the right variable is being controlled, the right target is known, and that the tolerance is correct. In SPC, the process gives information that leads to a useful change in the process—hence, the term *passive* statistical method. On the other hand, experimental design is known as an *active* statistical method. Information is extracted for process improvement based on tests done on the process, changes made in the input, and observations of the output. Consequently, experimental design should precede SPC, except when specifications are given by the customer.

Statistically-designed experiments provide a structured plan of attack. They are more efficient than one-variable-at-a-time experiments, complement SPC, and force the experimenter to organize thoughts in a logical sequence. Experimental design can be used to:

Improve a process by increasing its performance and eliminate troubles.

Establish statistical control of a process variable; that is, identify the variables to control the process.

Improve an existing product or develop a new product.

Throughout this chapter and the next, the following terminology will be used:

Factor: A variable such as time, temperature, operator, and so forth, that is changed and results observed.

Level: A value that is assigned to change the factor. For example, two levels for the factor temperature could be 110° C and 150° C.

Treatment condition: The set of conditions (factors and their levels) for a test in an experiment.

Replicate: A repeat of a treatment condition. Requires a change in the setup.

Repetition: Multiple results of a treatment condition.

Randomization: Treatment conditions are run in a chance order to prevent any buildup in the results.

Orthogonal array: Simplified method of putting together the treatment conditions so that the design is balanced and factors can be analyzed singly or in combination.

Interaction: Two or more factors that, together, produce a result different than their separate effects.

Basic Statistics

For any group of data, two parameters are of greatest interest, the mean and variance. For a group of data, $X_1, X_2, ..., X_n$, where n is the number of observations in the group, the mean or average is a measure of the central tendency of the group of data; that is,

$$\overline{X} = \frac{1}{n} \sum_{i=1}^{n} X_i$$

The variance is a measure of the dispersion about the mean of the group of data; that is,

$$s_X^2 = \frac{\sum_{i=1}^{n} \left(X_i - \overline{X} \right)^2}{n-1} = \frac{\sum_{i=1}^{n} X_i^2 - \frac{1}{n} \left(\sum_{i=1}^{n} X_i \right)^2}{n-1}$$

The standard deviation is often stated as the square root of the variance. The variance is also referred to as the mean square, MS, which is the sum of the squares, SS, divided by the number of degrees of freedom, ν; that is,

$$s_X^2 = MS = \frac{SS}{\nu}$$

The variance consists of n quantities $(X_i - \overline{X})$ in the numerator; however, there are only $n-1$ independent quantities, because a sample statistic is used rather than the population parameter. In this case, $\overline{X}$ is used rather than μ. Thus, the number of degrees of freedom, ν, is given by

$$\nu = n - 1$$

As the sample size of a population increases, the variance of the sample approaches the variance of the population; that is,

$$MS = \lim_{n \to \infty} \frac{\sum_{i=1}^{n} \left(X_i - \overline{X} \right)^2}{n-1} = \frac{\sum_{i=1}^{n} \left(X_i - \mu \right)^2}{n}$$

EXAMPLE PROBLEM

The ages of four adults are 31, 33, 28, and 36. Determine the mean, sum of squares, degrees of freedom, mean square (variance), and standard deviation of the data.

$$\overline{X} = \frac{1}{n}\sum_{i=1}^{n} X_i = \frac{1}{4}(31 + 33 + 28 + 36) = 32$$

$$SS = \sum_{i=1}^{n}\left(X_i - \overline{X}\right)^2 = (-1)^2 + (+1)^2 + (-4)^2 + (+4)^2 = 34$$

$$v = n - 1 = 4 - 1 = 3$$

$$MS = s_X^2 = \frac{SS}{v} = \frac{34}{3} = 11.33$$

$$s_X = \sqrt{MS} = \sqrt{11.33} = 3.37$$

Hypotheses

Hypotheses testing is a statistical decision-making process in which inferences are made about the population from a sample. A probability statement is made regarding the population. Thus, hypotheses testing is subject to error. No difference, change, guilt, and so forth, is assumed between the samples until shown otherwise.

Primarily, hypotheses testing is concerned only with whether or not two samples from identical populations differ—that is, whether or not their respective means differ. Statistical hypotheses are stated in null form as

$$H_0 : \mu_1 = \mu_2 \text{ or } \mu_1 - \mu_2 = 0$$

The probability of error is shown in Table 19-1.

A Type I error occurs if the null hypothesis is rejected when, in reality, it is true. Conversely, a Type II error occurs if the null hypothesis is accepted when, in reality, it is false. If either a Type I or II error occurs, alternative hypotheses are stated as

$$H_0: \mu_1 \neq \mu_2 \quad \text{(nondirectional, both tails)}$$
$$H_0: \mu_1 > \mu_2 \quad \text{(directional, right tail)}$$
$$H_0: \mu_1 < \mu_2 \quad \text{(directional, left tail)}$$

Alternative hypotheses are quantified by assigning a risk to the relative degree of Type I or II errors. The degree of risk in making a decision can be alternatively stated as the confidence in a decision. Types of decisions, their risk and/or confidence, and the consequences of the decision are generalized in Table 19-2.

TABLE 19-1
Probability of Error for Hypothesis Testing

	SAMPLE SAYS	
Decision	**Parts Are Different (Reject H_0)**	**Parts Are the Same (Accept H_0)**
Parts are really different (reject H_0)	No error (OK)	Type II (α) error (10%, or 0.10)
Parts are really the same (accept H_0)	Type I (α) error (5%, or 0.05)	No error (OK)

TABLE 19-2
Level of Confidence and Consequences of a Wrong Decision

Designation	Risk α	Confidence $1 - \alpha$	Description
Supercritical	0.001 (0.1%)	0.999 (99.9%)	More than $100 million (large loss of life, e.g., nuclear disaster)
Critical	0.01 (1%)	0.99 (99%)	Less than $100 million (a few lives lost)
Important	0.05 (5%)	0.95 (95%)	Less than $100 thousand (no lives lost, injuries occur)
Moderate	0.10 (10%)	0.90 (90%)	Less than $500 (no injuries occur)

When decisions are needed on process or system improvement, product improvement, and new products, the consequences of the decision need to be evaluated and assigned an appropriate risk and/or confidence.

t Test

The *t* test utilizes the *t* distribution to test the hypotheses of a sample from a population when the sample size is small. It compares two averages by separating difference, if there is one, from variance within the groups. Also, it can compare an average for one sample to a population mean or reference value. The *t* test assumes that the population is normally distributed. Furthermore, the *t* test can be used only when one or two samples are available for testing. For more samples, the *F* test, which is discussed in the next section, is used.

The *t* Distribution

Consider a normal random variable with mean, μ, and standard deviation, σ. If a small sample of a response variable $(y_1, y_2, \ldots, y_n)$ is taken from this normal distribution, the average, $\bar{y}$, and standard deviation, s, of the sample might not be closely related to μ or σ, respectively. The symbol X is defined as a control variable, and y is defined as a response variable with the relationship

$$y = b_1 X_1 + b_2 X_2 + \ldots + b_k X_k$$

Thus, when the sample size is small, the random variable

$$T = \frac{\bar{y} - \mu}{s/\sqrt{n}}$$

is governed by a t probability distribution with ν degrees of freedom, where $\nu = n - 1$. When n is small, the random variable T is not governed by a standard normal distribution; however, as n approaches infinity, the t distribution approaches a standard normal distribution, as depicted in Figure 19-1. Consider a t distribution for a random sample with ν degrees of freedom, as shown in Figure 19-2. A value t on the abscissa represents the $100(1 -)$ percentile of the t distribution, where the critical value α is the area under the curve to the right of t.

The value t is often designated by $t_{\alpha,\nu}$ to indicate the critical value and number of degrees freedom associated with the test. This is analogous to the terminology used in the Z test for a normal random variable when the sample size is large.

One-Sample *t* Test

The null statistical hypothesis for the one-sample t test is stated as

$$H_0 : \mu = \mu_0 \quad \text{or} \quad \mu - \mu_0 = 0$$

where the test statistic is

$$t = \frac{\bar{y} - \mu_0}{s/\sqrt{n}}$$

If the null statistical hypothesis is false, alternative statistical hypotheses are stated as

$$H_0: \mu \neq \mu_0 \quad \text{(nondirectional, both tails)}$$
$$H_0: \mu > \mu_0 \quad \text{(directional, right tail)}$$
$$H_0: \mu < \mu_0 \quad \text{(directional, left tail)}$$

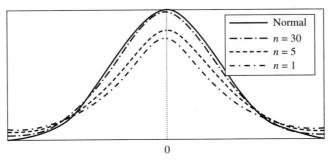

Figure 19-1 **Normal and *t* Probability Distribution Functions**

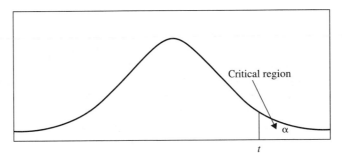

Figure 19-2 **Critical Region of *t* Distribution**

and the corresponding critical regions are given by

$$t \geq t_{\alpha/2,\nu} \quad \text{or} \quad t \leq -t_{\alpha/2,\nu}$$

$$t \geq t_{\alpha,\nu}$$

$$t \leq -t_{\alpha,\nu}$$

Values for $t_{\alpha,\nu}$ have been tabulated for various ranges of α and ν in Table B of the appendix.

EXAMPLE PROBLEM

A lawnmower-manufacturing company would like to advertise that their top-of-the-line, self-propelled mower can go 250 hours before experiencing starting problems (more than two pulls) and subsequent service. During year-round field tests of 10 identical lawnmowers at a proving ground in a warm climate, the 10 lawnmowers required service after 205, 430, 301, 199, 222, 124, 89, 289, 260, and 214 hours. Based on this data, can the manufacturer make this advertising claim?

$$n = 10$$
$$v = n - 1 = 9$$
$$\mu_0 = 250$$

$$\bar{y} = \frac{1}{n}\sum_{i=1}^{n} y_i = \frac{1}{10}(2333) = 233.3$$

$$s = \sqrt{\frac{\sum_{i=1}^{n} y_i^2 - \frac{1}{n}\left(\sum_{i=1}^{n} y_i\right)^2}{n-1}} = \sqrt{\frac{626,625 - \frac{1}{10}(2333)^2}{9}} = 95.64$$

$$t = \frac{\bar{y} - \mu_0}{s/\sqrt{n}} = \frac{233.3 - 250}{95.64/\sqrt{10}} = -0.552$$

At levels $\alpha = 0.01$, 0.05, and 0.10, $t_{\alpha,v}$ equals 2.821, 1.833, and 1.383, respectively, from Table B of the appendix. The manufacturer would like to claim $\mu > 250$, so the alternative hypothesis is $\mu < 250$, and the critical (rejection) region is $t \le -t_{\alpha,v}$. Because $t \ge -t_{\alpha}$, for all levels, the alternative hypothesis cannot be rejected, and hence the manufacturer cannot make the claim. After looking at the actual data, the primary reason the manufacturer cannot make the claim is the large spread in the data.

Two-Sample t Test

Consider two normal random variables with means μ_1 and μ_2 and respective standard deviations σ_1 and σ_2. If a small sample of n_1 random variables $(y_{11}, y_{12}, \ldots, y_{1n1})$ is taken from the first normal distribution, the mean, $\bar{y}_1$, and standard deviation, s_1, of the sample might not be close to μ_1 or σ_1, respectively. Similarly, if a small sample of n_2 random variables $(y_{21}, y_{22}, \ldots, y_{2n2})$ is taken from the second normal distribution, the mean, $\bar{y}_2$, and standard deviation, s_2, of the sample might not be close to μ_2 or σ_2, respectively.

The null statistical hypothesis for the two-sample t test is stated as

$$H_0: \mu_1 - \mu_2 = \mu_0$$

The test statistic is

$$t = \frac{\bar{y}_1 - \bar{y}_2}{s_p\sqrt{1/n_1 + 1/n_2}}$$

where the "pooled" estimator is given by

$$s_p = \sqrt{\frac{v_1 s_1^2 + v_2 s_2^2}{v_1 + v_2}}$$

and the degrees of freedom for each sample are

$$V_1 = n_1 - 1$$
$$V_2 = n_2 - 1$$

If the null statistical hypothesis is false, alternative statistical hypotheses are stated as

$$H_0: \mu_1 - \mu_2 \neq \mu_0 \quad \text{(nondirectional, both tails)}$$
$$H_0: \mu_1 - \mu_2 > \mu_0 \quad \text{(directional, right tail)}$$
$$H_0: \mu_1 - \mu_2 < \mu_0 \quad \text{(directional, left tail)}$$

and the corresponding critical (rejection) regions are given by

$$t \geq t_{\alpha/2, V} \quad \text{or} \quad t \leq - t_{\alpha/2, V}$$
$$t \geq t_{\alpha, V}$$
$$t \leq - t_{\alpha, V}$$

where the total degrees of freedom are $V = V_1 + V_2$.

EXAMPLE PROBLEM

A study was done to determine the satisfaction with the implementation of a telephone-based class registration system at a small liberal arts college. Twenty undergraduate students were interviewed and asked to rate the current system (sample 1) of seeing an advisor and registering in person. Complaints for the current system included long lines, closed classes, and set hours. The new telephone-based system (sample 2), which is in its infancy, was rated by eight seniors. Complaints for the new system included loss of personal contact, unfamiliarity with the system, and computer downtime. The ratings were done on a scale of 1 to 100, with the following results:

Sample	Data									
1	65	70	92	54	88	83	81	75	40	95
	99	100	64	77	79	81	50	60	95	75
2	55	71	95	88	66	79	83	91		

Based on this data, use $\alpha = 0.05$ to determine whether the college should proceed with implementing the new system.

$$n_1 = 20$$
$$n_2 = 8$$
$$v_1 = n_1 - 1 = 19$$
$$v_2 = n_2 - 1 = 7$$
$$v = v_1 + v_2 = 26$$

$$\bar{y}_1 = \frac{1}{n_1} \sum_{i=1}^{n_1} y_{1i} = \frac{1}{20}(1523) = 76.15$$

$$\bar{y}_2 = \frac{1}{n_2} \sum_{i=1}^{n_2} y_{2i} = \frac{1}{8}(628) = 78.50$$

$$s_1 = \sqrt{\frac{\sum_{i=1}^{n_1} y_{1i}^2 - \frac{1}{n_1}\left(\sum_{i=1}^{n_1} y_{1i}\right)^2}{n_1 - 1}} = \sqrt{\frac{121,327 - \frac{1}{20}(1523)^2}{19}} = 16.78$$

$$s_2 = \sqrt{\frac{\sum_{i=1}^{n_2} y_{2i}^2 - \frac{1}{n_2}\left(\sum_{i=1}^{n_2} y_{2i}\right)^2}{n_2 - 1}} = \sqrt{\frac{50,602 - \frac{1}{8}(628)^2}{7}} = 13.65$$

$$s_p = \sqrt{\frac{v_1 s_1^2 + v_2 s_2^2}{v_1 + v_2}} = \sqrt{\frac{19(16.78)^2 + 7(13.65)^2}{19 + 7}} = 16.00$$

$$t = \frac{\bar{y}_1 - \bar{y}_2}{s_p \sqrt{1/n_1 + 1/n_2}} = \frac{76.15 - 78.50}{16.00\sqrt{1/20 + 1/8}} = -0.351$$

At $\alpha = 0.05$, $t_{\alpha,v}$ equals 1.706 from Table B of the appendix. The college would like to claim $\mu_2 > \mu_1$ or $\mu_1 - \mu_2 < 0$. The critical (rejection) region is $t \leq - t_{\alpha,v}$. Because $t \geq - t_{\alpha,v}$, for an $\alpha = 0.05$ test, the school should not implement the new system.

F Test

Completely randomized designs are a basic type of experimental design. Completely randomized design involve a single-treatment variable (factor) applied at two or more levels. A random group of subjects are assigned (selected) to different treatment levels. Subjects must be selected from the same population, that is, same process using different levels of one variable of the process.

For a test involving three factor levels, three two-sample t tests for factor levels 1 and 2, 2 and 3, and 1 and 3 would need to be performed. Therefore, for three t tests with each $\alpha = 0.05$, the probability of a correct decision is given by

$$(1 - \alpha)(1 - \alpha)(1 - \alpha) = (1 - 0.05)(1 - 0.05)(1 - 0.05) = 0.86$$

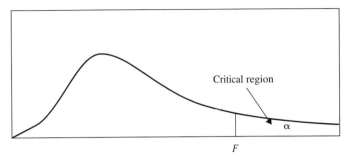

Figure 19-3 Critical Region of F Distribution

when three t tests are considered. Similarly, for a test involving four factor levels, six t tests would need to be performed, and the probability of a correct decision is 0.817. Thus, for more than two factors or levels, a more efficient technique is used to compare the means of more than two samples. Comparison between the means of more than two groups is accomplished by the use of the F distribution and *analysis of variance* (ANOVA).

The *F* Distribution

Consider an F distribution, as shown in Figure 19-3. Similar to the t distribution, a value F on the abscissa represents the $100(1 - \alpha)$ percentile of the F distribution where the critical value α is the area under the curve to the right of F. In a terminology similar to the t test, the critical value for F is designated by $F_{\alpha, v1, v2}$ where α, v_1, and v_2 are the risk, degrees of freedom for the numerator, and degrees of freedom for the denominator, respectively. For simplicity, the mathematical expression for the F distribution function is not stated here.

Analysis of Variance

The observations of an experiment with more than two factor levels are tabulated as shown in Table 19-3. For completeness in the formulation that follows, the number of observations are different at each factor level.

   In general, the samples selected are known as the levels, the specimens in each level are known as observations, or replicates, and the number of variables under study at a time is the number of factors. For the data in Table 19-3, there is only one level for each factor—thus, the term *factor level* in the table. The observations of an experiment can be written in a mathematical model as

$$y_{ij} = \mu + f_i + \varepsilon_{ij}$$

TABLE 19-3
Data for Factor Level Experimental Design

Factor Level	Data			
1	y_{11}	y_{12}	. . .	y_{1n_1}
2	y_{21}	y_{22}	. . .	y_{2n_2}
•	•	•	•	•
•	•	•	•	•
•	•	•	•	•
a	y_{a1}	y_{a2}	. . .	y_{an_a}

where y_{ij} = jth observation at the ith factor level ($i = 1, \ldots, a, j = 1, \ldots, n_i$)
μ = mean value for all of the observations
f_i = difference due to treatment (factor effect) at each factor level ($i = 1, \ldots, a$)
ε_{ij} = error or noise within factor levels ($i = 1, \ldots, a, j = 1, \ldots, n_i$)
a = number of factor levels
n_i = number of observations at each factor level ($i = 1, \ldots, a$)

In general, the observations of the experiments are assumed to be normally and independently distributed with the same variance in each factor level. Thus, the sum of the factor effects f_i can be defined as

$$\sum_{i=1}^{a} f_i = 0$$

From the preceding equation, the null statistical hypothesis for the F test is stated as

$$H_0 : f_1 = f_2 = \ldots = f_a = 0$$

If this hypothesis is false, an alternative hypothesis is stated as

$$H_0 : f_i \neq 0 \text{ for at least one } i$$

Testing for the validity of the hypotheses is accomplished by analysis of variance (ANOVA). The total variability in the data is given as

$$\sum_{i=1}^{a} \sum_{j=1}^{n_i} \left(y_{ij} - \frac{T}{N} \right)^2 = \sum_{i=1}^{a} \sum_{j=1}^{n_i} \left[\left(y_{ij} - \frac{A_i}{n_i} \right) + \left(\frac{A_i}{n_i} - \frac{T}{N} \right) \right]^2$$

where the total number of observations, total of the observations under the ith factor level, and total of the observations under all factor levels are given by

$$N = \sum_{i=1}^{a} n_i$$

$$A_i = \sum_{j=1}^{n_i} y_{ij}$$

$$T = \sum_{i=1}^{a} A_i$$

respectively. After expanding the square in the relationship for the total variability and simplifying the equation, the total variability in the data can be expressed as

$$SS_T = SS_F + SS_E$$

where the total sum of squares, sum of squares due to the factor, and sum of squares due to the error are given by

$$SS_T = \sum_{i=1}^{a} \sum_{j=1}^{n_i} y_{ij}^2 - \frac{T^2}{N}$$

$$SS_F = \sum_{i=1}^{a} \frac{A_i^2}{n_i} - \frac{T^2}{N}$$

$$SS_E = SS_T - SS_F$$

respectively. If there is a large difference among the means at different factor levels, SS_F will be large. The variability due to changing factor levels and error can be obtained by comparing the magnitude of SS_F and SS_E. To facilitate this, the mean squares of the factor and error are calculated by normalizing the sum of squares by their respective number of degrees of freedom; that is,

$$MS_F = \frac{SS_F}{v_F}$$

$$MS_E = \frac{SS_E}{v_E}$$

where the degrees of freedom for the factor and error are given by

$$v_F = a - 1$$

$$v_E = N - a$$

TABLE 19-4

Results for One-Factor Experimental Design

Source	Sum of Squares	Degrees of Freedom	Mean Square	F	F_{α, v_1, v_2}	Significant (yes/no)
Factor	SS_F	v_F	MS_F	F	F_{α, v_F, v_E}	
Error	SS_E	v_E	MS_E			
Total	SS_T					

respectively. Analysis of variance is a technique to determine significant factors based on the F test that is used to compare ratio of factor variance with error variance; that is,

$$F = \frac{MS_F}{MS_E}$$

If $F > F_{\alpha, v_1, v_2}$, where $v_1 = v_F$ and $v_2 = v_E$, it can be said that the factor-level means are different for a level α test. Results of the F test for a one-factor experiment can be nicely depicted using a format similar to Table 19-4.

EXAMPLE PROBLEM

Consider the following data for four levels of a factor.

Level	Data					Total A	$\overline{y}$	s^2
1	26	25	32	29	30	142	28.4	8.30
2	34	31	26			91	30.3	16.33
3	15	16	25	18	13	87	17.4	21.30
4	12	15	13	11		51	12.8	2.92

Based on these data, use $\alpha = 0.05$ to determine if there is any significant difference in the data.

$$a = 4$$

$$n_1 = 5, \ n_2 = 3, \ n_3 = 5, \ n_4 = 4$$

$$N = \sum_{i=1}^{a} n_i = n_1 + n_2 + n_3 + n_4 = 17$$

$$v_F = a - 1 = 3$$

$$v_E = N - a = 13$$

$$A_i = \sum_{j=1}^{n_i} y_{ij}; \ A_1 = 142, \ A_2 = 91, \ A_3 = 87, \ A_4 = 51$$

$$T = \sum_{i=1}^{a} A_i = 371$$

$$SS_T = \sum_{i=1}^{a} \sum_{j=1}^{n_i} y_{ij}^2 - \frac{T^2}{N} = 9117 - \frac{371^2}{17} = 1020.50$$

$$SS_F = \sum_{i=1}^{a} \frac{A_i^2}{n_i} - \frac{T^2}{N} = \frac{142^2}{5} + \frac{91^2}{3} + \frac{87^2}{5} + \frac{51^2}{4} - \frac{371^2}{17} = 860.65$$

$$SS_E = SS_T - SS_F = 159.85$$

$$MS_F = \frac{SS_F}{v_F} = \frac{860.65}{3} = 286.88$$

$$MS_E = \frac{SS_E}{v_E} = \frac{159.85}{13} = 12.30$$

$$F = \frac{MS_F}{MS_E} = 23.33$$

At $\alpha = 0.05$, with $v_1 = v_F$ and $v_2 = v_E$, F_{α, v_1, v_2} equals 3.41 from Table C-2 of the appendix.

Source	Sum of Squares	Degrees of Freedom	Mean Square	F	F_{α, v_1, v_2}	Significant (yes/no)
Factor	860.65	3	286.88	23.33	3.41	Yes
Error	159.85	13	12.30			
Total	1020.50					

Because $F > F_{\alpha, v_1, v_2}$, it can be stated that the factor-level means are different.

One Factor at a Time

Consider an experimental design with N_F factors with two levels for each factor, as shown in Table 19-5. At treatment condition 1, all the factors are run at level 1 to obtain the benchmark or reference value. The next treatment condition is to run factor A at level 2 while the other factors are kept at level 1. For the third treatment condition, factor B is run at level 2 while the other factors are kept at level 1. This sequence is continued until all factors arc run at level 2 while holding the other factors at level 1.

The change in response due to a change in the level of the factor is known as the *effect* of a factor. The main effect of a factor is defined as the difference between the average

TABLE 19-5

Effects and Data for a One-Factor-at-a-Time Experimental Design

Treatment Condition	FACTORS/LEVELS						Response (Results)
	A	B	C	D	...	N_F	
1	1	1	1	1	...	1	y_0
2	2	1	1	1	...	1	y_A
3	1	2	1	1	...	1	y_B
4	1	1	2	1	...	1	y_C
5	1	1	1	2	...	1	y_D
•	•	•	•	•	•	•	•
•	•	•	•	•	•	•	•
•	•	•	•	•	•	•	•
n_{tc}	1	1	1	1	...	2	y_{N_F}

response at the two levels. In order to determine the effect of each factor, the responses at level 2 are compared to the reference value (level 1); that is,

$$e_A = y_A - y_0$$
$$e_B = y_B - y_0$$
$$e_C = y_C - y_0$$

and so on, for each factor. In this manner, the factors that have a strong effect on the response can be easily determined. In addition, the sign of the effect indicates whether an increase in a factor level increases the response, or vice versa.

As can be seen, this type of experimental design varies one factor at a time and evaluates its effect. To understand this concept, it is necessary to look at an example of a one-factor-at-a-time experiment that is neither balanced nor efficient.

EXAMPLE PROBLEM

An experiment involves maximizing a response variable. Three factors (speed, pressure, and time) are compared at two levels. The factors and levels are given in the following table.

Factors	Level 1	Level 2
Speed (m/s)	25	35
Pressure (Pa)	50	75
Time (min)	5	10

At treatment condition 1, all the factors are run at level 1 to obtain the benchmark value. The table below shows the results for a one-factor-at-a-time experimental design. The next treatment condition is to run speed at level 2 while pressure and time are kept at level 1. For the third treatment condition, pressure is run at level 2 while speed and time are kept at level 1. Similarly, treatment condition 4 is run with time at level 2, while speed and pressure are run at level 1.

Treatment Condition	FACTORS/LEVELS			Response (Results)
	Speed	Pressure	Time	
1	1 (25 m/s)	1 (50 Pa)	1 (5 min)	2.8
2	2 (35 m/s)	1 (50 Pa)	1 (5 min)	3.4
3	1 (25 m/s)	2 (75 Pa)	1 (5 min)	4.6
4	1 (25 m/s)	1 (50 Pa)	2 (10 min)	3.7

The effects of speed, pressure, and time are:

$$e_S = y_S - y_0 = 3.4 - 2.8 = 0.6$$
$$e_P = y_P - y_0 = 4.6 - 2.8 = 1.8$$
$$e_T = y_T - y_0 = 3.7 - 2.8 = 0.9$$

It appears that pressure, time, and perhaps speed have a strong positive effect on the process. In other words, increasing any of the factors increases the response.

Orthogonal Design

Orthogonality means that the experimental design is balanced. A balanced experiment leads to a more efficient one. Table 19-6 shows an orthogonal experimental design for three factors with two levels each.

Although there are more treatment conditions, the design is balanced and efficient. Treatment conditions 1, 2, 3, and 5 are the same as treatment conditions 1, 2, 3, and 4 for the one-factor-at-a-time experiment in the previous section. A review of this particular design shows that there are four level 1s and four level 2s in each column. Although different designs have a different number of columns, rows, and levels, there will be an equal number of occurrences for each level. The idea of balance produces statistically-independent results. Looking at the relationship between one column and another, we find that for each level within one column, each level in any other column will occur an equal number of times. Therefore, the four level 1s for factor *A* have two level 1s and two level 2s for factor *B*, and two level 1s and two level 2s for factor *C*. The effect of

TABLE 19-6

Effects and Data for an Orthogonal Experimental Design

Treatment Condition	FACTORS/LEVELS			Response (Results)
	A	B	C	
1	1	1	1	y_{111}
2	2	1	1	y_{211}
3	1	2	1	y_{121}
4	2	2	1	y_{221}
5	1	1	2	y_{112}
6	2	1	2	y_{212}
7	1	2	2	y_{122}
8	2	2	2	y_{222}

factor A at each level is statistically independent, because the effects of factor B and factor C for each level are averaged into both levels of the factor A. Statistical independence is also true for factor B and factor C.

In order to obtain the main effects of each factor/level, the results must be averaged. The average of the response for factor A due to level i ($i = 1, 2$) is given by

$$\overline{A}_i = \frac{1}{(2)^{N_F - 1}} \sum y_{ijk \cdots m}$$

Similarly, the average of the response for factor B due to level j ($j = 1, 2$) is

$$\overline{B}_j = \frac{1}{(2)^{N_F - 1}} \sum y_{ijk \cdots m}$$

and so on, for all the factors. While the number of treatment conditions increased by a factor of two, the number of values that were used to calculate the factor/level average increased by a factor of four. This improvement in the number of values used to determine the average makes the orthogonal design very efficient in addition to being balanced.

The main effects of factors A and B are then given by

$$e_A = \overline{A}_2 - \overline{A}_1$$
$$e_B = \overline{B}_2 - \overline{B}_1$$

and so on, for all the factors.

EXAMPLE PROBLEM

The following table shows an orthogonal experimental design for the same experiment given in the previous section for a one-factor-at-a-time experimental design.

Treatment Condition	FACTORS/LEVELS			Response (Results)
	Speed	Pressure	Time	
1	1 (25 m/s)	1 (50 Pa)	1 (5 min)	2.8
2	2 (35 m/s)	1 (50 Pa)	1 (5 min)	3.4
3	1 (25 m/s)	2 (75 Pa)	1 (5 min)	4.6
4	2 (35 m/s)	2 (75 Pa)	1 (5 min)	3.8
5	1 (25 m/s)	1 (50 Pa)	2 (10 min)	3.7
6	2 (35 m/s)	1 (50 Pa)	2 (10 min)	2.7
7	1 (25 m/s)	2 (75 Pa)	2 (10 min)	3.1
8	2 (35 m/s)	2 (75 Pa)	2 (10 min)	4.4

The average of the response for the factors due to each level i is:

$$\overline{S}_1 = \frac{1}{4}(2.8 + 4.6 + 3.7 + 3.1) = 3.550$$

$$\overline{S}_2 = \frac{1}{4}(3.4 + 3.8 + 2.7 + 4.4) = 3.575$$

$$\overline{P}_1 = \frac{1}{4}(2.8 + 3.4 + 3.7 + 2.7) = 3.150$$

$$\overline{P}_2 = \frac{1}{4}(4.6 + 3.8 + 3.1 + 4.4) = 3.975$$

$$\overline{T}_1 = \frac{1}{4}(2.8 + 3.4 + 4.6 + 3.8) = 3.650$$

$$\overline{T}_2 = \frac{1}{4}(3.7 + 2.7 + 3.1 + 4.4) = 3.475$$

The main effects of speed, pressure, and time are then given by

$$e_S = \overline{S}_2 - \overline{S}_1 = 3.575 - 3.550 = 0.025$$
$$e_P = \overline{P}_2 - \overline{P}_1 = 3.975 - 3.150 = 0.825$$
$$e_T = \overline{T}_2 - \overline{T}_1 = 3.475 - 3.650 = -0.175$$

Based on these calculations, an increase in pressure (level 1 to level 2) has a strong effect on the process, whereas the small effects of speed and time are most likely due to the natural variation in the process. Clearly, this information is better than that obtained from the one-factor-at-a-time approach.

Point and Interval Estimate

In any statistical study, one of the objectives is to determine the value of a parameter or factor. Analysis and calculations yield a single point or value, which is called a *point estimate*. The true value is usually unknown; therefore, an *interval estimate* is needed to convey the degree of accuracy. It is the range or band within which the parameter is presumed to fall and is

$$CI = \bar{y} \pm t_{\alpha/2}\sqrt{s^2/n}$$

where CI = confidence interval.

EXAMPLE PROBLEM

Data for 24 observations has an average of 25.2 mm and a variance of 2.6 mm. Determine the interval that the point estimate lies within with 95% confidence. From the t table for 23 degrees of freedom and $\alpha/2 = 0.025$, the $t_{\alpha/2}$ value is 2.069. The confidence interval is

$$CI = \bar{y} \pm t_{\alpha/2}\sqrt{s^2/n} = 25.2 \pm 2.069\sqrt{2.6/24} = 24.5 \text{ to } 25.9 \text{ mm}$$

t Reference Distribution

The t reference distribution is a technique to determine which factor levels are significant. In the previous example problem, it was found, from the F test, that the levels were significant, but it was not known which ones were significant. The t reference distribution uses the pooled variance of the data to find an interval estimate of the data. If two averages are outside this distribution, then they are different; if they are inside, there is no difference. The equation is similar to the confidence interval one. Both can be derived from the control limit equation for the $\bar{X}$ chart. The equation is

$$Ref.\ Dist. = \pm t_{\alpha/2}\sqrt{s_p^2/n}$$

EXAMPLE PROBLEM

Using the t reference distribution, determine which pairs of levels are significant in the example problem on page 534.

$$\bar{n} = \frac{1}{4}(5 + 3 + 5 + 4) = 4.25$$

$$s_p^2 = \frac{4(8.30) + 2(16.33) + 4(21.30) + 3(2.92)}{4 + 2 + 4 + 3} = 12.29$$

Ref. Dist. $= \pm 2.160\sqrt{12.29/4.25} = \pm 3.67$

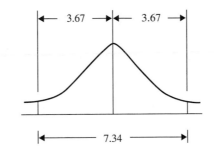

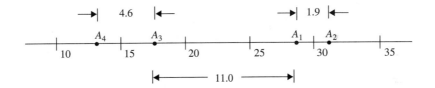

From the graph it is evident that there are no differences between A_1, A_2 or A_3, A_4, because the reference distribution of 7.34 easily covers these values. However, there is a difference between A_1, A_3; A_1, A_4; A_2, A_3; and A_2, A_4, because it does not cover these values.

There are a number of different ways to compare the factor levels from a significant F test. The t reference distribution is just one of them.

Two Factors

Consider an experiment run N times with two factors A and B, with a and b levels, respectively. The observations are tabulated in Table 19-7. For simplicity, the number of observations are the same at each factor and level.

TABLE 19-7
Data for Two-Factor Experimental Design

Factor A Levels	FACTOR B LEVELS			
	1	2	...	b
		Data		
1	$y_{111}, ..., y_{11n}$	$y_{121}, ..., y_{12n}$	...	$y_{1b1}, ..., y_{1bn}$
2	$y_{211}, ..., y_{11n}$	$y_{221}, ..., y_{22n}$	...	$y_{2b1}, ..., y_{2bn}$
•	•	•	•	•
•	•	•	•	•
•	•	•	•	•
a	$y_{a11}, ..., y_{a1n}$	$y_{a21}, ..., y_{a2n}$	...	$y_{ab1}, ..., y_{abn}$

These observations can be written in a mathematical model as

$$y_{ijk} = \mu + (f_A)_i + (f_B)_j + (f_{AB})_{ij} + \varepsilon_{ijk}$$

where $\quad y_{ijk}$ = kth observation at the ith and jth levels of factors A and B, respectively ($i = 1, ..., a, j = 1, ..., b, k = 1, ..., n$)

μ = mean value for all of the observations

$(f_A)_i$ = difference due to treatment (factor effect A) at each factor A level ($i = 1, ..., a$)

$(f_B)_j$ = difference due to treatment (factor effect B) at each factor B level ($j = 1, ..., b$)

$(f_{AB})_{ij}$ = interaction between factors ($i = 1, ..., a, j = 1, ..., b$)

ε_{ijk} = error or noise within factors and levels ($i = 1, ..., a, j = 1, ..., b, k = 1, ..., n$)

a = number of levels for factor A

b = number of levels for factor B

n = number of observations for each run (replicate)

The total number of observations, total of the observation under the ith and jth levels for factors A and B, total of the observations under the ith level for factor A, total of the observations under the jth level for factor B, and total of the observations under all factor levels are given by

$$N = abn$$

$$A_{ij} = \sum_{k=1}^{n} y_{ijk}$$

$$A_{Ai} = \sum_{j=1}^{b} A_{ij}, \quad A_{Bj} = \sum_{i=1}^{a} A_{ij}$$

$$T = \sum_{i=1}^{a} A_{Ai} = \sum_{j=1}^{b} A_{Bj}$$

respectively. After expanding the square in the relationship for the total variability in the data and simplifying the equation, the total variability in the data can be expressed as

$$SS_T = SS_A + SS_B + SS_{AB} + SS_E$$

where the total sum of squares, sum of squares due to factor A, sum of squares due to factor B, sum of squares due to the interaction between factors A and B, and sum of square due to the error are given by

$$SS_T = \sum_{i=1}^{a} \sum_{j=1}^{b} \sum_{k=1}^{n} y_{ijk}^2 - \frac{T^2}{N}$$

$$SS_A = \sum_{i=1}^{a} \frac{A_{Ai}^2}{bn} - \frac{T^2}{N}, \quad SS_B = \sum_{j=1}^{b} \frac{A_{Bj}^2}{an} - \frac{T^2}{N}$$

$$SS_{AB} = \sum_{i=1}^{a} \sum_{j=1}^{b} \frac{A_{ij}^2}{n} - \frac{T^2}{N} - SS_A - SS_B$$

$$SS_E = SS_T - SS_A - SS_B - SS_{AB}$$

respectively. The mean squares are calculated by normalizing the sum of squares by the respective number of degrees of freedom. The mean squares for factors A and B, interaction between factors, and error are given by

$$MS_A = \frac{SS_A}{v_A}, \quad MS_B = \frac{SS_B}{v_B}$$

$$MS_{AB} = \frac{SS_{AB}}{v_{AB}}$$

$$MS_E = \frac{SS_E}{v_E}$$

where the degrees of freedom for the factor and error are given by

$$v_A = a - 1, \quad v_B = b - 1$$

$$v_{AB} = (a - 1)(b - 1)$$

$$v_E = N - ab$$

TABLE 19-8
Results for a Two-Factor Experimental Design

Source	Sum of Squares	Degrees of Freedom	Mean Square	F	F_{α, ν_1, ν_2}	Significant (yes/no)
Factor A	SS_A	ν_A	MS_A	F_A	F_{α, ν_A, ν_E}	
Factor B	SS_B	ν_B	MS_B	F_B	F_{α, ν_B, ν_E}	
Factor AB	SS_{AB}	ν_{AB}	MS_{AB}	F_{AB}	$F_{\alpha, \nu_{AB}, \nu_E}$	
Error	SS_E	ν_E	MS_E			
Total	SS_T					

respectively. The ratio of the variance in factor A, factor B, and the interaction between factors A and B to the error variance is given by

$$F_A = \frac{MS_A}{MS_E}, \quad F_B = \frac{MS_B}{MS_E}$$

$$F_{AB} = \frac{MS_{AB}}{MS_E}$$

respectively. If $F_A > F_{\alpha, \nu_1, \nu_2}$, where $\nu_1 = \nu_A$ and $\nu_2 = \nu_E$, it can be said that factor A is significant for a particular value of α. Similarly, if $F_B > F_{\alpha, \nu_1, \nu_2}$, where $\nu_1 = \nu_B$ and $\nu_2 = \nu_E$, it can be said that factor B is significant for a particular value of α. Furthermore, if $F_{AB} > F_{\alpha, \nu_1, \nu_2}$, where $\nu_1 = \nu_{AB}$ and $\nu_2 = \nu_E$, it can be said that the interaction between factors A and B is significant for a particular value of α.

Results for a two-factor experimental design shown in Table 19-8 are depicted using a format similar to Table 19-4.

EXAMPLE PROBLEM

Consider an experiment on the volatility of a fluid with two factors, concentration (factor A) and temperature (factor B). Determine the significance of each factor for a level $\alpha = 0.05$. The results (response is volatility) of the experiment are given in the following table.

	FACTOR B LEVELS		
Factor A Levels	1	2	3
1	41, 38	43, 49	46, 47
2	42, 43	46, 45	48, 49

In order to obtain the significance of each factor and their interaction, the sum of the squares, degrees of freedom, mean square, and F are calculated first. These results are summarized in the following table.

Source	Sum of Squares	Degrees of Freedom	Mean Square	F	F_{α, ν_1, ν_2}	Significant (yes/no)
A	6.75	1	6.7500	1.6535	5.99	No
B	90.50	2	45.2500	11.0816	5.14	Yes
AB	6.50	2	3.2500	0.7959	5.14	No
Error	24.50	6	4.0833			
Total	128.25	11				

Based on these calculations, the effect of concentration on the volatility of the fluid is significant, whereas the effects of temperature and the interaction between concentration and temperature are not significant at a level $\alpha = 0.05$.

Full Factorials

Factorial experiments are suitable when there are many factors of interest in an experiment. Consider an experiment consisting of three factors, A, B, and C, with a and b levels for each factor, respectively. In a factorial experiment, all possible combinations of the factors are investigated. For example, when there are only two levels for each factor, all of the possible combinations (treatment conditions) can be represented using a sign table, as shown in Table 19-9.

In Table 19-9, the plus and minus signs represent the high and low levels for each factor, respectively. The method of determining the sign for the factors is to first make treatment condition (TC) 1 all negative. Then, use the equation 2^{c-1} to determine the number of consecutive like signs in a column, where c is the column number. Thus for the A column, with $c = 1$, $2^{c-1} = 2^0 = 1$; for the B column, with $c = 2$, $2^{c-1} = 2^1 = 2$; and for the C column, with $c = 3$, $2^{c-1} = 2^2 = 4$. Once the columns for the individual factors have been determined, the columns for the interactions are the multiplication of the respective columns. Thus, the sign for the AB interaction for TC 1 is $(-)(-) = +$; TC 2 is $(+)(-) = -$; TC 7 is $(-)(+) = -$; and TC 8 is $(+)(+) = +$. For the ABC interaction, multiply the signs of the three individual factors for each TC. Thus, the sign for the ABC interaction for TC 3 is $(-)(+)(-) = +$. Similar tables can be developed for more than three factors and more than two levels; however, if each factor had three levels, a different terminology would need to be used.

The procedure for determining the sum of squares, mean square, and so forth, is similar to the procedure presented in the previous section for two factors. However, because

TABLE 19-9
Signs for Effects and Data for a Three-Factor Experimental Design

Treatment Condition	FACTORS							Response (Results)
	A	B	C	AB	AC	BC	ABC	
1	−	−	−	+	+	+	−	$y_{11}, y_{12}, \ldots, y_{1n}$
2	+	−	−	−	−	+	+	$y_{21}, y_{22}, \ldots, y_{2n}$
3	−	+	−	−	+	−	+	$y_{31}, y_{32}, \ldots, y_{3n}$
4	+	+	−	+	−	−	−	$y_{41}, y_{42}, \ldots, y_{4n}$
5	−	−	+	+	−	−	+	$y_{51}, y_{52}, \ldots, y_{5n}$
6	+	−	+	−	+	−	−	$y_{61}, y_{62}, \ldots, y_{6n}$
7	−	+	+	−	−	+	−	$y_{71}, y_{72}, \ldots, y_{7n}$
8	+	+	+	+	+	+	+	$y_{81}, y_{82}, \ldots, y_{8n}$

of the increase in the number of factors, a simplified terminology is used. The sum of all responses at each treatment condition and total of all responses are given by

$$A_i = \sum_{j=1}^{n} y_{ij}$$

$$T = \sum_{i=1}^{8} A_i$$

respectively, where n is the number of runs (repetitions) per treatment condition. The sum of the responses due to each factor and level is then given by

$$A_+ = \sum_{+A's} A_i = A_2 + A_4 + A_6 + A_8, \qquad A_- = \sum_{-A's} A_i = A_1 + A_3 + A_5 + A_7$$

$$B_+ = \sum_{+B's} A_i = A_3 + A_4 + A_7 + A_8, \qquad B_- = \sum_{-B's} A_i = A_1 + A_2 + A_5 + A_6$$

$$C_+ = \sum_{+C's} A_i = A_5 + A_6 + A_7 + A_8, \qquad C_- = \sum_{-C's} A_i = A_1 + A_2 + A_3 + A_4$$

$$AB_+ = \sum_{+AB's} A_i = A_1 + A_4 + A_5 + A_8, \qquad AB_- = \sum_{-AB's} A_i = A_2 + A_3 + A_6 + A_7$$

$$AC_+ = \sum_{+AC's} A_i = A_1 + A_3 + A_6 + A_8, \qquad AC_- = \sum_{-AC's} A_i = A_2 + A_4 + A_5 + A_7$$

$$BC_+ = \sum_{+BC's} A_i = A_1 + A_2 + A_7 + A_8, \qquad BC_- = \sum_{-BC's} A_i = A_3 + A_4 + A_5 + A_6$$

$$ABC_+ = \sum_{+ABC's} A_i = A_2 + A_3 + A_5 + A_8, \qquad ABC_- = \sum_{-ABC's} A_i = A_1 + A_4 + A_6 + A_7$$

The total sum of squares, sum of squares for each factor, sum of squares due to interaction between factors, and sum of squares due to the error are given by

$$SS_T = \sum_{i=1}^{abc} \sum_{j=1}^{n} y_{ij}^2 - \frac{T^2}{N}$$

$$SS_A = \frac{A_+^2 + A_-^2}{n(2)^{k-1}} - \frac{T^2}{N}, \quad SS_B = \frac{B_+^2 + B_-^2}{n(2)^{k-1}} - \frac{T^2}{N}, \quad SS_C = \frac{C_+^2 + C_-^2}{n(2)^{k-1}} - \frac{T^2}{N}$$

$$SS_{AB} = \frac{AB_+^2 + AB_-^2}{n(2)^{k-1}} - \frac{T^2}{N}, \quad SS_{AC} = \frac{AC_+^2 + AC_-^2}{n(2)^{k-1}} - \frac{T^2}{N}$$

$$SS_{BC} = \frac{BC_+^2 + BC_-^2}{n(2)^{k-1}} - \frac{T^2}{N}, \quad SS_{ABC} = \frac{ABC_+^2 + ABC_-^2}{n(2)^{k-1}} - \frac{T^2}{N}$$

$$SS_E = SS_T - SS_A - SS_B - SS_C - SS_{AB} - SS_{BC} - SS_{AC} - SS_{ABC}$$

respectively, where k is the number of factors ($k = 3$ for this development). The mean squares are calculated by normalizing the sum of squares by the respective number of degrees of freedom. The mean squares for each factor, interaction between factors, and error are given by

$$MS_A = \frac{SS_A}{v_A}, \quad MS_B = \frac{SS_B}{v_B}, \quad MS_C = \frac{SS_C}{v_C}$$

$$MS_{AB} = \frac{SS_{AB}}{v_{AB}}, \quad MS_{AC} = \frac{SS_{AC}}{v_{AC}}, \quad MS_{BC} = \frac{SS_{BC}}{v_{BC}}, \quad MS_{ABC} = \frac{SS_{ABC}}{v_{ABC}}$$

$$MS_E = \frac{SS_E}{v_E}$$

where the degrees of freedom for each factor, interaction between factors, and the error are given by

$$v_A = a - 1, \quad v_B = b - 1, \quad v_C = c - 1$$
$$v_{AB} = (a-1)(b-1), \quad v_{AC} = (a-1)(c-1), \quad v_{BC} = (b-1)(c-1)$$
$$v_{ABC} = (a-1)(b-1)(c-1)$$
$$v_E = N - abc$$

respectively. The ratio of the variance in each factor and the interaction between factor to the error variance is given by

$$F_A = \frac{MS_A}{MS_E}, \quad F_B = \frac{MS_B}{MS_E}, \quad F_C = \frac{MS_C}{MS_E}$$

$$F_{AB} = \frac{MS_{AB}}{MS_E}, \quad F_{AC} = \frac{MS_{AC}}{MS_E}, \quad F_{BC} = \frac{MS_{BC}}{MS_E}, \quad F_{ABC} = \frac{MS_{ABC}}{MS_E}$$

respectively. If $F_A > F_{\alpha,v_1,v_2}$, where $v_1 = v_A$ and $v_2 = v_E$, it can be said that factor A is significant for a particular value of α. If $F_{AB} > F_{\alpha,v_1,v_2}$, where $v_1 = v_{AB}$ and $v_2 = v_E$ it can be said that the interaction between factors A and B is significant for a particular value of α. Similar comparisons can be made for factors B and C, and the interactions between factors A and C; B and C; and A, B, and C.

As previously stated, the change in response due to a change in the level of the factor is known as the factor effect. The effect of each factor is obtained by averaging the response from each level and then evaluating the difference between each average; that is,

$$e_A = \frac{A_+ - A_-}{n(2)^{k-1}}, \quad e_B = \frac{B_+ - B_-}{n(2)^{k-1}}, \quad e_C = \frac{C_+ - C_-}{n(2)^{k-1}}$$

$$e_{AB} = \frac{AB_+ - AB_-}{n(2)^{k-1}}, \quad e_{AC} = \frac{AC_+ - AC_-}{n(2)^{k-1}}, \quad e_{BC} = \frac{BC_+ - BC_-}{n(2)^{k-1}}$$

$$e_{ABC} = \frac{ABC_+ - ABC_-}{n(2)^{k-1}}$$

Interaction between the factors is said to exist when the difference in response between the levels of one factor is different at all levels of the other factors. For a large interaction, the corresponding main effects are small. In other words, prominent interaction effect may overshadow the significance of the main effect. Hence, knowledge of interaction is often more useful than the main effect.

Results for a full factorial experimental design including factor effect and significance are depicted in Table 19-10.

TABLE 19-10
Results for Three-Factor Experimental Design

Source (Factor)	Effect	Sum of Squares	v	Mean Square	F	F_{α,v_1,v_2}	Significant (yes/no)
A	e_A	SS_A	v_A	MS_A	F_A	$F_{,\alpha v_A, v_E}$	
B	e_B	SS_B	v_B	MS_B	F_B	$F_{,\alpha v_B, v_E}$	
C	e_C	SS_C	v_C	MS_C	F_C	$F_{,\alpha v_C, v_E}$	
AB	e_{AB}	SS_{AB}	v_{AB}	MS_{AB}	F_{AB}	$F_{,\alpha v_{AB}, v_E}$	
AC	e_{AC}	SS_{AC}	v_{AC}	MS_{AC}	F_{AC}	$F_{,\alpha v_{AC}, v_E}$	
BC	e_{BC}	SS_{BC}	v_{BC}	MS_{BC}	F_{BC}	$F_{,\alpha v_{BC}, v_E}$	
ABC	e_{ABC}	SS_{ABC}	v_{ABC}	MS_{ABC}	F_{ABC}	$F_{,\alpha v_{ABC}, v_E}$	
Error		SS_E	v_E	MS_E			
Total		SS_T					

EXAMPLE PROBLEM

Consider an experiment with three factors, each at two levels. Determine the significance of each factor for a level $\alpha = 0.05$ and the factor effects. The results of the experiment are given in the following table.

Treatment Condition	FACTORS							Response (Results)
	A	B	C	AB	AC	BC	ABC	
1	−	−	−	+	+	+	−	30, 28
2	+	−	−	−	−	+	+	28, 31
3	−	+	−	−	+	−	+	25, 37
4	+	+	−	+	−	−	−	36, 33
5	−	−	+	+	−	−	+	50, 45
6	+	−	+	−	+	−	−	45, 48
7	−	+	+	−	−	+	−	38, 41
8	+	+	+	+	+	+	+	44, 37

In order to obtain the significance and effect of each factor and their interaction, the sum of the squares, degrees of freedom, mean square, and F are calculated first. These results are summarized in the following table.

Source (Factor)	Effect	Sum of Squares	v	Mean Square	F	F_{α, v_1, v_2}	Significant (yes/no)
A	1.00	4.00	1	4.00	0.248	5.532	No
B	− 1.75	12.25	1	12.25	0.760	5.532	No
C	12.50	625.00	1	625.00	38.760	5.532	Yes
AB	1.25	6.25	1	6.25	0.388	5.532	No
AC	− 1.00	4.00	1	4.00	0.248	5.532	No
BC	− 2.75	110.25	1	110.25	6.837	5.532	Yes
ABC	− 0.25	0.25	1	0.25	0.016	5.532	No
Error		129.00	8	16.125			
Total		891.00	15				

Based on these calculations, factor C has a strong effect on the experiment; for example, increasing factor C from level 1 to level 2 increases the response by 12.50. The interaction between factors B and C is also significant.

Fractional Factorials

The perfect experimental design is a full factorial, with replications, that is conducted in a random manner. Unfortunately, this type of experimental design may make the number of experimental runs prohibitive, especially if the experiment is conducted on production equipment with lengthy setup times. The number of treatment conditions is determined by

$$TC = l^f$$

where TC = number of treatment conditions
l = number of levels
f = number of factors

Thus, for a two-level design, $2^2 = 4$; $2^3 = 8$; $2^4 = 16$; $2^5 = 32$; $2^6 = 64,...$, and for a three-level design $3^2 = 9$; $3^3 = 27$; $3^4 = 81$; .... If each treatment condition is replicated only once, the number of experimental runs is doubled. Thus, for a three-level design with five factors and one replicate, the number of runs is 486.

Table 19-11 shows a three-factor full factorial design. The design space is composed of the seven columns with + or −, and the design matrix is composed of the three individual factor columns A, B, and C. The design matrix tells us how to run the TCs, whereas the design space is used to make calculations to determine significance.

Three-factor interactions with a significant effect on the process are rare, and some two-factor interactions will not occur or can be eliminated by using engineering experience and judgment. If our engineering judgment showed that there was no three-factor

TABLE 19-11

Signs for Effects for a Three-Factor Experimental Design

Treatment Condition	FACTORS							Response (Results)
	A	B	C	AB	AC	BC	ABC	
1	−	−	−	+	+	+	−	y_1
2	+	−	−	−	−	+	+	y_2
3	−	+	−	−	+	−	+	y_3
4	+	+	−	+	−	−	−	y_4
5	−	−	+	+	−	−	+	y_5
6	+	−	+	−	+	−	−	y_6
7	−	+	+	−	−	+	−	y_7
8	+	+	+	+	+	+	+	y_8

TABLE 19-12
Signs for Effects for a Fractional Factorial

Treatment Condition	FACTORS			Response (Results)
	A	B	C = AB	
5	−	−	+	y_5
2	+	−	−	y_2
3	−	+	−	y_3
8	+	+	+	y_8

interaction (*ABC*), we could place a Factor *D* in that column and make it part of the design matrix. Of course, we would need to have a high degree of confidence that factor *D* does not interact with the other columns, *A, B, C, AB, AC,* or *BC*. Similarly, we could place a Factor *E* in the column headed *BC* if we thought there was no *BC* interaction. This approach keeps the number of runs the same and adds factors.

Another approach is to reduce the number of runs while maintaining the number of factors. If we assume no two-factor or three-factor interactions, we can set *C = AB*. This approach is accomplished by selecting the rows that have *C* and *AB* of the same sign, as shown in Table 19-12.

The error term for a fractionalized experiment can be obtained by replication of the treatment conditions or by pooling the nonsignificant effects (see Chapter 20).

Examples

There are numerous examples of organizations employing design of experiments in new product development, improvement of existing products, process improvement, and improvements in service organizations. The following examples give a wide range of organization that were capable of improving some aspect of their company or product by using design of experiments.

1. Evans Clay of McIntyre, Georgia, won the 1996 RIT/USA Today Quality Cup for small business by using design of experiments to increase production of kaolin clay by more than 10%, which helped the company post a profit for the first time in five years.[1] Evans Clay produces processed clay used to strengthen fiberglass used in boats and auto parts and used by the paper manufacturers. Evans Clay had not kept pace with changing times and were in serious financial danger having not posted a profit for several years. Their problem was that one of their two mills consistently produced less processed clay

---

[1] 1995 RIT/USA Today Quality Cup for Small Business.

than the other mill. To address the problem, Evans Clay conducted a robust design of experiment with numerous factors and levels: hammer configurations, air pressure, air flow, nozzles, dust collector bags, and the "horn" (used to produce sonic blasts to dislodge dust and increase air flow). The result of the design of experiments was to change the frequency of the horn blasts and to replace the dust collector bags made of polydacron with ones made of gortex that allow more air flow. As a result of their work, production increased by 10% and a profit was posted for the first time in five years.

2. John Deere Engine Works of Waterloo, Iowa, used design of experiments to eliminate an expensive chromate-conversion procedure used in the adhesion of their green paint to aluminum.[2] This change resulted in an annual savings of $500,000.

3. Nabisco Corporation had a problem with excessive scrap cookie dough and out-of-roundness conditions. They performed a factorial design to identify the important factors and the insignificant ones.[3] As a result, they saved 16 pounds of cookie dough per shift and eliminated the out-of-roundness condition.

4. A team of employees at Wilkes-Barre General Hospital in Northeastern Pennsylvania won the 2001 RIT/USA Today Quality Cup for health care using a simple experimental design technique.[4] Prior to the team's work, 3 out of every 100 open-heart surgery patients developed infections that could cost $100,000 per patient, involving weeks on a ventilator, more surgery, and increased death rate. The team from Wilkes-Barre General Hospital found that a $12.47 prescription antibiotic ointment reduced the rate of infection from 3 out of a 100 patients to less than 1 out of 100 patients. After studying nearly 2000 patients over three years, statistics showed that application of the ointment reduced the infection rate from 2.7% to 0.9%.

5. Eastman Kodak of Rochester, New York, used design of experiments to determine that they only needed to retool an existing machine instead of making a large capital investment in a new machine.[5] As a result, machine set-up times were reduced from 8 hours to 20 minutes, scrap reduced by a factor of 10, repeatability increased to 100%, and $200,000 was saved on the capital investment in a new machine.

6. Two 9th grade students from Farmington High School in Farmington, Michigan, used design of experiments to test the AA battery life for their remote-control model cars.[6] The students used 2^3 factorial design with three control factors and two levels for each factor: AA battery (high cost and low cost), connector design type (gold-plated contacts and standard contacts), and battery temperature (cold and ambient). A battery box with

---

[2] Rich Burnham, "How to Select Design of Experiments Software," *Quality Digest* (November 1998): 32–36.

[3] *Ibid.*

[4] George Hager, "Low-Cost Antibiotic Saves Patients Pain, Thousands of Dollars," *USA Today* (May 9, 2001): 3B.

[5] Rich Burnham, "How to Select Design of Experiments Software," *Quality Digest* (November 1998): 32–36.

[6] Eric Wasiloff and Curtis Hargitt, "Using DOE to Determine AA Battery Life," *Quality Progress* (March 1999): 67–72.

contacts and a test circuit constituted the experimental set-up. The students also performed an ANOVA, resulting in the battery cost being a significant factor and the other two factors not significant and possibly indistinguishable from experimental error. Their recommendations included increasing the sample size and studying the effects of noise levels.

7. K2 Corporation of Vashon, Washington, used design of experiments to reduce the high scrap rate in their new ski's complex design.[7] This resulted in a press downtime from 250 hours per week to only 2.5 hours per week.

8. Hercules Corporation had a problem with tin and lead leakage into circuit boards during plating causing costly rework or scrapping.[8] They performed a six-factor, sixteen-experiment design of experiments to find a correlation between anti-tarnish level and de-lamination. As a result, a slightly acidic rinse water was used, which eliminated the seepage problem.

As the previous examples show, design of experiments is used by a vast array of organizations, from industries to companies in the service sector, and even by young adults for a science project.

Conclusion

In order for experimental design to be a powerful and useful technique, careful attention must be given to the following considerations: [9]

Set good objectives.
>   Selection of factors and number of factors.
>   Selection of the value for the levels of each factor and number of levels.
>   Selection of response variable.

Measure response variable quantitatively.

Replicate conditions to dampen noise.

Run the experiments in a random order to eliminate any biasing.

Block out known (or unwanted) sources of variation.

Know (beforehand) which effects will be aliased from interactions.

Use results from one design of experiments to the next experiment.

Confirm results with a second experiment.

---

[7] Rich Burnham, 32–36.

[8] Ibid.

[9] Mark J. Anderson and Shari L. Kraber, "Eight Keys to Successful DOE," *Quality Digest* (July 1999): 39–43.

When performing the actual experiment, scientific procedures should be followed to ensure the validity of the results. Once the experiment has been performed, the statistical methods presented in this chapter should be implemented to arrive at conclusions that are objective rather than subjective.

TQM Exemplary Organization[10]

Founded in 1970, ADAC Laboratories designs, manufactures, markets, and supports products for nuclear-medicine imaging, radiation-therapy planning, and managing health care information. Many of the company's products are regulated by the Food and Drug Administration, which requires adherence to strict safety standards. ADAC, with 710 employees, has installed about 5,000 systems at more than 2,500 hospitals, clinics, and other sites around the world. These systems are extremely complex, comprising several thousand parts, the vast majority purchased from suppliers.

From 1990 through 1996, the company's share of the domestic nuclear medicine market increased from 6% to 50% and it became the market leader in Europe. ADAC executives credit the application of quality management principles and practices with significantly improving the company's financial health. Now, ADAC is leveraging its continuous-improvement capabilities to compete in new markets that it has targeted to expand its business.

The company's corporate planning process yields a strategic plan for the next three to five years and an annual business plan. Consistent with ADAC's primary core value, "Customers come first," the planning process begins with a thorough, fact-based analysis of customer requirements. This analysis uses data gathered from a variety of sources, including surveys, lost-order information, interviews conducted by customer-contact employees, logs of service calls, and focus groups. Results are integrated with those from analyses of competitive forces, risks, company capabilities, and supplier capabilities.

Short- and long-term strategies are then distilled into the "vital few," key business drivers that focus and align plans and continuous improvement efforts over the next year. In turn, each department translates the strategic directions and business drivers into specific requirements and action plans. These are the basis for MISS "most important tasks," or top priority improvements set for functional units and for individual employees. Alignment of plans is ensured by cross-functional work sessions at which MISS are presented.

Most workers participate on highly-empowered teams, and all manufacturing employees are members of self-directed work teams. All employees receive training on customer and supplier models, problem solving, and basic statistical analysis. An integral

---

[10] Malcolm Baldrige National Quality Award, 1995 Manufacturing Category Recipient, NIST/Baldrige Homepage.

element of ADAC's standardized problem-solving process, bench marking is used regularly by all continuous improvement teams to set performance goals and to gauge the effectiveness of its management processes.

ADAC's quality system has yielded highly leveraged improvements, helping the company to compete and to increase market share. ADAC consistently brings products to market faster than its larger competitors. For three recent product releases in its nuclear medicine business, ADAC was at least 8 months and as many as 21 months ahead of its nearest competitor. From 1990 to 1995, company revenues have nearly tripled, and the portion of the revenues accounted for by operating expenses has decreased to less than 30%, from almost 40%.

Significant gains in supplier performance also have been achieved. In 1992, ADAC instituted a program to certify its suppliers. The company purchases some 5,000 different types of parts. By the end of 1995, 70% of the parts received by ADAC came from certified suppliers. Purchased parts rejected during assembly have decreased from about 18 per camera in 1993 to about four per camera in 1996.

Efficiency gains have lowered the direct labor costs for producing each of its imaging cameras, from an average of almost $15,000 at the start of 1994 to less than $9,000 by the end of 1995. Nonconformance rates, as measured at final inspection, have fallen by about 40%.

As a result of performance gains and product improvements, the volume of service calls during the first 30 days after the installation of a new imaging system (an especially critical period when customers are forming their perceptions of quality) has been cut in half. A 1995 independent survey rated the first-month reliability of ADAC cameras as best in the industry. If customers do encounter serious problems, however, they can expect a quick and effective response. For example, if a system breaks down, ADAC technicians will have it back in operation within an average of 17 hours after receiving a customer's call, or less than a third of the time it took in 1990.

As designed, ADAC's business system is delivering increases in customer satisfaction, as ascertained through surveys. Customer-retention rates have increased from 70% in 1990 to 93% in 1995, and service-contract renewals have risen to 95%, from 85%. In independent, annual surveys of nearly 2,000 clinics and hospitals, nuclear medicine customers consistently have rated ADAC best at addressing their needs, and the gap between ADAC and its competitors has been widening. In 1994 and 1995, ADAC was the only company to score above five on this particular indicator of customer satisfaction, which is measured on a scale of 1 to 6. On all eight measures of service satisfaction from speed of phone response to preventive maintenance, ADAC was the sole leader in five categories and tied for the top spot in the remaining ones.

Exercises

1. Using the judicial system as an example, explain Type I and II errors in hypothesis testing.

2. Identify the appropriate level of risk for the following items and justify your answer.

(a) Space shuttle
(b) X-ray machine
(c) Camera
(d) Canned soup
(e) Pencil
(f) Computer keyboard
(g) Chair
(h) Running shoe
(i) Automobile
(j) Fresh vegetables
(k) Child's toy
(l) Golf club
(m) Baby food
(n) Restaurant food
(o) Haircut
(p) Breast implants
(q) Child's soccer game
(r) Driving to work
(s) Taking an airplane flight

3. A law enforcement organization claims that their radar gun is accurate to within 0.5 miles per hour for a court hearing. An independent organization hired to test the accuracy of the radar gun conducted 12 tests on a projectile moving at 60 miles per hour. Given data in the following table, determine if the radar gun can be used in court. State the hypothesis and base your comments on an appropriate α level.

Data
63   61.5   59   63.5   57.5   61.5   61   63   60   60.5   64   62

4. An organization developing a new drug to combat depression is performing testing on ten subjects. After giving 10 mg of the drug to each subject for 30 days, psychological tests are given to evaluate the drug's performance. The results of the test on a 100 scale are given in the following table. If the mean and variance of the psychological test prior to taking the drug was 61 and 89, respectively, comment on the performance of the drug using the two-sample t test with $\alpha = 0.01$.

Data									
88	73	66	95	69	73	81	48	59	72

5. Given data in the following table for wave-soldering nonconformities, determine if there are any differences between the two processes. Based on various α levels, would you recommend a change to the proposed process?

Process	Data											
Current	8	9	6	8	7	6	7	8	9	8	7	6
Proposed	10	9	8	8	9							

6. An archeologist has recently uncovered an ancient find. Based upon carbon dating of bones and tools found at the site, the following data has been acquired. Use an α level of 0.10 to determine whether the bones and tools are from the same time period. Also determine whether the bones or tools are from the early Bronze Age, which dates back to before 3000 BC.

Artifact	Data (BC)				
Bones	2850	3125	3200	3050	2900
Tools	2700	2875	3250	3325	2995

7. Using the information in the following table for three levels of a factor, determine if there is any significant difference in the data for $\alpha = 0.05$. If significance occurs, determine the appropriate levels using the t reference distribution.

Level	Data							
1	12	14	13	14	15	13		
2	17	16	16	15	14	15	15	
3	11	9	10	12	11	7	11	9

8. Because of an influx of nonconforming bolts, an aircraft manufacturer decides to check the ultimate strength of four different size bolts in their last order using a tensile testing machine. Based on the following data, use an appropriate α level to determine if there is significance. Furthermore, if the ultimate strength should be greater than 120 kip/in^2, identify the bolt size(s) that you feel may be nonconforming.

Bolt Diameter (in)	Strength (kip/in²)			
0.250	120	123	122	119
0.375	131	128	126	140
0.500	115	124	123	120
0.625	118	119	121	120

9. An engineer at a casting company performed an experiment to determine which factor (quenching temperature, alloy content, or machine tool speed) had the largest effect on the surface roughness. The following table gives the levels for each factor in the experiment. Using a one-factor-at-a-time experiment, determine which factor has the most effect on surface roughness if the responses are $y_0 = 1.10$ μ in, $y_A = 1.20$ μ in, $y_B = 0.80$ μ in, and $y_c = 1.60$ μ in.

Factor	Description	Level 1	Level 2
A	Quenching temperature (°F)	800	400
B	Machine tool speed (in/s)	0.005	0.01
C	Nickel Alloy content (%)	1	4

10. Repeat Exercise 9 using an orthogonal experiment if the responses are $y_{111} = 1.10$ μ in, $y_{211} = 0.80$ μ in, $y_{121} = 0.90$ μ in, $y_{221} = 0.70$ in, $y_{112} = 1.05$ μ in, $y_{212} = 1.35$ μ in, $y_{122} = 1.10$ μ in, and $y_{222} = 1.40$ μ in. Compare your results to Exercise 9 and comment on the effect of each factor on the machining process.

11. A university administrator is interested in determining the effect of SAT score and high school GPA on a university student's GPA. The university GPAs for 12 students are given in the following table. For an α level of 0.10, comment on the significance of SAT score, high school GPA, and their interaction on university GPA.

	SAT SCORE	
High School GPA	**Greater than 1050**	**Less than 1050**
Greater than 3.0/4.0	3.57, 3.75, 3.42	2.98, 2.59, 3.17
Less than 3.0/4.0	3.10, 3.22, 3.08	3.24, 2.55, 2.76

12. An insurance company is analyzing the cost of a femur fracture and tibia fracture at two hospitals. Given the following costs in dollars, determine if there is a significant difference in the cost of surgery at each hospital using an appropriate α level and comment on the results.

	TYPE OF SURGERY	
Hospital	**Femur Fracture**	**Tibia Fracture**
A	1325, 1250	900, 850
B	1125, 1075	1050, 1025

13. Develop a table similar to Table 19-9 for an experiment with four factors.

14. Formulate a full factorial experiment to determine what factors affect the retention rate in college. Identify four factors each at two levels that you feel influence retention rate. For example, one factor could be external work with two levels, 20 and 40 hours per week.

15. Three factors, each at two levels, are studied using a full factorial design. Factors and levels are given in the following table.

Factor	Description	Level 1	Level 2
A	Formulation	I	II
B	Cycle Time (s)	10	20
C	Pressure (lb/in^2)	300	400

Responses in the following table are for each treatment condition as depicted in Table 19-9. Set up a full factorial design and evaluate the significance and factor effects of this study for α levels of 0.10 and 0.05. Based on your results, comment on reducing this study to a fractional factorial experiment.

	TREATMENT CONDITION							
Replicate	*1*	*2*	*3*	*4*	*5*	*6*	*7*	*8*
1	1	2	3	4	6	6	7	9
2	2	4	5	6	8	8	9	11

16. Reduce the full factorial experiment in Exercise 14 to a three-factor fractional factorial experiment by using your experience and personal judgment. For instance, eliminate the four-factor interaction and some of the two- and three-factor interactions. Construct a table similar to Table 19-12.

17. Working individually or in a team, design a full factorial experiment and determine responses for one or more of the following items and one of your own choice. Your experiments should have at least three factors at two levels each and two replicates.

 (a) Accuracy of weather forecaster
    (examples of factors are time of day, location, channel, and so forth)
 (b) Quality of pizza
    (examples of factors are type of establishment, price, temperature, and so forth)
 (c) Computer mouse performance
    (examples of factors are ergonomics, sensitivity, price, and so forth)
 (d) Television remote control channel switching
    (examples of factors are time of day, gender, age, and so forth)

20

Taguchi's Quality Engineering

Introduction

Most of the body of knowledge associated with the quality sciences was developed in the United Kingdom as design of experiments and in the United States as statistical quality control. More recently, Dr. Genichi Taguchi, a mechanical engineer who has won four Deming Awards, has added to this body of knowledge. In particular, he introduced the loss function concept, which combines cost, target, and variation into one metric with specifications being of secondary importance. Furthermore, he developed the concept of robustness, which means that noise factors are taken into account to ensure that the system functions correctly. Noise factors are uncontrollable variables that can cause significant variability in the process or the product.

Loss Function

Taguchi has defined quality as the loss imparted to society from the time a product is shipped. Societal losses include failure to meet customer requirements, failure to meet ideal performance, and harmful side effects. Many practitioners have included the losses due to production, such as raw material, energy, and labor consumed on unusable products or toxic by-products.

The loss-to-society concept can be illustrated by an example associated with the production of large vinyl covers to protect materials from the elements. Figure 20-1 shows three stages in the evolution of vinyl thickness. At (1), the process is just capable of

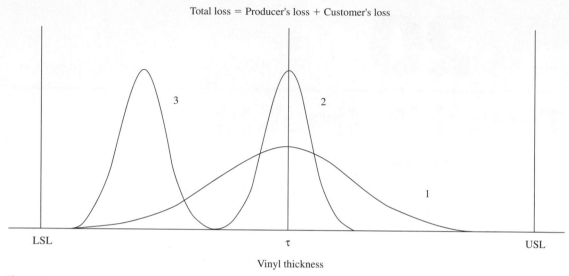

Total loss = Producer's loss + Customer's loss

LSL $\qquad$ τ $\qquad$ USL

Vinyl thickness

Figure 20-1 Loss to Society
Reproduced, with permission, from *Taguchi Methods: Introduction to Quality Engineering* (Allen Park, Mich.: American Supplier Institute, Inc., 1991).

meeting the specifications (USL and LSL); however, it is on the target *tau*, τ.[1] After considerable effort, the production process was improved by reducing the variability about the target, as shown at (2). In an effort to reduce its production costs, the organization decided to shift the target closer to the LSL, as shown at (3). This action resulted in a substantial improvement by lowering the cost to the organization; however, the vinyl covers were not as strong as before. When farmers used the covers to protect wheat from the elements, they tore and a substantial loss occurred to the farmers. In addition, the cost of wheat increased as a result of supply-and-demand factors, thereby causing an increase in wheat prices and a further loss to society. The company's reputation suffered, which created a loss of market share with its unfavorable loss aspects.

Assuming the target is correct, losses of concern are those caused by a product's critical performance characteristics deviating from the target. The importance of concentrating on "hitting the target" is documented by Sony. In spite of the fact that the design and specifications were identical, U.S. customers preferred the color density of shipped TV sets produced by Sony–Japan over those produced by Sony–USA. Investigation of this situation revealed that the frequency distributions were markedly different, as shown in Figure 20-2. Even though Sony–Japan had 0.3% outside the specifications, the

---

[1] Taguchi uses the symbol *m* for the target.

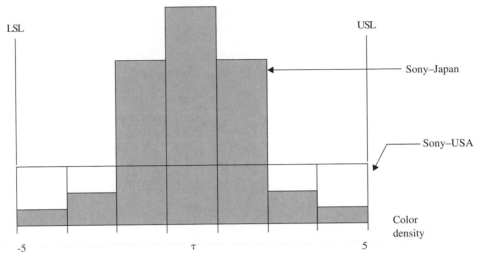

Figure 20-2 Distribution of Color Density for Sony–USA and Sony–Japan
Source: *The Asahi*, April 17, 1979.

distribution was normal and centered on the target. The distribution of the Sony–USA was uniform between the specifications with no values outside specifications. It was clear that customers perceived quality as meeting the target (Japan) rather than just meeting the specifications (USA). Ford Motor Company had a similar experience with transmissions.

Out of specification is the common measure of quality loss. Although this concept may be appropriate for accounting, it is a poor concept for all other areas. It implies that all products that meet specifications are good, whereas those that do not are bad. From the customer's point of view, the product that barely meets specification is as good (or bad) as the product that is barely out of specification. It appears the wrong measuring system is being used. The loss function corrects for the deficiency described above by combining cost, target, and variation into one metric.

Nominal-the-Best

Although Taguchi developed more than 68 loss functions, many situations are approximated by the quadratic function which is called the nominal-the-best type. Figure 20-3(a) shows the step function that describes the Sony–USA situation. When the value for the performance characteristic, y, is within specifications the loss is $0, and when it is outside the specifications the loss is A. The quadratic function is shown at 20-3(b) and describes the Sony–Japan situation. In this situation loss occurs as soon as the performance characteristic, y, departs from the target, τ.

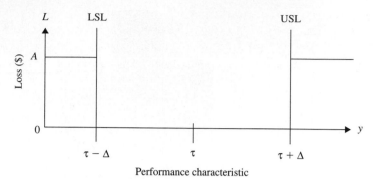

(a) Step function (Sony − USA)

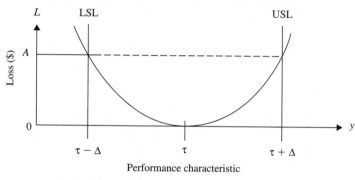

(b) Quadratic function (Sony − Japan)

Figure 20-3 Step and Quadratic Loss Functions

The quadratic loss function is described by the equation

$$L = k(y - \tau)^2$$

where L = cost incurred as quality deviates from the target
       y = performance characteristic
       τ = target
       k = quality loss coefficient

The loss coefficient is determined by setting $\Delta = (y - \tau)$, the deviation from the target. When Δ is at the USL or LSL, the loss to the customer of repairing or discarding the product is $A. Thus,

$$k = A/(y - \tau)^2 = A/\Delta^2$$

EXAMPLE PROBLEM

If the specifications are 10 ± 3 for a particular quality characteristic and the average repair cost is \$230, determine the loss function. Determine the loss at $y = 12$.

$$k = A/\Delta^2 = 230/3^2 = 25.6$$

Thus, $L = 25.6 \, (y - 10)^2$ and at $y = 12$,

$$
\begin{aligned}
L &= 25.6(y - 10)^2 \\
&= 25.6(12 - 10)^2 \\
&= \$102.40
\end{aligned}
$$

Average Loss

The loss described here assumes that the quality characteristic is static. In reality, one cannot always hit the target, τ. It is varying due to noise, and the loss function must reflect the variation of many pieces rather than just one piece. Noise factors are classified as external and internal, with internal being further classified as unit-to-unit and deterioration.

A refrigerator temperature control will serve as an example to help clarify the noise concept. External noise is due to the actions of the user, such as the number of times the door is opened and closed, amount of food inside, the initial temperature, and so forth. Unit-to-unit internal noise is due to variation during production such as seal tightness, control sensor variations and so forth. Although this type of noise is inevitable, every effort should be made to keep it to a minimum. Noise due to deterioration is caused by leakage of refrigerant, mechanical wear of compressor parts, and so forth. This type of noise is primarily a function of the design. Noise factors cause deviation from the target, which causes a loss to society.

Figure 20-4 shows the nominal-the-best loss function with the distribution of the noise factors. An equation can be derived by summing the individual loss values and dividing by their number to give

$$\bar{L} = k[\sigma^2 + (\bar{y} - \tau)^2]$$

where $\bar{L}$ = the average or expected loss.

Because the population standard deviation, σ, will rarely be known, the sample standard deviation, s, will need to be substituted. This action will make the value somewhat larger; however, the average loss is a very conservative value.

The loss can be lowered by first reducing the variation, σ, and then adjusting the average, $\bar{y}$, to bring it on target, τ. The loss function "speaks the language of things," which

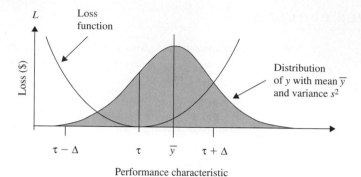

Figure 20-4 Average or Expected Loss
Reproduced, with permission, from Madhav S. Phadke, *Quality Engineering Using Robust Design* (Englewood Cliffs, N.J.: Prentice Hall, 1989).

is engineering's measure, and money, which is management's measure. Examples where the nominal-the-best loss function would be applicable are the performance characteristics of color density, voltage, dimensions, and so forth.

EXAMPLE PROBLEM

Compute the average loss for a process that produces steel shafts. The target value is 6.40 mm and the coefficient is 9500. Eight samples give 6.36, 6.40, 6.38, 6.39, 6.43, 6.39, 6.46, and 6.42.

$$s = 0.0315945 \qquad \bar{y} = 6.40375$$

$$\bar{L} = k\left[s^2 + (\bar{y} - \tau)^2\right]$$

$$= 9500\left[0.0315945^2 + (6.40375 - 6.40)^2\right]$$

$$= \$9.62$$

Other Loss Functions

There are two other loss functions that are quite common, smaller-the-better and larger-the-better. Figure 20-5 illustrates the concepts.

As shown in the figure, the target value for smaller-the-better is 0, and there are no negative values for the performance characteristic. Examples of performance characteristics are radiation leakage from a microwave appliance, response time for a computer, pollution from an automobile, out of round for a hole, etc.

In the larger-the-better situation, shown in Figure 20-5(b), the target value is ∞, which gives a zero loss. There are no negative values and the worst case is at $y = 0$. Actually,

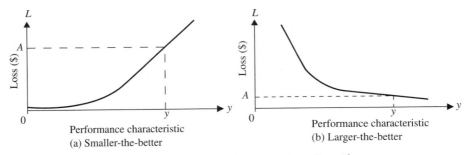

Figure 20-5 Smaller-the-Better and Larger-the-Better Loss Functions

TABLE 20-1

Summary of the Equations for the Three Common Loss Functions

Nominal-the-best	$L = k(y - \tau)^2 \qquad$ where $k = A/\Delta^2$
	$\bar{L} = k\,(\text{MSD}) \qquad$ where $\text{MSD} = [\Sigma\,(y - \tau)^2]/n$
	$\bar{L} = k[\sigma^2 + (\bar{y} - \tau)^2]$
Smaller-the-better	$L = ky^2 \qquad$ where $k = A/y^2$
	$\bar{L} = k\,(\text{MSD}) \qquad$ where $\text{MSD} = [\Sigma\,y^2]/n$
	$\bar{L} = k[\bar{y}^2 + \sigma^2]$
Larger-the-better	$L = k(1/y^2) \qquad$ where $k = Ay^2$
	$\bar{L} = k\,(\text{MSD}) \qquad$ where $\text{MSD} = [\Sigma\,(1/y^2)]/n$
	$\bar{L} = k[\Sigma\,(1/y^2)]/n$

larger-the-better is the reciprocal of smaller-the-better, and because of the difficulty of working with ∞, some practitioners prefer to work with the reciprocal. Thus, a larger-the-better performance characteristic of meters/second becomes a smaller-the-better performance characteristic of seconds/meter. Examples of performance characteristics are bond strength of adhesives, welding strength, automobile gasoline consumption and so forth.

Summary of the Equations

Table 20-1 gives a summary of the equations for the three common loss functions. It also shows the relationship of the loss function to the mean squared deviation (MSD).

These three common loss functions will cover most situations. After selecting one of the loss functions, one point on the curve needs to be determined in order to obtain the coefficient. It is helpful to work with accounting to obtain this one point. Knowing the coefficient, the equation is complete and can be used to justify the use of resources and as a benchmark to measure improvement. It is much easier to use the loss function to obtain cost information than to develop an elaborate quality cost system. Cost data are usually quite conservative; therefore, it is not necessary for the loss function to be perfect for it to be effective.

Sometimes the loss function curves are modified for particular situations. For example, larger-the-better can be represented by one-half the nominal-the-best curve. Another situation occurs where the performance characteristic is weld strength. In such a case the larger-the-better curve can terminate at the strength of the parent metal rather than ∞. If the three common loss functions do not seem to be representative of a particular situation, then individual points can be plotted.

Orthogonal Arrays[2]

Orthogonal arrays (OA) are a simplified method of putting together an experiment. The original development of the concept was by Sir R. A. Fischer of England in the 1930s. Taguchi added three OAs to the list in 1956, and the National Institute of Science and Technology (NIST) of the United States added three.

An orthogonal array is shown in Table 20-2. The 8 in the designation OA8 represents the number of rows, which is also the number of treatment conditions (TC) and the de-

TABLE 20-2
Orthogonal Array (OA8)[*]

TC	1	2	3	4	5	6	7
1	1	1	1	1	1	1	1
2	1	1	1	2	2	2	2
3	1	2	2	1	1	2	2
4	1	2	2	2	2	1	1
5	2	1	2	1	2	1	2
6	2	1	2	2	1	2	1
7	2	2	1	1	2	2	1
8	2	2	1	2	1	1	2

[*]Taguchi uses a more elaborate system of identification for the orthogonal arrays. It is the authors' opinions that a simple system using OA is more than satisfactory.

---

[2] Orthogonal arrays, interaction tables, and linear graphs in this chapter are reproduced, with permission, from *Taguchi Methods: Introduction to Quality Engineering* (Allen Park, Mich.: American Supplier Institute, Inc., 1991).

grees of freedom. Across the top of the orthogonal array is the maximum number of factors that can be used, which in this case is seven. The levels are designated by 1 and 2. If more levels occur in the array, then 3, 4, 5, and so forth, are used. Other schemes such as −, 0, and + can be used.

The orthogonal property of the OA is not compromised by changing the rows or the columns. Taguchi changed the rows from a traditional design so that TC 1 was composed of all level 1s and, if the team desired, could thereby represent the existing conditions. Also, the columns were switched so that the least amount of change occurs in the columns on the left. This arrangement can provide the team with the capability to assign factors with long setup times to those columns. Orthogonal arrays can handle dummy factors and can be modified. Refer to the bibliography for these techniques.

To determine the appropriate orthogonal array, use the following procedure:

1. Define the number of factors and their levels.
2. Determine the degrees of freedom.
3. Select an orthogonal array.
4. Consider any interactions.

The project team completes the first step.

Degrees of Freedom

The number of degrees of freedom is a very important value because it determines the minimum number of treatment conditions. It is equal to the sum of

(Number of levels - 1) for each factor.

(Number of levels - 1)(number of levels - 1) for each interaction.

One for the average.

An example problem will illustrate the concept.

EXAMPLE PROBLEM

Given four two-level factors, *A, B, C, D*, and two suspected interactions, *BC* and *CD*, determine the degrees of freedom, df. What is the answer if the factors are three-level?

$$df = 4(2 - 1) + 2(2 - 1)(2 - 1) + 1 = 7$$
$$df = 4(3 - 1) + 2(3 - 1)(3 - 1) + 1 = 17$$

At least seven treatment conditions are needed for the two-level, and 17 conditions are needed for the three-level. As can be seen by the example, the number of levels has

TABLE 20-3

Maximum Degrees of Freedom for a Four-Factor, Two-Level Experimental Design

Design Space				df
A	B	C	D	4
AB	AC	AD	BC	6
BD	CD			
ABC	ABD	ACD	BCD	4
ABCD				1
Average				1
			Sum	16

considerable influence on the number of treatment conditions. Although a three-level design provides a great deal more information about the process, it can be costly in terms of the number of treatment conditions.

The maximum degrees of freedom is equal to

$$\mathrm{df} = l^f$$

where l = number of levels
        f = number of factors

For the example problem with two levels, df $= 2^4 = 16$. Table 20-3 shows the maximum degrees of freedom.

In the example problem, it was assumed that four of the two-factor interactions (*AB, AC, AD,* and *BD*), four of the three-factor interactions (*ABC, ABD, ACD,* and *BCD*), and the four-factor interaction (*ABCD*) would not occur. Interactions are discussed later in the chapter.

Selecting the Orthogonal Array

Once the degrees of freedom are known, the next step, selecting the orthogonal array (OA), is easy. The number of treatment conditions is equal to the number of rows in the OA and must be equal to or greater than the degrees of freedom. Table 20-4 shows the orthogonal arrays that are available, up to OA36. Thus, if the number of degrees of freedom is 13, then the next available OA is OA16. The second column of the table has the number of rows and is redundant with the designation in the first column. The third col-

TABLE 20-4
Orthogonal Array Information

OA	Number of Rows	Maximum Number of Factors	MAXIMUM NUMBER OF COLUMNS			
			2-Level	3-Level	4-Level	5-Level
OA2	4	3	3	—	—	—
OA8	8	7	7	—	—	—
OA9	9	4	—	4	—	—
OA12	12	11	11	—	—	—
OA16	16	15	15	—	—	—
OA16[1]	16	5	—	—	5	—
OA18	18	8	1	7	—	—
OA25	25	6	—	—	—	6
OA27	27	13	—	13	—	—
OA32	32	31	31	—	—	—
OA32[1]	32	10	1	—	9	—
OA36	36	23	11	12	—	—
OA36[1]	36	16	3	13	—	—
.	.	.	.	.	.	.
.	.	.	.	.	.	.
.	.	.	.	.	.	.

Adapted, with permission, from Madhav S. Phadke, *Quality Engineering Using Robust Design* (Englewood Cliffs, NJ: Prentice Hall, 1989).

umn gives the maximum number of factors that can be used, and the last four columns give the maximum number of columns available at each level.

Analysis of the table shows that there is a geometric progression for the two-level arrays of OA4, OA8, OA16, OA32, . . . , which is $2^2, 2^3, 2^4, 2^5, \ldots$, and for the three-level arrays of OA9, OA27, OA81, . . . , which is $3^2, 3^3, 3^4, \ldots$. Orthogonal arrays can be modified. Refer to the references for more information.

Interaction Table

Confounding is the inability to distinguish among the effects of one factor from another factor and/or interaction. In order to prevent confounding, one must know which columns to use for the factors. This knowledge is provided by an interaction table, which

TABLE 20-5
Orthogonal Array OA8

TC	1	2	3	4	5	6	7
1	1	1	1	1	1	1	1
2	1	1	1	2	2	2	2
3	1	2	2	1	1	2	2
4	1	2	2	2	2	1	1
5	2	1	2	1	2	1	2
6	2	1	2	2	1	2	1
7	2	2	1	1	2	2	1
8	2	2	1	2	1	1	2

TABLE 20-6
Interaction Table for OA8

Column	1	2	3	4	5	6	7
1	(1)	3	2	5	4	7	6
2		(2)	1	6	7	4	5
3			(3)	7	6	5	4
4				(4)	1	2	3
5					(5)	3	2
6						(6)	1
7							(7)

is shown in Table 20-6. The orthogonal array (OA8) is repeated in Table 20-5 for the convenience of the reader.

Let's assume that factor A is assigned to column 1 and factor B to column 2. If there is an interaction between factors A and B, then column 3 is used for the interaction, AB. Another factor, say, C, would need to be assigned to column 4. If there is an interaction between factor A (column 1) and factor C (column 4), then interaction AC will occur in column 5. The columns that are reserved for interactions are used so that calculations can be made to determine whether there is a strong interaction. If there are no interactions, then all the columns can be used for factors. The actual experiment is conducted using the columns designated for the factors, and these columns are referred to as the design matrix. All the columns are referred to as the design space.

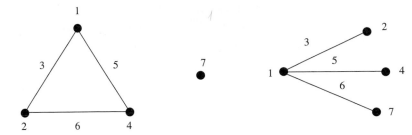

Figure 20-6 Linear Graphs for OA8

Linear Graphs

Taguchi developed a simpler method of working with interactions using linear graphs. Two are shown in Figure 20-6 for OA8. They make it easier to assign factors and interactions to the various columns of an array. Factors are assigned to the points. If there is an interaction between two factors, then it is assigned to the line segment between the two points. For example, using the linear graph on the left in the figure, if factor *B* is assigned to column 2 and factor *C* is assigned to column 4, then interaction *BC* is assigned to column 6. If there is no interaction, then column 6 can be used for a factor.

The linear graph on the right would be used when one factor has three two-level interactions. Three-level orthogonal arrays must use two columns for interactions, because one column is for the linear interaction and one column is for the quadratic interaction. The linear graphs—and, for that matter, the interaction tables—are not designed for three or more factor interactions, which rarely occur. Linear graphs can be modified; refer to the references for modification techniques. Use of the linear graphs requires some trial-and-error activity, and a number of solutions may be possible, as shown by the example problem.

EXAMPLE PROBLEM

An experimental design has four two-level factors (*A, B, C, D*) where only main effects are possible for factor *D* and there is no *BC* interaction. Thus, only interactions *AB* and *AC* are possible, and they can be assigned the line segments 3 and 5, 3 and 6, or 5 and 6, with their apex for factor *A*. Factors *B* and *C* are then assigned to the adjacent points. Column 7 or a line segment that does not have an interaction is used for factor *D*. A number of solutions are possible; one is shown here. The one chosen might well be a function of the setup time when the experiment is run. Column 5 is not used, so it is given the symbol *UX* for unexplained, and calculations for this column should show no effect (very small variation).

Orthogonal Array OA8

TC	B 1	A 2	AB 3	C 4	UX 5	AC 6	D 7
1	1	1	1	1	1	1	1
2	1	1	1	2	2	2	2
3	1	2	2	1	1	2	2
4	1	2	2	2	2	1	1
5	2	1	2	1	2	1	2
6	2	1	2	2	1	2	1
7	2	2	1	1	2	2	1
8	2	2	1	2	1	1	2

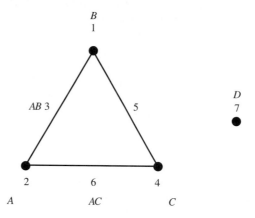

Interactions

The fourth step in the procedure is to consider interactions. Figure 20-7 shows the graphical relationship between two factors. At (a) there is no interaction because the lines are parallel; at (b) there is some interaction; and at (c) there is a strong interaction. The graph is constructed by plotting the points A_1B_1, A_1B_2, A_2B_1, and A_2B_2 drawing lines B_1 and B_2. Taguchi's approach to interactions are given in the following list.

1. Interactions use degrees of freedom; therefore, more treatment conditions are needed or fewer factors can be used.

2. Orthogonal arrays are used in parameter design to obtain optimal factor/levels for robustness and cost in order to improve product and process performance. On the other hand, statistics are applied in pure and applied research to find relationships and a mathematical model. The emphasis is different—one engineering and the other mathematical.

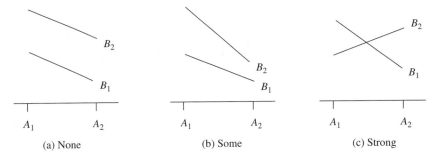

Figure 20-7 **Interaction Between Two Factors**

3. Interactions are primarily between control factors and noise factors. Control and noise factors are discussed later.

4. As long as interactions are relatively mild, main effect analysis will give the optimal results and good reproducibility.

5. OA12 (two-level) and OA18 (three-level) are recommended so that if interactions are present, they are dispersed among all the factors.

6. Engineers should strive to develop a design that uses main effects only.

7. Control factors that will not interact should be selected. For example, the dimensions length and width will frequently interact, whereas the area may provide the same information and save two degrees of freedom.

8. Energy-related outputs, such as braking distance, should be selected whenever possible. This concept is discussed in the next section.

9. An unsuccessful confirmation run may indicate an interaction.

The appendix gives the common orthogonal arrays with their interaction tables and linear graphs. OA12 and OA18 do not have linear graphs, because the effect of any interactions are dispersed within the array.

Signal-to-Noise (S/N) Ratio

Another of Taguchi's contributions is the signal-to-noise (S/N) ratio. It was developed as a proactive equivalent to the reactive loss function. Figure 20-8 illustrates the concept of the S/N ratio. When a person puts his/her foot on the brake pedal of a car, energy is transformed with the intent to slow the car, which is the signal. However, some of the energy is wasted by squeal, pad wear, heat, and so forth. The figure emphasizes that energy is neither created nor destroyed. At the bottom of the figure the concept is written in the form of a ratio.

Signal factors ($\bar{y}$) are set by the designer or operator to obtain the intended value of the response variable. Noise factors (s^2) are not controlled or are very expensive or

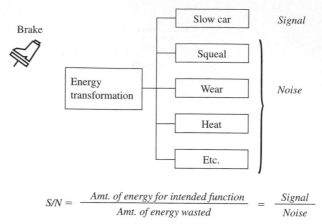

$$S/N = \frac{\text{Amt. of energy for intended function}}{\text{Amt. of energy wasted}} = \frac{Signal}{Noise}$$

Figure 20-8 Concept of Signal-to-Noise (S/N) Ratio

difficult to control. Both the average, $\bar{y}$, and the variance, s^2, need to be controlled with a single figure of merit. In elementary form, S/N is $\bar{y}/s$, which is the inverse of the coefficient of variation and a unitless value. Squaring and taking the log transformation gives

$$S/N_N = \log_{10}(\bar{y}^2/s^2)$$

Adjusting for small sample sizes and changing from Bels to decibels by multiplying by ten yields

$$S/N_N = 10\log_{10}\big[(\bar{y}^2/s^2) - (1/n)\big]$$

which is the nominal-the-best S/N_N ratio. The average and sample standard deviation are squared to eliminate any negative averages and to use the variance, which is an unbiased measure of the dispersion. By taking the log transformation, the calculated value becomes a relative one.

The S/N units are decibels (dB), which are tenths of a Bel and are a very common unit in electrical engineering. Why use decibels? If someone says that the voltage is 6 volts too low, does it indicate a problem? Of course, it depends if you are describing a 745,000-volt power line or the battery in your car. It makes more sense to say that your car battery voltage is 50% low or is only half of the target value of 12 volts. A useful system for describing this condition is logarithms. Another advantage of using decibels as the unit of measure is that they are a relative measure. For example, the difference between 74 dB and 71 dB is the same as the difference between 7 dB and 10 dB. Both are twice as good or bad. Decibels also are not affected by different units. Temperature in Celsius or in Kelvin will give different answers but the same amount of change. Table 20-7 shows some linear and percent changes for the decibel change. The percent

TABLE 20-7
Decibel, Linear, and Percent Change

dB Change (log)	Linear Change (nonlog) 10^8	Percent Change
0.001	1.00	0
0.5	1.12	12
1.0	1.26	26
1.5	1.41	41
2.0	1.59	59
3.0	2.00	100
6.0	4.00	300
10.0	10.00	900

change is found by subtracting the linear change from 1.000, dividing by 1.000, and multiplying by 100. Thus, a 2.0-dB change is

$$\frac{(1.59 - 1.000)}{1.000} 100 = 59\%$$

There are many different S/N ratios. Six basic ones are

1. Nominal-the-best
2. Target-the-best
3. Smaller-the-better
4. Larger-the-better
5. Classified attribute
6. Dynamic

We will discuss those ratios that parallel the loss function.

Nominal-the-Best

The equation for nominal-the-best was given in the initial discussion. It is used wherever there is a nominal or target value and a variation about that value, such as dimensions, voltage, weight, and so forth. The target (τ) is finite but not zero. For robust (optimal) design, the S/N ratio should be maximized. The nominal-the-best S/N value is a maximum when the average is large and the variance is small. When the average is off target on the high side, the S/N_N value can give more favorable information; when off target on the low side, the value can give less favorable information. Taguchi's approach is to reduce variation and then bring the average on target. Another S/N_T ratio, called target-the-best, eliminates these problems provided the target is known.[3]

EXAMPLE PROBLEM

Determine the S/N ratio for a process that has a temperature average of 21°C and a sample standard deviation of 2°C for four observations.

$$S/N_N = 10 \log_{10}\left[(\bar{y}^2/s^2) - (1/n)\right]$$
$$= 10 \log_{10}\left[(21^2/2^2) - (1/4)\right]$$
$$= 20.41 \text{ dB}$$

The adjustment for the small sample size in the example problem has little effect on the answer. If it had not been used, the answer would have been 20.42 dB.

Smaller-the-Better

The S/N_S ratio for smaller-the-better is used for situations where the target value (τ) is zero, such as computer response time, automotive emissions, or corrosion. The equation is

$$S/N_S = -10 \log_{10}[MSD] = -10 \log_{10}\left[(\Sigma y^2)/n\right]$$

The negative sign is used to ensure that the largest value gives the optimum value for the response variable and, therefore, robust design. Mean standard deviation (MSD) is given to show the relationship to the loss function.

EXAMPLE PROBLEM

A bread-stuffing producer is comparing the calorie content of the original process with a new process. Which has the lower content and what is the difference? Results are

| Original | 130 | 135 | 128 | 127 |
| Light | 115 | 112 | 120 | 113 |

---

[3] Thomas B. Barker, *Engineering Quality by Design* (New York: Marcel Dekker, 1990).

$$S/N_S = -10 \log_{10}\left[(\Sigma y^2)/n\right]$$
$$= -10 \log_{10}\left[(130^2 + 135^2 + 128^2 + 127^2)/4\right]$$
$$= -42.28 \text{ dB}$$

$$S/N_S = -10 \log_{10}\left[(\Sigma y^2)/n\right]$$
$$= -10 \log_{10}\left[(115^2 + 112^2 + 120^2 + 113^2)/4\right]$$
$$= -41.22 \text{ dB}$$

$$\Delta = |-41.22 - (-42.28)| = 1.06 \text{ dB}$$

Light is lower in calories by 26%.

Larger-the-Better

The third S/N ratio is larger-the-better. It is used where the largest value is desired, such as weld strength, gasoline mileage, or yield. From a mathematical viewpoint, the target value is 00. Like the loss function, it is the reciprocal of smaller-the-better. The equation is

$$S/N_L = -10 \log_{10}[\text{MSD}] = -10 \log_{10}\left[\Sigma (1/y^2)/n\right]$$

EXAMPLE PROBLEM

Using the existing design, the lives of three AA batteries are 20, 22, and 21 hours. An experimental design produces batteries with values of 17, 21, and 25 hours. Which is the better design and by how much? What is your next step?

$$S/N_L = -10 \log_{10}\left[\Sigma(1/y^2)/n\right]$$
$$= -10 \log_{10}\left[\left(\frac{1}{20^2} + \frac{1}{22^2} + \frac{1}{21^2}\right)/3\right]$$
$$= 26.42 \text{ dB}$$

$$S/N_L = -10 \log_{10}\left[\Sigma(1/y^2)/n\right]$$
$$= -10 \log_{10}\left[\left(\frac{1}{17^2} + \frac{1}{21^2} + \frac{1}{25^2}\right)/3\right]$$
$$= 26.12 \text{ dB}$$

$$\Delta = |26.42 - 26.12| = 0.3 \text{ dB}$$

The new design is 7% better. It is suggested that more data be collected.

Although signal-to-noise ratios have achieved good results, they have not been accepted by many in the statistical community. The controversy has focused more attention on variation or noise, whereas in the past the entire focus was on the average or signal. It is our opinion that with computer programs, it is quite easy to use three metrics—average, variance, and signal-to-noise. Also, note that the advantages of the log transformation can be used with the average and the variance.

Parameter Design

Introduction

There are three product-development stages: product design, process design, and production. These stages are shown in Table 20-8, along with the three previously discussed sources of variation or noise: environmental variables, product deterioration, and production variations. Only at the product design stage are countermeasures possible against all the sources of variation.

The cornerstone of Taguchi's philosophy is robust design. Figure 20-9 illustrates the three design components: system design, parameter design, and tolerance design, with robust design encompassing the latter two. System design is composed of traditional research and development. Until recently, Japan spent approximately 40%, 40%, and 20% and the United States spent 70%, 2%, and 28%, respectively, of their time and money on the three design components.

System design is the development of the prototype. It uses engineering and scientific knowledge to define initial setting of product and process parameters. Knowledge of customer requirements is important at this stage.

Parameter design is the selection of the optimal conditions (parameters), so that the product is least sensitive to noise variables. The idea is to start with inferior-grade, low-

TABLE 20-8
Product Development Stages

Product Development Stages	SOURCES OF VARIATION (NOISE)		
	Environmental Variables	Product Deterioration	Production Variations
Product design	0	0	0
Process design	X	X	0
Production	X	X	0

0—Countermeasures possible; X—Countermeasures impossible

Adapted, with permission, from Raghu N. Kackar, "Taguchi's Quality Philosophy: Analysis and Commentary," *Quality Progress* (December 1986): 21–29.

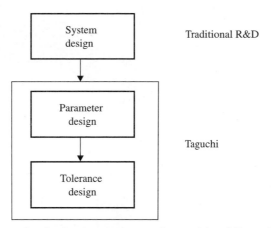

Figure 20-9 Robust Design is the Cornerstone of Taguchi's Philosophy

cost components and raw materials. Nothing is more foolish than research using high-priced materials and components. Variability is reduced by identifying control and noise factors and treating them separately in order to innovate and develop a product that is high in quality and low in cost. The concept uses OAs, response tables, and the metrics of S/N ratios, variances, and averages to obtain the appropriate parameters.

An excellent example of robust design is provided by the Ina Tile Company. Figure 20-10 shows a cross section of an 80-meter-long kiln for baking tiles. The kiln, purchased from West Germany, had quality problems because the tiles at the center were baked at a lower temperature than the outer tiles, which resulted in nonuniform dimensions. One hundred percent inspection was used to screen for improper dimensions; however, this activity was very expensive. The kiln could be redesigned to give uniform dimensions, but the redesign would be very expensive and there was no guarantee that it would correct the problem. It was decided to run an experiment using an OA8 design with seven variables at two levels. The results showed that by increasing the lime content of the clay from 1% to 5%, the excessive dimensional variation was eliminated. Lime is an inexpensive material in the content of the clay. It was also found that an expensive material in the process could be reduced.

Parameter Design Example

An example of an improved product at the design stage is illustrated by the development of a paper feeder for a copy machine. It is important that the prototype, as illustrated by the schematic in Figure 20-11, be constructed so that experiments can be run on the factors. The first step for the project team is to determine the performance characteristic from the customer's viewpoint, which most likely will be "no multi-sheets and no misses." Next, the factors and their levels for the control factors are determined. The team decides to use a three-level design with four control factors. They

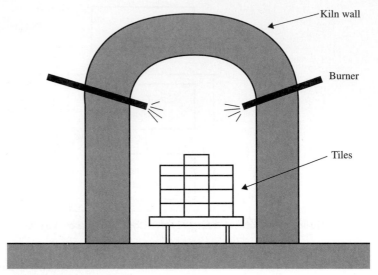

Figure 20-10 Ina Tile Company
Reproduced, with permission, from Madhav S. Phadke, *Quality Engineering Using Robust Design* (Englewood Cliffs, NJ: Prentice Hall, 1989).

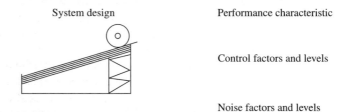

Figure 20-11 Parameter Design Concept Using a Paper Feed Device

are factor *A*—spring tension with the levels low, medium, and high; factor *B*—roller diameter with the levels small, medium, and large; factor *C*—speed with the levels slow, medium, and fast; and factor *D*—roller durometer with the levels soft, medium, and hard. The third step is for the team to determine the noise or uncontrollable factors that can, however, be controlled in an experiment. Note that uncontrollable factors can also be very expensive to control. The team identifies three noise factors and decides to experiment using two levels. They are factor *K*—paper weight with the levels 12 and 20 lb; factor *L*—moisture with the levels 30% RH and 80% RH; and factor *M*—number of sheets with the levels 1 and 100. Not all sources of noise can be included because of lack of knowledge. Additional information on the inclusion of noise factors is given later.

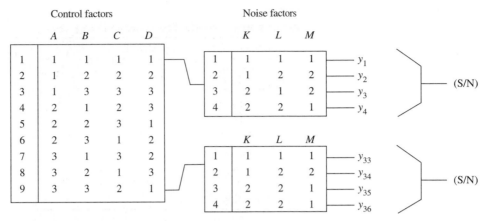

Figure 20-12 Parameter Design Concept
Adapted, with permission, from Raghu N. Kackar, "Taguchi's Quality Philosophy: Analysis and Commentary," *Quality Progress* (December 1986): 21–29.

The experimental design that results from the preceding example is shown in Figure 20-12. Basically there are two arrays: the control factor array, which is also called the inner, or controllable, array, and the noise array, which is also called the outer, or uncontrollable (except in the experiment), array. An OA9 with its nine treatment conditions is used for the inner array, and an OA4 with its four treatment conditions is used for the outer array. Treatment condition 1 is set up with all level 1s, and four runs are made—one for each of the noise treatment conditions. These four runs produce four results y_1, y_2, y_3, and y_4, which are combined to produce the S/N_1 ratio for TC 1 of the control factors. This process is repeated for the other nine treatment conditions of the control factors. The results are then used in a response table to determine the strong factors and their levels.

A number of case studies will be used to illustrate the approach. Each case builds on the preceding ones.

Case I: Iron Casting

This case illustrates the basic technique using a two-level, smaller-the-better performance characteristic with the maximum number of factors. Wirco Castings, Inc., designed an experiment to evaluate the percent of casting that required finish grinding, with the objective of reducing this labor-intensive operation. It was decided there were seven factors that influenced the grinding operation, and they are shown in Table 20-9, along with their levels. Noise factors were not considered to be important, so they were not included in this experiment.

TABLE 20-9
Factors and Levels for Iron Casting Design

Factors	Level 1	Level 2
A. Sand compact	A_1 = 55 mm	A_2 = 49 mm
B. Iron temperature	B_1 = FT	B_2 = Chill
C. Clay addition	C_1 = 6.5 lb	C_2 = 16 lb
D. Mold hardness	D_1 = 1000 lb/in.^{2}	D_2 = 750 lb/in.^{2}
E. Mulling time	E_1 = 4 min	E_2 = 1.7 min
F. Seacoal addition	F_1 = 6.7 lb	F_2 = 15 lb
G. Sand addition	G_1 = 0	G_2 = 150 lb

DESIGN AND RESULTS

An OA8 was used for the design, as shown in Table 20-10 with the treatment condition results. Each treatment condition was run and produced 16 molds with 4 cavities per mold, for a total of 64 castings per TC.

The effect of each factor and its levels are calculated here:

$A_1 = (89 + 55 + 38 + 44)/4 = 56.5$ $A_2 = (83 + 16 + 66 + 55)/4 = 55.0$

$B_1 = (89 + 55 + 83 + 16)/4 = 60.8$ $B_2 = (38 + 44 + 66 + 55)/4 = 50.8$

$C_1 = (89 + 55 + 66 + 55)/4 = 66.3$ $C_2 = (38 + 44 + 83 + 16)/4 = 45.3$

$D_1 = (89 + 38 + 83 + 66)/4 = 69.0$ $D_2 = (55 + 44 + 16 + 66)/4 = 42.5$

$E_1 = (89 + 38 + 16 + 55)/4 = 49.5$ $E_2 = (55 + 44 + 83 + 66)/4 = 62.0$

$F_1 = (89 + 44 + 83 + 55)/4 = 67.8$ $F_2 = (55 + 38 + 16 + 66)/4 = 43.8$

$G_1 = (89 + 44 + 16 + 66)/4 = 53.8$ $G_2 = (55 + 38 + 83 + 55)/4 = 56.8$

Calculations for level 2 can be simplified by subtracting level 1 from the total.

RESPONSE TABLE AND GRAPH

Values from the preceding calculations are placed in a *response table*, as shown in Table 20-11. The absolute difference, Δ, between level 1 and level 2 is calculated and placed in the table. A *response graph*, as shown by Figure 20-13, can also be constructed to aid in visualizing the strong effects. This graph is Paretoized, with the largest difference on the left and the smallest difference on the right.

A simple rule is used as a guideline to analyze which of the factors has a strong effect on the process and which is merely a natural variation. Take the largest difference,

TABLE 20-10
Orthogonal Array and Results for Iron Castings

TC	A 1	B 2	C 3	D 4	E 5	F 6	G 7	Results %
1	1	1	1	1	1	1	1	89
2	1	1	1	2	2	2	2	55
3	1	2	2	1	1	2	2	38
4	1	2	2	2	2	1	1	44
5	2	1	2	1	2	1	2	83
6	2	1	2	2	1	2	1	16
7	2	2	1	1	2	2	1	66
8	2	2	1	2	1	1	2	55

TABLE 20-11
Response Table for Iron Casting

	A	B	C	D	E	F	G
Level 1	56.5	60.8	66.3	69.0	49.5	67.8	53.8
Level 2	55.0	50.8	45.3	42.5	62.0	43.8	57.8
Δ	1.5	10.0	21.0	26.5	12.5	24.0	4.0

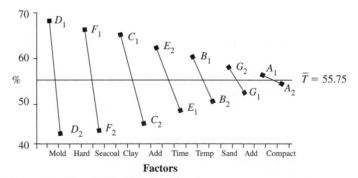

Figure 20-13 Response Graph for Iron Casting

which in this case is 26.5, and divide in half, to give 13.3. All differences equal to or above 13.3 are considered to be strong effects. Because this experiment is a smaller-the-better performance, the strong factors and their levels are D_2, F_2, and C_2.

CONFIRMATION RUN

The next step is to predict the outcome of the confirmation run using the equation

$$\hat{\mu} = \overline{T} - (\overline{T} - D_2) - (\overline{T} - F_2) - (\overline{T} - C_2) = D_2 + F_2 + C_2 - (N - 1)\overline{T}$$

where $\hat{\mu}$ = estimate of the response for y

$\overline{T}$ = overall average of the response data

Calculations are

$$\overline{T} = \Sigma y/n = (89 + 55 + 38 + 44 + 83 + 16 + 66 + 55)/8 = 55.8$$

$$\hat{\mu} = D_2 + F_2 + C_2 - (N - 1)\overline{T}$$
$$= 42.5 + 43.8 + 45.3 - (3 - 1)\,55.8$$
$$= 20.0\%$$

A fundamental part of the Taguchi approach is the confirmation run. For this experiment the factors and their levels are D_2, F_2, C_2, E_1, B_1, G_2, and A_1, and the result from the confirmation run was 19.2%, which is very close to the predicted value. TC 6 also had good results at 16%, using most of the same factors and their levels. Thus, the experiment is a success, and the new parameters are the strong effects of D_2, F_2, and C_2. The levels of the other four factors might not make any difference. If the confirmation run does not show good producibility, like this case, then (1) the factor levels may have been set too close, (2) an important factor was missing, or (3) interactions were present due to the improper selection of control factors.

As a result of this experiment, less finish grinding was needed, thereby reducing the workforce from six to five people. In addition, the parameter changes resulted in a reduction in scrap from 8% to 4% and in smoother castings.

Although the S/N ratio and variance have good additivity, the percent nonconforming should not be outside the range of 20% to 80%. Fortunately, in this experiment, the data were within that range. If such had not been the case, an omega transformation would have been made on each of the eight results. For information on the omega transformation, see the references.

Case II: Grille[4]

This case is a two-level design with a smaller-the-better performance characteristic and interactions. Automotive grille opening panels were shipped to Chrysler by a supplier

---

[4] Adapted, with permission, from P. I. Hsieh and D. E. Goodwin, "Sheet Molded Compound Process Improvement," *Fourth Symposium on Taguchi Methods* (Allen Park, Mich.: American Supplier Institute, Inc., 1986).

TABLE 20-12
Factors and Levels for Grille

	Variable	Level 1	Level 2
A	Mold pressure	Low	High
B	Mold temp.	Low	High
C	Mold cycle	Low	High
D	Cut pattern	Method I	Method II
E	Priming	Method I	Method II
F	Viscosity	Low	High
G	Weight	Low	High
H	Mat'l thickness	Process I	Process II
I	Glass type	Type I	Type II

and assembled in the car prior to painting. Surface imperfections in the finish (pops) caused a first run capability of 77% conforming, and the condition was not detected prior to painting. A joint supplier/customer team, using the problem-solving techniques of flow process and cause-and-effect diagrams, decided on a two-level design with nine control variables and five potential interactions, as shown in Table 20-12.

Five potential interactions were possible: *AB, AC, AD, BF,* and *FH.*

Because there are 15 degrees of freedom, an OA16 was needed. A modified linear graph was used to determine the experimental design, which is shown in Table 20-13. No factor or interaction was assigned to column 15, so it is labeled unexplained, *UX.*

The experiment was run with two repetitions per TC and a response table calculated as shown in Table 20-14. Using the one-half guideline, the factors *E, A,* and *C* and the interactions *FH, AC,* and *BF,* are the strong effects. It is also noted that *UX* has a strong effect.

The interactions are plotted to determine the level for those factors involved in the interactions. Using the results in Table 20-13, the calculations are

$$A_1C_1 = (56 + 10 + 2 + 1 + 3 + 1 + 50 + 49)/8 = 21.5$$
$$A_1C_2 = (17 + 2 + 4 + 3 + 4 + 13 + 2 + 3)/8 = 6.0$$
$$A_2C_1 = (1 + 3 + 3 + 2 + 3 + 4 + 0 + 8)/8 = 3.0$$
$$A_2C_2 = (0 + 3 + 12 + 2 + 4 + 10 + 0 + 8)/8 = 4.9$$

$$B_1F_1 = (56 + 10 + 17 + 2 + 1 + 3 + 0 + 3)/8 = 11.5$$
$$B_1F_2 = (2 + 1 + 4 + 3 + 3 + 2 + 12 + 2)/8 = 3.6$$
$$B_2F_1 = (3 + 1 + 4 + 13 + 3 + 4 + 4 + 10)/8 = 5.3$$
$$B_2F_2 = (50 + 49 + 2 + 3 + 0 + 5 + 0 + 8)/8 = 14.6$$

TABLE 20-13

Experimental Design Using an OA16 and Results for Grille

1	2	3	4	5	6	7	8	9	10	11	12	13	14	15		
A	B	AB	F	G	BF	E	C	AC	H	I	D	AD	FH	UX	R1	R2
1	1	1	1	1	1	1	1	1	1	1	1	1	1	1	56	10
1	1	1	1	1	1	1	2	2	2	2	2	2	2	2	17	2
1	1	1	2	2	2	2	1	1	1	1	2	2	2	2	2	1
1	1	1	2	2	2	2	2	2	2	2	1	1	1	1	4	3
1	2	2	1	1	2	2	1	1	2	2	1	1	2	2	3	1
1	2	2	1	1	2	2	2	2	1	1	2	2	1	1	4	13
1	2	2	2	2	1	1	1	1	2	2	2	2	1	1	50	49
1	2	2	2	2	1	1	2	2	1	1	1	1	2	2	2	3
2	1	2	1	2	1	2	1	2	1	2	1	2	1	2	1	3
2	1	2	1	2	1	2	2	1	2	1	2	1	2	1	0	3
2	1	2	2	1	2	1	1	2	1	2	2	1	2	1	3	2
2	1	2	2	1	2	1	2	1	2	1	1	2	1	2	12	2
2	2	1	1	2	2	1	1	2	2	1	1	2	2	1	3	4
2	2	1	1	2	2	1	2	1	1	2	2	1	1	2	4	10
2	2	1	2	1	1	2	1	2	2	1	2	1	1	2	0	5
2	2	1	2	1	1	2	2	1	1	2	1	2	2	1	0	8

$$F_1H_1 = (56 + 10 + 4 + 13 + 1 + 3 + 4 + 10)/8 = 12.6$$
$$F_1H_2 = (17 + 2 + 3 + 1 + 0 + 3 + 3 + 4)/8 = 4.1$$
$$F_2H_1 = (2 + 1 + 2 + 3 + 3 + 2 + 0 + 8)/8 = 2.6$$
$$F_2H_2 = (4 + 3 + 50 + 49 + 12 + 2 + 0 + 5)/8 = 15.6$$

These values are plotted in Figure 20-14. Analysis of the AC interaction shows that A_2 and C_1 give the best interaction results; however, C_2 gives the best results from a factor viewpoint, as seen in Table 20-14. If we use C_1, the gain will be 1.7 (4.6 − 2.9) from the interaction, but there will be a loss of 6.7 (12.1 − 5.4) from the factor. Thus, A_2 and C_2 will give the optimum results. For the BF interaction, the best values are at B_1 and F_2, although B_2 and F_1 are close. The decision may be based on some criterion other than "pops." The level chosen for F influences the choice of the level for H. Thus, if F_2 is chosen, then H_1 would be used; if F_1 is chosen, then H_2 would be used. The preceding analysis could just as well have started with the FH interaction rather than the BF interaction.

The confirmation run gave a first-time capability of 96%, for a savings of $900,000 per year. Future experiments are planned to find the reason for UX being too high.

TABLE 20-14
Response Table for Grille

Factor	Level 1	Level 2	Difference
E	14.31	3.19	11.12
A	13.75	3.75	10.00
C	12.06	5.44	6.62
D	7.19	10.31	3.12
B	7.56	9.94	2.38
I	7.50	10.00	2.50
H	7.62	9.88	2.26
F	8.38	9.12	0.74
G	8.62	8.88	0.26
FH	14.12	3.38	10.74
AC	13.19	4.31	8.88
BF	13.06	4.44	8.62
AD	6.81	10.69	3.88
AB	8.06	9.44	1.38
UX	13.25	4.25	9.00

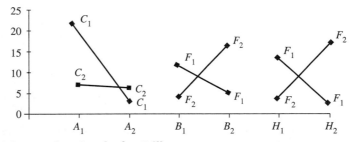

Figure 20-14 Interaction Graphs for Grille

Case III: Tube[5]

This case is a three-level control array and a two-level noise array, with a larger-the-better performance characteristic using the average and a signal-to-noise ratio. The experiment involves the joining of a small flexible tube to a rigid plastic connector, with

[5] Adapted, with permission, from Diane M. Byrne and Shin Taguchi, "The Taguchi Approach to Parameter Design," *Quality Progress* (December 1987): 19–26.

the objectives of minimum assembly effort and maximum pull-off force in pounds; the focus is on the latter. A project team determines the control factors and their levels, and they are listed in Table 20-15.

An OA9 is used for the four control factors, and an OA4 is used for the three noise factors. The layout, along with the results of the experiment, are shown in Table 20-16. For

TABLE 20-15
Factors and Levels for Tube

Control Factors	Levels		
A. Interference	Low	Med.	High
B. Wall thickness	Thin	Med.	Thick
C. Insertion depth	Shal.	Med.	High
D. % adhesive	Low	Med.	High

Noise Factors	Levels	
E. Time	24 h	120 h
F. Temp.	72°F	150°F
G. RH	25%	75%

TABLE 20-16
OA9 and OA4 Layout with Experimental Results for Tube

TC	A	B	C	D	E_1 F_1 G_1	E_1 F_2 G_2	E_2 F_1 G_2	E_2 F_2 G_1	S/N_L	$\bar{y}$
1	1	1	1	1	15.6	19.9	19.6	20.0	25.3	18.8
2	1	2	2	2	15.0	19.6	19.8	24.2	25.5	19.7
3	1	3	3	3	16.3	15.6	18.2	23.3	25.0	18.4
4	2	1	2	3	18.3	18.6	18.9	23.2	25.8	19.8
5	2	2	3	1	19.7	25.1	21.4	27.5	27.2	23.4
6	2	3	1	2	16.2	19.8	19.6	22.5	25.6	19.5
7	3	1	3	2	16.4	23.6	18.6	24.3	26.0	20.7
8	3	2	1	3	14.2	16.8	19.6	23.3	24.9	18.5
9	3	3	2	1	16.1	17.3	22.7	22.6	25.6	19.7

TABLE 20-17
S/N and $\bar{y}$ Response Table for Tube

S/N$_L$			Δ
$A_1 = 25.3$	$A_2 = 26.2$	$A_3 = 25.5$	0.9
$B_1 = 25.7$	$B_2 = 25.9$	$B_3 = 25.4$	0.5
$C_1 = 25.3$	$C_2 = 25.6$	$C_3 = 26.1$	0.8
$D_1 = 26.0$	$D_2 = 25.7$	$D_3 = 25.2$	0.8

$\bar{y}$			Δ
$A_1 = 18.9$	$A_2 = 20.9$	$A_3 = 19.6$	2.0
$B_1 = 19.8$	$B_2 = 20.5$	$B_3 = 19.2$	1.3
$C_1 = 18.9$	$C_2 = 19.7$	$C_3 = 20.8$	1.9
$D_1 = 20.6$	$D_2 = 20.0$	$D_3 = 18.9$	1.7

TC 1, there are four observations for the three noise factors. These observations are 15.6, 19.9, 19.6, and 20.0; their average is 18.8.lb, and their signal-to-noise ratio for larger-the-better is 25.3 lb. The process is repeated for the other eight treatment conditions.

The response table is shown in Table 20-17 for S/N and $\bar{y}$, along with the maximum difference between the levels. A better evaluation of the factors and their levels can be seen in the response graph given in Figure 20-15. For factor A, interference, level 2 (medium) is obviously the best one for both S/N and $\bar{y}$; for factor B, wall thickness, level 2 (medium) is best for $\bar{y}$, but there does not appear to be a clear choice for the S/for factor C, insertion depth, level 3 (deep) is best for both S/N and $\bar{y}$; and for factor D, percent adhesive, level 1 (low) is best for both S/N and $\bar{y}$.

A summary of results is shown in Table 20-18; it includes cost and ease of assembly, as well as information on the noise factors. For factor B, wall thickness, level 1 (thin wall thickness) was selected for its lower cost and ease of assembly as well as for the fact that the S/N did not show any difference. It should be noted that these factors and their levels are least sensitive to the three noise factors; therefore, it is a robust design. The predicted equation was

$$\bar{T} = \Sigma y/n = (18.8 + 19.7 + \ldots + 19.7)/8 = 19.7$$
$$\hat{\mu} = \bar{T} + (A_2 - \bar{T}) + (B_1 - \bar{T}) + (C_3 - \bar{T}) + (D_1 - \bar{T}) = A_2 + B_1 + C_3 + D_1 + (N - 1)\bar{T}$$
$$= 20.9 + 19.8 + 20.8 + 20.6 - (4 - 1)19.7$$
$$= 23.0$$

The S/N ratio could also have been used for the prediction. Results of the confirmation run were very close to the predicted value and also close to TC 5, which is the same combination except for the difference in the B level. The actual combination was not run

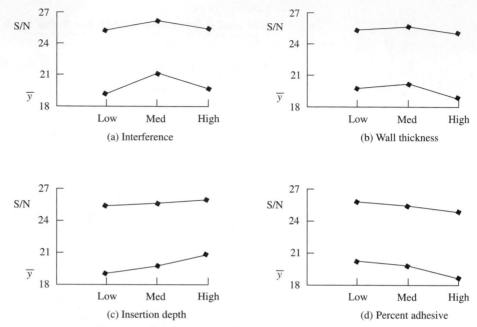

Figure 20-15 Response Graph for S/N and ȳ for Tube

during the experiment, this tendency is often the case with highly-fractionalized experiments. In addition, the operators were quite pleased with the ease of assembly.

Treating Noise

Before continuing to the next case, let's discuss ways to treat noise. There are three techniques:

1. *Repetition*. When the process is very noisy, it is necessary to run only a few repetitions.

2. *Strongest*. When there is one strong noise factor, then two levels for that factor will be sufficient. For example: If temperature is a strong noise factor, it would be set at, say, 20° and 40°, and there would be two runs for each TC.

3. *Compounded*. When neither repetition nor strongest is applicable, then compounded is used. It requires an initial experiment for noise using a prototype or some units from production. The objective is to determine the extremes. Table 20-19 shows an OA4 with results for three noise factors and the response table next to it. The two extreme noise situations are

$$N_1 = U_1, V_2, \text{ and } W_2$$
$$N_2 = U_2, V_1, \text{ and } W_1$$

Each of these techniques can be used to minimize the number of runs while maintaining the concept of the noise array.

TABLE 20-18
Summary of Results

Factors	Levels	Assembly Effort	Pull-off Force	Cost Rating	Overall Rating
Interference	1. Low	8.1	18.9	Least	—
(A)	2. Medium	8.3	20.9	—	×
	3. High	8.7	19.6	Most	—
Wall	1. Thin	7.8	19.8	Least	×
Thickness (B)	2. Medium	8.3	20.5	—	—
	3. Thick	8.4	19.2	Most	—
Insertion	1. Shallow	7.7	18.9	Least	—
Depth (C)	2. Medium	8.3	19.7	—	×
	3. Deep	9.1	20.8	Most	—
Percent	1. Low	8.3	20.6	Least	×
Adhesive (D)	2. Medium	8.4	20.0	—	—
	3. High	8.4	18.9	Most	—
Conditioning	1. 24 h		18.0		
Time (E)	2. 120 h		21.6		
Conditioning	1. 75°F		18.1		
Temp. (F)	2. 150°F		21.5		
Conditioning	1. 25%		19.9		
R.H. (G)	2. 75%		19.7		

TABLE 20-19
Compounded Noise Example for Three Noise Factors

TC	U	V	W	y		Level	U	V	W
1	1	1	1	50		1	30.0	47.5	45.0
2	1	2	2	10		2	42.5	25.0	27.5
3	2	1	2	45		Δ	12.5	22.5	17.5
4	2	2	1	40					

Case IV: Metal Stamping[6]

This case is a two-level design with a noise array and a nominal-the-best performance characteristic that is the distance from the center of the hole to the edge of a metal stamping. The target value is 0.40 in. Three control factors and their levels and three noise factors and their levels are determined by the team and are shown in Table 20-20. The experiment is run using an OA4 for the control array and a OA4 for the noise array. This layout along with the results are shown in Table 20-21.

TABLE 20-20

Control and Noise Factors with Their Levels for Metal Stamping

Control Factors	Level 1	Level 2
A. Roller Height	Sm	Lg
B. Material Supplier	SAE	SQC
C. Feed Adjustment	I	II
Noise Factors	**Level 1**	**Level 2**
U. Amount of Oil	Sm	Lg
V. Material Thickness	Low	High
W. Material Hardness	Low	High

TABLE 20-21

Experimental Design with Results for Metal Stamping

TC	A 1	B 2	C 3	U_1 V_1 W_1	U_2 V_2 W_1	U_2 V_1 W_2	U_1 V_2 W_2	– y	S/N_N
1	1	1	1	0.37	0.38	0.36	0.37	0.370	33.12
2	1	2	2	0.35	0.39	0.40	0.33	0.368	20.92
3	2	1	2	0.45	0.44	0.44	0.46	0.448	33.39
4	2	2	1	0.41	0.52	0.46	0.42	0.443	19.13

---

[6] Adapted, with permission, from *Taguchi Methods: Introduction to Quality Engineering* (Allen Park, Mich.: American Supplier Institute, Inc., 1991).

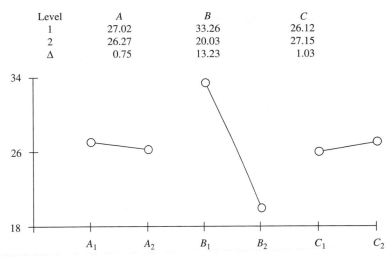

Level	A	B	C
1	27.02	33.26	26.12
2	26.27	20.03	27.15
Δ	0.75	13.23	1.03

Figure 20-16 Response Table and Response Graph for the S/N Ratio

The nominal-the-best strategy is to identify two types of control factors:

1. Those that affect variation and that are to be minimized. They are determined first using the S/N ratio.
2. Those that affect the average and are called adjustment or signal factors. They are used to adjust the average, $\bar{y}$, to the target, τ.

Figure 20-16 shows the response table and response graph for the S/N ratio. A strong effect is given by factor B, with level 1 the appropriate level. Thus variation is minimized by using either level of factors A and C and factor B_1. Figure 20-17 shows the response table and response graph for the average, $\bar{y}$. A strong effect is given by factor A, which is the roller height. Thus the adjustment factor becomes the roller height, and it is adjusted to obtain the target value of 0.400. This adjustment or signal factor can make the design very robust by providing this additional capability for the process or the product. An excellent example of this concept for a product is the zero-adjustment feature of a bathroom scale.

Regular analysis for the average, as used in this case, is appropriate when there is a small change in the average. If you like the log transform concept, then $10 \log \bar{y}$ could be used. Sensitivity analysis, Sm, is used when there is a large change in the average, which is true in research. The equation is

$$Sm \text{ (dB)} = 10 \log_{10} (T^2/n)$$

Level	A	B	C
1	0.369	0.409	0.412
2	0.446	0.411	0.408
Δ	0.077	0.002	0.004

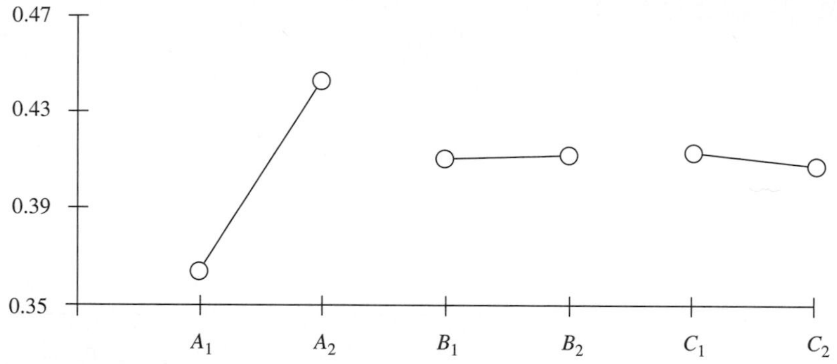

Figure 20-17 Response Table and Response Graph for the Average

The expression T^2/n is the sum of squares for the average, SS_{avg}, which is a common measure used in traditional design of experiments.

Regular analysis for the S/N ratio, such as used in this case, is appropriate when variability in relation to the average, $\bar{y}$, is measured in terms of a plus or minus percentage of $\bar{y}$. However, when variability in relation to the average is measured in terms of plus or minus absolute units and negative values are possible, then use the equation

$$S/N_N = -10 \log_{10} s^2$$

This situation occurs in few cases.

Tolerance Design

Tolerance design is the process of determining the statistical tolerance around the target. During the parameter-design stage, low-cost tolerancing should be used. Only when the values are beyond the low-cost tolerancing limits is this concept implemented. Tolerance design is the selective tightening of tolerances and/or upgrading to eliminate excessive variation. It uses analysis of variance (ANOVA) to determine which factors contribute to the total variability and the loss function to obtain a trade-off between quality and cost.

Percent Contribution

In order to determine the percent contribution of the factors to the total variability, the iron casting case is used as the learning vehicle. The first step is to calculate the sum of squares for each of the factors and the total:

$$SS_A = \Sigma\left(A^2/n\right) - T^2/n = \left(\frac{226^2}{4} + \frac{220^2}{4}\right) - \frac{446^2}{8} = 4.5$$

$$SS_B = \Sigma\left(B^2/n\right) - T^2/n = \left(\frac{243^2}{4} + \frac{203^2}{4}\right) - \frac{446^2}{8} = 200$$

$$SS_C = \Sigma\left(C^2/n\right) - T^2/n = \left(\frac{265^2}{4} + \frac{181^2}{4}\right) - \frac{446^2}{8} = 882$$

$$SS_D = \Sigma\left(D^2/n\right) - T^2/n = \left(\frac{276^2}{4} + \frac{370^2}{4}\right) - \frac{446^2}{8} = 28,405$$

$$SS_E = \Sigma\left(E^2/n\right) - T^2/n = \left(\frac{198^2}{4} + \frac{248^2}{4}\right) - \frac{446^2}{8} = 313$$

$$SS_F = \Sigma\left(F^2/n\right) - T^2/n = \left(\frac{271^2}{4} + \frac{175^2}{4}\right) - \frac{446^2}{8} = 1152$$

$$SS_G = \Sigma\left(G^2/n\right) - T^2/n = \left(\frac{215^2}{4} + \frac{231^2}{4}\right) - \frac{446^2}{8} = 32$$

$$SS_{\text{Total}} = \Sigma y^2 - T^2/n = \left(89^2 + 55^2 + \cdots + 55^2\right) - 446^2/8 = 3987.5$$

These values are placed in an ANOVA table, as shown in Table 20-22, along with their degrees of freedom, which for a two-level is 1 $(2 - 1)$. This information is given in the first three columns. Note that the smaller the difference in the response table, the smaller the SS. The fourth column is the mean square (MS) column for each factor, and its equation is

$$MS = \frac{SS}{df}$$

Because the number of degrees of freedom is 1, the MS value is the same as the SS value. If this were a three-level design, the number of degrees of freedom would have been 2: one for the linear component and one for the quadratic component, as shown in Table 20-24.

The last column in the table, labeled F, has not been completed. This value is determined by the equation

$$F = \frac{MS_{\text{factor}}}{MS_{\text{error}}}$$

TABLE 20-22
ANOVA for the Iron Casting Case

Source	df	SS	MS	F
A	1	4.5	4.5	
B	1	200.0	200.0	
C	1	882.0	882.0	
D	1	1404.5	1404.5	
E	1	312.5	312.5	
F	1	1152.0	1152.0	
G	1	32.0	32.0	
Total	7	3987.5	3987.5	

We do not have a value for MS_{error}. If the treatment conditions had been repeated, a value for the error could have been obtained. Regardless, a pooling-up technique can be used to obtain an estimate.

The pooling-up technique maximizes the number of significant factors. In other words, a factor can be classified as significant when, in truth, it is not. This action is referred to as the alpha error, or risk. Opposite to the alpha error is the beta error, or risk, which can classify a factor as being nonsignificant when, in truth, it is significant. The F-test, developed by Fischer, is used to determine significance at a designated alpha risk, which is usually 0.05.

The pooling-up procedure is to F-test the factor with the smallest SS against the next largest. If not significant, the SS is pooled and tested against the next largest. The process is continued until a factor is significant or one-half the total number of degrees of freedom is used.

Calculations for the first step using factors A and G and the iron casting case are

$$F = \frac{MS_G}{MS_e} = \frac{SS_G/df}{SS_A/df} = \frac{32/1}{4.5/1} = 7.11, \text{ thus, n.s.}$$

An F table for an alpha value of 0.05 and 1 degree of freedom for both the numerator and the denominator gives a critical value of 161. Because the calculated value is less than the critical value, the factor is not significant (n.s.). The next step is to pool the SS for the factors G and A and test against the next factor. Calculations are

$$F = \frac{MS_B}{MS_e} = \frac{SS_B/df}{SS_{B,G}/df} = \frac{200/1}{36.5/2} = 10.93 \text{ n.s.}$$

TABLE 20-23
Percent Contribution for the Iron Casting Case

Source	df	SS	MS	F	SS'	%
A	[1]	4.5				
B	[1]	200.0				
C	1	882.0	882.0	11.2[*]	803.2	20.1
D	1	1404.5	1404.5	17.8[*]	1325.7	33.2
E	1	312.5	312.5	4.0 n.s.	233.7	5.9
F	1	1152.0	1152.0	14.6[*]	1073.2	26.9
G	[1]	32.0				
Pooled e	3	236.5	78.8		551.7	13.8
Total	7	3987.5			3987.5	99.9

[*]Significance at 95% confidence, $F(0.05; 1, 3) = 10.1$.

From an F table, the critical value for 1 and 2 degrees of freedom is 18.5, which is greater than the calculated value, so factor B is also not significant. Factor B is now pooled with the other two factors to obtain SS of 236.5 and MS of 78.8. However, since one-half the total degrees of freedom was obtained, the pooling process is complete.

The F column for the ANOVA is completed and shown in Table 20-23. F values in the column are compared with the critical F, which is obtained from the F table and shown at the bottom of the table. Three of the factors are significant at an alpha of 0.05 and one factor is nonsignificant. Two additional columns, labeled SS', which is the pure SS after the error is subtracted, and %, which is the percent contribution, are shown in the table. Calculations for SS' are

$$SS'_C = SS_C - \left(MS_e * \mathrm{df}_C\right) = 882.0 - 78.8(1) = 803.2$$

$$SS'_D = SS_D - \left(MS_e * \mathrm{df}_D\right) = 1404.5 - 78.8(1) = 1325.7$$

$$SS'_E = SS_E - \left(MS_e * \mathrm{df}_E\right) = 312.5 - 78.8(1) = 233.7$$

$$SS'_F = SS_F - \left(MS_e * \mathrm{df}_F\right) = 1152.0 - 78.8(1) = 1073.2$$

$$SS'_e = SS_e - \left(MS_e * \mathrm{df}_{C,D,E,F}\right) = 236.5 + 78.8(4) = 551.7$$

Values for the percent contribution for each factor are obtained by dividing by the total and are shown in the last column. The percent contribution for the error is 13.8, which is satisfactory. If the percent contribution for the error is a high value, say, 40% or more, then some important factors were omitted, conditions were not precisely controlled, or measurement error was excessive.

TABLE 20-24
Percent Contribution for the Tube Case

Source		SS	df	MS	F	SS'	%
Intr.	(L)	[0.73500]	[1]				
	(Q)	5.28125	1	5.28125	15.2149[*]	4.93419	25.9
Tube	(L)	[0.48167]	[1]				
	(Q)	2.20500	1	2.20500	6.3525	1.85789	9.8
Ins. dp.	(L)	5.46260	1	5.46260	15.7374	5.11549	26.9
	(Q)	[0.07031]	[1]				
% Adh.	(L)	4.68167	1	4.68167	13.4876	4.33456	22.8
	(Q)	[0.10125]	[1]				
e		0.0	0				
Pooled e		1.38843	4	0.34711		2.77687	14.6
Total		19.01875	8			19.01875	100.0

[*]$F_{1,4}$ ($\alpha = 0.05$) = 7.7088.

Tables 20-24 and 20-25 provide further illustration of the percent contribution technique for two of the cases discussed in this chapter.

Case I: TV Power Circuit[7]

A TV power circuit specification is 115 ± 15 volts. If the circuit goes out of this range, the customer will need to correct the problem at an average cost for all TV sets of $45.00. The problem can be corrected by recalibration at the end of the production line for a cost of $1.60. Using the loss function, the customer's loss is

$$L = k(y - \tau)^2$$
$$A_0 = k(\Delta_0)^2$$
$$k = A_0/\Delta_0^2$$

---

[7] Adapted, with permission, from *Quality Engineering: Dynamic Characteristics and Measurement Engineering* (Allen Park, Mich.: American Supplier Institute, 1990).

TABLE 20-25
Percent Contribution for the Grille Case

Source	df	SS	MS	F	SS'	%
A	1	800.000	800.000	11.728**	731.788	11.04
B	[1]	[45.125]				
AB	[1]	[15.125]				
F	[1]	[4.500]				
G	[1]	[0.500]				
BF	1	595.125	595.1215	8.725**	526.913	7.95
E	1	990.125	990.125	14.515**	921.913	13.91
C	1	351.125	351.125	5.148**	282.913	4.27
AC	1	630.125	630.125	9.128**	561.913	8.48
H	[1]	[40.500]				
I	[1]	[50.000]				
D	[1]	[78.125]				
AD	1	120.125	120.125	1.761	51.913	0.78
FH	1	924.500	924.500	13.553**	856.288	12.92
UX	1	648.000	648.000	9.500**	579.788	8.75
e	16	1335.000	83.438			
Pooled e	23	1568.873	68.212		2114.571	31.9
Total	31	6628.000			6628.000	100.0

*Significance at 95% confidence, $F(0.05; 1, 23) = 4.28$.
**Significance at 99% confidence, $F(0.01; 1, 23) = 7.88$.

The manufacturer's loss function is

$$L = k(y - \tau)^2$$

Substituting gives

$$A = \frac{A_0}{\Delta_0^2} (\Delta)^2$$

Thus,

$$\Delta = \Delta_0 \sqrt{\frac{A}{A_0}}$$

$$= 15 \sqrt{\frac{1.60}{45.00}}$$

$$= 2.6 \text{ or about } 3 \text{ V}$$

The tolerance is ± 3 V, and the specifications are 112 V to 118 V. If the TV circuit is outside the specifications, it is recalibrated at a cost of $1.60.

Case II: Butterfly[8]

The plastic butterfly for the carburetor of a small engine has experienced a rash of complaints due to breakage. A larger-the-better loss function showed a loss of $39.00 at an average strength of 105 lb/in.^{2} and a standard deviation of 30 lb/in.^{2} for the defective items. Four factors of the plastic-molding process are identified by the project team, along with the experiment goal of $\bar{y} = 160$ lb/in.^{2} and $s = 16$ lb/in.^{2}. Table 20-26 shows the factors, range of interest, and the low-cost tolerancing. A new temperature-control system was recently installed on the machine, and its tolerance is ± 0.1%.

The parameter design resulted in a feed rate (*FR*) of 1200, a first rpm (*1R*) of 480, a second rpm (*2R*) of 950, and a temperature (*T*) of 360. A confirmation run was made using an OA9 with the low-cost tolerances as the outer levels and the parameter as the nominal. In other words, the three levels were 960, 1200, and 1440 for *FR*; 432, 480, and 528 for *IR*; 855, 950, and 1045 for *2R*; and 360, 360, and 360 for *T*. The results were $\bar{y} = 168.5$ lb/in.^{2} and $s = 28.4$ lb/in.^{2}, which was a substantial improvement, but

TABLE 20-26

Factors, Range of Interest, and Low-cost Tolerancing for Butterfly

Factor	Range of Interest	Low-cost Tolerance
A. Feed rate (*FR*)	1000–1400 g/min	± 20%
B. First rpm (*1R*)	400–480 rev/min	± 10%
C. Second rpm (*2R*)	850–950 rev/min	± 10%
D. Temp. (*T*)	320–400°F	± 0.1%

---

[8] Adapted, with permission, from Thomas B. Baker, "Quality Engineering by Design: Taguchi's Philosophy," *Quality Progress* (December 1986): 32–42.

the goal of $s = 16$ was not met. From the confirmation run, the percent contribution was calculated,

Feed rate	17.9%
First rpm	65.5%
Second rpm	9.4%
Residual (error)	7.3%
Total	100.1%

Temperature did not contribute to the percent contribution, so it is not included.

The next step is the rational (selective) reduction in tolerances by the project team. Variances are additive and standard deviations are not; therefore, calculations are made using variance. We have a variance of 806.6 (28.4^2) and need 256.0 (16^2). Thus, the variance needs to be reduced by 256.0/806.6, or 0.317 of its current value. Using this value, the factors, and the percent contribution, we can write the equation

$$0.317 = \left[(FR)^2 0.179 + (IR)^2 0.655 + (2R)^2 0.094 + e^2 (0.073) \right]$$

where $e^2 = 1$ and is the residual or error.

The solution to the equation is by trial and error. After deliberation, the project team decides that the feed rate can be reduced by 33% of its original value; the calculations are

$$0.317 = (0.33)^2 0.179 + \cdots$$
$$(0.33)^2 0.179 = 0.020$$
$$0.317 - 0.020 = 0.297 \text{ left}$$

The project team decides that the first rpm can be reduced by 50% of its original value; the calculations are

$$0.297 = \cdots + (0.50)^2 0.655 + \ldots$$
$$(0.50)^2 0.655 = 0.164$$
$$0.297 - 0.164 = 0.133 \text{ left}$$

The remaining factor is the second rpm. Removing the residual of 7.3%, the result is 0.060(0.133 − 0.073). The calculations are

$$(2R)^2 0.094 = 0.060$$
$$2R = 0.80$$

TABLE 20-27

New Tolerances for Butterfly

Factor	Old		New
FR	±20%	20(0.33)	±6.6%
1R	±10%	10(0.50)	±5.0%
2R	±10%	10(0.80)	±8.0%

New tolerances are shown in Table 20-27. If these need modification, the preceding process can be repeated with different values.

Levels for the final run are

FR	6.6% of 1200 = 80 (1120, 1200, 1280)
1R	5.05% of 480 = 24 (456, 480, 504)
2R	8.0% of 950 = 76 (874, 950, 1026)

Using an OA9 and these levels, the results were $\bar{y} = 179.9$, $s = 12.1$, and S/N = 45.0, which is almost 200% better than the original. The appropriate parameter settings and realistic tolerance settings are now known. From the loss function graph, the average loss is $2.00 per engine, for a savings of $370,000 for 10,000 engines. Statistical process control (SPC) is used to maintain the target and variation.

Noise can be based on (1) percent of the parameter, as in this case, (2) experience, or (3) standard deviation (Taguchi recommends 1σ for a two-level and 1.22σ for a three-level). A two-level design would occur when the tolerance is unilateral or one-directional or only the upper and lower specifications are used without the nominal or target. It should be noted that the rational reduction concept was not developed by Taguchi.

Case III: Control Circuit[9]

This case concerns the tolerance design of a control circuit after the parameter design has determined the factors and their target or nominal values. The design team decides to establish the tolerance levels at $\pm 1\sigma$. Table 20-28 shows the 12 factors with their nominal and tolerance specifications.

---

[9] Source: Robert Moesta, American Supplier, Inc.

TABLE 20-28

Factors and Levels for the Tolerance Design of the Control Circuit

Factors	Units	Level 1 $-\sigma$	Target or Nominal	Level 2 $+\sigma$
Resistor A	kilohms	2.09	2.20	2.31
Resistor B	ohms	446.5	4.700	493.5
Capacitor C	microfarads	0.65	0.68	0.71
Resistor D	kilohms	95.0	100.0	105.0
Capacitor E	microfarads	8.0	10.0	12.0
Transistor F	hfe	90.0	180.0	270.0
Resistor G	kilohms	9.5	10.0	10.5
Resistor H	kilohms	1.43	1.50	1.57
Resistor I	kilohms	9.5	10.0	10.5
Resistor J	kilohms	9.5	10.0	10.5
Transistor K	hfe	90.0	180.0	270.0
Voltage L	volts	6.2	6.5	6.8

The design team established a target for the performance characteristic of 570 cycles and functional limits of ± 150 cycles, with the loss at the limit of $100.00. Using these values, the average loss equation is

$$\overline{L} = 0.004444\left[\sigma^2 + (y - 570)^2\right]$$

The experiment was run using an OA16, which is shown in Table 20-29 along with the results. Note that three of the columns are unexplained or classified as error. From the results, the percent contribution is determined using the ANOVA and pooling-up technique, as shown in Table 20-30. Note the error includes the last three columns plus the pooling of factors E, H, and J. The error percent contribution is very low at 1.3%.

The mean squared deviation for the total is calculated from the percent contribution table using the equation

$$MSD_T = \frac{SS_T}{df_T} = \frac{105,361.5}{15} = 7024.1$$

TABLE 20-29
OA16 with Results for Control Circuit

TC	A	B	C	D	E	F	G	H	I	J	K	L	e	e	e	Data
1	1	1	1	1	1	1	1	1	1	1	1	1	1	1	1	523
2	1	1	1	1	1	1	1	2	2	2	2	2	2	2	2	430
3	1	1	1	2	2	2	2	1	1	1	1	2	2	2	2	674
4	1	1	1	2	2	2	2	2	2	2	2	1	1	1	1	572
5	1	2	2	1	1	2	2	1	1	2	2	1	1	2	2	609
6	1	2	2	1	1	2	2	2	2	1	1	2	2	1	1	534
7	1	2	2	2	2	1	1	1	1	2	2	2	2	1	1	578
8	1	2	2	2	2	1	1	2	2	1	1	1	1	2	2	527
9	2	1	2	1	2	1	2	1	2	1	2	1	2	1	2	605
10	2	1	2	1	2	1	2	2	1	2	1	2	1	2	1	707
11	2	1	2	2	1	2	1	1	2	1	2	2	1	2	1	541
12	2	1	2	2	1	2	1	2	1	2	1	1	2	1	2	669
13	2	2	1	1	2	2	1	1	2	2	1	1	1	2	1	430
14	2	2	1	1	2	2	1	2	1	1	2	2	2	1	2	480
15	2	2	1	2	1	1	2	1	2	2	1	2	2	1	2	578
16	2	2	1	2	1	1	2	2	1	1	2	1	1	2	1	668

This amount is then apportioned to each of the factors based on its percent contribution and placed in the *MSD* column of Table 20-31. Using the loss function equation, $L = k(MSD)$, the quality loss for each factor is determined and placed in the loss column of the table. Calculations for factor *A* are

$$MSD_A = MSD_T(\%_A/100) = 7024.1(3.1/100) = 217.7$$

$$L_A = k(MSD_A) = 0.004444(217.7) = \$0.97$$

Calculations are repeated for the other factors and placed in the table. The total quality loss is $31.22, shown at the bottom of the table.

The next step in the process is to evaluate the upgrade performance of the factors. With electronic components, a higher quality component is obtained by reducing the tolerance. For example, factor *A*, a resistor, changes from a 5% tolerance to a 1% tolerance, and Δ in the loss function equation is 5/1 = 5. Thus, Δ^2 is 25. This information is shown

TABLE 20-30
Percent Contribution for Control Circuit

Source	df	SS	MS	SS'	%
A	1	3,335.1	3,335.1	3,247.1	3.1
B	1	6,280.6	6,280.6	6,192.6	5.9
C	1	10,764.1	10,764.1	10,676.1	10.1
D	1	14,945.1	14,945.1	14,857.1	14.1
E	[1]	27.6			
F	1	715.6	715.6	627.6	0.6
G	1	36,960.1	36,960.1	36,875.1	35.0
H	[1]	150.0			
I	1	29,842.6	29,842.6	29,754.6	28.2
J	[1]	27.6			
K	1	1,580.1	1,580.1	1,492.1	1.4
L	1	410.1	410.1	322.1	0.3
e	[3]	322.8			
e (pooled)	6	528.1	88.0	1320.3	1.3
Total	15	105,361.5		105,361.5	100.0

TABLE 20-31
Quality Loss by Factor

Factor	Type	%	MSD	Loss—$
A	Resistor	3.1	217.7	0.97
B	Resistor	5.9	414.4	1.84
C	Capacitor	10.1	709.4	3.15
D	Resistor	14.1	990.4	4.40
E	Capacitor	0.0		
F	Transistor	0.6	42.1	0.19
G	Resistor	35.0	2458.4	10.93
H	Resistor	0.0		
I	Resistor	28.2	1980.8	8.80
J	Resistor	0.0		
K	Transistor	1.4	98.3	0.44
L	Voltage	0.3	21.1	0.09
e	Error	1.3	91.3	0.41
Total		100.0		$31.22

in Table 20-32. Also shown are the upgraded *MSD*, new loss, and quality gain; for factor *A* the calculations are

$$MSD'_A = MSD_A/\Delta^2 = 217.7/25 = 8.7$$
$$L'_A = k(MSD'_A) = 0.004444(8.7) = \$0.04$$
$$\text{Gain}_A = \$0.97 - \$0.04 = \$0.93$$

The final step in the process is to make the upgrade decision by comparing the quality gain to the upgrade cost to obtain the net gain. As shown in Table 20-33, a resistor upgrade is inexpensive and a transistor upgrade is expensive; this information affects the final decision. For factor *A* the net gain calculations are

$$\text{Net gain} = \text{quality gain} - \text{upgrade cost}$$
$$= \$0.93 - \$0.06$$
$$= \$0.87$$

Of course, because $0.87 is saved per unit, the upgrade decision is "yes."

TABLE 20-32
Upgrade Performance

Factor	Type	Loss—$	Upgrade Effect	Upgrade Factor	Upgraded MSD'	New Loss—$	Quality Gain—$
A	Resistor	0.97	5%-1%	25	8.7	0.04	0.93
B	Resistor	1.84	5%-1%	25	16.6	0.07	1.77
C	Capacitor	3.15	5%-1%	25	28.4	0.13	3.02
D	Resistor	4.40	5%-1%	25	39.6	0.18	4.22
E	Capacitor						
F	Transistor	0.19	12%-3%	16	2.6	0.01	0.18
G	Resistor	10.93	5%-1%	25	98.3	0.44	10.49
H	Resistor						
I	Resistor	8.80	5%-1%	25	72.2	0.35	8.45
J	Resistor						
K	Transistor	0.44	12%-1%	16	6.1	0.03	0.41
L	Voltage	0.09					
e	Error	0.41					
Total		31.22					

TABLE 20-33
Upgrade Decision for Control Circuit

Factor	Type	Quality Gain—$	Upgrade Cost—$	Net Gain—$	Make Upgrade?
A	Resistor	0.93	0.06	0.87	Yes
B	Resistor	11.77	0.06	1.71	Yes
C	Capacitor	3.02	1.00	2.02	Yes
D	Resistor	4.22	0.06	4.16	Yes
E	Capacitor				No
F	Transistor	0.18	2.00	(1.82)	No
G	Resistor	10.49	0.06	10.41	Yes
H	Resistor				No
I	Resistor	8.45	0.06	8.40	Yes
J	Resistor				No
K	Transistor	0.41	1.00	(0.59)	No
L	Voltage				No
e	Error				
Total			1.30	27.57	

As a result of this tolerance design, there was a substantial improvement in cost and performance. Upgrade costs were $1.30 and the net gain was $27.57 per unit. The C_{pk} went from 0.6 to 2.2.

Conclusion

The Taguchi approach has built on traditional design of experimental methods to improve the design of products and processes. These unique and relatively simple concepts result in substantial improvements in quality at lower costs.

TQM Exemplary Organization[10]

Based at Armstrong's corporate headquarters in Lancaster, Pa., their Building Products Operations, BPO, employs about 2,400 people, 85% of whom work at the operation's

---

[10] Malcolm Baldrige National Quality Award, 1995 Manufacturing Category Recipient, NIST/Baldrige Homepage.

seven manufacturing plants in six states. BPO makes and markets hundreds of products for both home and commercial interiors and industry. The world's largest manufacturer of acoustical ceilings, BPO accounted for nearly one-fourth of Armstrong's sales in 1994.

Within BPO, overall responsibility rests with its ten-member Quality Leadership Team, (QLT) composed of senior executives and headed by the BPO President. The QLT places its emphasis on leadership and fully shares its responsibility for identifying and realizing improvement opportunities with the entire organization.

The QLT performs fact-based assessments of how well it stacks up against its competitors in each of BPO's eight market segments. Then, the team defines BPO's "full potential" in each segment. Drawing on this and other information, such as the results of customer surveys, the QLT sets goals and devises action plans so that BPO will grow to reach its full potential. Along with organization-wide goals, each of the eight functional units develops and deploys action plans to every BPO employee. Relevant BPO goals and supporting process objectives are incorporated into the various incentive plans that now cover more than 93% of hourly and salaried workers.

In each of the past five years, over half of the BPO workforce has participated on the more than 250 improvement teams operating at any given time. The objectives of teams range from correcting specific operational problems at one plant to improving key business processes that enhance the entire organization. At each plant, the Quality Improvement Team, led by the facility's top manager, monitors the progress of all team efforts and reports on the results to the QLT. All Quality Improvement Teams are required to develop specific action plans and set goals that will have a measurable impact on one or more of BPO's five "key business drivers"—customer satisfaction, sales growth, operating profit, asset management, and high performance organization (human resources capabilities).

Across eight market categories in 1994, at least 97% of customers gave BPO an overall rating of good or better. As it pursues increasingly ambitious levels of customer satisfaction, BPO also is reducing operating costs. Scrap rates, for example, have been cut by 38% since 1991. Manufacturing output per employee has jumped 39% over the same span, exceeding company goals.

Over the past few years, BPO has made substantial investments to optimize its information gathering and analytical capabilities. It also has stepped up its benchmarking studies, conducting 89 in 1994, or more than twice the number performed during the previous year. The principal return on these efforts, according to the company, has been an ever-improving understanding of the dynamics of BPO's markets, competitors' performance, and its own business results. At all seven manufacturing plants, employees are organized into natural work teams or business unit teams whose individual members can perform a variety of jobs. As of 1995, six plants pay workers for mastering new skills and knowledge. Six plants also offer gain sharing, which links measures of safety, customer satisfaction, process effectiveness, and other aspects of performance areas to a portion of each employee's compensation.

In 1985, the company established a supplier quality management process that has entailed assessing the quality systems of 135 suppliers. Overall, notices of nonconformance sent to suppliers have been declining, falling 32% from 1992 to 1994. Over the same span, on-time delivery has improved from 93% in 1992, when the arrival time window for carriers was four hours, to 97.3% in 1994, even though BPO had reduced the window to 30 minutes.

Since 1991, BPO's "cost of quality"—the company's composite indicator of the price it pays as a result of waste and nonconformance—has dropped by 37%, contributing $16 million in additional operating profit in 1994 alone. In 1994 overall, BPO reduced operating costs by a company record $40 million, while maintaining or increasing its share in each of its markets. Employees shared in those accomplishments. BPO set industry safety records—employees worked more than 3 million hours without a lost time injury—and the company made its highest-ever gain sharing and incentive payouts.

Exercises

1. The specifications of a steel shaft are 6.40 ± 0.10 mm. The device sometimes fails when the shaft exceeds the specification. When failure occurs, repair or replacement is necessary at an average cost of $95.00.

   (a) What is the loss coefficient k?
   (b) What is the loss function equation?
   (c) What is the loss at 6.45 mm?

2. The specifications for an electronic device are 24 ± 0.4 A and the average repair cost is $32.00.

   (a) Determine the loss function.
   (b) Determine the loss at 24.6 A.

3. Determine the average loss for the information in Exercise 2 if 13 samples give 24.2, 24.0, 24.1, 23.8, 24.3, 24.2, 23.9, 23.8, 24.0, 23.6, 23.8, 23.9, and 23.7.

4. For an out-of-round condition (smaller-the-better) of a steel shaft, the true indicator readings (TIR) for eight shafts are 0.05, 0.04, 0.04, 0.03, 0.04, 0.02, 0.04, and 0.03 mm.

   (a) If the average loss at 0.03 is $15.00, what is the loss function?
   (b) What is the loss at 0.05?
   (c) What is the average loss?

5. When the tensile strength of a plastic part is 120 lb/in.^{2}, there is an average loss of $34.00 due to breakage. Determine the average loss for sample tests of 130, 132, 130, 132, and 131.

6. A new process is proposed for the manufacture of steel shafts, as given in the example problem on page 566. Data are 6.38, 6.40, 6.41, 6.38, 6.39, 6.36, 6.37.

    (a) What is the expected loss?
    (b) Is the new process better than the process of the example?
    (c) What future improvements might be tried? Hint: Compare average with target and the standard deviations of both processes.

7. Given three two-level factors and three suspected two-factor interactions, determine the degrees of freedom and the OA.

8. If a three-factor interaction was also suspected in Exercise 7, what are the degrees of freedom and the OA? What type of OA is this design?

9. What are the degrees of freedom and OA if the factors in Exercise 7 are three-level? Why does a three-level design require so much more design space?

10. An experimental design has five two-level factors (A, B, C, D, E), where only main effects are possible for factor C and there are no suspected AB and three-factor or higher interactions. Using a linear graph, assign the factors and their interactions to the columns of the OA.

11. Using a linear graph, assign the factors and their interactions to the columns of the OA determined in Exercise 7.

12. Using a linear graph, assign the factors and their interactions to the columns of the OA determined in Exercise 9.

13. A new process has been developed and the temperature results are 21°C for the average and 0.8°C for the sample standard deviation ($n = 5$).

    (a) What is the S/N ratio for nominal-the-best?
    (b) How much improvement has occurred? Compare to the example problem answer of 20.41 dB on page 578.
    (c) If you change the units of the example problem and this exercise, will you get the same results? Prove your conclusion.

14. Suppose the results of the new process for the bread stuffing example problem are 125, 132, 138, 137, 128, and 131. What conclusions can be drawn?

15. The yield on a new chemical process for five days is 61, 63, 58, 57, and 60 and the old process had recent yields of 54, 56, 52, 56, 53, 51, 54, 53, and 52. Is the new process better? If so, how much better?

16. The results for a larger-the-better experimental design that was run in random order with seven factors are as follows:

TC	A 1	B 2	C 3	D 4	E 5	F 6	G 7	R1	R2
1	1	1	1	1	1	1	1	19	25
2	1	1	1	2	2	2	2	20	24
3	1	2	2	1	1	2	2	24	22
4	1	2	2	2	2	1	1	22	25
5	2	1	2	1	2	1	2	26	20
6	2	1	2	2	1	2	1	25	26
7	2	2	1	1	2	2	1	25	20
8	2	2	1	2	1	1	2	25	21

(a) Determine the response table, response graph, strong effects, and prediction for the average and the S/N ratio.
(b) If the confirmation run is 27.82, what can you say about the experiment? If the confirmation run is 27.05, what can you say about the experiment?

17. The results of a nominal-the-best experimental design are as follows:

TC	A 1	B 2	C 3	N1	N2	$\bar{y}$	S/N
1	1	1	1	1.75	1.84	1.80	29.01
2	1	2	2	1.34	2.13	1.74	9.84
3	2	1	2	2.67	2.43	2.55	23.54
4	2	2	1	2.23	2.73	2.48	16.92

(a) Determine the response table, response graph, and strong effects.
(b) Analyze your results in terms of adjustment factors and variation factors.

18. The results for a smaller-the-better saturated experimental design using an OA16 with 15 factors where the factors A, B, …, O are located in columns 1, 2, …, 15, respectively, are as follows:

R1	R2	R3	R4
0.49	0.54	0.46	0.45
0.55	0.60	0.57	0.58
0.07	0.09	0.11	0.08
0.16	0.16	0.19	0.19
0.13	0.22	0.20	0.23
0.16	0.17	0.13	0.12
0.24	0.22	0.19	0.25
0.13	0.19	0.19	0.19
0.08	0.10	0.14	0.18
0.07	0.04	0.19	0.18
0.48	0.49	0.44	0.41
0.54	0.53	0.53	0.54
0.13	0.17	0.21	0.17
0.28	0.26	0.26	0.30
0.34	0.32	0.30	0.41
0.58	0.62	0.59	0.54

(a) Determine the response table, response graph, strong effects, and prediction for the average and the S/N ratio.
(b) If the results of the confirmation run are 0.13, 0.07, 0.06, 0.08, what can you say about the experiment?

19. The results of a larger-the-better experimental design with an outer array for noise are as follows:

TC	A	B	C	D	N1	N2
1	1	1	1	1	7.9	11.9
2	1	2	2	2	7.3	12.1
3	1	3	3	3	8.6	10.5
4	2	1	2	3	10.6	11.2
5	2	2	3	1	12.0	13.7
6	2	3	1	2	8.5	11.9
7	3	1	3	2	8.7	10.9
8	3	2	1	3	6.5	11.9
9	3	3	2	1	8.4	15.0

(a) Determine the response table, response graph, strong effects, and prediction for the S/N ratio.

(b) What value for the confirmation run would you consider satisfactory?

20. The results of a smaller-the-better experimental design are as follows:

TC	B 1	A 2	AB 3	C 4	UX 5	AC 6	D 7	S/N
1	1	1	1	1	1	1	1	32.1
2	1	1	1	2	2	2	2	33.6
3	1	2	2	1	1	2	2	32.8
4	1	2	2	2	2	1	1	31.7
5	2	1	2	1	2	1	2	31.2
6	2	1	2	2	1	2	1	33.7
7	2	2	1	1	2	2	1	32.3
8	2	2	1	2	1	1	2	33.6

(a) Determine the response table, response graph, and strong effects.

(b) Explain the results.

21. Determine the percent contributions of Exercise 16.

22. Determine the percent contributions of Exercise 20.

23. The confirmation run for the experimental design of an electronic device gave the following percent contributions for unpooled factors from an OA12 design. Also given is the upgrade effect and the upgrade cost.

Factor	Type	df	%	Ungrade Effect	Upgrade Cost—$
A	Capacitor	1	41.0	5%-1%	1.81
B	Resistor	1	12.4	5%-1%	0.15
C	Transistor	1	32.1	12%-3%	3.92
D	Resistor	1	20.9	5%-1%	0.15
e	Error	7	5.6		
		11			

If the total SS is 1301.2 and $k = 0.05$, determine the net gain per unit from upgrading.

24. A four-factor experiment gives the following percent contributions for the confirmation run: A (43%), B (9%), C (28%), D (13%), and residual (7%). If the variance is currently 225 and the desired value is 100, determine two possible reduction schemes.

25. Design and conduct a Taguchi experiment for

   (a) Growth of a house plant
   (b) Flight of a paper airplane
   (c) Baking brownies, chocolate-chip cookies, and so forth
   (d) Making coffee, popcorn, etc.
   (e) Any organization listed in Chapter 1, Exercise 5

Appendix

TABLE A

Factors for Computing Central Lines and 3 σ
Control Limits for Variables Charts

Sample Size	CHART FOR AVERAGES		CHART FOR STANDARD DEVIATIONS		
	Factors for Control Limits		Factor for Central Line	Factors for Control Limits	
n	A_2	A_3	C_4	B_3	B_4
2	1.880	2.659	0.7979	0	3.267
3	1.023	1.954	0.8862	0	2.568
4	0.729	1.628	0.9213	0	2.266
5	0.577	1.427	0.9400	0	2.089
6	0.483	1.287	0.9515	0.030	1.970
7	0.419	1.182	0.9594	0.118	1.882
8	0.373	1.099	0.9650	0.185	1.815

Sample Size	CHART FOR RANGES					Chart for Medians
	Factor for Central Line	Factors for Control Limits				
n	d_2	D_3	D_4	D_5	D_6	A_5
2	1.128	0	3.267	0	3.865	2.224
3	1.693	0	2.574	0	2.745	1.265
4	2.059	0	2.282	0	2.375	0.829
5	2.326	0	2.114	0	2.179	0.712
6	2.534	0	2.004	0	2.055	0.562
7	2.704	0.076	1.924	0.078	1.967	0.520
8	2.847	0.136	1.864	0.139	1.901	0.441

TABLE B
Critical Values, $t_{\alpha,\nu}$ of t Distribution

ν	0.25	0.10	0.05	0.025	0.01	0.005	0.001	0.0005
					α			
1	1.000	3.078	6.314	12.706	21.821	63.657	318.31	636.62
2	0.816	1.886	2.920	4.303	6.965	9.925	22.326	31.598
3	0.765	1.638	2.353	3.182	4.541	5.841	10.213	12.924
4	0.741	1.533	2.132	2.776	3.747	4.604	7.173	8.610
5	0.727	1.476	2.015	2.571	3.365	4.032	5.893	6.869
6	0.718	1.440	1.943	2.447	3.143	3.707	5.208	5.959
7	0.711	1.415	1.895	2.365	2.998	3.499	4.785	5.408
8	0.706	1.397	1.860	2.306	2.896	3.355	4.501	5.041
9	0.703	1.383	1.833	2.262	2.821	3.250	4.297	4.781
10	0.700	1.372	1.812	2.228	2.764	3.169	4.144	4.587
11	0.697	1.363	1.796	2.201	2.718	3.106	4.025	4.437
12	0.695	1.356	1.782	2.179	2.681	3.055	3.930	4.318
13	0.694	1.350	1.771	2.160	2.650	3.012	3.852	4.221
14	0.692	1.345	1.761	2.145	2.624	2.977	3.787	4.140
15	0.691	1.341	1.753	2.131	2.602	2.947	3.733	4.073
16	0.690	1.337	1.746	2.120	2.583	2.921	3.686	4.015
17	0.689	1.333	1.740	2.110	2.567	2.898	3.646	3.965
18	0.688	1.330	1.734	2.101	2.552	2.878	3.610	3.922
19	0.688	1.328	1.729	2.093	2.539	2.861	3.579	3.883
20	0.687	1.325	1.725	2.086	2.528	2.845	3.552	3.850
21	0.686	1.323	1.721	2.080	2.518	2.831	3.527	3.819
22	0.686	1.321	1.717	2.074	2.508	2.819	3.505	3.792
23	0.685	1.319	1.714	2.069	2.500	2.807	3.485	3.767
24	0.685	1.318	1.711	2.064	2.492	2.797	3.467	3.745
25	0.684	1.316	1.708	2.060	2.485	2.787	3.450	3.725
26	0.684	1.315	1.706	2.056	2.479	2.779	3.435	3.707
27	0.684	1.314	1.703	2.052	2.473	2.771	3.421	3.690
28	0.683	1.313	1.701	2.048	2.467	2.763	3.408	3.674
29	0.683	1.311	1.699	2.045	2.462	2.756	3.396	3.659
30	0.683	1.310	1.697	2.042	2.457	2.750	3.385	3.646
40	0.681	1.303	1.684	2.021	2.423	2.704	3.307	3.551
60	0.679	1.296	1.671	2.000	2.390	2.660	3.232	3.460
∞	0.674	1.282	1.645	1.960	2.326	2.576	3.090	3.291

TABLE C–1

Critical Values, F_{α, v_1, v_2}, of F Distribution ($\alpha = 0.1$)

v_2	\multicolumn{13}{c}{v_1 (NUMERATOR)}
	1	2	3	4	6	8	10	12	15	20	50	100	∞
1	4052	4999	5403	5625	5859	5981	6056	6106	6157	6209	6300	6330	6366
2	98.5	99.0	99.2	99.2	99.3	99.4	99.4	99.4	99.4	99.4	99.5	99.5	99.5
3	34.1	30.8	29.5	28.7	27.9	27.5	27.2	27.1	26.9	26.7	26.4	26.2	26.1
4	21.2	18.0	16.7	16.0	15.2	14.8	14.5	14.4	14.2	14.0	13.7	13.6	13.5
5	16.3	13.3	12.1	11.4	10.7	10.3	10.1	9.89	9.72	9.55	9.24	9.13	9.02
6	13.7	10.9	9.78	9.15	8.47	8.10	7.87	7.72	7.56	7.40	7.09	6.99	6.88
7	12.2	9.55	8.45	7.85	7.19	6.84	6.62	6.47	6.31	6.16	5.86	5.75	5.65
8	11.3	8.65	7.59	7.01	6.37	6.03	5.81	5.67	5.52	5.36	5.07	4.96	4.86
9	10.6	8.02	6.99	6.42	5.80	5.47	5.26	5.11	4.96	4.81	4.52	4.42	4.31
10	10.0	7.56	6.55	5.99	5.39	5.06	4.85	4.71	4.56	4.41	4.12	4.01	3.91
11	9.65	7.21	6.22	5.67	5.07	4.74	4.54	4.40	4.25	4.10	3.81	3.71	3.60
12	9.33	6.93	5.95	5.41	4.82	4.50	4.30	4.16	4.01	3.86	3.57	3.47	3.36
13	9.07	6.70	5.74	5.21	4.62	4.30	4.10	3.96	3.82	3.66	3.38	3.27	3.17
14	8.86	6.51	5.56	5.04	4.46	4.14	3.94	3.80	3.66	3.51	3.22	3.11	3.00
15	8.68	6.36	5.42	4.89	4.32	4.00	3.80	3.67	3.52	3.37	3.08	2.98	2.87
16	8.53	6.23	5.29	4.77	4.20	3.89	3.69	3.55	3.41	3.26	2.97	2.86	2.75
17	8.40	6.11	5.18	4.67	4.10	3.79	3.59	3.46	3.31	3.16	2.87	2.76	2.65
18	8.29	6.01	5.09	4.58	4.01	3.71	3.51	3.37	3.23	3.08	2.78	2.68	2.57
19	8.18	5.93	5.01	4.50	3.94	3.63	3.43	3.30	3.15	3.00	2.71	2.60	2.49
20	8.10	5.85	4.94	4.43	3.87	3.56	3.37	3.23	3.09	2.94	2.64	2.54	2.42
22	7.95	5.72	4.82	4.31	3.76	3.45	3.26	3.12	2.98	2.83	2.53	2.42	2.31
24	7.82	5.61	4.72	4.22	3.67	3.36	3.17	3.03	2.89	2.74	2.44	2.33	2.21
26	7.72	5.53	4.64	4.14	3.59	3.29	3.09	2.96	2.81	2.66	2.36	2.25	2.13
28	7.64	5.45	4.57	4.07	3.53	3.23	3.03	2.90	2.75	2.60	2.30	2.19	2.06
30	7.56	5.39	4.51	4.02	3.47	3.17	2.98	2.84	2.70	2.55	2.25	2.13	2.01
40	7.31	5.18	4.31	3.83	3.29	2.99	2.80	2.66	2.52	2.37	2.06	1.94	1.80
60	7.08	4.98	4.13	3.65	3.12	2.82	2.63	2.50	2.35	2.20	1.88	1.75	1.60
120	6.85	4.79	3.95	3.48	2.96	2.66	2.47	2.34	2.19	2.03	1.70	1.56	1.38
200	6.76	4.71	3.88	3.41	2.89	2.60	2.41	2.27	2.13	1.97	1.63	1.48	1.28
∞	6.63	4.61	3.78	3.32	2.80	2.51	2.32	2.18	2.04	1.88	1.52	1.36	1.00

TABLE C–2
Critical Values, F_{α, v_1, v_2}, of F Distribution ($\alpha = 0.05$)

v_2							v_1 (NUMERATOR)						
	1	**2**	**3**	**4**	**6**	**8**	**10**	**12**	**15**	**20**	**50**	**100**	**∞**
1	161	200	216	225	234	239	242	244	246	248	252	253	254
2	18.5	19.0	19.2	19.2	19.3	19.4	19.4	19.4	19.4	19.4	19.5	19.5	19.5
3	10.1	9.55	9.28	9.12	8.94	8.85	8.79	8.74	8.70	8.66	8.58	8.55	8.53
4	7.71	6.94	6.59	6.39	6.16	6.04	5.96	5.91	5.86	5.80	5.70	5.66	5.63
5	6.61	5.79	5.41	5.19	4.95	4.82	4.74	4.68	4.62	4.56	4.44	4.41	4.36
6	5.99	5.14	4.76	4.53	4.28	4.15	4.06	4.00	3.94	3.87	3.75	3.71	3.67
7	5.59	4.74	4.35	4.12	3.87	3.73	3.64	3.57	3.51	3.44	3.32	3.27	3.23
8	5.32	4.46	4.07	3.84	3.58	3.44	3.35	3.28	3.22	3.15	3.02	2.97	2.93
9	5.12	4.26	3.86	3.63	3.37	3.23	3.14	3.07	3.01	2.94	2.80	2.76	2.71
10	4.96	4.10	3.71	3.48	3.22	3.07	2.98	2.91	2.85	2.77	2.64	2.59	2.54
11	4.84	3.98	3.59	3.36	3.09	2.95	2.85	2.79	2.72	2.65	2.51	2.46	2.40
12	4.75	3.89	3.49	3.26	3.00	2.85	2.75	2.69	2.62	2.54	2.40	2.35	2.30
13	4.67	3.81	3.41	3.18	2.92	2.77	2.67	2.60	2.53	2.46	2.31	2.26	2.21
14	4.60	3.74	3.34	3.11	2.85	2.70	2.60	2.53	2.46	2.39	2.24	2.19	2.13
15	4.54	3.68	3.29	3.06	2.79	2.64	2.54	2.48	2.40	2.33	2.18	2.12	2.07
16	4.49	3.63	3.24	3.01	2.74	2.59	2.49	2.42	2.35	2.28	2.12	2.07	2.01
17	4.45	3.59	3.20	2.96	2.70	2.55	2.45	2.38	2.31	2.23	2.08	2.02	1.96
18	4.41	3.55	3.16	2.93	2.66	2.51	2.41	2.34	2.27	2.19	2.04	1.98	1.92
19	4.38	3.52	3.13	2.90	2.63	2.48	2.38	2.31	2.23	2.16	2.00	1.94	1.88
20	4.35	3.49	3.10	2.87	2.60	2.45	2.35	2.28	2.20	2.12	1.97	1.91	1.84
22	4.30	3.44	3.05	2.82	2.55	2.40	2.30	2.23	2.15	2.07	1.91	1.85	1.78
24	4.26	3.40	3.01	2.78	2.51	2.36	2.25	2.18	2.11	2.03	1.86	1.80	1.73
26	4.23	3.37	2.98	2.74	2.47	2.32	2.22	2.15	2.07	1.99	1.82	1.76	1.69
28	4.20	3.34	2.95	2.71	2.45	2.29	2.19	2.12	2.04	1.96	1.79	1.73	1.65
30	4.17	3.32	2.92	2.69	2.42	2.27	2.16	2.09	2.01	1.93	1.76	1.70	1.62
40	4.08	3.23	2.84	2.61	2.34	2.18	2.08	2.00	1.92	1.84	1.66	1.59	1.51
60	4.00	3.15	2.76	2.53	2.25	2.10	1.99	1.92	1.84	1.75	1.56	1.48	1.39
120	3.92	3.07	2.68	2.45	2.17	2.02	1.91	1.83	1.75	1.66	1.46	1.37	1.25
200	3.89	3.04	2.65	2.42	2.14	1.98	1.88	1.80	1.72	1.62	1.41	1.32	1.19
∞	3.84	3.00	2.60	2.37	2.10	1.94	1.83	1.75	1.67	1.57	1.35	1.24	1.00

TABLE C–3
Critical Values, F_{α,ν_1,ν_2}, of F Distribution ($\alpha = 0.01$)

ν_2	ν_1 (NUMERATOR)												
	1	**2**	**3**	**4**	**6**	**8**	**10**	**12**	**15**	**20**	**50**	**100**	**∞**
1	39.9	49.5	53.6	55.8	58.2	59.4	60.2	60.7	61.2	61.7	62.7	63.0	63.3
2	8.53	9.00	9.16	9.24	9.33	9.37	9.39	9.41	9.42	9.44	9.47	9.48	9.49
3	5.54	5.46	5.39	5.34	5.28	5.25	5.23	5.22	5.20	5.18	5.15	5.14	5.13
4	4.54	4.32	4.19	4.11	4.01	3.95	3.92	3.90	3.87	3.84	3.80	3.78	3.76
5	4.06	3.78	3.62	3.52	3.40	3.34	3.30	3.27	3.24	3.21	3.15	3.13	3.10
6	3.78	3.46	3.29	3.18	3.05	2.98	2.94	2.90	2.87	2.84	2.77	2.75	2.72
7	3.59	3.26	3.07	2.96	2.83	2.75	2.70	2.67	2.63	2.59	2.52	2.50	2.47
8	3.46	3.11	2.92	2.81	2.67	2.59	2.54	2.50	2.46	2.42	2.35	2.32	2.29
9	3.36	3.01	2.81	2.69	2.55	2.47	2.42	2.38	2.34	2.30	2.22	2.19	2.16
10	3.28	2.92	2.73	2.61	2.46	2.38	2.32	2.28	2.24	2.20	2.12	2.09	2.06
11	3.23	2.86	2.66	2.54	2.39	2.30	2.25	2.21	2.17	2.12	2.04	2.00	1.97
12	3.18	2.81	2.61	2.48	2.33	2.24	2.19	2.15	2.10	2.06	1.97	1.94	1.90
13	3.14	2.76	2.56	2.43	2.28	2.20	2.14	2.10	2.05	2.01	1.92	1.88	1.85
14	3.10	2.73	2.52	2.39	2.24	2.15	2.10	2.05	2.01	1.96	1.87	1.83	1.80
15	3.07	2.70	2.49	2.36	2.21	2.12	2.06	2.02	1.97	1.92	1.83	1.79	1.76
16	3.05	2.67	2.46	2.33	2.18	2.09	2.03	1.99	1.94	1.89	1.79	1.76	1.72
17	3.03	2.64	2.44	2.31	2.15	2.06	2.00	1.96	1.91	1.86	1.76	1.73	1.69
18	3.01	2.62	2.42	2.29	2.13	2.04	1.98	1.93	1.89	1.84	1.74	1.70	1.66
19	2.99	2.61	2.40	2.27	2.11	2.02	1.96	1.91	1.86	1.81	1.71	1.67	1.63
20	2.97	2.59	2.38	2.25	2.09	2.00	1.94	1.89	1.84	1.79	1.69	1.65	1.61
22	2.95	2.56	2.35	2.22	2.06	1.97	1.90	1.86	1.81	1.76	1.65	1.61	1.57
24	2.93	2.54	2.33	2.19	2.04	1.94	1.88	1.83	1.78	1.73	1.62	1.58	1.53
26	2.91	2.52	2.31	2.17	2.01	1.92	1.86	1.81	1.76	1.71	1.59	1.55	1.50
28	2.89	2.50	2.29	2.16	2.00	1.90	1.84	1.79	1.74	1.69	1.37	1.53	1.48
30	2.88	2.49	2.28	2.14	1.98	1.88	1.82	1.77	1.72	1.67	1.55	1.51	1.46
40	2.84	2.44	2.23	2.09	1.93	1.83	1.76	1.71	1.66	1.61	1.48	1.43	1.38
60	2.79	2.39	2.18	2.04	1.87	1.77	1.71	1.66	1.60	1.54	1.41	1.36	1.29
120	2.75	2.35	2.13	1.99	1.82	1.72	1.65	1.60	1.55	1.48	1.34	1.27	1.19
200	2.73	2.33	2.11	1.97	1.80	1.70	1.63	1.57	1.52	1.46	1.31	1.24	1.14
∞	2.71	2.30	2.08	1.94	1.77	1.67	1.60	1.55	1.49	1.42	1.26	1.18	1.00

TABLE D
Orthogonal Arrays, Interaction Tables, and Linear Graphs

Reproduced, with permission, from *Taguchi Methods: Introduction to Quality Engineering* (Allen Park, Mich.: American Supplier Institute, Inc., 1991).

Orthogonal Array (OA4)

TC	COLUMN		
	1	2	3
1	1	1	1
2	1	2	2
3	2	1	2
4	2	2	1

Linear graph for OA4

Orthogonal Array (OA8)

TC	COLUMN						
	1	2	3	4	5	6	7
1	1	1	1	1	1	1	1
2	1	1	1	2	2	2	2
3	1	2	2	1	1	2	2
4	1	2	2	2	2	1	1
5	2	1	2	1	2	1	2
6	2	1	2	2	1	2	1
7	2	2	1	1	2	2	1
8	2	2	1	2	1	1	2

Interaction Table for OA8

Column	COLUMN						
	1	2	3	4	5	6	7
1	(1)	3	2	5	4	7	6
2		(2)	1	6	7	4	5
3			(3)	7	6	5	4
4				(4)	1	2	3
5					(5)	3	2
6						(6)	1
7							(7)

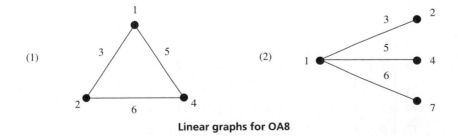

Linear graphs for OA8

Orthogonal Array (OA9)

TC	COLUMN			
	1	2	3	4
1	1	1	1	1
2	1	2	2	2
3	1	3	3	3
4	2	1	2	3
5	2	2	3	1
6	2	3	1	2
7	3	1	3	2
8	3	2	1	3
9	3	3	2	1

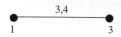

Linear graph for OA9

Orthogonal Array (OA12)

TC	COLUMN										
	1	2	3	4	5	6	7	8	9	10	11
1	1	1	1	1	1	1	1	1	1	1	1
2	1	1	1	1	1	2	2	2	2	2	2
3	1	1	2	2	2	1	1	1	2	2	2
4	1	2	1	2	2	1	2	2	1	1	2
5	1	2	2	1	2	2	1	2	1	2	1
6	1	2	2	2	1	2	2	1	2	1	1
7	2	1	2	2	1	1	2	2	1	2	1
8	2	1	2	1	2	2	2	1	1	1	2
9	2	1	1	2	2	2	1	2	2	1	1
10	2	2	2	1	1	1	1	2	2	1	2
11	2	2	1	2	1	2	1	1	1	2	2
12	2	2	1	1	2	1	2	1	2	2	1

Orthogonal Array (OA16)

TC	1	2	3	4	5	6	7	8	9	10	11	12	13	14	15
							COLUMN								
1	1	1	1	1	1	1	1	1	1	1	1	1	1	1	1
2	1	1	1	1	1	1	1	2	2	2	2	2	2	2	2
3	1	1	1	2	2	2	2	1	1	1	1	2	2	2	2
4	1	1	1	2	2	2	2	2	2	2	2	1	1	1	1
5	1	2	2	1	1	2	2	1	1	2	2	1	1	2	2
6	1	2	2	1	1	2	2	2	2	1	1	2	2	1	1
7	1	2	2	2	2	1	1	1	1	2	2	2	2	1	1
8	1	2	2	2	2	1	1	2	2	1	1	1	1	2	2
9	2	1	2	1	2	1	2	1	2	1	2	1	2	1	2
10	2	1	2	1	2	1	2	2	1	2	1	2	1	2	1
11	2	1	2	2	1	2	1	1	2	1	2	2	1	2	1
12	2	1	2	2	1	2	1	2	1	2	1	1	2	1	2
13	2	2	1	1	2	2	1	1	2	2	1	1	2	2	1
14	2	2	1	1	2	2	1	2	1	1	2	2	1	1	2
15	2	2	1	2	1	1	2	1	2	2	1	2	1	1	2
16	2	2	1	2	1	1	2	2	1	1	2	1	2	2	1

Interaction Table for OA16

Column	1	2	3	4	5	6	7	8	9	10	11	12	13	14	15
							COLUMN								
1	(1)	3	2	5	4	7	6	9	8	11	10	13	12	13	14
2		(2)	1	6	7	4	5	10	11	8	9	14	15	12	13
3			(3)	7	6	5	4	11	10	9	8	15	14	13	12
4				(4)	1	2	3	12	13	14	15	8	9	10	11
5					(5)	3	2	13	12	15	14	9	8	11	10
6						(6)	1	14	15	12	13	10	11	8	9
7							(7)	15	14	13	12	11	10	9	8
8								(8)	1	2	3	4	5	6	7
9									(9)	3	2	5	4	7	6
10										(10)	1	6	7	4	5
11											(11)	7	6	5	4
12												(12)	1	2	3
13													(13)	3	2
14														(14)	1
15															(15)

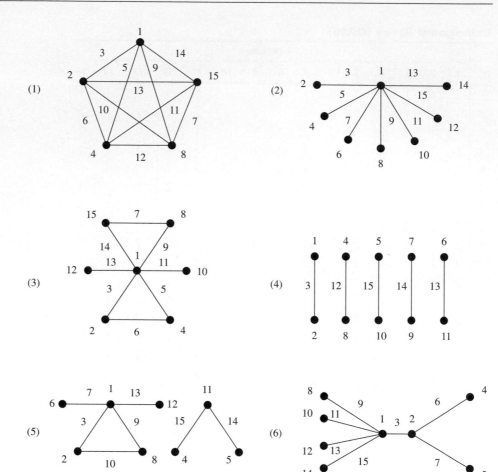

Linear graphs for OA16

Orthogonal Array (OA18)

TC	COLUMN							
	1	2	3	4	5	6	7	8
1	1	1	1	1	1	1	1	1
2	1	1	2	2	2	2	2	2
3	1	1	3	3	3	3	3	3
4	1	2	1	1	2	2	3	3
5	1	2	2	2	3	3	1	1
6	1	2	3	3	1	1	2	2
7	1	3	1	2	1	3	2	3
8	1	3	2	3	2	1	3	1
9	1	3	3	1	3	2	1	2
10	2	1	1	3	3	2	2	1
11	2	1	2	1	1	3	3	2
12	2	1	3	2	2	1	1	3
13	2	2	1	2	3	1	3	2
14	2	2	2	3	1	2	1	3
15	2	2	3	1	2	3	2	1
16	2	3	1	3	2	3	1	2
17	2	3	2	1	3	1	2	3
18	2	3	3	2	1	2	3	1

Orthogonal Array (OA27)

TC	COLUMN												
	1	2	3	4	5	6	7	8	9	10	11	12	13
1	1	1	1	1	1	1	1	1	1	1	1	1	1
2	1	1	1	1	2	2	2	2	2	2	2	2	2
3	1	1	1	1	3	3	3	3	3	3	3	3	3
4	1	2	2	2	1	1	1	2	2	2	3	3	3
5	1	2	2	2	2	2	2	3	3	3	1	1	1
6	1	2	2	2	3	3	3	1	1	1	2	2	2
7	1	3	3	3	1	1	1	3	3	3	2	2	2
8	1	3	3	3	2	2	2	1	1	1	3	3	3
9	1	3	3	3	3	3	3	2	2	2	1	1	1
10	2	1	2	3	1	2	3	1	2	3	1	2	3
11	2	1	2	3	2	3	1	2	3	1	2	3	1
12	2	1	2	3	3	1	2	3	1	2	3	1	2
13	2	2	3	1	1	2	3	2	3	1	3	1	2
14	2	2	3	1	2	3	1	3	1	2	1	2	3
15	2	2	3	1	3	1	2	1	2	3	2	3	1
16	2	3	1	2	1	2	3	3	1	2	2	3	1
17	2	3	1	2	2	3	1	1	2	3	3	1	2
18	2	3	1	2	3	1	2	2	3	1	1	2	3
19	3	1	3	2	1	3	2	1	3	2	1	3	2
20	3	1	3	2	2	1	3	2	1	3	2	1	3
21	3	1	3	2	3	2	1	3	2	1	3	2	1
22	3	2	1	3	1	3	2	2	1	3	3	2	1
23	3	2	1	3	2	1	3	3	2	1	1	3	2
24	3	2	1	3	3	2	1	1	3	2	2	1	3
25	3	3	2	1	1	3	2	3	2	1	2	1	3
26	3	3	2	1	2	1	3	1	3	2	3	2	1
27	3	3	2	1	3	2	1	2	1	3	1	3	2

Interaction Table for OA27

Column	COLUMN											
	2	**3**	**4**	**5**	**6**	**7**	**8**	**9**	**10**	**11**	**12**	**13**
1	3 4	2 4	2 3	6 7	5 7	5 6	9 10	8 10	8 9	12 13	11 13	11 12
2		1 4	1 3	8 11	9 12	10 13	5 11	6 12	7 13	5 8	6 9	7 10
3			1 2	9 13	10 11	8 12	7 12	8 13	6 11	6 10	7 8	5 9
4				10 12	8 13	9 11	6 13	7 11	5 12	7 9	5 10	6 8
5					1 7	1 6	2 11	3 13	4 12	2 8	4 10	3 9
6						1 5	4 3	2 12	3 11	3 10	2 9	4 8
7							3 12	4 11	2 13	4 9	3 8	2 10
8								1 10	1 9	2 5	3 7	4 6
9									1 8	4 7	2 6	3 5
10										3 6	4 7	2 7
11											1 13	1 12
12												1 11

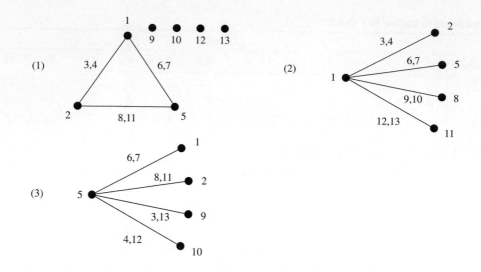

Linear graphs for OA27

References

ANDERSON, DAVID, *Management Information Systems*, New Jersey: Prentice Hall, Inc., 2000.

ASQ/AIAG TASK FORCE, *Fundamental Statistical Process Control*. Troy, MI: Automobile Industry Action Group, 1991.

ASQ QUALITY COST COMMITTEE, *Guide for Reducing Quality Costs*, 2nd ed. Milwaukee, WI: American Society for Quality, Inc., 1987.

ASQ QUALITY COST COMMITTEE, *Principles of Quality Costs*. Milwaukee, WI: American Society for Quality, Inc., 1986.

BESTERFIELD, DALE H., *Quality Control*, 6th ed. Upper Saddle River, NJ: Prentice Hall, 2001.

BOSSERT, JAMES L., *Quality Function Deployment: A Practioner's Approach*. Milwaukee, WI: ASQ Quality Press, 1991.

BRASSARD, MICHAEL, *The Memory Jogger Plus +. Featuring the Seven Management and Planning Tools*. Methuen, MA: GOAL/QPC, 1996.

CAMP, ROBERT C., *Benchmarking: The Search for Industry Best Practices That Lead to Superior Practice*. Milwaukee, WI: ASQ Quality Press, 1989.

CASCIO, JOSEPH, WODSIDE, GAYLE, and MITCHELL, PHILLIP, *ISO 14000 Guide. The New International Environmental Management Standards*. New York: McGraw-Hill, 1996.

CHASE, G. W., *Implementing TQM in a Construction Company*. Washington D.C.: Associated General Contractors of America, 1993.

CHRYSLER/FORD/GENERAL MOTORS SUPPLIER QUALITY REQUIREMENTS TASK FORCE. *Quality System Requirements QS-9000*. Troy, MI: Automobile Industry Action Group, 1994.

CHRYSLER/FORD/GENERAL MOTORS TASK FORCE, *Potential Failure Mode and Effects Analysis (FMEA)*. Troy, MI: Automobile Industry Action Group, 1995.

COVEY, STEPHEN R., *The 7 Habits of Highly Effective People*. New York, NY: Simon & Schuster, 1989.

CROSBY, PHILIP B., *Quality Without Tears*. New York: McGraw-Hill Book Company, 1984.

DEMING, W. EDWARDS, *Quality, Productivity, and Competitive Position*. Cambridge, MA: Massachusetts Institute of Technology, 1982.

DUNCAN, ACHESON J., *Quality Control and Industrial Statistics*, 5th ed. Homewood, IL: Richard D. Irwin, 1986.

FEIGENBAUM, A. V., *Total Quality Control*. New York: McGraw-Hill Book Company, 1961.

FISHER, DONALD C., *The Simplified Baldrige Award Organization Assessment*. New York: The Lincoln-Bradley Publishing Group, 1993.

GATES, BILL, *The Road Ahead*, New York: Viking Penquin, 1995.

GOETSCH, DAVID L., and STANLEY B. DAVIS, *ISO 14000 Environmental Management*, New Jersey, Prentice Hall, Inc., 2001.

GOODEN, RANDALL L., *Product Liability Prevention, Mil*waukee, WI: ASQ Quality Press, 2000.

HICKS, CHARLES R., *Fundamental Concepts in the Design of Experiments*. New York: Holt, Rinehart and Winston, 1973.

ISHIKAWA, K., *What Is Total Quality Control?* Englewood Cliffs, NJ: Prentice Hall, Inc., 1985.

JORDAN, JAMES A. JR and FREDERICK J. MICHEL, *The Lean Company—Making the Right Choices*, Dearborn, MI, Society of Manufacturing Engineering, 2001.

JURAN, JOSEPH M., Editor, *Quality Control Handbook*, 4th ed. New York: McGraw-Hill Book Company, 1980.

KNOUSE, STEPHEN B., Editor, *Human Resources Management Perspectives on TQM Concepts and Practices*. Milwaukee, WI: ASQ Quality Press, 1996.

LEBOW, ROB, *A Journey into the Heroic Environment*. Rocklin, CA: Prima Publishing, 1990.

MARTIN, E. WAINRIGHT, et. al., *Managing Information Technology*, New Jersey: Prentice Hall, 1999.

NAKAJIMA, SEIICHI, *Total Productivity Maintenance*, Portland, OR: Productivity Press Inc., 1988.

PEACE, STUART GLEN, *Taguchi Methods: A Hands-On Approach*. New York: Addison-Wesley Publishing Company, Inc., 1992.

PEACH, ROBERT W., Editor, *The ISO 9000 Handbook*. Fairfax, VA: CEEM Information Services, 1992.

SCHMIDT, WARREN H., AND JEROME P. FINNIGAN, *The Race Without a Finish Line*. San Francisco, CA: Jossey-Bass Publishers, 1992.

SCHOLTES, PETER R., *The Team Handbook*. Madison, WI: Joiner Associates, Inc., 1988.

SCHOLTES, PETER R., *The Team Handbook. How to Use Teams to Improve Quality*. Madison, WI: Joiner Associates, Inc., 1992.

TAGUCHI, G., *Introduction to Quality Engineering*. Tokyo: Asian Productivity Organization, 1986.

WHEELER, DONALD J., *Understanding Industrial Experimentation*. Knoxville, TN: Statistical Process Controls, Inc., 1988.

WIERSEMA, FRED, *Customer Intimacy*, Santa Monica, CA: Knowledge Exchange, 1996.

WINCHELL, WILLIAM, *TQM: Getting Started and Achieving Results with Total Quality Management*. Dearborn, MI: Society of Manufacturing Engineers, 1992.

Index